WESTERN CIVILIZATION SINCE 1500

Joseph R. Strayer PRINCETON UNIVERSITY

Hans W. Gatzke YALE UNIVERSITY

E. Harris Harbison LATE OF PRINCETON UNIVERSITY

Edwin L. Dunbaugh HOFSTRA UNIVERSITY

WESTERN

CIVILIZATION SINCE 1500

 HARCOURT BRACE JOVANOVICH, INC.

New York / Chicago / San Francisco / Atlanta

MAPS BY J. P. TREMBLAY

Note: Pages 38–521 in *Western Civilization Since 1500* are the same
      as pages 344–827 in *The Mainstream of Civilization*
      by Joseph R. Strayer, Hans W. Gatzke, E. Harris Harbison,
      and Edwin L. Dunbaugh (Harcourt Brace Jovanovich, Inc.).

ISBN: 0-15-595260-9

LIBRARY OF CONGRESS CATALOG CARD NUMBER: 78-141610

PRINTED IN THE UNITED STATES OF AMERICA

Preface

It requires a certain amount of courage to try to cover five centuries of history in a single volume, even though we have limited ourselves to the history of western civilization. We have been helped by the fact that we could draw on our earlier two-volume work, *The Course of Civilization*.

Western Civilization Since 1500 consists of Chapters 16 through 34 of the one-volume version of that work, *The Mainstream of Civilization*. A new introductory chapter summarizes the major developments in European civilization before 1500, and the Epilogue has been revised to carry the narrative through 1970.

As before, we have deliberately omitted certain details so that we could discuss as fully as possible the basic characteristics of each period in the history of modern western civilization. We have tried to emphasize connections and interrelations—the ways in which politics, economics, art, scholarship, and religion all influence one another. We have tried to capture the flavor of each age—the unique combination of beliefs, activities, and institutions that distinguish one society from another. The illustrations and the inserts in the text have been selected to give some idea of the diverse and ever-changing ways in which men have looked at and lived in their world. Finally, we have tried to consider the most difficult of all historical questions—the nature of and the reasons for change in human communities. Why and how do new institutions, new activities, new ideas rise and flourish? Why do they fade away? There are no easy answers to these problems; all we can do is to suggest lines of inquiry that the reader may wish to pursue.

Obviously it is easier to assess the characteristics and achievements of earlier periods than those of the age in which we live. The English Revolution of the seventeenth century ended long ago; the communist revolutions of the twentieth century continue to develop in strange and unpredictable ways. Obviously, also, it is more important to know details about the nature and background of problems that are still with us than details about problems that were solved (at least partially) long ago. For these reasons the book broadens as it reaches the nineteenth century. More information is provided and more events are described in the hope that the reader will better understand the present state of the world.

We trust that no one will passively accept our interpretations or believe that our book is an adequate summary of the modern period of western civilization. Our work is only an introduction, an attempt to persuade the reader to think deeply about history and to study it in detail. We are convinced that historical-mindedness is a necessity of human life. Consciously or unconsciously, we all base our estimates of the future on our knowledge of the past. It is important, then, that our knowledge of the past be as accurate and as deep as possible.

We lament the untimely death of one of the original members of the group, Professor E. Harris Harbison. We have tried to revise his material to make it fit the new pattern of this book. He would have done the job better, but without the foundation that he gave us the job could not have been done at all.

The authors are greatly indebted to the following historians who critically read their earlier work and made many valuable comments and suggestions: Frederick A. Allen, University of Colorado; Erich S. Gruen, University of California at Berkeley; William W. Hallo, Yale University; Raymond F. Kierstead, Yale University; William C. McDermott, University of Pennsylvania; John F. Oates, Duke University; Robert O. Paxton, Columbia University; Orest Ranum, Johns Hopkins University; Harald A. T. Reiche, Massachusetts Institute of Technology; Righton Robertson, Jr., University of Maryland; John L. Teall, Mount Holyoke College; and Charles T. Wood, Dartmouth College.

J. R. S.
H. W. G.
E. L. D.

Contents

List of Maps

COLOR MAPS

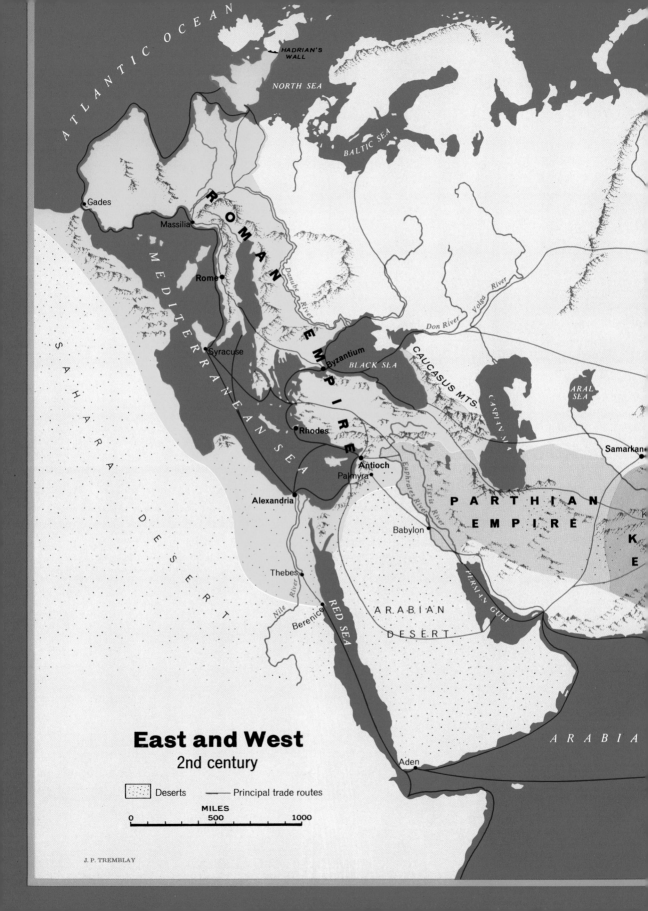

ATLANTIC OCEAN

HADRIAN'S WALL

NORTH SEA

BALTIC SEA

• Gades

• Massilia

ROMAN

Danube River

• Rome

MEDITERRANEAN SEA

SAHARA

DESERT

Volga River

Don River

• Syracuse

EMPIRE

Byzantium

BLACK SEA

CAUCASUS MTS.

CASPIAN SEA

ARAL SEA

• Rhodes

• Antioch

Palmyra

Euphrates River

Tigris River

Samarkan

PARTHIAN

• Alexandria

EMPIRE

K

E

• Babylon

PERSIAN GULF

Thebes •

Nile River

ARABIAN

DESERT

Berenice •

RED SEA

ARABIA

Aden •

East and West

2nd century

Deserts   —— Principal trade routes

MILES

0   500   1000

J. P. TREMBLAY

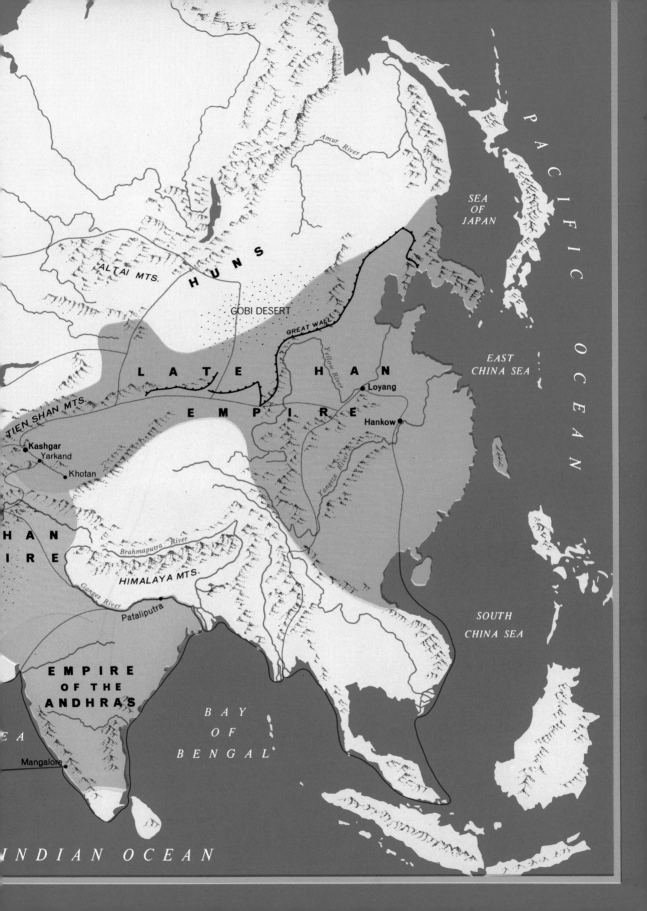

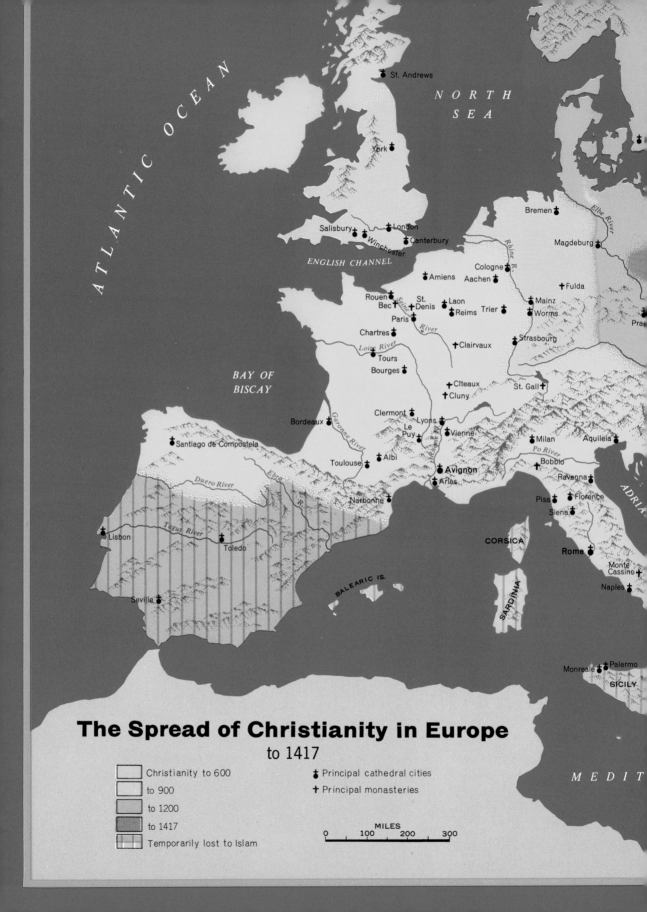

ATLANTIC OCEAN

NORTH SEA

† St. Andrews

York ⚲

Bremen ⚲

Elbe River

Magdeburg ⚲

Salisbury ⚲ ⚲ ✝ London
Winchester ⚲ Canterbury

ENGLISH CHANNEL

Cologne ⚲
Aachen ⚲
Rhine R.
† Fulda

Amiens ⚲

Rouen ⚲
Bec ✝   St.
Denis ✝   Laon ⚲
Reims ✝   Trier ✝
Mainz ⚲
Worms ⚲

Paris ⚲

Seine River

Pra⚲

Chartres ⚲
✝ Clairvaux
Strasbourg ⚲

Loire River

Tours ✝
Bourges ⚲

✝ Cîteaux
✝ Cluny
St. Gall ✝

BAY OF
BISCAY

Garonne River

Clermont ⚲
Bordeaux ⚲   Lyons ⚲
Le ⚲
Puy   Vienne ⚲

Milan ⚲
Aquileia ✝

Santiago de Compostela ⚲

Toulouse ⚲   ✝ Albi

Avignon ⚲
Arles ⚲

Po River
Bobbio ✝
Ravenna ✝

Ebro R.

Duero River

Narbonne ⚲

Pisa ⚲   ✝ Florence
Siena ✝

ADRIA

Lisbon ✝
Tagus River
Toledo ⚲

CORSICA

Rome ⚲

Seville ⚲

BALEARIC IS.

SARDINIA

Monte
Cassino ✝

Naples ✝

MEDIT

Monreale ⚲   ✝ Palermo

SICILY

The Spread of Christianity in Europe
to 1417

▢ Christianity to 600	⚲ Principal cathedral cities
▢ to 900	✝ Principal monasteries
▢ to 1200	
▢ to 1417	
▢ Temporarily lost to Islam	

MILES
0   100   200   300

BALTIC SEA

Novgorod

Moscow

Gnesen

Vistula River

Volga River

Kiev

ROMAN CHURCH
GREEK CHURCH

Cracow

Dnieper River

Don River

enna

Gran

Danube River

BLACK SEA

Tigris River

Constantinople

Thessalonica

AEGEAN
SEA

Euphrates River

CYPRUS

CRETE

ANEAN SEA

Nile R.

J. P. TREMBLAY

European Civilization

15th century

AREAS OF WARFARE

- Fall of Granada, 1492
- Wars of the Roses, 1454-85
- Hussite Wars, 1420-36
- Hundred Years' War, 1338-1453

▲ Members of the Hanseatic League
═══ Principal trade routes

MILES

0   100   200   300

NORWAY

ATLANTIC OCEAN

SCOTLAND
Edinburgh

NORTH SEA

DENMARK

IRELAND
Dublin

ENGLAND

Oxford   Cambridge

London

ENGLISH CHANNEL

Hamburg
Lübeck
Bremen
Brunswick
Magdeburg
Elbe River

Leiden
Rotterdam
Bruges
Ghent
Brussels
Antwerp
Louvain
Cologne
Erfurt
Leipzig
HOLY RO
Prague
Trier
Mainz
Noyon
Paris
Nuremberg
Regensbu
EMPIRE

FRANCE

Fontainebleau
Loire River
Tours

BAY OF BISCAY

Bordeaux

Angoulême

Dijon
BURGUNDY
Basel
Augsburg
Zurich
Constance
Lyons
Geneva
Trent

Milan
Po River
Venice
Ferrara
Bologna
ADR

Avignon
Genoa
PAPAL STATES

Marseilles
Pisa
Florence
Siena
Perugia

PORTUGAL
Lisbon

Duero River
CASTILE
Escorial
Madrid
Tagus River
Ebro
NAVARRE
ARAGON
Barcelona

Seville
GRANADA

CORSICA

SARDINIA
(ARAGON)

Rome

Palermo
SICILY
(ARAGON)

MEDI

BALTIC SEA

Novgorod

Moscow

Königsberg

Danzig

Thorn

Vistula River

Volga River

POLAND – LITHUANIA

Kiev

River

Cracow

Dnieper River

Don River

nna

Buda

H U N G A R Y

Danube River

BLACK SEA

O
T
T
O
M
A
N

Constantinople

Salonika

*AEGEAN
SEA*

E
M
P
I
R
E

Tigris River

Euphrates River

RHODES

CYPRUS

CRETE

ANEAN SEA

Nile R.

J. P. TREMBLAY

PACIFIC OCEAN

ARCTIC
OCEAN

Deshnev, 1648

STANOVOI

NORTH AMERICA

ROCKY MTS.

North Pole

HUDSON
BAY

River

Mississippi

GREENLAND

URAL

GULF OF
MEXICO

Jamestown,
1607

Plymouth,
1620

St. Lawrence R.

Quebec, 1609

New Amsterdam, 1625

NEWFOUNDLAND

ENGLAND

NETH.

EUROPE

Jamaica,
1655

WEST INDIES

CARIBBEAN
SEA

FRANCE

Danube R.

BLACK
SEA

Curaçao

PORTUGAL

SPAIN

MEDITERRANEAN SEA

Guadeloupe, 1635

Martinique, 1635

Barbados, 1624

ATLANTIC OCEAN

Nile River

SOUTH AMERICA

Amazon River

Niger River

AFRICA

ANDES MTS.

Congo River

Colonization 17th century

JAPAN

PACIFIC OCEAN

EAST CHINA SEA

Amur River

Lake Baikal

River

Yeniseisk, 1618

C H I N A

Yellow River

Yangtze River

otsk, 48

S I A

A R A L SEA

SPIAN SEA

Brahmaputra

HIMALAYA Mts.

Ganges R.

Indian River

I N D I A

Calcutta, 1690, 1700

SOUTH CHINA SEA

PHILIPPINE IS.

S P I C E I S. (MOLUCCAS)
AMBOINA

E A S T I N D I E S

BAY OF BENGAL

JAVA

AUSTRALIA

Madras, 1639
Pondicherry, 1674

Bombay, 1661, 1665

ARABIAN SEA

INDIAN OCEAN

J. P. TREMBLAY

The Westward Expansion of the United States 1776-1853

ROCKY

BRITISH

CEDED TO GREAT BRITAIN 1818

CESSION B' GREAT BRITA 1818

OREGON TERRITORY 1846

Columbia River

ROUTE OF THE FORTY-NINERS

SOUTH PASS

OREGON TRAIL

Missouri River

SIERRA NEVADA MTS.

Great Salt Lake

Salt Lake City

Carson City

Sutter's Mill
Sacramento

San Francisco

MEXICAN CESSION, 1848

• Cheyenne

Platte River

LOUISIANA PURCHASE, 1803

SANTA FE T

P A C I F I C   O C E A N

Colorado River

GADSDEN PURCHASE, 1853

• Santa Fe

ANNEXATION OF TEXAS, 1845

GULF OF CALIFORNIA

M E X I C O

Rio Grande

Alamo, 1836

Palo Alto, 1846

Resaca de la Palma, 1846

Monterrey, 1836

Buena Vista, 1847

MOUNTAINS

The Westward Expansion of the United States 1776-1853

- - - - - Stagecoach lines   ⊥⊥⊥ Canals   +++ Railroads   • Centers of population

Deserts

■ Forts

MILES

0   100   200   300

NORTH AMERICA

LAKE SUPERIOR

Northwest Territory

LAKE MICHIGAN

LAKE HURON

Battle of Lake Erie 1813

Detroit

Toledo

Chicago

Cleveland

LAKE ERIE

L. ONTARIO

Lundy's Lane, 1814
Chippewa, 1814

Buffalo

Plattsburg, 1814

VT. N.H.

NEW YORK

Albany

MASSACHUSETTS

Boston

CONN. RHODE ISLAND

New Haven

New York

Newark

Trenton

NEW JERSEY

Philadelphia

DEL.

PENNSYLVANIA

Harrisburg

1800
1810
1820

1790

Baltimore

MD.

Washington, 1814

Springfield

CUMBERLAND ROAD

Indianapolis

Columbus

1840

1830

1850

Washington

Richmond

VIRGINIA

Ohio River

St. Louis

Kansas City

WESTWARD EXPANSION TO 1783

APPALACHIAN MTS.

NORTH CAROLINA

Mississippi River

Memphis

SOUTH CAROLINA

Atlanta

Charleston

GEORGIA

Savannah

Mississippi Territory

FLORIDA PURCHASE, 1819

New Orleans, 1815

New Orleans

Galveston

GULF OF MEXICO

ATLANTIC OCEAN

St. Lawrence River

J. P. TREMBLAY

Napoleonic Europe 1812

- Napoleonic Empire
- States under French control
- States allied to France
- → Routes of Napoleon

MILES
0   100   200   300

BALTIC SEA

Tilsit

3DOM Friedland
PRUSSIA

DUCHY

6 - 07

OF

WARSAW

Vistula River

Austerlitz

Wagram

Vienna

STRIAN EMPIRE

BESSARABIA

Danube River

Moscow

Borodino

1812

RUSSIAN EMPIRE

Volga River

Dnieper River

Don River

BLACK SEA

OTTOMAN EMPIRE

Tigris River

Euphrates River

AEGEAN
SEA

NCES

1798

ANEAN SEA

1799

Abukir Bay

Nile R.

J. P. TREMBLAY

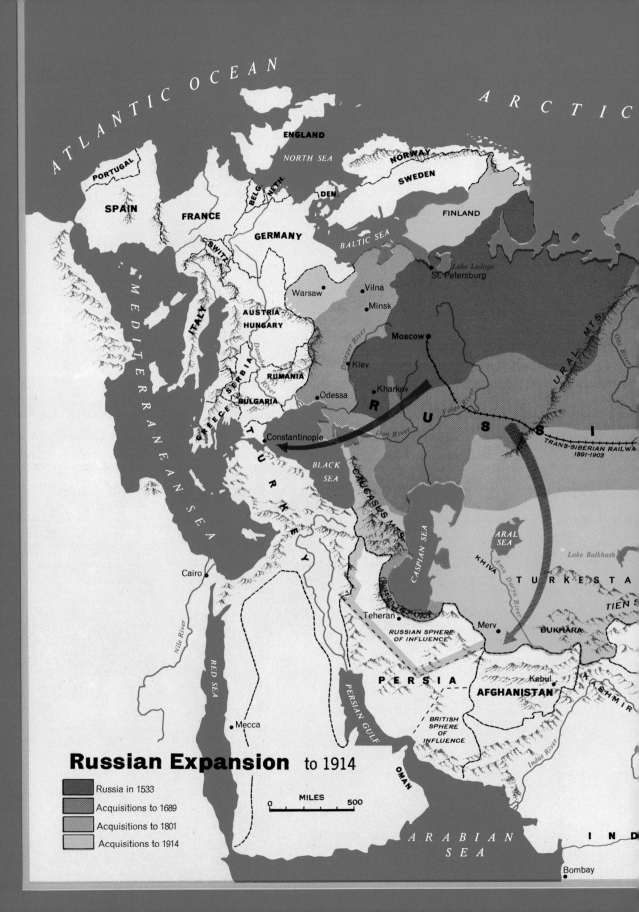

Russian Expansion to 1914

ATLANTIC OCEAN

ARCTIC

NORTH SEA

ENGLAND

PORTUGAL

NORWAY

SWEDEN

SPAIN

FRANCE

BELG. NETH.

DEN.

GERMANY

FINLAND

SWITZ.

BALTIC SEA

Lake Ladoga

St. Petersburg

Warsaw

Vilna

Minsk

ITALY

AUSTRIA
HUNGARY

Dnieper River

Moscow

URAL MTS.

Ob River

Kiev

MEDITERRANEAN SEA

SERBIA

RUMANIA

Danube River

Kharkov

R   U   S   S   I

Odessa

BULGARIA

GREECE

Volga River

TRANS-SIBERIAN RAILWAY
1891-1903

Constantinople

Don River

TURKEY

BLACK SEA

CAUCASUS MTS.

CASPIAN SEA

ARAL SEA

Lake Balkhash

KHIVA

Amu Darya River

TURKESTAN

TIEN S

Cairo

RUSSIAN SPHERE
OF INFLUENCE

Teheran

RUSSIA 1921

Merv

BUKHARA

Nile River

RED SEA

PERSIA

Kabul

KASHMIR

AFGHANISTAN

PERSIAN GULF

Mecca

BRITISH
SPHERE
OF
INFLUENCE

Indus River

OMAN

IND

ARABIAN SEA

Bombay

Russian Expansion to 1914

- Russia in 1533
- Acquisitions to 1689
- Acquisitions to 1801
- Acquisitions to 1914

MILES

0   500

ALASKA
(Russian, 1787?- 1867)

BERING SEA

O C E A N

P A C I F I C

OKHOTSK SEA

N   E M P I R E

SAKHALIN

Russian,
(1875-1905)

KURILE IS.
(Russian, 1711-1875)

Amur River

Lake
Baykal

MANCHURIA

ALTAI MTS.

Vladivostok

RUSSIAN SPHERE OF INFLUENCE

OUTER MONGOLIA

SEA
OF
JAPAN

J A P A N

Tokyo

KOREA

Seoul

Peking

Port Arthur
(Russian, 1898-1905)

Yellow River

C H I N A

EAST
CHINA SEA

Shanghai

Yangtze River

Brahmaputra

River

O C E A N

LAYA
AL

MOUNTAINS

BHUTAN

Mekong River

ges River

Calcutta

BURMA

SIAM

FRENCH
INDO-CHINA

Hong Kong

SOUTH
CHINA SEA

J. P. TREMBLAY

BAY OF
BENGAL

World Population

Distribution

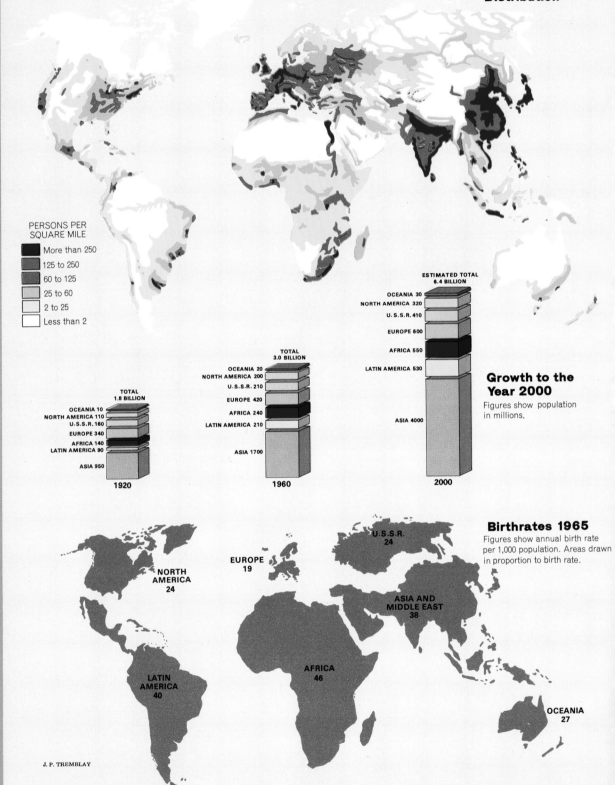

PERSONS PER
SQUARE MILE

- More than 250
- 125 to 250
- 60 to 125
- 25 to 60
- 2 to 25
- Less than 2

**ESTIMATED TOTAL
6.4 BILLION**

OCEANIA 30
NORTH AMERICA 320
U.S.S.R. 410
EUROPE 600
AFRICA 550
LATIN AMERICA 530
ASIA 4000

2000

Growth to the Year 2000

Figures show population in millions.

**TOTAL
3.0 BILLION**

OCEANIA 20
NORTH AMERICA 200
U.S.S.R. 210
EUROPE 420
AFRICA 240
LATIN AMERICA 210
ASIA 1700

1960

**TOTAL
1.8 BILLION**

OCEANIA 10
NORTH AMERICA 110
U.S.S.R. 160
EUROPE 340
AFRICA 140
LATIN AMERICA 90
ASIA 950

1920

Birthrates 1965

Figures show annual birth rate per 1,000 population. Areas drawn in proportion to birth rate.

U.S.S.R. 24
EUROPE 19
NORTH AMERICA 24
ASIA AND MIDDLE EAST 38
LATIN AMERICA 40
AFRICA 46
OCEANIA 27

J. P. TREMBLAY

WESTERN CIVILIZATION SINCE 1500

Prologue

Three words appear repeatedly in this book that look simple and are actually very difficult to define. They are "civilization," "western," and "modern." It is easy enough to use them; it is not so easy to say what they mean. What is civilization? When and how did a distinct type of civilization—western civilization—develop in Europe? And when did this western civilization begin to manifest traits that we call "modern"?

Every group of scholars that is interested in man and society gives a different meaning to the word "civilization". Even historians are by no means in full agreement, though during the last century a good many of them have reached a consensus. When they speak of a civilization, they mean a society in which there is some degree of economic and political organization, some measure of occupational specialization, and a set of beliefs or values that is accepted by most members of the society. Organization, specialization, and common beliefs in turn generate a distinct pattern of living that can be recognized, despite frequent change, over long periods of time.

Organization in its simplest form provides security against external and internal enemies, some control of the environment (for example, irrigation, community building, or collective agricultural operations), and some reasonably

The remains of Mycenae, an ancient Peloponnesian city first excavated in 1876–77. Mycenae represented an example of the earliest stage of true Greek civilization from 1600–1100 B.C.

stable means of exchanging products. Without this minimum degree of organization each family or small group of families has to strive for self-sufficiency and so is doomed to live at a bare subsistence level. No one will stop procuring his own food and spend his time making cloth unless he has some assurance that he can exchange that cloth—safely and regularly—for food. And if everyone has to give over his days to hunting animals or collecting grain, then no one is likely to become a very good cloth-maker. Conversely, as soon as a group of people has attained an acceptable level of security and has set up regular procedures for exchanging goods, then individual members of the group can develop specialized skills. Effective organization, even in a small community, can stimulate a high degree of specialization. A few thousand Greeks working together in a city-state managed to produce or acquire almost every object they wanted in the entire Mediterranean world, in spite of the poverty of their soil and their lack of other natural resources. A few thousand North American Indians divided into small, wandering bands barely managed to survive, though they lived in a much richer country.

Organization requires a certain amount of cooperation from the people who make up the community. Cooperation is not achieved by coldly rational appeals to self-interest, nor can it be maintained simply through threats and punishments. If, however, men share common beliefs, they are likely to cooperate in carrying out the tasks of their society. So long as a group believes that it is working toward generally accepted goals through forms of organization that seem right and proper, it will attain at least some of its objectives and it will survive as a group. Once a group, or some members of a group, loses this assurance, either an altered set of beliefs or a restructured society will emerge. One of the problems faced by every civilization is how to maintain common beliefs and common values in the face of technical, economic, and social change. Internal decay, resulting from a loss of common beliefs and values, is the real destroyer of civilizations; external attack usually knocks over only empty shells.

The Ancient Middle East

We find the earliest examples of organization, specialization, and cooperation based on common beliefs in the city-states of the great river valleys of Eurasia—first in the Tigris-Euphrates valleys of Mesopotamia, next in the Nile valley of Egypt and the Indus River valley of India, and last in the Yellow River valley of China. "City-state" is too grandiose a term for the earliest settlements; they were hardly more than big villages. But the emergence of the village itself marks an important stage in organization and specialization; it was the product of a social and economic revolution that took place at the end of the Stone Age, about 7000 B.C. When men began to grow their food in cleared fields instead of relying on hunting and food-gathering, when they settled in one place rather than roaming over a wide area, when they built permanent homes instead of throwing up temporary shelters, they experienced a more pressing need for organization and richer opportunities for specialization. A sedentary population is more vulnerable to external attacks and suffers more from internal disputes than a migratory population. It cannot solve its problems simply by

moving away from an exposed site or by splitting up into smaller groups. The members of a village using primitive agricultural techniques have to cooperate in clearing and planting fields, herding animals, and controlling the water supply. At the same time the existence of a settled community means that there is a permanent market in which specialized craftsmen can produce and exchange goods. Even in the very earliest settlements we find a differentiation of social, economic, and political roles. There is a governing group, a priestly group, a merchant group, an artisan group, and an agricultural group. One man may of course play several roles—ruler and priest, or priest and businessman—but the differentiation in roles is already well advanced.

The big villages grew into cities, and the cities into states. The influence of an urban center spread farther and farther into the countryside until it touched the area dominated by another urban center. The frictions that developed when two spheres of influence met often led to war, and a series of wars in turn sometimes resulted in the establishment of a fairly large kingdom. War itself was likely to speed up the development of political institutions, and the creation of a kingdom required an elaboration of all forms of organization. The creation of a kingdom also required a conscious attempt to build up common beliefs and loyalties. The victors might, for example, substitute their gods for the gods of the defeated, or they might simply subordinate the gods of the defeated to the greater gods (who had proved their greatness by giving victory), or the victors and the vanquished might decide that they had been worshiping the same gods under different names. A good deal of local variation was tolerated, so long as special respect was paid to the ruler's god, or to the ruler as an embodiment of that god.

4

We cannot, in this brief introduction, trace the long history of the kingdoms that grew up in India and in China. China, for some time, had few contacts with the rest of the world. India was in fairly close touch with Mesopotamia; but while Indian ideas reached the countries to the west, they were absorbed into existing patterns of thought and did not persist as a separate cultural tradition. On the other hand, the kingdom of Egypt and the various kingdoms and empires that succeeded one another in the Mesopotamian area laid the foundation for the ancient Mediterranean civilization out of which western civilization was to grow. And just as important as Egypt and Mesopotamia were the border states that grew up in Asia Minor and Persia, and in the contested lands that lay between Egypt and the successive masters of the Tigris-Euphrates area. The Hebrews and the Phoenicians are the best known of these border peoples, and when we remember that the Phoenicians invented (or at least perfected) the alphabet and that the Jewish tradition lies at the root of two great world religions, we see what significant contributions could be made by even the smaller communities of the Middle East.

There were some striking differences among the peoples of the ancient Middle East. The king of Egypt was a god, owner of the whole country, master of all its inhabitants. The Mesopotamian kings were only servants of the gods, and their subjects had full rights over their own property and considerable freedom of action. Egypt built in stone, Mesopotamia in brick. The chief agricultural problem in the Nile valley was irrigation; the chief problem in Mesopotamia was drainage. There are dozens of other examples, but behind the diversity was a degree of uniformity. With a very few exceptions, all the societies of the Middle East were agricultural

The Ancient Near East

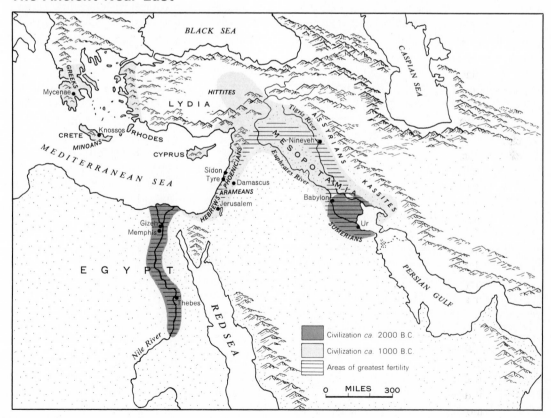

societies. A vast number of agricultural workers supported a much smaller population of artisans and traders, and an even smaller elite of priests, bureaucrats, nobles, and members of the royal family. No one family of agricultural workers could produce much of a surplus, but the surplus from the labors of many thousands of workers could be funneled into very narrow channels and used to produce great works of art for gods and kings, and a luxurious level of living for the upper classes. The surplus could also be used to finance wars, and every kingdom—even the little kingdom of the Hebrews—went through a phase of empire-building. Through war, through migration, and through trade there was a considerable amount of mixing of peoples and an extensive exchange of ideas and techniques. In fact, the real problem is not to explain the uniformity of the social structure or the diffusion of ideas, but rather to explain why a few ideas did not spread very far. Every Middle Eastern society had invented or borrowed the technique of writing; yet only a small number of the border peoples accepted the immense improvement in writing made possible by the invention of the alphabet. Many peoples, notably the Egyptians, were intensely interested in religion, yet none of them adopted the rigid monotheism of the Jews. But such cases were rare, and their rarity simply demonstrates that there was a common fund of experience and knowledge in the ancient Middle East that could be drawn on by all the peoples of the area.

This fund of experience and knowledge was rich and varied. By the end of the second millennium B.C., political organization had reached a stage where vast areas and hundreds of thousands of people could be governed from a single center, where power could be safely delegated to provincial administrators, where large armies could be raised and kept in the field year after year. Economic organization had produced not only a host of local traders and specialized artisans but a class of merchants who traveled thousands of miles every year. Masterpieces of architecture, sculpture, and painting had been produced and some religious writers had expressed ideas that are still significant. Some knowledge of astronomy, arithmetic, and geometry had been acquired. In short, by 1000 B.C. the ancient Middle East had achieved a level of civilization that many parts of the world would not surpass for centuries.

The Greeks

On the western edge of this Middle Eastern civilization lived the Greeks. They were almost certainly invaders from the north who had settled in the Greek peninsula, the Aegean islands, and the coast of Asia Minor about 2000 B.C. The physical features of the area, in which small patches of fertile land are cut off from one another by rocky hills and barren mountains, encouraged the establishment of many small kingdoms. Each king had a fortified palace or town from which he could protect the farmers in his district. The invasions continued for many centuries and the first settlers naturally viewed the successive newcomers with hostility. Persistent warfare strengthened the tendency toward political fragmentation. The Greeks were never able to unite; they clung to their separate states until Alexander the Great forced them to become part of a Mediterranean empire.

Geography had another effect on Greek life: it almost forced the Greeks to become a maritime people. Every path led toward the sea; almost every Greek grew up with the smell of salt water in his nostrils. Inland one could make only a bare living from the thin soil, but overseas were rich countries that could provide cheap food and attractive luxuries. Soon after the first invasions, certainly by 1700 B.C., we hear of Greek sailors in the Aegean seeking unoccupied land, trading with wealthy neighbors, sacking enemy towns. The early Greek traders had many competitors and few commodities to offer in foreign markets, but in the long run they managed to dominate the commerce of the eastern Mediterranean. Greek colonies along the coasts of Thrace, the Black Sea, and southern Italy supplied grain to the older settlements. As a result, the farmers of the homeland could concentrate on raising grapes and olive trees that

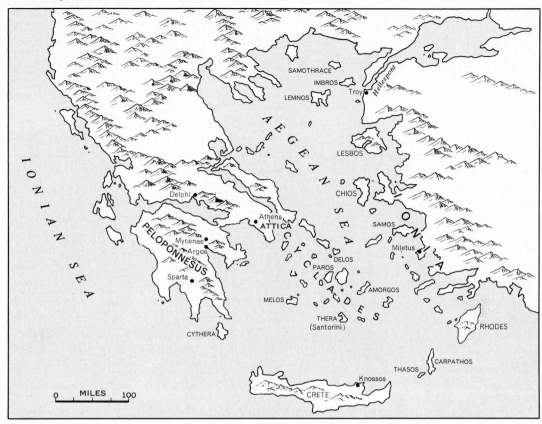

flourished on the hillsides where grain would never grow. Exports of wine, olive oil, pottery, and metal work, together with shipping and middlemen's profits, produced a favorable balance of trade. It took a long while to work out this trading system, but even in the second millennium B.C. the Greeks were clearly trying to build up their commerce, and by the eighth century B.C. they had become the most successful merchants of the Mediterranean.

Finally, geography put the Greeks into close contact with some of the most advanced peoples of the Middle East. At the time of the first Greek settlements, a remarkable civilization was flourishing on the island of Crete. Called Minoan, after a legendary King Minos, this civilization had been influenced by all the peoples of the Middle East, and especially by Egypt. But the

Minoans had added a quality of grace and elegance that was all their own. Instead of the heavy, massive buildings and statues of Egypt that dwarfed the observer, the Minoan style was restrained, sensitive, proportioned to the human body. The Minoans may have passed these qualities on the Greeks; certainly they influenced the Greeks in many ways. Even more than the Greeks, the Minoans had to be a maritime people. Their ships frequented the Aegean; they traded with the Greeks; they may even have established a sort of overlordship over some of the little Greek kingdoms. Later (about 1480 B.C.) a great disaster struck Crete, perhaps a terrific volcanic explosion. The people who rebuilt the ruined palaces and cities wrote a primitive form of Greek, which would suggest that roles had been reversed and that the Greeks were

Minoan Civilization on Crete			"Dark Ages"	Dominance of City-states of Asia Minor	Dominance of Athens and Sparta		Hellenistic Era
Arrival of Greeks	Mycenaean Civilization in Aegean Area						

Decline of
City-state System and
Conquest by Macedon

now lords of Crete. In any case, the earliest form of Greek civilization—the Myceanean—had many affinities with the Minoan civilization.

The Greeks who settled along the western coast of Asia Minor also learned from their immediate neighbors. Asia Minor was fully integrated into the ancient Middle Eastern civilization, and it was from this region that the Greeks acquired some of their earliest ideas about astronomy, mathematics, and philosophy. They also learned the use of coined money, a notable invention made about 700 B.C. in a kingdom of Asia Minor. Using coins instead of weighing out chunks of precious metals made trade easier, an advantage that the mercantile-minded Greeks appreciated.

The peak of the influence of Asia Minor on the Greeks came centuries after the peak of Minoan influence. In between lies a dark period during which the Greeks almost vanish from view, probably because new invasions from the north had shattered the old Mycenaean society. When the Greeks reappear, they are still divided into small kingdoms built around a fortified town; they are still bothered by their agricultural problems; and they are still trying to expand their overseas trade. Two new—or if not new, greatly strengthened—traits appear: an insatiable curiosity about everything in the world and a willingness to try out new ideas and new forms of organization.

The Greeks seem to have realized that small states could survive in a world of large states only by making the fullest use of their human resources. Under a monarchical or aristocratic government, most citizens were barred from the political process and hence were unable to devote their full energies to the common welfare. So there was a trend toward democracy, a system in which more men could hold responsible positions in the army and in government. In

Athens by the fifth century B.C. every citizen could vote and hold office. Slaves and natives of other cities (perhaps half the population) were still excluded, but Athens and Greek city-states like Athens provided more political freedom than any other contemporary government.

Curiosity, and the stimulation of individual talents through the responsibilities and opportunities offered to all free citizens, encouraged men to speculate about social and natural phenomena. The Greeks argued and wrote about politics and ethics, about philosophy and poetry, about mathematics and science. They tried to find out first principles and general laws that could be applied universally. They borrowed many of their facts from other peoples, but they had an ability to generalize that their predecessors had lacked. Their one weakness was to rely too much on logical reasoning—formal logic was a Greek invention—and to generalize too rapidly on the basis of incomplete evidence. A good example of the Greek mind at work is Euclid's geometry (c. 300 B.C.). Many of his propositions had been known before (for example, the square on the hypotenuse) but had never been properly proved nor fitted into a coherent, consistent, logical system. Yet Euclid's whole system rests on axioms, truths that he thought were so self-evident that they needed no proof. In philosophy, Plato's emphasis on the importance of abstract ideas and Aristotle's theory of development through impressing form on matter were brilliant intuitions that were to lead to centuries of discussion, but they were based on logical argument rather than on observation.

The free Greek spirit also expressed itself in art and in literature. Man is always the measure, but man at the height of his powers. Temples are built to a human scale; the gods are glorified human beings just as heroic men are demigods. Drama deals with the fate of man in an

Athens, the Acropolis.

unfriendly world, and especially with the fate of men who lack moderation and a sense of the fitness of things. History—again an area where the Greeks improved greatly on earlier work—deals with the triumphs and failures of individuals.

There was a darker side to the Greek character, a side that expressed itself in the frenzies of secret religious rites and in the violence of Greek political life. One reason why the Greeks stressed rationality, moderation, and a sense of proportion was that they were painfully aware

that they were often emotional, overly ambitious, and wildly partisan. The Greek city-states were never able to work together, even when their very existence was threatened. The Persian Empire, the last of the great Middle Eastern monarchies, very nearly overran the Greek world in the fifth century B.C. because the Greek cities fought individually instead of under a common command. The elation that followed the defeat of Persia may have encouraged Greek artists and writers to produce their masterpieces; it certainly led politicians to incredible excesses. Athens and

Sparta, the two states that had done most to defeat Persia, began playing crude power politics in an attempt to gain the leadership of Greece. Athens tried to build a maritime empire; Sparta countered by forming an alliance system on the mainland. The long and bitter Peloponnesian war that followed (431–404 B.C.) left the Greeks so exhausted that they could not resist the next threat to their independence.

That threat came from Macedon, a half-Greek kingdom that lay to the north of the Aegean. Philip of Macedon defeated a badly organized Greek alliance in 338 B.C. Philip's son, Alexander the Great (336–323 B.C.), permitted the Greeks a large measure of local autonomy but made it clear that they were expected to cooperate in building up an eastern empire. Since he succeeded in conquering all the ancient Middle East (Asia Minor, Syria, Egypt, Mesopotamia, Persia) plus western India, the Greeks had plenty of chances to cooperate.

Alexander had no respect for Greek politicians, but he had great respect for Greek culture. All through his vast empire he built new cities on the Greek model (such as Alexandria in Egypt) or installed Greeks or Hellenized* natives as the rulers of old cities. Greek became the language of the upper classes; Greek art and literature furnished the models for artists and writers. True, Greek culture never spread beyond the large cities, and even there the Greek veneer was sometimes very thin. Yet the Greeks left an indelible mark on a large part of the ancient world. Alexander's early death made little difference; the generals who divided his empire continued his policy of Hellenization. For almost a thousand years the ruling group and the literate classes of the Middle East followed a tradition that was largely Greek. One example of this pervasive Greek influence will suffice: Although Jesus almost surely spoke Aramaic and certainly did not speak Greek, the New Testament was written in Greek.

Actually, the political collapse of Greece during and after the war between Athens and Sparta was not quite so disastrous as it is sometimes said to have been. Plato wrote after the defeat of Athens; Aristotle was the tutor of Alexander. Euclid composed his geometry about 300 B.C. The greatest achievements of Greek science, such as the measurement of the circumference of the earth or the hypothesis that the earth moved around the sun, came in Alexandria during the Hellenistic period. The Greeks had lost none of their ingenuity, though they had lost the self-confidence that came from being free citizens of free cities. The philosophies that they developed during the Hellenistic period emphasized withdrawal from the world, the simple life, the search for internal harmony. The most suc-

Pericles on Athens and Sparta

This oration, inserted by the Greek historian Thucydides in his *History of the Peloponnesian War* does not give Pericles' exact words, but it does express admirably the pride of the Athenians in their city and its form of government.

We are called a democracy, for the administration is in the hands of the many and not of the few. But . . . the claim of excellence is also recognized, and when a citizen is in any way distinguished, he is preferred to the public service, not as a matter of privilege, but as the reward of merit. . . . Our city is thrown open to the world, and we never expel a foreigner or prevent him from seeing or learning anything of which the secret, if revealed to an enemy, might profit him. . . . In the matter of education, whereas the Spartans from early youth are always undergoing laborious exercises which are to make them brave, we live at ease, and yet are equally ready to face the perils which they face. . . . For we are lovers of the beautiful, yet simple in our tastes, and we cultivate the mind without loss of manliness. . . . Such is the city for whose sake these men fought and died; . . . and every one of us who survive should gladly toil on her behalf.

From Pericles' Funeral Oration, in Thucydides, *The History of the Peloponnesian War,* trans. by B. Jowett in Francis R. B. Godolphin, ed., *The Greek Historians* (New York: Random House, 1942), Vol. I, pp. 648–50.

---

*The Greeks called themselves Hellenes (as they still do). Alexander tried to Hellenize (make Greek) his empire. The period following Alexander's conquests is known as the Hellenistic Age.

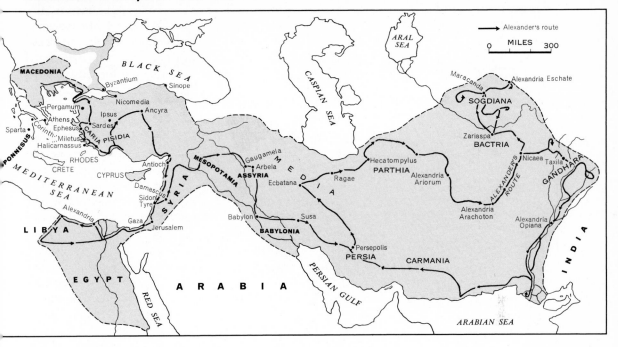

Alexander's Empire 336–323 B.C.

cessful of these philosophies—Stoicism—did teach that men should perform public functions when duty called them, but the Stoics also believed that no one should seek public office and that a private citizen could lead a better life than a statesman. On the other hand, a sense of the insignificance of the private citizen in a great empire made the Greeks less arrogant and more tolerant of other peoples than they had been. Hellenistic philosophy emphasized the brotherhood of all men and the existence of a universal law. All these ideas—withdrawal from the world, self-control, a sense of duty, the equality of all men under a single law—passed from the Hellenistic philosophers to the new lords of the Mediterranean world, the Romans.

The Romans

The Romans were one of various Italic peoples, closely related to the Greeks, who had settled in the Italian peninsula during the second millen-

nium B.C. They had more good land than the Greeks, fewer good harbors, and no chain of islands to lure them out to sea. Rome and its neighboring communities remained agricultural while the Greeks were building their commercial empire. But Rome was surrounded by enemies, and the Romans learned almost as early as the Greeks that a small community could survive in a hostile world only if it could get the whole-hearted support of all its inhabitants. The Romans learned this lesson even better than the Greeks. Not only did they eventually give the right to vote and to hold office to all free Romans; they also extended Roman citizenship to residents of their military colonies and to some of their allies. Conquered cities were allowed to keep their own autonomous governments so long as they helped Rome in time of war. Thus Rome was able to extend its authority over the Italian peninsula and to draw a large, well-disciplined army from the growing population of free Roman citizens and free citizens of allied cities.

The test of this system came when the expanding Roman state moved into the sphere of influence of an expanding North African state—Carthage. Carthage was a Phoenician settlement that had become far more powerful than the mother country itself; it controlled what is now Tunisia, much of Sicily, and the eastern part of Spain. Rome defeated Carthage in two long and perilous wars (264–241 and 218–202 B.C.), largely because Rome could always raise one more army, while Carthage, even though it won many victories, eventually exhausted its resources. With the collapse of Carthage, Rome became master of the western Mediterranean. But it was hard for the dominant power in the West to avoid friction with the states of the East. One by one, Rome defeated the kingdoms that had grown out of Alexander's empire. Macedon, Greece, Asia Minor, Syria, and, last of all, Egypt came under Roman rule. Meanwhile Julius Caesar completed the process of subduing all the countries bordering on the Mediterranean by conquering Gaul (France) in a series of campaigns that lasted from 59 to 52 B.C. Britain and a small part of western Germany were added latter, but the basic work of building a Roman Mediterranean empire had all been accomplished before the birth of Christ.

The structure of the Roman state was severely strained by the annexations that followed the defeat of Carthage and the eastern kingdoms. Rome continued to be generous with grants of Roman citizenship, but most citizens lived far from Rome. Since the Roman constitution was still that of a city-state, power theoretically lay in the hands of assemblies of all citizens. But since Rome never developed the idea of representation, power actually lay in the hands of the inhabitants of the city of Rome. A citizen who could not get to Rome could not vote. The populace of Rome was not well informed and was easily swayed by cheap oratory, bribes, and threats of force. For some generations it followed the lead of the Senate, an assembly of rich landholders, heads of patrician families, and ex-officials. Most office-holders and generals were selected from senatorial families and took their seats in the Senate when their terms had expired. The leaders of the Senate were ruthless and selfish men who made fortunes out of provincial governorships and army commands. So long as the most prominent senators remained more or less united, they were able to preserve a fair degree of stability. After 100 B.C., however, they began to quarrel more and more openly over the spoils of office. Each faction sought the support of the Roman voters. Elections became so corrupt and tumultuous that eventually they could not be held at all. Riots in the city became civil wars that spread throughout the state. Just at the moment when Rome was completing the task of uniting the Mediterranean world, rival military commanders threatened to destroy that unity.

In the end, however, one general became supreme. The Gallic wars had given Julius Caesar great personal prestige and control over an army of veterans. He used these assets to eliminate his rivals and to begin the rebuilding of the Roman government. His assassination (44 B.C.) put an end to those efforts and triggered a new round of civil wars. But Caesar's grandnephew and heir, Octavian, succeeded, after years of intrigue and battle, in destroying all his opponents. By 27 B.C. he was in full control of the Roman world. As the restorer of peace and prosperity, he was hailed by the Senate as Augustus (the revered, the majestic one). And as Augustus he became the first Roman emperor.

Augustus' power rested on his command of the army (emperor is merely the English form of the Latin *imperator,* commander-in-chief) and on his position as First Citizen (less politely, boss) in the Roman political structure. But the early Empire was far from being a monolithic despotism. Popular assemblies soon withered away, but the Senate retained a good deal of its political influence and continued to administer some of the more peaceful provinces. Neither Augustus nor his immediate successors had a bureaucracy large enough to rule all parts of the Empire directly. The emperor was there to keep the peace and to intervene where trouble seemed to be looming, but not to take over local administration.

In the old Roman fashion, most of the work of government was done by allied or subject city-states, with only general supervision by imperial authorities. Where city-states did not exist, as in parts of Gaul and Spain, they were created by Roman governors. This division of the West into city-states was one of the most important results of Rome's conquest of the Mediterranean world. Through the city-state the culture of Rome and of Greece flowed into less developed areas. Because the business of a city-state had to be conducted in Latin and according to Roman forms, knowledge of Latin and of Roman laws and institutions began to spread throughout non-Roman populations. The lasting influence of Rome on western Europe was not due to authoritarian controls; it was due to the fact that it was to everyone's advantage to learn Roman ways.

The East was another matter. Here was an older civilization that felt culturally superior to Rome, however weak it might be militarily. There could be no Latinization of the East, but for several centuries there was a fruitful interchange of ideas between the Greek-speaking and Latin-speaking halves of the Empire. In the East as in the West, Roman law and administrative techniques made a strong impression. In return, the West took from the East literary and artistic standards, and a wide assortment of philosophies and religions. There was one important omission in the exchange of ideas: The Latin part of the Empire never showed much interest in Greek science. But on the whole, by the end of the first century A.D. the organization of society and the ways of living and thinking were much the same throughout the Mediterranean world. A Roman citizen was as much at home in Beirut or Alexandria as he was in Marseilles or Naples.

Religious writers have said for many centuries that Jesus chose to be born in the reign of Augustus because then, for the first time, the civilized world was at peace and was so well unified that it was ready to receive the new revelation. Certainly the Roman Empire had created a home for and a need for Christianity. Jesus lived and died among the Jews, but his message quickly reached the Greek-speaking peoples of the East and took only a little longer to become known in Italy and Gaul. Paul's letters take us right around the Mediterranean coast—Galatians, Ephesians (Asia Minor), Philippians, Thessalonians (Macedonia), Corinthians (Greece), and finally Romans. As for the need, both Greeks and Romans had long been dissatisfied with their old religions and had grown increasingly unhappy as the individual became lost in the vast multitudes of the Empire.

Philosophies such as Stoicism could help a few men—in fact, Stoicism became almost an official creed for the Roman governing class—but Stoicism was too cold and rational for most people. For those who wanted more assurance that the individual was significant and that the world was meaningful, there were the mystery religions, cults in which a god sacrificed himself for his people and through his own resurrection assured the salvation and his followers. While the mystery religions offered consolation to many, they offended thoughtful and fastidious men. They bore traces of dark origins—magical incantations and animal sacrifices—and they had polytheistic tendencies. A very fearful man might belong to two or three cults at the same time; he might worship Isis and Osiris in Egypt, and the Great Mother in Asia Minor.

Christianity grew out of the pure monotheism of the Jews; it rejected all other religions and showed its confidence in the truth of its message by its intolerance. For the poor and the humble, it was enough to know that God was a loving Father who had sent His only Son to redeem mankind through His death on the cross. For the educated classes, Christianity was free of the inconsistencies and crudities that marred other religions. One could talk about Christianity in the language of Greek philosophy or

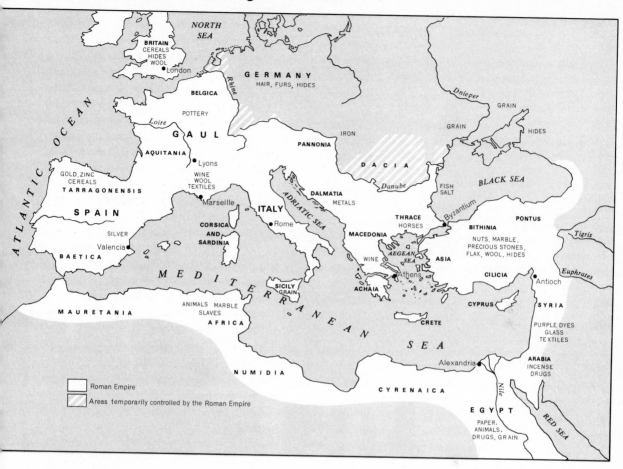

of Roman law—as Paul did, and as the author of the Fourth Gospel did. Christianity spread slowly through the Empire, but it spread steadily, and occasional persecutions did nothing to stop it.

The Roman Empire flourished in the first century, in spite of palace squabbles and some detestable emperors. It flourished even more in the second century, when the "Five Good Emperors" ruled and when the Roman administrative system was perfected. A decline began about 190 A.D. with the death of Marcus Aurelius, a Stoic and the last of the "Good Emperors." But for fifty years more the Empire suffered no disastrous set-backs, and it was in those years that Roman law saw its classical period.

The Romans had long realized that the early laws of their own city were archaic and could not be applied throughout a world empire. They were quite ready to allow subject peoples to use their own laws in their own communities. But what was to be done when citizens of different communities sued each other, or sued a Roman? Obviously some common rules must be found that would be acceptable to men of different origins and traditions. For generations Roman lawyers tried to formulate these general rules, encouraged by the emperors and by the Stoic belief in universal law. They sought justice and equity, and they came as close to achieving these ends as any jurists have ever done. The "law of nations" that they worked out became the common law of the Empire; even the Romans

Ulpian was one of the great Roman jurists of the early third century A.D. These passages were quoted by Justinian's lawyers at the beginning of the *Digest,* an authoritative treatise on Roman law.

Justice is a constant and perpetual will to give every man his due. The principles of law are these: to live virtuously, not to harm others, to give his due to everyone. Jurisprudence is the knowledge of divine and human things, the science of the just and the unjust.

Law is the art of goodness and justice. By virtue of this we [lawyers] may be called priests, for we cherish justice and we profess knowledge of goodness and equity, separating right from wrong and legal from the illegal. . . .

of Rome found that this new jurisprudence was superior to their old customs. And as the whole Mediterranean world came under the same law, the old distinctions between Roman citizens, allies, and subjects became meaningless. Soon after 200 A.D. almost every inhabitant of the Empire was considered a Roman citizen.

Roman law was the most lasting achievement of the Empire. The basic principles had been worked out by 235 A.D., but the law continued to grow until it was summarized and codified in the sixth century by the emperor Justinian. Justinian's Code, in turn, became the basic text for medieval and early modern lawyers. The law of most European states has been strongly influenced by Roman law, and Europeans inherited the Roman fascination with legal problems. In no other civilization have men trained in the law exerted the influence that they did in Rome and still do in Europe and countries of European origin.

Just as the Empire was reaching a peak of administrative efficiency and legal learning, it was struck by a series of disasters from which it never recovered. Civil wars devastated many provinces and opened the way for invasions by barbarians pressing on the frontiers. Poverty and insecurity weakened the cities so that they could no longer perform their old functions in local government. For fifty years—235 to 285 A.D.—the Empire was almost in a state of anarchy, and the partial recovery that came after 285 was achieved only by making the emperor a military dictator.

The most obvious reason for this collapse was political. Rome had never worked out a regular, generally accepted way of choosing a new emperor. A competent emperor could nominate his successor, but the choice of a weak emperor was ignored. In the latter case, senior generals fought for the throne, and the frontiers were neglected while the armies destroyed each other. In the third century the generals were particularly aggressive, and even the few able emperors who emerged could not survive long enough to restore order.

Lack of fixed rules of succession was a problem, but it had been a problem in the first century when the Empire was strong. Economic weakness probably created greater difficulties. During the centuries of expansion, Rome had lived off the plunder of conquered lands; a Rome with fixed boundaries had to live off its own resources. These resources were not great. The mines, the forests, and the soil around the rim of the Mediterranean were nearly exhausted, and the Romans had not settled in large numbers in the richer lands to the north. There was relatively little manufacturing for anything but local markets. Rome had an unfavorable balance of trade, because of its desire for luxury goods from the Orient, and the resulting drain of money depressed prices in the Empire. Most citizens were very poor, so the cities had trouble collecting the taxes needed for local government. Most citizens produced goods only for a local market, or for a great landlord in their district; the collapse of the Empire could not make their position worse and might make it better by removing imperial (as opposed to local) taxes. And for the soldiers (who were recruited from the poorest classes and were miserably underpaid), the one chance for wealth was to support a general who was claiming the throne. There would be loot during the campaign and gifts after the final victory. In fact, a good many

A Roman emperor and his soldiers struggling with barbarians, from a 3rd-century sarcophagus.

generals had the imperial purple forced upon them by soldiers who simply wanted a chance to raid the treasury.

Finally, there was a psychological problem that had begun long before and that grew worse with every century—the feeling that the individual did not count, that nothing mattered, that no change (or at least no change for the good) would ever happen, that there was no use trying to keep the machinery going. This feeling, as we have seen, stimulated interest in the mystery religions, but all the religions, even Christianity, counseled withdrawal from the world rather than participation in war and politics. Only a handful of soldiers, public officials, and aristocrats imbued with the old Roman traditions really wanted to keep the Empire going. It is remarkable that they succeeded, though they succeeded only at a price. That price was the transformation of the Empire into an absolute mon-

archy. The cities lost their autonomy. Peasants, artisans, and even minor officials were bound to their jobs for life. The emperor became an oriental despot whose will was law.

These measures, begun by Diocletian (285–305), preserved a united Empire for over a century. It was not a wasted century, in spite of the growing rigidity of the social and political structure. Diocletian's successor, Constantine (307–337), first tolerated and then actively encouraged the Christian Church. He certainly believed in the Christian God; he may also have realized that Christianity represented the most vital force in the Empire. The leading writers and thinkers were Christian, and Christian art was replacing the decaying classical style. Constantine also built a new capital, named for himself, at the strategic point where the Black Sea empties into the Aegean. Constantinople, with its almost impregnable fortifications, preserved the independence of the eastern part of the Empire for over a thousand years.

Constantine's heirs completed the process of making Christianity the official religion of the Empire. They also completed the process of barbarizing the army. For a long time the only Romans in the army had been peasants from the more backward provinces; now the peasants, bound to the soil, could no longer be used to fill the ranks. For a long time barbarians from across the frontiers had been enlisted as auxiliary troops; now they formed the bulk of the army. By 400 A.D. almost every "Roman" general and

almost all the soldiers were Germans. These men were not disloyal, so long as they were paid, but they had no particular attachment to the Empire and no great understanding of Roman ways.

As a result, when the next crisis came, a large part of the Empire simply disintegrated. An invasion of central Europe by the Huns (an Asian people) set the Germanic tribes milling about and pushed some of them up against the Rhine-Danube frontier. There they met some resistance, but not enough to stop all of them all of the time. Most Romans had lost their old enthusiasm for the Empire, and their initiative

The Late Roman Empire *ca.* 395 A.D.

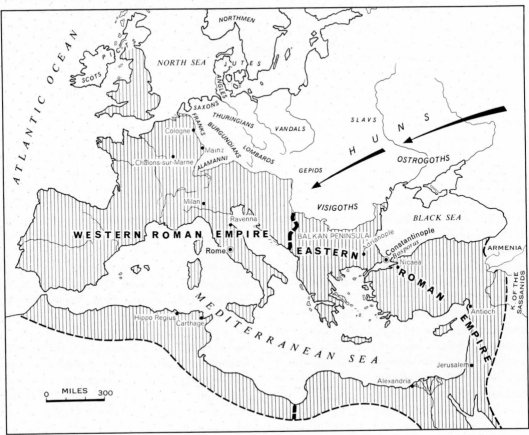

and sense of responsibility had been stifled by generations of despotic rule. The Germanized Roman army was not always eager to fight other Germans, and in any case it was not large enough to defend the whole frontier. So the Germans moved in, usually without much fighting or looting, and occupied most of the West. The last emperor in the West was deposed in 476 A.D.; after that Spain, Gaul, Britain, and Italy came under the rule of Germanic kings.

The End of Mediterranean Unity

This collapse of the Empire in the West was, curiously enough, the first step in creating a distinctively western civilization. For the East did not fall to the Germans, partly because Constantinople formed a shield for the provinces of Asia Minor, Syria, and Egypt, partly because the economic situation was better in the East, partly because the government in the East had a little more political skill and a little more courage. An emperor continued to rule in Constantinople and for a time preserved the fiction that the western kings were his deputies. But the fiction had no substance and was soon forgotten, not because the Germanic kings were hostile to the emperor, but because they simply did not understand what the Empire was. The Roman machinery of government in the West ran down and stopped; the cities dwindled and died; the number of educated men decreased sharply; and commerce with the East declined. The West could no longer draw on the cultural or physical resources of the East. It remained to be seen what the West could do with its own resources.

Those resources were potentially quite valuable. They included the fertile northern plains that the Romans had neglected or had never occupied, a large and steady supply of water power (also neglected by the Romans), and large deposits of iron and other metals. They included the highly developed Latin language (far richer than the primitive Germanic dialects), Latin literature and philosophy, and Roman law (though the latter barely escaped with its life). Last, they included the Christian Church, which did its best to preserve Roman traditions of organization and learning. The only great loss to the West (and even this was repaired after some centuries) was the loss of Greek works in mathematics, logic, and science. Even before the collapse of the Empire in the West, fewer and fewer Romans had taken the trouble to learn Greek. After the collapse, the Greek texts practically disappeared.

The West had valuable resources, but it was a long time before they could be exploited. The Latin-speaking majority was apathetic; the ruling German minority was ignorant and inexperienced. Large-scale organization and widespread cooperation became almost impossible. Germanic kings, who had ruled only a few thousand warriors, did not know how to govern large kingdoms. They could not preserve the Roman bureaucracy or the Roman tax system; they simply delegated their authority in each county to counts who struggled vainly to keep the peace. The vast majority of the population made its living from agriculture, but agricultural techniques were primitive (especially in the north) and there was a chronic shortage of food. There was relatively little long-distance trade. The working political and economic unit was a small rural district in which no one lived more than a day's journey from the local market and the neighborhood court.

The one large-scale organization that did survive, the Catholic Church, had trouble in preserving its unity and in reaching the people. The Church had always been a city-centered institution. The bishops and most of the clergy lived in the cities; the faithful came to the cities to hear services and to receive the sacraments. There were few rural parishes, and almost none north of the Alps. Now the cities were dying and the Church had to deal with a vast rural population—half-Christian, Latin-speaking peasants and heathen Germans. It took time to convert the Germans; it took about three centuries to establish rural parishes throughout the Germanic kingdoms. Until this was done, most men had little contact with Christianity and Christianity had little influence on their behavior.

By the time of the Empire's collapse, it had been generally accepted that the pope, bishop of Rome and successor of St. Peter, was head of the Church, or at least head of the Latin-speaking part of the Church. This preeminence might be contested by the patriarch of Constantinople, but it was never challenged in the West. After the breakdown of the Empire, however, the pope had difficulty in exercising any administrative authority. A bishopric was a profitable position, and barbarian kings named as bishops friends and relatives who were often ignorant and vicious men. Even when good bishops were appointed, the kings tried to dominate them and ignored requests and pleas from the pope to respect the privileges and property of local churches.

The most helpful allies of the popes were the monks, men who had renounced the world and who lived in tightly organized religious communities under the rule of an abbot. They formed a disciplined force in an age when discipline was rare; they were more respected and less often harassed by secular rulers than the rest of the clergy; they were, on the whole, obedient to the pope. During the seventh and eighth centuries the popes began to use the monks to strengthen the Church. Monks were sent as missionaries to the heathen Anglo-Saxons, and the Anglo-Saxons, with the zeal of new converts, soon sent missionaries to the Low Countries and to Germany. The churches founded by missionary monks proved more obedient to the pope than churches in areas that had long been nominally Christian, such as Gaul. Eventually a reform movement spread from the missionary areas into the rest of western Europe. The character and learning of the bishops improved and the influence of the pope increased. But the reform succeeded only because it was supported by the kings, and the Church remained very loosely organized and subject to local pressures. It was only after the year 1000 that the pope began to gain administrative control over the Church.

Meanwhile the Mediterranean area, the center of the old classical civilization, suffered new blows after a temporary recovery under the emperor Justinian (527–565). Justinian resolved to restore the splendor and the unity of the Roman Empire. His building program (including Hagia Sophia in Constantinople) and his codification of Roman law left enduring monuments of his ability and his ambition. But his effort to reconquer the West was a complete disaster. He succeeded only in destroying the Gothic kingdom of Italy, the most advanced Germanic state, and in exhausting the resources of his eastern provinces. Italy soon fell into the hands of another Germanic people, the Lombards, who were far less capable rulers than the Goths had been. Syria, Egypt, and North Africa were oppressed by heavy taxation and were angered by Justinian's obvious willingness to sacrifice their interests in order to strengthen himself in the West. In theological disputes, Justinian steadily supported doctrines of the Latin Church and opposed those of Egyptian and Syrian theologians. Since religion was almost the equivalent of patriotism for the easterners, loyalty to the emperor was shaken. Justinian forced his bishops, most of whom were Greeks, to follow his policy, but in doing so he simply released long-suppressed feelings of resentment against domination by a Greek-speaking minority. During the crisis of the fifth century the East had held together. In the crisis that was soon to come, the Egyptians and Syrians made almost no effort to preserve their ties to the Empire.

The new crisis was caused by the rise of a new religion—Islam. The prophet Mohammed (571–632 A.D.) had gradually convinced his fellow Arabs that he had received a revelation from God that superseded all earlier revelations. He accepted much of Jewish and Christian tradition, but he emphasized strict monotheism (in opposition to the Christian doctrine of the Trinity) and the joys of Paradise and the pains of hell (in opposition to Jewish uncertainties concerning the afterlife). His religion was simple and easily taught. No priest or theologian was necessary. To become a Moslem—that is, a convert to Islam—one had only to believe in Allah and in his prophet Mohammed, to accept Mohammed's sayings (the Koran) as the word of God, and to pray each day and fast for one month of the year.

Mohammed was not only a prophet; he was a political and military leader. Before his death he had united most of the scattered Arab tribes. His successors, the caliphs, used this united force to conquer the Middle East. Syria, Egypt, and North Africa fell after brief struggles. Persia, weakened by repeated wars with the Roman Empire, came under Moslem domination at the same time. Not all the conquered peoples became converted, but enough of them accepted Islam so that new armies could be raised for new wars. In the West the Moslem armies took Morocco, overran most of Spain, and raided Gaul. In the East they pushed as far as the Indus valley. In just about a century the Moslems had created an empire larger than that of Rome at its greatest extent.

The Mediterranean world was now split into three unequal fragments. Largest and richest were the lands of the Moslem caliphate. The remnant of the Roman Empire now included only Greece,

the Balkans, and Asia Minor, but it was a wealthy and well-organized state. Because it now was completely centered on Constantinople, whose old name was Byzantium, this fragment of the old Roman state is usually called the Byzantine Empire. Finally, there was western Europe, poor, backward, and barbarous.

The shock of Justinian's wars and of the Moslem wars of conquest separated the West even more sharply from its old neighbors than had the earlier Germanic invasions. Not all contacts were broken, of course. Trade between East and West continued; the Byzantine Empire for a long time held enclaves in Italy and sent embassies to western courts; pope and patriarch remained in communion with each other until the eleventh century. But the West was profoundly suspicious of the Byzantines, who seemed arrogant, oversophisticated, and unreliable, and it was profoundly hostile to the Moslems, who were raiding Italy and southern

The Growth of the Islamic Caliphate   632–750

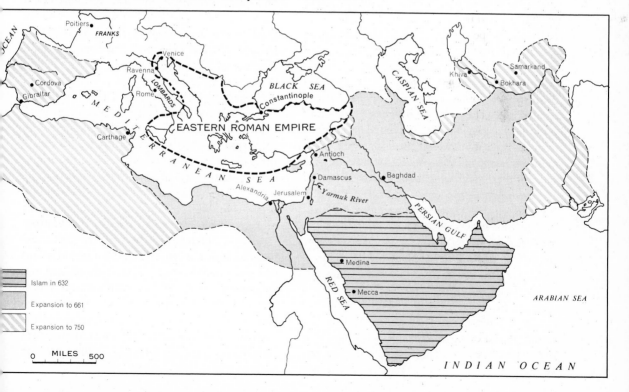

The Coronation of Charlemagne

Now when the king upon the most holy day of the Lord's birth was rising to the mass after praying before the tomb of the blessed Peter the Apostle, Leo the Pope, with the consent of all the bishops and priests and of the senate of the Franks and likewise of the Romans, set a golden crown upon his head, the Roman people also shouting aloud. And when the people had made an end of chanting praises, he was adored by the pope after the manner of the emperors of old. For this was also done by the will of God. For while the said Emperor abode at Rome certain men were brought to him who said that the name of Emperor had ceased among the Greeks, and that there the Empire was held by a woman called Irene, who had by guile laid hold on her son the Emperor and put out his eyes and taken the Empire to herself. . . . Which when Leo the Pope and all the assembly of the bishops and priests and abbots heard, and the senate of the Franks and all the elders of the Romans, they took counsel with the rest of the Christian people, that they should name Charles king of the Franks to be Emperor, seeing that he held Rome the mother of empire where the Caesars and Emperors always used to sit.

From *Chronicle of Moissac,* trans. by J. Bryce, *The Holy Roman Empire* (New York: Macmillan and St. Martin's Press, 1911), p. 54.

Gaul. On the other hand, neither Byzantines nor Moslems saw much advantage in trying to expand relations with an undeveloped and poverty-stricken area. For several centuries western imports from the East, whether of goods or of ideas, remained at a low level.

Another result of Justinian's wars and the Moslem conquests was the destruction of the Germanic kingdoms that touched the Mediterranean. The Franks, whose strength lay on the lower Rhine and in northeastern Gaul, were far enough removed from the Mediterranean turmoil to escape damage, and they gradually picked up fragments of other kingdoms in southern France, northeastern Spain, and northern Italy. By the end of the eighth century the Franks were dominant in western Europe. The little Anglo-Saxon kingdoms in Britain had not yet united to form an English state; there was only a bare beginning of political organization in Scandinavia, and not even a beginning among the Slavs of central Europe. But the Frankish kings ruled lands that stretched from the Ebro to the Elbe and from the North Sea to Rome. Given the strength of local feeling and the weakness of Germanic administrative methods, this was far too large an area to remain long united. But for about a century the Frankish empire held together, and during that century some decisive steps were taken in founding a distinctively western civilization.

This fruitful period is usually called the Carolingian Age, after the most famous of Frankish kings, Charlemagne or Charles the Great (768–814). Charlemagne, however, in many ways simply continued the work of his father and grandfather, and many of his own plans (especially in cultural matters) were fulfilled only in the reigns of his son and grandsons. The basic policy, from the beginning to the end of the Carolingian dynasty, was close cooperation between king and pope. The kings protected the pope from his enemies and supported missionary work in Germany. They encouraged reform in Gaul and closer connections between pope and bishops. They also encouraged a great increase in the number of rural parishes. As a result, the Church in the West improved the quality of its personnel, began to improve its administrative system, and had more frequent contact with the mass of the population. In fact, it was only with the Carolingian period that most men north of the Alps began to have a real chance to practice the Christian religion.

In return, the Church gave its spiritual support to the Carolingians and called on its prelates to take an active part in the administration of the kingdom. Since the clergy by this time were the only educated class, their assistance was absolutely necessary if the government was to operate. Moreover, the bishops and abbots were usually more loyal to the king than to the counts (the district governors), and they were often used by the Carolingians to balance the influence of local strong men. Finally, since the prelates were drawn from all parts of Europe, they helped to spread a common culture across the continent.

This common culture was the most lasting achievement of the Carolingian Age. Charles and his successors were eager to improve the education of the clergy, and with their encouragement a basic curriculum was established that was followed in all church schools. The Latin classics had to be studied to improve skill in the use of the language; as a result, books that were on the verge of disappearing were recopied and preserved. The Bible had to be explained in detail, so copies of the Bible were multiplied and errors in earlier texts were corrected. The Church Fathers furnished the authoritative explanations of the Scriptures, and again a vast effort of copying and emendation was needed. Added to this was a reform in handwriting that made reading much easier. It was only in the Carolingian Age that a large enough number of men in western Europe began to understand and to use their Latin and Christian intellectual heritage to help mold western society.

The culmination of the papal-Carolingian alliance came in 800 A.D. when the pope crowned Charles emperor in St. Peter's Church in Rome. This act symbolized Charles' supremacy in the West and his role as protector of the Church. It added somewhat to his moral authority over his subjects, though it did not increase his political power. On the other hand,

Charlemagne presents a model of his new church at Aix-la-Chapelle to the Virgin. Scene from a panel of the shrine at Aix.

it irritated the Byzantine emperor and thus helped to widen the rift between eastern and western Europe. The revival of a "Roman" Empire also created problems that were to plague the West for centuries. What authority did the emperor have over Italy, and especially Rome? If the pope could make an emperor, could he then depose him? And if a pope could depose an emperor, could he not also depose kings?

Revival in the West

In the years that followed Charlemagne's death, however, the problems of the Empire became submerged in the greater problem of whether any political unit could survive. Internal strife among the Franks and a new wave of invasions from the north, east, and south threatened all forms of organization. Charlemagne's grandsons, after a bloody civil war, split the family lands into three shares. One grandson took France; another took the nucleus of what became Germany; the eldest received a middle kingdom, including the Netherlands, Belgium, Lorraine, part of Switzerland, Provence, and North Italy. This long, narrow strip lacked cohesion, and soon the kings of France and Germany began to fight over fragments of the middle kingdom, a fight that has continued into our own century. Meanwhile the Scandinavian Vikings began to raid and then conquer parts of Ireland, England, France, and Germany; the Magyars (a group of Asian nomads) occupied the Hungarian plain and plundered Germany and North Italy; and the Moslems terrorized the coasts of Italy and southern France. Under the impact of war and invasion the Carolingian Empire dissolved. The Empire split into kingdoms, the kingdoms into principalities, the principalities into counties, and the counties into castellanies (small areas ruled by the lord of a castle).

The fragmentation went farthest in France and in western Germany, and by 900 A.D. a new type of political organization was beginning to appear—a type that was later to be known as feudalism. In feudalism the actual work of government was done by a lord assisted by a band of armed retainers. Some lords ruled only the district around a castle; some were able to unite several castellanies; a very few lords (for example, the Duke of Normandy) had effective power over many counties. But large or small, the territory ruled by a lord was an autonomous political unit. There was a face-saving theory by which the lord owed allegiance and obedience to the king, or to some superior (a duke or a count) who stood between him and the king. This theory was to be helpful later in furnishing an excuse for reconstituting large political units, but in the tenth century it was meaningless. The chain of obedience was broken at many points, and each break marked the existence of an independent lordship.

The retainers of the lords were knights, men who never had independent political power but who gradually emerged as a landlord class. Most lords had a great deal of land, worked by free or unfree peasant farmers, while their castles were small and crowded. So it was easier to give a knight some land and the services of the peasants who worked the land than it was to support him in the lord's household. By 1100 most knights possessed estates, or even whole villages, and they gradually acquired a sort of police-court jurisdiction over their peasants. But the knights always remained politically dependent on greater men—barons, counts, or kings.

Feudalism was a rudimentary form of organization in which the ruler treated his rights of government as if they were private property. It was, however, a type of government that met the needs of the time. The effective political unit—county or castellany—corresponded fairly closely with the working economic unit—a district centered around a few local markets. Local defense could be better secured by a local lord than by a distant king. Since the lord thought of his government as his private property, it was to his interest to improve that government, thereby making it more profitable. In time, feudal government became far more effective and far more popular than either the Germanic kingships or the late Carolingian monarchy had been. Most modern European states grew out of feudal states.

The immediate advantage of feudalism was that it gave increased security to many parts of the West. Inside the larger lordships relative peace prevailed, and frontier skirmishing and the quarrels of petty lords did far less damage than civil wars among Frankish kings had done. Feudal lords did their share in beating back the invasions of the Northmen and the Moslems, though kings and popes also won significant victories over these intruders. (The Magyar threat was blunted largely by the efforts of the king of Germany.) Altogether, in the century after the year 1000, there were very few major wars and almost no large-scale invasions of Europe.

Increased security, limited though it was, meant increased population. An increased population, in turn, required more food, and so stimulated improvements in agricultural techniques. These improvements produced enough food to support a rapid growth of the urban and professional classes. Industry and commerce expanded; for example, fine woolen cloth made in Flanders could be exchanged with Byzantines and Moslems for eastern luxuries. Political stability and economic expansion brought the West above the subsistence level for the first time in centuries.

Just as significant as increased production was the increased influence of the Church. It had taken a long time for Christianity to get under the skins of the people of the West. The slow extension of the parish system, the setbacks caused by repeated invasions by non-Christian peoples, the ignorance of many of the clergy, and the weak administrative system of the Church were all responsible for this lag. But during the eleventh century the Northmen and the Magyars were converted, and a new reform movement, much more widespread than that of the Carolingians, improved the quality of the clergy and increased the administrative authority of the pope. Laymen became more devout (if not more virtuous), more eager to demonstrate their attachment to the faith, and more willing to accept the leadership of the Church. For the first time in centuries the West had ideals and goals that commanded the ardent support of almost all members of society.

The Civilization of Western Europe in the Middle Ages

These improvements in the condition of western Europe after the year 1000 created a burst of energy that lasted for more than two centuries. One of the first problems was to find land for the increasing population. Even though the towns were growing, they absorbed only about ten percent of the population. Everyone else had to make a living by farming. All over Europe forests were cleared and swamps and marshes were drained. The Germans began to push into the half-empty Slavic lands that lay between the Elbe and Oder rivers. Some peasant families traveled hundreds of miles in order to obtain small farms on this eastern frontier. The Norman Conquest of England in 1066 was not just a military adventure: northern France was overpopulated; England was underpopulated; and most of William's army was composed of poor knights looking for land. The less well-known Norman Conquest of southern Italy and Sicily was also accomplished by poor knights who could not make a living in their own country. And the long, slow reconquest of Spain from the Moslems was spurred on by the existence of empty land in the disputed area that lay between the little Christian kingdoms of the north and the Moorish states of the south.

Another problem was to make governments strong enough to put down internal disorder. In pursuit of this goal, however, rulers ran head-on into one of the strongest movements of the eleventh and twelfth centuries: the drive to reform the Church. No government could operate without the help of the clergy; members of the clergy were better educated, more competent as administrators, and usually more reliable than laymen. Kings and the greater feudal lords naturally wanted to control the appointment of bishops and abbots in order to create a corps of capable and loyal public servants. On the other hand, the reformers wanted a Church that was completely independent, a Church that would instruct and admonish lay rulers rather than serve them. The conflict between the two points of view led to a struggle that

Principles of Gregory VII

ca. 1075

This document was certainly drawn up in Gregory's circle, and probably by the pope himself. It expresses the views of those who were trying to increase papal power in both Church and state.

1. That the Roman church was founded by the Lord alone.
2. That only the Roman pontiff is rightly called universal.
3. That he alone can depose or reestablish bishops.
4. That his legate, even if of inferior rank, is above all bishops in council; and he can give sentence of deposition against them. . . .
12. That it is permitted to him to depose emperors. . . .
18. That his decision ought to be reviewed by no one, and that he alone can review the decisions of everyone.
19. That he ought to be judged by no one.
20. That no one may dare condemn a man who is appealing to the apostolic see.
21. That the greater cases of every church ought to be referred to him.
22. That the Roman church has never erred nor will ever err, as the Scripture bears witness.
23. That the Roman pontiff, if he has been canonically ordained, is indubitably made holy by the merits of the blessed Peter. . . .
24. That by his precept and license subjects are permitted to accuse their lords. . . .
27. That he can absolve the subjects of the unjust from their fealty.

From *Dictatus Papae Gregorii VII,* trans. by E. Lewis, *Medieval Political Ideas* (New York: Knopf, 1954), Vol. II, pp. 380–81.

lasted for half a century, from the 1070's to the 1120's.

The leading figures in the struggle were the pope and the king of Germany. Germany had suffered less from civil war and invasion than had France and had consequently been less severely fragmented. The king had some power in most parts of the country, largely through the support given him by bishops and abbots whom he had appointed. In 962 a German king was strong enough to conquer northern Italy and to revive the title of emperor, which had lapsed after Charlemagne's Empire had collapsed. Almost all German kings after 962 were also emperors, titular rulers of northern Italy, and protectors of Rome and of the pope. In this last capacity they frequently installed men of their own choice in the papal office and on at least one occasion deposed a pope.

Such a situation was obviously intolerable to the reformers. Pope Gregory VII (1073–1085) forbade the emperor to interfere in papal elections; henceforth the pope was to be chosen only by the cardinals. Gregory also tried to keep the emperor from naming bishops and abbots. The emperor Henry IV (1056–1106) in turn tried to depose the pope. Gregory then released Henry's subjects from allegiance to their ruler and a rebellion broke out in Germany. Henry was so weakened that he had to seek the pope's forgiveness at Canossa (1077). This was not a complete victory for Gregory (Henry later succeeded in driving him from Rome), but it did prove that some concessions would have to be made by lay rulers. Eventually a compromise was reached by the successors of Gregory and of Henry, a compromise that paralleled agreements reached between the pope and other rulers. Papal independence and papal administrative authority over the Church were clearly recognized. Royal influence over the appointment of bishops was admitted, and many bishops continued to act as advisers and officials of kings. The pope, however, could give orders to and discipline any bishop.

The net result of the struggle was to put the Church in a position rarely enjoyed by a religious organization. It was completely independent of the state. It had shown that it had enough support among men of all classes to shake the structure of any government that opposed it. The Church had taken over the leadership of western Europe.

An early demonstration of this leadership was the First Crusade (1095–1099). Pope Urban II

Choir of the Cathedral of Beauvais, 1247–72. The builders tried to make this the highest church in France; the choir was a success, but the nave collapsed and was never finished.

had many reasons for inaugurating the movement. Sending belligerent knights and nobles to fight the Moslems would distract them from their petty wars in Europe. If western warriors could help the Byzantines to regain some of their lost provinces, the quarrels between the Greek and the Roman Churches, which had culminated in the mutual excommunications of pope and patriarch in 1054, might be healed. Finally, Urban earnestly desired that the Holy Land be under Christian rule. His appeal for an expedition to the East had enormous and unexpected success. Men from all parts of the West responded to Urban's summons and under the leadership of a papal legate marched through Europe, Asia Minor, and Syria to capture the city of Jerusalem. No secular ruler could have raised such an army or persuaded men from so many different countries to cooperate. Only the pope could make full use of the religious fervor of the people. For two centuries the protection of the Holy Land through Crusades was a primary goal of western Christians, and in the interests of the Crusades the pope could intervene in every aspect of European life.

The new energy of the West, guided by the Church, also led to remarkable achievements in art and scholarship. A vast number of churches were built between 1000 and 1300 A.D., and a completely new architectural style emerged. The earlier Romanesque churches still had some affinities with buildings of the late Roman Empire, but about the middle of the twelfth century the first Gothic churches appeared in northern France. The new style was marked by height and light, with emphasis on vertical rather than horizontal lines and on enlarging window space as far as possible. To fill the windows, stained glass was needed; to adorn the exterior and especially the portals, large numbers of statues were required. All the arts worked together to make the Gothic style one of the most beautiful ever imagined by the human mind.

In scholarship it was much the same story. By the twelfth century there was a sharp increase in the number of students and a desire to go beyond the work of the late Roman Empire. To teach large numbers of students, a new institution had to be invented—the university. To acquire new knowledge, texts that had been neglected or little used had to be studied. At Bologna the study of Roman law, as codified under Justinian, became the principal pursuit. Thousands of men from all parts of Europe studied at Bologna and carried home with them new ideas about the nature of the state and the meaning of justice. At Paris, the emphasis was on theology, and on logic as an indispensable tool in the understanding of theology. Since only a few basic texts on logic were known, a search was made for new material. This material could be found only in Greek, or in Arabic translations from the Greek. Several generations of devoted scholars spent their lives in turning these books into Latin. In the process, all of Aristotle's logical works were recovered, and much more besides. The Greek scientific and mathematical tradition, amplified by the Arabs, became, for the first time, part of the intellectual heritage of the West. The Romans had neglected science, but from the twelfth century on western Europeans showed an increasing interest in scientific studies.

For the scholars at Paris, however, theology, not physics or mathematics, was the "queen of the sciences." With great effort they managed to weave all their knowledge together into a pattern of Christian theology and philosophy. The final synthesis was achieved by St. Thomas Aquinas (1225–1274). Thomas believed that all learning, even that of the pagans, was inspired by the Divine Reason, and that it was impossible for a truth known by natural reason to contradict a truth known by revelation. Thus a great deal of Greek and Moslem scholarship could be absorbed into western thought.

The Church led Europe, but it could not do everything. It admitted that lay governments were necessary to keep the peace and to repress crime. It taught that the chief duty of a ruler was to do justice. This view was reinforced by the revival of legal studies and by the self-interest of kings and princes. In the twelfth and thirteenth centuries the best way to strengthen a state was to improve the administration of justice

Feudal France late 11th century

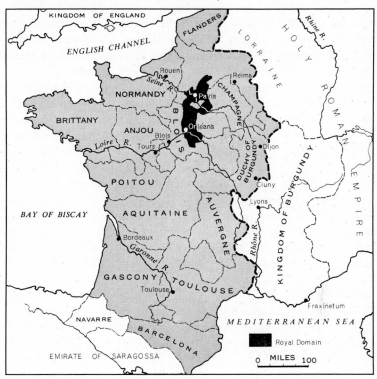

and to persuade or force subjects to come to the law courts. More firmly than any other political units that had existed before, the European states that began to emerge in the twelfth century were based on law.

The process of state-building went farthest and fastest in England and France. England had avoided fragmentation, partly because it was a small country, partly because the old Anglo-Saxon aristocracy that might have set up autonomous provincial governments was wiped out by the Norman Conquest. The new Norman aristocracy was created by the king, was dependent on him, and had very limited powers. The kings had land, officers, and courts in every part of England. So it was very easy for them to develop a reasonably efficient financial administration that centered royal revenues in one place. It was almost as easy to attract people to the royal courts. The kings sent their judges around on regular circuits; they protected the possessions of all free men; they used the jury to determine the facts in law suits instead of depending on such superstitious practices as trial by battle. By 1200 uniform taxes had been imposed on the country and all cases of any importance went to royal courts.

The king of France had greater difficulties. At first he ruled directly only a small district running north and south of Paris. Even in this limited area there were unruly and disobedient lords; outside it were the feudal principalities (Normandy, Flanders, Burgundy, and others) where he had no power at all. His first job was to get full control of the Paris region; this was done early in the twelfth century. Next was the delicate task of finding ways of annexing the great lordships. Some came in by way of marriages between royal princes and heiresses; a few of the smaller ones came by purchase; but the most effective means was judgment by the king's court. Respect for the court grew during the twelfth century; by the thirteenth century a lord who defied its jurisdiction or disobeyed its orders could be punished by confiscation of his lands. King John of England lost the duchy of Normandy in this way—a lesson that made a deep impression on other lords. By 1285 the greater part of France was ruled directly by the king, and the part that was still held by feudal lords was reasonably obedient to him.

France, however, was less unified than England. In England there was one law and one system of courts. In France each province was allowed to keep its old laws and courts even after it was annexed to the crown. English royal courts dealt directly with the people. The French royal court at Paris dealt largely with appeals from provincial officials and feudal lords. Imperfect unity in turn reduced royal income. General taxes in France started a century later than in England, and even then strongly entrenched local privileges cut down the yield. France had four or five times the population of England, but the revenues of the two kings were often about the same.

Other countries were less advanced. The Spanish kingdoms were still occupied with their struggle against the Moors; the Scandinavian kingdoms were still unstable; the Slavic kingdoms were just beginning to get organized. Germany and Italy had been shattered by the struggle between pope and emperor. The typical political unit in Germany was to be the principality, and in Italy the city-state. But even in these areas there had been improvement since the period of invasion and civil war that followed the collapse of the Carolingian Empire. Almost everywhere secular rulers—kings, princes, city magistrates—were repressing internal violence and providing greater security for all classes.

The thirteenth century, which was on the whole a peaceful and prosperous period for the West, was a time of troubles for eastern Europe. Crusaders who had originally planned to attack the Moslems in the Holy Land were misled by Venetian politicians and Byzantine exiles and instead took the city of Constantinople (1204). The Greeks held on to fragments of their empire and eventually drove the westerners out of the

capital city (1261), but the restored Byzantine Empire was never very strong. It could not resist the advance of the Turks, which began in the fourteenth century, and the Byzantines became even more suspicious of the West than they had been.

Russia was hit even harder. In the thirteenth century the Mongols started the greatest series of invasions in the history of the Asian nomads. They took China, Persia, and Mesopotamia and drove clear across Russia to the frontiers of Hungary. Russia had been Christianized by the Greek Church and had drawn most of its intellectual and artistic tradition from the Byzantines. Now the Russian princes were forced into the northern forests, and even there they had to pay tribute to the Mongols. Contacts with Constantinople decreased; contacts with the West almost ended. Russia turned in on herself, proud of her orthodox faith and her old traditions, suspicious of all outsiders.

Thus the division between East and West that had begun centuries before was accentuated. The Byzantines could not forget the conquest of 1204, and the heirs of the Byzantine emperors were to be Turkish sultans, not Christian kings from the West. Russia had become isolated and for many generations was to look south and east to the camps of the Mongol khans, rather than west to Latin Christendom. The Moslems succeeded in converting the Mongols who had occupied their lands, but in the process they too became somewhat orientalized and withdrawn. Moslem civilization of the twelfth century had been much more akin to western civilization than was the Moslem civilization of the fourteenth century.

The Crisis of the Later Middle Ages

The West once more stood alone. But it was in a far stronger position than it had been when the old Mediterranean world broke into fragments. By the thirteenth century the main outlines of what we call medieval civilization were well established. This medieval civilization was clearly a western civilization, unlike any that had existed before and unlike any of its contemporaries. Its ideals were largely Christian; its intellectual tradition was a unique combination of Greek, Roman, and Moslem thought, with some Jewish and even some Hindu influence. The West had an art that was entirely its own and habits of thinking that were becoming more and more original. It had built new institutions—the Church, the law-based monarchy, the university. It had improved its technology and had reached an economic level not inferior to that of earlier civilizations. In fact, per capita income in western Europe in the thirteenth century was probably higher than it had been in the same area in the best days of the Roman Empire. But this western civilization was no richer, no stronger, no more impressive in its intellectual and artistic production than contemporary civilizations in China, India, or the Moslem world. It was still based largely on peasant agriculture; industrial production was still low; even the rich lived under conditions that would appal a slum-dweller today. As for the poorest peasants and textile-workers, their lives were short, miserable, and hopeless. By modern standards, western Europe in the thirteenth century was an underdeveloped society.

Moreover, western civilization was beginning to show signs of strain. The strain appeared first in the Church, which in exercising its leadership had found itself more and more involved in worldly affairs and less and less able to understand the affairs in which it was involved. For example, the Church drew most of its income from the land and did not fully understand the behavior and the problems of the urban classes. The Church had encouraged rulers to seek peace and justice but failed to see that their very success in this endeavor was strengthening men's loyalty to secular rulers. The Church still sought independence from lay authority but thirteenth-century popes confused independence with their desire for a particular political configuration in Italy, one in which there was no strong state in the peninsula. In resisting the emergence of a strong Italian state they drifted into a long series of wars with German emperors, who by this time held Sicily and Naples and were trying to unite these southern territories with Lombardy

and Tuscany. During the wars (1229–1268) the popes taxed the clergy to support papal armies, gave indulgences to their supporters, and called on the kings of France and England for assistance. By playing politics, the papacy became politicized; by relying on secular rulers, the papacy lost much of the independence that it was trying to preserve; by preventing the creation of a strong Italian state, the papacy created such anarchy that the fourteenth-century popes had to abandon Rome and take refuge in France. By 1300 there was much less respect for the Church as an institution than there had been in 1200.

Western Europe remained more attached to the Christian faith than to the institution that embodied that faith. Two new religious orders, the Dominicans and the Franciscans, founded early in the thirteenth century, tried to reach the people who were alienated from or neglected by the rest of the clergy. These orders gained considerable support from townspeople, intellectuals, and secular administrators. But while they helped to preserve the faith they had little influence on men's conduct. Western Europeans became more worldly, more selfish, more critical of the administration of the Church. The conflict between belief and behavior, the contrast between revivalistic piety and cynical resistance to papal orders, led to a dangerous instability in society.

Meanwhile secular governments were growing in power and prestige. The thirteenth century was on the whole a peaceful age; even the papal-imperial wars were fought mostly on a local level and only occasionally led to large-scale battles. If men did not settle their quarrels by fighting, they had to settle them by law suits; and the more cases that came to the courts, the stronger the governments became. In these circumstances it was easy to transfer loyalty from a Church that did not seem to be doing its job very well to secular states that did seem to be. The show-down came at the end of the century when major wars broke out again between France and Flanders, England and Scotland, and France and England. The kings of England and France ordered their clergy to pay taxes to support these wars, even though the clergy were supposed to be free from secular burdens. The pope at first forbade the clergy to pay, but this prohibition caused such a storm of protest that he had to admit that the clergy could be taxed for defense of the state. A few years later the king of France arrested a bishop on charges of treason. When the pope ordered the bishop's release and criticized the king's behavior, an agent of the king tried to arrest the pope on trumped-up charges of heresy. The attempt very nearly succeeded, and the ensuing propaganda attack against the pope became so nasty that in the end the papacy fully absolved the king and his ministers. In a head-on collision between Church and state, the Church had backed down.

The Black Death in England

Then that most grievous pestilence penetrated the coastal regions by way of Southampton and came to Bristol, and people died as if the whole strength of the city were seized by sudden death. For there were few who lay in their beds more than three days or two and a half days; then that savage death snatched them about the second day. In Leicester, in the little parish of St. Leonard, more than three hundred and eighty died; in the parish of the Holy Cross, more than four hundred, and in the parish of St. Margaret, more than seven hundred. . . .

And the price of everything was cheap, because of the fear of death, there were very few who took any care for their wealth, or for anything else. For a man could buy a horse for half a mark [about 7 shillings] which before was worth forty shillings, a large fat ox for four shillings, a cow for twelve pence, a heifer for sixpence, a large fat sheep for four pence. . . . And the sheep and cattle wandered about through the fields and among the crops, and there was no one to go after them or collect them. They perished in countless numbers everywhere, for lack of watching . . . since there was such a lack of serfs and servants, that no one knew what he should do. For there is no memory of a mortality so severe and so savage. . . . In the following autumn, one could not hire a reaper for less than eight pence [per day] with food, or a mower at less than twelve pence with food.

From Henry Knighton, *Chronicle,* in *The Portable Medieval Reader,* ed. by J. B. Ross and M. M. McLaughlin (New York: Viking, 1949), pp. 218–19.

The people, including a large number of the clergy, had supported their king rather than the pope. The threat of a Church-inspired rebellion against a disobedient ruler was no longer credible.

These events put an end to the leadership that the Church had exerted in lay affairs for two centuries. Logically, the victorious states should have succeeded to that leadership. But the states were not quite ready to assume the responsibility. Their administrative structures were not yet complete; for example, no state had a foreign office or a war department. There was still a good deal of localism that limited the effectiveness of actions by the central governments. Worst of all, no state was able to solve a host of new problems that arose in the fourteenth century, and at times even the strongest states, such as England, were almost as discredited as the Church. Therefore, the state does not emerge as the controlling force in western civilization until the end of the fifteenth century, and this emergence may be taken as one sign of the beginning of the modern period. Meanwhile, Europe floundered for a century and a half with no leadership of any kind.

The problems of the fourteenth century were grave enough to perplex the ablest men. The economy had reached its limits; until new techniques, new industries, and new markets were discovered, Europe could neither produce more from its own resources nor acquire more from other areas. Population was pressing heavily on the land. Many peasants were barely at subsistence levels, but the labor market of the overcrowded cities offered them no relief. Landlords were finding it hard to live on their rents and had to borrow money at high rates of interest. So did most kings and princes. But the bankers from whom they borrowed were no better off; almost all of them went bankrupt during the century. In short, western Europe had entered a long and serious economic depression.

Population pressure was relieved by the Black Death, an outbreak of bubonic plague that entered Europe in 1347, swept through the West in a great arc—Italy, France, England, Germany— and returned several times during the century.

In the areas that were hardest hit a third or more of the population died. The psychological shock of such a mortality rate and the economic shock of adjusting to a completely new population pattern were enormous. Peasants were better off, since they could now concentrate their work on the richest lands; artisans were worse off, since they had lost many customers and had to pay higher prices for food. It took a long time to strike a new balance between rural and urban producers. Meanwhile, society was dangerously unstable. There were frequent revolts by peasants eager to exploit their advantageous position, and by artisans trying to avoid loss of income and status.

With no economists and only a few badly trained doctors, governments could not have been expected to do much about the problems of depression and disease. They might, however, have avoided war. But in an age when many men were suffering from diminishing incomes, pressures for war were great. Nobles and landed gentry, who raised and commanded companies of soldiers, could make a good living out of army wages and could always hope for a windfall—the plundering of a town, for example, or the ransom of a prominent prisoner. Merchants and mariners could try to eliminate their competitors. Kings could add new provinces to their domains and could forget their other problems in the excitement of conflict. Uncertain boundaries and attempts by feudal lords, such as the count of Flanders, to assert their independence from higher authorities were also excuses for fighting. The thirteenth century had been relatively peaceful; the fourteenth and early fifteenth centuries were periods of almost constant warfare.

The longest and most costly war was the Hundred Years' War between England and France, which lasted officially from 1337 to 1453. Actually, neither country could afford continuous fighting and the war was interrupted by long truces. Nevertheless, it used up most of the income of the two governments and devastated large areas of France. Other wars, in Scandinavia, Germany, Italy, and Spain, were less spectacular but caused a great deal of suffering.

The net result of all these conflicts was to confirm patterns that were already emerging in the thirteenth century. Germany remained a divided land ruled by many independent princes, of whom the Habsburg rulers of Austria were the strongest. Northern Italy remained a region of city-states, now wealthier than most of the other cities of Europe because the Italians had gained a virtual monopoly over the eastern trade. The district around Rome claimed by the pope was almost in a state of anarchy, and southern Italy was occupied by a decaying monarchy. The three Spanish kingdoms of Portugal, Castile, and Aragon had driven the Moors to the southernmost tip of the peninsula, and marriages that would lead to the union of Castile and Aragon were being prepared. Most important of all, the outcome of the Hundred Years' War confirmed the unity of France and forced the English to give up their hopes of holding territory on the continent. When a peasant girl, Joan of Arc, became convinced that her religious duty and her loyalty to the French royal house required her to drive out the English, and then secured enough support to persuade armies to follow her against the invaders, it became clear that the English were facing forces they could not defeat. It is too early to speak of nationalism, but dislike of English rule had brought the French very close to nationalistic ideas. The English burned Joan as a heretic in 1431, but twenty years later they had lost all their French lands except Calais.

The wars also tended to sharpen an already-existing difference between the institutions of England and those of other kingdoms. England was a unitary state, not an assemblage of provinces. Therefore England had a single representative assembly, the Parliament, instead of an assembly for each province or region. Representative assemblies had been introduced into most European states by thirteenth-century rulers who had found them useful instruments for influencing public opinion. Occasionally the assemblies were asked to give advice on policy or the making of statutes; more frequently, they were asked to consent to taxation. But where there were many provincial assemblies the opposition of one province made little difference; and

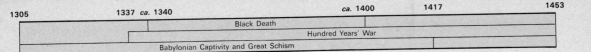

		Black Death				
			Hundred Years' War			
	Babylonian Captivity and Great Schism					

where the pressure of war was greatest, as in France, there was a tendency to let the king collect taxes for defense without bothering about getting consent. The English Parliament, on the other hand, spoke for the whole country and England never had to face a dangerous invasion. The representatives of the propertied classes—the landowners and businessmen—who sat in Parliament agreed on basic issues, so class disputes did not weaken the assembly. Moreover, the members of Parliament were drawn from among the same men who collected local taxes and who, as Justices of the Peace, maintained order in the towns and counties. The government needed the support of these men, especially since it was weakened by factions among the nobility and by civil wars that resulted in the death of five of the nine kings who ruled between 1307 and 1485. All English governments in this period had to seek public support and the appearance of legitimacy. Parliament could give both. Therefore, Parliament became an essential part of the machinery of government; no statute could be enacted and no tax imposed without its consent. On the continent, representative assemblies seldom played an important role in government, and what influence they did have dwindled in the fifteenth century. The English Parliament survived both the disorders of the fifteenth century and the strong monarchs of the sixteenth century and by the seventeenth century occupied a unique position in Europe.

Futile wars, heavy taxes, bad administration,

An English court in the later Middle Ages. This miniature is one of four vellum leaves surviving from a law treatise of the reign of Henry IV, early 15th century. At the top are the five judges of the Court of King's Bench; below them are the king's coroner and attorney. On the left are the jury and in front, in the dock, is a prisoner in fetters, with lawyers on either side of him. In the foreground more prisoners, chained to each other, wait their turn, watched over by jailers. On the center table stand the ushers, one of whom seems to be swearing in the jury.

and factional quarrels had decreased respect for secular governments. But the Church was unable to profit from this decline, because the Church suffered from similar troubles. Early in the fourteenth century, French influence, coupled with disorders in Italy, persuaded the popes to abandon Rome for Avignon, a city just across the Rhône from France. There they stayed for over seventy years (1305-1378). This "Babylonian Captivity" hurt the prestige of the Church. The Avignon popes were good administrators but not good spiritual leaders; they were suspected (wrongly) of being puppets of the king of France; and a pope who was not at Rome hardly seemed a true pope. But worse was to follow. Pope Gregory XI moved back to Rome and died there in 1378. His successor, Urban VI, who was chosen under some pressure from the Roman mob, soon succeeded in angering the cardinals. They fled back to Avignon, repudiated their choice of Urban, and elected a rival pope, Clement VII. All attempts to heal the dispute failed, and for forty years there were two lines of popes, one at Rome and one at Avignon. This Great Schism left Europe completely confused and divided. No one was entirely sure who the rightful pope was and everyone was disgusted by the bickering between the two camps. Heresy, belief in witchcraft, and cynical immorality flourished. The Great Schism was one of the events that prepared the way for the Protestant Reformation.

In the darkest days of the fourteenth century it looked as if the western civilization that had so recently emerged was about to collapse. But there was a surprising toughness in European society. Almost everything seemed to be working badly, but almost nothing stopped working altogether. The Church continued to function, and the vast majority of the people remained fervently Christian. Kings and ministers might be overthrown, but monarchies endured. The nobility gained power because it commanded the armed

The Great Schism 1378–1417

forces, but it remained dependent on central governments because the governments paid the troops. There was no new fragmentation of the European political structure such as had occurred after the death of Charlemagne. War and plague did not stop the production of goods nor the exchange of commodities. In fact, in some areas per capita production actually increased as peasants concentrated on the best land and as artisans moved into country districts where they were less hampered by urban regulations on hours of labor and techniques of production. Pessimism about the state of the world did not kill the intellectual life of the universities. Some of the most subtle theological reasoning of all time appeared in the fourteenth century, as did the first really original European contributions to scientific theory. For example, scholars at Oxford worked out a close approximation to the correct law of accelerated motion. This continuing interest in science was especially important because other peoples, notably the Moslems, were losing

interest in the subject. Between 1300 and 1500, western Europe gained a practical monopoly of the study of science.

During the same period some notable advances in technology were made. Ocean-going sailing ships were perfected and voyages were made to distant Atlantic islands, such as the Azores. Blast-furnaces were improved, so that the production of iron increased. The discovery of gunpowder did not immediately change the art of war, because early cannon were too clumsy for anything but siege operation, but it did put new demands on the art of metallurgy. In light industry new types of textiles were developed and the first mechanical clocks appeared. It was not yet true that western technology was superior to that of any other region, but it was true that the West was experimenting with a very broad range of technologies. There was growing interest in rather complicated machinery—for example, blast-furnace bellows driven by water-power and multiple pumps to pull water out of deep mines. Both the wide range of skills and the fascination with machinery were to be important influences in the future.

There was a great potential for growth in western civilization in the fifteenth century. Many men were aware of this potential; they felt that if they could just get back on the right track all their troubles would vanish. One of the most common words in the writings and speeches of the period was "reform." And it was through the effort to reform its society that western Europe entered the modern age.

Suggestions for Further Reading

W. H. McNeill, *The Rise of the West** (1963). In spite of its title this excellent book deals largely with the ancient world. G. V. Childe, *What Happened in History?** (1964), is a good summary of ancient history before the Greeks. M. Rostovtzeff, *A History of the Ancient World,* 2 vols. (1926), is a little out-of-date, but the superb illustrations and the emphasis on social and economic history make it worth consulting. The book covers Greece and Rome as well as the ancient Middle East.

M. I. Finley, *The Ancient Greeks** (1963), is a good introduction to Greek history. The standard textbook is G. W. Botsford and C. A. Robinson, *Hellenic History* (4th ed., 1957). M. Grant, *The World of Rome** (1961), M. P. Charlesworth, *The Roman Empire** (1951), and H. Mattingly, *Roman Imperial Civilization* (1959), are all worth reading.

F. Lot, *The End of the Ancient World** (1953), is a classic study of the collapse of the Roman Empire. L. M. Duchesne, *Early History of the Christian Church,* 3 vols. (1912–1924), is still one of the best surveys of the subject.

C. Dawson, *The Making of Europe** (1932), is an excellent account of the early Middle Ages. It should be supplemented by F. L. Ganshof, *Feudalism** (3rd Eng. ed., 1964), and by R. Latouche, *The Birth of the Western Economy** (1961). R. W. Southern, *The Making of the Middle Ages** (1953), is a first-rate account of the culture of the High Middle Ages. On institutions, see R. Lopez, *The Birth of Europe* (1967), and J. R. Strayer and D. C. Munro, *The Middle Ages* (5th ed., 1970).

W. K. Ferguson, *Europe in Transition* (1962), and D. Hay, *Europe in the Fourteenth and Fifteenth Centuries* (1967), are good introductions to the problems of Europe in the later Middle Ages.

---

* Available in paperback edition.

1

The Revival of Europe

During the course of the fourteenth century economic depression, plague, and war had weakened western Europe. Secular rulers, who in 1300 had seemed close to establishing absolute monarchies, had lost much of their power over the privileged classes and thus much of their ability to maintain law and order. The prestige of the Church had declined during the Babylonian Captivity and the Great Schism. Most men believed in monarchy as the best form of government; almost all believed in the Church as the only source of salvation. But with both these traditional authorities functioning badly, there seemed to be little hope for religious reform or a revival of security and prosperity. Everyone desired peace, a healing of the schism in the Church, better government, and increased production and trade. But no one knew how to begin, and there was a note of hopelessness in the writings of even the most ardent reformers of the period.

By the end of the fifteenth century, a startling change had taken place. The economic depression had ended; new industries at home and new trade-routes overseas had opened up new opportunities and created new wealth. Kings and princes had clearly gained the upper hand over the privileged classes, especially in France, Spain, and England. The papal schism was ended and Rome was once more the capital of Western

The Exchange at Antwerp, founded in 1531, was the center of European trade and finance until the end of the century.

Christendom. New forms of learning based on an intensive study of the classics were competing with or modifying older studies. New forms of art were challenging the late Gothic style. Most important, there was a note of optimism and confidence, of excitement and enjoyment. There was talk of a "new age" dawning, a "dark age" past, a rebirth of the best qualities of classical civilization. By 1500 the basic characteristics of our "modern" world were becoming visible: its dynamic economy and fluid society, its sovereign nation-states and international anarchy, its secular ideals, and its intellectual and moral values.

We can now see that the political and economic revival of Europe was led by the North, while intellectual, literary, and artistic innovations were largely the work of Italy. But this difference was less obvious in the fifteenth century than it was later, and in the transition from the medieval to the modern world the Italians had the great advantage of being the first to realize that a transition was taking place. They were the ones who talked of a new age, of a break with the barbarous past; they were the ones who believed that a new civilization could be created that would be a worthy heir of Greece and Rome. As a result, in the two centuries between the death of Dante (1321) and the sack of Rome by mutinous imperial troops (1527), Italy exerted increasing influence over the rest of Europe. Italians set the style in architecture, sculpture, and painting; they dictated the literary taste that Europe was to follow for generations. They developed a genuinely new social ideal, that of "the gentleman," and the educational ideal of a "liberal education." Italy was the school of Europe. Northerners flocked there by the thousands, and Italians, in turn, appeared in every northern court, even in remote Muscovy.

There were several reasons for Italy's leadership in the change from medieval to early modern ways of life. Italy had always been somewhat different from the rest of Europe during the Middle Ages. It was never completely feudalized, and it early rejected most feudal institutions. It rejected a unified monarchy under the German emperor even more decisively. Scholasticism never dominated Italian thinking, nor did the Gothic style ever dominate Italian art. Since the medieval tradition in Italy was weak, it could easily be rejected. Yet the Italian cities had great wealth, large populations, and complete independence. If they wanted to reject medieval forms and try new experiments in art, literature, and politics, they could be powerful instruments of social change.

The City-states of Northern Italy

The northern Italian cities were dominated by international trade. A third of the population of Florence lived by importing wool from agricultural countries and selling finished cloth all over Europe and the Levant. Almost all the population of Venice depended directly or indirectly on trade in oriental goods such as silk and spices. In such communities capitalists—the banker, the export merchant, the large-scale manufacturer—were the most important figures.

The Italian towns controlled the countryside around them as northern European towns did not. They had broken the power of the landed nobility and had absorbed the defeated class into their own communities. Peasant villages and small market-towns had been annexed by large urban centers. Thus city-states were created—that is, a strong city government controlled not only its own immediate area but hundreds of square miles of rural territory.

Class divisions were sharp in these city-states. At the top were the wealthy merchants and bankers—the *popolo grasso,* or "fat people," as they were called. Beneath them were the lesser bourgeoisie, the *popolo minuto,* or "little people"—craftsmen, shopkeepers, and petty businessmen. And beneath them was a growing proletariat of workers. Outside the town walls was the peasantry, who had no political influence and little hope of improving their condition. Conflict was constant between the *popolo grasso* and the *popolo minuto,* and occasionally the workers themselves rose in brief, short-lived rebellions, as they did in Florence in 1378. Generally an oligarchy representing the big business interests managed to maintain political control. But the

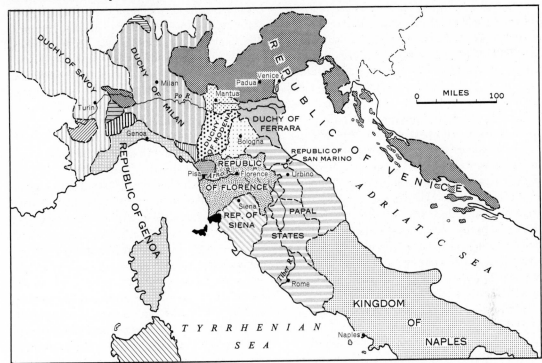

oligarchs did not always agree among themselves, nor did they always preserve internal security or financial stability. During the fourteenth century quarrels among oligarchs and conflicts between classes became so frequent and so disturbing that town after town called in an outsider and gave him absolute power to restore law and order. These men set up military dictatorships and held on to their power through a combination of ruthlessness and shrewdness. They shed the blood of political opponents without hesitation or scruple, but they were generally careful to improve the city's public utilities, strengthen its defenses, devise an efficient system of taxation, provide police protection, and above all, foster business. Thus the rise of big business led to irreconcilable personal and class struggles, and these in turn to "the age of the despots."

War and Diplomacy

Oligarchs and despots, realizing that the merchants and shopkeepers disliked military service, replaced citizen militias with mercenary troops called *condottieri.* These troops were not very reliable; they were loyal to their generals rather than to their employers. The generals tried to preserve their military assets by avoiding pitched battles and trying to win wars by clever maneuvers and negotiations. But while they did not fight very much, they did have a monopoly of military power and some generals displaced weak despots or divided city governments.

What distinguished northern Italy most sharply from the rest of Europe was the total independence of its city-states from any central government. From Venice, oldest and proudest of the city-states, on down to towns of a few thousand inhabitants, city governments acted as if they were subject to no superior power. Motivated by economic and political self-interest, each city-state engaged in endless wars, making and breaking alliances, and jealously watching the most powerful state of the moment to make sure that it did not become strong enough to conquer the peninsula. About the middle of the fifteenth century the Italian city-states began to maintain resident ambassadors at the courts of foreign states to keep rulers in constant touch with governments that might one day become either useful allies or dangerous enemies. At about the same time a kind of "balance of power" began to operate among the five leading states in Italy—Venice, Milan, Florence, the Papal States, and the Kingdom of Naples—in response to an unwritten understanding that no one of the five must be allowed to gain a preponderance of power. When France and Spain intervened in Italy at the close of the fifteenth century, both these practices—the basic machinery of modern diplomacy and the balancing of power among a group of sovereign states—spread to the larger stage of Europe. By the mid-sixteenth century, resident ambassadors were common throughout central and western Europe, and a rough balance of power had been established between the ruling dynasties of the two most powerful states, France and Spain.

Milan, Venice, and Florence

Behind these generalizations lie the striking variety and individuality of the Italian cities of this era. Milan, the largest city of the Po Valley, was perhaps the most typical. It submitted early to a despot and about 1400 a Milanese ruler, Gian Galeazzo Visconti, came as close as any strong man of the time to eliminating his rivals and uniting northern Italy. He failed, but the fear he inspired persisted, and no other despot managed to come so close to dominating northern Italy.

Venice, the greatest commercial power of the peninsula, was absorbed in her widespread Mediterranean interests and was relatively isolated from Italian politics until she began to acquire territory on the mainland in the later fifteenth century. Her republican constitution was the oldest and her government the most stable in Italy. There was no despot in Venice—her doge, or duke, was a figurehead—but a tight-knit commercial aristocracy ran the city, through a small and tough-minded executive committee, the Council of Ten. Perhaps because the energies of the whole population were so absorbed in commerce, there were no real revo-

lutions and few conspiracies in Venetian history. Her constitution stood as a model of republican stability to other Italians.

Florence, like Venice, was proud of being a republic among the welter of despotisms and was especially proud of having helped to frustrate Gian Galeazzo Visconti's attempt to snuff out republican liberties in Italy. But in every other respect Florence and Venice were unlike. Venice lived primarily by her commerce; Florence primarily by her banking and industry. The most astute bankers and the finest textiles in Europe were both to be found in Florence. The energies of Venetians were directed outward toward the sea; the energies of Florentines were focused on industry and politics within the city walls. Venetian society and Venetian government exhibited a high degree of stability, whereas nothing seemed stable in Florence. Revolution seemed to be the chief outdoor sport and constitution-making the chief indoor sport. During the fourteenth and early fifteenth centuries the Florentines tried everything from dictatorship to radical democracy; they compromised on oligarchy and finally ended with boss rule. In 1434 a new-rich party within the oligarchy, led by one of the city's wealthiest and shrewdest bankers, Cosimo de' Medici, gained power. For almost sixty years Cosimo and his grandson, Lorenzo the Magnificent (d. 1492), ran the city by manipulating its republican constitution. Cosimo was a banker who had been forced to play politics in order to save his financial interests. Lorenzo was a more typical despot, only incidentally concerned with the family banking business. But each devoted his energy, his money, and his taste to the job of protecting, expanding, and beautifying the city. The most glittering example of Italy's golden age was Florence under the Medici.

Italian Urban Civilization

In these busy, crowded cities of northern Italy a new sort of society and a new set of social ideals grew up, quite unlike feudal society and chivalric ideals. Birth and status counted for almost nothing. The chivalric virtues of loyalty and honor seemed irrelevant. Here were urban communities built upon advanced industrial methods and a division of labor, and dependent on the continental market for their economic existence. Competition was keen at every level, from managing a shop or fashioning an altar piece to serving as banker to the pope or running a city government. Careers were open to talent everywhere, and it was talent, education, and determination that counted, not birth or ownership of land. The man who ended his life as a famous painter, a widely read author, a wealthy banker, or an infamous despot may well have begun life as a poor peasant or a humble artisan. Self-reliance, rational calculation, ingenuity in adapting means to ends, imagination, and boldness—these were the qualities that carried men to the top. And there was always room at the top for creative and brilliant minds, if they had also the will to achieve fame. All these qualities were summed up in a word often on the lips of artists, writers, and statesmen: *virtù*. This was the quality that made a man a true man (Latin: *vir*). It did not mean "virtue" in the modern sense, but rather "virtuosity," that combination of genius and determination that makes for greatness in artistic creation, statesmanship—or crime.

Individualism

The first mark of this society, at its upper levels at least, was individualism. For the typical Italian city-dweller, few of the old authorities carried the weight they once had carried. He owed no allegiance to a feudal lord. His gild could not regulate his business practices so closely as it might have done two centuries earlier. The city government demanded strict obedience, it is true, but he had a large say in how this government was run and could lay down limits that not even a despot could overstep without facing trouble. He recognized no worldly power of king or emperor or pope within the boundaries of his city-state. And although the city-dweller professed himself a good Christian and a hater of heresy, he generally despised the clergy and tended to accept their authority only when it was backed by strong ecclesiastical sanctions.

Thus in the fifteenth century there was a new emphasis on man as a private person, mainly concerned with himself, his family, his friends, and his own self-development. Such individualism sometimes went to extremes, as it did in the case of Benvenuto Cellini (1500–71), a sculptor who described his violent and colorful career in a famous *Autobiography*. Cellini assumed that the ordinary laws of morality were made for ordinary people and that they neither could nor should be enforced in the case of geniuses like himself. He also assumed that autobiography, a literary form that had been very rare in the Middle Ages, was a natural form of expression and one that would find eager readers. He begins his book: "All men of whatsoever quality they be, who have done anything of excellence, . . . ought to describe their life with their own hand." Later he remarks, "I make no profession of writing history. It is enough for me to occupy myself with my own affairs." Cellini was obviously interesting to himself, and he was sure he was interesting to others.

Secularism

The second mark of this new society was its predominantly secular tone. This does not mean that it was pagan or anti-Christian. It means that the things of this world increasingly occupied the time and attention of the Italian townspeople—the balance of profit and loss, well-built houses and fine clothes, rich food and drink, the enjoyment of leisure—and that the ascetic and otherworldly ideals of the medieval Church seemed more and more remote to them. Their tastes and attitudes are evident in the marvelously realistic stories of Boccaccio's popular *Decameron* (*ca.* 1350). The heroes and heroines are not exactly irreligious or critical of Christian ideals, but they despise the hypocrisy of priests and monks, and they rejoice in the triumph of clever people of the world over clerical busybodies.

The secularism of Italian society can thus be broken down into two components: preoccupation with worldly pursuits, and contempt for those who professed the ascetic ideal but did not live up to it. There were a few pagans or

Minters making silver thalers (from which comes our word *dollar*). A heated metal disk has been placed on a die with the tongs, another die has been placed on top of the disk, and the minter is striking the top die with an iron mallet. Detail from a painting by Hans Hesse, Church of St. Anne, Annaberg, Saxony.

atheists. But most men simply thought more constantly of this world than of the next, without denying the ultimate importance of the next. There was a latent conflict between the older and the new ideals, a conflict that troubled many writers and artists. In fact, tension between worldly and otherworldly ideals was more typical of the period than was the frank and untroubled enjoyment of temporal pleasures.

Humanism

The third mark of Italian urban society was its enthusiasm for classical antiquity. This enthusiasm came to be called Humanism—from the Latin *humanitas,* as used by Cicero to describe the literary culture proper to a well-bred man. The Middle Ages had always lived in the shadow of Rome, and interest in classical literature was nothing new. John of Salisbury in the twelfth century had a first-rate knowledge of Latin literature, and the greatest medieval poet, Dante, made it his conscious concern to blend the best of both classical and Christian ideals throughout the *Divine Comedy.* However, Francesco Petrarca, or Petrarch (1304–74), is rightly called the father of a new Humanism. His enthusiasm for Cicero, his love for Rome (he said he wished he had been born in the ancient world instead of his own), and his feel for the style of classical Latin were contagious. Within a generation or two after his death Petrarch's followers were busily digging out classical manuscripts from monasteries, writing letters to one another in impeccable Ciceronian Latin, pouring contempt on the Latin style of medieval scholastic philosophers, and, most important, getting jobs as secretaries at the papal Curia and the courts of the despots, or as teachers to the children of the ruling classes in the cities. These professional Humanists were something new in European society. Generally they were laymen who made a living by their learning, not clerics or monks devoting spare time to classical study. They were self-made men who were selling a new type of scholarship to their contemporaries—and who found the market very good. Enthusiasm for the classics was heightened after 1395, when refugee scholars from Constantinople began to teach Greek to eager students in Florence and elsewhere. And by the end of the fifteenth century a few Italians were even beginning to learn Hebrew and Arabic. Humanism was both a scholarly movement and a social fad. The Humanists revived the study of classical Latin, Greek, and Hebrew, and they got the ruling classes of the Italian cities excited about what they were doing.

The Humanists initiated a revolution in educational theory and practice. Formal education in the Middle Ages had been dominated by the clergy and directed mainly to the production of clerics. The nobility had their own program of training knights to hunt and fight and behave properly at court. But neither of these systems of education offered much to the sons of business and professional town-dwellers, and already there were town schools, primarily for laymen, that taught arithmetic and medieval Latin grammar. The Humanists of the fifteenth century rediscovered what Greco-Roman writers had meant by the "liberal arts": the liberating effect on mind and imagination of the study of great literature and philosophy. To this they added the chivalric emphasis on outdoor activity and athletic skill and so formed a new pattern of education. The result was a program designed to produce well-rounded and well-read laymen, able to write classical Latin and perhaps Greek, well-mannered and at home in polite society,

Petrarch on Mortal and Immortal Ends

I do not think my way of looking at it is so unreasonable as you imagine. My principle is that, as concerning the glory which we may hope for here below, it is right for us to seek it while we are here below. One may expect to enjoy that other more radiant glory in heaven, when we shall have there arrived, and when one will have no more care or wish for the glory of earth. Therefore, as I think, it is in the true order that mortal men should first care for mortal things; and that to things transitory things eternal should succeed; because to pass from those to these is to go forward in most certain accordance with what is ordained for us, although no way is open for us to pass back again from eternity to time.

From Petrarch, as quoted in *Petrarch's Secret*, trans. by W. H. Draper (London: Chatto and Windus, 1911), p. 176.

physically strong and well groomed, skillful in the art of war. "We call those studies liberal," wrote one Humanist educator, "which are worthy of a free man . . . that education which calls forth, trains, and develops those highest gifts of body and of mind which ennoble men." In practice this education too often degenerated into a narrowly literary training, floundering in the grammatical details of dead languages and consciously aristocratic in its ideals. But at its best it passed on to later generations, including our own, the goal of turning out well-balanced human beings, devoted to both classical and Christian ideals, and able to become better businessmen or lawyers or statesmen because of their liberal education.

Historical Self-consciousness

The fourth and final mark of this urban society was its historical self-consciousness. The historical sense of the Middle Ages was not highly developed. The crucial events of the Christian drama had already happened, and time now had only to run on and out to its conclusion in the Last Judgment. There had been no essential change since the days of Constantine: The emperor was still theoretically the temporal head of Christendom, and the pope, Christ's Vicar, was the spiritual head. The passage of time would not bring further significant change.

Petrarch and his Humanist successors in the fifteenth century revolutionized this conception of the past. They became more interested in this world and its history. Their enthusiasm for classical antiquity enabled them for the first time to see the ancient world as a civilization that had run its course. It had been born, it had flourished, and it had died. They talked of the "Fall of Rome" and of a "Dark Age" that had followed. Above all, they talked of a "rebirth," or "revival," that was beginning in their own age. Rome had had its Golden Age and had fallen; darkness had succeeded, but now the light was beginning to dawn once more. The Humanists and their followers were highly conscious of their position in history and of their historical mission.

The "Renaissance"

While the Italian Humanists were sure that they lived in an age of rebirth, they were not nearly so sure of the profound implications of their work as were later historians. Chief of these was the Swiss Jacob Burckhardt, who wrote a brilliant book called *The Civilization of the Renaissance in Italy* (1860). Thanks to Burckhardt, western historians accepted the idea that there was a "Renaissance," or rebirth, after the Middle Ages, that it marked a sharp break with medieval ideals and practices, and that it was centered in Italy. There was much truth in Burckhardt's thesis, but he exaggerated both the sharpness of the breach with the medieval past and the uniqueness of Italy in comparison with the rest of Europe.

The term "Renaissance" is most useful when it is applied to the revolutionary change in the arts, in literature, and in the concept of man that took place in Italy in the fourteenth, fifteenth, and early sixteenth centuries. It is less useful when applied to political and ecclesiastical history because it is hard to say what "rebirth" means in these areas. And it is quite useless when

applied to economic and social history, in which changes are always slow and in which the important developments began as far back as the eleventh century. Historians of art and literature are relatively sure of what "Renaissance" means; other historians are unsure in varying degrees to the point of total doubt. This does not mean that artistic and literary developments had no connection with economic and social change. It means simply that the word "Renaissance" is best used to describe the revolution in artistic and literary taste and skill that occurred at the close of the Middle Ages.

Literature, Philosophy, and Scholarship

Wherever there were classical models to fall back on, the tendency at first was for both writers and artists to lose themselves in simple imitation, in the first flush of excited rediscovery. It was easy, for instance, for Humanists to imitate the letter-writing, the orations, the moral essays, and even the poetry of the Romans—and they did, *ad nauseam,* in the early fifteenth century. When it became possible for educated Florentines to read Plato in the original Greek, the Medici fostered an informal group of scholars who became known as the Platonic Academy. Their leading members, Marsilio Ficino (1433–99) and Pico della Mirandola (1463–94), tried to reconcile Platonism and Christianity, as the Schoolmen had tried to reconcile Aristotelianism and Christianity. It was the one serious attempt at philosophical synthesis during the Renaissance, and it was a failure. But enthusiasm for Plato and Platonism was infectious and had widespread influence on poets and painters throughout Europe in the next century. In fact, Plato dominated the imagination of the Renaissance as Aristotle had dominated the thought of the Schoolmen.

All was not mere imitation in Italian thought and writing, however. Modern critical scholarship, in the sense of careful linguistic and historical analysis of the literary remains of the past, dates from the Renaissance, and particularly from one of the keenest minds of the age, Lorenzo Valla (*ca.* 1405–57). Valla analyzed the language and the historical background of the so-called Donation of Constantine, one of the main bulwarks of the popes' claims to temporal power, and proved beyond a shadow of a doubt that the document was a clumsy forgery of the Dark Ages. He further compared several Greek manuscripts of the New Testament with the accepted Latin translation, the Vulgate, and showed that the translation was full of errors and distortions. The critical spirit and scholarly technique which he inaugurated influenced Erasmus, Pierre Bayle, and Voltaire and resulted in the "scientific" scholarship of the nineteenth century.

Social and Political Thought

Much of Renaissance thought about the relation of man to man simply paraphrased the ethics and political theories of the Greeks and Romans. But sometimes a man wrote freshly from his own experience and spoke directly to the members of his own society. For example, Leon Battista Alberti (1404–72) in his book *On the Family,* described the interests and ideals of the Florentine families he knew: prudence and thrift, strong family feeling and little concern for larger causes outside, appreciation of comfort, planning and foresight, and pride in owning a house in the city and an estate in the country to produce all the family's food. It is one of the earliest idealized portraits of what will later be called the bourgeois virtues.

A social stratum just above that described by Alberti is sketched in Baldassare Castiglione's (1478–1529) *The Courtier,* based on his memories of the court of the Duke of Urbino. If Alberti painted the good householder for future generations, Castiglione painted the gentleman—graceful, attractive, courteous, liberally educated, noble in spirit if not necessarily in birth, at home either on the field of battle or among cultivated ladies. The concept of "the gentleman" owed much to chivalry and other traditional sources, but Castiglione presented it as a genuinely fresh ideal in the history of European civilization.

In the case of Niccolò Machiavelli (1469–1527), wide reading in the classics illuminated years of practical political experience.

A Great Historian's Conception of the Renaissance

In the Middle Ages both sides of human consciousness—that which was turned within as that which was turned without—lay dreaming or half awake beneath a common veil. The veil was woven of faith, illusion, and childish prepossession, through which the world and history were seen clad in strange hues. Man was conscious of himself only as member of a race, people, party, family, or corporation—only through some general category. In Italy this veil first melted into air; an *objective* treatment and consideration of the state and of all the things of this world became possible. The *subjective* side at the same time asserted itself with corresponding emphasis; man became a spiritual *individual,* and recognised himself as such. In the same way the Greek had once distinguished himself from the barbarian, and the Arabian had felt himself an individual at a time when other Asiatics knew themselves only as members of a race. It will not be difficult to show that this result was owing above all to the political circumstances of Italy. . . . At the close of the thirteenth century Italy began to swarm with individuality; the charm laid upon human personality was dissolved; and a thousand figures meet us each in its own special shape and dress. Dante's great poem would have been impossible in any other country of Europe.

From Jacob Burckhardt, *The Civilization of the Renaissance in Italy,* 1860 (London: Allen & Unwin, 1878), Part II, Ch. 1, p. 129: "The Development of the Individual."

Machiavelli's career as ambassador and secretary of the Florentine government helped him to understand the Roman historian Livy, and Livy helped him to understand the power politics of his own age. Exiled by the Medici from Florence in 1512, he began to read widely and to reflect on what makes states expand and grow, what are the causes of political breakdown, how political leaders get and hold power, what can be learned from the past.

Machiavelli set down his reflections in a long, rambling book, *Discourses on Livy,* and in a briefer and more famous essay, *The Prince.* He made it clear that he was describing things as they were, not as they ought to be. Ideal states he

left to others; in the world as it is, power is what counts. The Roman Republic, he thought, was the best example in history of successful state-building. Its constitution was a masterly blend of monarchy, aristocracy, and democracy; it had good laws and a good citizen army; its religion supported the civic virtues of justice, prudence, and courage, not those of patience and humility; its rulers knew that the good of the state came before the dictates of individual morality. And so Rome, unlike any Italian city-state of Machiavelli's day, had been able to

unite the whole of Italy and to endure for centuries.

But Machiavelli realized that this ideal, real though it once had been, might be too difficult for a corrupt and divided group of Italian city-states to revive. Perhaps a prince of real *virtù,* with the courage of a lion and the cunning of a fox, might be able to learn the laws of politics from history and experience and use them to build a strong state in Italy. He would know that men in their collective relations with one another are bad, and therefore he would not be held back by any moral scruples. If others broke faith with him, as they certainly would, the prince must be prepared to break faith with them for the good of his state. Fortune might frustrate his work, but a man of *virtù* had at least an even chance of overcoming bad luck. If his generation had both the intelligence and the will, Machiavelli believed, something could be done about the helpless state of Italy, which was by now falling under the heels of France and Spain.

Machiavelli's *Prince* was to become a grammar of political and diplomatic practice to heads of state as remote as Mussolini and Hitler. In its origin it was a perfect example of the fruitful combination in Renaissance thought of classical "rebirth" and contemporary "new birth," of historical example and practical experience. Both his disillusioned analysis of things as they were and his passionate plea for reform were entirely characteristic of the age.

The Arts

The influence of classical examples was strong also in the visual arts, but here original elements were even more noticeable than in social and political thought. Roman buildings survived, of course, all over Italy. Brunelleschi (1377?–1446), the greatest architect of his generation, absorbed their spirit and designed new churches in semi-classical style after 1420, thus inaugurating a return to the classical from the Gothic style in architecture. The late Roman sculpture that was dug up (hardly any of the Greek works of the classical age were yet known) inspired sculptors to imitation. But there were no ancient paintings to look at (Pompeii was not unearthed until the eighteenth century), and so Italian painters had to depend on the inspiration of their medieval predecessors and their own genius in elaborating their art.

Italian Renaissance painting developed mainly out of the late medieval tradition known as Gothic naturalism. The dominant interest of fourteenth-century writers, artists, and philosophers was in the concrete, individual thing as it actually existed, not so much in the general idea or eternal truth behind and in all things, which had been the typical concern of earlier

---

Machiavelli on the Policy of Princes

You must know, then, that there are two methods of fighting, the one by law, the other by force: the first method is that of men, the second of beasts; but as the first method is often insufficient, one must have recourse to the second. It is therefore necessary for a prince to know well how to use both the beast and the man.

A prince being thus obliged to know well how to act as a beast must imitate the fox and the lion, for the lion cannot protect himself from traps, and the fox cannot defend himself from wolves. One must therefore be a fox to recognise traps, and a lion to frighten wolves. Those that wish to be only lions do not understand this. Therefore, a prudent ruler ought not to keep faith when by so doing it would be against his interest, and when the reasons which made him bind himself no longer exist. If men were all good, this precept would not be a good one; but as they are bad, and would not observe their faith with you, so you are not bound to keep faith with them.

From Machiavelli, *The Prince*, in *The Prince and the Discourses*, ed. by Max Lerner (New York: Modern Library, 1940), Ch. 18, p. 64.

---

medieval thinkers. Late medieval artists and writers tried to represent nature and man more and more realistically—to model a leaf as it actually appeared in nature, to chisel the features of a real man or woman, to sketch the character of a person in concrete detail, as both Boccaccio and Chaucer did with such success in their collections of tales. In fifteenth-century painting, particularly in the Netherlands, this effort resulted in the most astonishing skill in representing the smallest details of visual reality.

It was an Italian painter, however, who first realized that photographic realism is not enough, that the artist must conceive the human figure as a whole, place it in three-dimensional perspective, and arrive at a more sophisticated realism that sacrifices minute details to organic unity. This painter was Masaccio (1401–*ca.* 1428), the founder of Renaissance painting and one of the great innovators in the history of the art.

God separating the waters from the earth. From the ceiling of the Sistine Chapel, by Michelangelo.

Italian painting of the fifteenth and sixteenth centuries is far too rich in content and varied in technique for us to describe in detail. Some of its general characteristics may be suggested, however. The first thing that strikes the historical observer is the separation of painting and sculpture from architecture. It was as if the sculptured prophets and many-colored saints had stepped down from their niches and stained-glass windows in the great medieval cathedrals to be reincarnated in bronze statues in Italian public squares or painted portraits in Italian palaces. Painting and sculpture were no longer arts subordinate to architecture. Painters began to adorn the walls of monasteries and houses with frescoes. After they had learned from Flemish artists the technique of painting with oils, the Italians went on to develop the easel painting, meant to be hung in a palace or house and to be enjoyed for its own sake. Donatello (1368?–1466), in his *David,* was the first to model a free-standing nude figure, and from then on to the great works of Michelangelo (1475–1564) sculptors developed their art with no thought but of its own perfection. The zest of solving fresh problems infected architects as well as painters and sculptors. Brunelleschi went far beyond classical or medieval models in designing and building his famous dome over the transept of the cathedral in Florence (1420–36). Architecture, sculpture, and painting each went its own way. An individual artist might turn his hand to all three, and a painter might borrow ideas from sculpture. But in each case the artist could create as he pleased without subjecting one art to another.

The second characteristic worth noting was the heightened individuality and social prestige of the artist. A famous passage in Cellini's *Autobiography* describes the unveiling of his bronze statue of Perseus in the central square of Florence in 1554. "Now it pleased God," he wrote, "that on the instant of its exposure to view, a shout of boundless enthusiasm went up in commendation of my work, which consoled me not a little." Such a shout might have greeted the proclamation of a crusade in the eleventh century or the triumphant conclusion of a world war in the twentieth. But the public appreciation of a work of art, the assumption that great art is the product of individual "genius," which is something to be nurtured—these were as characteristic of the Renaissance as they were atypical of ages before and after. The artist was to the age of the Renaissance what the saint was to the Middle Ages and what the scientist was to be to the modern world. Italy's Golden Age was the golden age of the artist and the writer.

In seeking a higher realism, Italian painters studied the laws of spatial perspective about the same time that Humanists were restudying the temporal or historical perspective of their day. As a result the artists pictured real persons whom they knew, in recognizable space. Some of them spent their lives probing the psychological depths of human beings and trying to put on canvas what they found. The chief of these was the lonely scientific and artistic genius, Leonardo da Vinci (1452–1519), whose curiosity about the secrets of nature was as insatiable as his curiosity about the nature of man. In painting *The Last Supper* he chose not the moment when Christ breaks the bread and remarks, "This is my body . . . ," as a medieval artist might have done, but the more humanly dramatic and startling moment when He announces, "One of you will

Freud on Michelangelo's Moses

The Moses of legend and tradition had a hasty temper and was subject to fits of passion. It was in a transport of divine wrath of this kind that he slew an Egyptian who was maltreating an Israelite, and had to flee out of the land into the wilderness; and it was in a similar passion that he broke the Tables of the Law, inscribed by God Himself. . . . But Michelangelo has placed a different Moses on the tomb of the Pope, one superior to the historical or traditional Moses. He has modified the theme of the broken Tables; he does not let Moses break them in his wrath, but makes him be influenced by the danger that they will be broken and calm that wrath, or at any rate prevent it from becoming an act. In this way he has added something new and more than human to the figure of Moses; so that the giant frame with its tremendous physical power becomes only a concrete expression of the highest mental achievement that is possible in a man, that of struggling successfully against an inward passion for the sake of a cause to which he has devoted himself.

From Sigmund Freud, "The Moses of Michelangelo," 1914, *On Creativity and the Unconscious* (New York: Harper, 1958), p. 37.

betray me." The resulting psychological crisis experienced by each disciple is carefully portrayed. The climactic episode of the Creation, as Michelangelo painted it on the ceiling of the Sistine Chapel in St. Peter's, was the creation of Adam—an almost superhuman man at the threshold of self-consciousness, languid, wondering, awakening—almost as if he were a symbol of the man of the Renaissance. According to some interpreters, Michelangelo chose to portray Moses at the moment when he has caught sight of his people's idolatrous Golden Calf and is struggling to control himself.

These few examples typify the Renaissance point of view. The central concern is man here in this world, troubled, striving, with unknown possibilities. Thus Renaissance art is humanistic in the broader, more philosophical meaning of the word. Not that the artists rejected God or ignored nature. God is still there, and Renaissance landscapes are charming. But God is seen through man, through man's heroism and his tragedy; and generally nature is of interest only as background or setting to the human drama. The most important question is what is to become of man. Pico della Mirandola, in a famous *Oration* on man's dignity (1486), pictured God as giving man something he had given to no other creature, the unique gift of freedom:

> Thou, constrained by no limits, in accordance with thine own free will, in whose hands We have placed thee, shalt ordain for thyself the limits of thy nature. . . . We have made thee neither of heaven nor of earth, neither mortal nor immortal, so that with freedom of choice and with honor, as though the maker and molder of thyself, thou mayest fashion thyself in whatever shape thou shalt prefer.

Every other creature had its pattern and its limits, but to Pico man's nature and destiny were in his own hands. The men of the Renaissance had not lost belief in God, but they were convinced, in a way their medieval ancestors would not have understood, that man was on his own.

The greatness of Italian art lay in the fact that it reflected all the tensions and contradictions in the prevailing attitudes toward man. There was no party line in Renaissance art; there were no premature solutions of sharp differences, no accepted syntheses. Some artists were realists, others idealists. Donatello modeled despots as he saw them, with hard and observant realism, while Raphael (1483–1520) a generation later idealized the peasant girls he knew as calm and self-possessed Madonnas of ethereal beauty. Some artists were scientists and psychologists like Leonardo, who tried to peer into the souls of men and women, while others were like the Venetian Titian (1477–1576), who was more interested in the external marks of character and the glorious play of color on the objects about him. Michelangelo, perhaps the most typical as well as the greatest artist of them all, gave his life to attempting the impossible: to reconciling the classical ideal of harmony, balance, and "nothing in excess," with the limitless strivings and boundless love of Christian piety. This attempt to reconcile the Greco-Roman and Hebraic-Christian worlds was the central striving

of the Renaissance. It failed, but the failure left an imperishable record in the arts.

Natural Science

The Renaissance contributed relatively little to the progress of natural science, but this little was important. The Humanists in general were more interested in man than in nature and more absorbed in literature than in mathematics and physics. Nevertheless the northern Italian cities of the fourteenth and fifteenth centuries contributed significantly to the scientific tradition that reached and influenced Galileo in the seventeenth century.

In the techniques that directly concerned man and his comfort the Italians made notable progress. As craftsmen, mechanics, and engineers, they were the best in Europe. In the science of perspective, their painters worked out the mathematical principles of representing figures in space. Their artists and doctors together advanced the knowledge of human anatomy beyond where it had been left by the Greeks. The *Notebooks* of Leonardo da Vinci, a landmark in the history of both art and science, show how closely the two interests were related in the fifteenth-century mind. His studies of anatomical detail, for instance, are of equal interest to painters and doctors. Furthermore, the medieval interest in science survived in the northern Italian universities, particularly Padua. There the study of mathematics flourished and the arguments over Aristotelian laws of motion, which had been begun at the University of Paris, continued. Padua eventually passed on to Galileo a theory of scientific method in something like its modern form.

The Councils and the Papacy

Italian energy and enthusiasm did something to dissipate the pessimism of the late fourteenth century. But Europe was still profoundly Christian and could not be entirely satisfied until its religious problems were solved. Of the three difficulties that faced the Church in 1400—the schism, heresy, and administrative reform—only one was completely overcome. By the mid-fifteenth century there was only one pope in Rome, even if the prestige of his office had been sadly tarnished. The most dangerous heresies had been walled off or driven underground, but the religious atmosphere was still heavy with discontent and revolt. And the more men talked of religious and financial reforms in the Church, the more impossible it seemed to effect them.

The Great Schism had imposed an almost intolerable psychological burden on Europe. In theory there could not possibly be two true Vicars of Christ, yet there was no way of being sure which of the two claimants was the real successor. Men felt as if they were in a sinking ship: "If we remain in it," a contemporary wrote, "we must perish with it, and if we stray outside, salvation escapes us, since outside the ship there is no salvation." Many Lollards and other heretics had strayed outside. Those who remained on board tried desperately to find some solution.

The stubborn behavior of the two lines of popes at Rome and Avignon, in refusing to resign or to submit to arbitration, had increased antipapal feeling among both clergy and laity throughout Europe. In 1395 the French became so exasperated with their own pope that the French clergy, egged on by the government, withdrew their obedience from him for five years. This was the first sign of a policy that was to have an ominous future: secession from papal jurisdiction by the clergy of a large nation under the pressure of the secular government. Even in the fifteenth century it seemed possible that Christendom might dissolve into independent national churches.

The Conciliar Movement

As early as 1379, the year after the schism developed, scholars at the University of Paris had suggested a more conservative and practical scheme than the withdrawal of obedience. They urged that a general council of the Church be called. The leading advocates of the idea at the university worked out a revolutionary conception of the Church to support their proposal. The Church, they argued, was not the papacy but the whole body of believers. Thus the Church's authority was embodied in a council representing all the faithful, with the pope as a limited monarch responsible to this representative assembly. The so-called fullness of power, which canon lawyers claimed for the pope, was a usurpation. Authority in the Church came from the bottom up, not from the top down. This conciliar theory of the constitution of the Church was to have strong appeal to secular rulers who were looking for a club to hold over the papacy. It was also to have a strong attraction for reformers during the next century.

In 1408 most of the cardinals of both sides deserted their popes and summoned a general council to meet at Pisa the next year. For a moment, a group of cardinals without a pope confronted two popes without any cardinals, but the result was simply the election of a third pope. Unfortunately, neither the Roman nor the Avignonese pope resigned, as had been hoped. After five more years of confused negotiations, the new emperor, Sigismund, compelled the Pisan pope, John XXIII, to summon a genuinely representative assembly.

This great council, which met at Constance in Switzerland from 1414 to 1418, made a strong impression on the imagination of the age. It healed the schism by bullying John XXIII into resigning, persuading the Roman pope to resign after he had gone through the formality of summoning and approving the council himself, and deposing the Avignonese pope, who by now had fled to Spain and was supported only by Aragon. In 1417 the council elected a new pope, Martin V, who soon commanded the allegiance of all western Christendom. The council was less successful in instituting reform. The English and German delegates worked in vain to have reform considered before the election of a new pope; the Latin nations were more anxious to heal the schism first and let reform come later. Once Martin V was elected, interest flagged in even the mild report of a committee to study abuses, and the council dispersed without every really facing the complicated malpractices in the hierarchy. On the other hand, the council dealt energetically, though shortsightedly, with the problem of heresy.

John Hus being burned at the stake in 1415. He wears a fool's cap with pictures of the devil and the word "heresiarch" (leader of heretics).

John Hus

The danger-spot in 1414 was Bohemia. Here during the preceding century the emperor Charles IV had helped to foster a national and cultural awakening among the Czechs. But Czech scholars ran into two obstacles: a corrupt and leaderless Church, and a steady influx of Germans into the cities and into the University of Prague. Since the Czechs tended to be reformers, while the Germans generally supported the *status quo* in the Church, the gifted group of Czech preachers and teachers who attacked ecclesiastical abuses soon found themselves leading a movement that was as much patriotic as it was religious. In 1402 a brilliant young leader appeared in John Hus (*ca.* 1369–1415). The burden of his preaching was that faith must be based on the Bible as the only source of authority, that Christ, not the pope, was the true Head of the Church, and that a man is saved by God through Christ, not by trusting in ceremonies and in a mediating priesthood now thoroughly corrupt. Hus knew the ideas of Wiclif, whose books had been brought to Bohemia by Czech students returning from England, but he had developed his basic theories independently. By 1414 Hus had been excommunicated by the Roman pope, but he was at liberty and his ideas were accepted by a majority of the Czech people.

Hus eagerly seized the opportunity to journey to Constance to present his case before the council. He was almost immediately imprisoned for heresy. The emperor, who had granted him a safe-conduct, withdrew his protection the moment the dreaded charge of heresy was made. The conciliar leaders would have preferred a public recantation that could have been publicized throughout Bohemia, but Hus stood firm. In the dramatic trial that followed, the essential issue was whether the Bible and a man's conscience are the ultimate religious authority, as Hus argued, or whether the Catholic Church represented by the clerical hierarchy is the sole authority, as the council declared. Hus was condemned and burned at the stake outside the walls of Constance in May 1415. His follower, Jerome of Prague, was burned on the same spot the following spring.

Before the council disbanded, civil and religious warfare had broken out in Bohemia. It lasted for almost twenty years. The upshot was an agreement in 1436 between the more conservative Hussites and the Church. This agreement recognized a national church in Bohemia with local control over ecclesiastical appointments and with its own liturgical practices, notably the right to offer the cup as well as the bread to the laity in the Eucharist. For the first time the Church had made an agreement on equal terms with condemned heretics after excommunicating them and solemnly preaching a crusade against them. Wiclif's Lollards had been driven underground in England, but the Hussite heresy had simply been walled off in Bohemia.

The restored papacy, which owed its existence to the Council of Constance, was more successful in defeating the conciliar movement than it was in extirpating heresy. The fathers had decreed at Constance that general councils must be summoned regularly, eventually once every ten years. But the superior diplomacy and the more efficient administrative machinery of the Roman papacy made this provision a dead letter within a few years. Leading churchmen

and secular rulers ceased to support the conciliar ideal, and by the time Nicholas V became pope (1447–55) the threat that the Church might be transformed into a limited monarchy was over. Never again was there a general council of the church that the pope could not control.

The popes' triumph over the councils left the papacy stronger in some respects but weaker in others. No one within the Church itself could challenge the papal "fullness of power," but the victory had been bought by making wide concessions to powerful secular rulers. In opposing the reforming element in the councils, the popes had isolated themselves from clerical and lay leaders of opinion, particularly in the north of Europe. As a result, the popes depended on the support of lay rulers and could not resist their efforts to control the clergy within their own realms. In 1438 the king of France summoned an assembly of the French clergy and issued a solemn decree known as the Pragmatic Sanction of Bourges. This decree strictly limited the pope's power of appointment and taxation in France and in effect set up a national, or "Gallican," Church, as it was called. In later years the popes were able to persuade the French monarchs to modify this one-sided action by "concordats," or agreements, between the papacy and the French crown. But in these agreements the monarchy always retained its control over appointments to the higher clergy. With some differences, the kings of England and Spain established similar limitations on papal power during the fourteenth and fifteenth centuries. In Germany, where there was no central government strong enough to stand up to the pope, papal rights of appointment, taxation, and jurisdiction were not limited as they were in the stronger monarchies. The popes had eliminated all rivals for power within the church, only to be faced by much more greedy and formidable rivals outside the Church—the monarchs.

The Renaissance Papacy

The eighty years between the accession of Nicholas V to the papacy (1447) and the sack of Rome (1527) are often called the period of the Renaissance Papacy. It was a brilliant but tragic era in the history of the Church. Some of the popes of the period were patrons of Humanism and the arts, notably Nicholas V, founder of the Vatican Library, and Julius II (1503-13), builder of St. Peter's. Pius II (1458-64) had been Aeneas Sylvius, a celebrated Humanist, before his election. Two were particularly noted for their wars: Sixtus IV (1471-84), who was rumored to have died of rage at the conclusion of a peace settlement; and Julius II, who was known to his generation as "the Warrior Pope." More than one was notorious for his nepotism, or favoritism to relatives. Roderigo Borgia, Alexander VI (1492-1503), was by far the worst of the lot. His mistresses lived openly with him, his voracious Spanish relatives got whatever they asked for, and his notorious son, Cesare Borgia, made a bloody attempt to become the ruler of all northern Italy with his father's help. All the accumulated evils of many years seemed to become intensified in the papal court: simony, nepotism, immorality, involvement in secular politics and warfare. Innocent III two centuries before had been immersed in secular diplomacy, but it had been on a European-wide scale and the excuse had always been the advancement of the Church's cause. Now the scale of involvement was limited in effect to the Italian peninsula, and the popes were generally motivated by a narrow family interest. As time went on, the papacy became thoroughly Italianized, perhaps out of fear of another schism. (Since the end of the schism in 1417, only one non-Italian pope has been chosen, in 1522.) Most secular rulers came to assume that as ruler of the Papal States the pope would act like any Italian despot, at the dictates of his own personal and family interests—with the unfair competitive advantage, of course, that he was considered to be the Vicar of Christ. But even when the papacy seemed to be simply another Italian principality it was sustained by the basic belief that the office was greater than the man, that the moral character of the pope did not lessen his authority in spiritual matters.

The open corruption of the papal Curia during the fifteenth century, however, had much to do with the Protestant revolt that began in 1517. As one historian has put it, the popes of the Renaissance tried to substitute splendor for reform. In the hands of an intelligent and devoted Humanist like Nicholas V this was not an unworthy ideal. To him it meant reconciling Christianity with the best in ancient civilization and rebuilding Rome as the capital of a revived Christendom. But this ideal did not satisfy the mystical and moral strivings of thousands of the faithful, particularly those outside Italy. Significantly it was under a cultivated son of Lorenzo de' Medici, Pope Leo X (1513-21), that most of Germany was lost to the papacy, and under an illegitimate son of Lorenzo's brother, Pope Clement VII (1523-34), that England was lost.

Economic Growth in the North

While Italy was building city-states on the wealth derived from its old monopoly of Mediterranean trade, northern and western Europe was building nation-states based on new industries and new trade-routes. The cumulative effects of technological change began to stimulate the northern economy during the fifteenth century. Thus slow improvements in building and rigging sailing ships made possible the great voyages of Vasco da Gama and Columbus. The first gave the Atlantic countries an increasing share of the lucrative trade in oriental goods. The second gave the same countries a monopoly of the wealth of a New World. Even though Italian trade remained close to its old level, it was dwarfed by the much greater trade of Portugal and Spain, of France, England, and the Netherlands.

In Europe, new and very profitable industries began to appear. To follow only one thread, improved techniques in metallurgy made it possible to take full advantage of the discovery of gunpowder and to make cannons for sieges and naval warfare. More metal was needed: Mining methods had to be improved and blast-furnaces had to be enlarged to enable metal-workers to use the increased supply of ore. The Atlantic states gained control of world sea-lanes, not only because their ships were slightly better than those of their rivals but because they were more powerfully armed with naval cannons. On land the use of siege cannons weakened the nobles, strengthened the monarchs, and so increased security. The noble's castle was no longer a secure retreat, and no ordinary noble could afford the vast cost of heavy guns. If they were to maintain their military tradition, the nobles had to become officers in the armies of kings and princes who could afford to buy the new weapons. They were not always well-disciplined officers, but they were no longer independent war-lords.

As we have seen, the invention of printing from movable type also depended on advances in metallurgy. And that invention, in the middle of the fifteenth century, had even more revolutionary effects than the invention of the cannon. So long as books had to be laboriously copied by hand, only a few men could aspire to higher learning. But as printing presses spread rapidly from the Rhine Valley to Italy, the Netherlands, France, Spain, and England, Europeans had a

Pope Sixtus IV (1471–84), who reorganized the Vatican Library, appoints the well-known humanist Platina as Librarian. Painting by Melozzo da Forli.

flood of books available at prices that would have been unbelievable a century earlier. There were "standard editions" of the Bible, the Fathers, and the classical writers in both Greek and Latin, scientific works, devotional treatises, and popular manuals in the vernacular languages. Like all mechanical inventions, printing brought both good and evil in its train. The "standard editions" could multiply errors as well as corrections, and the pamphlets that were now so easy to print and circulate in large numbers could mislead as well as inform. But one thing was clear: Learning would never again be the monopoly of a small upper class in European society. Anything human beings had written could now be multiplied and placed quickly and cheaply in the hands of anyone who could read.

Industry and Agriculture

New industries such as cannon-founding and printing required large initial investment in plant and machinery. They were organized from the

start as capitalistic enterprises—that is, enterprises in which accumulated wealth was deliberately used to produce more wealth. In addition to capital, these industries needed and attracted free laborers from town or country who could be employed for a wage and dismissed when business slacked off.

Even in the country capitalistic methods calculated to produce a profit were occasionally being applied to the land. Landlords had long realized that raising sheep for wool might be more profitable than accepting a customary rent. Legally or illegally, many of them, particularly in England, managed to fence off, or "enclose," lands formerly reserved for the common use of villagers, or to convert ploughed land to pasture. Since tending sheep required far fewer man-hours than raising food on the same amount of land, many families were displaced from the soil. Occasionally "improving landlords" turned to more intensive cultivation of the soil in order to produce a larger cash crop of food for the growing urban markets, often riding roughshod

The Financial Empire of Jakob Fugger ca. 1485-1525

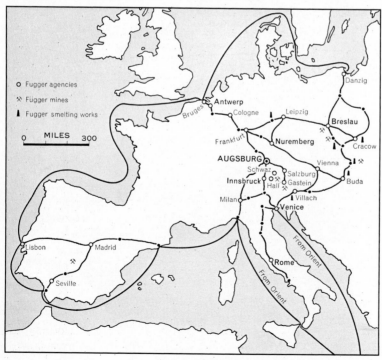

over the preference of villagers for timeworn methods.

In short, capitalism was being applied to industry and agriculture wherever individual entrepreneurs saw profit to be made in producing books, weapons, clothing, or food for sale in the open market. For some peasants and workers this meant new opportunity. Many an ambitious peasant was able to better his position, as Martin Luther's father did by becoming a miner. But a great deal of misery and unemployment also resulted from the breaking down of customary economic relationships, the eviction of peasants from their holdings, and the movement of population to the new industrial centers. "Sturdy beggars" and "vagabonds" were a constant problem to sixteenth-century town governments.

Wealth derived from the new industries and commerce tended to concentrate in a few hands in a few places. For a brief period the most powerful banking house was that of the Fuggers of Augsburg in South Germany. Jakob Fugger (1459–1525) invested in Austrian mines and Spanish colonies and was banker to the pope. On the whole, however, from about 1476 to 1576 Antwerp was the Wall Street of northern Europe, with Lyons not far behind. Then, for a century after 1576, it was Amsterdam. The wealth that poured in from the Orient and the New World had a way of gravitating to the commercial centers of the Netherlands. Where the investment market was freest, where the largest and most aggressive firms transacted most of their business, here were the nerve centers of European finance. Italy was losing its old place as the banking center of Europe. Financial power was clearly shifting to the North.

Political Consolidation and Centralization

The most highly developed monarchies of western Europe—England and France—had undergone a severe crisis in the fourteenth century. The successors of Edward I and Philip the Fair allowed their political ambitions to outstrip their financial resources. The Hundred Years' War (1338–1453) exhausted both France and England, and plague and social revolt added their toll of misery to war. The monarchs were not equal to the strain. As the fifteenth century opened, France was ruled by a king who had periods of insanity (Charles VI), and England was ruled by a usurper who owed his throne to his fellow barons and to Parliament (Henry IV). The future did not seem very bright for the monarchies that had been so painfully built up in the twelfth and thirteenth centuries.

The later fifteenth century, however, saw a remarkable recovery of monarchical institutions in western Europe. As people grew more and more weary of war, violence, and anarchy, the forces striving to restore some semblance of law and order rallied to the support of the monarchs in France, the Spanish kingdoms, and England. Even weak rulers profited from the demand for peace and strong government. And economic revival made it easier to support stronger armies and more effective bureaucracies.

France

At times during the Hundred Years' War the authority of the French king had almost disappeared, but there had been considerable recovery before the war ended in 1453. Charles VII was not a great king, but he was clever enough to make use of the widespread enthusiasm aroused by Joan of Arc to expel the English and to restore law and order to the French countryside. In 1438, by the Pragmatic Sanction of Bourges, he asserted his authority over the French clergy. In the 1440's he solved the financial problem of the crown by obtaining consent to a wide-based tax on land called the *taille;* he then continued to levy the tax on his own authority. He organized a small standing army (at most, 25,000 men) under direct royal control, gained the support of wealthy merchants who supplied him with a siege train of heavy artillery, and methodically ousted the English from all their strongholds on the Continent except Calais.

Louis XI (1461–83) carried on his father's work and left the monarchy stronger than it had been since Philip IV. Louis, a slovenly and superstitious man with a morbid fear of death, had none of the majesty of kingship. He was called "the Spider" because he preferred to trap his enemies in diplomatic webs rather than to fight them. Machiavelli admired him, with reason. The greatest threat to the French monarchy was the powerful state that the dukes of Burgundy had built up on France's eastern frontier, including the wealthy provinces of the Netherlands as well as Burgundy proper. Louis never actually defeated his rival, Charles the Bold, Duke of Burgundy (1467–77), but he shrewdly helped Charles defeat himself. In the end the duke was killed in battle against the Swiss. The richest part of his inheritance, the Netherlands, fell to the Emperor Maximilian (1493–1519) through his marriage with Mary, daughter of Charles the Bold; but the strategically located Duchy of Burgundy went to the king of France. At home, Louis encouraged trade and kept a firm rein on the nobles and higher clergy. His successor Charles VIII (1483–98) married the heiress of Brittany and so brought the last remaining feudal duchy under direct royal control.

With France fully under control, Charles felt strong enough to invade Italy (1494) in order to assert his claims to Naples as heir of the Angevins. Spain, which also had claims in Italy, quickly reacted, and foreign armies fought over the peninsula for half a century. The Italian city-states were helpless; even if they had been united they probably could not have resisted such powers as France and Spain. As it was, Spain gradually gained a dominant position in Italy, and with the loss of independence Italian life lost much of its vigor and excitement. On the other hand, France was not greatly weakened by its losses in the Italian wars, an indication of the monarchy's new strength.

Spain

The Iberian Peninsula had suffered almost as severely as France from war and anarchy in the early fifteenth century. From 1085 to 1212 the petty Christian kingdoms of northern Spain had fought heroically to reconquer the peninsula from the Moslems in a movement known in Spanish history as the Reconquista. By the fifteenth century these kingdoms had coagulated into three monarchies: Portugal in the West, Castile in the center, and Aragon on the Mediterranean coast. The Kingdom of Granada, a small strip in the South, was the last remnant of Moslem rule. In 1469 a momentous marriage took place between Ferdinand of Aragon (1479–1516) and Isabella of Castile (1474–1504). The marriage brought no organic fusion of the political institutions of the two states, but husband and wife followed a common foreign policy and their heir could properly be called king of "Spain." A new national monarchy had been born from a dynastic union.

Isabella re-established the authority of the crown in Castile and with her husband led a successful "crusade" to expel the Moors (as the Moslems in Spain were called) from Granada in 1492. The victory touched off a wave of national patriotism and religious intolerance, which had been slowly gathering force during the later fifteenth century. In 1492 all Jews in both kingdoms were ordered either to become Christians or leave the land, and ten years later, in spite of promises of toleration when Granada fell, all Moors in Castile were offered the same choice. In 1478 some Dominicans had persuaded the pope to authorize Ferdinand and Isabella to set up the Spanish Inquisition. This dreaded instrument became a powerful weapon of national unification when the monarchs directed it against the "converted" Jews and Moors. There was thus a note of religious fervor and racial hatred, which was lacking elsewhere, in the birth of Spain as a great power.

A second marriage was greatly to affect Spain's European destiny in the sixteenth century. The Emperor Maximilian and his wife, Mary of

Burgundy, had a son, Philip, who was heir to Austria through his Habsburg father and to the Netherlands through his mother. Philip married Joanna, the daughter of Ferdinand and Isabella. Their son Charles, born in 1500, eventually became king of Spain (1516–56) and ruler of the Netherlands, Austria, Milan, Naples, and the Spanish possessions in America. In 1519 he was also elected emperor as Charles V. Thus Spain was thrust out into the full stream of European politics and world empire by coming under the Habsburg dynasty in 1516.

Spain was not a wealthy country, nor were its two halves, Castile and Aragon, ever thoroughly amalgamated. Even today Catalonia is markedly different from Castile. But the Spanish armies soon proved themselves the best in Europe during campaigns in Italy and the Netherlands, and Columbus' discoveries brought in a stream of gold and silver from the New World that surpassed all European dreams of wealth. As a result, Spain was to become the leading power in Europe in the sixteenth century.

England

The Hundred Years' War had been a heavy burden on England. But her most severe trial followed the end of the war, when her restless nobility and professional soldiery returned from France to plunge into thirty more years of intermittent civil strife in the Wars of the Roses (1454–85). When it was all over, the first of the Tudors was on the throne as Henry VII (1485–1509), by right of conquest and a dubious hereditary claim. The bloodshed and violence of the wars had sickened the people, and plots and counterplots had killed off most of the leaders of the nobility. Taking advantage of the opportunity to restore the monarchy, Henry proved himself one of the ablest rulers in English history. He kept England out of foreign wars, encouraged trade, restored the sources of royal revenue, and eliminated all pretenders to the throne. His son,

Henry VIII (1509–47), inherited a full treasury, a united nation, and (for its day) an efficient administration. Henry VIII soon wasted the treasury surplus in war with France, but he and his overbearing minister, Cardinal Wolsey, did manage to concentrate power in their own hands. Henry VIII's England could compare well with either France or Spain in governmental efficiency and potential military strength, even though it had only about half Spain's population and a fifth that of France.

The Monarchs and the Nobility

Louis XI, Ferdinand and Isabella, and Henry VII all had common problems which they met in strikingly similar ways. The chief obstacle in the path of rebuilding royal authority in the later fifteenth century was the military, political, and economic strength of the great nobles in each country (the kings were wise enough never to attack the social prestige of the nobility). The monarchs used various expedients in their cold war with overmighty subjects. The key to success was to make the royal council an effective agency of central government. Councillors were selected from among nobles who were loyal to the king and from members of the upper middle class who sought power and promotion. Key councillors, often at their own expense, developed groups of agents who kept them informed about internal and external threats to the security of the state. At the same time the Council, or one of its committees, was given supreme judicial power so that it could act quickly in any emergency. Thus in England the Secretaries of State, who were the most influential members of the Council, were well aware of plots against the throne through their close contacts with local authorities, with English ambassadors abroad, and with a network of spies. The Star Chamber, the judicial arm of the Council, could be used to suppress any manifestations of aristocratic independence, and the ordinary courts almost never failed to convict men accused by the Council. In France and Spain the Council was equally well informed and had even greater judicial power.

The Monarchs
and the Representative Assemblies

A second possible obstacle to royal absolutism was the representative assembly: the Estates General in France, the Cortes in the Spanish kingdoms, and Parliament in England. These assemblies had reached the peak of their influence in the fourteenth century. In the fifteenth century, everywhere but in England, they declined. This was due more to the ineffectiveness of assemblies than to the hostility of monarchs. Except in England, provincial feeling was so strong that it was difficult to reach agreement on any issue. Assemblies were more ready to grumble than to act. In France, for example, the Estates General, in spite of repeated requests, neither supported nor proposed clear-cut alternatives to royal policies. It is also true that the kings had weakened the Estates by depriving them of their financial powers; old taxes were continued and new ones imposed by royal authority alone. Thus the Estates General of France were weak and useless and gradually ceased to meet. In Spain, the monarchs played off class against class by summoning only the representatives of the cities when they needed money, thus depriving the townsmen of the possible aid of the great nobles. Anxious to support royal authority, the town representatives usually consented readily to whatever taxes the king demanded. Deprived of any real power, the Cortes of Castile, like the Estates General of France, met less and less frequently after the end of the fifteenth century. In England Henry VII apparently had little respect for Parliament and, after the first years of his reign, seldom summoned it. But, since the English Parliament could speak for all the privileged classes and all parts of the country, it was more difficult to ignore than the weak and divided assemblies of other countries. In England provincial rivalries scarcely existed; landowners and the bourgeoisie usually cooperated, and no general tax could be levied without Parliamentary consent. When Henry VIII got into trouble with the pope, he summoned Parliament to give him support; this use of Parliament as an accomplice had unanticipated results. By 1600, thanks to the frequent use Henry Tudor and his successors made of it, Parliament had become a more powerful force in English government than ever before. By that time the representative assemblies on the Continent, in states governed by absolute monarchs, had become hollow forms.

The Monarchs and the Church

The final obstacle to the development of monarchical power was the Church. Against this obstacle the kings moved cautiously. Louis XI was proud to be called "Most Christian King" of France, Ferdinand and Isabella were proud to be known as the "Catholic Kings," and Henry VIII was especially proud of his title "Defender of the Faith," which the pope granted him in 1521. But on the three crucial questions of appointment of the higher clergy, taxation of the clergy, and the appeal of ecclesiastical cases to Rome not one of the monarchs admitted the full papal claims. The kings of England and France had established their right to tax their own clergy by 1300. The French kings had asserted their right to control clerical appointments in the Pragmatic Sanction of Bourges, and the pope had granted Francis I the right to nominate the higher clergy and to settle the bulk of ecclesiastical disputes in France in the Concordat of Bologna in 1516. Even the "Catholic Kings" of Spain asserted and maintained their right to appoint, to tax, and to reform the clergy within their kingdoms, despite papal objections. Thus long before the Protestant Reformation there were "national churches" in Europe that looked to the authority of the secular ruler in matters of appointment, taxation, and even jurisdiction, although not in doctrine.

These tendencies in western Europe toward the consolidation of territory and the centralization of political power also appeared in the kingdoms of Norway and Sweden; they appeared too in Russia, where Ivan the Dread (1534–84) ruthlessly broke the power of the aristocracy. In

Italy, however, there was no central government to be strengthened (much to the despair of observers like Machiavelli). In the German Empire the central government was a sham. There was no imperial army, no system of imperial taxation, no imperial supreme court with overriding authority. An attempt at the close of the fifteenth century to give the Empire these advantages was almost a total failure. When Charles V became emperor in 1519, his real strength lay in the fact that he was duke of Austria, lord of the wealthy towns of the Netherlands, and king of Spain, with its well-equipped armies and overseas treasure. Becoming emperor added something to his prestige, much to his responsibilities, but little to his power. Many German princes expanded their territories at the expense of weaker neighbors and increased their authority within their principalities by methods very similar to those of the kings of western Europe. But in 1500 there was no central authority in Germany strong enough to resist papal exactions, foreign intervention, or the spread of heresy.

This lack of central authority was to be of crucial importance for the future. On the one hand, it meant that the Protestant Reformation, once it started, could not be brought under control. On the other, it meant that the emperor had to rely on his own hereditary domains in meeting a new threat that came from the East. The Turks had advanced steadily after the fall of Constantinople in 1453. The greatest of their sultans, Suleiman the Magnificent (1520–66), captured Belgrade, won most of Hungary in the battle of Mohacs (1526), and almost took Vienna in 1529. With a divided Germany behind him and a dangerous enemy facing him in the Danube Valley, the emperor could not play his old role of defender of Christendom until he had built a new state out of the old Habsburg territories.

Suggestions for Further Reading

1. General

J. Burckhardt's great "essay," *The Civilization of the Renaissance in Italy** (1860), is still the starting point for study. J. A. Symonds, *The Renaissance in Italy,** 7 vols. (1875), is more readable but less scholarly than Burckhardt. W. K. Ferguson, *The Renaissance in Historical Thought* (1948), traces the development of the idea of "rebirth" from the humanists themselves through Burckhardt to the present. The same author has also written a good brief survey, *The Renaissance** (1940). The introductory volume to the *Rise of Modern Europe* series (edited W. L. Langer), by E. P. Cheyney, *The Dawn of a New Era: 1250–1453** (1936), treats economic, political, and cultural phenomena which were to have significance for later centuries. The next volume in the series is M. P. Gilmore, *The World of Humanism: 1453–1517** (1952). Both make excellent use of recent monographic material and offer critical bibliographies. D. Hay, *The Italian Renaissance* (1961), is a new work of considerable value.

2. Italian Society and Politics

A. W. O. von Martin, *Sociology of the Renaissance** (1941), is a good example of the approach to the Renaissance of modern social historians. There is interesting material on Renaissance businessmen and bankers in M. Beard, *A History of the Business Man* (1938), and R. de Roover, *The Medici Bank* (1948). I. Origo, *The Merchant of Prato* (1957), is an enjoyable study of a small-town businessman. G. Mattingly, *Renaissance Diplomacy* (1955), traces the origins of modern diplomacy in Italy in a fascinating way. There are histories of all the major Italian states, but the most important for an understanding of the Renaissance are those on Florence. F. Schevill, *A History of Florence** (1936), is the best brief treatment in English. Based on this is the same author's briefer *The Medici** (1949).

---

* Available in paperback edition.

H. Baron, *The Crisis of the Early Italian Renaissance,** 2 vols. (1955), is an important recent study of Florentine politics and culture in the early fifteenth century. Perhaps the best single volume on Machiavelli is F. Chabod, *Machiavelli and the Renaissance** (1958). D. Merejkowski's novel, *The Romance of Leonardo da Vinci** (trans. 1902), gives a vivid and unforgettable picture of Italian society based on sound historical scholarship.

3. Literature and Art

Most of the general works listed above contain discussion of the literary and artistic achievements of the age. The classic literary history, still well worth reading, is F. de Sanctis, *History of Italian Literature* (1870; trans. 1931). G. Highet, *The Classical Tradition** (1949), traces Greek and Roman influences on western literature. P. O. Kristeller, *Renaissance Thought** (1961), is a brief but penetrating analysis. The best introduction to the educational theories of the humanists is W. H. Woodward, *Vittorino da Feltre and Other Humanist Educators** (1905). Of the many works on Italian Renaissance art, two by masters of their subjects may be mentioned: B. Berenson, *The Italian Painters of the Renaissance** (rev. ed., 1930), and E. Panofsky, *Renaissance and Renascences in Western Art,* 2 vols. (1959). An older handbook, still useful, is H. Wölfflin, *The Art of the Italian Renaissance** (1903; edited as *Classic Art,* 1952). A. C. Krey, *A City That Art Built* (1936), is an interesting brief attempt to relate cultural flowering to economic and political circumstances in Florence.

4. Contemporary Writings

It is easy to become acquainted with the thought of Renaissance writers because of the number of readily available translations. Two source collections are particularly good: *The Renaissance Philosophy of Man** (edited E. Cassirer, 1948), which includes Pico's *Oration,* and *The Portable Renaissance Reader** (edited J. B. Ross and M. M. McLaughlin, 1953), which includes a selection from Alberti's *On the Family.* There are many editions of Boccaccio's *Decameron,* Cellini's *Autobiography,* and Castiglione's *The Courtier.* N. Machiavelli, *The Prince and the Discourses** (trans. 1940; Modern Library), is the most convenient edition. C. B. Coleman has edited *The Treatise of Lorenzo Valla on the Donation of Constantine* (1922), and E. A. McCurdy has edited *The Notebooks of Leonardo da Vinci,* 2 vols. (1938). *The Vespasiano Memoirs** (trans. 1926) offer contemporary thumbnail sketches of humanists, artists, and princes. B. Burroughs has recently edited Vasari's *Lives of the Artists** (1961).

5. The Church

There is a full account of the Councils of Constance and Basel and of the Renaissance popes in the five-volume work by an Anglican bishop, M. Creighton, *A History of the Papacy from the Great Schism to the Sack of Rome* (1882–94). The best account, however, based on the Vatican archives, is the still larger work of the Swiss Catholic, L. Pastor, *History of the Popes,* 40 vols. (trans. 1891–1953). On conciliar ideas, see B. Tierney, *Foundations of the Conciliar Theory* (1955), and E. F. Jacob, *Essays in the Conciliar Epoch* (1953).

6. Technological and Economic Growth in the North

L. Mumford, *Technics and Civilization** (1934), is always stimulating but often inaccurate in detail. On printing, see: P. Butler, *The Origin of Printing in Europe* (1940); D. C. McMurtrie, *The Book: The Story of Printing and Bookmaking* (3rd rev. ed., 1943); and E. P. Goldschmidt, *The Printed Book of the Renaissance* (1950). R. Ehrenberg, *Capital and Finance in the Age of the Renaissance* (trans. 1928), is a study of the Fuggers. The Fugger Newsletters of the later sixteenth century are available in *News and Rumor in Renaissance Europe.**

---

* Available in paperback edition.

7. Political Centralization

The best brief account in English is in M. P. Gilmore, *The World of Humanism** (1952). There are informative chapters on this and related subjects in both the *Cambridge Medieval History,* Vols. VII and VIII (1932, 1936), and the *New Cambridge Modern History,* Vols. I and II (1957, 1958). There is a good popular biography of Louis XI by P. Champion (1927). R. B. Merriman, *The Rise of the Spanish Empire in the Old World and in the New,* Vol. II (1936), is the best account of Spanish consolidation. S. T. Bindoff, *Tudor England** (1950), is a good introduction of recent interpretations of English history. See also G. R. Elton, *The Tudor Revolution in Government** (1953). On Germany, see H. Holborn, *A History of Modern Germany: The Reformation* (1959). On the Turks, see P. Wilter, *The Rise of the Ottoman Empire* (1938).

---

* Available in paperback edition.

2

Reform and Revolution in Western Christendom

The Need for Reform in the Western Church

At the opening of the sixteenth century, the Roman Church was in greater danger than it had been at any time since the Great Schism. Faced by the growing power of secular rulers who were limiting the papacy's powers of taxation, jurisdiction, and appointment, and caught in the maelstrom of Italian power politics, the popes of the fifteenth century had found themselves threatened by leagues of Italian princes and by pressure from more distant and more powerful rulers. The popes had no military power of their own. Moreover, by 1500 they were regularly in debt, with little prospect of finding an easy way out of their financial straits. Even able and devoted Vicars of Christ might have had difficulty defending the independence of the papacy and raising its moral prestige. But this was the era of the Renaissance popes—at best, worldly-minded administrators, at worst, corrupt and immoral men with secular tastes and interests. Some, like Alexander VI, used the contributions of the faithful to carve out princi-

Martin Luther and His Friends (ca. 1530), by Lucas Cranach the Elder. Luther (far left), the Swiss reformer Ulrich Zwingli (right, in cap), and other leaders of the Reformation seem to be shielded by Frederick the Magnanimous, Elector of Saxony.

palities for their illegitimate sons. Most of them, under financial pressure, sold justice in their courts and appointments to office in their councils.

Bishops and archbishops throughout Europe were generally of noble blood, and many of them had been nominated by monarchs or by the pope for loyal service rather than for their piety or administrative ability. Some held more than one bishopric, although this was contrary to canon law, and some rarely visited their sees (one bishop visited his only once, when he was buried there). Even conscientious bishops found that their power to appoint the clergy and to reform abuses within their dioceses had diminished. Many powers that properly belonged to the bishop had either fallen into the hands of local laymen or had been "reserved" by the pope. The ignorance and immorality of the parish clergy were bywords among contemporary writers. The parish priest in general was no better or worse than he had been for centuries, but moral sensitivity to clerical misconduct had been rising. Furthermore, the tithes that the priest levied and the fees that he charged for baptisms, marriages, and burials were burdensome to laymen. Dislike of the clergy was widespread, ranging from amused contempt to bitter hatred. Despite serious efforts at reform, the moral tone of many monastic orders was low. Monastic life no longer attracted the pious, as it had several centuries earlier, and monasteries

A cartoon by Holbein makes the point that the handing over of the indulgence letter was timed so as not to anticipate the dropping of the money into the coffer. We see in this cartoon a chamber with the pope enthroned. He is probably Leo X because the arms of the Medici appear frequently about the walls. The pope is handing a letter of indulgence to a kneeling Dominican. In the choir stalls on either side are seated a number of church dignitaries. On the right one of them lays his hand upon the head of a kneeling youth and with a stick points to a large ironbound chest for the contributions, into which a woman is dropping her mite. At the table on the left various Dominicans are preparing and dispensing indulgences. One of them repulses a beggar who has nothing to give in exchange, while another is carefully checking the money and withholding the indulgences until the full amount has been received. In contrast he shows on the left the true repentance of David, Manasseh, and a notorious sinner, who address themselves only to God.

From R. H. Bainton, *Here I Stand* (Nashville: Abingdon-Cokesbury Press, 1950), pp. 72–73.

now had to search out recruits to keep their numbers up.

The most dangerous abuses were those practices that could be interpreted as the selling of spiritual benefits. The Church was rich in land but poor in the newer forms of wealth. It cost money to maintain such a large institution, and the clergy had a right to ask for a fair share of the growing wealth of Europe. But the methods used to raise money and the purposes for which the money was spent (such as waging war to add territory to the Papal States) outraged many believers. Papal demands for money were passed from the bishops to the parish clergy to the people. Thus some priests demanded the best garment of a deceased parishioner as a "mortuary

fee" and had regular tables of charges for other religious rites. Even worse were the abuses that the pope allowed to creep into the sale of indulgences.

Indulgences

Indulgences, in fact, were the raw nerve of the Church's whole financial system. An indulgence was a remission of the temporal penalty for sin imposed by a priest in the sacrament of penance. It was granted on condition of true contrition for the sin and in consideration of some pious deed performed, such as going on a crusade or a pilgrimage. During the Middle Ages a money "contribution" became the normal consideration, and the necessity for contrition was often forgotten by the believer. In the fourteenth century the popes developed the doctrine that Christ and the saints had accumulated a "treasury of merits" from which Christ's Vicars could dispense benefits to the faithful through indulgences. In the fifteenth century Sixtus IV, on the strength of this doctrine, claimed the power to release the souls of the dead from the penance they were undergoing in Purgatory as the temporal penalty for their sins. This claim helped make the indulgence trade even more lucrative. It was hard to withhold a contribution that would release the soul of a dead parent from years of suffering in the next world. In theory, contrition was still necessary, and the money was a "contribution." But many laymen concluded that the Church was selling salvation at a price—and was then wasting the money on petty wars and luxurious living.

Criticism of the Church was not new. Though the Church was divinely instituted, everyone knew that it was administered by fallible human beings—that is, by sinners. The moral state of the clergy was probably no worse in 1500 than, say, in 1100. But the world of 1500 was far different from that of 1100, and it is well to review some of the main differences in order to understand why criticism now constituted a real danger to the Church.

The European world of 1500 was more secular in its interests and ideals, as we have seen. The artist, the despot, the sea captain, and the businessman were pursuing careers that seemed more exciting than sainthood, and the medieval interpretation of life in this world as a pilgrimage to life after death seemed unsatisfying, even though it was not yet openly rejected. Granted that salvation was the goal of mankind, some men began to ask, was renunciation of the world the only, or even the surest, way to gain that goal?

At the same time, though, the fifteenth century was an age of increasing secular interests among some; it was an age of heightened religious sensitivity and piety among others. Both the worldly-minded and the devout were becoming critical of the growing complexity of the Church's sacraments and ceremonies. Popular piety of the late Middle Ages had nurtured a luxuriant growth of religious practices that seemed to verge on superstition and idolatry. The cult of the saints and the veneration of relics became a kind of obsession. As the number of sacred symbols and ceremonies multiplied, their religious significance almost disappeared. A fifteenth-century French artist painted a sensual, photographic portrait of the French king's mistress as the Virgin Mary, apparently without being conscious of any blasphemy. As a modern historian has put it, the religious atmosphere of the later Middle Ages was "supersaturated," and the most observant church leaders of the fifteenth century grew worried. They saw that the Church was becoming dangerously vulnerable to radicals who might ask: What is the core of Christianity? Is it to venerate an image of St. Anthony, to avoid meat on Fridays, and to go on a pilgrimage? Or, rather, is it to love one's neighbor and to live a Christlike life?

A final reason why ecclesiastical abuses were so dangerous to the Church in 1500 was that there were now secular rulers strong enough to use the cry for reform for their own purposes. We have seen that the monarchs of western Europe were already appointing and taxing the clergy. The upper classes all over Europe coveted the wealth of the Church. Many secular rulers, should they so decide, now had the power to confiscate the Church's lands, buildings, and revenues in the name of reform. Reform by royal command sometimes had good results. In Spain, Cardinal Jiménez de Cisneros, strongly backed by Ferdinand and Isabella, instituted many reforms in the Spanish clergy at the opening of the sixteenth century. But there was always the danger that reform by a secular power might result in state control of the Church and confiscation of its property.

Failure of Fifteenth-Century Reform Movements

Various schemes for reform had been advanced in the fifteenth century. In the Rhineland, the Brethren of the Common Life, a group of laymen who devoted themselves to communal living and biblical piety, emphasized direct, intimate communion with God in their communities and schools. In Florence between 1494 and 1498 one of the most remarkable preachers of the age, the Dominican monk Girolamo Savonarola, moved multitudes to repentance and for a time had the crowds making bonfires of their wigs, make-up, and other "vanities." These reformers still held to the medieval conception of reform. According to that conception, the Church itself was divinely constituted and so could not be "reformed," but the individuals who composed it could and should be regenerated. The leaders at the councils of Constance and Basel were reformers of a more modern sort. They meant to reform the institution itself by making the pope a limited monarch. Hus wanted to reform both the individual and the institution by returning to the Bible as the standard of Christian living and ecclesiastical practice.

Each of these differing conceptions of reform was to take root and bear seed in one way or another during the sixteenth century. But before 1500 the impetus of each movement was soon spent and the institutional abuses remained untouched. The councils failed to make permanent changes in the constitution of the Church, and both Hus and Savonarola were executed as heretics. Whenever attempts at reform threatened to undermine the status of the clergy as mediators between God and man, or the power of the pope as the Vicar of Christ, they were declared heretical and stamped out. It seemed that the strength of vested interest and the dead weight of authority were so strong that the Church would never be roused from its complacency.

Christian Humanism

A new and hopeful type of reform movement—Christian Humanism—emerged in the sixteenth century. Under the inspiration of the classical revival in Italy, a number of scholars in northern Europe began to recommend a return to the best of both the classical and the Christian traditions through a study of the classics and the Bible. They argued that if men could appreciate the ethical perfection of Socrates and Jesus, of Plato and Paul, then the absurdities of scholastic hair-splitting and the irrelevance of many ecclesiastical practices would become evident. Reform would inevitably follow from a better understanding of the simplicity of primitive Christianity—and of the noble ideals of the Greeks and Romans, which they felt to be complementary rather than antagonistic to Christianity. Let the Church take for its guides the Bible and the early Fathers rather than the scholastic theologians of the Middle Ages. Abuses would disappear if laymen and clerics alike would recognize that Christianity was an attitude of mind and a way of life, not a complex set of dogmas and ceremonies.

This program was fundamentally conservative, designed to save the Church from itself. Its leaders were almost without exception loyal to Rome. It was obviously optimistic in its estimate of human nature. It rated the power of reason and education very high. It encouraged historical and literary studies in the hope that they would reveal earlier and purer practices. Cardinal Jiménez in Spain set scholars to producing a monumental edition of the Bible that presented the original Hebrew and Greek texts in parallel columns with the Latin. In Germany, Johann Reuchlin defended the study of Hebrew literature as a means of understanding the Old Testament, even though a group of Dominicans wished to destroy all Hebrew books. In France, Lefèvre d'Etaples studied the Epistles of Paul and translated the New Testament into French (1523) in an effort to enlighten his contemporaries and further the cause of reform. For Sir Thomas More in England, study and reform were also closely related. In his famous *Utopia,* More wrote a searching analysis of the most glaring social, political, and ecclesiastical evils of his day from the point of view of a scholar steeped in Plato and the Gospels as well as in the monastic tradition of the Middle Ages.

Erasmus

The acknowledged leader of these Christian Humanists was Erasmus of Rotterdam (*ca.* 1466–1536). Erasmus' enthusiasm for the Greco-Roman classics matched his enthusiasm for the Bible and early Christian writings. He devoted his life to scholarship in the conviction that sound learning would help save the Church. He edited the New Testament in the original Greek (1516), with a preface urging that it be translated into all the vulgar tongues, and he published editions of the early Church Fathers. His hundreds of letters and his briefer books were even more influential. In them, with lively humor, underlying seriousness, and an unsurpassed command of the Latin language, he argued for what he called "the philosophy of Christ," the love of God and neighbor that he saw as the essence of Christianity. He feared that the Church of his day had obscured this essential truth with useless forms and ceremonies. In a typical passage he ridiculed monkish ideas of religion. When the final reckoning comes, one monk will point to his fastings and ceremonies for credit, "another will boast that for sixty years he never touched money, except when his fingers were protected by two pairs of gloves." Christ will interrupt their boasts and say, "Whence comes this new race of Jews? I promised the inheritance of my Father, not to cowls, prayers, or fasts, but to works of charity." This device of imagining how Christ himself would judge the world of the 1500's was characteristic of Christian Humanism.

Christian Humanism offered the last chance of peaceful reform. But it was a movement that needed time, patience, and understanding to be successful. It was to influence every effort to reform the Church during the next century, both Protestant and Catholic, but as a practical program it was doomed to failure. It was too exclusively intellectual. The times were revolutionary and the remedies that Europe was to adopt were both sterner and simpler than Erasmus' "philosophy of Christ."

Luther's Revolt from Rome

On October 31, 1517, an Augustinian friar serving as Professor of Bible in the little University of Wittenberg in Saxony posted ninety-five theses, or propositions, for academic debate on the subject of indulgences. The author, Martin Luther (1483-1546), was outraged by the unscrupulous salesmanship of a Dominican friar

Erasmus' Preface to His Edition of the New Testament

I utterly dissent from those who are unwilling that the sacred Scriptures should be read by the unlearned translated into their vulgar tongue, as though Christ had taught such subtleties that they can scarcely be understood even by a few theologians, or, as though the strength of the Christian religion consisted in men's ignorance of it. The mysteries of kings it may be safer to conceal, but Christ wished his mysteries to be published as openly as possible. I wish that even the weakest woman should read the Gospel—should read the epistles of Paul. And I wish these were translated into all languages, so that they might be read and understood, not only by Scots and Irishmen, but also by Turks and Saracens. To make them understood is surely the first step. It may be that they might be ridiculed by many, but some would take them to heart. I long that the husbandman should sing portions of them to himself as he follows the plough, that the weaver should hum them to the tune of his shuttle, that the traveller should beguile with their stories the tedium of his journey.

From Erasmus, "Paraclesis," *Novum Instrumentum*, trans. by Frederic Seebohm, in *The Oxford Reformers* (New York: Dutton, 1914), p. 203:

named Tetzel who had been hawking indulgences in Magdeburg. "So soon as coin in coffer rings," Tetzel was reported as preaching, "the soul from Purgatory springs." The proceeds from this particular sale of indulgences were meant to go toward the building of St. Peter's church in Rome, though most of it actually ended up in the pockets of the Archbishop of Mainz and of the Fugger banking firm. Luther's theses were immediately printed and debated not only in Wittenberg but all over Germany. The sensation they caused marked the start of the Protestant Reformation.

Luther's chief propositions were:

There is no divine authority for preaching that the soul flies out of purgatory immediately the money clinks in the bottom of the chest. . . . It is certainly possible that when the money clinks in the bottom of the chest, avarice and greed increase. . . . All those who believe themselves certain of their own salvation by means of letters of indulgence, will be eternally damned, together with their teachers. . . . Any Christian whatsoever, who is truly repentant, enjoys plenary remission from penalty and guilt, and this is given him without letters of indulgence.

At the time, Martin Luther was a strong-willed, keen-minded, high-strung man in his early thirties. He had become increasingly dissatisfied with the emphasis his teachers laid on good works. He had been a most conscientious friar; he had fasted and prayed and confessed without end. If good works could win a man salvation, surely they should win it for him, he thought. Yet performing the acts commanded by the Church gave him no inner sense of forgiveness, only a growing sense of guilt, despair, and deepening spiritual crisis. Peace came to him when he suddenly understood, as in a revelation, what St. Paul had meant when he said that a man is saved not by doing the works of the Jewish law but by his faith in Christ. The ceremonies and religious practices of the medieval Church seemed to Luther a new Jewish law. Man is too corrupted by sin to meet the demands of such a law by his own efforts, and so he must rely on his faith in God's mercy. It is unthinkable that a man can buy God's favor by doing a good deed or performing some sacramental act. In the matter of saving a man's soul, Luther concluded, God does everything, man can do nothing.

It took Luther some time to work out the revolutionary implications of this thought. If man is saved by faith alone, then all ceremonies and sacraments, all pilgrimages and indulgences, everything the medieval Church called good works, are at best irrelevant and at worst dangerous. Indulgences were the first good work at which he struck. Within a short time after his attack their sales dropped off sharply in Germany. When the Dominicans, chief sellers of the indulgences, persuaded Pope Leo X to condemn his theses, Luther was gradually driven to deny the authority of the pope. Soon afterward, when he came to believe that John Hus had been right on certain matters in spite of his condemnation by the Council of Constance, he denied the authority of general councils as well. By April 1521 Luther was standing before the Emperor Charles V at an imperial diet at Worms and declaring that he was bound by the authority of the Scripture and his own conscience rather than by that of either pope or council. He could not recant any of his writings, he added, because his conscience was "captive to the Word of God" and because it was "neither safe nor right to go against conscience." The Bible and conscience—these were to be the two chief pillars of Protestant Christianity.

Luther was not burned at Worms, as Hus had been at Constance. His safe-conduct was respected and he was allowed to return to the protection of his ruler, Frederick, the Elector of Saxony. For twenty-five years, till his death in 1546, he taught, preached, and wrote at Wittenberg. Meanwhile the revolt against the papacy that he had started gathered momentum and spread over northern Europe. In the end, the unity of Western Christendom was permanently destroyed.

Luther on Good Works

Good works do not make a man good, but a good man does good works. A bishop is not a bishop because he consecrates a church, but he consecrates a church because he is a bishop. Unless a man is already a believer and a Christian, his works have no value at all. They are foolish, idle, damnable sins, because when good works are brought forward as ground for justification, they are no longer good. Understand that we do not reject good works, but praise them highly. . . . When God in his sheer mercy and without any merit of mine has given me such unspeakable riches, shall I not then freely, joyously, wholeheartedly, unprompted do everything that I know will please him? I will give myself as a sort of Christ to my neighbor as Christ gave himself for me.

From Martin Luther, "On the Freedom of a Christian Man," trans. by R. H. Bainton, *Here I Stand* (Nashville: Abingdon-Cokesbury, 1950), pp. 230–31.

Lutheran Principles

In breaking with the papacy, Luther was guided by three main principles: salvation by faith, not by works; the ultimate authority of the Bible; and the priesthood of all believers. The three were closely related. It was through study of the Bible that Luther came to his belief in salvation by faith, and it was to the Bible that he always appealed against the authority of tradition or the papacy. His greatest literary work was a German translation of the Bible (completed in 1532), which he wrote in order that God's Word might be put into the hands of every devout person in Germany who could read. There was no essential difference between a priest and a layman, he insisted. A dedicated layman reverently reading the Scripture was closer to divine truth than a worldly pope proclaiming dogma for the Church. Christ had meant every believer to be a priest to his neighbor; He had not intended a special few to act as mediators between man and God. A Christian can serve God as well by being an honest merchant or a faithful housewife as by becoming a monk or a nun. Thus Luther encouraged the dissolution of the monastic orders, and in order to dramatize his convictions he married a nun and became the happy father of six children.

Luther's original protest had been a purely religious matter, rooted in his own spiritual experience. But to gain support he had to appeal to the nationalistic and financial grievances of his fellow Germans. "What has brought us Germans to such a pass that we have to suffer this robbery and this destruction of our property by the Pope?" he asked in 1520. "If the kingdom of France has resisted it, why do we Germans suffer ourselves to be fooled and deceived?" Luther appealed to princes eager to confiscate church property, to businessmen restive under papal taxation, to German patriots resentful of the Italians who dominated the papacy and the College of Cardinals, and to devout laymen and conscientious priests who were shocked by the corruption in the Church. His principles of salvation by faith and of serving God in one's secular calling appealed especially to laymen, who found in them a way of reconciling Christian

Luther on the Church

Thus it may come to pass that the Pope and his followers are wicked and not true Christians, and not being taught by God, have no true understanding, whereas a common man may have true understanding. Why should we then not follow him? Has not the Pope often erred? Who could help Christianity, in case the Pope errs, if we do not rather believe another who has the Scriptures for him? Therefore it is a wickedly devised fable—and they cannot quote a single letter to confirm it—that it is for the Pope alone to interpret the Scriptures or to confirm the interpretation of them. They have assumed the authority of their own selves. And though they say that this authority was given to St. Peter when the keys were given to him, it is plain enough that the keys were not given to St. Peter alone, but to the whole community. . . . Moreover, if the article of our faith is right, "I believe in the holy Christian Church," the Pope cannot alone be right; else we must say, "I believe in the Pope of Rome," and reduce the Christian Church to one man, which is a devilish and damnable heresy. Besides that, we are all priests, as I have said, and have all one faith, one Gospel, one Sacrament; how then should we not have the power of discerning and judging what is right or wrong in matters of faith?

From Martin Luther, "Address to the Christian Nobility of the German Nation," *Luther's Primary Works*, ed. by H. Wace and C. A. Buchheim (London: Hodder and Stoughton, 1896), pp. 170–71.

devotion with an active concern about worldly affairs. High-minded and low-minded motives were inextricably mixed in the minds of those who accepted Luther's arguments.

Luther had no intention of breaking away from the true Church of Christ or of setting up a rival organization. But after 1520 he was convinced that the Church founded by Christ and the Apostles had wandered from the true path somewhere in the Middle Ages, and that the bishop of Rome was not the Vicar of Christ, but rather the Anti-Christ. Much of the dogma and ritual of the Church of his day, Luther believed, was the work of men, not of God. Such accretions must be stripped away, leaving only the pure faith of the Apostles and the early Church Fathers. In his zeal for reform, Luther actually set up a new church under the protection and control of secular rulers in Germany. In this church there were two sacraments (Baptism and Holy Communion) in place of seven, a simplified ritual in German rather than Latin, and more emphasis on the congregation's participation in the service. But Luther never wavered in his belief that he was not setting up another "church" but that he was purifying *the* Church. There could be only one true Church Catholic, into which all men were received in Baptism. Either the pope was right when he excommunicated Luther as a heretic in 1520, or else Luther was right when he burned the bull of excommunication. At first there were not two churches, one "Catholic" and the other "Lutheran," but an irreconcilable argument over the nature of the one true Church.

The Spread of Lutheranism

Luther's ideas were spread by his students and by his books, which poured from the new

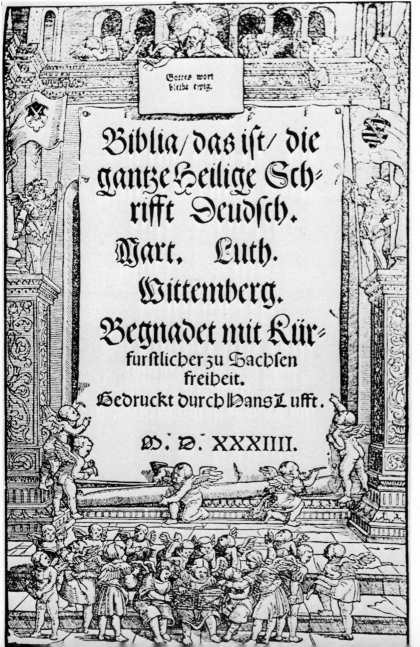

Title page of the first German translation of the Bible, by Martin Luther, printed in 1534 with the approval of the Elector of Saxony.

The Spread of Protestantism 16th century

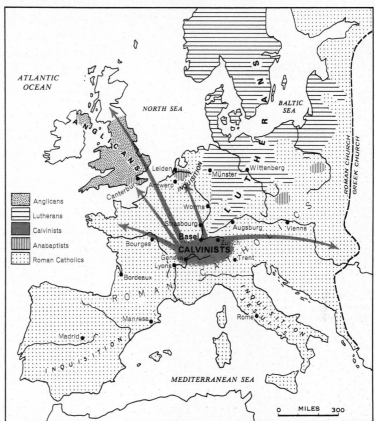

printing presses in both German and Latin. Many priests and monks were among his first converts, and his views were particularly popular among the middle classes of the German cities and the princes of northern and central Germany. The Humanists at first greeted his attack on indulgences with joy, but as Luther became more violent most of them retreated to the fold of the Roman Church. They wanted reform not revolution, as Erasmus made clear when he finally and reluctantly broke with Luther in 1524. To Erasmus, Luther was a fanatic; to Luther, Erasmus was only half a Christian.

The peasants were excited by Luther's message at first, but he lost most of them after the Peasants' Rebellion of 1524–25. This was the largest and bloodiest of the many peasant uprisings that resulted from complex economic and

social causes during the later Middle Ages. The rebels' chief aim was to abolish serfdom and the burdens of the manorial system. "Therefore do we find in the Scripture that we are free," they argued, "and we will be free." Luther was close enough to his peasant origins to sympathize with their demands, but the freedom he was interested in was an inner religious freedom, freedom from an ecclesiastical system, not from social or political bondage. At last, the atrocities committed by the peasants turned him against them, and he wrote a bitter condemnation of the uprising. The rebellion itself was finally put down with atrocities that went beyond even those of the rebels. The peasants felt that Luther had betrayed them, but the middle and ruling classes welcomed his social conservatism. After 1525 he and his followers fought as hard against radicals on

SOYRGOINVS
INVENTOR

Sketches of Calvin drawn by a student, perhaps during a lecture.

was unable to bring political or military pressure to bear on cities and states that had turned Lutheran. From 1522 to 1559 Charles and his son Philip were caught up in a series of conflicts with France that absorbed much of their energy and income. Meanwhile Charles and his brother Ferdinand were also trying to stem the tide of Turkish conquest in the Mediterranean and the Danube Valley. The French in the West and the Turks in the East, sometimes in alliance with each other, allowed the emperor only a few intervals of peace in which to turn his attention to the religious division of Germany.

By the time of Luther's death in 1546, the German cities and principalities were about evenly divided between the two faiths. In 1547, during a peaceful interlude in his international struggles, Charles V finally found an opportunity to attack the Lutheran states. A confused war followed which proved that neither side could destroy the other, and in 1555 the emperor reluctantly allowed his brother Ferdinand, who was ruler of Austria and later emperor, to conclude the Religious Peace of Augsburg. This peace allowed the city-states and princes of the Empire to choose between Lutheranism and Catholicism and bound them to respect each other's rights. *Cuius regio, eius religio,* as someone later summed up the principle: The ruler determines the religion for the region. People who disliked the ruler's choice might migrate to another state. Lutherans were allowed to keep any church lands they had seized before 1552, but it was agreed that every Catholic bishop or abbot who turned Protestant in the future would have to resign his title and leave his lands in Catholic hands. This last clause was difficult to interpret and caused trouble later. The chief flaw in the settlement, however, was the exclusion of Calvinists, whose numbers were growing rapidly, from the benefits of the peace.

The Peace of Augsburg was the first official recognition, however grudging, that Western Christendom had been rent asunder and would have to continue as a house divided. It was not religious toleration, but it was a step along the way. In the end, northern Germany became mostly "Protestant" (as Lutherans had been

their left, who wanted to carry the religious revolt too far, as they did against the Roman Catholics on their right, who wished to wipe out Lutheranism.

There was at first no effective resistance in Germany to the spread of Luther's ideas. The emperor Charles V never wavered in his orthodoxy, but the task of holding together his scattered dominions proved so difficult that he called since 1529, when they presented a "protest" at an imperial diet); southern Germany remained mostly "Catholic." The division remains today about as it was in 1560. Outside Germany, Lutheran ideas spread widely but took root only in Scandinavia, where the kingdoms of Denmark, Norway, and Sweden became Lutheran before mid-century. Perhaps because Luther spoke so forcefully in the German idiom to his fellow Germans, his teaching was not so well adapted to export as was the teaching of John Calvin.

Calvinism

Luther's University of Wittenberg was not the only center from which reform ideas radiated. Other important centers were Zurich, Basel, Strasbourg, and especially Geneva. In these southern German and Swiss cities there developed a type of Protestantism closely related to Lutheranism but different in emphasis—more rational and systematic, more organized and disciplined, laying more stress on moral conduct and political action, less on the inner relation of man to God. The members of this second family of Protestant churches are generally called "Reformed" churches, in contrast with the "Lutheran."

Among the early Swiss and South German reformers were Ulrich Zwingli of Zurich (1484–1531) and Martin Bucer of Strasbourg (1491–1551). Neither man agreed entirely with Luther. Zwingli took a more radical position on the sacraments, arguing that Communion was essentially a memorial service commemorating the Last Supper. Bucer tried to reconcile various Protestant groups and was more tolerant than most of the other reformers.

More influential than either Zwingli or Bucer was John Calvin (1509–64). Calvin had been trained as a lawyer and a Humanist in his native France before he became converted to Protestantism and settled down as a pastor in Geneva. He learned much from Luther, as well as from Zwingli and Bucer. Through these influences and through his early training, he became the chief theologian and organizer of

second-generation Protestantism. His *Institutes of the Christian Religion* served as the basic handbook of Protestant principles for two centuries. It was a clear, well-organized, well-written book in both its Latin and its French versions, and its argument had all the logic a trained lawyer could bring to it. Calvin's two polar principles were the absolute sovereignty of God and the radical depravity of man. No acts of sinful man can merit salvation; God, through his inscrutable will, has chosen some to be saved and some to be damned. The effect of this doctrine on Calvin's followers was not to induce resignation and despair but to stimulate moral activity and strenuous effort as God's instruments. Good works could not save a Calvinist—but they might be evidence that God was working through him.

Calvin on Predestination

Predestination we call the eternal decree of God, by which he has determined in himself, what he would have to become of every individual of mankind. For they are not all created with a similar destiny; but eternal life is foreordained for some, and eternal damnation for others . . . .

In conformity, therefore, to the clear doctrine of the Scripture, we assert, that by an eternal and immutable counsel, God has once for all determined, both whom he would admit to salvation, and whom he would condemn to destruction. We affirm that this counsel, as far as concerns the elect, is founded on his gratuitous mercy, totally irrespective of human merit; but that to those whom he devotes to condemnation, the gate of life is closed by a just and irreprehensible, but incomprehensible, judgment. . . .

How exceedingly presumptuous it is only to inquire into the causes of the Divine will; which is in fact, and is justly entitled to be, the cause of everything that exists . . . . For the will of God is the highest rule of justice; so that what he wills must be considered just, for this very reason, because he wills it.

From John Calvin, *Institutes of the Christian Religion*, trans. by John Allen (Philadelphia: Westminster Press, 1930), book III, Ch. 21, pars. 5, 7; Ch. 23, par. 2.

Good works were a "sign" that a man was probably one of the Elect.

As time went on, Calvin's church in Geneva became the model for Presbyterian or Reformed churches in France, England, Scotland, the Netherlands, the Rhineland, Bohemia, and Hungary—later in North America and Dutch South Africa. Calvin advocated that each local congregation have a ruling body composed of both ministers and laymen (presbyters, or elders) who were to watch carefully over the moral conduct and beliefs of the faithful. These officials then met in synods which linked up the Reformed congregations of a whole district or nation. Thus in place of the Roman Catholic hierarchy of bishops and priests under the pope, and in place of Luther's state-churches, Calvin devised a peculiarly tough and flexible system of church government that resisted control by the state, maintained strict discipline, and, in

the lay elders, included a potentially democratic element. Unlike Lutheranism, Calvinism met the two conditions for successful export all over Europe: It possessed a systematic theology and it offered a practical substitute for medieval church organization.

By the 1550's Calvinism was spreading rapidly. Except in a few cities like Geneva, the nerve center of the movement, and in Scotland, Calvinists never became a majority. But the Calvinist minorities were stubborn, well organized, and widely distributed over Europe. Calvinism left a deep imprint on English society in the form of Puritanism, on France through the Huguenots, on Hungary, and on the Dutch Netherlands. Calvinist minorities formed a kind of revolutionary international society throughout Europe in the later sixteenth century. Like their chief rivals, the Jesuits, the Reformed ministers were often able to elicit a religious loyalty that

The more rigid Protestants objected to all religious paintings and sculpture as leading to idolatry. In this engraving of 1579, Calvinists are pulling down statues of saints and destroying stained glass windows.

transcended loyalty to secular rulers and nations. Calvinism was the militant, international form of Protestantism.

The Radicals

Some reformers wanted to move much further and faster along the road of religious revolution than Luther, Zwingli, or Calvin. Throughout Germany workers and peasants had been hard hit by the economic changes of the fourteenth and fifteenth centuries. Often their discontent took on a religious coloring, combining easily with what survived of earlier heresies—Waldensian, Lollard, and Hussite, for example. These uneducated men and women took most of Luther's ideas literally—the Bible as ultimate authority, the priesthood of all believers, the freedom of true Christians from manmade ecclesiastical laws and organizations. During the 1520's in Switzerland and in the upper Rhine Valley particularly, little groups of such people came together proclaiming that a true church of Christians was a voluntary association of converted believers, not an official or established institution like that of the Lutherans, Calvinists, or Catholics. Most of them believed that until a man came of age and knew what he was doing, he should not be admitted to the church through baptism. Thus, since they had to rebaptize most of their converts, their enemies called them Anabaptists, or rebaptizers. Their ritual was simple, and generally they took the Bible literally. Most of them would not take an oath in a law court, accept public office, or serve as soldiers; some practiced communism of goods on the model described in the second chapter of Acts. They were cruelly persecuted by Catholics and conservative Protestants alike as dangerous heretics and social radicals. A small but violent minority gave temporary excuse for such persecution by capturing the city of Münster and conducting a reign of terror there for over a year (1534–35). But generally they were pacifists and eager to suffer as their models, the Apostles, had done. After the 1530's the Anabaptists were to be found mainly in the Netherlands, Bohemia, Poland, and England, having been stamped out in southern Germany where they had originated.

In addition to such "evangelical" groups, which tried to return to the first-century Gospel even more literally than Luther, there were other religious radicals. Some, continuing the medieval mystical tradition, believed in following an inner voice rather than the letter of the Scripture, as did the Quakers in the next century. Others were more rationalistic, anticipating the doctrine that the nineteenth century was to call Unitarianism, the belief that there is only one God, not a Holy Trinity, and that Jesus was not God but man at his best. No one in the sixteenth century went quite this far, but the physician Michael Servetus (1511–53) combined an emphasis on the humanity of Christ with mystical and rationalistic ideas. He was imprisoned by the Catholic Inquisition, escaped, and in 1553 was burned at the stake in Geneva as a result of Calvin's influence.

The ideas of these religious radicals, who went too far not only for Roman Catholics but for Luther and Calvin, were of great importance in the religious history of the Anglo-Saxon peoples. It was in England during the seventeenth century and later in the English colonies in America that Anabaptist ideas were fully realized. There the doctrine that the church should be a voluntary association, "a free church in a free state," organizing itself and electing its pastor, was accepted without any restrictions. Modern Baptists (who believe in adult baptism only), Congregationalists (who emphasize the autonomy of local congregations of Christians), and Quakers (who rely on the "inner light" and tend toward pacifism) all look back to the religious radicals of the sixteenth century as their remote ancestors. American Protestant conceptions of the place of the church in society derive more from Anabaptism than from either Luther or Calvin.

Anglicanism

The peculiarity of the English Reformation is that it was initiated by a king for reasons that had almost nothing to do with religion. Henry

VIII cut England off from the papacy much as the king of France had cut his realm off from the papal obedience in 1395. But in England the jurisdictional breach with Rome was followed by a decisive religious change.

In 1527, ten years after Luther had posted his ninety-five theses, both England and her king seemed entirely orthodox. Parliament had restricted papal rights of appointment and jurisdiction in England, but England had not gone so far toward developing a national, or "Anglican," Church as France had in "Gallicanism." Lutheran ideas, strongly opposed by the king, had taken only shallow root in England among a few merchants, monks, and university scholars. There was some anticlericalism among the people and some patriotic dislike of the pope, but no organized movement of revolt. Henry, however, found himself in a personal quandary that was to lead him into direct conflict with the pope, Clement VII. After eighteen years of married life, Henry's wife, Catherine of Aragon, had given him only one living child, a daughter. He knew that the lack of a male heir might well throw England into a new War of the Roses, and he knew that Catherine could bear him no more children. Furthermore, he was infatuated with a lady of the court named Anne Boleyn. Henry therefore asked the pope to annul his marriage with Catherine so that he might marry Anne. It was not hard to find technical grounds for the annulment (Catherine had been briefly married to Henry's older brother), but it was hard to persuade the pope to acquiesce, because he was in the power of the emperor, Charles V, and Charles was the nephew of Catherine.

Henry, a strong-willed man convinced that he was right, was skillful in political manipulation. In 1529 he summoned Parliament, determined to make the nation his accomplice in whatever he might have to do. He and his chief minister, Thomas Cromwell, deftly built up anticlerical sentiment in Parliament and forced the English clergy to acknowledge that the king was "Supreme Head of the Church in England." Then Henry threatened to withdraw all revenue and obedience from the pope. When Clement still refused to grant the annulment, Henry carried out his threat. He had the marriage annulled in England by Thomas Cranmer, whom the pope had just named as Archbishop of Canterbury, married Anne, and then, in 1533–34, had Parliament cut all ties between the Roman papacy and England by a series of statutes. Conscientious monks, priests, and laymen who resisted this separation were executed; the most prominent martyr was Sir Thomas More (1478–1535), author of *Utopia* and chancellor of England from 1529 to 1532, who was proclaimed a saint in the twentieth century. Henry was now a kind of pope of the Church in England, except that as a layman he never claimed the power to administer the sacraments.

A Catholic, Sir Thomas More, on the Church

The true Church of Christ is the common known church of all Christian people not gone out nor cast out. This whole body both of good and bad is the Catholic Church of Christ, which is in this world very sickly, and hath many sore members, as hath sometime the natural body of a man. . . . The Church was gathered, and the faith believed, before any part of the New Testament was put in writing. And which was or is the true scripture, neither Luther nor Tyndale [translator of the New Testament into English] knoweth but by the credence that they give to the Church. . . . The Church was before the gospel was written; and the faith was taught, and men were baptised and masses said, and the other sacraments ministered among Christian people, before any part of the New Testament was put in writing. . . . As the sea shall never surround and overwhelm the land, and yet it hath eaten many places in, and swallowed whole countries up, and made places now sea that sometime were well-inhabited lands, and hath lost part of his own possession in other parts again; so though the faith of Christ shall never be overflown with heresies, nor the gates of hell prevail against Christ's Church, yet in some places it winneth in a new people, so may there in some places by negligence be lost the old.

From *The Workes of Sir Thomas More*, 1557, pp. 527, 852, 853, 921.

Between 1535 and 1539 he and his agents demonstrated the extent of his authority by dissolving the 550 monasteries in England, turning their inmates out into the world, and confiscating their lands. Because Henry needed ready money to carry on a war with France, most of these lands were eventually sold to nobles, gentry, and merchants. The result, probably unforeseen, was to bind a whole new class of landowners to the English crown and to the new religious settlement.

In breaking with the papacy, Henry had no intention of breaking with orthodox Catholic belief and practice. He made it clear to his people that the breach with Rome meant no letting down of the bars against heresy, whether Lollard, Lutheran, or Anabaptist. It was impossible, however, to seal England off from the influx of Protestant tracts and ideas, and Henry himself approved the distribution to churches of an English translation of the Bible. By the time of his death in 1547, the Protestant wing of the English clergy led by Archbishop Cranmer was growing in power. During the brief reign of Henry's sickly son Edward VI (1547–53) the government moved rapidly toward building a church that was more Protestant in doctrine and ritual. Cranmer gathered together the most impressive parts of the ancient liturgies of the Catholic Church and translated them into majestic English in the Book of Common Prayer. This collection served as the rallying point of Anglicanism, as Luther's hymns did for Lutherans and Calvin's *Institutes* for Calvinists.

This new official Protestantism had no time to take root among the people. In 1553 Catherine of Aragon's daughter Mary, the most honest and least politic of all the Tudors, came to the throne. She tried to vindicate her mother and atone for her father's sins by turning the clock back to 1529, abolishing all antipapal legislation, and restoring England to the papal obedience. But she outraged her people's patriotism by marrying a foreigner, Philip II of Spain, son and heir presumptive of Charles V, and she shocked their humanity by allowing three hundred Protestants to be burned for heresy in about three years. The courage with which Cranmer and more

obscure victims went to their deaths, together with the arrogance of Philip's courtiers, left an indelible impression on the English people. Patriotism and Protestantism became identified in the public mind.

When Anne Boleyn's daughter, Elizabeth I (1558–1603), came to the throne, there was little possibility that she would keep England in the Catholic camp. Elizabeth cautiously guided her Parliaments and her bishops into a compromise religious settlement. She accepted the title of "Supreme Governor" of the Church in England, but she saw to it that the Book of Common Prayer could be read and used by both moderate Catholics and Protestants; for the rest, she refused "to make windows into men's souls," as she put it. After the pope excommunicated her in 1570 she was forced to treat zealous Catholics in England as traitors, but she was almost as annoyed with the "Puritans," who wished to go much further than she in purifying the Anglican Church of Catholic traditions. The Puritans were strong in Parliament, but when they became obstreperous Elizabeth clapped some of them into jail. The idea that patriotism required independence from Rome became dominant during her reign, and in the end England was the largest single state to secede permanently from the Roman obedience. The secession cost less in bloodshed than it did elsewhere, largely because of the firm control that Henry VIII and Elizabeth exercised over the pace of religious change in England.

Anglicanism was the most conservative form of Protestantism. In fact, many Anglicans today follow Henry VIII in insisting that their church is not "Protestant" at all. In Anglican theory it was the Roman papacy which in effect had "seceded" from the Catholic tradition during the Middle Ages, and it was Henry VIII and Cranmer who restored the true continuity between the Church of the Fathers and the Church of the sixteenth century. In England itself the Anglican position was a broad middle ground between a Catholic minority that wished to bring England back to Rome and a Puritan minority that wished to build a more radically Protestant church in England.

The Catholic Reformation

Luther, Calvin, Cranmer, and the radical reformers thought of what they were doing as a "reformation" of the Church, and to this day the movement is generally called the Protestant Reformation. To Roman Catholics, however, the movement was a "revolt" against the divine authority of the Vicar of Christ, a religious revolution. From this point of view the only true "reformation" was the successful effort finally made by the Roman Church to reform

Contemporary engraving of St. Ignatius Loyola, founder of the Jesuits.

B. IGNATIVS LOYOLA FVNDATOR Soc. IESV.

Ut cognoscamus in terra viam tuam, in omnibus gentibus salutare tuum. Psal. 66.

itself, partly in response to the Protestant attack, partly as a result of internal pressures. Historians call this movement the Catholic Reformation, or the Counter Reformation.

This movement was both a religious revival and a counterattack on Protestantism. Before Luther appeared on the scene, some distinguished members of the clergy founded the Oratory of Divine Love at Rome in the hope of beginning a spiritual revival among the clergy. They directed their efforts toward the monastic orders and the papal court itself. In the course of the sixteenth century they succeeded in transforming the atmosphere at the Vatican. After the bloody sack of Rome in 1527 by undisciplined imperial troops, better popes were chosen, who in turn appointed better cardinals. In the second half of the century, several of the popes were zealous, almost fanatical, men who would have seemed utterly out of place in the Renaissance papacy a century earlier. Politics still influenced religion and certain administrative abuses persisted, but the popes of the later sixteenth century were spiritual leaders, not Italian princes.

The driving forces behind the Catholic Reformation, especially the political forces, originated in Spain. Years of crusading against the Moors had given Spanish Catholicism a peculiarly intense quality lacking in the rest of Europe. King Philip II of Spain (1556–98), the son of Emperor Charles V, was a devoted Catholic who felt that it was Spain's destiny to stand as the bulwark of Roman Catholicism against the Protestants in Europe. He tended to give orders to the popes rather than to take orders from them, but during his reign Spanish armies and navies, Spanish diplomacy, and Spanish saints constituted the hard core of a revived and militant Catholicism all over Europe.

The most powerful single agency in restoring papal power, in rolling back the tide of Protestantism, and in carrying Catholic missions overseas was a new order founded by one of the most single-minded and influential saints in Christian history, a Spaniard of Basque descent named Ignatius of Loyola (1491–1556). While he was fighting the French in the service of his king, Ignatius' leg was fractured by a cannon ball.

During a long and painful convalescence, he devoured the lives of the saints, which were the only reading matter at hand, and decided to enlist as a kind of Christian knight in the service of the Virgin Mary. During a lengthy period of trial and temptation he perfected the "spiritual exercises" which he later passed on to generations of followers. These exercises consisted in the believer's concentrating his imagination on the most vivid details of Hell and of the life and death of Christ in order to strengthen his will and to direct it toward salvation. While Ignatius was a student at the University of Paris (about the same time as Calvin), he enlisted ten friends who became the nucleus of a new order. This new order, which was approved by the pope in 1540, was the Society of Jesus. Its members became known as Jesuits.

The rules of the new order were designed to develop a flexible, disciplined, and efficient body of ecclesiastical shock troops for the papacy. The Jesuit wore no distinctive habit; he dressed as his job might require, as priest, teacher, missionary, or secret agent. He swore a special oath of obedience to the pope. He was carefully selected and trained for the most dangerous and difficult tasks the Church might require, from serving as confessor to a king, to venturing into Protestant countries where he might be executed as a traitor, to voyaging to foreign lands as remote as Brazil or India. The Jesuits were spectacularly successful. They strengthened the pope's control over the Church itself; they ran the best schools in Europe; and during the late sixteenth century they won back most of Bohemia, Poland, Hungary, and southern Germany from Protestantism.

The Roman Church strengthened itself against the Protestant attack in other ways as well. A general council was held at Trent in three sessions between 1545 and 1563 to define Catholic dogma and to reform abuses. Since the papal representatives and the Jesuits controlled the deliberations from the beginning, there was no danger of a revolt against the papacy as there had been in the councils of a century before. In reply to the central doctrines of Protestantism, the council declared that salvation is by both faith and works and that final religious authority is in the Bible and tradition as interpreted by the Roman Church. The worst financial and administrative abuses in the ecclesiastical organization were reformed, and seminaries were set up for the training of priests. The council defined the Church's teachings much more sharply than they had ever been defined before and re-established the absolute supremacy of the pope over the clerical hierarchy. Rome had lost much in the struggle with heresy, but the Catholic Church of 1563 was far better able to cope with future heresies than it had been in 1500. New forms of the Inquisition had been established in Spain (1480), the Netherlands (1523), and Italy (1542), and a system of censorship of printed books was instituted for the Church as a whole in 1559 and approved by the Council of Trent, which issued an "Index" of books that the faithful were forbidden to read.

The Roman Church had found a new religious vitality and had closed its ranks against the Protestant threat. By the second half of the sixteenth century a relatively monolithic Catholic Church, reorganized from within and backed by Spain, the strongest military power in Europe, faced the divided Protestants on somewhat better than even terms.

Summary and Significance

It is not easy to sum up the significance of the Protestant and Catholic Reformations. They were religious movements, phrased in theological terms, rooted deep in the religious experience of men like Luther and Loyola, and resulting in a religious fragmentation of Western Christendom that has lasted to the present day. But Luther's angry protest against indulgences would not have had such far-reaching results had not the economic, social, and political conditions been just right. The religious upheaval was intermingled with the growth of capitalism, of secularism, of national sentiment, and of absolutism in government. It is very difficult to say precisely what was cause and what was effect. We can only say that while German princes, for example, took advantage of purely religious protests to confiscate church property for their own interests, religious reformers also took advantage of purely secular events, like Henry VIII's desire to get rid of his wife, to advance the Protestant cause.

One thing is clear. The era of reform and revolution in the Church temporarily arrested the trend toward the secularization of culture that had begun in the last centuries of the Middle Ages. The century that followed Luther's death was a religious age; its most serious arguments were religious arguments; its wars were intensified by religious fanaticism; and most of its leading figures were either men of religion or men considerably affected by religion. Intensified interest in religion introduced a new and intolerant "ideological" element into the familiar economic and political causes of conflict in European society. The hatred among Catholic, Lutheran, Calvinist, and Anabaptist was as profound in the sixteenth century as the hatred among fascist, communist, and democrat in the twentieth, and for somewhat the same reasons. No man could believe that he or his family or his society was safe so long as opposing religious groups were allowed to exist. Only in time did it become evident that differing religious beliefs did not necessarily lead to civil war and the collapse of the state. Religious toleration was an eventual result of the Reformation but not of the efforts of the reformers.

For over a century the long-run effects of the Protestant Reformation on the economic, political, and cultural development of Europe have been vigorously debated by historians. It has been argued and denied that Protestantism,

with its emphasis on serving God in one's secular calling and with its appreciation of the bourgeois virtues of honesty, thrift, and self-discipline, provided the necessary religious sanction for the development of capitalism. It has been argued and denied that Lutheranism aided the growth of divine-right monarchy whereas Calvinism provided a spur toward the development of constitutionalism, and Anabaptism toward the development of modern socialism. It has been argued and denied that Protestantism wrecked the development of art by destroying religious sculpture and paintings and by rejecting most religious symbolism. And it has been argued and denied that by dissolving monasteries and thus destroying educational foundations Protestants set back elementary education many years. Both the good and the bad in modern capitalism, modern nationalism, and modern secularism have been attributed to Protestantism by one historian or another.

The historical data are far too complex for dogmatic judgments in such matters. The permanent schism of Western Christendom and the temporary intensification of religious motives in European politics can justly be attributed to the Protestant movement. Beyond this, all that can be said surely is that Protestantism allied itself with developments that had their origins far back, sometimes intensified them and accelerated their growth, occasionally blocked or countered their expansion. Capitalism, democracy, nationalism, and the secularization of culture appeared in Catholic as well as Protestant lands, and none of these phenomena can be explained by a simple chain of causes leading back to Luther and his revolt from Rome.

Suggestions for Further Reading

1. The Religious Upheaval

The best attempt at a synthetic treatment of social, political, and religious developments is still P. Smith, *The Age of the Reformation** (1920), a lively and opinionated book. H. J. Grimm, *The Reformation Era* (1954), does religious developments fuller justice than Smith and is abreast of recent

---

* Available in paperback edition.

scholarship, particularly on Luther. There are briefer treatments of the period in general in R. H. Bainton, *The Reformation of the Sixteenth Century** (1952), G. L. Mosse, *The Reformation** (1953), and E. H. Harbison, *The Age of Reformation** (1955).

The mental and emotional climate of the fifteenth century is vividly described in J. Huizinga, *The Waning of the Middle Ages** (trans. 1924); the piety of the period is examined in A. Hyma, *The Christian Renaissance* (1924). There are two perceptive biographies of Erasmus, by P. Smith* (1923) and J. Huizinga* (trans. 1952). Erasmus' best-known writings are available in modern editions: *The Praise of Folly* (edited H. H. Hudson, 1941) and *Ten Colloquies of Erasmus** (edited C. R. Thompson, 1957).

The best short biography of Luther in English is R. H. Bainton, *Here I Stand** (1950). H. Boehmer, *Road to Reformation** (1946), is another excellent Protestant account of Luther's development to 1521. H. Grisar, *Martin Luther: His Life and Work* (1935), is the best brief Catholic biography. There is no better biography of Calvin in English than W. Walker, *John Calvin* (1906), but this older account may be brought up to date by using the fine, broader survey of J. T. McNeill, *The History and Character of Calvinism** (1954). Modern translations of the writings of Luther, Calvin, and other reformers are appearing fast—for instance, in the *Library of Christian Classics*. These are too numerous to list here. H. E. Fosdick's anthology, *Great Voices of the Reformation* (1952), is a useful selection of passages from the works of the reformers from Wiclif to Wesley.

There is no standard work on the radicals. Good introductions to different aspects of the "left wing" of the Reformation are offered in F. H. Littell, *The Free Church* (1958), R. H. Bainton, *The Travail of Religious Liberty** (1951), and N. Cohn, *The Pursuit of the Millennium* (1957).

On the origins of the Anglican Church there are two brief and authoritative accounts: F. M. Powicke, *The Reformation in England* (1941), and T. M. Parker, *The English Reformation to 1558** (1950). G. Mattingly, *Catherine of Aragon** (1941), is a very perceptive and readable biography. A good Catholic account is by P. Hughes, *The Reformation in England* (3 vols., 1950–54).

An excellent discussion of the Catholic Reformation is H. Daniel-Rops, *The Catholic Reformation** (2 vols., 1961). Another good treatment is P. Janelle, *The Catholic Reformation* (1949). The best biography of St. Ignatius is by the Jesuit, P. Dudon (1949). For a less favorable treatment, see R. Fülöp-Miller, *The Power and Secret of the Jesuits* (1930). H. Jedin is engaged in writing a definitive *History of the Council of Trent,* the first volume of which has appeared in translation (1957).

2. Results of the Reformation

On the economic, political, and cultural consequences of the Reformation there are wide differences of opinion. A famous essay of M. Weber, *The Protestant Ethic and the Spirit of Capitalism** (1905), became the starting point of a long controversy about the economic significance of Protestantism, which still continues sporadically. *Protestantism and Capitalism: The Weber Thesis and Its Critics** (edited R. W. Green, 1959), is a convenient collection of selections from the literature of this controversy. R. H. Tawney, *Religion and the Rise of Capitalism** (1926), is a stimulating essay in the Weber tradition; H. M. Robertson, *Aspects of the Rise of Economic Individualism* (1933), is severely critical of Weber. E. Troeltsch, *Social Teaching of the Christian Churches,** 2 vols. (1912), is difficult but rewarding reading on the economic, social, and political theories of Catholics, Lutherans, Calvinists, and "the sects." The same author's *Protestantism and Progress** (1906) maintains that the Reformation was still largely "medieval" and that the Enlightenment was the true beginning of "modern" times. K. Holl, *The Cultural Significance of the Reformation** (1911) is more inclined to view Luther as the prophet of modern Germany and of twentieth-century culture in general. For a readable and perceptive survey of the period, see A. G. Dickens, *Reformation and Society in Sixteenth-Century Europe** (1966).

---

* Available in paperback edition.

A 16th-century sailing ship, with its navigator (left center) sighting the sun to determine his latitude. The foremast (right) is square-rigged for running with the wind. The mainmast and the mizzenmast astern (left) are lateen-rigged for better tacking against the wind.

3

The Age of
Discovery and
the Greatness
of Spain

The Protestant Reformation struck a
Europe that was already in the throes of a
different sort of revolution. That revolution was
launched by Portuguese voyages down the northwest coast of Africa; it quickened with the
discovery of America and the sea route to India;
and it continued unabated throughout the sixteenth century. For Europeans this was an age
of discovery without parallel. For the first time
they found themselves in direct contact with all
the continents on the globe and with all the
civilized peoples who inhabited them. That
contact began to have a profoundly disturbing
effect on the economy and the politics of Europe
just as the Peace of Augsburg was bringing a
respite from religious strife.

The Development of
Oceanic Commerce

In 1400 Europeans knew scarcely more about
the earth than the Romans had. The oceans
around the Continent were still impenetrable
barriers; the only long journeys ever taken by
Europeans had been across the Eurasian steppes.
Franciscan friars and the Polos of Venice had
shown that China could be reached by land and
that the steppes linked Europe and Asia. But
after the collapse of the Mongol Empire in the

fourteenth century the routes across the steppes were no longer safe for missionaries or merchants. Arab sailors now became the middlemen between the Orient and Europe. They brought the spices and textiles of India and the East Indies to Alexandria and Beirut, whence the Venetians distributed them to the rest of Europe. The Europeans themselves had no direct contact with the East.

By the end of the sixteenth century an almost incredible geographical revolution had taken place. Arnold J. Toynbee defines it as "the substitution of the Ocean for the Steppe as the principal medium of world-communication." Europeans had mastered both the technological and the psychological problems of making long voyages over the sea. Their ships had crossed and recrossed the Atlantic Ocean, rounded the southern tips of Africa and South America, pushed into the Indian Ocean, and crossed the Pacific. Before this time men had believed that there was far more land than water on the surface of the globe. Now explorers were discovering that there was far more water than land, and that the water could serve as a highway to any coast in the world for men who knew how to use its winds and ride its waves. The Mongol Empire had rested on mastery of the steppes. The empires of the future would rest on mastery of the oceans. When the first ship to circumnavigate the globe finished its voyage in 1522, Europe had begun to cast a web of communication and influence around the earth. During the next four centuries that web was to draw all the civilizations of the world under the influence of Europe.

Conditions for Maritime Discovery

By the year 1000, Norsemen from Iceland and Greenland had coasted North America in small, open boats. They were too few, however, to make any permanent settlement, and their discoveries were unknown to the rest of Europe. Before Europeans could make a sustained drive to push out across the Atlantic they needed better ships, surer aids to navigation, and stronger motivation.

Better ships were long in coming. Oar-propelled galleys had already mastered the Medi-

terranean, and by the thirteenth century Genoese and Venetian galleys were venturing out into the Atlantic to Morocco and Flanders. But on the open seas mariners needed sails rather than oars and broad, round hulls rather than long, narrow galleys. By the fifteenth century the Portuguese had devised a craft capable of long ocean voyages: the squat, three-masted caravel, with two masts generally square-rigged and one mast lateen-rigged. The caravel preserved the advantage of both the European square-rig, which was better for running before the wind, and the Arab lateen-rig, which was better for sailing close to the wind. It was slower than the galley, but it had more space for cargo and more elbowroom for seamen on long voyages.

Galleys had generally stayed close to land, hugging the shoreline. Before ships could venture straight out to sea, shipmasters needed some way of determining their direction and their whereabouts. The compass gave them a sense of direction in dark weather; the astrolabe enabled them to determine their latitude with fair accuracy; and improved portulan charts gave them confidence that they could return to port. (No precise way of determining longitude was known until the eighteenth century.)

City-states were the original bases for long-range navigation. Venetian and Genoese merchants linked the Black Sea and Egypt with Italy and England, and the Germans of the Hanseatic League traded from Russian Novgorod to French Bordeaux. But transoceanic exploration, trade, and colonization required a broader base for support. The new monarchies of western Europe were better situated geographically than the Italian or German city-states to open up the Atlantic. They also had advantages in manpower, resources, and political centralization. After 1400 the larger monarchies gradually replaced the cities as the major centers of commercial enterprise.

It is not easy to determine the motives that prompted Europeans—rather than Chinese or Moslems—to "discover" the rest of the world by taking to the sea. The Moslems had been crossing the Indian Ocean for centuries, and the Chinese regularly sailed up and down the East Asian coast and into the Indian Ocean; but neither people tried to go farther. Certainly the crusade ideal influenced Portuguese and Spanish rulers. To convert the heathen and to weaken Islam by placing Christian allies in the Moslem rear was the goal of many explorers. Crusading zeal was not the main impetus of the great discoveries, but it could be used to inspire enthusiasm for dangerous ventures and to sanctify more worldly motives.

Of those more worldly motives, the need to find precious metals to pay for eastern imports was the most compelling. In an age without refrigeration, the spices that helped preserve meats and make them more palatable—pepper from India, cinnamon from Ceylon, ginger from China, nutmeg and cloves from the East Indies—were luxuries that were almost necessities. The long journey from India or the Moluccas and the Arab-Venetian trade monopoly made such spices expensive. But Europeans needed them more keenly than Asians needed anything Europe had to offer except gold and silver; so there was a steady flow of precious metals from Europe eastward. This drain limited the supply of specie (hard coins) in Europe at a time when it was increasingly needed as currency. Before credit systems became widely used in the seventeenth and eighteenth centuries, the only practical way to provide the money needed by burgeoning commerce and industry was to increase the supply of bullion. Fifteenth-century rulers hardly saw the problem in these terms, but they were acutely aware of their need for gold. They knew that they had to have hard cash in their treasury to hire soldiers, equip navies, and maintain bureaucracies.

By the late fifteenth century a restless, energetic, and bold seafaring population was scattered along Europe's Atlantic coastline. Resourceful sailors, fishermen, and merchants had developed the techniques and the ships for making long voyages. They had religious and economic motives strong enough to overcome their superstitious fears of what lay beyond known waters, and their governments were often ready to back them. Europe needed Asia more than Asia needed Europe, and Europeans believed that it would not be too difficult to reach Asia

Toynbee on the Age of Discovery

Since A.D. 1500 the map of the civilized world has indeed been transformed out of all recognition. Down to that date it was composed of a belt of civilizations girdling the Old World from the Japanese Isles on the north-east to the British Isles on the north-west. . . . The main line of communication was provided by the chain of steppes and deserts that cut across the belt of civilizations from the Sahara to Mongolia. For human purposes, the Steppe was an inland sea. . . . This waterless sea had its dry-shod ships and its quayless ports. The steppe-galleons were camels, the steppe-galleys horses, and the steppe-ports "caravan cities." . . . The great revolution was a technological revolution by which the West made its fortune, got the better of all the other living civilizations, and forcibly united them into a single society of literally world-wide range. The revolutionary Western invention was the substitution of the Ocean for the Steppe as the principal medium of world-communication. This use of the Ocean, first by sailing ships and then by steamships, enabled the West to unify the whole inhabited and habitable world.

From Arnold J. Toynbee, *Civilization on Trial* (New York: Oxford U. Press, 1948), pp. 67–70.

by sailing due west. Ptolemy in the second century had underestimated the size of the globe and had overestimated the span of Asia, and the geographers of the fifteenth century, accepting his miscalculations, were convinced that Japan and China lay only a few thousand miles west of Europe. The journey seemed possible, and the material and psychological environment was favorable for an age of discovery.

Portuguese Exploration

Perhaps the most interesting figure of the whole age stands at its very beginning: Prince Henry the Navigator (1394–1460), the younger son of King John I of Portugal. Prince Henry was obsessed with the desire to learn more about Africa; he devoted his life to organizing, equipping, and sending out fleets that pushed farther and farther down the African west coast. In a remarkable observatory at Sagres on Cape St.

Vincent, the southwestern tip of Portugal, he brought together the scientific and the seafaring knowledge of his day. We know he had vague notions of outflanking Islam by reaching lands that the Moslems had never touched, but his main objective was to find gold.

After Henry's death the impetus of exploration was lost for a time. But Henry's grand-nephew, King John II (1481–95), speeded up the effort to find an all-water route to India that would short-circuit the Venetian-Arab monopoly. By 1488 Bartholomew Dias had discovered the Cape of Good Hope, and in 1497 Vasco da Gama rounded the cape with four ships, reached Calicut on the Malabar Coast of India in 1498, and was back in Lisbon with two of his ships in 1499. In 1500 a larger fleet, commanded by Cabral, touched the coast of Brazil and then headed for India in Da Gama's wake.

This first contact by sea with India was to have momentous consequences, but neither side was particularly impressed by the other on first meeting. The Hindus had only contempt for the bedraggled sailors who had spent months aboard Da Gama's ships, and the Europeans soon made it clear that they found nothing to respect in the civilization of India. When the Hindus asked Da Gama what he sought in India, he is said to have replied laconically, "Christians and spices."

During the sixteenth century the Portuguese strove to build a commercial empire in the Indian Ocean. Affonso de Albuquerque, the brutal but able Portuguese governor from 1509 to 1515 and the real founder of that empire, understood the relationship between trade, sea power, and strategic bases. He seized Goa on the western coast of India to serve as his headquarters, Malacca on the Strait of Malacca to control the trade between the Spice Islands and the Indian Ocean, and Ormuz to dominate the Persian Gulf. He failed to capture Aden, a base from which he could have strangled the Arab-Venetian trade through the Red Sea. He was as ruthless in disciplining his own men as he was in terrorizing Hindu princes and fighting Arab seamen. At Albuquerque's death in 1515 the Portuguese had a large share of the spice trade (though not a

monopoly) and controlled strategic bases all the way from Africa to the East Indies.

It was easy for the Portuguese and other Europeans to seize footholds in India because the Moslem and Hindu princes of the coastal districts were weak, and the Mogul Empire of the North had little power in the South. The Portuguese, however, established only trading posts, not colonies of settlement, in India, and even the trading posts soon ceased to be very profitable. The early voyages had made large profits for their backers. But the cost to the Portuguese government of equipping fleets and maintaining fighting forces soon ate up the profits. Portugal was a relatively small and poor country, with a small merchant class. Italians, German, and Flemish bankers soon dominated the Portuguese trade, and the spices that arrived at Lisbon were sent on directly to Antwerp, which proved to be a better point from which to distribute them to Europe. The burden of empire was already proving heavy when Portugal, as we shall see, fell into the grip of Spain in 1580.

Columbus and Spanish Exploration

In 1484, before the Portuguese had reached the Cape of Good Hope, a Genoese sailor named Christopher Columbus had tried in vain to persuade King John II of Portugal to back him in a voyage of exploration to the west. Columbus was convinced by all the evidence at hand that it would be comparatively easy to reach Cipangu (Japan) by sailing due west. But for years he was unable to persuade any monarch to back him. At last the rulers of Spain, who had conquered the Moorish Kingdom of Granada in January 1492, were free to turn their attention elsewhere. And so it was under Castilian auspices that Columbus sailed on his famous voyage. It took the Portuguese almost a century of patiently organized effort to reach the Old World eastward, while the Spanish reached the New World westward in one brilliant voyage. There was a large element of luck in the founding of Spain's empire in the New World.

Columbus touched land in the Bahamas on October 12, 1492, thinking he had struck some

East meets West. A Japanese screen painting showing a Portuguese sailor playing a game of go with a Japanese friend in the sterncastle of a native ship.

small islands in the Japanese archipelago. Throughout four voyages and until his death in 1506, he remained convinced, in the face of increasingly puzzling evidence, that it was the Old World of Japan and China that he had discovered. And so, although it was Columbus who named the "Indians" he found on the shores of Haiti and Cuba, it was the Florentine Amerigo Vespucci who gave his name to the continents Columbus had discovered. Amerigo, director of the Medici branch bank in Seville, sailed on both Spanish and Portuguese voyages and described what he saw in letters that were widely read throughout Europe. In one he referred to the great southern continent in the west as *Mundus Novus,* a New World. Later map-makers labeled the two new continents "America," for the man who first realized that it was a new, not an old, world that was opening up to view.

The Treaty of Tordesillas, 1494

Since both Spain and Portugal were seeking the same lands, they soon had to appeal to the pope for an adjudication of their rival claims to unoccupied and heathen lands around the globe. The pope, Alexander VI, was a Spaniard, and the line of demarcation that he drew in 1493 a hundred leagues west of the Cape Verde Islands was favorable to Spain. Portugal, however, gained a diplomatic victory through a treaty with Spain in 1494—the Treaty of Tordesillas. By this treaty a line was drawn from pole to pole 370 leagues west of the Cape Verde Islands, separating Portugal's claims to the east from Spain's to the

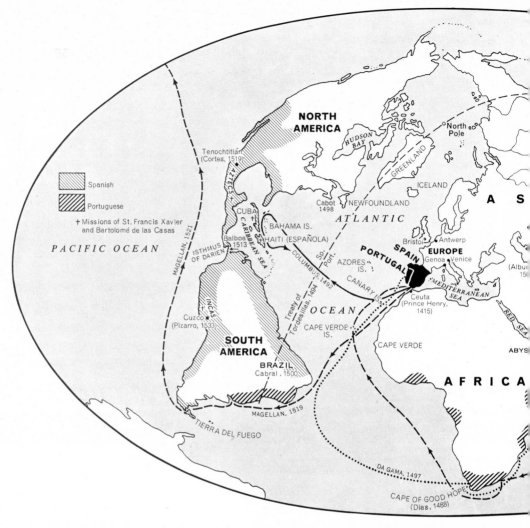

west. The Portuguese assumed that the line applied only to the Atlantic (it gave them Brazil, though they did not know this in 1494). The Spanish preferred to believe that the line extended round the world, cutting it in half as a knife cuts an orange. They hoped that this interpretation might give them the Moluccas, the heart of the Spice Islands, but later (1527) Spain sold all her claims to these islands to Portugal.

Magellan

By 1512 the Portuguese were in the Moluccas, and in 1513 the Spaniard Balboa sighted the Pacific from the Isthmus of Darien in Central America. In the years to come, the Spanish, the English, and others tried again and again to discover a strait through the New World by which they might sail westward into the Pacific and reach the Spice Islands. The Portuguese navigator Magellan was convinced that he could do just that by rounding the southern tip of South America. He knew, of course, that Portugal would never back him in such an expedition, so in 1519 he sailed with Spanish backing. It was the third of the truly great voyages—along with those of Columbus and Da Gama. Magellan negotiated the straits that are named for him and got across the Pacific after incredible hardships, only to be killed by natives in the Philip-

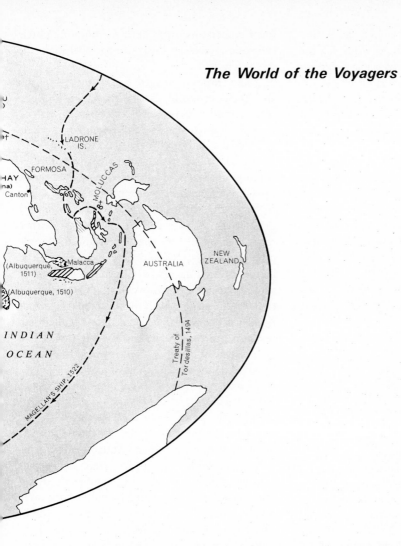

pines. His navigator, Sebastian del Cano, brought one of the five original ships back to Lisbon by way of the Cape of Good Hope in 1522, the first ship to sail round the world.

The Spanish Empire in the West

From 1520 to 1550 the conquistadors of Spain carved out an empire in the West. As the Spaniards on the Caribbean islands began to hear exciting tales of wealthy, half-civilized empires, they turned from exploration to conquest. The most notable of the conquistadors were Hernando Cortes, who in 1519–21 conquered the formidable Aztec Empire in Mexico with 600 men, 16 horses, and a few cannons, and Francisco Pizarro, who in 1533–34 conquered the Inca Empire in Peru with even fewer followers. Their firearms, steel swords, and horses gave the Spaniards an advantage over the more primitively armed groups that faced them, but it was primarily their daring, their discipline, and their fanatical faith that accounted for their fantastic successes.

Within a generation Spanish soldiers, lawyers, and friars unexpectedly found themselves the undisputed rulers of vast stretches of territory and hundreds of thousands of human beings. Often the new ruling class simply stepped into the place of former conquerors like the Aztecs and Incas, living on the tribute from subject populations that had supported their predecessors. But the Spaniards needed labor to exploit the new lands fully, and the Indians were unwilling to change their ways to meet Spanish demands. Thus when sugar became an important crop, Negro slaves had to be imported from Africa to do the work. The industry most favored by the Spanish government, however, was the mining of gold and silver. After the discovery of enormously rich silver mines in both Mexico and Peru in 1545, the extraction and shipment of silver became the main business of the Spanish Empire as a whole. Every spring after 1564 the plate fleet of twenty to sixty vessels gathered at Havana harbor to be convoyed by warships to Seville. And every year the Spanish government waited anxiously until the bullion, which everyone agreed was the key to national strength, was safely in harbor.

The empire that grew out of these exploits and these economic activities was a kind of compromise between what the Spanish settlers, the Christian friars, and the Spanish government at Madrid would each have liked to see develop in America. The settlers, many of them former conquistadors, would have liked to set themselves up as manorial lords living on the forced labor of the natives, unmolested by any political direction from Madrid. The Franciscans and other friars, particularly the great Dominican, Bartolomé de las Casas, would have liked to see the natives treated as fellow Christians and fellow subjects of the Spanish crown. Las Casas worked tirelessly to protect both the legal and the moral rights of the Indians in the face of relentless pressure from the settlers to exploit them. The government in Spain was determined to centralize all decision-making in Seville or Madrid, and to protect the natives so far as possible, as the friars urged.

The theory of the Spanish Empire, as it had unfolded by the end of the sixteenth century, was remarkably sensible and humane by contemporary standards. The settlers were allowed to command the forced labor of the subject Indians, but this labor was regulated by public authority, not by private right. There were abuses, sometimes serious, and the long arm of the home government was often awkward and exasperatingly slow in dealing with local problems. But as time went on the Spanish came close to accomplishing what the Portuguese failed to accomplish in the East and what the English never attempted in North America: the Christianization and Europeanization of a whole population. The Spaniards took seriously the papal bulls of 1493 which gave them the heathen peoples of the New World to convert and nurture in the Christian faith. In theory, the natives were considered Christians and subjects of the king (unlike the unfortunate Negroes, who were dismissed as the slaves of West African kings). The gulf between Spaniard and native was never entirely closed, in either religion or culture. But

Las Casas on the American Indians

It has been written that these peoples of the Indies, lacking human governance and ordered nations, did not have the power of reason to govern themselves—which was inferred only from their having been found to be gentle, patient and humble. It has been implied that God became careless in creating so immense a number of rational souls and let human nature, which He so largely determined and provided for, go astray in the almost infinitesimal part of the human lineage which they comprise. From this it follows that they have all proven themselves unsocial and therefore monstrous, contrary to the natural bent of all peoples of the world.

. . . Not only have [the Indians] shown themselves to be very wise peoples and possessed of lively and marked understanding, prudently governing and providing for their nations (as much as they can be nations, without faith in or knowledge of the true God) and making them prosper in justice; but they have equalled many diverse nations of the world, past and present, that have been praised for their governance, politics and customs, and exceed by no small measure the wisest of all these, such as the Greeks and Romans, in adherence to the rules of natural reason.

From Bartolomé de las Casas, *Apologética historia de las Indias,* in *Introduction to Contemporary Civilization* (New York: Columbia U. Press, 1954), 2nd ed., Vol. I, p. 499.

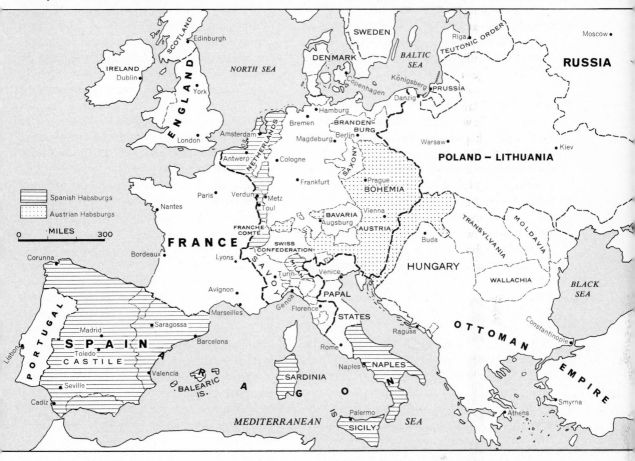

Spanish and Portuguese in the end became the
languages of all Latin Americans, and Roman
Catholicism the dominant religion. Intermarriage
was so common that the mestizos, or descendants
of mixed marriages, eventually became more
numerous than the pure-bred of either race. The
Spanish (and the Portuguese in Brazil) made
a serious attempt to convert a New World to
western civilization.

Spain Under Philip II

In the later sixteenth century Spain was the
dominant power in Europe as well as in America.
The accession of the Habsburg Charles to the
throne of Spain in the early sixteenth century

had thrust the Spanish into the full stream of
European politics and diplomacy at a moment
when the Protestant revolt was beginning to
spread, the Turks were expanding up the Danube
Valley, and the job of exploring and colonizing
America was demanding a huge expenditure of
energy. To roll back the threats of heretics and
infidels while conquering a new world was a
heavy task for a state so recently formed. But
for a brief and brilliant time, the Spanish under
the Emperor Charles V (1516–56) and his son,
King Philip II (1556–98), were almost equal
to the challenge. The sixteenth and early seventeenth centuries were the golden age of Spain.

In 1555–56 Charles V divided his family
holdings between his brother Ferdinand and his
son Philip. To Ferdinand went the Habsburg

possessions in Austria and the imperial crown (still elective in theory, but by now always bestowed on a Habsburg). To Philip went the crowns of Castile and Aragon, with Castile's possessions in the New World, the Kingdom of Naples and the Duchy of Milan (which meant control of Italy), and the Netherlands. Thus for a century and a half after 1556 there were "Austrian Habsburgs" and "Spanish Habsburgs," separate ruling houses but houses that cooperated closely in matters of dynastic policy. Except for the Netherlands, which might well have gone to Ferdinand because of the Netherlands' close cultural and geographical ties with the Empire, the possessions of Philip II formed a more tight-knit and centralized state than his father's holdings.

Philip II was thoroughly Spanish in speech, thought, and character. After the conclusion of peace with France in 1559, he returned from the Netherlands to Spain to remain until his death almost forty years later. He caught the imagination of his people as few of their rulers had done. To the Spanish he is still "Philip the Prudent," one of their greatest kings. Distrustful of his advisers, unable to delegate authority even in minor matters, slow in coming to a decision, strongly Catholic in religion (his enemies would have said "bigoted"), convinced of his divine right to govern Spain as an absolute ruler strictly accountable to God but to no one else, Philip devoted his country to the ideal of a restored Catholic Christendom with the Spanish monarchy as its leading power and defender. For centuries the Spanish had fought the Moors. To Philip, the crusade would continue against half-converted Jews and Moors at home and against Turks and Protestants abroad until the Christian Commonwealth of the Middle Ages had been restored. Meanwhile the Catholic faith would be carried to the New World. Since Spain was the divinely chosen agent of this mission, what was in the interest of Spain was naturally in the interest of Christendom as a whole. Or so it appeared to Philip and to most of the Spanish nobility.

If ever there was a monarchy and a ruling class with a sense of destiny, it was the Spanish of the sixteenth century. This spirit was evident in the Spanish Jesuits who guided the Council of Trent and helped to reconvert much of central Europe to Catholicism, in the Spanish friars who labored to convert the American Indians, in the conquistadors who toppled native empires in the New World, and in the tough Spanish infantry who for over a century defeated every foe they met in Europe. Philip II's Spain was the strongest military power on the Continent, the strongest naval power in the Atlantic, and the wealthiest state in Europe. Spain was the nerve center of the Catholic Reformation. No wonder the terror of the Spanish name lived on into the seventeenth century long after Spanish strength had begun to waste away.

Economic Policy

The economic basis of Spain's predominance was the gold and silver that flowed to Seville in a swelling stream from the New World. Early in the sixteenth century the bullion imported was almost entirely gold. But after the discovery in 1545 of the rich mines in Peru and Mexico, it was mostly silver. The value of the treasure that reached Spain rose enormously between 1500 and 1600. In very round figures the average yearly value of bullion imports at the beginning of the century was something under $300,000; by about 1550 the value had increased 15 times; and by 1600 over 40 times, to about $12,000,000. Then a steady decline set in, until about 1660 the average was down to around $1,200,000. The Spanish crown received about a quarter of the total as its share.

This influx of precious metals, combined with internal financial problems, led to a steep rise in prices. At first the rise was slow and generally stimulating to Spanish industry and commerce. But it had become precipitous by the middle of the century, amounting to a severe inflation that struck first Spain and then the rest of western and central Europe as the metal flowed out of the Iberian Peninsula (in spite of all government prohibitions). It has been estimated that prices quadrupled in Spain in the course of the century. Since prices rose faster than taxes could be increased, Philip II was forced to repudiate his government's debts three times, in 1557, 1575, and 1596. (His successors had to follow the same course in 1607, 1627, and 1647.) The effect of inflation on Spanish industry was eventually disastrous. Since prices always rose faster in Spain than elsewhere, it was relatively more expensive to manufacture goods in Spain than in other countries. This meant that Spanish producers could not sell their goods abroad and that cheaper foreign products captured the Spanish market. In the short run, Spain's silver enabled her to maintain her supremacy in Europe by paying her armies in cash and buying what goods she needed abroad. In the long run, this policy helped to ruin her industry and commerce, and even to undermine her agriculture. There were other reasons for Spain's economic troubles in the seventeenth century, such as the expulsion of her best farmers, the Moriscoes, as the converted Moors were called. But the influx of precious metals was probably the major reason for both the rapid rise and the equally rapid decline of Spain as the leading power in Europe. Spain lived for a century on the windfall of American treasure, but when the supply of bullion dwindled in the seventeenth century she found that the real sinews of her national strength—native industry and agriculture—were ruined.

Religious Policy

Philip II's religious policy was the most narrowly intolerant of his time. He abhorred heresy and unbelief with a holy hatred and said he would rather be king in a desert than in a land of heretics. He feared Islam as the ancient enemy both of Christendom and of his people. In his eyes and in those of most of his countrymen, the Moors who had been forcibly Christianized after the conquest of Granada in 1492 were still Moslems at heart. Furthermore, they were more prosperous than most Spanish farmers, and they were reputedly in league with the Moslems of North Africa. In 1566 Philip ordered them to stop using the Arabic language and learn Castilian, to give up their Moorish dress, and to stop taking hot baths, as was their custom. In 1569 the exasperated Moriscoes broke into

On Philip II of Spain

The pallor of his complexion was remarked on by all observers, and most of them drew the proper conclusion, namely, that it indicated a weak stomach and lack of exercise. Reddened eyes were a penalty of his excessive devotion to the written word both day and night. . . . Reading and writing occupied the major portion of Philip's day. . . . He had taken deeply to heart his father's injunction to direct everything himself, and never to give his full confidence even to the most faithful of his ministers, and the natural result was that his time was completely occupied with receiving and answering reports and letters. . . . Reports, reports, and even more reports; Philip was literally submerged with them in his later years, and moreover he did not stop at reading them; he annotated them, as he went along, with comments on matters as absurdly trifling as the spelling and style of the men who had written them—all in that strange, sprawling hand of his, one of the most illegible hands of an age more than usually replete with chirographical difficulties.

From R. B. Merriman, *The Rise of the Spanish Empire* (New York: Macmillan, 1934), Vol. IV, pp. 21–24.

a revolt, which was savagely suppressed. They were driven out of Andalusia and scattered over Spain. In the years after 1609 they were hounded from the country entirely. Their numbers and importance have sometimes been exaggerated, but there is no doubt that their loss helped to weaken the Spanish economy.

At the height of the revolt of the Moriscoes in 1570, the Turks captured Cyprus from the Venetians. Once again Europe trembled before the threat of Islamic expansion. Philip II immediately allied with the pope and the Venetians to counter the danger, and in October 1571 a Spanish and Venetian fleet won a famous victory over a large Turkish fleet at Lepanto in the Gulf of Corinth. Nothing decisive came of the battle because the Christian forces were unable to follow up their victory. But the event had considerable importance for European morale because it was the first time a Turkish fleet had been defeated.

Philip's prestige probably never stood higher in Europe than in the years immediately following Lepanto. He was popular at home, and his defeat of the Turks gave him the undisputed political leadership of Catholic Europe. France, potentially the strongest monarchy in Europe, was torn by civil war during most of his reign and so was unable to contest his leadership. England had just undergone a serious rebellion in 1569 and her queen had been excommunicated by the pope in 1570. Meanwhile the Empire was safely in the hands of Philip's Habsburg cousins. It seemed as if his dream of a resurgent Catholic Christendom dominated by Spain was about to become a reality.

This dream was shattered during the last quarter of the sixteenth century by the revolt of the Netherlands, the rise of English sea power, and the accession of a Protestant to the throne of France. In his struggle with the embattled forces of Protestantism in northern Europe, Philip overreached himself, exhausted his resources, and started his nation on its long decline.

The Revolt of the Netherlands

The Netherlands were the wealthiest and most densely populated of Philip II's dominions. The 3 million people dwelling beside the mouths of the Rhine and the Meuse had lived by their industry and commerce since the early Middle Ages. The looms of the southern provinces turned out great quantities of linen and woolen cloth, while the fisheries and shipping of the northern provinces steadily increased in value. The comfortable houses of Bruges, Ghent, Antwerp, and Amsterdam were built with the profits of this flourishing industry and trade.

The seventeen provinces of the Netherlands had been united in a personal union by the dukes of Burgundy. But when Charles V inherited the territories in 1519 through his grandmother, Mary of Burgundy, there was little in the way of national feeling or common institutions to bind them together. Charles, who was brought up in Flanders and spoke Flemish as his native language, was the closest thing to a native ruler the Netherlands had ever had, but he regularly sacrificed their interests to his broader imperial aims. During his reign the faint beginnings of a Netherlandish national consciousness appeared.

The provinces were a crossroads for ideas as well as for commerce. The Humanism of Erasmus as well as the teachings of Luther took early root in the Netherlands, to be followed by Anabaptist ideas. But in the 1550's a militant, disciplined Calvinism spread rapidly and soon became the dominant form of Protestantism. When Philip II took over the rule from his father in the fall of 1555, Calvinists constituted tight-knit minorities in most of the cities of the seventeen provinces.

Within ten years after his accession, Philip had alienated most of the nobility and bourgeoisie of the provinces. Native nobles were displaced in favor of Spaniards in the governing council, a policy that hurt the pride of the upper classes. A threat to enforce the laws against heresy with new efficiency and severity sent a chill of terror through the Calvinist merchants and ministers. Madrid was almost a thousand miles away from Brussels, and Philip's Spanish-Catholic mind was even more remote from the interests and concerns of his busy, prosperous Dutch and Flemish subjects, whether they were Calvinist or Catholic. The revolt that ensued was partly a provincial reaction against centralization, partly a patriotic movement directed against foreign rule, and partly a religious protest against an inquisitorial Catholicism.

In 1566 Calvinist mobs began to break images of the saints and smash stained-glass windows in Catholic churches throughout the Netherlands. Philip decided to make a frightful example of the iconoclasts. He sent the Duke of Alva and about 10,000 Spanish regulars to the Netherlands with orders to bring the troublemakers either to the block or to the stake. Alva set up what came to be called a "Council of Blood" and boasted (with some exaggeration) that within the six years of his residence in the Netherlands (1567–73) he had executed upwards of 18,000 people. In addition to spilling so much blood, Alva and his council confiscated large amounts of property and imposed a 10 percent sales tax that almost strangled the trade of the country during the year or two it was in force. The Netherlanders never forgot these six years. Instead of crushing the opposition to Philip, Alva's policy solidified their resistance, at least for a time.

William the Silent and Dutch Independence

By 1572 the resistance movement had found a leader in William the Silent, Prince of Orange, the wealthiest landowner in the provinces. William was no military genius—he lost almost every battle he fought against the Spanish—but he had political wisdom, integrity, and patience, a rugged kind of patriotism, and a deep hatred of religious fanaticism, whether Calvinist or Catholic. He tried his best to hold the Calvinists in check, keep all seventeen provinces united against the Spanish, and still find a solution that would leave Philip as titular ruler. For a few years it looked as if he might succeed. In 1576 Calvinist excesses provoked a frightful sack of Antwerp by Spanish troops known as the "Spanish Fury." This was enough to frighten all seventeen provinces into an agreement to stick together. The agreement was called the Pacification of Ghent.

Within three years, however, both Protestant and Catholic radicals had got out of hand, moderates had lost influence, and animosity between Catholics and Protestants had begun to undermine the universal hatred of Spain. The almost unanimous opposition to Alva gradually gave way to a savage civil war in which the Calvinists, the best-disciplined minority, took over leadership of the opposition to Philip. Most of the Catholics rushed back into the arms of Spain for protection. The seventeen provinces split in two as Calvinists fled to the Dutch provinces in the north beyond the great rivers, where they were better able to defend themselves, and Catholics fled to the Walloon provinces in

the south, where Spanish troops could be maintained and supplied from the upper Rhine. In 1579 the Dutch provinces in the north formed the Union of Utrecht. This union ultimately became the foundation of the United Provinces, or Dutch Netherlands, which formally declared their independence of Philip II in 1581. And so the unanticipated result of the revolt of 1566 was that the seven northern provinces broke away from Spanish rule while the ten southern provinces remained under Habsburg control and eventually (in 1830) became the kingdom of Belgium.

The Rise of the United Provinces

The Dutch Netherlands had to fight for their independence for two generations after 1581. They got some help from French and English troops at various times, but the price that the

The Division of the Netherlands 1581

French Duke of Anjou and the English Queen Elizabeth asked for their help was often dangerously high. In the long run it was dogged determination, geography, and the rivalry of their enemies that won the Dutch their independence. William the Silent was assassinated in 1584, but his descendants carried on his tradition of able and disinterested leadership as *stadtholders* (regents) of one or more of the seven provinces. The "United Provinces" never formed more than the loosest sort of political federation, but the Dutch fought with stubbornness when they had to. The Duke of Parma, who became Philip's representative in the Netherlands in 1578, was one of the best military commanders of his day, but he was unable to reconquer the provinces beyond the bend of the Rhine and Meuse, especially since he lacked control of the sea. The Dutch "Sea Beggars," or privateers, won as many battles against the Spanish on the water as William's armies lost on the land. When Philip's Invincible Armada was broken up in 1588 by the English and the weather, reconquest of the northern provinces became impossible. Finally, in 1648, the king of Spain recognized the independence of his former Dutch subjects.

By this time the new Dutch state had miraculously become one of the great powers of Europe. Most long wars exhaust even the victors, but the Dutch came out of this war the most powerful industrial and commercial nation in Europe. By the early seventeenth century they were building more ships each year than all other nations combined (2,000, it was said), and they were better ships than any others. During the first half of the seventeenth century the Dutch captured more and more of the carrying trade not only of Europe but of the world. Their rates were cheaper, their business methods more efficient, their handling of cargo more skillful. The goods that they offered for exchange were constantly being improved, thanks partly to the influx of skilled textile workers from the impoverished Spanish Netherlands. Antwerp (in the Spanish Netherlands) had been ruined by the Spanish soldiery and blocked off from the sea through the closing of the Scheldt River by the Dutch. Thus Amsterdam (in the United Provinces) took Antwerp's position as the commercial and financial center of Europe. Until their own vulnerability to attack by land became evident after 1660, the Dutch had no rivals who could contest their power.

The sheer geographical extent of Dutch commercial operations was remarkable. Dutch ships handled much of the grain trade of the Baltic and a large part of the carrying trade of England, France, Italy, and Portugal. When Philip II seized the crown of Portugal in 1580 and stopped the Dutch from visiting Lisbon (whence the Dutch were accustomed to distribute Portuguese spices to the rest of Europe), the Dutch with characteristic daring went out to the source of the spices themselves in the Moluccas. In 1602 the Dutch East India Company was formed and soon established its headquarters at Batavia on the island of Java. By the middle of the century the Dutch had seized the richest part of Portugal's eastern empire— the Moluccas, Malacca, and Ceylon. For over a century the company paid very large dividends, mainly by ruthlessly monopolizing the production of spices and limiting it to keep up prices. In 1652 the Dutch founded a colony at the Cape of Good Hope. A few years earlier they had come close to ousting the Portuguese from Brazil. By 1614 they had a settlement on Manhattan Island named New Amsterdam which became the center for a large Dutch carrying trade in the New World. And when the French and British embarked on overseas trade and colonization, they found not only the Spanish and the Portuguese but the Dutch ahead of them all over the world.

So it was an industrial and commercial giant that Philip II conjured up when he set out to crush his rebellious subjects in the Netherlands. The revolt of the Netherlands may be considered as a kind of dress-rehearsal-in-miniature for those larger popular and patriotic revolts against absolute monarchy, beginning with the Puritan Rebellion in England and continuing through the American and French revolutions, that marked the next two centuries. There are many differences between these movements, but there are many similarities in the mixture of economic, patriotic, and religious grievances, the blindness of the monarchs, and the ultimate triumph of "middle-class" interests.

Elizabethan England

Philip of Spain was almost as unfortunate in his dealings with England under Queen Elizabeth I as he was in his dealings with the Netherlands. England was crucial to his plans. If he could have added control of England to his control of Spain, Milan, and the Netherlands, France would have been encircled and the vital sea routes between Spain and the Netherlands would have been safer. For a few years (1554–58), while Philip was married to Queen Mary of England, it seemed as if the Emperor's dream would be realized: England had been brought within the Habsburg orbit and restored to Roman Catholicism. But Elizabeth's accession to the throne in 1558 changed everything.

Queen Elizabeth I (1558–1603) is generally accounted the greatest of the Tudors and one

Queen Elizabeth at a formal session of Parliament. The bishops are seated to her right, the Lords to her left; the Commoners stand outside the bar with the Speaker in the center.

of England's ablest rulers, though to some critics she was simply a stingy and narrow-minded woman. Whatever the judgment, England was immeasurably stronger at her death than at her accession, and she died beloved by the great majority of her people. At twenty-five, when she came to the throne, she had already lived through disgrace, humiliation, and even danger of execution during her sister Mary's reign. She had seen how Mary had lost the love of her people by marrying a foreigner and by burning heretics. These early experiences left her a strong-willed and shrewd young woman, aware of how precarious both her own situation and that of her nation were, determined to put politics before religion and to follow a purely national policy.

Her instinct was always to temporize and compromise. As the daughter of Henry VIII and Anne Boleyn, she could never allow England to submit to papal authority. But she wanted a religious settlement that would not alienate patriotic Catholics, and she hoped she could deceive the Catholic powers of Europe for a time into thinking that she could be won back to Rome. On the other hand, she resented the attempt of the Puritan minority to dictate a radical religious settlement and a risky, pro-Protestant foreign policy. However, she never completely broke with her patriotic Puritan subjects and never lost their loyalty, even when she punished them for advocating radical measures. Elizabeth's policy was nationalist first and Protestant second, but the long-term result was to encourage that fusion of patriotism and Protestantism which became a permanent characteristic of English public opinion after her death.

She compromised and temporized in her foreign policy as well. Her instinct was to avoid clear-cut decisions, to keep a dozen intrigues afoot so that there were always avenues of escape from any policy, and to avoid war at almost any cost. The chief danger at her accession was from French influence on Scotland. The French had long been allies of the Scots, and Mary Stuart, Queen of Scots, was married in 1558 to the heir to the French crown. A year later John Knox, who had become a Calvinist, returned to his native Scotland from Geneva and began a religious revolution. Catholicism and French influence on the Scots were both undermined. Moreover, since Mary Stuart's husband was now king of France, it was clear that France would make every effort to defeat the Calvinists. For once Elizabeth made a rapid decision: to ally with the Calvinist party in Scotland and keep the French out. By 1560 Knox, the Kirk (Church), and the pro-English party were in control, and the French had lost all influence in Scotland. The way was paved for the union of the English and Scottish crowns in 1603.

Mary Queen of Scots

Mary Stuart returned to Scotland in 1561 after her husband's death. She was a far more charming and romantic figure than her cousin Elizabeth, but she was no stateswoman. A convinced Catholic, she soon ran head-on into the granitelike opposition of Knox and the Kirk. Her marriage to her cousin Lord Darnley turned out badly and she became involved in a plot resulting in his murder. In 1567 she was forced to abdicate, and in the following year she fled from Scotland and sought protection in England from Elizabeth. No visitor could have been more unwelcome. Mary, as Henry VII's great-granddaughter, had the best hereditary claim to be Elizabeth's heir, but she was a Catholic and a foreigner. Elizabeth would never formally recognize her as her successor, nor would she marry in order to produce another heir, nor would she do anything to harm her fellow sovereign, except keep a close watch on her through her agents. This policy exasperated Elizabeth's Puritan advisers and left Mary free to become the center of almost every French or Spanish plot against Elizabeth's life during the next twenty years.

The Anglo-Spanish Conflict

Though there were many sources of friction between them, Elizabeth and Philip of Spain remained on relatively good terms for over twenty-five years. As time went on, however, it became increasingly difficult to keep the peace. England was a small country with less than half the population of Spain, but during the quarter-century of peace that Elizabeth's cautious temporizing gave her people, English industry, commerce, and shipping expanded considerably. For reasons we have already suggested, the Spanish were unable to produce the goods needed by their colonies. And Spanish shipping was incapable of supplying the insatiable colonial demand for African slaves. An aggressive merchant named Sir John Hawkins was the first Englishman to carry both goods and slaves direct to the Spanish settlements in the Caribbean, in 1562. It was

profitable but dangerous work. In 1569 he and his cousin, Sir Francis Drake, were almost wiped out by a Spanish fleet. In revenge, Drake seized the annual silver shipment from Peru on its way across the Isthmus of Panama. In 1577–80 he followed Magellan's route around the world and demonstrated the vulnerability of the Spanish Empire. Meanwhile English sailors were boldly probing the coasts of North America in a vain search for a Northwest Passage that would short-circuit the Portuguese route to the Indies. Like their fellow Protestants, the Dutch, the English were contesting the Spanish-Portuguese monopoly of overseas trade.

It was the revolt of the Netherlands, however, that finally brought England and Spain to blows. For centuries the economic ties between England and the Low Countries had been close. The English people sympathized with Alva's

The Spanish Armada, by an unknown artist. Some of the Spanish ships, like the galleass in the foreground, had both oars and sails.

victims, and English Sea Dogs cooperated informally with Dutch Sea Beggars to prey on Spanish shipping and to cut Spanish communications by sea with the Netherlands. Philip's ambassadors in England became deeply involved in one plot after another against Elizabeth's life, usually with the object of setting Mary Stuart on the throne. In 1587 Elizabeth reluctantly consented to Mary's execution when confronted with unmistakable evidence of her complicity in these plots. Philip immediately planned an attack on England. In 1588 he sent his "Invincible Armada" north to hold the Channel while Parma ferried his Spanish veterans across to conquer England for Spain.

The story of the defeat of the Armada has become an allegory of the triumph of a young, vigorous nation over an old and senile nation. The Spanish ships were large and slow, equipped with inferior cannons, and commanded by a landlubber. The fleet was conceived as a means of transporting troops, not of fighting battles at sea. The English ships that put out from Plymouth to harry the Spanish up the Channel were smaller and more maneuverable, trained to fire their cannons at longer range. When the Spanish reached Calais and anchored there, Parma had still not completed his plans. The English sent in fire ships among the Spanish ships as they lay at anchor, drove them northward in panic, and attacked them fiercely off Gravelines. Stormy weather completed what the English had begun. Hardly half the galleons that had left Spain made their way back northward and westward around Scotland and Ireland. The victory gave a lift to the morale of Englishmen and of Protestants everywhere. It ended all further thought of Spanish conquest of England—or reconquest of the Netherlands, for that matter. It did not mean the end of Spanish sea power, which was still greater than that of any other country. But when peace was finally signed in 1604, the English, with the Dutch, stood close to the Spaniards as powers on the sea.

The French Wars of Religion

One obvious reason for Spain's ascendancy in the later sixteenth century was the fact that France, traditionally the chief obstacle to Habsburg expansion, was torn by a series of civil and religious wars that prostrated the monarchy and devastated large areas of the country between 1562 and 1593. Almost overnight France was transformed from an aggressive national monarchy into an object of intervention by neighboring states.

The Causes of the Civil War

France, with a population about double that of Spain, was the largest nation in Christian Europe under a single government. But, impressive as the French monarchy was, it was far from

---

The Armada

When the Spanish Armada challenged the ancient lords of the English on their own grounds, the impending conflict took on the aspect of a judicial duel in which as was expected in such duels, God would defend the right. . . . So when the two fleets approached their appointed battleground, all Europe watched. For the spectators of both parties, the outcome, reinforced, as everyone believed, by an extraordinary tempest, was indeed decisive. The Protestants of France and the Netherlands, Germany and Scandinavia saw with relief that God was, in truth, as they had always supposed, on their side. The Catholics of France and Italy and Germany saw with almost equal relief that Spain was not, after all, God's chosen champion. From that time forward, though Spain's preponderance was to last for more than another generation, the peak of her prestige had passed. . . . So, in spite of the long, indecisive war which followed, the defeat of the Spanish Armada really was decisive. It decided that religious unity was not to be reimposed by force on the heirs of medieval Christendom, and if, in doing so, it only validated what was already by far the most probable outcome, why, perhaps that is all that any of the battles we call decisive has ever done.

From Garrett Mattingly, *The Armada* (Boston: Houghton Mifflin, 1959), pp. 400–01.

having absolute power. There was still a powerful and turbulent aristocracy in France, and French provinces clung jealously to local customs and privileges. The country was imperfectly unified; there was no body that could speak for the whole realm, as Parliament could for England. Class differences were sharp and the bureaucracy was overworked, corrupt, and inefficient.

Into this half-established absolute monarchy the strong irritant of religious conflict was injected about the middle of the century in the form of militant Calvinism. The rational theology and disciplined organization of Reformed Christianity—not to mention the superb French style of Calvin's writings—appealed widely to many nobles and bourgeois throughout France. The French Calvinists were nicknamed Huguenots. On the eve of the civil wars they boasted about 2,500 churches. They probably never numbered more than a sixth of the population (some scholars say as low as a twelfth), but they were an aggressive and well-organized minority, sure of their faith, and confident of the support of a few nobles, such as Admiral Coligny, at the very top of the social hierarchy. Arrayed against them were strongly Catholic noble families, and, more important, the University of Paris and the Paris *parlement*. Most important of all was the fact that the Concordat of Bologna had given the kings of France full control over the appointment of the higher clergy as well as considerable indirect control of papal taxation and jurisdiction. In short, established authority consistently opposed religious change, and consequently the Huguenots remained a permanent minority in France.

The Course of the Wars

The wars that broke out in France in 1562 were at once social, political, and religious. When Henry II died in 1559, the royal authority fell into the hands of the Queen Mother, Catherine de' Medici, during the reigns of her three weakling sons, Francis II (1559–60), Charles IX (1560–74), and Henry III (1574–89). Catherine was an astute woman who put politics before religion and did her best to keep the feuding factions at court and the religious fanatics throughout the country from flying at each other's throats. But she lacked formal authority and by now the animosities had become bitter. Calvinists allied themselves with discontented nobles and upholders of local autonomy. On the other side were Catholics, royal agents, and defenders of the *status quo*. Fanatics on both sides appealed for foreign aid, the Huguenots to the English, the Dutch, and the Germans, the Catholics to Spain. Both England and Spain sent troops, mostly at the beginning and again at the end of the wars.

Fighting was of the savage and bitter kind that characterizes civil wars. The Catholics won most of the pitched battles but were unable to wipe out the Huguenots. In 1572 Catherine was persuaded by the Catholic fanatics that one sharp blow might end all the trouble. At two o'clock on the morning of St. Bartholomew's Day, Catholic armed bands set upon the Huguenots in Paris, where many of their leaders were gathered for the wedding of the king's sister to the Protestant, Henry of Navarre. Coligny and many others were killed. The slaughter spread quickly to other French cities, and before it was over probably 10,000 Protestants had been massacred. This was the most spectacular of innumerable atrocities on both sides. It horrified Protestants throughout Europe and, according to one story, made Philip II laugh aloud. But it had little effect on the conflict in France.

Henry of Navarre

The wars dragged on for twenty more years, becoming more and more confused and purposeless until the Huguenot Henry of Navarre came

Massacre of St. Bartholomew's Day, 1572, a painting by an eye-witness, François Dubois.

to the throne in 1589 as Henry IV (1589–1610). He had a difficult time making good his claim to the crown against a Catholic League which held Paris and against troops of Philip II which intervened from the Spanish Netherlands under Parma. In the end he found that the only way he could capture Paris was to renounce his faith and become a Catholic, which he did in 1593. He did not forget his former fellow Protestants, however. By the Edict of Nantes in 1598 the Huguenots were granted freedom of conscience, freedom of worship in specified places, equal civil rights, and control of some 200 fortified towns throughout France. In short, the edict simply recognized a religious stalemate, and zealots on both sides of the religious fence considered it only temporary. But it constituted the first formal recognition by a European national monarchy that two religions could be allowed to exist side by side without destroying the state, and growing numbers of Frenchmen who preferred civil peace at any price to the anarchy and fanaticism of the past forty years supported it. With the conclusion of peace with Spain and the publication of the Edict of Nantes in 1598, France was ready to resume the building of a strong monarchy.

The General Character of the Later Sixteenth Century

The age of Philip II and of Elizabeth of England has been called the Age of Religious Warfare. It is true that religion was often the spark that set aflame the combustible materials of sixteenth-century society, but early nationalism, economic instability, and social unrest also played their part. A more precise description of the period might be the Age of Religious Politics. Until the Reformation, European politics and diplomacy had grown slowly less religious and more secular. Now for a century, thanks to the religious schism, politics and diplomacy became once more strongly motivated and embittered by religion. The monarchies were faced by religious ideologies that often commanded fiercer loyalties than could the dynasties themselves. A Jesuit might scheme and work and die for an ideal that obviously transcended all state boundaries. In the same way a Scottish Presbyterian, a Dutch Calvinist, and a French Huguenot might have more in common than subjects of the same king. Thus religious differences sometimes undermined the power of monarchs, as they did in France and the Netherlands. And sometimes religious zeal reinforced loyalty to the dynasty, as it did in Spain and among English Protestants. Perhaps the best symbol of this Age of Religious Politics was the Escorial, which Philip II built for his residence near Madrid. The building was half-palace, half-monastery; and the private chamber of the king was connected directly with the chapel of the monastery. A century later a palace would be built at Versailles that would express the spirit of a quite different age.

"Golden Ages"

In spite of internal and external conflicts, the late sixteenth and early seventeenth centuries witnessed a "golden age" of literature and the arts in three of the nations we have been considering. Shakespeare's plays and Spenser's poetry in Elizabethan England, Cervantes' *Don Quixote* and Velasquez' paintings in Spain of the early seventeenth century, and Vondel's poetry and Rembrandt's portraits in Holland of the mid-seventeenth century represent a kind of summit of achievement in the history of the arts in these three nations. Shakespeare (*ca.* 1564–1616), Cervantes (1547–1616), and Vondel (1587–1679) are still the greatest figures in the literary history of their native countries, and, though England produced no great painter, Frans Hals (*ca.* 1580–1666) and Rembrandt van Rijn (1606–69) are the towering figures in Dutch painting, as El Greco (*ca.* 1548–1614) and Velasquez (1599–1660) are in Spanish.

In each case the artistic flowering accompanied or, as in Spain, immediately followed a period of heroic national struggle, effort, and

Religion and Patriotism

A Spanish ambassador reporting the words of a French Catholic in 1565:

Nowadays Catholic princes must not proceed as they once did. At one time friends and enemies were distinguished by the frontiers of provinces and kingdoms, and were called Italians, Germans, Frenchmen, Spaniards, Englishmen, and the like. Now we must say Catholics and heretics, and a Catholic prince must consider all Catholics of all countries as his friends, just as the heretics consider all heretics as friends and subjects whether they are their own vassals or not.

An English Protestant writing in 1589:

All dutiful subjects in this land desire with all their hearts the continuance of God's religion; the preservation of Queen Elizabeth; and the good success of the English navy. These particulars, I grant, are not expressed in flat in the Lord's Prayer; but they are contained within the compass of, and may be deduced from the petitions of that excellent prayer. Whosoever doubteth this is void of learning.

As quoted in Erich Marks, *Die Zusammenkunft von Bayonne* (Strassburg: K. J. Trübner, 1889), p 14; as quoted in Benjamin Hanbury, *Historical Memorials Relating to the Independents* (London: Congregational Union of England and Wales, 1839–44), Vol. I, p. 71.

achievement. It is tempting to say that ages of national expansion and excitement, times of heroism and "crusade," provide great artists with the stimulation and the receptive audiences they need. On a more mundane level, it is clear that "golden ages" depend on the existence of a class of people with enough education, wealth, and leisure to appreciate luxuries like books and paintings. The historian can record the existence of such classes and the occurrence of heroic national effort in England, Spain, and the Dutch Netherlands during these years. But he cannot account satisfactorily for Shakespeare's extraordinary appreciation of the complexities of human motivation, Cervantes' sympathy for all sorts and conditions of men, or Rembrandt's penetration of the depths of the religious soul. All these are manifestations of purely individual genius. Nor can he account for the appearance in France during a time of troubles of three writers who have profoundly influenced the French mind: Montaigne (1533–92), Descartes (1596–1650), and Pascal (1623–62). The historian can explain something about the conditions and characteristics of "golden ages." He cannot explain the appearance of genius.

Suggestions for Further Reading

1. Geographical Discovery

Two brief general studies provide a good introduction to the subject: J. H. Parry, *Europe and a Wider World, 1415–1715* (1949), and C. E. Nowell, *The Great Discoveries and the First Colonial Empires** (1954). W. C. Abbott, *The Expansion of Europe,* 2 vols. (1918), is an older but still valuable general account, including consideration of the effect of the discoveries upon Europe. *The Great Age of Discovery* (edited A. P. Newton, 1932) is a collection of reliable articles by various authors. Sir Percy Sykes, *A History of Exploration* (1934), surveys the whole subject from ancient times on; H. H. Hart, *Sea Road to the Indies* (1950), describes the Portuguese exploits; J. B. Brebner, *The Explorers of North America, 1492–1806** (1933), and A. P. Newton, *The European Nations in the West Indies, 1493–1688* (1933), treat exploration in particular areas. E. Sanceau has written a good modern biography of Henry the Navigator (1947). S. E. Morison, *Admiral of the Ocean Sea,** 2 vols. (1942), is the best account of Columbus. C. McK. Parr, *So Noble a Captain* (1953), is a reliable account of Magellan. E. Sanceau, *The Land of Prester John* (1944), traces Portuguese interest in Abyssinia. The best correctives for older Anglo-Saxon notions of Spanish colonizing are C. H. Haring, *The Spanish Empire in America* (1947), and L. Hanke, *The Spanish Struggle for Justice in the Conquest of America* (1949). R. L. Reynolds, *Europe Emerges** (1961), is a good analysis of European expansion in general.

2. Spain

R. B. Merriman, *Rise of the Spanish Empire in the Old World and in the New,* 4 vols. (1918–34), is a superbly written and scholarly account of Spain in Europe and overseas to the death of Philip II. J. H. Elliott, *Imperial Spain, 1469–1716** (1964), is a remarkable book. R. Trevor Davies, *The Golden Century of Spain, 1501–1621** (1937), and *Spain in Decline, 1621–1700** (1956), are well-informed, interesting, sometimes controversial accounts. J. H. Parry, *The Spanish Theory of Empire in the Sixteenth Century* (1940), studies the effect of empire upon the Spanish monarchy. E. J. Hamilton, *American Treasure and the Price Revolution in Spain, 1501–1650* (1934), is the starting point for study of sixteenth-century inflation.

3. The Netherlands

The most scholarly brief account of the Dutch rebellion and its consequences is in the two books of P. Geyl, *The Revolt of the Netherlands, 1555–1609** (1932), and *The Netherlands Divided, 1609–1648* (1936). There is a beautifully written popular biography of William the Silent by C. V. Wedgwood* (1944).

---

* Available in paperback edition.

4. Elizabethan England

There is a wealth of well-written, scholarly books on the period. Sir John Neale, author of three brilliant volumes on the parliamentary history of the reign, has written the best biography of Elizabeth, *Queen Elizabeth I** (1952). E. Jenkins, *Elizabeth the Great** (1959), adds insight on the purely personal side. C. Read's thorough biographies, *Mr. Secretary Walsingham,* 3 vols. (1925), and *Mr. Secretary Cecil* (Lord Burghley), 2 vols. (1955, 1960), provide intimate knowledge of the politics of the period. A. L. Rowse has written with zest on Elizabethan society in *The England of Elizabeth** (1950) and *The Expansion of Elizabethan England** (1955). J. A. Williamson, *The Age of Drake** (3rd ed., 1952), is by a master of naval history; and G. Mattingly, *The Armada** (1959), is one of those rare books, a definitive treatment of its subject which is at the same time magnificent reading. A good brief survey is S. I. Bindoff, *Tudor England** (1959).

5. France

It is more difficult to find good reading in English on France than on England in the sixteenth century. L. Batiffol, *The Century of the Renaissance* (trans. 1916), is an older general account of France in the sixteenth century. J. E. Neale, *The Age of Catharine de' Medici** (1943), is very useful, as is H. Pearson, *Henry of Navarre* (1963). There is a brief modern account of the period in F. C. Palm, *Calvinism and the Religious Wars* (1932). J. W. Thompson, *The Wars of Religion in France, 1559–1576* (1909), is older but still useful. A. J. Grant, *The Huguenots* (1934), is both scholarly and brief. W. F. Church, *Constitutional Thought in Sixteenth Century France* (1941), discusses with discernment the conflict of medieval and modern ideas of government during the civil wars.

---

* Available in paperback edition.

4

Political and Economic Crises of the Seventeenth Century

The Siege of Magdeburg in 1631 by Habsburg and Catholic League forces under General Tilly. This siege resulted in one of the bloodiest massacres of the Thirty Years' War.

The seventeenth century saw the culmination of a long, slow process that has engaged our attention many times in preceding chapters: the emergence of the modern, sovereign territorial state from the feudal and ecclesiastical society of the Middle Ages. This process began with the building of strong "feudal monarchies" in the thirteenth century. After a lapse in the fourteenth century, it made further headway in the "new monarchies" of the later fifteenth century. After a further lapse marked by civil and religious wars following the Reformation, it produced, by the end of the seventeenth century, two contrasting types of modern state: the absolute monarchy of France, and the constitutional monarchy of England. The making of the modern state was a process of defining and concentrating political power. From a theoretical point of view, it meant defining the concept of "sovereignty" ever more clearly. From the practical point of view, it meant fixing supreme power in some organ of the state, either in the monarchy (as in France and most other states) or in the representative assembly (as in England and a few other states).

Decisive changes also took place in international relations. The seventeenth century witnessed the slow decline of Spain, the rise of France to European hegemony, the heyday of Dutch prosperity and power, the emergence of England as a major power, the final disintegration of the German Empire, and the appearance of Russia on the stage of European diplomacy. For the first time, economic theories began to influence statesmen, and so the seventeenth century saw the last of the "religious" wars and the first

Hobbes' Leviathan

When Thomas Hobbes published his tough-minded book on the state in 1651, he chose his title from the Book of Job. "Leviathan" is the fearful and powerful aquatic beast, either a crocodile or a whale, described by Job in Chapter 41. The crowned ruler pictured above is likened by the artist to this beast, described in the verse of Job quoted above his head: "There is no power on earth that may be compared to him." The book and its title page are good landmarks of the making of the modern state. Hobbes calls the sovereign power of a state, usually conferred on one man, "that great Leviathan, or rather (to speak more reverently) that mortal God, to which we owe under the immortal God, our peace and defence."

of the "commercial" wars. Europe continued to expand abroad, but now it was the Dutch, the English, and the French who were the leaders, not the Spanish and the Portuguese. Finally, a "scientific revolution" gave Europeans a radically new way of understanding and controlling natural processes (see Chapter 6).

The Mercantile Economy of Early Modern Europe

We have already seen that important changes in the European economy had begun in the fifteenth century. By the seventeenth century the cumulative effects of these changes were so great that historians have spoken of them as a "Commercial Revolution." Contemporaries were also aware that a change had taken place, but it was only in 1776 that Adam Smith found a name for the economy of the early modern period. He called it the mercantile system. This was a system based on commerce, as opposed to the agricultural system of the Middle Ages. Certainly the volume and value of European trade had increased enormously. And the countries that were assuming political leadership in Europe were becoming the centers of trade. The main routes now focused on London, Amsterdam, and Paris rather than on Lisbon and Seville. In England, France, and the Netherlands, the merchant was far more important than the industrialist and far more influential than the farmer. Smith's phrase is accurate; the economy was a mercantile economy.

New Types of Economic Organization

By the end of the sixteenth century it had become apparent that the gild system, designed for local workers, could not supply the growing demands of cities, courts, and armies. New organizations were needed for large-scale commerce and industry. Usually it was the merchants, the men who had the money and who knew the markets, who did the work of organizing.

One method was simply to transform a gild, so that a few masters dominated production and all other gild members were reduced to the status of workers. Another technique was called the putting-out system. For example, in the textile industry an entrepreneur would buy wool, pass it out to peasants to be spun into thread, carry the thread to others to be woven into cloth, take the cloth to the dyers, and finally sell the finished product. This system had the double advantage of bypassing the gild restrictions in the towns and of tapping new sources of cheap labor in the countryside. In the same way English merchants bought Swedish iron, gave it out to Sheffield tool-makers, and sold the product abroad. (The English were the best precision-tool-makers in Europe.) The putting-out system dominated the textile industry from the sixteenth to the eighteenth centuries.

Another type of organization was the gathering-in system (we call it the factory system). In industries like printing, cannon-founding, mining, and shipbuilding, for example, and even in some textile processes such as silk-weaving and calico-printing, it was more efficient to gather workers together at some central place where their work could be directly supervised and coordinated. In both the putting-out and the gathering-in systems, it was almost invariably the merchant, not the manufacturer or the technician, who did the organizing.

Joint Stock Companies

Another important innovation was the joint stock company. The first associations of merchants were "regulated companies"—groups of men who secured a monopoly on trade to a given area, but each of whom traded on his own account. They were associations of men, not of capital. What was needed, however, was a type of association that would attract the investments of men who had neither the desire nor the ability to qualify as active traders in a regulated company. The answer was the joint stock company, an amazingly flexible institution that was to be the parent of many other economic and political institutions on both sides of the Atlantic.

Europe's Growing Population

This chart is an attempt by a historian to show at a glance the changes in population density per square mile in certain European countries during a period of four hundred years. Since there was no census anywhere in Europe before the nineteenth century, the author is careful to point out that "the estimates are rough approximations only." Such charts are helpful, but since they are based on very inadequate data, the reader must always remember that they convey an undue sense of definiteness and precision.

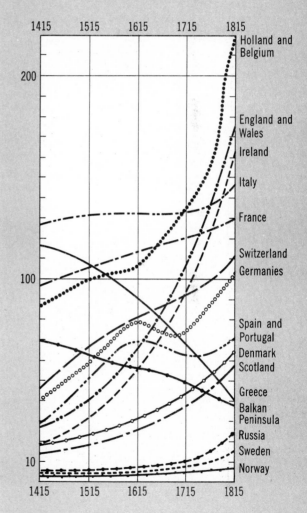

Redrawn from Geoffrey Bruun, *Europe in Evolution, 1415–1815* (Boston: Houghton Mifflin, 1945), pp. 240–41.

The Center of European Economy early 17th century

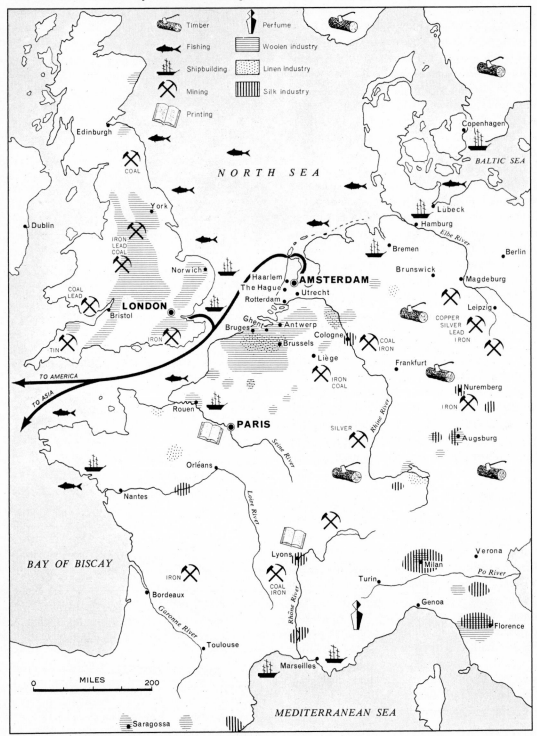

The joint stock company began as an association of investors, not of traders. Individuals bought shares in a venture, such as a trading voyage, and shared in the profits in proportion to their investment. When the association continued beyond a single venture, it became a joint stock company. This device had two advantages: It enabled anyone from a modestly wealthy man to Queen Elizabeth to invest in a business enterprise like Drake's voyages, and it associated businessmen with courtiers and statesmen at a time when both business sense and influence at court were necessary to the success of commercial ventures. The joint stock idea originated in southern Europe, but it was first applied to large-scale overseas enterprise in England in the Russia Company of 1553. The English East India Company, the companies that founded Virginia and Massachusetts, and the Bank of England were all joint stock companies. In the end, the joint stock company became the dominant form of commercial organization.

An equally striking change was the change from town to king as the regulator of economic activity. The unit of economic activity in the Middle Ages, apart from agriculture, was the town or the city-state. As stronger monarchs appeared at the end of the Middle Ages, urban economy was steadily absorbed into the national economy throughout much of Europe, except in Italy and Germany. The monarch stepped into the shoes of medieval town officials and regulated trade and production much as municipal governments had done, but on a larger scale.

Mercantilism

The aim of this regulation was to advance the common good, not to increase the wealth of individuals. But a king's definition of the common good was the strength and security of his realm, and during the seventeenth century monarchs began to believe that these ends could be attained by following an economic doctrine called mercantilism. This doctrine, in its simplest form, assumed that there is only a certain stock of wealth in the world at any given time, and if one country gains wealth another loses it. To prevent loss, home industries and shipping should be encouraged and colonies founded to provide raw materials that would otherwise have to be bought from foreigners. Most important, however, was regulating trade so as to increase a country's stock of precious metals. This was not an unreasonable precaution in an age when credit devices were in their infancy and when, in case of war, a country had to have a reserve of gold and silver to pay its suppliers and soldiers.

The obvious way to build such a reserve— short of discovering new mines or capturing a Spanish plate fleet—was for a nation to export more than it imported. Foreign buyers would have to settle their balances in precious metals. And so mercantilism called for tariffs to discourage imports and various benefits to encourage export industries. But some exports—gold and silver, scarce raw materials, and skilled workmen, for example—weaken a state and should therefore be forbidden. Logically, mercantilist theory called for the abolition of all internal tariffs and all internal barriers to trade, though it was impossible to accomplish this except in England. At the core of mercantilism was the conviction that trade is the most important of all economic activities and that the regulation of trade is the government's most important economic concern.

Mercantilists favored the acquisition of colonies that enhanced the strength of the mother country by furnishing tropical products or by buying home manufactures. But they had no use for colonies that raised crops or produced manufactured goods that competed with the home country's products, nor for colonies that traded directly with other nations. The integration of colonies into the home economy was a cardinal principle of the mercantilists.

We have necessarily made mercantilism seem more clear-cut and consistent than it actually was in practice. It differed from one country to another, in response to the interests of the ruling group. In France the system is often called *Étatisme,* or state-ism. The hand of the government was very heavy in France, government intervention in commercial enterprise was direct and positive, regulation was minute, and rela-

An Englishman on the Importance of Trade

ca. 1630

Although a kingdom may be enriched by gifts received, or by purchase taken from some other nations, yet these are things uncertain and of small consideration when they happen. The ordinary means therefore to encrease our wealth and treasure is by foreign trade, wherein we must ever observe this rule; to sell more to strangers yearly than we consume of theirs in value. For suppose that when this kingdom is plentifully served with the cloth, lead, tin, iron, fish and other native commodities, we do yearly export the overplus to foreign countries to the value of twenty-two hundred thousand pounds; by which means we are enabled beyond the seas to buy and bring in foreign wares for our use and consumptions, to the value of twenty hundred thousand pounds; by this order duly kept in our trading, we may rest assured that the kingdom shall be enriched yearly two hundred thousand pounds, which must be brought to us in so much treasure; because that part of our stock which is not returned to us in wares must necessarily be brought home in treasure. . . .

Behold then the true form and worth of foreign trade, which is, the great revenue of the king, the honour of the kingdom, the noble profession of the merchant, the school of our arts, the supply of our wants, the employment of our poor, the improvements of our lands, the nursery of our mariners, the walls of the kingdoms, the means of our treasure, the sinews of our wars, the terror of our enemies.

From Thomas Mun, *England's Treasure by Foreign Trade* (New York: Oxford U. Press, 1933), p. 5.

tively little initiative was left to individual enterprise. In England mercantilism also meant regulation of the economy in the government's interest. But even before 1688, and especially afterward, the English government was more responsive to the pressures of businessmen than was the French. It is often very difficult to tell whether English economic policy represented the interest of the state as a whole or the interests of individual entrepreneurs. In the United Provinces, where the federal government was in effect a government of businessmen, the interest of the state and the interests of the business community practically coincided. Dutch mercantilism was not so much the regulation of trade by the state as it was the control of economic policy by organized business. In the rest of Europe, however—in Spain, Portugal, Austria, Prussia, and Sweden—mercantilism represented primarily the interest of the monarchy and so followed the French model more than the Dutch.

The Rise in Prices

The rise in prices continued in the seventeenth century, though not so rapidly as in the later sixteenth century. The rise was not uniform in all parts of Europe, and in the present state of research it is hard to generalize. A reasonable estimate is that prices more than doubled between 1500 and 1600 in Europe as a whole, then rose another 20 percent by 1700, and another 10 percent by 1800. This inflationary tendency had both social and political results. The social results are much disputed by historians, but most agree that there was a good deal of social mobility and restlessness. Older noble families, dependent on fixed incomes, went through an economic crisis which lessened, for a time, their prestige and power. Well into the seventeenth century there were always many impoverished nobles and gentry in England, France, and Spain who were ready to join an overseas voyage or a continental war. On the other hand, the classes that lived by trade, large industry, or capitalistic farming did well, bought land, and often gained titles of nobility. Thus a new aristocracy was pushing its way into the ranks of the privileged and taking its place beside the older families.

We have already seen something of the political effects of the rise in prices. Generally speaking, prices tended to rise faster than government income, and almost every major government in the seventeenth century had to face severe financial crises. In Spain the price rise was more severe than elsewhere, and the burden of military commitments was very heavy. The result was, as we have seen, that the government was forced to repudiate its debt about every twenty years from 1550 to 1650. The French government was somewhat more successful in raising the money it needed for its wars and its court, but its taxation system was antiquated and trouble was simply postponed to the eighteenth century. In England the Stuarts were never able to build a sound system of government finance because they lost the confidence of Parliament, which controlled the major part of the royal revenue. But after 1688 a government that had gained the confidence of Parliament as well as the business community was able to construct an exceptionally strong system of public finance that included parliamentary taxation, a national bank, and a permanent public debt. In large measure this system was modeled on Dutch governmental finance, the most successful of the age. Since the rulers of the United Provinces were representatives of the business community, they had little difficulty, at least for a century, in raising the money and credit they needed for their overseas empire-building and their wars. In an age dominated by trade, a state that had a flourishing commerce and could command the confidence of its merchants could weather any financial storm. A state that had little commerce, or in which commerce was growing slowly while merchants were discouraged, was likely to find itself in financial difficulties.

European Expansion in the Seventeenth Century

Europe continued to expand overseas in the seventeenth century. We have seen how the Dutch were drawn by their war of independence to take to the sea, and how by the end of the seventeenth century they had ousted the Portuguese from their empire in the East. Early in the century two new competitors for commerce and colonies appeared: the English and the French. Neither of them was strong enough to attack established colonies, such as those of Spain, directly. As a rule they went to areas untouched by Spaniards and Portuguese and developed a new and rival kind of empire. Meanwhile the Russians moved overland to stake out their claim to the northern half of Asia.

The East

First the English and then the French followed Vasco da Gama's route to the East. The English East India Company was founded in 1600, the Dutch in 1602, the French in 1664. The Dutch discouraged English trade with the Spice Islands—they killed ten English merchants in 1623—so the English withdrew to India. There they set up "factories," or trading posts, on the Portuguese model. Until the break-up of the Mogul Empire in central India early in the eighteenth century, it was never possible for Europeans to penetrate very far into the subcontinent of India. Their footholds on the coast depended entirely on sea power for support; and as Portuguese sea power declined in the seventeenth century and as the Dutch busied themselves farther east, the English were able to establish themselves at Bombay, Madras, and Calcutta. Meanwhile, the French at Pondicherry had become their most important potential rivals. The stage was set for a struggle in the next century between the British and the French East India companies over the commerce and riches of India.

The Caribbean

In the Caribbean the Dutch, the English, and the French were all searching for footholds around the periphery of the Spanish settlements. After an unsuccessful attempt to take Brazil from the Portuguese, the Dutch seized Curaçao as a base from which to raid Spanish commerce. The English settled Barbados in 1624 and acquired Jamaica in 1655. Meanwhile, the French settled Guadaloupe and Martinique. All these islands rapidly became rich sugar-producing areas, thanks to slave labor. So the English and the French, who came to the Caribbean to trade and buccaneer in the Dutch manner, stayed on to become plantation-owners in the Spanish manner. The English and French sugar islands were the darlings of mercantilists at home. The planters cultivated a crop that could not be grown in Europe; they developed no industries to compete with home industries; and they were entirely dependent on their mother countries for shipping. Not surprisingly, the sugar islands were the center of attention among financiers and diplomats for over a century.

The chronic dearth of manufactured goods and slaves in the Spanish colonies meant that foreign smugglers who could slip by the Spanish navy were always welcome. As Portuguese control of the slaving stations on the western coast of Africa relaxed, the Dutch and English stepped in to supply the Spanish West Indies with the Negroes needed on their sugar plantations. The brutality of this trade has become a byword, but it aroused no protest whatever in any European nation during the seventeenth and early eighteenth centuries.

North America

In North America a new kind of colonial expansion was beginning that was to have more far-reaching results than West Indian sugar-planting, though it was long overshadowed by the economic success of the tropical islands. There were many reasons why the Dutch, the English, and the French at the opening of the seventeenth century became interested in North America. For some time their sailors had been searching for a northwest passage to the Indies. Their ships were already engaged in cod-fishing on the Newfoundland Banks. It was evident that North America could supply vast quantities of furs and timber. There might be precious metals to be mined, and it might turn out that sugar could be grown farther north than the Caribbean. Permanent settlements could support all these economic activities and at the same time help turn the flank of the Spanish in the New World.

Sir Walter Raleigh's unsuccessful attempt to found a colony in Virginia during the 1580's, however, had revealed some of the difficulties of settling the land the Spanish had left unoccupied. Colder climate, poorer soil, and hostile natives discouraged a plantation type of economy. To plant a permanent colony in North America a whole labor force would have to be transported and supported, perhaps for years, until the settlement became self-sufficient. This called for a large investment of capital and a large number of settlers. Furthermore, it called for strong belief and determination.

The Dutch, the French, and the English

It was the English and, to a lesser degree, the French, not the Dutch, whose determination proved strongest. The Dutch explored the Hudson in 1609 and settled New Amsterdam on Manhattan Island in 1621, but their colony of New Netherland never became more than a center for maritime trade and the export of furs. Unsupported by the company that founded it, it fell to the English in 1664. The French were more successful. From Cartier, who discovered the St. Lawrence in 1535, to La Salle, who coursed the Mississippi in 1682, their explorers were more adventurous, their fur-traders better able to adapt to the country, and their Jesuit missionaries more determined, than the representatives of any other European nation in the New World. In 1605 there were French settlers in Acadia and in 1608 Champlain founded Quebec. By 1640 there were perhaps 3,000 Frenchmen in Canada; by the end of the century about 10,000.

The growth was slow for several reasons. The settlement of French Canada was marked by paternalism and relatively little individual initiative. Only when the French government actively encouraged Frenchmen to emigrate, as it did under Colbert in the 1660's and 1670's, did the colony grow appreciably. Since land was granted in large blocks, or *seigneuries,* to a few proprietors under semifeudal conditions, there was little inducement for peasants to emigrate. The government strictly prohibited the Huguenots, who wanted to emigrate, from going to Canada (they went to the English colonies instead). A fairly solid block of settlements grew up in the St. Lawrence Valley, but the slow-growing colony of *seigneurs* and *habitants* (as the peasants were called) was soon far outdistanced by the English settlements to the south.

The founding of the English colonies in North America was the result of a peculiarly favorable set of historical circumstances in the mother country. The idea that colonization meant wealth had been skillfully sold to ordinary Englishmen by enthusiasts and businessmen before Queen Elizabeth's death. London and

Bristol merchants were ready for colonizing ventures and able to organize such ventures by means of joint stock companies. The constitutional and religious conflicts that troubled England through most of the seventeenth century provided many people with both material and idealistic motives for wishing to emigrate. Finally the English government, whether it was that of the Stuarts or of their revolutionary opponents, encouraged but did not interfere with colonizing projects. In particular, it put no bar in the way of religious minorities that wished to emigrate.

The first successful colony, planted at Jamestown by the Virginia Company in 1607, had a difficult time until the settlers discovered that by concentrating on a single crop, tobacco, they could buy the goods they needed from England. The little band of religious dissenters who landed at Plymouth in 1620 lost half their number during the first winter and survived only by sheer heroism. But the Massachusetts Bay Company, which founded Boston, was able to profit by the Pilgrims' experience. In 1630 it transported 900 settlers across the ocean in a large and well-planned operation. Within ten years the population had increased to about 14,000 in Massachusetts and within twenty years there were about 20,000 in New England as a whole. This population had developed a surplus of food for export, and had plenty of fur, fish, and timber to ship back to the mother country. By the end of the century more colonies had been established, either as offshoots of the original settlements or by royal grants to "proprietors," until there were twelve in all (the thirteenth was added in 1732). By 1700 it has been estimated that there were almost 200,000 English settlers in North America, as compared with about 10,000 French. It was already clear that most North Americans would someday speak English.

English and French Colonies

The English colonies were more divided and less well controlled by the home government than the French. New France was under one central administration at Quebec, whereas the English colonies were under twelve separate governments. Each of the twelve eventually elected representative assemblies that controlled local legislation and taxation. The royal governors were not responsible to these assemblies, but, since they were generally dependent on the assemblies for their salaries, their power was strictly limited. In the 1660's Parliament did its best to impose strict mercantilist theories on the colonies—for example, by ruling that certain exports must be sent directly to England in English or colonial ships. These measures caused complaints, and after the Revolution of 1688 the English government gradually became less insistent on asserting its authority. The colonists accepted parliamentary regulation of their trade so long as the regulations were not too strictly enforced, but they became more and more accustomed to running their own affairs to suit themselves.

Without conscious design, the English in the seventeenth century fashioned a new kind of colonial empire in North America, quite different from either the Portuguese or the Spanish. The Portuguese Empire (and, to a large degree, the Dutch) was based on armed trade. The Spanish Empire was based on the efforts of a ruling class of soldiers, planters, and missionaries to convert the natives and exploit their labor. But the Protestant English (and Protestant Dutch) were never particularly interested in converting the natives. They never felt responsible for the Indians as the Spanish did, partly because there was no possibility of exploiting their labor. So they simply displaced the natives from the land on which they settled. The English transferred a whole European population to a new environment and permitted it to blend the traditional institutions it brought from home with the innovations and improvisations evoked by the new surroundings. Not surprisingly, these innovations tended toward economic, political, and religious freedom. The breeze was blowing in this direction in England, and it was blowing even more strongly in the colonies.

The Russians in Siberia

While the French and the British in North America were pushing westward from the Atlantic seaboard toward the Pacific, the Russians were pushing eastward from the Ural Mountains across Siberia toward the Pacific. The two movements were strikingly similar in many respects, but the Russians had no ocean to cross at the start and they reached the Pacific first. In 1581, groups of Cossacks—"pioneers," or "frontiersmen," who had earlier pushed back the Tartars and Turks and had settled in the lower valleys of the Dnieper, the Don, and the Volga—began to move eastward from the Urals under a leader, Ermak, who became famed in song and story. Like the French in Canada, the Cossacks were mainly in search of furs, particularly sable, and so they followed the dark pine-forest, not the steppe, to the south. The great rivers of Siberia—the Obi, the Yenisei, and the Lena—flow north into the Arctic Ocean, but in their upper reaches they branch out so that they almost touch one another. Thus the Cossacks could move easily across the continent by water. The movement was not planned or organized. The settlers simply flowed eastward through the sparsely settled wastes of Siberia in search of furs, occasionally stopping to form widely separated settlements, and reached the Pacific in the early 1640's, barely two generations after the movement began. The distance covered was greater than that across North America, but there were no wide mountain barriers until near the end and no serious resistance from natives until the Cossacks met the Chinese in the Amur Valley. There the Russians were checked by a superior, civilized state, and in 1689, by the first treaty concluded between Russia and China, the Russians withdrew from the Amur basin. They remained behind the Stanovoi Mountains for the next 170 years.

Like the English, the Cossacks were in search of freedom as well as furs, and their early communities in Siberia were often wild and lawless, like the later towns of the American "Wild West." But the tsar's government soon reached out across the vast distances to establish its administration and to tax the lucrative fur trade—more like the French than the English government in North America. By 1700 there were perhaps half again as many Russian settlers in Siberia as there were French and British in North America. By the end of the century, Russian traders were venturing across the Bering Strait into Alaska and down the North American coastline in search of seals. Thus long before the English colonists in America had reached the Pacific, the Russians, by a combination of individual daring and government backing, had staked out a claim to the northern half of Asia and had even reached out to touch the shores of the Western Hemisphere.

France: In Search of Order and Authority, 1598–1661

Seventeenth-century France still felt the effects of the anarchy and violence that had prevailed for almost half a century before the Edict of Nantes in 1598. Three weakling kings had tarnished the prestige of the monarchy, and the great nobles had become powerful and unruly. Merchants and manufacturers had been hard hit by the wars, and the peasants had suffered heavily from the ravages of undisciplined soldiers. The mass of the people, weary of disorder, were now ready to submit to any authority that would give them security.

Jean Bodin, the most penetrating political thinker of the tragic years just past, had seen what was needed. In his book *The Republic,* which he published in 1576, Bodin argued that in any well-ordered state, supreme power or sovereignty must be clearly lodged somewhere in some organ of the state, preferably the monarchy. Sovereignty he defined as the power "to lay down the law to subjects in general without their consent." Bodin did not think of this power as arbitrary or capricious: the sovereign was still subject to the laws of God and of nature. But he insisted that sovereign power must not be limited by any human agency—that is, it must be "absolute" to be effective. He insisted that it could not be divided—for instance, among king, Estates General, and *parlements.* It must be recognized as legitimately residing in one person or one political institution. No one had defined sovereignty so clearly before or argued so persuasively for it as the only remedy for feudal anarchy and civil war. Bodin's prescription for France's ills was fulfilled in the French absolute monarchy that became the model and envy of most of Europe.

Henry IV and Sully

The first steps toward restoring the power of the monarchy and the prosperity of the land were taken by Henry IV and his minister, Sully. Henry, first of the Bourbon dynasty, was a popular king—courageous, vigorous, humorous, tolerant, and sound in his judgment of men. But he spent much of his time in hunting and love-making and left the routine business of government to Sully and others. Sully was a puritanical Huguenot with a keen sense of economy and a hatred of dishonesty. He improved the financial condition of the monarchy, partly by avoiding expensive wars and partly by patching up the tax-collecting system. The French taxation system was inefficient, corrupt, and inequitable. The taxes were "farmed"—that is, the right to collect them was granted to private collectors who paid the government a fixed sum and then collected all they could. The burden fell most heavily on the peasant, since the nobles were exempt from major taxes. Sully could do nothing to make the system more just (nor could any French minister down to the Revolution), but he could make it work better by discharging dishonest and inefficient tax farmers. (It has been estimated that as a rule hardly half the taxes collected in France at this time reached the treasury.) Moreover, the reestablishment of internal peace and order, which allowed agriculture and commerce to recover, helped to increase the government's revenues, especially from customs duties. When Henry IV was assassinated by a Catholic fanatic in 1610 there was a sizable surplus in the treasury.

The Estates General of 1614

Within a few years the work of Henry and Sully was in ruins. Under the regency of Henry's widow, Marie de' Medici, the treasury surplus was sopped up by rapacious courtiers, and Spain began once more to intervene in French affairs,

sometimes in a strange alliance with the Huguenots. In 1614 the Estates General were summoned to one of their rare meetings, but the deliberations soon turned into a struggle between the First and Second Estates (the clergy and the nobility) and the Third Estate (the bourgeoisie and many provincial royal officers). Neither group was willing to take responsibility; neither had the power to demand reform. The assembly dissolved with a strong declaration that "the king is sovereign in France, and holds his crown from God only." It was not to meet again until 1789, on the eve of the Revolution.

Richelieu

In 1614 Henry IV's son, Louis XIII, was still only fourteen years old, a neurotic youth passionately addicted to hunting. He was soon to be married to Anne of Austria, daughter of Philip III of Spain, as a symbol of France's subjection to Habsburg influence. There was not much to be hoped for from the monarch himself—except that he might choose and support some able first minister. The man was already in sight—a brilliant young bishop named Richelieu—but it took him several years to become a cardinal (in 1622) and head of the king's council (in 1624). From 1624 to his death in 1642 Richelieu was the real ruler of France. Richelieu, rather than any member of the Bourbon dynasty, founded absolute monarchy in France.

There is no mystery about Richelieu, as there is about many other great figures in history. He had the clearest and most penetrating mind of any statesman of his generation. And he made his purpose perfectly plain: to enhance the power and prestige of the French monarchy beyond any possibility of challenge. He came to his task with a marvelous grasp of political and diplomatic possibilities, an infallible memory, and an inflexible will unhampered by moral scruples. Richelieu admired Machiavelli's writings, and the heart of his political creed was *raison d'état*—the doctrine that the good of the state is the supreme good, and that any means may be used to attain it. He would coolly send an innocent man to his death in order to frighten other troublemakers, enhance the authority of the monarchy, and so save bloodshed in the end. "In judging crimes against the state," he argued, "it is essential to banish pity." He was not irreligious, but the workings of his mind were overwhelmingly this-worldly. "Man is immortal; his salvation is hereafter," he once argued against some conscientious scruples of the king, but "the state has no immortality, its salvation is now or never." While his cardinal's robes helped protect him against assassination, his policy was that of an astute secular statesman who put public order before religious zeal. His reputation for diabolical cleverness went even beyond the reality and helped him to bewilder his enemies and gain his ends.

Richelieu had three concrete objectives that had to be carried out more or less simultaneously. First, he meant to break the political and military power of the Huguenots. Second, he meant to crush the political influence of the great nobles. And finally, he meant to destroy the power of the Habsburgs to intervene in French internal affairs.

The Edict of Nantes had allowed the Huguenots to garrison about 200 towns, the chief of which was La Rochelle on the west coast. Richelieu persuaded Louis XIII that he would never be master in his own house until he had wiped out this "empire within an empire." Rumors that the government had decided to attack provoked the Huguenots to rebel, and Richelieu proceeded to besiege and capture La Rochelle. At the Peace of Alais in 1629, which settled the dispute, Richelieu was unexpectedly generous in his terms. He had no respect whatever for what he contemptuously called "the allegedly Reformed religion," but he allowed the Huguenots the right to worship as they pleased once he had attained his primary objective of

Three studies of Richelieu, by Philippe de Champaigne.

eliminating their political and military autonomy. He did not wish to alienate Protestants abroad who could help him in a war with Spain and Austria, and he hoped he could make loyal and useful citizens out of the Huguenots. In this he was successful. The Huguenots served the crown in the war that followed against the Habsburgs and stuck loyally by the monarchy in the crisis of the Fronde.

Richelieu's attack on the political power of the nobility was less successful than his attack on the Huguenots, but it was just as determined. Until the very end of his career, he was constantly threatened by aristocratic intrigues. In response to this threat, he developed a network of spies, set up a special tribunal to try noble lawbreakers, and sternly forbade dueling, a privilege that marked the freedom of the aristocracy from ordinary restraints. He gradually weeded the great nobles out of provincial governorships and put more local administrative responsibilities on direct representatives of the crown. These representatives, called *intendants,* were usually drawn from the *noblesse de la robe,* ennobled office-holders of middle-class ancestry. They were therefore more dependent on the monarchy than the older nobility. Richelieu did nothing to lessen the economic or social privileges of the French nobility, but he did curtail its political power.

Richelieu was no financier, nor did he have any interest in bettering the condition of the common people. He spent large sums on rebuilding the armed forces and even more in actual warfare against Spain. He left the government's finances and the nation's peasants in worse condition than he had found them. But through his subtle diplomacy and his well-timed intervention in the Thirty Years' War, he made France, instead of Spain, the leading European power.

Mazarin and the Fronde

Richelieu's death in 1642 (Louis XIII died a few months later, in 1643) put his work to a severe test. Louis XIV was a child of five when his father died, and so his mother, Anne of Austria, was appointed regent. Fortunately she left the business of government to the man whom Richelieu had picked and trained to succeed himself, an Italian cardinal named Mazarin. Mazarin had the subtlety and political skill of his master but not his inflexible will; he was both more adaptable and, as a foreigner, less popular than Richelieu. His two main objectives were to continue the war against Spain until the Habsburgs were beaten and to maintain the prestige of the monarchy at the level to which Richelieu had raised it. The nobility hated him as a foreign upstart, however, and the bourgeoisie hated him for the high taxes he imposed to carry on the war. The result was the last serious rebellion to take place against the monarchy until the French Revolution—a complicated and uncoordinated movement of resistance known as the Fronde (1648–52).

The word "Fronde" referred to a game of slinging clods at passing coaches, which was played by the more unruly children of Paris. The rebellion was like the game; it was annoying, but in the end it did not keep the monarchy from driving along the road to absolutism. The leaders were fundamentally loyal to the king, and they did not wish to risk upsetting the established social order. Each group was trying to modify the structure of government so that it could have a little more influence. But no group could agree with others on a joint program, with the exception of the purely negative policy of exiling Mazarin. Thus the *parlements,* which began the struggle when Mazarin reduced the interest paid on the public debt, stood for the privileges of the old, more or less hereditary corporations of bureaucrats who controlled the highest courts in the land. They wanted the king to rule with their advice, rather than with that of favorites and privy councillors. The nobles, who joined the rebellion later, had no intention of letting the *parlements* become dominant in government; they wanted to get rid of the *intendants* and regain their old powers as provincial governors. In the provinces, many men rebelled to protect or enlarge local privileges, but they often found it hard to decide whether they should support a *parlement* or a noble governor.

The result might have been different if anyone had dared draw on the deep-seated resentment of the lower classes—a resentment that had been expressed during the first half of the century in many local riots against taxation and misgovernment. But while a few theorists talked of liberty and democracy, no one was willing to take the chance of unleashing forces that might not be controllable. Unlike the contemporary English rebellion, in which the middle and lower classes accepted radical doctrines and defeated the king (see p. 129), the Fronde remained dominated by the nobility and the upper bourgeoisie. Each group approached the brink of making unlimited war on the king even at the risk of social revolution, and each drew back in horror. This innate conservatism, combined with lack of unity among the leaders, led to the disintegration of the rebellion. There was very little hard fighting; by the end of 1652, Mazarin, who had had to flee the country, was once more back in the saddle. Most Frenchmen drew the lesson that a strong monarchy was preferable to futile civil war. The young king, Louis XIV, was to profit from this reaction when he came of age. Meanwhile, he remembered with loathing the violence and instability of the Fronde. He came to hate Paris, despise the mob, and fear the nobles when they were unrestrained by a firm royal hand.

In spite of the Fronde and the tax burden that continued to oppress the common people, Mazarin carried on the war with Spain until the proud Spaniards were forced to ask for terms in 1659. Maria Theresa, daughter of Philip IV of Spain, was married to Louis XIV. Both the treaty and the marriage symbolized the humiliation of Spain and the triumph of France as the leading power in Europe. Mazarin died in 1661, and Louis XIV announced to his ministers that he would henceforth be his own prime minister. Now the work of Richelieu had come to full fruition. The French monarchy no longer had anything to fear from Huguenots and nobles at home or from Habsburgs abroad. It was an absolute monarchy, endowed with a fuller sovereignty than any other yet seen in European history.

England: In Search of Civil and Religious Liberty, 1603–60

While Richelieu and Mazarin were laying the foundations of absolute monarchy by divine right, leaders in England were slowly developing a constitutional, parliamentary monarchy. Richelieu could see clearly where he was going, but the goal was never clear to English leaders during their century of conflict with the crown. Englishmen groped their way toward a conception of sovereignty as something rooted in law rather than in personal authority, something to be lodged in the hands of an assembly that represented the community, or at least its more wealthy and influential members. England was not alone in its resistance to absolute monarchy, but the result in other countries, such as Poland, was anarchy and confusion. Only in England was a representative assembly able to increase its power without wrecking the state. When Queen Anne came to the throne in 1702 the English government was both a stronger and a more popular government than it had been in 1603 when James I succeeded Elizabeth I. The example of England, particularly as reflected in the writings of John Locke, was to have an enormous influence on western history during the next two centuries.

England, on the periphery of European civilization, had always been peculiar in its political development. For instance, although the strong monarchy of the Tudors (1485–1603) was part of a general European trend, the survival and strengthening of Parliament under such a monarchy was without parallel elsewhere. The Tudors continued to use Parliament in legislation and taxation whereas rulers on the Continent found representative assemblies either useless or obstructive. Parliament, particularly the House of Commons, slowly acquired a corporate feeling and a sense of being an integral part of the national government. The House of Commons, it will be remembered, represented both the mercantile classes in the towns and the gentry in the country. The knights and squires had been increasing in numbers, wealth, and political influence since the dissolution of the monasteries.

They governed England at the local level as justices of the peace (the English monarchy had no paid bureaucrats like the French *intendants*), and they dominated the lower house of Parliament by sitting as representatives not only of the counties but of many boroughs as well. The House of Commons in which they sat had grown steadily in wealth and influence, until one member could boast in 1628 that the lower house could buy the House of Lords three times over.

Thus the English Parliament in the early seventeenth century represented the nation, above class differences and local interests, in a way no other representative assembly in Europe did. There were no provincial estates in England as there were in France, and the class lines between peers, gentry, and wealthy burgesses were not so sharply drawn as the line between nobility and Third Estate on the Continent. English merchants were continually buying land and becoming gentlemen, and younger sons of the nobility often went into the professions. This meant that if the monarch should ever fall out with Parliament—and with the social groups it represented—he would not be able to play class against class or district against district.

The Tudors

Queen Elizabeth had had arguments with her Parliaments, but the threat from abroad and the political good sense of both the queen and the opposition kept these arguments from becoming dangerous. It was generally recognized that only Parliament could make a law or impose

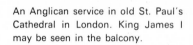
An Anglican service in old St. Paul's Cathedral in London. King James I may be seen in the balcony.

a tax. It was also recognized that making policy, especially foreign policy, lay outside the competence of Parliament and within the sphere of what was called the royal prerogative.

The Tudors felt, however, that it was sometimes wise to confirm royal policy by parliamentary statute, particularly in the delicate field of religion. Henry VIII used Parliament to break with Rome; Mary had asked Parliament to restore England to the Roman obedience by statute, and Elizabeth had broken with the pope once more by statute. Elizabeth's Parliaments tried more than once to reform the Anglican Church in a Puritan direction and to nudge the queen on foreign policy—presumptuous acts for which Elizabeth scolded them sharply. But she was too popular for Parliament ever to make a real issue of the conflict and too astute ever to demand a clear definition of her prerogative. Tudor "despotism" was a popular despotism, and Tudor rulers found that they could exercise their sovereign power most effectively in cooperation with Parliament.

James I and Parliament

The Stuarts, who ruled from 1603 to 1714, either could not or would not cooperate with Parliament. James I (1603–25), the son of Mary Queen of Scots, was a well-meaning but pedantic intellectual who never understood the social structure or the political realities of the kingdom he inherited from Elizabeth. His aims were praiseworthy—peace with Spain, toleration of the Catholic minority in England, union of England and Scotland, and a strong but benevolent monarchy—but he did not inspire confidence as a political leader. Moreover, many of his ministers were incompetent. Unlike Elizabeth, who often concealed her imperious will in cloudy and ambiguous language, James liked to have things dangerously clear. He had written a book, *The True Law of Free Monarchies,* in which he insisted that kings owed their position to God alone,

were responsible only to God, and in fact were themselves like gods on earth.

His belief in a monarchy "free" of restraints, free to do as it pleased for the common good, did not appeal to the classes represented in Parliament. The Tudors had long ago ended the threat of aristocratic violence, and peace with Spain in 1604 removed the danger of foreign conquest. Only their own king could now attack the beliefs or interfere with the property rights of Englishmen. Parliament, fearing royal tyranny, began to criticize James' acts. James, fearing parliamentary intervention in policy matters, began to scold Parliament. The delicate Tudor balance was destroyed.

Friction rapidly developed over three related issues: religion, finance, and foreign policy. The Puritan majority in the House of Commons wished to "purify" the Anglican Church of everything that savored of Catholic practice, from "popish" ritual to the authority of bishops. James was convinced that the Presbyterian system of church government, which he had known in his youth in Scotland, would not only destroy royal control of the church, but would threaten the monarchy itself. "No bishop, no king," he remarked within a year of his arrival in England. Parliament, annoyed by the extravagance of James' court and dubious about his policies, denied him enough money to meet the rising costs of government. James replied by raising money without parliamentary approval—for example, by increasing the customs duties on his own authority. When his right to take such actions was contested, the courts ruled in his favor—probably correctly, since the king controlled foreign trade as part of his control of foreign policy. But the seeming subservience of the courts to the royal will further disturbed Parliament.

Meanwhile James was following a foreign policy that exasperated the Puritan majority in Parliament. He was too friendly with Spain for the Puritan taste, he did little to defend Protestants abroad against the rising tide of Catholicism, and he finally tried to marry his son Charles to the Spanish Infanta. When James chided the House of Commons in 1621 for even discussing his foreign policy, the House bristled and passed a unanimous Protestation defending its right to discuss "the arduous and urgent affairs concerning the King, State, and defence of the realm, and of the Church of England." This was revolutionary talk. James tore the resolution from the Commons' *Journal,* but he could not undo what had been done. The House of Commons, which Queen Elizabeth had kept under the control of her privy councilors, was now taking the initiative under leaders of its own. An aggressive and powerful element among James' subjects was demanding a voice in politics which he was utterly unwilling to grant.

Charles I and the Puritan Rebellion

The situation rapidly worsened during the first four years of the reign of Charles I (1625–29). Charles tried to please Parliament by attacking Catholic countries, but his incompetent favorite, the Duke of Buckingham, failed to capture Cadiz in Spain or to relieve the French Huguenots at La Rochelle. Parliament had urged war but had not granted adequate taxes, so the government tried to pay for the wars by levying a forced loan and by imprisoning those who objected to paying. Parliament in 1628 drew up a formal protest in the form of a Petition of Right, which they finally compelled Charles to approve. Its two main provisions were that no one should henceforth be compelled to pay any tax or loan "without common consent by Act of Parliament," and that no one should be imprisoned without cause shown.

Next year the House of Commons was roused to fury before Charles dissolved it. It declared that anyone who introduced anything savoring of Catholic practices in the Anglican Church was "a capital enemy to this kingdom and commonwealth," and that anyone who advised or submitted to the levying of taxes without parliamentary consent was "a betrayer of the liberties of England." The issue of "sover-

England During the Puritan Rebellion   1642–46

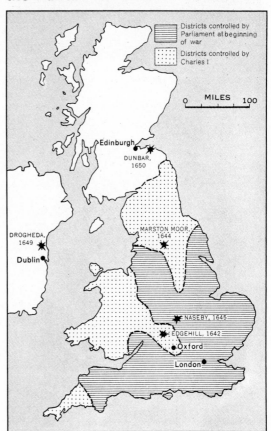

eignty" had finally been raised, and the word itself was being debated by lawyers and parliamentary orators. Where did the supreme power in England lie—in the king or in Parliament? The old answer, that it lay in the "king-in-Parliament," would no longer do. The royal prerogative and "the liberties of England" were no longer reconcilable.

Charles I now took things into his own hands and ruled without Parliament for eleven years (1629–40). He was less intelligent and more stubborn than his father. James had always yielded before conflict became irreconcilable. Rather than yield, Charles was to resort to duplicity and falsehood in the crises ahead of him, and as a result he ended his life on the scaffold, trusted by almost no one. Trying to duplicate Richelieu's

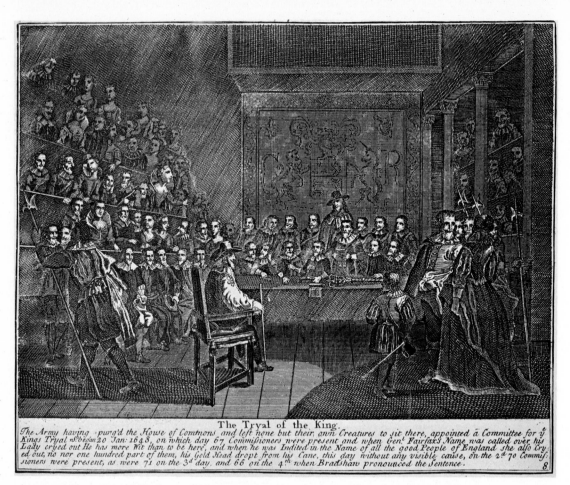

The Tryal of the King.

The Army having purg'd the House of Commons and left none but their own Creatures to sit there, appointed a Committee for y Kings Tryal w.h began 20 Jan: 1648, on which day 67 Commissioners were present and when Gen.l Fairfax's Name was called over, his Lady cry'ed out He has more Wit than to be here, and when he was Indited in the Name of all the good People of England she also cry: ed out, no nor one hundred part of them, his Gold Head dropt from his Cane, this day without any visible cause, on the 2.d 70 Commiſ: sioners were present, as were 71 on the 3.d day, and 66 on the 4.th when Bradshaw pronounced the Sentence. 8

The trial of Charles I in 1649, from a 17th-century engraving. As the royalist artist pointed out, the court was named by the radical minority left after the purge of the House of Commons, and not all the members named attended.

brilliant work across the Channel, he chose tough-minded advisers: Thomas Wentworth, Earl of Strafford, in political affairs, and William Laud, Archbishop of Canterbury, in ecclesiastical affairs. With them and others, Charles devised new methods of nonparliamentary taxation that provided enough money to run the government so long as it stayed out of war. Laud began a movement back toward more ritual and formality in the Anglican service, a movement the Puritans regarded as an attempt to restore Catholicism. All opposition, whether to arbitrary taxation or to innovations in worship, was sternly suppressed by the courts. Everything went well until Laud tried to force the Anglican Book of Common Prayer on stubbornly Presbyterian Scotland.

Before long an angry and well-led Scottish army was encamped in northern England. Charles and Strafford, finding themselves unable to raise an army to fight the Scots, had to summon Parliament to get the money to buy them off.

The Long Parliament, which met in November 1640 and was not dissolved until 1653, became a workshop of revolution. It sent Strafford and Laud to the scaffold. It passed an act stating that a Parliament must be summoned at least every three years. It outlawed all nonparliamentary taxation and abolished the special royal courts (the Court of Star Chamber and the Court of Ecclesiastical Commission), which had been the chief instruments of the "Eleven Years' Tyranny." In other words, in less than a year (1640–41) Parliament had made absolute monarchy impossible in England. This much of its work won unwilling approval from Charles, since sentiment for it was virtually unanimous. But when the more radical Puritans in Parliament went on to abolish bishops in the Anglican Church, a party began to form around Charles in opposition to the parliamentary majority. And thus a civil war broke out in 1642 and lasted until 1649.

Enough has been said to suggest that the Puritan Rebellion was primarily a war of ideas, not of classes or of districts or even of interests, though the interests of merchants and gentry who were outraged by nonparliamentary taxation were certainly involved. Generally the towns, the middle class, and the economically advanced southeastern counties of England supported Parliament, while many rural areas, aristocrats, and the backward northwest supported Charles. But nobles, squires, and artisans from all parts of England were to be found on both sides. Unlike the Fronde, in which narrow interest groups failed to work out programs with broad appeal, the Puritan Rebellion offered a real alternative to the established order: parliamentary monarchy instead of benevolent absolutism, and a Presbyterian Church governed by elected "presbyters," or elders, instead of an Anglican Church governed by bishops appointed by the crown. Unlike the Fronde again, the Puritan Rebellion was able to attract and to accept men with really radical ideas—men who wanted neither a monarchy nor an established church.

As the civil war intensified, Parliament proved to be more successful than the king in raising money and in building a strong army. A brilliant cavalry officer named Oliver Cromwell formed a "New Model Army" largely from among his fellow Independents, or Congregationalists. These Independents were generally of lower economic status than either Anglicans or Presbyterians. They were unsophisticated, Bible-reading Puritans of strict morals who believed in independent congregations democratically organized, with little or no national organization. Cromwell and his army finally defeated the king's forces in 1645, only to fall out with the Pres-

Democratic Ideas in the English Revolution

After it was sure of victory, the Parliamentary Army began to worry about a proper government for England. A Council of the Army, including representatives of the ordinary soldiers, held a series of debates at Putney in 1647 on a constitution for the country. One of the basic issues was whether all men could vote.

Major Rainborough: I think that the poorest he that is in England hath a life to live, as the greatest he, and therefore truly, sir, I think it's clear, that every man that is to live under a government ought first by his own consent to put himself under that government, and I do think that the poorest man in England is not at all bound in a strict sense to that government that he hath not had a voice to put himself under.

[General Ireton argued that only those with property should vote.]

Sexby [a representative of the soldiers]: I see that though liberty were our end, there is a degeneration from it. We have ventured our lives to recover our birthrights and privileges as Englishmen, and by the arguments urged there is none. There are many thousands of us soldiers that have ventured our lives; we have had little property . . . yet we have had a birthright. But it seems now, except a man hath a fixed estate in this kingdom, he hath no right in this kingdom. I wonder we were so much deceived.

From *Puritanism and Liberty*, ed. A. S. P. Woodhouse (London: J. M. Dent and Sons, Ltd., 1938), pp. 53, 69.

byterians, who had dominated Parliament since the Anglicans withdrew in 1642 to join Charles. With Parliament and the army at loggerheads about what to do with the king and about what sort of government to set up in England (many in the army wanted a truly democratic regime), the king was able to escape and make one last bid for victory before being finally defeated by Cromwell in 1648. Cromwell and the Independents in the army were determined now to get at what they considered the root of the trouble. They "purged" Parliament of its Presbyterian members, executed King Charles I in 1649, abolished monarchy and the House of Lords, and set up a republic, or "Commonwealth," with the "rump" of the Long Parliament as its government and Cromwell as its moving spirit.

Cromwell

Cromwell proved to be a revolutionary leader unlike almost any other in western history. He was a deeply religious man who tried in vain to avoid becoming a dictator. Yet he was ruthless and determined when he felt his policies were threatened. He massacred the Catholic Irish when they rebelled, defeated the Scots when they intervened in favor of the son of Charles I, fought a commercial war with the Dutch in 1652–54, and boldly dissolved what was left of the Long Parliament in 1653. In a few short years he had decisively won a civil war, united the British Isles under one government for the first time, made England again the terror of the seas, and apparently wiped the slate clean for any political experiment he wished to try. The rest of his career until his death in 1658, however, was a tragic search for answers to insoluble problems: how to guarantee religious toleration to all kinds of Protestants except determined Anglicans, and

An allegorical engraving showing Cromwell triumphant.

at the same time how to develop some constitutional basis for his government. Cromwell tried to rule through a written constitution (the first in the history of any major state) and with the assent of a Parliament. He took the title of Lord Protector instead of king, but he quarreled with his Parliaments as bitterly as the Stuarts had quarreled with theirs. At one point Cromwell had to set up an open military dictatorship to keep his Parliament from disbanding his army and persecuting his coreligionists. The plain fact was that most Englishmen were not ready for religious toleration, especially toleration of the radical religious minorities that made up Cromwell's army.

Furthermore, it became more and more evident that it was impossible in England to break utterly with history and to set up a new sort of government simply by writing a constitution. There was already a "constitution" deeply ingrained in the English political tradition, although it was nowhere written down in full. Soon after Cromwell's death even his own supporters saw that the only possible remedy for military dictatorship was to restore Parliament, and that the only way to restore Parliament was also to restore the monarchy. In 1660 the monarchy, Parliament, and the Anglican Church were all restored when a "Convention Parliament" invited Charles II to return from France and take up the crown.

The Restoration

At first glance nothing more remained in England after twenty years of civil war and revolutionary experiment than had remained in France after the defeat of the Fronde. To this day Englishmen refer to the events we have described as the "Puritan Rebellion." They do not call it a revolution because it was succeeded by the "Restoration." But one thing at least had been decided: There was to be no absolute monarchy in England. All acts of the Long Parliament before the outbreak of civil war were still valid, and these acts put severe limitations on royal power, even if the balance of power between king and Parliament was still uncertain. Strafford and Laud had tried to do for Charles I

what Richelieu and Mazarin had done for Louis XIV, but all three Englishmen died on the scaffold while all three Frenchmen died in their beds. The turmoil of the first half of the seventeenth century left most Englishmen with certain half-expressed convictions whose effects can be traced in English history for generations. Among these convictions were a fear of allowing any one individual to acquire too much political power, a deepened respect for government by law rather than by personal command, a reverence for Parliament as the defender of individual rights against arbitrary despotism, and a distaste for standing armies.

The early seventeenth century was a brilliant age in the history of English literature, including Shakespeare's mature work, the Authorized, or King James, Version of the Bible (1611), and Milton's formative years. It was also a brilliant period in political thinking, as statesmen and pamphleteers argued for royalist, parliamentary, or radical principles of government.

Perhaps Thomas Hobbes' *Leviathan* (1651) best represented the political insights and fears, if not the greatest hopes, of these turbulent years. Writing in the midst of civil war, Hobbes pictured the life of man without government

Hobbes on Might and Right

The Laws of Nature (as Justice, Equity, Modesty, Mercy, and in sum doing to others as we would be done to), of themselves, without the terror of some Power to cause them to be observed, are contrary to our natural Passions, that carry us to Partiality, Pride, Revenge, and the like. And Covenants, without the Sword, are but Words, and of no strength to secure a man at all. Therefore notwithstanding the Laws of Nature (which everyone hath then kept, when he has the will to keep them, when he can do it safely), if there be no Power erected, or not great enough for our security, every man will and may lawfully rely on his own strength and art for caution against all other men.

From Thomas Hobbes, *Leviathan,* 1651 (New York and London: Everyman, 1914), p. 87.

as "solitary, poor, nasty, brutish, and short." Without some authority to enforce law, there is no society, no order, only "a war of every man against every man." Men in general are inclined to "a perpetual and restless desire of power after power." So they set up a sovereign power by agreement or contract (it makes no difference whether the sovereign is a king or a Parliament), by which all men agree to obey the sovereign, but only so long as he is able to maintain order. The sovereign is not bound by anything in the contract. No clearer argument for might as the necessary basis of all right had ever been written. Hobbes took Bodin's argument for a legitimate sovereign authority and subtly transformed it into justification of sheer arbitrary power. His book could be used equally well to support Charles I or Cromwell. In a sense the main effort of Englishmen during the seventeenth century was to find some way to refute Hobbes—to subject political power to the restraint of law and to increase its responsibility to the governed. They finally succeeded in 1688.

Germany: Disintegration and Disaster, 1618–48

While France was building the strongest monarchy in Europe and England was undergoing a constitutional crisis from which she was to emerge with new strength, the German-speaking peoples were caught up in one of the most futile and destructive wars in the history of Europe. The Thirty Years' War (1618–48) was really four successive wars that began in Bohemia, spread to the rest of the Empire, and finally involved most of the major powers on the Continent. It was a savage and demoralizing conflict that left "Germany" poorer and weaker than the western European states.

The Causes of the Thirty Years' War

The war sprang out of a complicated mixture of religious and political grievances. Lutherans and Catholics had not fought each other since the Peace of Augsburg (1555), but the Catholics were disturbed by the fact that, in spite of the provisions of the peace, most of the Catholic

bishoprics in northern Germany had fallen into Lutheran or secular hands. This gave some grounds for creating an ultra-Catholic movement headed by the Jesuits and the German Catholic princes, particularly Maximilian, Duke of Bavaria. The spread of Calvinism introduced a new source of friction, partly because Calvinists had been excluded from the Peace of Augsburg. When Maximilian roughly disciplined the Protestant town of Donauwörth, Frederick V, the Calvinist ruler of the Palatinate, a small state on the middle Rhine, took the lead in forming a Protestant Union among the German princes and cities in 1608. In reply, a Catholic League was organized the next year under the leadership of Maximilian. By 1609 two illegal military alliances faced each other within the Empire, each afraid of the other and each determined to keep the rival religion from making any further gains.

Revolt in Bohemia

As these examples show, each component of the Empire was a virtually independent state. The Habsburgs, who held the imperial title, realized that the only way to rebuild and expand imperial authority was to establish firm control over what had been their old family domains—Austria, Bohemia, and Hungary. Thus the Austrian Habsburg, Ferdinand of Styria, got himself elected King of Bohemia in 1617.

Bohemia was a flourishing kingdom in which two nationalities (Germans and Czechs) and several religions (Catholicism, Lutheranism, Calvinism, and remnants of the Hussite movement of two centuries earlier) lived fairly peaceably together under earlier Habsburg promises of toleration. Ferdinand, a zealous Catholic, began systematically to undermine this toleration and to re-Catholicize the country. This action provoked rebellion by the Bohemian Estates, which were dominated by a strong Protestant majority. In May 1618 two of Ferdinand's councilors were tossed from a castle window in Prague and civil war broke out between the Habsburg ruler and the Estates. The Estates raised an army, deposed Ferdinand, and offered the crown of Bohemia to Frederick V of the Palatinate. When Frederick unwisely accepted, the

Protestant Union became involved in defending the Bohemian Estates while Maximilian of Bavaria brought the Catholic League to the support of Ferdinand. In 1619 Ferdinand was elected emperor. Thus a war that might have remained a local affair soon spread throughout the Empire.

The Bohemian phase of the war was soon ended. The forces of the emperor and the League won an overwhelming victory in 1620. Frederick fled, and the emperor proceeded to work his will on the prostrate Bohemians. Half the property in the country changed hands through confiscation. The Jesuits, with strong secular backing, set out to reconvert the country to Catholicism, and within ten years they had succeeded. The prosperity of the country was ruined, Protestantism was stamped out or driven underground, and Czech nationalism was crushed for two centuries to come. The first round of the struggle had gone decisively to the Habsburgs and their Catholic allies.

Danish Intervention

The fall of Bohemia terrified German Protestants and elated the Catholics. The Spanish Habsburgs came to the aid of their fellow Catholics, and the armies of the League were everywhere triumphant. But in spite of the common danger, the Protestants could not unite. The Lutherans had been more afraid of a Calvinist victory in Bohemia than of an imperial triumph, and so Lutheran Saxony had actually helped Ferdinand put down the revolt. Although Frederick V was the son-in-law of James I, Protestant England gave no help because James and Charles were too involved in difficulties at home.

In 1625 the Protestant king of Denmark intervened, partly to save the cause of his coreligionists but primarily to pick up some territory in northern Germany. Within a year he was beaten in battle by a large army raised by the most inscrutable figure of the war, a wealthy war profiteer and professional soldier named Wallenstein, who had offered the emperor his services. Wallenstein had no religious convictions whatever, and his political aims have puzzled generations of historians. His immediate aim

seems to have been to build an imperial Habsburg military machine of such strength that it could not only eliminate all Protestant opposition but could operate independently of all other forces in the Empire, including the Catholic League. Before long Wallenstein and the League were as much at loggerheads on one side as Calvinists and Lutherans were on the other. Religion slowly receded in significance as the war became a struggle for the hegemony of Europe.

The high-water mark of Habsburg triumph and Catholic reaction was reached in 1629. Denmark withdrew from the war, leaving Wallenstein's army supreme. The Catholic League and Jesuit advisers persuaded Ferdinand to issue the Edict of Restitution, which restored to Catholic hands all ecclesiastical lands lost to Protestantism since 1552. It was evident that this edict could not be carried out without more bloodshed, because it meant that Catholic bishops were to be restored throughout northern Germany. Such an act would destroy the rough balance between Catholicism and Protestantism in Germany and weaken the northern states for the benefit of Austria and Bavaria. This threat finally roused the Lutherans inside and outside Germany to a sense of their peril.

Swedish Intervention: Gustavus Adolphus

In 1631 growing Habsburg power was blocked by the intervention of Sweden, a country that had not appeared before on the stage of international politics. Gustavus II (Gustavus Adolphus) was the ablest ruler of his generation. His country was sparse in population and resources, but he had cultivated its iron and timber industries, united the nation behind him, and built the best army of the day. It was not large, but it was well equipped (with the first uniforms and an improved musket), well disciplined, and inspired by high morale. Gustavus had already come close to making the Baltic a Swedish lake in wars with Denmark and Poland. He now stepped into the fray as the sincere champion of Lutheranism, hoping apparently to set up a federation of Protestant states in Germany under Swedish leadership.

Gustavus arrived too late to save Magdeburg from a terrible sack by the Habsburg Imperialists in May 1631, but in the fall of 1631 he overwhelmed the Imperialist armies at Breitenfeld in Saxony. He then marched triumphantly to the Rhine. Wallenstein whom the emperor had dismissed under pressure from the Catholic League, was recalled, only to be beaten by Gustavus at Lützen in 1632. Gustavus himself was killed in the battle, however, and by 1634 his army had finally been outnumbered and beaten, Wallenstein had been murdered by one of his staff, and another phase of the war had come to an end. Swedish intervention had saved German Protestantism but had not gained a decision. The most powerful state of all had been watching the course of events closely and was now to intervene with decisive results.

French Intervention: Richelieu

Since coming to power in 1624, Richelieu had kept in close touch with the progress of the war through his ambassadors and agents. But for ten years he did not feel that the French army was strong enough to intervene in Germany. His major purpose was to crush the Habsburgs, both Austrian and Spanish, and he was ready to ally with anyone, Protestant or Catholic, who was opposed to them. The Dutch, who went back to war with their old enemies the Spanish, were his first allies, and in 1631 he subsidized the invasion by Gustavus Adolphus. When the Swedes were finally defeated in 1634, Richelieu saw that he would have to intervene directly if he was to check Habsburg expansion in, and perhaps control of, Europe. And so in May 1635 he sent a French herald to Brussels to declare war on the king of Spain.

The Thirty Years' War had lasted for seventeen years with no decisive result, and it was to continue for thirteen more dreary years while French, Swedish, and Dutch armies fought against the Spanish and Austrian Habsburgs. In 1643 the French finally destroyed the legend of Spanish invincibility by crushing a Spanish army at Rocroi in the Netherlands. It was the first time in 150 years that a Spanish army had suffered a major defeat. The emperor's allies deserted him, and by 1648 the Swedes were threatening Vienna and storming Prague. The dream of Emperor Ferdinand II (who had died in 1637) of re-Catholicizing Germany and establishing a strong Habsburg monarchy in central Europe lay in ruins.

The Peace of Westphalia, 1648

A peace was finally worked out at the Congress of Westphalia (1643–48), Europe's first great peace conference and the first international gathering of importance since the Council of Constance (1414–18). But it was a far different gathering from that of two centuries earlier. The atmosphere and the business at hand were now entirely secular, and the communities represented

The Sack of Magdeburg

May 1631

Then was there naught but beating and burning, plundering, torture, and murder. Most especially was every one of the enemy bent on securing much booty. When a marauding party entered a house, if its master had anything to give he might thereby purchase respite and protection for himself and his family till the next man, who also wanted something, should come along. It was only when everything had been brought forth and there was nothing left to give that the real trouble commenced. Then, what with blows and threats of shooting, stabbing, and hanging, the poor people were so terrified that if they had had anything left they would have brought it forth if it had been buried in the earth or hidden away in a thousand castles. In this frenzied rage, the great and splendid city that had stood like a fair princess in the land was now, in its hour of direst need and unutterable distress and woe, given over to the flames, and thousands of innocent men, women, and children, in the midst of a horrible din of heartrending shrieks and cries, were tortured and put to death in so cruel and shameful a manner that no words would suffice to describe, nor no tears to bewail it.

From Otto von Guericke, in *Readings in European History*, ed. James Harvey Robinson (Boston: Ginn, 1906), Vol. II, pp. 211–12.

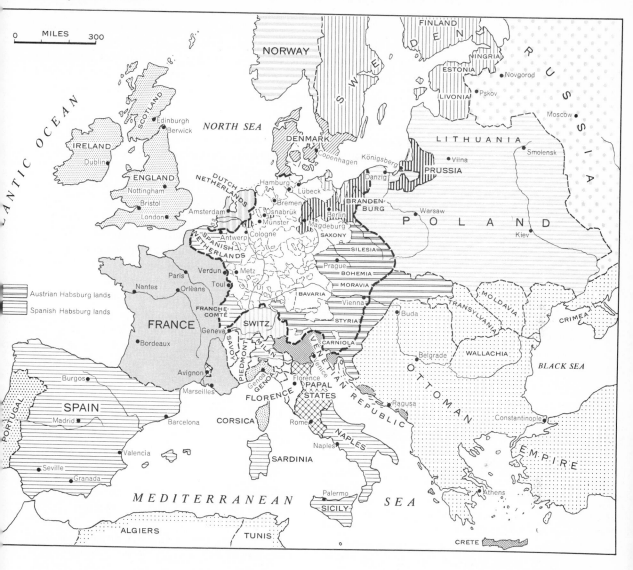

were sovereign territorial states that recognized no earthly superior and only the most shadowy common interests. "Christendom" had dissolved, and the word "civilization" would not be coined till the next century to express in secular terms what "Christendom" had once meant to Europeans in religious terms.

Almost every act of the Congress emphasized the importance of the sovereign state. For example, it recognized the right of each German principality to make alliances and to declare war on its own. This constituted practical recognition of the disintegration of the Empire into over 300 separate sovereignties. Switzerland and the Dutch Netherlands were finally recognized as sovereign states, independent of all ties to the Empire. France acquired some very ambiguous rights to Alsace, Sweden acquired strips of German territory along the shores of the Baltic and the North Sea, and the two German states of Brandenburg and Bavaria ended up with increased territory and prestige. As for religion, the old principle of *cuius regio, eius religio* was reaffirmed. Calvinism was simply added to Catholicism and Lutheranism as one of the recognized faiths. The ownership of church lands was settled as of 1624, meaning in general that northern Germany remained Protestant and southern Germany Catholic. France and Spain were unable to reach agreement, so their war continued until French victory was finally recognized in the Peace of the Pyrenees in 1659. France received some territory along the Pyrenees and in Flanders, and the Spanish princess, Maria Theresa, married Louis XIV. In general, the peace settlements of the middle of the century left France the strongest power in Europe, Spain prostrate, the Empire shattered, and a kind of power vacuum in the center of Europe.

The Social Results of the War

The Thirty Years' War was one of the most brutal and destructive wars of which we have record until the twentieth century. Armies robbed, raped, and murdered their way back and forth across Germany. The lack of any modern supply system meant that they had to live off the land. We have gruesome records of towns totally wiped out, cities reduced to a small fraction of their original population, and cultivated land reverting to waste. Starvation and disease killed more than the sword. It is impossible to be sure of the total decline in population, but some historians believe that Germany may have lost a third of its inhabitants. Others insist that the destruction was not so great as contemporary sources would suggest, and that recovery in farming districts was rapid. The social and psychological effects, however, were certainly frightful. A whole generation grew up accepting violence and brutality as normal. Superstition and witchcraft increased in influence. The fragmentation of the Empire into practically independent states hampered economic recovery. Cultural and political provincialism were to go hand in hand for the next two centuries in German history. In fact, it is almost impossible to find any good result that came out of the generation of aimless fighting in Germany known as the Thirty Years' War.

Suggestions for Further Reading

1. General Works on the Seventeenth Century

There are three very successful attempts at a synthetic treatment of the period: D. Ogg, *Europe in the Seventeenth Century** (5th ed., 1948), is a sound and interesting narrative of the major developments on the Continent, arranged by country. G. N. Clark, *The Seventeenth Century** (1931), is a more analytical discussion of different aspects of the period: for instance, population, industries, military organization, political thought, science, religion. C. J. Friedrich's volume in the *Rise of Modern Europe* series, *The Age of the Baroque, 1610–1660** (1952), combines narrative and analysis and makes use of recent interpretations of baroque style. C. J. Friedrich and C. Blitzer, *The Age of Power** (1957), is a brief and thoughtful survey of the century, based on Friedrich's larger work.

2. Mercantilism and Economic Growth

L. B. Packard, *The Commercial Revolution, 1400–1700* (1927), is the briefest reliable treatment of mercantilism. J. W. Horrocks, *Short History of Mercantilism* (1925), and P. W. Buck, *The Politics of Mercantilism** (1964), are somewhat longer studies. The fullest and best treatment is E. F. Heckscher, *Mercantilism*, 2 vols. (1935). H. Sée, *Modern Capitalism* (trans. 1928), is the best extensive discussion of the subject. F. L. Nussbaum, *History of the Economic Institutions of Modern Europe* (1933), summarizes

---

* Available in paperback edition.

the work of the great German historian of capitalism, W. Sombart. D. Hannay, *The Great Chartered Companies* (1926), is a good introduction to its subject. J. U. Nef, *War and Human Progress* (1950), argues that war is a detriment, not a stimulant, to technological and economic progress, particularly in this period.

3. Expansion Overseas

In addition to the works cited for Chapter 18 on geographical discovery, the following are useful on special topics: B. H. M. Vlekke, *The Story of the Dutch East Indies* (1945); L. B. Simpson, *The Encomienda in Spain* (1929); and H. A. Wyndham, *The Atlantic and Slavery* (1935). On the rivalry of France and England in America, the many fascinating volumes of Francis Parkman dating from the 1860's are still worth reading, especially the earlier ones. G. M. Wrong, *The Rise and Fall of New France*, 2 vols. (1928), is the standard modern account. *The Cambridge History of India*, 5 vols. (1922–37), is useful for reference.

4. France

J. Boulenger, *The Seventeenth Century**(trans. 1920), is a standard one-volume account in English. F. C. Palm, *The Establishment of French Absolutism, 1574–1610* (1928), and P. R. Doolin, *The Fronde* (1935), are good special studies. Of the many books on Richelieu, the most trustworthy short account is C. V. Wedgwood, *Richelieu and the French Monarchy** (1949). C. J. Burckhardt, *Richelieu: His Rise to Power** (1964), is a solid piece of work.

5. England

The classic one-volume account, Whiggish in sympathy and brilliantly written, is G. M. Trevelyan, *England under the Stuarts* (1904, 1946). The standard modern account is G. Davies, *The Early Stuarts, 1603–1660* (1937), in the *Oxford History of England* series. The detailed narrative history of S. R. Gardiner, published in 18 volumes (1863–1903) and covering the years 1603–56, is a major achievement of English historical scholarship to which all later accounts are indebted. C. V. Wedgwood has published three volumes of a history of the Puritan rebellion, *The King's Peace* (1955), *The King's War* (1958), and *A Coffin for King Charles* (1964). D. L. Keir, *The Constitutional History of Modern Britain, 1485–1937** (4th ed., 1950), and J. R. Tanner, *English Constitutional Conflicts of the Seventeenth Century** (1928), together constitute a good introduction to some of the more technical constitutional issues of the period. There are many biographies of Cromwell, but the best is still C. H. Firth, *Oliver Cromwell and the Rule of the Puritans in England* (1900, 1925). W. Notestein, *The English People on the Eve of Colonization, 1603–1630** (1954), is a good introduction to the social history of the period, and B. Willey, *The Seventeenth Century Background** (1934), a good introduction to its intellectual history. A. S. P. Woodhouse, *Puritanism and Liberty* (1938), is a selection of sources illustrating the ferment of democratic ideas during the rebellion. See also W. Haller, *The Rise of Puritanism** (1938), and M. Walzer, *The Revolution of the Saints* (1965).

6. Germany

There are good chapters on the Thirty Years' War in Ogg and Friedrich (Section 1, above), also in H. J. Grimm, *The Reformation Era* (1954), and H. Holborn, *A History of Modern Germany: The Reformation* (1959), both listed after Chapter 17. Far and away the best general account in English is C. V. Wedgwood, *The Thirty Years War** (1938). The scholars' argument over how destructive the war was may be followed in S. H. Steinberg's criticism of Wedgwood in *History,* Vol. 32 (1947), pp. 89–102. T. K. Rabb, *The Thirty Years' War** (1964), gives readings on the causes and effects of the war.

---

* Available in paperback edition.

5

Absolutism and Constitutionalism, 1660–1715

During the latter half of the seventeenth century France was the leading nation in Europe. Her population was twice that of Spain and over four times that of England. Her land was fertile and her commerce and industry were growing.

France Under Louis XIV

There were no disturbing arguments over forms of government; absolute monarchy was accepted by almost all Frenchmen as necessary, reasonable, and right. By the Peace of the Pyrenees (1659) the French army had displaced the Spanish as the strongest military machine on the Continent. As time went on, it seemed as if not only French generals, French military engineers, and French diplomatists but French architects, French painters, French dramatists, and French philosophers were the best in Europe. French fashions in dress dominated the Continent, the French language became the leading language of diplomacy and polite conversation, and the French court with its elaborate etiquette and ceremonial became the model for countless smaller courts throughout Europe. As Florence had been the nerve center of the Italian Renaissance and Spain of the Catholic Reformation, so France was the nerve center of late-seventeenth-century politics, diplomacy, and culture.

The palace of Louis XIV at Versailles.

How much of this predominance is to be attributed to the long reign of Louis XIV is one of those questions that historians can speculate about but never answer. No one doubts that French (and European) history would have run in different channels had Louis never lived—or had he not lived so long. He was born in 1638, became king in 1643, took the reins of power into his own hands in 1661 at twenty-three, and died in 1715 at the age of seventy-seven, leaving the throne to his great-grandson. By temperament and training Louis was the very incarnation of divine-right monarchy—the idea that hereditary monarchy is the only divinely approved form of government, that kings are responsible to God alone for their conduct, and that subjects should obey their kings as the direct representatives of God on earth. In an age that put its trust in absolute rulers, the achievements of the French people at the peak of their greatness cannot be separated from the personality of their ruler, even if it can be proved that many of those achievements were unrelated to, or even accomplished in spite of, the ruler.

Louis is said to have remarked, "I am the state." Even if the remark is apocryphal, the words reveal more of the true importance of his reign than anything else he said or wrote. Louis XIV set out early in his reign to personify the concept of sovereignty. He dramatized this aim

immediately after Mazarin's death by ordering his ministers thereafter to report to him in person, not to a "first minister." To be the real head of a large and complicated government required long, hard work, and Louis paid the price. His education was poor and he had little imagination, no sense of humor, and only a mediocre intelligence. But he had common sense, a knack of picking up information from others, and a willingness to work steadily at the business of governing. "If you let yourself be carried away

Louis XIV, by Hyacinthe Rigaud, 1701.

by your passions," he once said, "don't do it in business hours." Painstakingly he caught up all the threads of power in his own hands. All major decisions were made in four great councils, which he attended regularly. These decisions were then carried out by professional "secretaries" at the head of organized bureaucracies. In the provinces, the *intendants* more and more represented the direct authority of the central government in justice, finance, and general administration. Louis reduced the importance of the *parlements,* never summoned the Estates General, and, so far as such a thing was humanly possible in his century, built a government that was himself.

Colbert and the Economy

Colbert, Louis XIV's Controller-General of Finance, systematically ordered the economic life of the country under royal direction. He was an extreme mercantilist; everything he did was consciously or unconsciously meant to strengthen the country for war. He set up high protective tariffs to help home industry, fostered new export industries, encouraged the French colonies in Canada and the West Indies, and did everything he could to develop a powerful navy and a strong merchant marine. Some historians suspect that his minute regulation of industry and commerce did more to hinder than to help the French economy. But until the burden of foreign wars became heavy in the 1680's, national production and wealth were increasing. Colbert also cut down waste and corruption in the collection of taxes, as Sully had once done, but he was unable to make the burden of taxation much more equitable because of the exemptions held or purchased by members of the nobility and the bourgeoisie, the classes best able to pay. During the crisis of Louis' last war an attempt was made to tax these upper classes in order to stave off bankruptcy, but the attempt set no precedent.

The Nobility

The most dangerous potential opponents of royal absolutism, as Louis XIV knew from his own experience during the Fronde, were the members of the nobility. Louis completed Richelieu's work of destroying the political power of the French nobility. He excluded the nobles completely from all responsible positions in government and cheapened their status by increasing their numbers. An army commission came to be almost the only major outlet for a noble's ambition, which meant that the nobles as a class generally constituted a war party at court. All important positions in Louis XIV's government, such as the secretaryships and intendancies, were filled by men of bourgeois or recently ennobled families.

Louis did not attack the social privileges of the nobility; he used them to make the nobles utterly dependent on him. In 1683 he moved the court and government from the Louvre in Paris to Versailles, fifteen miles away. He had hated Paris since the riots of the Fronde, and now in the formal gardens and ornate chateaux of Versailles, which he had built on waste marsh and at considerable cost of human lives and treasure, he felt at home. It was an utterly artificial atmosphere, as far removed from reality as Versailles was physically removed from the bustle of Paris. Here the great nobles were compelled to live. Here a ball seemed as important as a battle, and holding the basin for the king's morning ablutions was a job as much to be coveted as commanding the king's armies. Instead of competing for political power, nobles squandered their fortunes and exhausted their energies in jockeying for social prestige. The regular rectangular shapes of the gardens, the balanced classical lines of the baroque architecture, the bright glint of mirrors and chandeliers, all these seemed to symbolize and emphasize the isolation of Versailles from nature, from the French nation, from the real world. Through all this Louis moved with impassive dignity. Years of self-conscious practice in kingship had given him a kind of public personality—cool, courteous, impersonal, imperturbable—which carried out perfectly the artificiality of the little world at Versailles. At his death he left to his successors a privileged nobility shorn of all political power and responsibility, demoralized by pleasure, and uneasily aware of its uselessness. It was a dangerous heritage.

Religious Policy

The only other potential opponents of Louis' absolutism were religious groups. The king had his differences with several popes who disliked his Gallican principles, but these quarrels never led to a real breach. Louis was always a good Catholic in a formal sense. He disliked and persecuted the Jansenists, an austere group of Catholic "puritans" who followed the teachings of St. Augustine on original sin and the need

---

Bishop Bossuet on Absolutism

Jacques Bénigne Bossuet was tutor to Louis XIV's son in the 1670's.

The royal power is absolute. With the aim of making this truth hateful and insufferable, many writers have tried to confound absolute government with arbitrary government. But no two things could be more unlike. . . . The prince need render an account of his acts to no one. . . . Without this absolute authority the king could neither do good nor repress evil. . . . God is infinite, God is all. The prince, as prince, is not regarded as a private person: he is a public personage, all the state is in him; the will of all the people is included in his. As all perfection and all strength are united in God, so all the power of individuals is united in the person of the prince. What grandeur that a single man should embody so much! . . . Behold this holy power, paternal and absolute; behold the secret cause which governs the whole body of the state, contained in a single head: you see the image of God in the king, and you have the idea of royal majesty. God is holiness itself, goodness itself, and power itself. In these things lies the majesty of God. In the image of these things lies the majesty of the prince.

From Jacques Bénigne Bossuet, "Politics Drawn from the Very Words of Scripture," in James Harvey Robinson, ed., *Readings in European History* (Boston: Ginn, 1906), Vol. II, pp. 275–76.

for grace and who criticized the Jesuits as compromisers with the world. Louis, whose confessors were Jesuits, thought the Jansenists subversive (they had been condemned by the pope) and impertinent (they disapproved of his numerous mistresses). After 1680, though never a particularly religious man, he seems to have become increasingly concerned about the fate of his own soul. When his queen, Maria Theresa, died in 1683, he gave up his mistresses and secretly married Madame de Maintenon, a pious Catholic whose parents were Huguenots. In 1685 he shocked Protestant Europe by revoking the Edict of Nantes, by which Henry IV had granted religious toleration to the Huguenots.

There were about a million Huguenots out of a total population of perhaps eighteen million in France at the opening of Louis XIV's reign. After Richelieu deprived them of their military and political privileges, they had become good citizens and had remained loyal to the crown during the Fronde. Many were successful in industry and the professions, though few had attained the civil and military positions that were theoretically open to them. The French Catholic clergy had long tried to persuade Louis XIV that the continued exercise of the Protestant religion in France was an insult to his dignity and authority, and as the king became more concerned about his salvation the idea of atoning for his sins of the flesh by crushing heresy became more attractive to him. The Edict was "interpreted" more and more strictly. Protestant children were declared of age at seven and converted to Catholicism, and any attempt by their parents to win them back was punished by imprisonment. Money was offered to converts, Protestant chapels were destroyed, and troops were quartered on prominent Huguenots to make life miserable for them. Finally Louis, aided and abetted by his Jesuit advisers, announced that since all the heretics had finally been reconverted to Catholicism there was no further need for the Edict of Nantes and it was therefore revoked. Protestant churches and schools were closed, and all Protestant children were baptized as Catholics. The Revocation was savagely enforced by imprisonment, torture, and condemnation to the galleys, but about 200,000 Huguenots managed to escape to England, the Dutch Netherlands, Brandenburg, and the New World, where their industry and skill contributed appreciably to the economic life of their new homes. To France the Revocation brought both economic and moral loss.

There were only two other examples of such brutal treatment of religious minorities in the seventeenth century: the systematic impoverishment and degradation of the Irish Catholics by their English conquerors, and the ruthless suppression of Bohemian Protestantism by the Habsburgs. But in both these cases, unlike that of France, national hatred complicated religious differences. The Revocation of the Edict of Nantes was an anachronistic act of religious intolerance that gained Louis XIV little and lost him much.

Arts and Literature

To dramatize his conception of kingship and to underscore the dependence on the monarch of all other persons and institutions in the state, Louis chose as his emblem Apollo, the sun god. The symbol of the sun, on whose rays all earthly life is dependent, was worked into the architecture and sculpture of the palace of Versailles. The Sun King patronized the arts and gave historians some reason to call his reign the "Augustan Age" of French culture. As befitted such a patron, the prevailing taste was classical, insisting on form, order, balance, and proportion. The ideals of literature and art were "order, neatness, precision, exactitude"—and these were presumed to be the ideals of all reasonable men of all ages.

Pierre Corneille (1606–84) was the father of French classical tragedy. In 1636 he had written Le Cid, the first of his powerful dramas which glorified will power and the striving for perfection. Corneille was still writing when Louis XIV began his personal reign, but he was soon eclipsed by his brilliant younger contemporary, Jean Racine (1639–99). Racine wrote more realistically about human beings in the grip of violent and sometimes coarse passions, bringing French tragedy to its highest point of perfection in the years between 1667 and 1677. Then he underwent a religious conversion and renounced playwrighting as an immoral occupation. Some who thrilled to his and Corneille's tragedies had little respect for the comedian Molière (1622–73), but Molière's wit and satire became the unsurpassable model for future French dramatists. From 1659 to his death in 1673 he was the idol of audiences at Versailles. All three playwrights concentrated on portraying the typical—the hero, the man of honor violently in love, the miser, the hypocrite, for instance—typical human beings who belonged to no particular time or place. As a result, French classical drama of the age of Louis XIV could be understood and appreciated by people everywhere, and French taste in writing came to be the dominant taste of other countries as well. So it was with architecture and the other arts. The baroque style, which ruled the design and decoration of the palace at Versailles, was intelligible and exportable. French artistic and literary standards became the standards of cultivated Europeans everywhere.

The Wars of Louis XIV

Richelieu and Mazarin had begun the process of strengthening the French army, but French military power reached its peak under Louis XIV. Le Tellier and his son Louvois were the ministers of war for almost fifty years. They subordinated the aristocratic officer class to the royal authority, developed a supply system, coordinated infantry and artillery, and, like Gustavus Adolphus, supplied the soldiers with uniforms. Vauban, one of the great military engineers of history, invented the fixed bayonet and perfected the art of building—and of destroying—fortifications. All in all, Louvois provided his master with the largest and best-equipped army in Europe: 100,000 men in peace and up to 400,000 in war.

Strengthening the army provided the king with great temptations to use his power in foreign wars. War would please the nobles, who profited by it and who had little outlet for their ambitions at home. War would exercise and justify the enormous standing army. Above all, successful war would enhance the glory of the

The Vanity of Louis XIV

He reigned, indeed, in little things; the great he could never reach: even in the former, too, he was often governed. The superior ability of his early ministers and his early generals soon wearied him. He liked nobody to be in any way superior to him. Thus he chose his ministers, not for their knowledge, but for their ignorance; not for their capacity, but for their want of it. He liked to form them, as he said; liked to teach them even the most trifling things. It was the same with his generals. He took credit to himself for instructing them; wished it to be thought that from his cabinet he commanded and directed all his armies.

Naturally fond of trifles, he unceasingly occupied himself with the most petty details of his troops, his household, his mansions; would even instruct his cooks, who received, like novices, lessons they had known by heart for years. This vanity, this unmeasured and unreasonable love of admiration, was his ruin.

From Louis de Rouvroy, Duke of Saint-Simon, *Memoirs*, trans. by Bayle St. John (London: 1876), Vol. II, p. 358; also published in T. C. Mendenhall *et al.*, eds., *Ideas and Institutions in European History, 800–1715* (New York: Holt, 1948), Vol. I, p. 302.

monarch, raise him still further above his subjects, and perhaps make him the arbiter not only of France but of Europe as well. No one better than Louis XIV exemplified a nineteenth-century historian's dictum, "All power tends to corrupt, and absolute power corrupts absolutely." For half a century Europe was ravaged by wars that were started to satisfy the megalomania of the French king. As Louis' thirst for power grew beyond all rational bounds, so did his enemies' fear of him.

The aims of Louis' earlier wars were relatively limited and understandable. With Spain's power broken and the Empire in a state of collapse, he wanted to annex the Spanish Netherlands (later Belgium), Franche-Comté, and bits of western German territories. He fought two wars for these objectives, but each time, after early victories he found himself thwarted by an alliance of other powers. By 1678 he had gained only Franche-Comté and a few border towns in Flanders.

For a time Louis tried legal chicanery in place of bullets to gain more territory. French courts called Chambers of Reunion were set up to "reunite" to France any land which at any time had been a dependency of a French territory. This process gave Louis control of the independent Protestant republic of Strasbourg in 1681, and it was long before European indignation subsided or Strasbourg became a contented part of France. The Revocation of the Edict of Nantes in 1685 was further evidence to European statesmen of Louis' intemperance, and in 1686 the defensive League of Augsburg was formed by the emperor, Spain, Sweden, and several German states. Europe was already at war when William of Orange, ruler of the Dutch Netherlands and Louis' most implacable enemy, became King William III of England in 1689. The circle was closed around France when the English and the Dutch joined the League.

This time France was on the defensive. At the very outset, in 1688, the French united their enemies by perpetrating one of the most senseless atrocities of the century, the systematic devastation of the Palatinate for no good political or military reason just before the occupying French troops withdrew. The War of the League of Augsburg was waged in India and America as well as in Europe, so it may be called the first of the modern world wars. After ten years of fighting, France agreed to the Peace of Ryswick (1697), by which she managed to retain her gains up to 1678 but was forced to renounce nearly all accessions after that date except Strasbourg. England came out of the war considerably stronger as a naval and military power; France came out of it a weaker power than she had been a decade earlier.

The War of the Spanish Succession, 1701–14

At the turn of the century all the fears and hatreds that had been built up during a genera-

The Conquests of Louis XIV 1661–1715

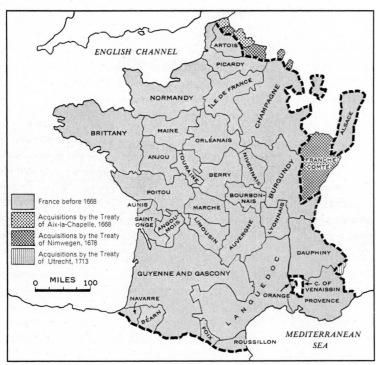

France before 1668

Acquisitions by the Treaty of Aix-la-Chapelle, 1668

Acquisitions by the Treaty of Nimwegen, 1678

Acquisitions by the Treaty of Utrecht, 1713

tion of fighting were concentrated in a fourth struggle, the War of the Spanish Succession (1701–14). This war, like that of 1688–97, was fought in America and India as well as in Europe. In its origins and its course, the older motives of dynastic ambition were mixed with the newer motives of commercial advantage and national sentiment. Religion now played no important part whatever.

In 1698 Charles II of Spain, who had for thirty years been a kind of walking medical exhibit of half a dozen fatal diseases, was finally dying. He was the last of the Habsburgs who had ruled Spain since 1516, and he had no direct heirs. The question was whether the Spanish Empire would fall to some member of the Austrian Habsburg family or to some member of the French Bourbon dynasty (both Louis XIV's mother and wife were Spanish Habsburg princesses) or would be partitioned or dismembered in some way. The English and the Dutch had obvious reasons for keeping France from gaining control of the Spanish colonial trade or of the Spanish Netherlands. Louis seemed willing to compromise and twice concluded secret treaties with the English and the Dutch to partition the Spanish dominions, but when news of the second treaty reached Madrid the dying king lost his temper. In order to preserve the Spanish Empire intact as a bulwark of Catholicism, he made a will leaving all his dominions to a grandson of Louis XIV. This grandson was proclaimed King Philip V of Spain shortly after the death of Charles II in November 1700.

Louis XIV soon decided to tear up the treaties by which he had accepted a more modest share of the Spanish Empire. He recognized the will of Charles II and sent French troops into the Spanish Netherlands. In 1701 William III of England concluded the Grand Alliance of the Hague by which the English, the Dutch, and the emperor bound themselves to fight until they had ended the threat of Bourbon control of Spain and of the Spanish colonies. Louis XIV had made his last and most arrogant bid for the dominance of Europe, but this time he was forced to fight for France's life against enemies who proved as arrogant and unyielding as he. Within a few years the large allied forces under the brilliant command of Prince Eugene of Savoy and the English Duke of Marlborough had beaten the French in four bloody battles (Blenheim, 1704; Ramillies, 1706; Oudenarde, 1708; Malplaquet, 1709). The English navy had trounced the French at sea, and the English had seized Gibraltar. An allied army had even dethroned Philip V in Spain for a time.

Louis XIV, his country exhausted, sued for peace on almost any terms, only to be met by an allied demand that he contribute French troops to expel his own grandson from Madrid. This was too much for even a badly beaten monarch and he refused, backed by a rising tide of national feeling in France. A similar national reaction in Spain in favor of their new Bourbon monarch, Philip V, resulted in the defeat of English and Austrian troops there. In 1710 a victory of the Tories over the Whigs, who had been the war party in England, brought in a government in London favorable to peace. And finally in 1712 the French won their only important victory of the war. In the end the allies paid the price for asking too much from Louis at the moment when he was almost helpless. The Peace of Utrecht (1713–14), which settled the war, was somewhat more favorable to France than it might have been if it had been signed four years earlier. Here at the very end of his career, the balance of power seemed to work in Louis XIV's favor by preventing the elimination of France from the ranks of the great powers.

The Peace of Utrecht, 1713–14

In theory, the Peace of Utrecht gave the French what they had fought for: Philip V remained on the throne of Spain, but on condition that the crowns of Spain and France should never be worn by the same monarch. In every other aim, however, the French were thwarted. They gave up all conquests east of the Rhine, failed to win the Spanish Netherlands, and lost their bid for control of the Spanish colonial trade. England was the chief winner. She took Newfoundland, Acadia (Nova Scotia), and Hudson's Bay Territory from France, and Gibraltar and

Minorca from Spain. In addition, the English received the *Asiento*—the right to supply Negro slaves to the Spanish colonies, a privilege that proved very lucrative and provided an excuse for a large-scale smuggling trade with the Spanish Empire. England came out of the war rich and powerful, her navy far and away the largest in Europe. France came out of it still a great nation, but with her people badly exhausted by high taxation and her government bankrupt and unpopular. The Austrian Habsburgs gained by being given the Spanish Netherlands (which now became the Austrian Netherlands), as well as Milan, Naples, and Sicily. Austria thus replaced Spain as the ruling power in Italy. Two new smaller powers, Brandenburg-Prussia and the Duchy of Savoy, came out of the war with increased territories and heightened prestige as a reward for having been on the winning side. A century and a half later Prussia was to unify Germany, and Savoy, as the Kingdom of Sardinia, was to take the lead in the unification of Italy. The Dutch kept the Scheldt River closed, thus blocking the outlet of the port of Antwerp. But they had suffered from the long strain of fighting against the French for half a century and were soon to disappear from the ranks of the great powers.

The Peace of Utrecht ended the first attempt by a European state to establish an overwhelming predominance of power since the days of Philip II of Spain. When Louis XIV died in 1715, rulers outside France breathed a sigh of relief; it was even said that the common people of his own land "openly returned thanks to God." His bid for European hegemony had been defeated by the workings of the balance-of-power principle, but the seeds of future war were unfortunately still deep in the European soil.

England: The Emergence of a Parliamentary Monarchy

While Louis XIV was putting the finishing touches on the institution of absolute monarchy in France, the English, without any very clear idea of where they were headed, were completing the foundation of a constitutional monarchy controlled by Parliament.

The restoration of the king, Parliament, and the Anglican Church in 1660 had established a kind of equilibrium between the crown and Parliament, but it was soon evident that it was a very unstable balance. Who was really to control the government—the king or the wealthy landowners and merchants who dominated Parliament? What was the religious settlement to be, and who was to have the last word in making it? Who was to control foreign policy? These three main questions of the past two generations —the questions of politics, religion, and foreign policy—still awaited final answers. It took almost two more generations of domestic intrigue and foreign war for the answers to be found.

Charles II, 1660–85

Charles II was quite unlike his father—witty, worldly-wise, attractive, a man of easy morals and shrewd political sense. He had lived long in exile in France, and his cousin, Louis XIV, was his model. His ultimate aim was to restore England to Catholicism and to set up an absolute monarchy on the French model, but he was too intelligent to ignore the difficulties in his way and too lazy to persist long in any determined policy. He was resolved not to risk exile or execution. He knew that if his goal was to be reached, it would be by intrigue, manipulation, and compromise, not by force or by open proclamation of his aims. The result was twenty-five years of infinitely complex party politics and secret diplomacy in which the issues were never very clear to the people or to members of Parliament, or even to the king's ministers themselves.

Cavalier Parliament, 1661–79

Parliament held a commanding position at the beginning of the reign. The "Cavalier Parliament," which met in 1661 and was not dissolved until 1679, was dominated by the landed nobility and gentry, who were now restored to their ancient influence in both local and national government. Both groups were strongly royalist for the moment, both determined to stamp out all remnants of religious and political radicalism. But at the same time they were not willing to see the crown recover any real financial independence of Parliament. In place of the old idea that "the king should live of his own," Parliament now granted Charles a regular income from customs and excise duties, but it was not enough. Charles found that he could not meet even the ordinary expenses of government, let alone the expenses of his extravagant mistresses, from his regular revenue. And there was certainly no money for foreign war unless Parliament approved the objectives. So for a time at least, Charles had to let Parliament have its way under the leadership of his father's adviser, Edward Hyde, Earl of Clarendon.

Parliament also had the last word in the religious settlement. The Cavalier Parliament was as strongly pro-Anglican as it was pro-royalist. In a series of statutes passed between 1661 and 1665 and known as the "Clarendon Code," Puritans who dissented from the established church were excluded from local government and Puritan ministers were rooted out of the Anglican clergy. Later legislation made it illegal for a dissenter to sit in Parliament, to serve in the army or navy, or to attend the universities at Oxford or Cambridge. Behind this attempt to discourage dissent was the fear that Puritans were inevitably political radicals. But while the Clarendon Code lowered the social position and narrowed opportunities for dissenters, it did not greatly decrease their numbers. Presbyterians, Congregationalists, Baptists, and Quakers (also Methodists a century later) formed permanent but peaceful minority groups. The dissenters remained antagonistic to the ruling Anglican majority, but they were even more bitterly opposed to Catholicism.

Charles did not like the Clarendon Code. He would have preferred a policy that tolerated both Puritans and Catholics, but Parliament would not stand for this. In 1672 Charles issued a "Declaration of Indulgence," which suspended the operation of the laws against both groups. But the next year Parliament forced him to withdraw the declaration and accept a severe Test Act excluding all but Anglicans from civil and military office. To the Anglican gentry in Parliament, Puritans were still radicals and Catholics still traitors.

Foreign Policy

Soon another rift appeared between king and Parliament, this one over foreign policy. In 1665 Parliament forced Charles into war with the Dutch but did not give him enough money to win it. When victories failed to develop, Clarendon was unfairly held responsible and was exiled. After Louis XIV began his attacks on the Spanish Netherlands in 1667, the ordinary Englishman began to see the military power of Catholic France as more of a threat than the commercial rivalry of the Protestant Dutch. But to Charles II Louis was still the ideal ally—powerful, wealthy, and an old personal friend.

In 1670 England once more allied herself with France against the Dutch, and Charles negotiated with Louis one of the most notorious deals in the history of English foreign policy, the secret Treaty of Dover. By this agreement Charles promised to declare his Catholicism and to reconvert England to Catholicism in return for French money and, if necessary, French troops. There is still argument about how sincere he was, but there is no doubt about the general objective of his foreign policy. Between 1675 and 1681 four more secret agreements were concluded between Charles and Louis in which Charles usually promised to thwart Parliament's anti-French moves in return for subsidies from France. The close understanding between Charles and Louis leaked out and gradually built up English fears of Catholicism and French dominance. The landed classes represented in Parliament were suspicious of Charles, far less royalist in sentiment than they had been in 1661, and ready to give way to panic if any incident should excite their fear of France and popery.

Whigs and Tories

In 1678 these accumulated fears were fanned into flame by a lurid incident known to history as the Popish Plot. A thoroughly disreputable character named Titus Oates concocted a story, accepted by almost the whole country, that there was a Jesuit plot afoot to murder the king and put his Catholic brother James, the Duke of York, on the throne with French help—"a damnable and hellish plot," Parliament called it, "for assassinating and murdering the king and rooting out and destroying the Protestant religion." Civil war seemed about to break out again. A "Country Party" led by the Earl of Shaftesbury campaigned at the polls and supported a bill to exclude the Duke of York from the succession to the throne. An Anglican and royalist "Court Party" rallied to the support of Charles II and his brother, though at first without very much enthusiasm. Members of the first group were called Whigs (a name hitherto applied to fanatical Scottish Presbyterians); members of the second group were called Tories (a name for Catholic outlaws in Ireland). The Whigs controlled the three brief Parliaments that followed the dissolution of the Cavalier Parliament in 1679, and innocent men went to their deaths for complicity in the Popish Plot. But the Whig leaders soon overplayed their hand, public opinion swung back in favor of the king, and it was now the turn of innocent Whigs to suffer. By 1681 Shaftesbury had fled abroad, the inventors of the Popish Plot were disgraced or executed, and Charles was stronger than ever before. Until his death four years later he ruled without Parliament, thanks to Louis' subsidies, with his brother James by his side.

The origin of political parties in the modern sense—groups organized for the purpose of electioneering and controlling government through a representative assembly—lies in these chaotic years of English history. Instead of civil war, the eventual outcome was the "two-party system," which came to be characteristic of English and American politics. Whigs and Tories were the remote political heirs of the Parliamentarians and royalists of the 1640's. In turn they became the ancestors of the Liberals and Conservatives, the Democrats and Republicans, of two centuries later.

James II, 1685–88

The Duke of York, who succeeded Charles II as James II in 1685, was a very different sort of person from his brother—a bigoted convert to Catholicism without any of Charles' political shrewdness or tendency to compromise. Within three short years (1685–88) he managed to infuriate almost every group of any importance in English political and religious life, and in the end he provoked the revolution that Charles had succeeded in avoiding. Made overconfident by early successes, he introduced Catholics into the high command of both army and navy and camped a standing army a few miles from London. He surrounded himself with Catholic advisers and attacked Anglican control of the universities. He claimed the power to suspend or dispense with acts of Parliament. In a vain attempt to win the support of Puritans as well as Catholics, he issued a Declaration of Indulgence along the lines of his brother's. By revoking borough charters and browbeating sheriffs he tried to ensure the election of a Parliament favorable to his policies. Louis XIV's Revocation of the Edict of Nantes in 1685 had already terrified Protestants in England. Their fears increased when the hope of a Protestant succession was suddenly destroyed by the unexpected birth of a son to James' Catholic queen.

The "Glorious Revolution" of 1688

In spite of the intense political tension, civil war did not break out in 1688 as it had in 1642. Englishmen still remembered the horrors of civil war, and this time there was only one side. James had literally no support of any significance, except for a handful of personal friends. He had alienated both Anglicans and nonconformists, Tories and Whigs, nobles and common people. The result, therefore, was a bloodless "revolution," a thoroughgoing political overturn which, as historians look back upon it, answered all the main questions of the century in favor of a limited, or parliamentary, monarchy and established the constitutional pattern of English public life that has persisted to the present time.

James II had two daughters by his first wife (Clarendon's daughter), both of whom remained Protestants. The elder, Mary, was married in 1677 to the stadtholder of the Dutch Republic, William of Orange, who was Louis XIV's

Contemporary engraving of the coronation of William III and Mary, King and Queen of England, in Westminster Abbey, 1689.

outstanding Protestant opponent on the Continent. In June 1688 a group of prominent and representative Englishmen, both Whigs and Tories, invited William to cross the Channel and save the Protestant cause in England. In the following November William landed on the southern coast of England with a Dutch army and marched slowly on London. There was almost no resistance. James II fled to France and a Convention Parliament declared that James had "abdicated" the throne by his flight. It then invited William and Mary to become joint sovereigns. A "Bill of Rights" was passed and the "Glorious Revolution" was accomplished.

The chief result of the Revolution was the establishment of parliamentary sovereignty over the crown. Parliament had made a king and could regulate the right of succession to the throne.

Though William was a strong-willed man, especially in matters of foreign policy, he knew that Parliament had the final say. Though the supporters of James II and his son intrigued and even staged two abortive rebellions, there was no second Restoration. Parliament could criticize, influence, and eventually make the government's policy.

The Bill of Rights emphatically denied the king's right to suspend acts of Parliament or to interfere with the ordinary course of justice. It furnished a base for the steady expansion of civil liberties in the generation after 1688. Toleration and freedom from arbitrary arrest were established by law; censorship of the press was quietly dropped. The king had to summon Parliament every year because he could not pay or control his armed forces without parliamentary consent. These regular meetings strengthened the parties and made the king dependent on their support. In 1707 the monarch vetoed a parliamentary bill for the last time.

Struggles for control of policy were now no longer between king and Parliament, but between factions in Parliament. The Revolution did not establish democracy, but it did establish control by the wealthy landed proprietors and merchants over both the central and local organs of English government. Generally speaking, the greater noble landowners, the bankers and the merchants, and most dissenters, were Whigs, while the smaller gentry, the Anglican parish clergy, and some great lords were Tories. But parties were still loosely organized, and small factions with selfish interests often held the balance of power. England was governed by shifting alliances among leaders of the propertied classes.

The Cabinet System

It took over a century for parliamentary leaders to work out a smooth and efficient way to run the government. The ultimate answer (after 1784) was to be the "cabinet system"—that is, government by a committee of leaders of the majority party in Parliament, holding the chief executive offices in the government, acting under the leadership of a "prime minister," and acknowl-edging primary responsibility to Parliament rather than to the crown for their actions. During the reigns of William and Mary (1689–1702) and Mary's sister, Queen Anne (1702–14), the first fumbling moves were made which led to such a system, though parliamentary leaders had as yet no sense of their goal, and monarchs still considered ministers to be responsible to them rather than to Parliament. The privy council had long been too large and unwieldy for effective deliberation, and a "cabinet council," or inner circle of important ministers, had developed under Charles II. The members of this "cabinet" slowly found that it was better to discuss major questions among themselves and to present a united front to the monarch. Sometimes a leading member of the "cabinet" was referred to as "prime minister." In order to gain Parliament's indispensable support in war or peace, both William and Anne occasionally found that it was better to choose their ministers not from both parties but from the majority party. By the time Queen Anne died in 1714 it had become evident that the real government of England was slowly falling into the hands of a cabinet of ministers who controlled a parliamentary majority, often by bribery, and felt themselves ultimately responsible to the political interests of this majority.

Religious Toleration

The Revolution also produced a certain measure of religious toleration. Broad-mindedness was becoming fashionable in educated circles, and both Anglicans and Puritans were now more afraid of Catholic France than they were of each other. Puritans had supported Anglicans against James II, and King William, who came from the most tolerant country in Europe, insisted on a religious truce. The result was the "Toleration Act" of 1689, which allowed dissenters to worship as they pleased and to educate their clergy and laity in schools of their own. Dissenters were still legally excluded from all civil and military offices, however, and there was no repeal of the long series of anti-Catholic statutes, although they were not enforced with any great rigor after 1689. Protestant fear that a Catholic might succeed to the throne was finally quieted by the Act of Settlement of 1701, which provided that the sovereign should always be an Anglican. The act also settled the succession, in case James II's two daughters should die without children, on the descendants of that daughter of James I who had married the ill-fated elector of the Palatinate before the Thirty Years' War. In this way the elector of Hanover came to the throne in 1714, when Queen Anne died, without issue, thus bringing the Stuart dynasty to a close.

War Against France

A third result of the Revolution was to unite crown and Parliament on foreign policy as they had never been united under the first four Stuarts, and thus to turn the energies of a generation of Englishmen from domestic conflict to foreign war. Once on the throne, King William had no difficulty bringing England into the Grand Alliance against Louis XIV, who was sheltering James II in exile. Parliamentary monarchy soon demonstrated that it was a more formidable foe than the absolute monarchy of the Stuarts had been. The English government was able to raise money to fight its wars in a way that was barred to all other European governments except the Dutch. The founding of the Bank of England in 1694 was an important event in the history of English public finance. Within a few days of its founding, it had raised over a million pounds of investors' money which it promptly lent to the government at 8 percent interest. So long as the government continued to pay the interest, the bank made no demand for repayment of this loan. Thus the present permanent, or "funded," national debt began. The merchants and tradesmen, large and small, who invested their money in the bank obviously had confidence in the government, and their investment bound them still more firmly to support the revolutionary settlement.

Throughout the next century English wealth combined with English sea power was to give the island kingdom a striking power out of all proportion to its area and population. During the reigns of William and Mary and of Anne, trade, which was more and more the foundation of English wealth, increased considerably. The Peace of Utrecht (1713) gave English sea power, the guarantor of English trade, an almost unrivaled position. The solution in 1689 of the chief political and religious differences between crown and Parliament touched off an almost explosive release of English energies which by 1763 had rocketed England to the hegemony of Europe.

Ireland and Scotland

The Revolution also did something to further the unification of the British Isles, though indirectly. England, Ireland, and Scotland all had the same king from 1603 on, but union went no further than the common crown. The two smaller kingdoms, especially Ireland, suffered greatly during the seventeenth century through involvement in England's religious and political divisions. The native Irish were Catholic to a man, and the Protestant English both despised them and feared them as potential allies of the Catholic Spanish and French. By settling Protestant colonists in Ulster, James I planted the present Protestant minority in Northern Ireland. But the Irish were generally loyal to the Stuart dynasty, and for that reason they suffered cruelly under Cromwell. After the Revolution James II tried to fight his way back to his throne by way of Ireland; this led to a savage and systematic persecution of the Catholic Irish by English (and Irish) Protestant landlords, comparable only to Louis XIV's brutal treatment of the Huguenots. The Irish were exploited and bled white economically, their priests were persecuted, and their Parliament was reserved for Protestants only.

The Scots had somewhat better fortune in the end, although they too suffered by being involved in England's troubles through the century. Scotland had gained little by giving a king to England in 1603. It remained a poor but proud neighbor of a larger kingdom, excluded from the benefits of English trade, jealously guarding its own law and its own Parliament, and firmly defending its Presbyterian Church against Anglican attacks. Although it was the Scots who had touched off the Puritan

Rebellion against Charles I, there was strong attachment to the native dynasty in Scotland, especially among Catholic clansmen of the Highlands. After 1649 and again after 1689 Scotland became a base for risings in support of the Stuarts. The Scots accepted the Revolution of 1688, but they did not accept the Act of Settlement of 1701. They threatened to choose a separate king of their own—possibly the exiled pretender James II—in case James' last daughter, Anne, died without issue. This frightened the English into serious negotiations. In 1707 an organic union between the two kingdoms was finally agreed upon and was confirmed by an Act of Union. Scotland retained her own law and her established Presbyterian religion, but she surrendered her separate Parliament in return for representation in the English Parliament. Scottish nationalists were (and still are) angry over their loss of independence, but Scotland gained much in the next century by becoming an integral part of the Kingdom of Great Britain. Scottish merchants, administrators, and philosophers were to play a prominent part during the eighteenth century in building the British Empire and in furthering the Enlightenment.

John Locke

The Puritan Rebellion and the Glorious Revolution together constituted the first of those revolutions in modern western states which ended absolute divine-right monarchy and eventually put the middle classes in control of government. English leaders did their best to insist to the outside world in 1688–89 that they were doing nothing new or revolutionary at all, but they never succeeded in persuading foreigners that they were merely conservative supporters of ancient English liberties. Europe was more interested in the interpretation of the Revolution by John Locke (1632–1704), a friend of the Earl of Shaftesbury, the founder of the Whig Party. In *Of Civil Government: Two Treatises* (1690) Locke set down in plain, common-sense fashion the general principles underlying the long English struggle for liberty which culminated in the Revolution of 1688. Even if the logic was not always clear, the reasonableness of the discussion had great influence throughout the eighteenth century.

Locke directed his attack explicitly against the divine-right theory of monarchy, and implicitly against the more pragmatic absolute theory of Thomas Hobbes. He began with the rights to "life, liberty, and property," which he said all men possess naturally, and went on to insist that the sole purpose of all government is to preserve these rights. Legislative and executive powers are to be strictly separated; if the executive becomes tyrannical and invades the rights of individuals, the people must curb it through their representative assembly—or if all else fails, they may revolt and set up a new government. In other words, an ultimate right of revolution always resides in the people, and the dissolution of government does not necessarily mean the dissolution of society. Locke's book was probably written before 1688 as a sort of program for

---

Locke on Government by Consent

Cf. "Bishop Bossuet on Absolutism," p. 447.

Men being, as has been said, by nature all free, equal, and independent, no one can be put out of this estate and subjected to the political power of another without his own consent, which is done by agreeing with other men, to join and unite into a community for their comfortable, safe, and peaceful living, one amongst another, in a secure enjoyment of their properties, and a greater security against any that are not of it. . . . When any number of men have so consented to make one community or government, they are thereby presently incorporated, and make one body politic, wherein the majority have the right to act and conclude the rest. . . . Absolute, arbitrary power, or governing without settled standing laws, can neither of them consist with the ends of society and government, which men would not quit the freedom of the state of Nature for, and tie themselves up under, were it not to preserve their lives, liberties, and fortunes, and by stated rules of right and property to secure their peace and quiet.

From John Locke, *Of Civil Government: Two Treatises*, 1690 (New York: Everyman, 1924), pp. 164–65, 186.

revolution, but it was not published until after the Revolution and so naturally became a kind of apology for what had been done. Inalienable rights, government by consent, separation of powers, the right of revolution—these were the ideas that Locke implied were at the heart of the Glorious Revolution. These were the ideas that seemed self-evident truths to Americans in 1776 and to Frenchmen in 1789 and that formed a link between the English, the American, and the French revolutions.

Eastern Europe, 1648–1721

The economy of early modern Europe was divided into two sharply defined halves by an imaginary line running north from the head of the Adriatic Sea, around the Bohemian mountains, and down the Elbe River to the North Sea. West of this line was an area that was increasingly affected by the growth of towns and trade. The majority of the population still lived on the land, but most peasants were free workers and many of them small landowners. Most serfs in the West had become agricultural laborers for pay, and most feudal nobles had become landlords who hired labor for wages (particularly in England) or simply lived on rents. Though still a minority, the bourgeoisie were increasingly influential in society and politics.

East of the line was a society still largely agrarian and feudal, an area of few large towns and an insignificant bourgeoisie. Here in Hungary, Bohemia, Poland, Prussia, and Russia, the landed estates were larger and the landed nobility more powerful politically than in the West. During the sixteenth and seventeenth centuries the nobles of eastern Europe managed to reduce the great majority of the peasants to a state of serfdom in which the peasant was bound to the land and forced to work from two to five days a week for his lord. One reason for this drive to enslave the peasant was that grain prices were rising in western markets and eastern landlords had every inducement to increase the production of their estates. Another reason was that the governments of eastern Europe were either dominated by nobles, as in Hungary and Poland, or favorable to the growth of serfdom because it supported the nobles who served the state, as in Prussia and Russia. In western Europe, command of money was increasingly the key to power and influence; in the East, ownership of land and command of compulsory services were still the secrets of power.

It is impossible to give more than a sketch of political and military developments in this vast area of eastern Europe between the end of the Thirty Years' War and the peace settlements of 1714–21.

Warfare was as common as in the West, and much more dangerous. States that arose with no natural frontiers on the flat plains of central and eastern Europe could easily be wiped out. Modernized armies were needed, but such armies could be created only by strong, centralized administrations and supported only by effective tax systems. Neither centralization nor taxation was easy. Eastern rulers were facing roughly the same obstacles to the growth of centralized government that western rulers had faced two centuries and more earlier: a powerful landed nobility, a church that held itself above dynastic interests and owned a large portion of the wealth of the land, an agrarian economy with limited commerce and infant industries, a bourgeoisie still too small to bear the weight of heavy taxation, and an ignorant and exploited peasantry tied to the land and thus incapable of meeting the need of new industries for labor. To build a "modern" state in the face of these difficulties was beyond the capacities of all but the ablest rulers.

The Holy Roman Empire

The one large political organization bridging eastern and western Europe was the Holy Roman Empire. But while there was still an emperor, and a diet, which met "perpetually" at Regensburg after 1663, the Empire was a political fiction. It had no central administration, no system of imperial taxation, no standing army, no common law, no tariff union, not even a common calendar. The Peace of Westphalia had recognized the sovereignty of the individual states, as well as the right of France and Sweden to take part in the deliberations of the diet. In the welter of political units—free cities, ecclesiastical principalities, counties, margravates, and duchies, together with one kingdom (Bohemia) —which made up the Empire, almost every petty princeling fancied himself a Louis XIV and fashioned a court modeled as closely as possible on Versailles. Already the Empire fitted Voltaire's description a century later as "neither Holy, nor Roman, nor an Empire."

The ruling families of a few of the larger states—Bavaria, Saxony, Hanover, Brandenburg, and Austria—were trying hard to expand their territories by war or marriage and to gain royal titles. Augustus the Strong of Saxony, in addition to fathering 365 children, managed to get himself elected king of Poland in 1696. In 1701 the Elector of Brandenburg got the emperor's consent to style himself king in Prussia. And in 1714 the Elector of Hanover became king of England. But only two great powers eventually grew out of the wreck of the Empire. These were Austria and Brandenburg-Prussia.

The Habsburgs and Austria

The attempt of Emperor Ferdinand II (1619–37) to revive and strengthen the Empire under Habsburg control was defeated in the Thirty Years' War. The Habsburgs thereafter turned to a policy which Ferdinand had also furthered, that of consolidating and expanding the hereditary lands of the family in Austria and the Danube Valley. Thus a centralized Habsburg monarchy might be developed that could hold its own with the states of the West. The Emperor Leopold I (1658–1705) was the chief architect of this policy, aided by some capable civil servants and one remarkable general, Prince Eugene of Savoy.

To weld a centralized monarchy together, Leopold had to reduce three separate areas—Austria, Bohemia, and Hungary—to some semblance of unity and obedience. In the Duchy of Austria and neighboring Tyrol, his lawyers were able to establish his ascendancy over a feudal nobility whose economic position was still strong. Bohemia, it will be remembered, had been reduced

to obedience to Vienna early in the Thirty Years' War. A new nobility owing its titles to the Habsburg ruler replaced the old, and the crown of Bohemia, previously elective, was made hereditary in the Habsburg family in 1627.

The real problem was Hungary. Although the Habsburgs had usually been the elected monarchs of the kingdom since early in the sixteenth century, hardly a third of Hungary was actually in Habsburg hands. The rest was either directly or indirectly ruled by the Ottoman Turks. To establish their authority in Hungary, the Habsburg monarchs in Vienna had to deal not only with the powerful Hungarian nobility and the Hungarian Protestants but with the Turks and the French as well. The nobles were wealthy and unruly; the Protestants were numerous and inclined to side with the Turks against the Catholic Habsburgs. The Ottoman Empire was not the power it had been in the sixteenth century, but since 1656 it had been undergoing a revival under a vigorous line of grand viziers of the Kiuprili family, who in the 1660's began a new thrust up the Danube Valley directed at their old enemies, the Habsburgs. Louis XIV, also an inveterate enemy of the Habsburgs, allied himself with the Turks and Hungarian rebels against his Austrian foes. Thus building a Danubian monarchy was as much a foreign as a domestic problem.

The Siege of Vienna, 1683

The crisis came in 1683. In July of that year a Turkish army of 200,000 laid siege to Vienna. For two months the fate of Christendom seemed to hang in the balance. Then volunteers began to flow in from all over the Continent to help the emperor in his extremity. The greatest pope of the century, Innocent XI, contributed moral and material aid, and King John Sobieski of Poland arrived with an army that helped rout the Turks by September. The retreat continued year after year as the impetus of Europe's last crusade carried on down the Danube Valley, until Eugene of Savoy broke Turkish military power at the battle of Zenta (1697).

The Peace of Carlowitz in 1699 gave the Habsburgs full control of Hungary. The Hungarian Protestants were crushed; many of them were executed for treason. The landowning nobility were left in full control of their serfs and in possession of many of their old privileges, in return for recognizing the ultimate sovereignty of the chancellery at Vienna. The Habsburgs were thus content with what one historian calls "a loose framework of centralized administration." They left local administration much as they found it, but they had established a strong monarchy in the Danube Valley where none had existed before.

The Treaties of Ryswick (1697) and Carlowitz (1699) thus marked the appearance on the European stage of two new great powers: England and Austria. Each had risen in response to Louis XIV's bid to make himself the heir of Habsburg power in Spain and Germany. The two illustrated how diverse great powers could be in the seventeenth century: England, a parliamentary monarchy controlled by a commercial and landed aristocracy, her strength based on commerce and sea power; Austria, a bureaucratic monarchy with agriculture and a standing army its most conspicuous sources of strength. At about the same time two more powers were just beginning to appear, each as distinct and different as England and Austria. These were Brandenburg-Prussia and Russia.

The Rise of Brandenburg-Prussia

The story of the rise of the Hohenzollerns in northern Germany is somewhat parallel to that of the Habsburgs in the South, except that the Hohenzollerns started with less and had farther to go. Their achievements owed proportionately more to the genius and patience of one man, Frederick William (1640–88), called the Great Elector.

The Hohenzollerns had been margraves of Brandenburg since 1417 (a margrave was count of a "mark," or frontier province). To this small territory around Berlin they had added by inheritance two other areas: Cleves and some neighboring lands on the Rhine (1614), and the Duchy of Prussia on the Baltic coast to the northeast (1618). When the Thirty Years' War broke out, there was nothing to suggest that the ruler of

these three scattered territories had any brighter a future than a dozen other German princes. His lands had no natural boundaries, no traditional ties with each other, poor soil, few resources, and sparse population, about a million and a half in all. Furthermore, they were especially hard hit by the Thirty Years' War. Swedish and Imperialist armies tramped back and forth across Brandenburg without hindrance, Berlin lost over half its population, and the Great Elector's dominions as a whole probably lost almost two-thirds of their people—a loss that took forty years to make up.

The Great Elector, 1640–88

Frederick William was twenty years old when he became elector in 1640 during the later years of the Thirty Years' War. Though he was a devoted Calvinist, he nevertheless respected the Lutheranism of his subjects and was genuinely tolerant in an age of intolerance and fanaticism. The helplessness of Brandenburg during the war taught him that his first and foremost task must be the development of an army, and to this end he set himself with unrelenting effort.

"A ruler is treated with no consideration if he does not have troops and means of his own," he advised his son in 1667. "It is these, Thank God! which have made me considerable since the time that I began to have them."

In 1640 he had a poorly equipped and ineffective army of 2,500 men. Before the end of the war in 1648 he had increased it to 8,000, and by his death in 1688 he had a peacetime force of 30,000, which was once expanded in wartime to 40,000. It was something of a miracle for a state with the meager population and resources of Brandenburg-Prussia to produce such a large, well-equipped, and well-trained standing army in so short a time. In forty years (1648–88) Brandenburg had become the strongest military power in Germany except for Austria. If there was any explanation, it was the single-minded devotion of the Great Elector to his goal and to any political, social, or economic policy that would help him reach it.

The first thing he had to do was to establish his authority over the Estates of Brandenburg

Frederick William, the Great Elector, as a young man; painting by his contemporary, Mathias Czwiczeic.

and Prussia, which had almost complete control of taxation. In Brandenburg the Great Elector was strong enough to imitate the practice of the king of France by simply continuing to raise taxes that had once been granted by the Estates, which were never summoned again after 1653. In Prussia the townsmen were more stubborn and the Junkers (or nobles) more unruly. Their leaders turned to Poland for support, and Frederick soon had a fight on his hands. The fight ended only after he had executed the ringleaders of the resistance. In the end Frederick set up a taxation system for the support of his army which was common to all his territories, administered by civil servants of his own choosing, and independent of local control. The nobility were shorn of their power in the Estates and pressed into service to the Hohenzollern state

as officers in the army. In return, the power of the Junkers over their serfs on their own estates was left untouched. Military strength, not social betterment, was the Great Elector's objective.

It could be argued, however, that much social betterment came indirectly from his building of a strong army, even if the Prussian peasants were sinking deeper into serfdom. The devastation of war was even worse than aristocratic oppression, and Frederick William protected a whole generation from invasion. He used his army as a weapon in diplomacy rather than in war by selling his support to one side or another in return for subsidies. The subsidies helped pay for the army, and the alliances seldom required much fighting. By pursuing this policy, the Great Elector and his immediate successors made substantial territorial gains. For example, by playing off Sweden against Russia, the Hohenzollerns gained Stettin and Pomerania in 1720. There was little sentiment and much shrewdness in this foreign policy, which showed its results in the steady growth of the army and the territorial expansion of the state.

Frederick William's economic policy was designed to develop his lands to the point where they could support his army without the need for foreign subsidies. He did much to revive and improve agriculture after 1648, and much to encourage industry and commerce. His tolerant policies made Brandenburg a haven for religious refugees—persecuted Lutherans, German Calvinists, and, above all, French Huguenots after the Revocation of the Edict of Nantes in 1685. These immigrants, together with Dutch, Swiss, and other newcomers, brought new skills in agriculture and industry, helped increase the population, and added considerably to the strength of the state. He welcomed even the more radical Protestant sects and the Jews, drawing the line only at admitting the Jesuits, whom he considered too intolerant.

The recognition of the Great Elector's son as King Frederick I in 1701 symbolized the appearance of a new power in Europe. Prussia (as the Hohenzollern lands came to be known) had devoted relatively more of its population, its resources, and its energies to military purposes than had any other German state during the later seventeenth century. It has been said that in Prussia the army created the state. The army was, in fact, the first institution common to all the elector's lands, and its bureaus were the models for many organs of the later civil government. But while the needs of the army were especially important in Prussia, they played a significant role in the development of every great power in Europe except England.

Sweden

While Prussia was growing in strength, her neighbors, Sweden and Poland, were declining, for different reasons. Sweden had burst upon the European horizon as a military power of first rank during Gustavus Adolphus' invasion of Germany (1630–32). During the latter part of the century the Baltic became a Swedish lake, and a Swedish empire grew up on both sides of the inland sea all the way from the Gulf of Finland to the North Sea. Iron ore and agriculture were the Swedes' chief resources, a technically superior musket their chief military advantage.

Swedish power, however, rested on shaky foundations. The country had a population of less than 2 million—that is, not much larger than Prussia and smaller than the Dutch Republic. Her lines of empire were over-extended, and her enemies—from Russia and Poland to Prussia and Denmark—were hungry for revenge.

When young Charles XII (1697–1718) came to the throne, a coalition of Russia, Poland, and Denmark pounced upon his Baltic territories. Charles XII proved to be a military genius and crushed his enemies in a series of lightning campaigns. But he became intoxicated by success and engaged in political adventures that far exceeded his country's resources. He marched

The Baltic: A Swedish Lake 1621–1721

deep into Russian territory and was totally defeated at Pultava in 1709. He failed to gain Turkish support, though he spent some years at the Ottoman court seeking an alliance. Finally, he lost his life in a raid on Norway in 1718. In the peace settlements of 1719–21, the Swedish empire outside Sweden was divided among Hanover, Denmark, Prussia, and Russia. Sweden settled down gracefully enough in the eighteenth century to her earlier role of second-class power.

Poland

The case of Poland was quite different, though the results were somewhat similar. Poland, formed in 1386 by the union of the crowns of Poland and Lithuania, was, after Russia, the largest state in Europe. Polish prosperity and culture had reached their peak in the sixteenth century, when the Polish people, linked by their Roman Catholic religion to western Europe, had felt some of the effects of the Renaissance, the Protestant revolt, and the Catholic Reformation. By the beginning of the seventeenth century, however, economic and political decline had set in. The Polish monarchy had always been elective. Until about 1572 the nobles had usually elected the legal heirs of their monarchs, but after this they began to choose anyone whom they believed they could control. By 1700 the real power in Poland lay in the hands of the nobility. The monarchy was almost powerless, though petty German princes still sought election to gain the prestige of a royal title. The peasants were the most depressed in Europe, sunk deep in serfdom. There was almost no bourgeoisie, since the towns had not flourished. Political power was concentrated in the diet, which by now represented only the nobility, since representatives of the towns no longer dared to attend.

The diet was notorious for its futility. By using the *liberum veto* any member might "explode" the diet—that is, dissolve the diet and wipe out everything it had done up to that moment. Of fifty-seven diets held in the century after 1652, all but nine were so "exploded"—one by a member who simply wanted to see what would happen. If legislation did succeed in running the gauntlet of this national assembly, there was still no way of getting it enforced in the provincial assemblies of lesser nobles or on the private estates of the landed barons. John Sobieski (1674–96), a native Pole of high integrity who made a serious effort to lead the country out of its weakness, was the last great king of Poland. After him the Polish crown became simply the prize of foreign intrigue, and Poland started down the path that led to extinction at the hands of her more powerful neighbors at the end of the eighteenth century.

Russia

Throughout the seventeenth century there was no great power east of Sweden, Poland, and the Ottoman Empire. The Grand Duchy of Moscow had fallen on evil days after the death of Ivan the Dread in 1584. Disputes about the succession to the tsar's crown led to a "Time of Troubles," and the accession of the Romanovs, who were to rule Russia from 1613 to 1917, at first did little to strengthen the state. In the 1650's a near revolution was provoked by a reforming patriarch of the Orthodox Church who ordered that the ritual and liturgy be revised in order to bring them closer to the original Greek text of the Bible. This order exasperated vast numbers of the uneducated masses to whom the Slavonic texts were sacrosanct. For many years after, "Old Believers" resisted the official religious policy of the government in spite of executions and exile. For the rest, Russia was a victim state through most of the century, often unable to defend her frontiers against invading Swedes, Poles, and Turks, and still cut off from access to either the Baltic or the Black Sea. English merchants had made contact with Moscow in the 1550's through the White Sea, and German merchants were even more active in the capital. But while Russia absorbed some of the technology (especially the military technology) of the West, it remained relatively untouched by cultural changes in the rest of Europe. Renaissance, Reformation, and scientific revolution, with all the ferment they brought to the West, remained almost unknown to the peoples living east of Catholic Poland.

Peter the Great, 1689–1725

In 1689 one of the most remarkable rulers in all European history came to power in Russia at the age of seventeen. He was a giant of a man, nearly seven feet tall (his enormous boots are still proudly preserved in the Kremlin), with large, skillful hands, inexhaustible energy, insatiable curiosity, and a hot temper. As a boy he had loved to play at war. He had also spent much of his time with the Dutch and Germans who lived in the "German Quarter" of Moscow, listening and learning. In these early years the great passion of his later life seems to have been born: to make Russia a great power by rapidly westernizing its technology, its civil and military institutions, and its popular customs. At his death in 1725 he had aggrandized, upturned, and exhausted his country and had earned the name by which he was to be known to later history: Peter the Great.

Peter's plans at first developed slowly. Using an unreformed army, he failed to capture Azov at the mouth of the Don from the Turks in 1695. Next year, after he had built a fleet on the river with Dutch help, Azov fell. Peter had learned a lesson: In order to build a navy and to modernize an archaic army, he would first have to learn a great deal from the West. From 1696 to 1698, thinly disguised as a private citizen, Peter visited Holland, England, and Germany. Here he learned how an utterly different society built its ships, made its munitions, ran its government, and conducted its diplomacy. He alternately shocked and amazed the Dutch and English who came to know him. Direct, spontaneous, and naive in temperament, he always had to try to do things for himself. He worked in the shipyards, eagerly questioned everyone he met on western technology, and caroused through the night in drunken orgies with his Russian companions. He hired over 700 technicians of various sorts to return with him to Russia.

In Vienna word reached him of a revolt of the *streltsi,* the barbarous and undisciplined palace guard which to Peter represented everything backward and reactionary about Russia. (The *streltsi* were in league with the "Old Believers" and were better at staging palace revolutions than at fighting an enemy.) Peter hastened back to Moscow and made a fearful example of the rebels, executing over a thousand of them and using torture on a scale that shocked even his countrymen, who were used to brutality. At the same time he forbade the wearing of beards and long robes by any Russian, as a sign of his determination to westernize even the personal habits and costumes of his subjects. His subjects wore beards because God was presumed to wear a beard and man was made in His image. But to Peter, beards symbolized the old Russia of reaction, rebellion, and religious orthodoxy. The clean-shaven look

Peter the Great, by Aert de Gelder.

An English Bishop's Impression of Peter the Great

1698

He is a man of very hot temper, soon inflamed and very brutal in his passion. He raises his natural heat by drinking much brandy, which he rectifies himself with great application. He is subject to convulsive motions all over his body, and his head seems to be affected with these. He wants not capacity, and has a larger measure of knowledge than might be expected from his education, which was very indifferent. A want of judgment, with an instability of temper, appear in him too often and too evidently.

He is mechanically turned, and seems designed by nature rather to be a ship carpenter than a great prince. This was his chief study and exercise while he stayed here. He wrought much with his own hands and made all about him work at the models of ships. . . .

After I had seen him often, and had conversed much with him, I could not but adore the depth of the providence of God that had raised up such a furious man to so absolute an authority over so great a part of the world.

From Gilbert Burnet, *History of His Own Time,* 1734, Vol. II, pp. 221–22.

was western. Typically, the tsar himself took a hand in shaving some of his courtiers.

There was nothing particularly original about what Peter did to reform the military, political, and social institutions of his country. He borrowed his ideas and techniques from what other statesmen were doing at the time in France, England, the Dutch Republic, Brandenburg, and Sweden. But his methods were more casual and informal, more brutal and ruthless, than were those of western countries.

His awareness of the need to build a large modernized army energized his reforms in all the other areas. An overwhelming defeat by the Swedes at Narva in 1700 spurred on Peter's efforts to improve his army. With the help of foreign officers and advisers he had trained a formidable force of over 100,000 by 1709, the year he annihilated Charles XII's forces at Pultava. At the time of his death the army numbered over 200,000 in a population of about 8 million. Years of warfare against the Turks were unsuccessful, and even Azov was lost once again. But decisive victories came in the North. In the Great Northern War Peter gained territory on the Gulf of Finland which had once belonged to Sweden. This gave him the "window on the sea," the direct contact with western Europe through the Baltic, which was his primary aim.

To man his army, Peter developed a conscription system. To pay for it was harder, since he could not borrow money. As expenses increased, he and his advisers taxed anything and everything they could think of: births, marriages, caskets, graves, and beards, among other things. By the end of his reign the combined burdens of heavy taxation, conscription for the army, and forced labor for industry and for building had resulted in a measurable decline in the population.

Political reforms followed military reforms, though more slowly. Peter's method of governing was informal and haphazard. To get something done, he would dash off a hastily written order and set up a commission to carry it out. Slowly, toward the end of his reign, some order was brought out of the resulting chaos. The first provincial governments were set up; the numerous commissions were brought under supervisory "colleges"; and a "senate," or central administrative body, was instituted to interpret the tsar's orders (which were sometimes confusing) and to carry out his will. A secret police also appeared to provide a check on all officials.

In Russia the imperial government did more and individuals or nonofficial groups did less than in any other European country. After 1700 no new patriarch was appointed, and the church was strictly subordinated to the state under a civilian official. When new industries were needed to support the army, government contractors founded them, using forced labor (serfs and criminals) granted by the tsar. One of Peter's most herculean achievements was to compel the ancient hereditary nobility to serve the state. He ordered many of the sons of the nobility to study abroad, then compelled them as well as their parents to serve for life either in the army, in the government, or in industry. At the same time he enlisted commoners for the service of the state, giving them land and titles of nobility. He thus created a "service nobility" out of older and newer classes. To support this service nobility, he allowed them a free hand in dealing with the serfs on their lands. A census for tax purposes resulted in greatly increasing the number of serfs in Russia by classifying doubtful cases as servile. After 1762 the nobles were freed from the obligation of service to the state, but it took another century for the peasants to become free from the galling form of serfdom prevailing in Russia. In central Europe a serf was usually bound to the land, but in Russia he could be sold apart from the land like a slave and was generally at the mercy of his master—a fact that made it easier for new industries to acquire forced labor but degraded the Russian serf to a level even below that of his fellows in Germany and Austria.

St. Petersburg

In 1707 Peter moved the seat of his government to a new city that he had built on conquered territory at the eastern end of the Gulf of Finland and had named in honor of his patron saint. St. Petersburg was a strange symbol of his work as a whole. It was a city unlike Moscow, without roots in the country's past, built new on a marsh by forced labor. The nobles were ordered to build houses in it and merchants were ordered to settle in it. This seaport city looked westward to Germany, Holland, and western Europe, not to the interior as landlocked Moscow had for centuries. The nobility and civil servants hated it at first, but in the end it became their capital—the political center of what has been called "a government without a people," and the social center of a westernized aristocracy out of all touch with the Russian peasant. As Versailles came to stand for the France of Louis XIV, so St. Petersburg (later called Petrograd and then Leningrad) came to stand for the Russia of Peter the Great—a powerful autocracy with few vital connections with the people.

Historians still differ sharply in estimating the value of Peter's work, but on some things they are fairly well agreed. The older Russian institutions were bankrupt, and western influences were beginning to have their effect even before Peter appeared on the scene. Peter hastened processes of change that were almost certain to have come in any case. He cannot be blamed for all the evil results that followed, since many of them (such as the intensification of serfdom) had their roots deep in the past and owed much of their growth to Peter's successors. Two things he did accomplish: He transformed Russia from a victim state into a great power, and he involved it irrevocably with the future development of Europe. Since his time, Russia has always been a factor in the European balance of power. Peter's westernizing policy ultimately provoked a strong nationalistic and orthodox reaction, leaving Russia divided to the present day between deep suspicion of everything foreign and eager admiration of western technology and culture. But never again was Russia able to turn its back on Europe.

Even more important than Peter's accomplishments were Peter's methods. His example created a tradition of dynamic autocracy. To future tsars and future dictators his reign was to be the classic example of what might be accomplished by a ruthless and demonic will.

Conclusion

The half-century between 1660 and 1715 thus saw significant changes in the political and social structure of Europe. Absolute divine-right monarchy reached the apogee of its development in the France of Louis XIV and was imitated from Madrid to St. Petersburg. It is difficult to imagine two more different personalities than Louis XIV of France and Peter of Russia, but their aims were essentially similar. A few smaller peoples like the Swiss had quietly rejected monarchy in favor of republican government, and the Dutch had become wealthy and powerful as a republic. But it took the English Revolution to demonstrate to Europe that there was a practical alternative to absolute monarchy that could serve great powers as well as small. So by 1715 the political alternatives of absolutism and constitutionalism were each embodied in a great power. At the same time there were important shifts of power within the European state system. The French bid for predominance failed, provoking the rise of England and Austria as great powers. Two great empires of the sixteenth century, the Spanish and the Ottoman, were in decline. Two peoples of limited resources and numbers, the

Dutch and the Swedes, had bid strongly for great-power status in the mid-seventeenth century, but by 1715 their strength was spent. Two new powers had appeared in the East to join the balance, the small military Kingdom of Prussia and the vast semibarbarous Tsardom of Russia. The rivalries of these states—England versus France, France versus Austria, Austria versus Prussia, Austria and Russia versus the Ottoman Empire—were to become the dynamic elements in eighteenth-century war and diplomacy.

Suggestions for Further Reading

1. General

The best general accounts of the period are F. L. Nussbaum, *The Triumph of Science and Reason, 1660–1685** (1953), and J. B. Wolf, *The Emergence of the Great Powers, 1685–1715** (1951), both in the *Rise of Modern Europe* series, with useful bibliographies. These are particularly helpful as introductions to the history of eastern Europe, on which it is hard to find good reading in English. A general study of an important subject begins with this period: Sir Ernest Barker, *The Development of Public Services in Western Europe, 1660–1930* (1944). On the general theme of this chapter, see: J. N. Figgis, *The Divine Right of Kings** (1896, 1922); C. J. Friedrich and C. Blitzer, *The Age of Power** (1957); and F. D. Wormuth, *The Origins of Modern Constitutionalism* (1949).

2. France Under Louis XIV

There are good chapters on Louis' reign in Ogg and Boulenger (Chapter 19). Two excellent short surveys are L. B. Packard, *The Age of Louis XIV** (1914), and M. P. Ashley, *Louis XIV and the Greatness of France** (1946). A. Guérard, *The Life and Death of an Ideal: France in the Classical Age** (1928), is a more thought-provoking and comprehensive discussion, including both politics and culture within its scope. J. E. King, *Science and Rationalism in the Government of Louis XIV, 1661–1683* (1949), is an important study. On economic history, the three books of C. W. Cole are the best introduction: *French Mercantilist Doctrines Before Colbert* (1913), *Colbert and a Century of French Mercantilism,* 2 vols. (1939), and *French Mercantilism, 1683–1700* (1943). C. Hill, *Versailles* (1925), is one of many books on the life of the court. W. H. Lewis, *The Splendid Century** (1954), is a recent popular account of all aspects of the reign, full of fascinating material. The best guides to the literary history of the period are the various works of A. A. Tilley.

3. England

G. N. Clark, *The Later Stuarts, 1660–1714* (1934), in the *Oxford History of England,* is a particularly fine synthesis. A more detailed narrative history of the period may be found in three books, all more or less Whig in sympathy: D. Ogg, *England in the Reign of Charles II,* 2 vols.* (1934); the same author's *England in the Reign of James II and William III* (1955); and G. M. Trevelyan, *England*

---

* Available in paperback edition.

under Queen Anne, 3 vols. (1930–34). A. Bryant, *Charles II* (1931), is more pro-Stuart. The most recent interpretation of the whole period of revolution in England is C. Hill, *The Century of Revolution, 1603–1714* (1961). There is a good modern biography of James II by F. C. Turner (1948), but none of William III. Sir John Pollock, *The Popish Plot* (1903, 1945), is the standard investigation of a tangled historical problem. On the economic history of the period, there is a good special study, *The Bank of England,* by Sir John Clapham, 2 vols. (1944), and a masterly brief sketch by Sir George Clark, *The Wealth of England, 1496–1760* (1947). Pepys' Diary is the most deservedly famous contemporary account of the Restoration period. It is perhaps read best in the abridgment of O. F. Morshead, *Everybody's Pepys* (1926).

4. Eastern Europe

In addition to the general accounts in Nussbaum and Wolf (Section 1, above), two books are particularly helpful as an introduction to the problems of eastern Europe: S. H. Cross, *Slavic Civilization Through the Ages* (1948), and O. Halecki, *Borderlands of Western Civilization* (1952). For Germany as a whole, see H. Holborn, *A History of Modern Germany, 1648–1840* (1964). On Habsburg history, P. Frischauer, *The Imperial Crown* (1939), follows the history of the house to 1792 and is mostly concerned with personalities. H. F. Schwarz, *The Imperial Privy Council in the Seventeenth Century* (1943), is concerned with constitutional matters. On Prussia, S. B. Fay, *The Rise of Brandenburg-Prussia to 1786** (1937), is very brief but also very good. J. A. R. Marriott and C. G. Robertson, *The Evolution of Prussia* (1915), is more detailed. F. Schevill has written an admiring biography of Frederick William, *The Great Elector* (1947). R. N. Bain, *Scandinavia: A Political History* (1905), and O. Halecki, *History of Poland** (1943), are useful national histories. J. A. R. Marriott, *The Eastern Question* (1917, 1940), is a reliable survey of the slow disintegration of the Ottoman Empire and of the resulting repercussions in Europe. The classic larger history of Russia is by V. O. Kluchevsky; the standard Marxist account is by M. N. Pokrovsky. There are good one-volume histories by G. Vernadsky (rev. ed., 1944), Sir Bernard Pares (new ed., 1953), and B. H. Sumner (rev. ed., 1947). B. H. Sumner, *Peter the Great and the Emergence of Russia** (1950), is a well-informed and judicious short account. R. J. Kerner, *The Urge to the Sea: The Course of Russian History* (1942), contains a valuable account of Russian expansion eastward to the Pacific. J. Blum, "The Rise of Serfdom in Eastern Europe," *American Historical Review,* Vol. LXII (July 1957), is a masterly examination of the differences in the economic development of eastern and western Europe. See also his *Lord and Peasant in Russia** (1961).

---

* Available in paperback edition.

An assembly of *philosophes:* Voltaire (1), Adam (2), Abbé Mauri (3), d'Alembert (4), Condorcet (5), Diderot (6), and Laharpe (7). Contemporary engraving by Jean Huber.

6

The Scientific Revolution and the Enlightenment

Until the seventeenth century the growth of civilized man's knowledge about the natural world around him had been slow, fumbling, and discontinuous. He had made many individual observations of natural phenomena and had derived some useful generalizations from these observations. But many generalizations were poorly stated and others were entirely erroneous. "Experiments" in the modern sense were all but unheard of, and most people felt that scientific speculation was both unsure and impractical.

The Scientific Revolution

By the eighteenth century a startling change had occurred. A large body of verifiable knowledge about nature had accumulated and has continued to accumulate at an increasing rate down to our own day. This knowledge has had revolutionary effects. Human society today has at its disposal more food, clothing, and shelter, faster ways of moving about the globe, quicker means of communicating across great distances, and more power than anyone could have dreamed of before about 1600. The characteristic mark of our civilization is that it is a "scientific civilization," and this quality began to be noticeable in the seventeenth century.

Discussion of a new method of inquiry—we call it the scientific method—began in the universities in the late thirteenth and fourteenth centuries and came to fruition in western Europe after 1600. The new method was essentially a combination of two elements: careful observation and controlled experimentation, and rational interpretation of the results of this observation and experimentation, preferably by use of mathematics. In Professor Whitehead's words, science is "a vehement and passionate interest in the relation of general principles to irreducible and stubborn facts."

When Galileo and others began to apply this method in physics and astronomy, a chain of brilliant "discoveries" resulted. These discoveries fired the imagination and enthusiasm of European thinkers. Scientific societies were organized, scientific journals began to appear, and "chain discoveries," each one resting on the results of the one preceding it, made their appearance. Science, hitherto the pursuit of occasional lonely individuals, became a social enterprise and has continued so to the present. Furthermore, it became fashionable. The humanists were little interested in science; Newton's work made a profound impression on every writer in Europe. Finally, the gap between the theories of the scholar and the practical knowledge of the technician began to close.

The Medieval Universe

Precisely *why* all this took place when and where it did is still a puzzle. The one thing that can be said is that ever since the twelfth century the people of western Europe had been interested in scientific problems. But the medieval answers to these problems were not very stimulating. For example, it was generally believed that the universe was a finite sphere with the earth at the center. Between the center and the outermost limits were nine transparent spheres that carried the stars, the planets, the sun, and the moon in their daily revolutions around the earth, which remained motionless. On earth all was change, corruptibility, and decay. In the heavens all was perfection and incorruptibility—the perfect sphericity of sun and moon, the unvarying circular motion of the heavenly bodies, and the music of the spheres produced by their motion. And so what was the rule on earth was not the rule in the heavens. There was an earthly physics and a heavenly physics, and the laws of the one were not those of the other.

Even in the Middle Ages, however, not all men were satisfied with this relatively simple picture of the universe. In the thirteenth and fourteenth centuries a small but increasing number of scholars began to question existing explanations. Many of them were Franciscans, inspired perhaps by their founder's sensitive feeling for nature. Stimulated by the current study of Greco-

The Scientific Revolution

ALFRED NORTH WHITEHEAD

A brief and sufficiently accurate description of the intellectual life of the European races during the succeeding two centuries and a quarter up to our own times is that they have been living upon the accumulated capital of ideas provided for them by the genius of the seventeenth century. . . . It is the one century which consistently, and throughout the whole range of human activities, provided intellectual genius adequate for the greatness of its occasions. . . . The issue of the combined labors of four men [Descartes, Galileo, Huyghens, and Newton] has some right to be considered as the greatest single intellectual success which mankind has achieved.

HERBERT BUTTERFIELD

The so-called "scientific revolution," popularly associated with the sixteenth and seventeenth centuries, but reaching back in an unmistakably continuous line to a period much earlier still . . . outshines everything since the rise of Christianity and reduces the Renaissance and Reformation to the rank of mere episodes, mere internal displacements, within the system of medieval Christendom.

From Alfred North Whitehead, *Science and the Modern World* (New York: Macmillan, 1925), pp. 57–58, 67; Herbert Butterfield, *The Origins of Modern Science* (London: Bell, 1949), p. vii.

Arabic science, a group of teachers at Oxford and Paris began to apply mathematical reasoning to problems of physics and astronomy, such as accelerated motion. Their speculations were continued by professors at the University of Padua in the fifteenth and sixteenth centuries. At Padua, a center of medical training for three centuries, the proper method of studying nature was vigorously debated in the course of arguments about Aristotle. Medieval universities had kept interest in science alive, and the first faint beginnings of the scientific revolution may be seen in Oxford, Paris, and Padua.

Most Europeans of 1500, however, did not question the standard Greek authorities. The normal state of everything in the universe was a state of rest: Things moved only if they were pushed or pulled by a mover—so said Aristotle. Galen, in the second century, had described the anatomy of the human body so convincingly that doctors still saw the human organs through his eyes. Ptolemy in the same century had worked out such an ingenious mathematical explanation of the observed irregularities in the movements of the planets that no one in 1500 thought it could be improved upon. All motion in the heavens was circular, Ptolemy assumed, but there were smaller circles, or "epicycles," whose centers moved around the circumference of larger circles, and on the circumferences of these smaller circles the planets moved. It took about eighty epicycles to do the job, but the system worked quite well in explaining the observed phenomena. There seemed to be very little reason at the close of the Middle Ages to try to improve on either the observations or the theories of these ancient writers.

The Background of Change

In the fourteenth, fifteenth, and sixteenth centuries, however, certain forces in European society were preparing the way for a change in the general view of nature. Artisans and craftsmen were becoming more skilled in their techniques. The invention of the lens and the development of the glass industry, to take but one example, contained the promise of vastly extending man's powers of observing natural processes. New techniques in shipbuilding led to voyages of discovery, which in turn stimulated interest in nature and turned men's attention to problems of navigation.

The Renaissance, with its emphasis on literature and art, was in some ways antiscientific. But humanism stimulated a passionate interest in man. Leonardo's studies of the anatomy of the body and Machiavelli's studies of the anatomy of society owed much indirectly to humanism. Furthermore, humanistic study revealed conflicting opinions among the ancients on matters of science, just at the moment when the authority of Galen and Ptolemy was becoming shaky for other reasons. Anatomical studies by artists and the increasing practice of dissection suggested that Galen had made mistakes in observation. Growing skill in mathematics exposed the clumsiness of Ptolemy's explanations. In the opening years of the sixteenth century, conditions were ripe for change.

1543: Vesalius and Copernicus

In 1543 two notable scientific works heralded the end of medieval science and the beginnings of a revolution in western man's conception of nature. Vesalius' *On the Structure of the Human Body* was for its day a marvelously careful description of human anatomy based on direct observation in dissection. Vesalius did not free himself completely from the authority of Galen, nor was there much theory in his book. But it was an influential example of the power of observation. Copernicus' *On the Revolutions of the Heavenly Bodies* was a brilliant mathematical treatise which showed that the number of Ptolemy's epicycles could be reduced to 34 if one assumed that the earth turned on its axis once a day and moved around the sun once a year. Unlike Vesalius, Copernicus was no observer. He learned during his study at Padua in the early years of the century that there was an ancient opinion that the earth moved, and he found that this assumption made everything simpler to explain mathematically. Since medieval theory decreed that "nature always acts in the simplest ways," the simpler explanation must be the truer. And so with no experimental or observational proof, Copernicus presented his readers with a theory of a universe in which the earth was no longer the center. The experimental and the theoretical sides of the modern scientific method were perfectly exemplified in Vesalius' and Copernicus' books, but they were not yet conjoined in one man or one work.

In 1600 a monk named Giordano Bruno was burned at the stake for preaching that the universe was not finite but infinite in extent, that it was filled with numberless suns and planets like our own, and that God was equally in every planet or atom in the cosmos. Bruno had been inspired by Copernicus, although Copernicus himself believed in the finite sphere of the fixed stars and the uniqueness of the earth. This intuition of the infinity of the universe spread gradually among all scientists.

Bacon and Descartes

The two major prophets of the Scientific Revolution were Francis Bacon (1561–1626) and René Descartes (1596–1650). Bacon, an English lawyer and essayist, waged a vigorous battle in his books against the deductive method of Scholasticism, which started from premises usually taken on authority and then deduced all the logical consequences. This method might help men to organize truths already known, he said, but it could never help them to discover new truths. Only inductive reasoning, which starts from direct observations of phenomena and goes on to develop the principles that explain these observations, can produce new truth. Bacon was as interested in controlling nature as in knowing its processes. He pictured an imaginary society of scientists whose end was to benefit mankind by conducting hundreds of experiments and discovering useful facts. Bacon failed to appreciate the importance of mathematical models in theoretical analysis (he was unconvinced by Copernicus), but his writings did dramatize the importance of empirical research. The founding in 1662 of the Royal Society of London, the first scientific society in England, owed much to Bacon's inspiration, and in a sense he was the remote ancestor of the great research laboratories and research teams of today.

Descartes, a French mathematician and philosopher, was strong where Bacon was weak and weak where Bacon was strong. To Descartes, the excitement of science lay in mathematical analysis and theory. In a famous autobiographical account, he told how the literature and philosophy he studied as a youth left him unsatisfied because they reached no certain conclusions, how mathematics charmed him by its precision and certainty, and how he set out to discover a "method of rightly conducting the reason and discovering truth in the sciences." In November 1619, in a moment of intuition, he saw the exact correspondence between geometry and algebra: the truth that any equation can be translated into a curve on a graph, and that any regular curve can be translated into an equation. This intoxicating vision suggested to him a new way of grasping ultimate truth. If only men would systematically doubt all notions based on authority or custom and start with clear and precise ideas they know to be true, the whole universe might be deduced from a few simple principles and thus comprehended as clearly as the coordinate geometry he had discovered.

Descartes was one of the first to believe that science could save humanity. His enthusiasm was infectious, but he moved too fast. He reduced the universe, including the body of man, to a mathematically intelligible machine. To do this he had to take mind out of the world of matter entirely and define it as a separate substance which comprehended the world of matter but did not exist in it. His generalizations in astronomy, physics, and anatomy were often premature, and his passion for system-building went beyond his capacity to check by experiment. But his enthusiasm for scientific "method," his insistence on systematic doubt of older beliefs, and his firm conviction that the universe was a machine that could eventually be explained by a single overarching mathematical theorem, all left a profound mark on the thinking of scientists in the next two centuries.

Experiment and Mathematics

Both Bacon and Descartes were overoptimistic. Bacon thought that a generation of determined experimentation would establish a solid structure of knowledge about the universe. Descartes thought that a universal science could be deduced fairly soon from a few basic mathematical axioms. Meanwhile, experimentation and mathematics were developing more slowly and more steadily in the hands of a growing host of scientists.

William Gilbert used what little was known of the mysterious force of electricity to deduce that the earth itself was a great magnet (1600). William Harvey, who had studied at Padua, proved that the blood must circulate from arteries to veins to heart to lungs and back to heart and then arteries again by measuring the amount of blood actually pumped out by the heart in a minute and arguing that it must go somewhere (1628). Later in the century the new microscope revealed the tiny capillaries that actually connect arteries to veins. Torricelli, Pascal, and others investigated the ancient proposition that "nature abhors a vacuum," a proposition that had been firmly believed by everyone from Aristotle to Descartes. In order to prove the falseness of the proposition, the new investigators created vacuums in test tubes, invented the barometer, and discovered the pressure of the atmosphere. All these advances evidenced a growing precision in observation and an increasing sophistication in controlling experiments.

At the same time mathematics was making rapid strides. The invention of decimals and of logarithms early in the century facilitated calculation; Pascal inaugurated the study of probability; and at the end of the century Newton and Leibniz crowned the work of many others by simultaneously inventing calculus, which provided the first method of analyzing regularly accelerating or decelerating motion.

Kepler

It was in astronomy and physics that experimental techniques and mathematical methods found their most fruitful union. The German astronomer, Johannes Kepler (1571–1630), was troubled by discrepancies in Copernicus' theory, which he nevertheless believed to be true. He worked from the observations of his master

Harvey Discovers the Circulation of the Blood (1629)

Since calculations and visual demonstrations have confirmed all my suppositions, to wit, that the blood is passed through the lungs and the heart by the pulsation of the ventricles, is forcibly ejected to all parts of the body, therein steals into the veins . . . flows back everywhere . . . from small veins into larger ones, and thence comes at last into the vena cava and to the auricle of the heart; all this too in such amounts that it cannot be supplied from the ingesta [food] and is also in greater bulk than would suffice for nutrition.

I am obliged to conclude that in all animals the blood is driven around a circuit with an unceasing, circular sort of motion, that this is an activity of the heart which it carries out by virtue of its pulsation, and that in sum it constitutes the sole cause for the heart's pulsatile movement.

From C. C. Gillispie, *The Edge of Objectivity* (Princeton: Princeton U. Press, 1960), p. 71.

Tycho Brahe, which were far more accurate than those available to Copernicus. Copernicus had clung to the old belief that all heavenly bodies moved in circles. But to Kepler it was obvious that the planets' orbits were not circles. For years he worried about the geometry of these orbits and finally tried the ellipse. The properties of the ellipse had been studied since the time of the Greeks, and Kepler quickly saw that his solution fitted the observations. The planets' orbits, he announced, are elliptical, with the sun in one of the two foci of the ellipse. Further, a line from the sun to a planet sweeps out equal areas of the ellipse in equal times, and the cube of the distance of each planet from the sun is proportional to the square of the time of its revolution. Here was astounding proof of the intuition of Descartes and others that nature in some mysterious sense was mathematical. A geometrical figure, studied for centuries as pure theory, was found to "fit" the facts of nature. The implication was that nature was perhaps really a machine, intelligible to careful observers equipped with the tools of mathematics.

Two of Galileo's telescopes, in the Tribuna di Galileo, Florence.

Galileo

The first fruits of Kepler's work appeared in 1609. During the same year an Italian, Galileo Galilei (1564–1642), professor at Padua and Pisa, turned a newly invented instrument, the telescope, on the heavens and soon afterward published an account of what he saw. The changeless perfection and perfect sphericity of the heavenly bodies had dissolved before his gaze. The moon had craters and mountains; there were moving spots on the sun; there were rings around Saturn; and Jupiter proved to have four moons of its

own. A bright new star had already appeared and been noted in 1572, and in 1577 a new comet had cut a path through what should have been crystalline spheres. The finite, spherical universe of the Middle Ages was shattered, and thoughtful men suspected strongly that they were looking out into boundless space, sparsely populated by stars like the sun and possibly by other solar systems as well. The old distinction between terrestrial and celestial physics was apparently dissolving. The moon was not a perfect globe and the sun was not changeless. Perhaps the same forces and laws operated both on earth and in the heavens. Nor was the earth any longer the motionless center of the universe. The earth was a planet circling the sun like Jupiter or any other, and round about the solar system were infinite, silent spaces.

This was too much for obscurantists in the Church. The Copernican theory had been denounced in 1616, and in 1632 Galileo himself was condemned by the Roman Inquisition, threatened with torture, and humiliated, though not actually mistreated. Though he was forced to recant, his brilliantly written dialogues contributed mightily to the overthrow not only of Ptolemy in favor of Copernicus, but also of Aristotle in favor of a new physics.

Galileo's physics was inspired by the speculations of the fourteenth-century Franciscans, but he went much further and was much more accurate in developing mathematical formulae to describe the laws of motion. He worked out the law of falling bodies. The result was a simple mathematical formula again: The distance covered increases as the square of the time. He saw that the path followed by a projectile is a regular curve, a parabola, produced by the operation of two forces on the projectile; the initial impetus and the pull of the earth. He came close to formulating the key concept of modern mechanics, the law of inertia: that all bodies tend to remain at rest or to continue in motion in straight lines unless acted upon by outside forces. From this deceptively simple proposition—so fundamentally different from Aristotle's conception of motion as the result of some mover's action—was to spring the law of gravitation.

Galileo came within an ace of discovering it, but the honor was to be reserved for one who was born in the year he died, 1642.

Newton

It was the genius of an Englishman, Sir Isaac Newton (1642–1727), that related Kepler's astronomy to Galileo's physics, destroyed all distinction between celestial and terrestrial physics, and accomplished at least part of Descartes' dream of establishing a "universal science." The basic intuition came to Newton while he was still a student in his twenties at Cambridge University. The thought occurred to him that the force which keeps the moon from flying off at a tangent and bends it into an orbit about the earth must be exactly the same force that pulls an apple from its branch to the ground. There must be a universal force of attraction between every body in the universe, and this force must be calculable—even if we do not

know exactly what it is in itself. Newton's earliest calculations came close enough to mathematical proof to persuade him that it was in truth the same force that operated on the moon and the apple, and that this force varied "directly as the product of the masses" involved and "inversely as the square of the distance" separating the bodies. For some time he seems to have lost interest in his "law," but twenty years later a scientist friend, Edmund Halley, urged him to work out and publish his theory. Newton developed the necessary mathematics (calculus) to prove his theory to his own satisfaction and published his conclusions, in Latin, in *The Mathematical Principles of Natural Philosophy* (1687). This proved to be not only one of the greatest books in the history of science but one of the most influential in the history of human thought.

To scientists Newton's law of gravitation provided a single, simple explanation of a grow-

Some of Newton's calculations to determine the orbit of the comet which his friend, Edmund Halley, observed in 1682. Together they proved that the comet, later named for Halley, followed a vast elliptical orbit which brought it near the sun about every seventy-five years (a famous appearance before William's conquest of England in 1066 was recorded in the Bayeux Tapestry). It was Halley who persuaded Newton to publish his conclusions about gravitation, and it was laborious calculations like these on which Newton's book was eventually based.

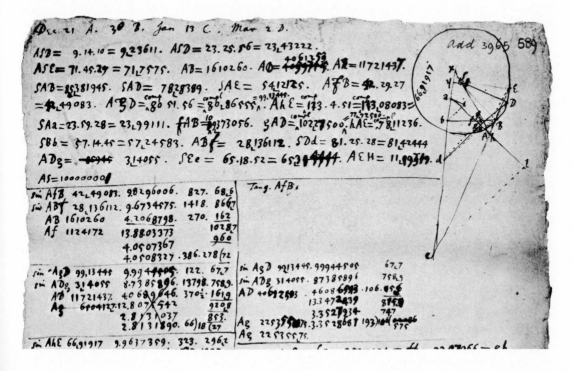

ing mass of data in astronomy and physics and laid the foundations of future research in both these sciences. Further, Newton gave scientific method its classic formulation in his "Rules of Reasoning":

> In experimental philosophy (i.e., science) we are to look upon propositions collected by general induction from phenomena as accurately or very nearly true, notwithstanding any contrary hypotheses (theories) that may be imagined, till such time as other phenomena occur, by which they may either be made more accurate or liable to exceptions.

Newton's support of the experimental, or inductive, approach was aimed at the premature generalizing of Descartes and his followers. But obviously he did not underestimate the value of mathematical theory, as Bacon had. In Newton the slow growing together of empirical observation and rational interpretation reached full maturity.

The Newtonian Universe

To the layman, who learned about Newton's work through popularizers, a new universe began to open up. It was a far cry from the small and finite medieval universe. It was a universe in which the significant objects were bodies or masses moving about in infinite space in response to regularly operating forces. Mass, force, and motion were the key concepts, and mathematics was the means of understanding them. Medieval man had been obsessed by the question "Why?" and had felt he understood whatever he encountered in nature once he had discovered its end or purpose. Seventeenth-century scientists limited themselves to asking "How?" and were satisfied when they found what appeared to be the immediate causes of natural processes. The world of Kepler, Galileo, and Newton was a vast machine, working according to laws that could be mathematically expressed, laws that were intelligible to anyone who followed the proper experimental and mathematical methods.

What was the place of God and of man in this universe? We shall see what the answers to this question were in the next century. But here we must observe that no seventeenth-cen-

tury scientist of prominence thought that he was reading God or man out of the universe in any sense. Descartes considered himself a good Catholic and was apparently not troubled by the dangers inherent in his sharp separation of the world of matter from the world of mind. Newton spent most of his energy in his later years in religious speculation. Contradictions were not necessarily evident to the first modern scientists and their readers.

Still, the religious view of life was weakening in the later seventeenth century, and the development of science was in part the result of this decline. The charters of the scientific societies and academies that sprang up throughout Europe during the century usually contained clauses stating that purely theological or political discussion would not be tolerated and that "ultimate" or "final" causes were no part of the group's concern. In the earliest history of the Royal Society of London, published in 1667, it is clear that scientific discussions offered a peculiar attraction to thoughtful men during a fanatical and bitter civil war like the Puritan Rebellion. Science was impartial politically and theologically; it did not stir men's tempers; it would not start religious wars; and above all, it was useful—it could benefit mankind. Scientific truth was an alternative to theological truth, more verifiable, more practical, more peaceful—or so at least some men argued. It was more than coincidence that modern science arose in a century that saw Europe's last violent struggles over religion.

One supremely sensitive philosopher felt the religious awe implicit in the new mechanistic picture of the universe. This was an obscure Dutch lens-grinder, Baruch Spinoza (1632–77). To Spinoza the new universe of mass, force, and motion, operating in strict obedience to inexorable laws, was God. There was no need, he thought, to consider God as above, behind, or beyond nature. God is not a "free cause" apart from natural law. He is not "Creator" or "Redeemer." He is natural law. "God never can decree, nor ever would have decreed, anything but what is; God did not exist before his decrees, and would not exist without them." Nature is "a fixed and immutable order," with "no particular goal in view." Man, like everything else, is part of this order. So Spinoza could write a book called *Ethics Demonstrated in the Geometrical Manner* and say, "I shall consider human activities and desires in exactly the same manner as though I were concerned with lines, planes, and solids." The wise man contemplates this natural order with serenity and delight: This was Spinoza's religion. Naturally such arguments were called atheistical, and Spinoza was considered a dangerous radical by his contemporaries.

For most men, however, the new science did not destroy the traditional religion. Rather it compelled them to consider the religious significance of a greatly expanded and complicated universe. The telescope was revealing the immense size of the cosmos, displacing the earth and even the sun from the center of the universe. The microscope was beginning to reveal the wonders of the world's minutiae—the capillaries, the bacteria, the cells, the foundations of life. No one felt the two infinites—the infinitely great and the infinitesimally small—so keenly or speculated so profoundly about their religious significance as Blaise Pascal (1623–62). "The whole visible world is only an imperceptible atom in the ample bosom of nature," he wrote. The universe, he said, is "an infinite sphere, the center of which is everywhere, the circumference nowhere." "The eternal silence of these infinite spaces frightens me." Yet to examine a mite—"with its minute body and parts incomparably more minute, limbs with their joints, veins in the limbs, blood in the veins, humors in the blood, drops in the humors, vapors in the drops"—is equally astonishing. "What is man in nature? A Nothing in comparison with the Infinite, an All in comparison with the Nothing, a mean between nothing and everything." And yet man is greater than anything in the universe because he comprehends all this, and because Christ died on the cross for him. In this way, Pascal related the new universe to Christianity. Other Christians were not so concerned about the new science, and other scientists were not so concerned to articulate a Christian interpretation.

The Culture of the Seventeenth Century

The Baroque Style in Art

The age of the scientific revolution was also the age of the "baroque" style in art—a style that sprang up in the later sixteenth century, reached its climax about the middle of the seventeenth, and came to its end around the middle of the eighteenth. The term *baroque* was invented by eighteenth-century critics who regarded seventeenth-century art as a grotesque corruption of Renaissance art. But modern critics consider the baroque a great achievement; one of them has called it "the high-water mark of European creative effort." As a style it is difficult to define because it reflected all the contrasts and contradictions of seventeenth-century culture in general: its religious ecstasy and its sensual worldliness, its credulity and its rationalism, its violence and its respect for order. Baroque painters and sculptors were influenced by all these contradictions. They portrayed voluptuous women in repose, military heroes in battle, and saints in ecstasy with equal skill and zest.

In general, the dominant notes of the baroque were a sense of tension and conflict and a liking for the grandiose and dramatic. The conflicts of man and the universe, of man and man, and of man within himself were conceived on a more heroic, and often a more tragic, scale than they had been in the Renaissance. Renaissance painters and writers had been interested in man himself. Baroque painters and writers were fascinated by man in his environment—typical men torn by conflicting passions, confronted by human and supernatural enemies, buffeted by elemental forces beyond their control.

There were instructive parallels between the thought-worlds of the artists and the thought-worlds of the scientists of the period. To Galileo and Newton, bodies or masses moving through space in response to conflicting forces such as gravitation and centrifugal force were the objects of study. To the great French dramatists of the age—Corneille, Racine, and Molière—the objects

of study were typical human beings acting and reacting in response to conflicting passions such as love and duty. Baroque painters were intrigued by space. Vermeer portrayed figures in a space that was bathed and suffused with light; Rembrandt spotlighted them in the midst of darkened space; and others pictured them floating through apparently infinite space (to baroque artists the supernatural was natural). The scientists' concern with "mass, force, and motion" seems closely related to the painters' and poets' concern with men caught in the tension between elemental forces in their whole natural or supernatural environment. The typical hero of baroque literature, it has been said, is Satan in Milton's *Paradise Lost*—swayed by colossal passions, moving through vast three-dimensional spaces, commanding many of the natural forces in the universe, but ultimately checked and frustrated by God.

The most typical product of baroque architecture was the royal palace: Versailles in France, Schönbrunn in Austria, or Blenheim, Marlborough's regal residence in England. The style was fundamentally Renaissance classical, but grander, more ornate, and more complicated. These palaces were designed to be the stage settings of worldly greatness. The vast reception rooms, the halls of mirrors, the great sweeping staircases, and the long vistas of the formal gardens were designed to enhance the drama of royalty and aristocracy. Even the churches of the period— such as Bernini's colonnades framing St. Peter's in Rome—suggested the majesty of God rather than his mercy.

But it was the operas that originated in Italy early in the seventeenth century that were the most original creation of the baroque. The union of dramatic action and a simpler musical style was a great popular success, and opera continued to grow as a distinct form of art down to the twentieth century. The grandiose and palatial stage settings (sometimes outdoors), the dramatic conflicts of the action, and the emotive power of the music exactly suited the taste of the period. Italian composers led the way until

Baroque ceiling of the Church of St. Ignatius, Rome, 1691–94.

the end of the seventeenth century: Monteverdi, the father of the opera, Frescobaldi, Scarlatti, and Vivaldi. But it was an Englishman, Henry Purcell, who wrote the most moving opera of the century, *Dido and Aeneas* (1687).

Seventeenth-Century Thought About Man

The seventeenth century developed conceptions about man that were based on Renaissance views but went beyond them. These conceptions may be conveniently summed up under three heads: individualism, relativism, and rationalism tempered by empiricism. We are speaking here of the thought of the most adventurous and best-educated minds, not of the many, whose thought-world was still largely "medieval."

Individualism

Radical thinkers of the seventeenth century took an increasingly individualistic view of man in society. The most intense Christian piety of the period—whether it was the Catholic devotion preached by St. François de Sales, the stern conscience of Puritans and Jansenists, or the warm inner conviction of German Pietists—was highly individualistic. The trend was equally evident in political theory. The fashion was to start with the individual and then to ask how society and the state could have originated and how they could be justified. Supporters of the divine right of kings were still numerous, but advanced thinkers were arguing that the state was based on a contract, either explicit or implicit, between the people and the ruler. Some, like Hobbes, argued that this contract, once made, was irrevocable. Others, like Locke, insisted that if the ruler broke the terms of the contract, which were usually thought to provide for good government, the people might depose him and set up a new ruler in his place. This idea of a "political contract" between ruler and people had some basis in the Old Testament and had been reinforced by feudal "contracts" between lords and vassals. It had been revived as a fighting idea by religious minorities when they were resisting the tyranny of rulers.

As time went on, the idea of a "social contract" took its place by the side of the "political contract." This was the idea that society itself was the result of a voluntary agreement among individuals who had been absolutely independent in their original "state of nature." The two ideas were mixed, somewhat confusedly, in Locke and later theorists. In both contracts, the individual with his rights and his natural independence logically came first; then came society or the state. In contrast, the Middle Ages had thought of society as an organism or a "body" in which individuals were mere "members." The more radical thinkers of the seventeenth century were coming to think of society as an artificial organization of independent individuals based on voluntary agreement or consent.

Relativism

The greatest thinkers of the Middle Ages were sure that the people of Christendom were God's chosen people and that the truth had been revealed once and for all to Christians. During the sixteenth and seventeenth centuries humanism, the voyages of discovery, and the development of science greatly weakened this assurance.

Humanism had shaken this assurance by revealing Greco-Roman civilization in clearer historical perspective. Here—in a society long since dead, but still alive in its literature, its art, and its historical records—was an alternative to the medieval Christian view of life. Modern historical studies—history, archeology, philology— were born during the Renaissance and were carried on with even greater skill during the seventeenth century. This steady development of the "historical sciences," as they would be called today, slowly impressed upon thoughtful Europeans that there had been other societies in other times with ideas and institutions quite different from those of the present. Thus the idea of relativism in time was born and grew.

The idea of relativism in space resulted from the geographical discoveries, as we have seen. The discovery in America of societies far less civilized than Europe and of societies in Asia more civilized in many respects than Europe had the

effect of shaking European provincialism. Perhaps the "noble savages" of the New World were happier than the more cultured but more corrupt Christians of Europe. Perhaps Christians had something to learn from Persian sages and Chinese philosophers. So at least increasing numbers of Europeans began to think in the seventeenth and eighteenth centuries.

As the temporal and geographical horizons of the European imagination widened, the vision of man's place in nature was complicated by scientific discovery, as we have seen in considering Bruno and Pascal. European Christians were not unique in time and space, as they had once thought, nor, perhaps, was man himself unique.

The intellectual results of historical study, geographical exploration, and scientific discovery are best seen in the work of Pierre Bayle (1647–1706), the great scholarly skeptic of the later seventeenth century. Bayle, originally a Huguenot, was briefly converted to Catholicism, but he renounced all orthodox belief when his brother died in a dungeon during an attempted forced conversion. He took up residence in the relatively tolerant Dutch Netherlands and devoted the latter part of his life to a crusade against superstition, religious intolerance, and dogmatism in general. In 1697 he published a great rambling book, a *Historical and Critical Dictionary,* which had enormous influence on eighteenth-century thinkers. Into this book he poured all the relativism and skepticism that he had acquired through his extensive historical study, his amateur knowledge of science (he was an admirer of Descartes), and his personal experience. He argued that atheists might be good citizens and that there was no necessary connection between a man's religious beliefs and the way he behaved. He insisted that there is nothing more abominable than to make conversions by force. He ridiculed the idea that stars and planets could influence human life and mercilessly attacked superstition on every front. He distrusted all historical authorities, including the writers of the Old Testament, unless he was sure that their account of events was inherently credible. His test of truth was reason—and few if any accounts of miracles met this test. All in all,

Bayle was the most thoroughgoing skeptic and the most destructive critic of his generation.

Rationalism and Empiricism

The leading thinkers of the seventeenth century were predominantly rationalistic. Reason was the faculty that distinguished man from the beast, and the triumphs of seventeenth century science proved that reason could be trusted. And so the conclusion was drawn that the man of reason could know and understand the world into which he was born if he made the right use of his mind.

This optimistic attitude was reflected in the growing belief in "natural law." The idea of a law of nature that served as a standard of moral behavior for all men at all times in all places originated with the Stoics and was developed by the medieval Schoolmen. During the Renaissance and the Reformation this idea went into eclipse, but the discovery of "laws of nature" like Kepler's laws of planetary motion helped to revive it in the seventeenth century. Cicero had given the idea classic formulation: "There is in fact a true law—namely, right reason—which is in accordance with nature, applies to all men, and is unchangeable and eternal. By its commands this law summons men to the performance of their duties; by its prohibitions it restrains them from doing wrong." This law was implanted in the minds of men by God himself. Its content was hazy, but it was understood to include respect for life and property, good faith and fair dealing, giving each man his due. These principles could always be discovered by reason, just as reason could discover the proof of a geometrical proposition. Hugo Grotius, in his book *On the Law of War and Peace* (1625), turned to this law of nature in an attempt to find some basis for a "law of nations" which would transcend the religious fanaticisms of the Thirty Years' War.

The best example of this kind of thinking, however, is John Locke's faith that there are certain "natural rights" vested in every individual in the "state of nature," notably life, liberty, and property. From this it follows logically, as conclusion from axiom, that men form societies and set up governments mainly to preserve these rights. Descartes had hoped to be able to deduce the universe from a few central mathematical principles; Locke in his *Second Treatise of Government* assumed that he could deduce society and government from a few simple axioms about man and natural law.

This enthusiastic rationalism in the study of man and society was qualified by an undercurrent of empiricism, of respect for sense-experience. Here again Locke led the way in his *Essay Concerning the Human Understanding.* Many of its readers thought that it did for the study of man what Newton had done for the study of nature. Locke argued that all our ideas come from experience. The mind at birth is a *tabula rasa,* a clean slate, on which our sense-experiences gradually imprint conceptions. There are no "innate ideas," and no self-evident axioms (as Descartes has assumed). The mind and its ideas can be explained only by the outside forces that act upon it.

This was the purest empiricism. Locke hoped that it would provide a weapon for getting rid of all the superstitions and prejudices that cluttered men's minds, but it could do even more than he anticipated. Logically, Locke's theory of the mind did away with original sin (which was held to be born into all men), with revelation (which did not come through the senses), with mathematical axioms, and with all "natural rights" (which were obviously innate and not based on experience). And so the rationalism of Locke's theory of society clashed with the empiricism of his theory of the mind—as the mathematical tendency clashed with the fact-finding tendency in seventeenth-century study of man in general. The eighteenth century was to inherit both: a strong faith in reason and natural law, together with a firm confidence in sense-experience. Out of these two a new blend was to come in the "Enlightenment."

The Enlightenment

The task which the leading thinkers of the eighteenth century set themselves was to popularize the methods and principles of seventeenth-century natural science and to apply these methods and principles to God, man, and society. Scientific discovery continued, but the work that attracted the most brilliant writers of the age was that of applying the new scientific method of analysis to long-festering human ills—economic, social, political, and ecclesiastical. Their concern was not so much to discover new truth about nature as to use the methods of natural science to reform society.

The eighteenth century's own name for this movement was the "Enlightenment." This term suggested the dawn of an age of light after a long night of darkness—the darkness of ignorance, superstition, intolerance, and slavery to the past. The new light was the light of science, as the poet Alexander Pope suggested:

> Nature and nature's laws lay hid in night;
> God said, "Let Newton be," and all was light.

Although there were "enlightened" writers and readers in every country of Europe from Russia to Spain and from England to Italy, the movement was centered in France, and more particularly in Paris. There were good reasons for this. After the death of Louis XIV (1715)

Voltaire on Superstition

Almost everything that goes beyond the adoration of a Supreme Being and submission of the heart to his orders is superstition. One of the most dangerous is to believe that certain ceremonies entail the forgiveness of crimes. Do you believe that God will forget a murder you have committed if you bathe in a certain river, sacrifice a black sheep, or if someone says certain words over you? . . . Do better, miserable humans; have neither murders nor sacrifices of black sheep. . . .

Notice that the most superstitious ages have always been those of the most horrible crimes. . . . The superstitious man is ruled by fanatics and he becomes one himself. On the whole, the less superstition, the less fanaticism, and the less fanaticism, the fewer miseries.

Translated from Voltaire, *Dictionnaire philosophique* (Reproduction of edition of 1776. Paris: Editions de Cluny, n.d.), III, pp. 218–25.

the French government became steadily more inept and ineffective, while the social tension between the privileged aristocracy and the less privileged but powerful wealthy middle class became more acute. Many leaders of the Enlightenment were of the middle class, and their writings often reflected middle-class interests. These men of letters were angered by bureaucratic stupidity and aristocratic arrogance; they wanted to get rid of privilege and obscurantism. They learned to write with clarity and wit so that they influenced not only their fellow-bourgeois but many members of the nobility as well. Government censorship could stop only the most blatant attacks; it was quite incapable of checking the criticism and satire that poured from the presses, particularly in the second half of the century.

For one interested in ideas, Paris was the most exciting place in Europe during the eighteenth century. Here the intellectuals were in close touch with one another, excited by the feeling that they were helping to guide a revolution of ideas without precedent in European history, and bound together in a crusade to put an end to all the barbarities and absurdities of the old order. Such an intellectual conspiracy could develop only in Paris, capital of the largest and most civilized state in Europe. Other countries were too small, too backward, or, in the case of England, too complacent to become major centers of "enlightened" thought and agitation.

Voltaire

As a movement the Enlightenment is often dated from Voltaire's visit to England (1726–29). Voltaire (1694–1778) (his real name was François Marie Arouet) became the central figure and moving spirit of the Enlightenment, in part at least as a result of this trip. He already had reason to dislike the old regime in France, having been imprisoned for a short time in the Bastille. In England he read Newton and Locke, and he sensed the relative freedom of English society compared with his own. After his return to France he published his *Philosophical Letters on the English* (1733), in which he passed on to his readers Newton's main principles in watered-down form, as well as Locke's theories of human nature and political freedom. He skillfully contrasted the rationality of Newton's method and the reasonableness of the English way of life with the more unreasonable aspects of church, state, and society in France.

These letters set the tone of "enlightened" propaganda in France for the next half-century. They were "philosophical"—that is to say, they reflected on the facts of life to discover their meaning and they searched constantly for general principles that might be useful to mankind in general. And so the men of the Enlightenment called themselves *philosophes,* observers of the human scene with breadth of view and a sense of the practical. They were popularizers in the best sense of the word, crusaders for the application of the best intellectual tools of the century to the most vexatious social problems of their own day. Voltaire was the greatest of them—the most prolific, the wittiest, the most readable, and perhaps the angriest. His prime targets were religious intolerance, religious bigotry, and superstition. The close union in France of religious persecution and theological obscurantism with a capricious monarchical despotism exasperated him.

"Ecrasez l'infâme" (crush the infamous thing), he cried, in letters, pamphlets, stories, and satires. In an essay on "religion" he described a vision he had had of a desert covered with piles of bones, the bones of "Christians slaughtered by each other in metaphysical quarrels." He went on to report a "philosophical" conversation with the shades of Socrates and Jesus, who both deplored the spectacle he had just seen. And he attacked intolerance in his own day as vigorously as the barbarism of the past.

When Voltaire died in 1778, he was the literary dictator of Europe, the first writer to have made a fortune from the sale of his own writings. He was laid to rest in Paris in a ceremony worthy of a king.

Montesquieu

The second leading figure of the Enlightenment, Montesquieu (1689–1755), tried to institute a "social science" by applying the methods of the natural sciences to the study of society.

In *The Spirit of the Laws* (1748) he suggested that forms of government were related to climate and other environmental factors, and he tried to discover what form of government best fitted a given set of environmental conditions. The book was not "scientific" by later standards, but it was the first serious attempt to relate a civilization to its environment. (Voltaire later elaborated the concept in his *History of Civilization,* 1754.) Montesquieu, like Voltaire, was impressed by Locke's theories about the English constitution. As a French nobleman he wished to limit the excesses of royal absolutism. He concluded that the ideal political form was a separation and balance of powers within government. This conclusion was to have great influence on the authors of the American Constitution.

Diderot and the Encyclopedia

The third major figure of the Enlightenment was Denis Diderot (1713–84), co-editor of a huge *Encyclopedia* designed to sum up human knowledge and provide a kind of handbook of enlightened philosophy for the educated world. Diderot was an enthusiast for science and technology, full of confidence in man and his abilities, a kind of prophet of a this-worldly religion of man. His interests were reflected in the titles and content of the *Encyclopedia,* which appeared in thirty-five volumes over the course of thirty years (1751–80). Much of the most trenchant writing of Diderot, Voltaire, and other *philosophes* was done in articles for the *Encyclopedia.* The book succeeded in becoming a bible of the "enlightened" everywhere. Through it ran pride in man's accomplishments, contempt for his follies, and confidence in his future.

Leading Ideas of the Enlightenment

There were many other leaders of the Enlightenment, but, rather than list names, it is more fruitful to outline the main ideas on which these people agreed and to sketch the relation of these ideas to religion and to social thought. These ruling ideas may be summed up in five words, each of which bore a heavy freight of meaning in the eighteenth century: reason, nature, happiness, progress, and liberty.

The Encyclopedia on "Philosopher"

Reason is to the philosopher what grace is to the Christian.

Grace causes the Christian to act, reason the philosopher.

Other men are carried away by their passions, their actions not being preceded by reflection: these are the men who walk in darkness. On the other hand, the philosopher, even in his passions, acts only after reflection; he walks in the dark, but by a torch.

The philosopher forms his principles from an infinity of particular observations. Most people adopt principles without thinking of the observations that have produced them: they believe that maxims exist, so to speak, by themselves. But the philosopher takes maxims from their source; he examines their origin; he knows their proper value, and he makes use of them only in so far as they suit him.

Truth is not for the philosopher a mistress who corrupts his imagination and whom he believes is to be found everywhere; he contents himself with being able to unravel it where he can perceive it. He does not confound it with probability; he takes for true what is true, for false what is false, for doubtful what is doubtful, and for probable what is only probable. He does more, and here you have a great perfection of the philosopher: when he has no reason by which to judge, he knows how to live in suspension of judgment.

From Denis Diderot, *Encyclopedia*, 1778, trans. by F. L. Baumer, in *Main Currents in Western Thought* (New York: Knopf, 1952), p. 374.

The eighteenth century believed as passionately in reason as the seventeenth, but with a difference. Voltaire's "reason" relied more on experience and less on mathematics than Descartes'. It was a weapon of skeptical inquiry based on observed facts rather than an instrument of deduction from axioms. To the Enlightenment, reason was the alternative to superstition and prejudice; it was the only sure guide to the principles that governed man and nature. Man's reason could discover the fundamental rationality of the universe, but it could also make human society more sensible. The *philosophes,* as shown by their writing for the *Encyclopedia,* were less interested in "pure science" than in technology, less concerned with system-building than with practical improvements. Reason was now a pragmatic instrument, applicable not only to astronomy and physics but to agriculture, government, and social relations.

"Nature" was one of the favorite words of the Enlightenment. It was not always clear just what the *philosophes* meant by it, but it was clear enough that to nearly all of them "nature" or "the natural" were the proper standards for measuring God and man. If a thing was according to "nature," it was reasonable and therefore good. Voltaire and his contemporaries brought the idea of natural law to the peak of its prestige and the beginning of its decline. One of them devised this definition of natural law:

> The regular and constant order of facts by which God rules the universe; the order which his wisdom presents to the sense and reason of men, to serve them as an equal and common rule of conduct, and to guide them, without distinction of race or sect, towards perfection and happiness.

There is order and law, then, throughout the universe—laws of economics, of politics, of morality, as well as of physics and astronomy. These laws can be discovered by reason. Men may ignore or defy them but they do so at their peril. To the enlightened the way to happiness lay in conformity to nature and nature's laws. The man who broke nature's laws was looked on by the enlightened of the eighteenth century somewhat as the heretic who broke God's laws was looked on by the clergy in the Middle Ages, as a rebel against the order of the universe.

The end in view now was happiness, not salvation—happiness here in this world, not joy in the next. The Enlightenment was thoroughly secular in its thinking. When Jefferson included "the pursuit of happiness" along with life and liberty as an inalienable human right, he was expressing the general agreement of the enlightened. The tendency of medieval Christianity to ignore misery in this life because it would be compensated for in the next angered the *philo-*

sophes, who insisted that Christian ideals, if they were worth anything at all, must be realized here and now. Voltaire and his fellows were humanitarians. They abominated torture and cruelty, slavery and the callous treatment of the insane. An Italian, Beccaria, was the first to point out that savage penalties do not stop crime and to demand more rational treatment of criminals. The *philosophes* were also cosmopolitan and even pacifist in temper. Some of the bitterest passages ever written about the insanity of war and the absurdity of blind patriotism were penned by Voltaire. The "happiness" which he and others talked about was often materialistic. But it corresponded closely with Christ's injunction to feed the hungry, clothe the naked, and visit the sick and imprisoned. To the enlightened this was far more important than saving anything so vague as one's own soul.

The *philosophes* were the first sizable group of educated Europeans to believe in progress. They took the older Christian idea of the spiritual progression of mankind from Creation through the Incarnation to the Last Judgment and secularized it. The progress of civilization, they believed, was now out of God's hands and in man's own. Once man had found the clue to discovering and using nature's laws in modern science and technology, progress was sure, inevitable, and swift. Both man and society were perfectible. Time was on man's side, they thought, not against him or even indifferent to him.

This was a major revolution in western thought. The Middle Ages could not have conceived of purely secular progress unrelated to God. Men of the Renaissance still felt themselves inferior to the heroic Greeks and Romans. But in a literary battle between "ancients" and "moderns" which began in 1687 the idea appeared that the "moderns" were as good as, and probably better than, the "ancients." By 1750 a French *philosophe* and economist, Turgot, suggested that the essential element in history was man's slow struggle upward to his crucial discovery of the scientific method. In 1794 Condorcet, a mathematician under sentence of death during the French Revolution, wrote a *Sketch for a Historical Picture of the Progress of the Human Mind,* which summed up all the optimism of his century. He saw "the strongest reasons for believing that nature has set no limit to the realization of our hopes" and foresaw "the abolition of inequality between nations, the progress of equality within nations, and the true perfection of mankind." Progress, he concluded, was now "independent of any power that might wish to halt it" and "will never be reversed." The scientific method cannot be lost, scientific knowledge of natural law will accumulate, and so progress can never cease. It was an intoxicating vision, a vision shared by the vast majority of the enlightened.

All the French *philosophes* were concerned about liberty. They were acutely aware of the limitations on liberty that prevailed inside France: restrictions on freedom of speech, freedom of religion, freedom of trade, freedom to choose a job, and freedom from arbitrary arrest. Looking at England through slightly rose-

Key Words in History

If we would discover the little backstairs door that for any age serves as the secret entranceway to knowledge, we will do well to look for certain unobtrusive words with uncertain meanings that are permitted to slip off the tongue or the pen without fear and without research; words which, having from constant repetition lost their metaphorical significance, are unconsciously mistaken for objective realities. In the thirteenth century the key words would no doubt be *God, sin, grace, salvation, heaven,* and the like; in the nineteenth century, *matter, fact, matter-of-fact, evolution, progress;* in the twentieth century, *relativity, process, adjustment, function, complex.* In the eighteenth century the words without which no enlightened person could reach a restful conclusion were *nature, natural law, first cause, reason, sentiment, humanity, perfectibility.* In each age these magic words have their entrances and their exits. And how unobtrusively they come in and go out! We should scarcely be aware either of their approach or their departure, except for a slight feeling of discomfort, a shy self-consciousness in the use of them.

From Carl L. Becker, *The Heavenly City of the Eighteenth-Century Philosophers* (New Haven: Yale U. Press, 1932), p. 47.

colored glasses, they envied Englishmen their economic, political, and religious liberty. Their concern about liberty was potentially the most explosive part of their thinking, but almost none of them felt that violence was necessary. Their belief in liberty was tied to their belief in reason. Reason would soon reveal the true natural laws governing everything from trade and government to religion. The artificiality of French society, French government, and French religious practices would become evident, and a benevolent despotism, enlightened by this knowledge, would set things right. Or so at least Voltaire and the majority of the Encyclopedists believed.

The Enlightenment and Religion

These ideas inevitably affected the religious thought of Europe. The fashionable belief among educated persons in the eighteenth century came to be Deism, the belief in a God who is Creator but not Redeemer. Like a watchmaker who designs and constructs a complicated piece of machinery to keep perfect time, so God created the universe and started it going and then stepped aside to let it run according to its natural laws. God does not concern Himself with redeeming men or society. The essence of religion is awe and reverence before the rationality and perfection of the universe—a feeling reflected in the hymns of Isaac Watts, which are still sung in many Protestant churches. To a Deist (Voltaire was a good example) all talk of revelation or miracle, all belief in the special intervention of God in the natural order, was false. All dogma and ritual was superstition, since man needed only his reason to understand God. The heart of natural religion was the morality common to all mankind. "Light is uniform for the star Sirius," Voltaire wrote, "and for us moral philosophy must be uniform." Obviously, Deism tended to undermine orthodox Christianity and to substitute for it a rational belief in God as First Cause and natural law as man's moral guide. A few of the French *philosophes* went further and pushed beyond Deism to atheism. Baron d'Holbach, for example, argued that there is nothing but matter in the universe, that man himself is a conglomeration of atoms, and that

everything that happens is determined by natural law. But in the end many Protestants were able to find a compromise between Christian beliefs and the Enlightenment's rationalism, humanitarianism, and tolerance. The result in the next century was Protestant Liberalism.

Others reacted against Deism in the direction of more intense piety. To the enlightened, religious fervor of any sort savored of the fanaticism that had caused the wars of religion, and so all enthusiasm was frowned on. But Deism could be understood only by the educated, and its cold rationality had no appeal to emotional natures. Hence the wide popularity of two warmly emotional Protestant movements, Pietism in Germany and Methodism in England and America. Both emphasized the importance of inner religious experience, of individual "conversion." Pietism was a second and milder Protestant Reformation, directed this time not against the pope but against both the dogmatically orthodox and those who were inclined to Deism in Germany. Individualistic, tolerant, and unconcerned about creeds or ceremonies, the Pietists attracted followers among both Catholics and Protestants.

John Wesley (1703–91) was the leader of a somewhat parallel revival of a warm, personal Christian piety in England in the years following his conversion in 1738. Finding his efforts resisted by the respectable Anglican clergy, he took his message directly to the people, addressing huge congregations outdoors or in remote chapels, teaching them to sing their way to heaven with the hymns of his brother Charles, and sending out streams of pamphlets from his printing presses to the congregations he had established. In the end Wesley was forced to establish a new denomination outside the Anglican Church—the Methodist (originally a term of derision directed at the "methodical" piety of Wesley's followers). Methodism touched thousands upon thousands of Englishmen at home and in the colonies who cared nothing for the arid intellectualism of many of the Anglican clergy in the eighteenth century. More than one historian has suggested that it was Methodism that kept the English lower classes from turning to revolutionary violence during the first impact of the Industrial Revolution.

Social and Political Thought

The *philosophes* were interested in social and political problems, but they were reformers not revolutionists. Their formula for reform was simple: Discover by reason and experience the natural laws that should operate in any given situation, clear away all artificial obstacles to their operation, and the result will be progress toward happiness and freedom. The first "economists" in the modern sense used this formula to launch an attack on mercantilism. In 1758 François Quesnay published his *Economic Survey,* which argued for the existence of natural economic laws that must be allowed to operate freely. In 1776 the Scot Adam Smith published his *Wealth of Nations,* which argued in parallel fashion that all nations would be wealthier if they removed restrictions on trade and let the the natural law of supply and demand govern the exchange of commodities. Quesnay was primarily interested in agriculture and Smith in commerce, but both came to the same conclusion: that economic laws, like other natural laws, should be respected, that interference with these laws is dangerous, and that the greatest happiness and freedom come from allowing these laws to operate freely.

The same line of reasoning in political theory led to the theory of enlightened despotism. The *philosophes* hoped that divine-right monarchy would become benevolent monarchy, that monarchs would gradually become "enlightened" (or perhaps engage enlightened *philosophes* as advisers) and so govern their people according to natural law rather than according to their own caprice. To Voltaire and most of his fellows, government should be for the people but not necessarily by the people. A smaller group believed that reason pointed in the direction of a constitutional monarchy like the English, a government based on natural rights and contract, with a separation of powers as a further guarantee of political liberty. Finally, to enlightened despotism and constitutional government there was added a third theory, the theory of democracy, still too radical to be of much immediate in-

fluence but of enormous importance for the future. This was the theory obscurely but excitingly preached in *The Social Contract* (1762) by Jean Jacques Rousseau (1712–78).

Rousseau

Rousseau was a native of Geneva who turned up in Paris after a troubled and wandering youth, came to know Diderot and others of the *philosophes,* and for a time tried to become one of them. He was never easy in their company, however. He trusted reason, but he relied even more on emotion. He trusted nature, but to him nature was the unspoiled simplicity of pre-civilized man, "the noble savage." In a kind of conversion which he experienced in 1749, he became convinced that mankind had lost more than it had gained by cultivating the arts and sciences, and so he surrendered his faith in progress. He grew more and more irritated by the artificiality of Paris society and finally broke with his former friends. Voltaire thought him mad, and Rousseau was haunted in his miserable later years by the illusion that he was being persecuted by everyone.

Rousseau was the great critic of the Enlightenment. By temperament he was a shy and sensitive misfit who vainly wanted "to belong." Deep down he felt himself to be good, but he felt too that he had been corrupted and humiliated by an artificial society to which he did not and could not belong. To what kind of society or state could he give himself, then? Only to a society in which there were no hereditary rulers, no privileged aristocracy, no one with any right to lord it over others, none but those who had freely consented to become members of the society and had given up to the group all their individual rights. Perhaps Rousseau had an idealized Geneva in mind as he wrote *The Social Contract*—a community in which all the citizens knew and trusted each other, in which the minority accepted the majority's view with good grace because both felt themselves part of the same community. At any rate, he developed a theory of liberty as willing obedience to laws that the individual himself had helped to make as an active and loyal citizen, even though he

Rousseau on the Social Contract

The problem is to find a form of association . . . in which each, while uniting himself with all, may still obey himself alone, and remain as free as before. This is the fundamental problem of which the Social Contract provides the solution: . . . the total alienation of each associate, together with all his rights, to the whole community. . . . Each man, in giving himself to all, gives himself to nobody. . . . Each of us puts his person and all his power in common under the supreme direction of the general will, and, in our corporate capacity, we receive each member as an indivisible part of the whole. . . . In order that the social compact may not be an empty formula, it tacitly includes the undertaking, which alone can give force to the rest, that whoever refuses to obey the general will shall be compelled to do so by the whole body. This means nothing less than that he will be forced to be free.

From Jean Jacques Rousseau, *The Social Contract* (New York and London: Everyman, 1913), book I, Chs. 6, 7, pp. 14–18.

might have been in the minority on any given issue. Locke and Montesquieu had thought that the way to obtain political liberty was to guarantee individual rights and to separate the organs of government so that no one of them could gain unrestricted control. Rousseau thought he would never feel free until he could find a community to which he could give up everything, on condition that all others did the same. In such a community there would be no division between rulers and ruled; the people would rule themselves. What magistrates there were would be mere servants of the community who could be instantly removed if they failed to carry out the people's will. If the people really governed themselves there should be no checks and balances, no separation of powers, no protection of rights.

Rousseau was picturing democracy in its essence: a tight-knit community of loyal and active citizens, unhampered by any checks on their collective will because they unreservedly accepted this general will as their own. His book was highly abstract and difficult to understand.

But when revolution actually flared up in France after his death, *The Social Contract* came into its own. It was not a work of the Enlightenment; its full force could be felt only in the new age of democratic revolution, nationalism, and Romanticism.

So the two centuries that saw the Scientific Revolution and the Enlightenment might well be called the most revolutionary centuries in western intellectual history. The true watershed between what we call "medieval" and "modern" thought about God, man, and nature runs somewhere through these two centuries. The world of Luther and Loyola, of Charles V and Philip II, was still organically related to the Middle Ages. The world of Newton and Locke, of Voltaire and Rousseau, was unmistakably the father of our own.

Arts and Letters
in the Eighteenth Century

The pervasive faith in the rationality, intelligibility, and order of the universe displayed by the scientists and philosophers of the age was reflected in the art and literature of the later seventeenth and early eighteenth centuries. Rationalism blended easily with classicism. The regularity and harmony of Newton's universe seemed to accord with the balance and proportion that Greek architects had admired as artistic ideals and with the rationality and restraint that the leading Greek and Roman writers had held up as literary ideals. The dictators of literary and artistic taste at the close of the seventeenth century were classicists, and when *philosophes* like Voltaire wrote dramas they accepted classical standards as unquestioningly as Corneille and Racine. Architects accepted classical rules of balance and unity with equal zeal in the "Georgian" buildings of England and the beautifully proportioned Place de la Concorde in Paris. Enthusiasm for classical antiquity reached its post-Renaissance climax in 1748 when the remains of the Roman city of Pompeii were discovered in startlingly well-preserved condition under the lava of Mt. Vesuvius.

An Age of Prose

The age of reason was an age of prose. Essays, satirical tales, novels, letters, and histories were the characteristic literary forms of the eighteenth century. Authors bent their energies to description and narrative rather than to suggestion and imagination. The essays of Addison and Steele, which began to appear in 1709, sketched a delightful picture of English rural society, while Jonathan Swift's *Gulliver's Travels* (1726) and Voltaire's *Candide* (1759) were more biting and satirical commentaries on human society. As the century progressed, the novel emerged as the favorite form of literary expression; the most mature example was Henry Fielding's *Tom Jones* (1749). Besides fiction, men read philosophy, economics, and history—of which Edward Gib-

bon's majestic *History of the Decline and Fall of the Roman Empire* (1788) was the most enduring example. Everything that could be done in prose—argument, satire, realistic description, historical narrative—was tried and done well by some French or British writer.

The elegance and aristocratic flavor of eighteenth century society can be seen in its painting, and especially in the portraits which were the most characteristic form of the art. The delicate-featured and exquisitely groomed women who look coolly down on the observer and the worldly, sometimes arrogant faces of their husbands under their powdered wigs suggest the artificiality of their society and sometimes the hardness of their characters. Furniture, table ware, and the great town and country

Canvassing for Votes, an English election campaign of the 18th century. Engraving by William Hogarth.

houses of wealthy merchants and nobles reflect the same elegance and aristocratic spirit.

Not all the books, the arts, and the crafts were meant for the enjoyment of the aristocracy, however. The eighteenth century saw the appearance of the first newspapers, written for a wide audience of educated readers. Willian Hogarth (1697–1764) made engravings of his realistic satirical sketches of English lower-class society and sold them by the thousands. Above all, the novelists, the dramatists, and the musicians began to appeal to a middle-class audience that went far beyond the limits of the aristocracy. After the 1770's the plays and operas in Paris were apt to have a keen, satirical edge and to be directed at bourgeois listeners. The heroes and heroines of the novels were more often of middle-class origins than either upper- or lower-class. Music began to move from the aristocratic salon into the public auditorium.

Music

The greatest cultural achievement of the eighteenth century was its music. The musical world of the early eighteenth century was dominated by two great Germans: Johann Sebastian Bach (1685–1750) and George Frederick Handel (1685–1759) (who spent most of his life in England). Together they realized all the dramatic and emotive possibilities of the baroque style, Handel in his oratorios for chorus and instruments, Bach in his richly varied works for keyboard instruments, chamber groups, orchestras, and choruses. In the latter part of the century the orchestra, which had originated in the seventeenth century, was expanded and strengthened, the pianoforte invented, and music brought more and more into touch with a wider public. Joseph Haydn (1732–1809), who wrote for both chamber groups and orchestras, developed the musical forms known as sonatas and symphonies. The other outstanding musical personality of the latter half of the century, Wolfgang Amadeus Mozart (1756–91), was possibly the most gifted musician who ever lived. An infant prodigy, he lived only thirty-five years and died in poverty, but within this short space of time he produced

string quartets, concertos, symphonies, and operas that were masterpieces of invention and form.

The Beginnings of Romanticism

Beneath the dominant tendency to respect rational structure and classical balance, however, there were countercurrents of revolts. We have already seen some evidence of these currents in Pietism and Methodism, and in Rousseau's distrust of an exclusive reliance on reason. More clearly than Rousseau, the Scottish philosopher David Hume (1711–76) criticized reason as a method of knowing truth and defended the validity in human experience of feeling, conscience, and habit. French and English novelists developed sentimentalism to a fine art, putting their heroines through heart-rending misfortune and mistreatment and trying at every turn to arouse the reader's anger, pity, love, or terror. The most influential was Samuel Richardson's 2,000-page tear-jerker, *Clarissa Harlowe* (1748), which influenced Rousseau in writing his *Nouvelle Héloïse* (1761). The strange, the unusual, the offbeat, and the fantastic began to come into fashion. Gothic architecture and literature began to be appreciated once more, and a collection of poems (1762) ostensibly by a medieval poet named Ossian was very popular, though it turned out to be a forgery.

In Germany, which never came totally under the sway of the French Enlightenment, a "Storm and Stress" movement in literature emphasized the great elemental emotions and denied the supremacy of reason. Johann Gottfried von Herder (1744–1803) worked out a philosophy of history that emphasized the uniqueness and peculiarity of each nation or race, the individuality of its genius, and the falsity of any view that denied this uniqueness in the name of universal reason. Johann Wolfgang von Goethe (1749–1832) at the start of his long literary career published *The Sorrows of Young Werther* (1774), a morbid tale ending in a suicide, which appealed to lovers of sentiment and sensibility. The greatest philosopher of the age, Immanuel Kant (1724–1804), a man who never traveled more than a few miles from Königsberg, his native city in East Prussia, launched a powerful attack on the rationalism of his age as too narrow and too dogmatic. Starting from David Hume's criticism of reason, Kant distinguished carefully between speculative (or scientific) reason and practical (or moral) reason in his very difficult book, *Critique of Pure Reason* (1781). The effect of his work was to enable Christians and idealists to make a new case for religion and morality based on the fact of man's conscience.

Taken together, these various tendencies heralded the beginnings of what was to be called Romanticism. The "Age of Reason" thus contained within itself the seeds of an age that would rely for its artistic, philosophical, and even social insight on emotion and conscience rather than on reason.

Suggestions for Further Reading

1. General

J. H. Randall, *The Making of the Modern Mind* (1926, 1940), is the most successful one-volume survey of the course of western thought, by a philosopher with a sense for historical context. To Randall, "the modern mind" is essentially the scientific mind. C. Brinton, *Ideas and Men* (1950)—the material since the Renaissance has been published as *The Shaping of the Modern Mind** (1953)—is a more informally written and engaging narrative by a historian. Both books are particularly good on the seventeenth and eighteenth centuries. P. Smith, *A History of Modern Culture, 1543–1776,** 2 vols. (1930–34), is full of fascinating material on everything from political theory and science to magic and witchcraft, but does little to develop a synthesis. G. R. Sabine, *A History of Political Theory* (1938), is the most penetrating one-volume survey, particularly full on English political thought in the seventeenth century and French in the eighteenth. A. O. Lovejoy, *The Great Chain of Being** (1936), is a classic account of the underlying western conception of the universe as a hierarchical structure of being, from the Greeks to the nineteenth century.

2. The Scientific Revolution

E. A. Burtt, *The Metaphysical Foundations of Modern Physical Science** (1924, 1955), and A. N. Whitehead, *Science and the Modern World** (1925, 1948), are famous philosophical inquiries into the origins of modern science, not easy reading, but rewarding to the serious student. A. R. Hall, *The Scientific Revolution** (1954), is the best modern account, well informed and critical. H. Butterfield, *The Origins of Modern Science, 1300–1800** (1949), is a more readable discussion of the subject for the lay reader written by a general historian. Alexandre Koyré writes absorbingly about the cosmological implications of the "revolution" in *From the Closed World to the Infinite Universe** (1957). C. C. Gillispie, *The Edge of Objectivity** (1960), is a brilliantly written essay on the growth of objectivity in the study of nature from Galileo to Einstein. R. G. Collingwood traces the chief western conceptions of the natural order from the Greeks to the present in *The Idea of Nature** (1945). C. J. Singer, *From Magic to Science** (1928), is still valuable for its interpretation of the origins of modern science. On the social background of scientific development, three books are particularly valuable: M. Ornstein, *The Role of Scientific Societies in the Seventeenth Century* (1928); D. Stimson, *Scientists and Amateurs: A History of*

---

* Available in paperback edition.

the Royal Society (1948); and G. N. Clark, *Science and Social Welfare in the Age of Newton* (1937). There are biographies and special studies, too numerous to list here, of every scientist mentioned in the text. But two studies of a famous case are worth noting: G. de Santillana, *The Crime of Galileo** (1955), and F. S. Taylor, *Galileo and the Freedom of Thought* (1938). The effect of scientific discovery on literature is the theme of M. Nicolson, *Science and Imagination** (1956).

3. Culture of the Seventeenth and Eighteenth Centuries

There is no full and reliable discussion in English on the baroque style in art, the basic studies being in German. The best introductions are in C. J. Friedrich, *The Age of the Baroque** (1952), and Chapter 6 of H. Leichtentritt, *Music, History, and Ideas* (1938). Friedrich's book, together with succeeding volumes in the *Rise of Modern Europe* series (see listings for Chapters 20 and 22), contain valuable accounts of literary and artistic movements in the two centuries. The latter third of G. N. Clark, *The Seventeenth Century* (1931), is devoted to art, literature, and philosophy. B. Willey's two volumes, *The Seventeenth Century Background** (1934) and *The Eighteenth Century Background** (1940), sketch a broad background for the study of English literature in the period. F. Fosca, *The Eighteenth Century* (1953), is probably the best introduction to the painting of the age. In addition to Leichtentritt (above), M. F. Bukofzer, *Music in the Baroque Era* (1947), is particularly interesting. There is no satisfactory general account of religious developments, but A. C. McGiffert, *Protestant Thought Before Kant* (1911), is a brief reliable account, and the various works of E. Troeltsch mentioned for Chapter 17 are always thought-provoking. M. J. Bradshaw, *The Philosophical Foundations of Faith* (1941), is illuminating on the religious attitudes of prominent seventeenth-century figures like Descartes. M. L. Edwards, *John Wesley and the Eighteenth Century* (1933), is one of many books on Methodism.

4. Contemporary Literature

The best way, as always, to gain a first-hand knowledge of the thought and feeling of the period is through a study of some of the paintings, the buildings, the literary and philosophical writings, and the musical works of the age. This becomes increasingly easy to do after the sixteenth century because of the availability of reproductions, records and cheap reprints. The student will have to make his own selection, but some of the following should be on any reading list (many editions of each except where specified): Descartes, *Discourse on Method**; Bacon, *New Atlantis*; Pascal, *Pensées**; Galileo, *Dialogue on the Great World Systems* (edited G. de Santillana, 1953); John Bunyan, *The Pilgrim's Progress**; John Locke, *Second Treatise of Government** and *Essay Concerning Human Understanding**; *Selections from Bayle's Dictionary* (edited E. A. Beller and M. D. Lee, 1952); Beccaria, *Essay on Crimes and Punishments** (trans. 1953); *The Portable Voltaire** (edited B. R. Redman, 1949); Rousseau, *Social Contract**; Henry Fielding, *Tom Jones**; Samuel Richardson, *Clarissa* (abridgment, Modern Library, 1950). *The Portable Age of Reason Reader** (edited C. Brinton, 1956) is an excellent selection of readings from the *philosophes*.

5. The Enlightenment

The most significant study of the transition from the seventeenth century to the eighteenth, from the Scientific Revolution to the Enlightenment, is P. Hazard, *The European Mind: The Critical Years, 1680–1715** (trans. 1952). There are excellent chapters on the Enlightenment in W. L. Dorn, *Competition for Empire** (1940), and in the *New Cambridge Modern History,* Vol. VII (1957), by A. Cobban. The most searching interpretation of the movement as a whole is E. Cassirer, *The Philosophy of the Enlightenment** (1932, trans. 1951), which emphasizes the break with older ways of thinking accomplished by the eighteenth century. C. L. Becker's charming lectures, *The Heavenly City of the Eighteenth-Century*

---

* Available in paperback edition.

*Philosophers** (1932), emphasize the continuity with the past. G. R. Havens, *The Age of Ideas: From Reaction to Revolution in Eighteenth-Century France** (1955), is a sound recent study. On the idea of progress, besides Becker, see J. B. Bury, *The Idea of Progress** (1920, 1932); R. F. Jones, *Ancients and Moderns** (1936); and C. Frankel, *The Faith of Reason: The Idea of Progress in the French Enlightenment* (1948). C. R. Cragg, *Reason and Authority in the Eighteenth Century* (1964), is an excellent account of the Enlightenment on the English side of the Channel, and D. Mornet, *French Thought in the Eighteenth Century* (1929), of enlightenment on the other. For the political thought of the *philosophes,* see K. Martin, *French Liberal Thought in the Eighteenth Century** (1929); and for the historical thought of Voltaire, Robertson, Hume, and Gibbon, see J. B. Black, *The Art of History* (1926).

---

* Available in paperback edition.

7

Aristocracy and Empire, 1715–1789

The seventy-five years between the death of Louis XIV (1715) and the outbreak of the French Revolution (1789) have a character of their own. This was a period of stability and equilibrium. There were no religious wars and no social upheavals (except for an uprising of serfs in far-off Russia), and there appears to have been somewhat less social mobility than in the seventeenth century. Monarchy was the most prevalent form of government, with divine-right monarchy evolving into "enlightened despotism."

Closely examined, however, the governments of the European states in the eighteenth century, both monarchies and republics, are better described as "aristocracies." Everywhere landed or moneyed minorities controlled or strongly influenced the governments of Europe. The Whig nobles and merchants who dominated the English Parliament, the French nobles and lawyers who dominated the royal councils and the law courts of France after the death of Louis XIV, the Junkers who commanded the Prussian armies, the landed nobles who made a farce of the Polish Diet, the "service nobility" which ceased to serve any but its own interests after the reign of Peter the Great in Russia, the wealthy bourgeois who

Maria Theresa of Austria with her husband, Emperor Francis I, and eleven of their children. The future Emperor Joseph II stands in the right center.

directly controlled the governments of the Dutch Republic and the German free cities—all were rich and well-born and thus fitted the eighteenth-century definition of aristocrats. Everywhere "aristocracy" was resurgent against absolute monarchy, and many of the gains of seventeenth-century monarchies were lost or compromised. Only where the monarch or the chief minister was a man of unusual ability was this revival of aristocratic activity turned to the benefit of the central government.

In this undeclared war between monarch and aristocrat a kind of compromise was generally reached. Eighteenth-century governments maintained an uneasy balance between centralization and decentralization, between absolute monarchy and aristocratic privilege. This might have been illogical, but strict adherence to basic principles had caused the bloody religious and civil wars of the last two centuries. Most men were glad to accept the structure of society and government as they found it after 1715. It was a glorious age to be alive in—if you were an "aristocrat." There was much abject poverty, injustice, and brutality in European society, but these could be forgotten if one centered one's attention on the brilliant "civilization" (the word first appeared in the 1770's) of the Paris salons or the London coffeehouses. To men who remembered the devastation of the Thirty Years' War or the

fanaticism of Cromwell's "saints," social stability and political equilibrium were worth a fairly high price in injustice.

International Relations

Equilibrium was also the rule in international relations. The defeat of Louis XIV's bid for a preponderance of power in Europe had been bloody and costly, and European statesmen were tacitly agreed that all such attempts to become "top dog" should be stopped at the outset. The balancing of power among the "great powers" of Europe—France, Britain, Austria, Prussia, and Russia (Spain, Holland, Sweden, Poland, and the Ottoman Empire could no longer qualify)—became the chief concern of diplomats.

The balance, of course, seldom remained steady for very long. Every country was constantly on the lookout for additional territory or for new colonies and trading opportunities abroad. In order to avoid large-scale wars like those needed to curb Louis XIV's ambitions, it became the custom for all the great powers to expect "compensation" whenever one of them was fortunate or daring enough to acquire new territory. This was hard on the weaker states, which were carved up to provide the "compensation," but it admittedly preserved the balance and often maintained the peace.

There were wars, and they were fairly frequent. But they were not so bloody or so exhausting as those of the seventeenth century. Generally they were "limited wars"—in two senses. First they were limited in the numbers of persons who took part in them or were affected by them. Eighteenth-century armies were professional armies, often recruited or kidnaped from the dregs of society or composed of foreign mercenaries. Except in Russia, where serfs made up most of the army, there was no general conscription, and the civilian was usually little affected by wars. Warfare consisted of elaborate maneuvering by highly disciplined professional units rather than bloody mass combat. There was little pillaging, even in enemy territory, because it was bad business to devastate a territory that might be annexed.

Wars were limited also in their objectives. There were no wars of annihilation. The enemy of today might be the ally of tomorrow, and it was thought well not to defeat any power too thoroughly because that would disturb the balance. The religious hatreds of the seventeenth century had cooled, and the passions of revolutionary liberalism and nationalism had not yet sprung into flame. The statesmen and generals fought for comparatively definite and concrete political and economic objectives, not for ideologies. When the objectives were attained—or when it became clear that they could not be attained immediately—the statesmen made peace or arranged a truce. There was no need to fight through to unconditional surrender. In spite of cut-throat competition for "empire"—in the form of land, population, colonies, or trade—the monarchs, bureaucrats, and aristocrats of the eighteenth century felt themselves part of a common civilization. The competition was a

Aristocracy

[By the 1760's] the world had become more aristocratic. Aristocracy in the eighteenth century may even be thought of as a new and recent development, if it be distinguished from the older institution of nobility. In one way it was more exclusive than mere nobility. A king could create nobles, but, as the saying went, it took four generations to make a gentleman. In another way aristocracy was broader than nobility. Countries that had no nobles, like Switzerland or British America, or countries that had few nobles of importance, like the Dutch provinces, might have aristocracies that even nobles recognized as such. . . . Aristocracy was nobility civilized, polished by that "refinement of manners" of which people talked, enjoying not only superiority of birth but a superior mode of life. It was a way of life as pleasing as any that mankind has ever developed, and which the middle classes were to imitate as much and as long as they could, a way of life characterized by dignified homes and by gardens and well-kept lawns, by private tutors and grand tours and sojourns at watering places, by annual migration between town and country and an abundance of respectful and unobtrusive servants.

From R. R. Palmer, *The Age of the Democratic Revolution* (Princeton: Princeton U. Press, 1959), pp. 29–30.

jockeying for power among cousins rather than a fight for survival against deadly enemies.

The picture of a stable, well-balanced eighteenth-century society which we have sketched could of course be compared to Newton's picture of the universe—a beautifully stable order of perfectly balanced gravitational pushes and pulls in which every mass moved along discoverable lines of force. But this picture must not be exaggerated. The eighteenth century was also a dynamic age. Its precarious equilibrium was an equilibrium among rapidly expanding forces. Wealth and trade were increasing; something like a revolution in agriculture was in the making, and a revolution in industry had begun. European economy and diplomacy were rapidly becoming global rather than continental, and the struggle for empire was reaching the farthest corners of the earth. For the first time, battles fought in America, Africa, and Asia began to tip the balance of power in Europe. The eighteenth century was not all order and stability. It was pregnant with revolution as well.

The years from 1715 to 1789 may conveniently be divided into three periods of about twenty-five years each: (1) a generation of peace and prosperity, 1715–40; (2) a period of worldwide warfare, 1740–63; and (3) an interval of enlightened despotism, aristocratic resurgence, and revolutionary stirrings, 1763–89.

Peace and Prosperity, 1715–40

After the peace settlements of 1713 in western Europe and of 1719–21 in eastern Europe, both governments and peoples were weary of war. The age that followed was unheroic, unexciting, and corrupt, like many other postwar periods. But peace restored law and order, and order stimulated an enormous expansion of trade, particularly in western Europe.

Increase of Trade and Wealth

Sea-borne commerce was the key to wealth in the eighteenth century. Thanks to the enterprise of their merchants and the technical skill of their mariners, the foreign trade of Britain and France increased about five times during the eighteenth century. In the case of Britain the sharpest increase was in colonial trade. This meant that Britain needed a larger merchant marine than her rivals and forced the British to build the strongest navy in the world to protect her overseas trade. In the case of France the greatest increase was in trade with other European nations. In both cases the accumulation of wealth in the hands of the upper classes was spectacular. For the first time the wealth of Europe began to eclipse the wealth of Asia. The two preceding centuries of exploration and establishment of overseas trading connections had begun to pay off handsomely in material benefits. The dinner table of a merchant of Liverpool, for instance, was graced by sugar from the West Indies, wine from Portugal, and tobacco from Virginia. His wife might wear calico

from India in summer and furs from Canada in winter. Their daughter might be married to the heir of a nobleman whose capacious Georgian house had been built on the combined profits from his land and his mercantile investments.

Many of the commodities, however, on which this thriving trade was based were derived from the labor of slaves or serfs. Only African slaves could stand the kind of work required on the sugar plantations of the West Indies or on the tobacco plantations of Virginia, and even they survived only about seven years, on the average. There was an almost insatiable demand for Negro slaves in the sugar islands, a demand that was met largely by English slave traders who procured their victims from the petty kings of the west coast of Africa, exchanged them for sugar in the West Indies, had the sugar converted into rum in New England, than used the rum to debauch native rulers and thus to secure more slaves in Africa. The serfs who toiled without recompense for their noble landlords in the grain-producing regions of eastern Europe were in much the same position in the economic order as the slaves of the West Indies. In short, a large part of the European economy was still based, as the economy of Greece and Rome had been, on servile labor.

There were signs in England, however, of the beginnings of revolutionary changes in both farming and industry. Eventually these changes were to result in an unprecedented expansion in the amount and variety of food, clothing, shelter, and luxuries which Europeans could produce. Historians speak of these changes as the "Agricultural Revolution" and the "Industrial Revolution," but since the results of these two new revolutions were seen most clearly in the nineteenth century, they will be discussed below.

Mississippi and South Sea Bubbles

European commercial capitalism was still expanding its field of operations in the early eighteenth century. The period of peace after 1713 encouraged both private financial speculation and wildcat commercial ventures. The years 1719 and 1720 saw the first large-scale example of a typically modern phenomenon, a cycle of boom-and-bust, or, as contemporaries called it, a "bubble."

The wars of Louis XIV had burdened both the French and the English governments with large debts. When a Scottish promoter named John Law showed up at the court of France after the death of Louis XIV and offered to solve the government's financial troubles, he was given *carte blanche* to manage the French economy as he saw fit. He set up a bank to issue paper currency and organized a Mississippi Company to trade with France's colony in Louisiana. The company boldly took over the government's debt, accepting government bonds in payment for shares of its own stock. Then it promoted a boom in the price of its stock by spreading tall tales of its commercial prospects. When the price finally reached forty times its original value, investors began to sell in order to cash in on their profits. Before long the price had plummeted, the bubble had burst, and Law had fled the country.

A similar episode occurred across the Channel in London. A South Sea Company had been organized to exploit the trade with the Spanish colonies provided for by the Peace of Utrecht. It too took over much of the government's debt, and it too deliberately promoted a boom in its own stock. In 1720, a few months after Law's failure, the South Sea bubble burst.

The collapse of the Mississippi and South Sea bubbles in 1719–20 hampered the development of joint stock companies and ruined a good many individual investors. But the underlying commercial purposes of the two companies were essentially sound, and when reorganized, both continued to make money for their investors for many years. French trade, particularly, was stimulated, although investors lost confidence in the French government. In contrast, the English government came to acknowledge the national debt as a public obligation and never again permitted private interests to assume responsibility for it, thus gaining the confidence of investors.

England Under Walpole

During the generation of peace that followed the death of Louis XIV, the English

worked out some of their internal political problems. As had been determined by the Act of Settlement, the Elector of Hanover succeeded Anne as ruler of England in 1714. Compared with the Stuarts, the first two Hanoverian monarchs, George I (1714–27) and George II (1727–60), were colorless figures. Both were stupid men who spoke little or no English. They interfered constantly in minor details of government, but neither was capable of grasping the larger issues. As a result, an "inner cabinet" of ministers became more and more responsible for policy decisions. Legally, the king was still free to choose his own ministers. Actually, he had to select men who could influence elections and control a majority in Parliament. These leading ministers began to meet at dinner to concert policy. They began to force out of office colleagues who disagreed with the group's majority, and they usually accepted the leadership of the ablest or most powerful among them in presenting their policy to the king. These informal practices vaguely foreshadowed the "cabinet system" and "prime minister" of the nineteenth century.

Robert Walpole, a country squire who had family connections with both the landed and the commercial aristocracies, is generally considered the first prime minister in English history, though he would not have acknowledged the title. For some twenty years, from 1721 to 1742, he was the manager of the Whig party in Parliament and the leading minister in the government. The first two Hanoverians by necessity chose their ministers from Whigs, since the Tories were tainted by affection for the Stuarts and had little strength in Parliament.

Walpole was a good-natured, hard-headed politician who understood the landed and financial "interests" represented in Parliament and knew how to hold a parliamentary majority together by tact, persuasion, and, if necessary, bribery and corruption. The fact that he was addicted to hard drinking and off-color stories helped rather than hurt him in managing the Whig merchants and landed gentry who controlled Parliament and ran local government as justices of the peace. Walpole's motto was, "Let sleeping dogs lie." He took care never to stir up any issue, at home or abroad, that might arouse passion and conflict. In 1733, for instance, he proposed a sensible scheme for raising more revenue from excise taxes and less from customs duties in order to discourage smuggling and encourage legitimate trade. But when his scheme was met by a storm of irrational abuse ("No excise, no popery, no wooden shoes" was one slogan), he dropped it. So far as the colonies were concerned, he followed a policy of "salutary neglect," leaving them to grow in population and wealth by their own efforts. In foreign affairs, he preserved the peace until 1739, when the London merchants and their spokesmen in Parliament (the "Patriots") forced him into a commercial war with Spain. Even then, he tried to keep the war as limited as possible.

On the whole, Walpole's ministry was a fruitful one for England. Both England and her colonies prospered; the credit of the government was never better; and the ruling aristocracy of landed and commercial wealth governed with a loose rein. When Voltaire visited England in 1726–29 he may have idealized English society and government somewhat. But there was without question more equality before the law in England, more personal freedom, more sense of

Sir Robert Walpole, leader of the Whig government from 1721 to 1742, talking to the Speaker of the House of Commons. Engraving after a painting by Hogarth.

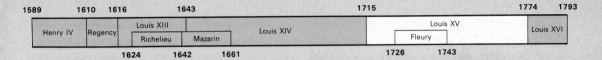

| 1589 | 1610 | 1616 | 1643 | | 1715 | | 1774 | 1793 |

Henry IV | Regency | Louis XIII | Mazarin | Louis XIV | | Louis XV / Fleury | Louis XVI
Richelieu | 1624 | 1642 | 1661 | | 1726 | 1743 |

public obligation in the ruling class, more security of property, and more widespread prosperity than anywhere else in Europe.

Louis XV and Cardinal Fleury

The generation of peace that brought strength to Britain brought weakness to France. Louis XIV's great-grandson Louis XV (1715–74) was a child of five when he came to the throne. The Regency that governed in his name for eight years had to make concessions to all the powerful elements in French society that had been kept in leash by the Sun King. The result was an aristocratic reaction in French government. Nobles began to reappear as policy-makers on the royal councils, and the *Parlement* of Paris boldly reasserted its ancient claim to register and enforce royal legislation or not, as it saw fit. The French monarchy remained as absolute as ever in theory, but after Louis XIV there was no strong hand to make the theory work. French government became inefficient and inconstant. Aristocratic privilege exasperated the middle classes and in the long run made it impossible for the government to avoid financial insolvency.

For a time the decline was arrested by Cardinal Fleury, the leading minister from 1726 to 1743. Fleury had ability, but he was no Richelieu. He was past seventy when he came to power, and his policy, much like Walpole's, was to preserve the peace, make cautious compromises, and avoid direct confrontation with the holders of power—in this case the nobility. He dissociated himself from the statesmanlike attempt of another minister to tax the nobility like everyone else, but he stabilized the currency, encouraged trade, and did all he could to make the old system of tax-farming work. His monarch was too debauched and incapable to set a more constructive course.

Fleury lost power in his last years, and when he died at the age of ninety, Louis XV decided that he would govern for himself without a prime minister. This simply meant that France now had a king who could neither govern himself nor let anyone else govern for him. Louis XV's best-known remark, "After me, the deluge," perfectly expressed his attitude. The aristocracy naturally took full advantage of this situation and greatly increased its influence. France remained the largest and potentially the most powerful nation in Europe. French trade and industry were growing at a rapid rate, but the government was run by royal mistresses and favorites (Mme. de Pompadour was the most prominent), and the French state could not make full use of its resources.

Declining Monarchies and Empires

Elsewhere in Europe, with few exceptions, monarchical institutions were in decline as they were in France during the generation after the Peace of Utrecht.

In Spain the Bourbon whom Louis XIV established on the throne, Philip V (1700–46), did something to curb the nobility and to encourage trade and industry. But the dry rot had eaten too deep into Spanish society and government to allow a real revival of the nation's greatness. Neither the Spanish economy, nor the army and navy, nor the colonies made any significant gains.

Austria was an unwieldy empire composed of three separate kingdoms (Austria, Bohemia, and Hungary) and two dependencies of quite different cultures and traditions (northern Italy and the Netherlands). The Habsburg Emperor Charles VI (1711–40) had to spend years in persuading his own subjects and foreign governments to accept a "Pragmatic Sanction" which provided that his daughter Maria Theresa (Charles had no sons) should succeed him as ruler of all his various lands. By the time of his death he had the agreement on paper of everyone concerned, but no one was sure just how long the agreement would be respected by greedy neighboring monarchs or restless Hungarian nobles.

Farther to the east, the Polish and Ottoman empires continued to decline. A desultory and trivial war over the succession to the Polish crown was fought between 1733 and 1738 by France and Spain against Austria and Russia. The Russian candidate for the throne won out, and all the losers were "compensated" by being given scraps of territory elsewhere—Spain in Naples and Sicily, for instance. At the same time Austria and Russia were once more at war with the Ottoman Turks. The Turks were to prove tougher than the Poles, but it was evident that both empires were destined for ultimate destruction.

The generation after Peter the Great's death in 1725 saw a series of palace revolutions that placed the Russian crown successively on the heads of half a dozen children or incompetent women. German, particularly Prussian, influence was very strong at the court. As in France, the nobles managed to free themselves from many of the restrictions placed on them by earlier and stronger monarchs. The Russian nobles extended the power that Peter had given them over their own serfs but tried to renounce the obligation to serve the state which he had imposed on them in return. In Russia, as in Hungary and Prussia,

King Stanislaus of Poland vainly tries to keep his crown on his head while Catherine II of Russia, Joseph II of Austria, and Frederick II of Prussia carve up his country, 1773. An engraving by Le Mire after Moreau le Jeune.

the peasant sank deeper and deeper into serfdom during the eighteenth century while the governments made one concession after another to the hereditary nobles in order to gain their favor. Until the accession of Catherine the Great in 1762 there was no strong hand at the helm of the Russian state, but Peter's work in raising his country to the position of a great power in European war and diplomacy proved to be permanent.

Frederick William I of Prussia

Probably the most successful ruler of his generation apart from Walpole—and for quite different reasons—was King Frederick William I of Brandenburg-Prussia (1713–40). While absolute monarchy seemed to be in decline elsewhere, this strange, uncouth, and furious man, who smoked tobacco and drank beer in Gargantuan quantities, continued the work of transforming one of the smallest and poorest states of Europe into a great military power. Following in the footsteps of the Great Elector, he centralized the administration in a so-called General Directory, pared civil expenditures to the bone, and worked his subordinates remorselessly, all with the object of building the best-disciplined and most formidable army in Europe. "Salvation is from the Lord," he remarked, "but everything else is my affair." When he was through he had increased the size of his army to over 80,000 men, twice what it had been under his father. But while Frederick William built the fourth largest and the most efficient army on the Continent, he drew back whenever he might have used it. He left his son a full treasury, an efficient civil bureaucracy, and a highly trained army—an army that had not fought a battle in over a generation.

He despised his son, Frederick, for his unmilitary habits and his taste for reading Voltaire and playing the flute. On occasions he would break the flute, burn the books, and even have the young man publicly beaten. When Frederick finally tried to flee the country with a friend, his father had the friend beheaded before his son's eyes and put the young man to work in the bureaucracy. Strange to say, the treatment

worked. Without losing his taste for literature and music, Frederick grew interested in administration and the army. He succeeded his father in 1740 as Frederick II (1740–86), better known to history as Frederick the Great.

Worldwide Warfare, 1740–63

The generally peaceful generation we have described was followed by a generation dominated by two wars, the War of the Austrian Succession (1740–48) and the Seven Years' War (1756–63), separated by a few years of intensive diplomacy. These wars grew out of two irreconcilable rivalries for power. One was the rivalry between the rising Hohenzollerns of Prussia and the more established Habsburgs of Austria for territory in central Europe. The other was the rivalry between Great Britain and France for trade and colonial empire in North America, the West Indies, Africa, and India. Twice these two rivalries became entangled with each other, although the partnerships changed between the wars. And in the final peace of 1763 England and Prussia gained at the expense of France and Austria.

The British Navy and the Prussian Army

These wars were to demonstrate that the most efficient fighting units in eighteenth-century Europe were the British navy and the Prussian army. The most obvious explanation of superiority in each case was the unrivaled excellence of the officers. But behind the two military arms were two sharply different societies and political systems, each well adapted to the particular sort of competition in which the nation found itself.

Great Britain had many advantages in the race for sea power. She was an island, safe from invasion by land, and therefore able to pour into ships the men and money that continental states had to pour into armies. Maritime enterprise was both profitable and patriotic; a seafaring career attracted enterprising younger sons of the nobility as well as yeomen and artisans. The reservoir of experienced sailors was larger in England than

France, her nearest rival, because the British had the largest merchant marine in the world. Finally, the government and the ruling classes recognized the importance of trade and sea power, and in spite of periods of neglect they supported naval construction and encouraged British shipping.

Britain's rival, France, had almost all the advantages England had—experienced sailors, a large merchant marine, warships superior in design even to the British, and colonial bases overseas. But she had long land frontiers and a tradition of pushing those frontiers to the east and of intervening in the affairs of central Europe. This situation created an impossible dilemma. France could not be both the greatest land power and the greatest sea power, and if the army was favored, as it usually was, then the navy suffered.

The Prussian army was the creation of the Hohenzollerns, who had shaped a society and designed a state to support it. The Prussian bureaucracy and fiscal system had grown out of institutions devised to provide direct support to the army. The Junkers had been taught that their calling was to serve the king, in the army by preference, in the civil service if necessary, and in return for their service they were given wide powers over the serfs who supported them. Enterprising members of the small middle class were also enlisted into the civil service, and serfs were conscripted when needed into the army. The proverbial discipline of the Prussian army pervaded to some degree both the society and the government. In England, central government by Parliament, local government by amateurs, and a considerable amount of freedom proved to be a good formula for producing sea power. In Prussia, centralized professional administration from above under an absolute monarch leading a disciplined aristocracy proved to be a successful formula for producing land power.

The War of the Austrian Succession, 1740–48

In 1740 Maria Theresa, a beautiful but inexperienced young woman, succeeded her father in the Habsburg dominions, to which her right of succession had been guaranteed by the Pragmatic Sanction. Frederick II of Prussia almost immediately threw his army into Silesia, one of her richest provinces, on the northeastern frontier of Bohemia. Frederick had published an anonymous little book against the immorality of Machiavelli, but he had learned some of the Florentine's precepts well. Silesia, with its million inhabitants, its linen industry, and its iron ore, would finally make Brandenburg-Prussia a great power. Both Maria Theresa and the European powers were caught off-guard. Frederick seized his opportunity, took what he needed, and spent the next twenty years defending his gain.

For a time it was not too difficult. Frederick's boldfaced aggression encouraged every enemy of the Habsburgs to join in the attack: Bavaria, Spain, and finally France. Strangely enough, Hungary, which resented Habsburg rule, proved to be Maria Theresa's salvation. When she went to Budapest with her infant son and made an

Empire

The agrarian and feudal states of the Continent were powerful because of their ownership of land and people. Conversely the masters of the maritime commonwealth were powerful chiefly because of their trade. The continental monarch could maintain his domination over the state only by means of a large army. In order to have as large an army as possible, he must, since the process of industrialization was too slow for him, seek to increase his territory. The rulers of the maritime powers, on the other hand, could control their states and their policies by means of movable wealth, with which they could hire soldiers and pay subsidies to their allies. What the conquest of a wealthy contiguous province meant to land powers like Prussia and Austria, the expansion of commerce meant to a maritime power like Great Britain. The acquisition of Silesia by Prussia produced an increment of wealth and power, much as the dislodgment of the French from the slave-trading stations of the African Gold Coast signified an expansion of British commerce and sea power. In both cases the policy was essentially predatory.

From Walter L. Dorn, *Competition for Empire, 1740–1763* (New York: Harper, 1940), pp. 9–10.

emotional appeal to the Hungarian Parliament, the chivalrous nobility rose tumultuously to her support. During the wars that followed, an able minister, Count Haugwitz, centralized the Habsburg administration and reorganized the army. Austria, a helpless victim state in 1740, was able to revive and become a formidable antagonist to the king of Prussia. Frederick's armies fought brilliantly, however, and the combined pressure of France, Bavaria, and Prussia—shaky though the alliance was—proved to be too much for Maria Theresa to overcome. In 1748 at Aix-la-Chapelle she agreed to a peace treaty that left Silesia in Frederick's hands.

Meanwhile the Anglo-French rivalry had also broken out into war. When war began between England and Spain in 1739, it was only a question of time before France would be drawn in. France and Spain cooperated closely in the eighteenth century. Both had Bourbon rulers, and France had a large economic stake in the Spanish Empire since she supplied the Spanish colonies with most of their manufactured goods. English and French interests clashed in America and in India. In North America the English felt threatened by the French military hold on Canada and Louisiana, while the French felt threatened by the pressure of the English colonies expanding northward and westward. In the West Indies there was rivalry over the sugar islands. In India the death of the last Mogul emperor in 1707 had led to the collapse of all central administration. Both the French and the British East India Companies were trying to influence native principalities, particularly around Madras and Pondicherry. From Canada to the Carnatic Coast of India, then, uneasy Frenchmen and Englishmen were ready to fly to arms.

In 1744 France declared war on Great Britain and immediately the war in Europe and the war overseas merged into one. In 1745 the American colonists captured Louisbourg in Canada, and in 1746 the French seized Madras. Nothing decisive came of the conflict, however, because the English could not yet make up their minds whether to concentrate their efforts on a land war on the Continent against France or on the war overseas. The former policy was denounced by the "Patriots" in Parliament as "Hanoverianism"—that is, a pandering to the interests of the monarch, George II, who was still Elector of Hanover in Germany. The English navy defeated the French; the French army defeated the English on the Continent; but neither side pressed its successes very far, neither on sea or on land. A typical "limited" war, the War of the Austrian Succession ended in a stalemate so far as Britain and France were concerned. The French gave up their conquest of Madras, and the English government, much to the disgust of the American colonists, gave back Louisbourg. The French came out of the war with no gains over either Austria or England. The English came out of it with a clearer sense of how they should fight their next war with France.

The Diplomatic Revolution

England had fought in the War of the Austrian Succession in loose agreement with her old ally, Austria. France had fought in a still looser alliance with Prussia (Frederick deserted his ally twice to make truces with Austria). During the years between 1748 and 1756, a "diplomatic revolution" took place in which the chief antagonists in the first general war of mid-century changed partners in preparation for the second. This "revolution" illustrates nicely the main characteristics of eighteenth century diplomacy.

The chief instigator of the "revolution" was Count Kaunitz, the Austrian chancellor. Burning with desire to crush Frederick and recover Silesia, he decided that the only practical way was to heal the ancient antagonism between Bourbons and Habsburgs and to gain the support of France—and if possible of Russia as well—in a new war against Prussia. Prussia, he was sure, could not last long against the three strongest powers on the Continent. Kaunitz worked carefully to bring Mme. de Pompadour around to his side, but it was a chain of calculations and miscalculations by other statesmen that actually brought France to agree to the alliance. The English ministry became worried about whether Austria had the will and desire to help England defend Hanover against France. Prussia was obviously better placed to defend Hanover, but when Frederick agreed to do so in return for British subsidies, the French were irritated. Since Frederick had made an agreement with France's ancient enemy, England, the French were now ready to reach an understanding with Frederick's enemy, Austria. Soon a coalition of France, Austria, and Russia was arranged and it looked as if Prussia's situation was hopeless. Frederick saw that his only chance was to catch his enemies off-guard, and, characteristically, he started the war with an offensive in 1756, almost a year earlier than his opponents had planned.

Conflict Overseas

War had already broken out between the British and the French overseas. In India, Joseph Dupleix had been trying since 1749 to make the French East India Company a political as well as a commercial power. By dominating native states, he hoped to increase the company's revenue and hamper British trade. The English East India Company soon became alarmed, and there were some armed clashes in which Dupleix' forces were defeated. In 1754 the company directors, afraid that Dupleix was leading them into serious conflict with the British, recalled him to France. Ironically, his idea of increasing the company's revenue through domination of native states was adopted by the British East India Company under its brilliant local leader, Robert Clive, and became the foundation of British territorial rule in India.

The situation in America was even more tense than in India. The French in Canada had used the interval of peace to build a chain of forts from the St. Lawrence down the Ohio to the Mississippi, and the British government had countered by sending ships and troops to the American colonies. The time was approaching when either the French or the English would have to abandon the North American continent —and there were now perhaps a million and

a half British subjects (including slaves) in North America and only about 60,000 French—the ratio had grown to twenty-five to one. British troops and colonists began to strike at the French forts. An attempt to capture Fort Duquesne, the most important link in the chain (on the site of modern Pittsburgh), was disastrously defeated in 1755, and England and France were at war.

So in 1756 Europe was once more deep in conflict—this time France, Austria, and Russia against England and Prussia. The largest navy in the world had little to fear, but the odds were very great against the best army in Europe. If Prussia were defeated and partitioned, as seemed likely, any British gains overseas might well be wiped out at the peace conference. The Anglo-French and the Austro-Prussian rivalries had become inextricably mingled.

The Seven Years' War, 1756–63

England made no headway in the war until the summer of 1757, when William Pitt became virtual prime minister. Pitt, one of Britain's greatest war ministers, shrewdly focused the nation's war efforts on conquests overseas. His policy represented the commercial aims of the London business community, but it also appealed to the pride of the ordinary Englishman in the navy and the growing colonial empire. Pitt concentrated power in his own hands, and his energy and his enthusiasm stimulated his subordinates to unheard-of efforts. The "year of miracles" (1759) demonstrated Pitt's remarkable ability to direct a complex series of operations and to choose first-rate commanders. In this one year Quebec fell, Guadaloupe was taken, French military power in India was broken, and the French fleet was crushed off Quiberon Bay. England's control of the seas enabled her to hold both Canada and India, a classic example of the strategic importance of sea power.

While Britain was destroying the French Empire abroad, Prussia was fighting for her life on the Continent. England's "year of miracles" was a year of near disaster for Prussia. Her army was badly defeated by the Russians at Kaunsdorf in 1759; the Prussians now needed a miracle just to survive. Only the divisions among his enemies allowed Frederick to prolong the war. Kaunitz had not promised enough of the spoils to France and Russia to stimulate an all-out effort from either country. Pitt's subsidies to German forces were just enough to pin the French down in bloody fighting in Westphalia. The war was unpopular in France and was putting a heavy strain on the already shaky French financial system. Austrian armies were poorly led and the Austrian government was almost as afraid of the Russian army in the Oder Valley as it was of the Prussian. So Frederick held on, though his resources were almost exhausted, until the "Hohenzollern miracle" occurred. The Empress Elizabeth of Russia died in 1762 and was succeeded by Peter III, a warm admirer of the king of Prussia. Peter promptly withdrew from the war, and Austria now had only a crippled and sulky France as a major ally. With no hope of winning a decisive victory, Maria Theresa decided to end the war. Peace was made in 1763, leaving Prussia in permanent possession of Silesia. To have preserved the *status quo* was a moral victory for Frederick. Prussia had clearly established herself as one of the great powers.

The death of an empress saved Frederick the Great from possible defeat. The death of a king indirectly robbed Britain of some of the fruits of victory. When George III succeeded his grandfather in 1760 he wished to prove himself thoroughly English, unlike the first two Georges. This meant withdrawing from all involvement in German affairs, contrary to Pitt's advice. By October, 1761, Pitt had been forced out of office. Lord Bute, George's Scottish favorite, deserted Frederick II and set himself to get peace with France at almost any price.

The Peace of Paris, 1763

The peace finally signed at Paris in January 1763 was overwhelmingly favorable to Great Britain, but it was not so severe on the French as Pitt would have wished. France received back from her conqueror most of her purely economic stakes around the world: her trading posts in India, her slave stations in West Africa, her sugar islands in the West Indies, and her fishing rights off Canada, together with two tiny islands off Newfoundland, St. Pierre and Miquelon. But her political and military power in India and on the North American continent was permanently broken. She agreed to maintain no more troops in India and to recognize the native rulers whom the British had set up. She ceded the whole of Canada and everything east of the Mississippi to Britain and handed over Louisiana west of the Mississippi to Spain. Henceforth the British had no serious competitors in North America.

Enlightened Despotism, 1763–89

During the twenty-five years that followed the Peace of Paris, the imagination of educated men was fired by the "enlightened" ideas and practices of a number of European monarchs. The ancient institution of monarchy seemed to take a new lease on life. The major ideas of the Enlightenment—reason, natural law, happiness, progress, liberty—began to filter through to the rulers. The later *philosophes* were questioning aristocratic and ecclesiastical privilege, unequal taxation, and the unfair treatment of certain social classes. Was it reasonable? Was it natural? These were the fashionable questions in "enlightened" quarters, and some of the crowned heads of Europe became troubled by them. Further, the mid-century wars had left almost every European state in need of reform and reconstruction. Law and order had to be restored, trade revived, and government treasuries refilled. So the practical needs of a postwar era, added to the ferment of new ideas, produced what was known as "enlightened despotism."

This apparently new kind of monarchy was in many ways a revival of older monarchical ideas, and a reaction against the power that the aristocracy had gained in the eighteenth century. In rooting out irrational customs and vested interests, enlightened despots could curb the power of the nobility and the clergy and attack local and provincial privileges just as monarchs before them had been doing for several centuries. The difference was in the way the enlightened despots justified what they did. They talked little about divine right or hereditary title and a great deal about following reason and serving the public. Frederick the Great called himself "merely the first servant of the state," liable at any moment to render an account of his service to his subjects. But this did not mean that he or any other monarch felt he was really responsible to his people. Monarchs might be "enlightened," but they were still "despots." As one contemporary economist observed, "Whenever old disorders have been eradicated speedily and with success, it will be seen that it was the work of a single enlightened person against many private interests."*

Few of the rulers who dominated the political horizon in the later eighteenth century measured up to the ideal of an enlightened despot. George III of England (1760–1820) and Louis XV of France (1715–74) were hardly enlightened in any sense of the word, although some of their policies were. Among the minor monarchs, Gustavus III of Sweden (1771–92) and Charles III of Spain (1759–88) had some claim to the title, but the three most prominent enlightened despots were Catherine the Great of Russia, Frederick the Great of Prussia, and Joseph II of Austria.

Catherine the Great of Russia

Catherine II (1762–96) was a German princess who became Empress of Russia through a conspiracy of her friends that led to the assassination of her husband, Tsar Peter III (1762). Uneasily conscious of being a usurper, she tried to make Russia great in an effort to endear herself to her people. She had to make concessions to preserve the support of the nobility, including lavish gifts to a long succession of lovers whom she used as her chief officers of state. She read

the books of the French *philosophes,* corresponded with Voltaire, persuaded Diderot to visit her court, and made much of her "enlightenment" for publicity purposes. In 1767 she excited her admirers by summoning a Legislative Commission to codify the laws of Russia and to give the nation a sort of constitution. The representatives were elected by every class in the land except serfs, and they came armed with statements of grievances. Very little came out of their deliberations, however: some slight religious toleration and some limitation of torture in legal proceedings. The members went home in 1768, and the Russian government was to make no further attempt to summon a representative assembly until the twentieth century.

The net result, in fact, of Catherine's reign was not enlightened government but the strengthening of the nobility and the extension of serfdom. In 1773–75 a vast and dangerous uprising of serfs broke out in the valley of the Volga, led by a Cossack named Pugachev. The revolt was directed at the local landlords and officials; and after it was broken and Pugachev had been brought to Moscow in an iron cage to be drawn and quartered, it was these landlords and officials who profited by the reaction. Peter the Great's idea of a service nobility had long been weakening. In 1785 Catherine freed the nobles from both military service and taxation and gave them absolute control over the serfs on their estates. Further, she gave away large tracts of crown land to noble favorites, thus subjecting hordes of relatively free peasants on these estates to serfdom. At the end of her reign it has been estimated that 34 million out of a population of 36 million Russians were in a state of serfdom—a state that was not very different from that of Negro slaves in the American colonies. The net result of Catherine's reign was to encourage the forces that were making Russia a state built on slavery.

Catherine was called "the Great" not because of her enlightenment—if any—but because of her conquests. Peter the Great had pushed his possessions out to the Baltic Sea in the northwest at the expense of Sweden. Catherine expanded the frontiers of her state many hundreds of miles to the west and south at the expense of Poland

---

* Quoted in R. R. Palmer, *The Age of the Democratic Revolution* (Princeton: Princeton University Press, 1959), p. 105.

Russia's Growth in Europe 1462-1796

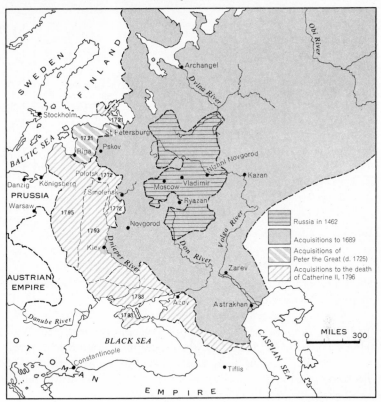

and the Ottoman Empire. Russians were concerned about the large Orthodox minority in Catholic Poland. Furthermore, during a large part of the seventeenth century, the Poles had threatened Moscow, and the Polish frontier was still only about 200 miles from the old Russian capital when Catherine came to the throne. The ancient Russian thirst for vengeance on the Poles was to be richly satisfied after 1763 when Catherine put one of her favorites, Stanislaus Poniatowski, on the Polish throne. From that time on Russia and Prussia made it their business to see that the anarchy and confusion of Polish politics continued and that any suggestion of constitutional reform or revival of the national spirit was snuffed out.

The Partitions of Poland

In 1772 Catherine and Frederick the Great arranged the first partition of Poland. Frederick

took West Prussia and so joined Prussia to Brandenburg territorially for the first time. Catherine took a generous slice of northeastern Poland. To preserve the balance of power they thought it wise to give Maria Theresa a share of the loot (Galicia). The pious empress hung back at first, but Frederick remarked that the more she wept for Poland, the more she took. This first partition shocked the Poles into a nationalistic revival. King Stanislaus himself was swept along by the patriotic fervor and forgot that he owed his throne to Catherine. In 1791 after the outbreak of the French Revolution, a remarkable reform constitution was instituted setting up a strong monarchy and abolishing the *liberum veto*. Catherine's answer was swift and ruthless. Early in 1792 she called off the war she was fighting against the Turks, rushed an army into Poland, abolished the new constitution, restored the old anarchy, and arranged a

The Partitions of Poland

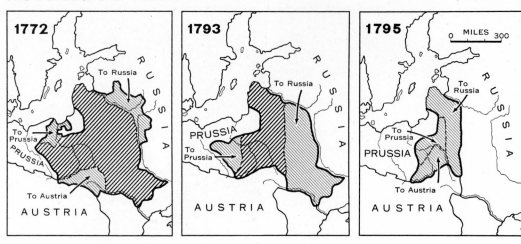

second partition of Polish territory in 1793, this time with Prussia alone.

These events were followed by a genuinely popular uprising in what was left of Poland, led by a Pole who had fought for the Americans in their revolution, Thaddeus Kosciusko. The end was inevitable. Kosciusko was captured by the Russians, the revolt collapsed, and Stanislaus was forced to abdicate. The Kingdom of Poland was wiped off the map in a third partition of 1795 among Russia, Prussia, and Austria. In the three partitions, Russia took almost two-thirds of the original Polish territory, and Prussia and Austria divided the remainder.

Catherine's successes against the crumbling Ottoman Empire were almost as decisive. In a series of wars running from 1768 to 1792 Catherine gained the Crimea and most of the northern shore of the Black Sea. The Treaty of Kuchuk Kainarji (1774) also gave Russia vague rights to protect Orthodox Christians in the Ottoman Empire—rights that were to be used later as excuses for Russian intervention in Turkish affairs. The Ottoman Empire escaped the fate of Poland because it was stronger internally and because its two chief enemies, Austria and Russia, were jealous of each other. But when Catherine died in 1796 there seemed to be little obstacle to a Russian advance to the Straits and the Mediterranean.

Frederick the Great of Prussia

Frederick II of Prussia (1740–86) had a somewhat better claim than Catherine to be considered "enlightened." He had a first-rate mind and a real grasp of what the *philosophes* were talking about. He invited Voltaire to Potsdam, and although they soon fell to quarreling over the merits of Frederick's poetry, they both agreed that it was the job of a king to combat ignorance and superstition among his people, to enhance their welfare, and to promote religious toleration. Frederick welcomed religious exiles of all sorts—even Jesuits expelled from France and Spain. He treated the Jews badly, but his general tolerance in religion was the best evidence of his enlightenment. He was a mercantilist in his economic policies; he sought national self-sufficiency and used protective tariffs to foster infant industries. Interested in the new scientific agriculture, he tried to encourage new methods by bringing new farmers to his kingdom. Some 300,000 immigrants entered Prussia during his reign. Finally, he rationalized and simplified the Prussian laws and court procedures—another typical objective of enlightened despotism.

In some respects, however, Frederick was not at all enlightened, though he was always a despot. He believed firmly in social rank and privilege. The Junkers served him well as officers in his army, and the army was the most important

Frederick the Great of Prussia visiting Voltaire at Potsdam, where the philosopher lived in the early 1750's. Engraving from a painting by Monsiaux.

organ of the state. In return for their services, he allowed the nobility to keep full control over the peasants on their estates. He strictly defined the ranks of noble, bourgeois, and peasant and made it difficult if not impossible for a man to move from one class to another. Prussian serfs were not so badly off as Russian and Polish serfs, but those who lived on private estates were almost as much at their lord's mercy. Frederick did something to improve the lot of serfs on his own estates, but otherwise he showed no taste for social reform.

In some respects the discipline, the machine-like efficiency, and the strict centralization of power in the Prussian monarchy was the result of a long Hohenzollern tradition, quite unrelated to the influence of the Enlightenment. The powerful state that Frederick II erected in twenty-three years of war (1740–63) and consolidated in twenty-three years of peace (1763–86) was the most striking political achievement of his time.

But twenty years after the strong hand of the despot was removed, Prussia proved to be an easy victim for Napoleon. The weakness of enlightened despotism, as well as its strength, lay in the fact that everything depended on the monarch.

Joseph II of Austria

The monarch with the best claim to be called an enlightened despot was Joseph II of Austria. Although he professed contempt for the *philosophes,* he was more thoroughly converted to the main tenets of the Enlightenment than any of his fellow monarchs. And he was probably more sincerely devoted to his people's welfare than any of the others.

Frederick II's seizure of Silesia in 1740 was the signal for a reorganization of the Habsburg Empire. During Maria Theresa's long reign (1740–80) an imperial bureaucracy was developed that was able to centralize in Vienna the administration of all the divisions of the empire except Hungary. All parts of the empire but Hungary were brought into a tariff union in 1775. The nobles were compelled to assume at least some of the burden of taxation. Maria Theresa did more for the serfs in her kingdom than any other ruler of her time by limiting the amount of labor they owed their lords and by curbing the lords' power to abuse them. In much of this she was aided and abetted by her son, Joseph, who became emperor and coregent after the death of her husband in 1765. But Joseph wished to move much further and faster than his mother. Until her death in 1780 he chafed under the compromises and conservatism that characterized Maria Theresa's policies, particularly in religion.

In the ten years of Joseph II's own rule (1780–90), literally thousands of decrees poured out from the imperial chancellery in Vienna. He proclaimed religious toleration for all Christians and Jews. He dissolved monasteries devoted solely to contemplation and turned their revenues over to the hospitals that were to make Vienna the medical center of Europe in the next century. He applied a system of equal taxation in proportion to income to everyone in the Habsburg dominions, regardless of rank or nationality. He imposed one language for official business, German, on all parts of the empire, including Belgium, Italy, and Hungary. Most significant of all, Joseph abolished serfdom. Early in his reign he issued a number of decrees that gave all serfs in the Habsburg dominions personal freedom—freedom to leave the land, to marry whom they pleased, to choose any job they liked. This much of Joseph's work was permanent. In later decrees he tried to relieve peasants who stayed on the land of all forced labor and to turn them into property-owners, but these decrees were repealed by his successors.

Joseph II made more and more enemies by his policy of centralization and reform: the clergy, the landed nobility, non-German parts of his empire like Hungary, even peasants who

The Growth of Brandenburg-Prussia   1640–1795

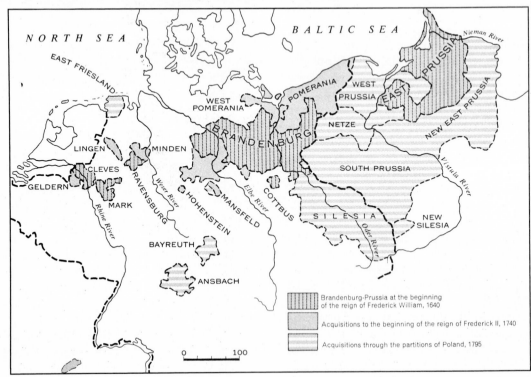

Brandenburg-Prussia at the beginning of the reign of Frederick William, 1640

Acquisitions to the beginning of the reign of Frederick II, 1740

Acquisitions through the partitions of Poland, 1795

failed to understand his intentions. In 1789, when revolution broke out in France, peasants in the Austrian Empire began to plunder and murder landlords to gain the rights Joseph had held out to them. In 1790 both Belgium and Hungary were in revolt against his rule. The Church was bitterly hostile to him. Joseph felt lonely and deserted. "I am the only one holding to the true course," he wrote his brother Leopold, "and I am left to labor alone . . . . I am without any assistance whatsoever." Worn out, he died in 1790, choosing as his own epitaph: "Here lies Joseph II, who was unfortunate in everything that he undertook."

It is clear why Joseph II has been called "the revolutionary Emperor." Like Peter the Great he had shown what a single determined will could accomplish in the face of stubborn private interests. Unlike Peter, he had been guided by the principles of reason, tolerance, and humanitarianism. But Joseph was a revolutionist without a party. He had to depend on an unimaginative bureaucracy and on the secret police which he found it necessary to set up. Enlightened despotism in his hands might have formed a bridge between divine-right monarchy and democratic revolution. But it also suggested that permanent revolution demanded a broader base of popular understanding and support than he had been able to command.

France, England, and the American Revolution, 1763–89

France and Great Britain were the centers of the Enlightenment, but neither had an enlightened despot as monarch. Perhaps as a result (such large generalizations are very difficult to prove), each suffered a revolution from below. The American colonists won their independence from England in the name of reason and natural rights, and the French bourgeoisie, fired by the same ideals, destroyed aristocratic privilege in France.

Abortive Revolution from Above in France

When the Seven Years' War ended in 1763, both the French and the British governments needed more revenues to carry the burden of their war debts and to meet the rising costs of administration. Louis XV proposed to continue a war tax that fell on nobles and commoners alike and to institute a new tax on office-holders. It was a statesmanlike proposal, but Louis' program was greeted by a storm of opposition from nobles and wealthy bourgeois alike. The *parlements* resisted the new taxes on the ground that they went against the "fundamental laws" of the kingdom and the "natural rights" of Frenchmen. Louis answered by abolishing the *parlements* and instituting a whole new system of law courts. It looked like a minor "enlightened" revolution, but it did not last. Louis XV died in 1774, and his son, Louis XVI, was neither strong enough nor determined enough to continue the fight against privilege. The old *parlements* were restored, the new taxes were dropped, and the financial problem was passed on to more cautious ministers. In the end, Louis XV's abortive reforms resulted in a further aristocratic reaction. After 1774 the nobility and the *parlements* came back so strongly from their defeat that the Bourbon monarchy became in effect their prisoner.

The Revolt of the British American Colonies

The political and social situation was different in England, but the course of events was somewhat similar. A reasonable attempt by the government to raise new revenue was met by a storm of opposition in the American colonies. As a result, the attitude of the English governing classes stiffened. Concessions either to the colonists abroad or to reformers at home became impossible, and an irreconcilable conflict broke out which ultimately split the British Empire.

For nearly half a century before the Seven Years' War the policy of the British government toward its American colonies, as we have seen, had been one of "salutary neglect." For all practical purposes, the thirteen colonies governed themselves. Governors were appointed by the ministry in London, but their salaries were paid by colonial legislatures that were in fact quite independent of the British Parliament. They were

Many Englishmen opposed the Stamp Act. This etching, made in 1761, shows the funeral procession of "Miss Americ-Stamp." The sign on the warehouse in the background reads "Goods Now Ship'd for America."

also elected more democratically than Parliament or than almost any other representative bodies in Europe. Before 1763 Parliament never tried to tax the colonies. It did impose customs duties on colonial trade, but the intent of these levies was not to raise revenue but to regulate trade and compel it to flow toward the mother country.

The Seven Years' War, by eliminating French military power from North America, made the colonists feel more confident and less dependent on Great Britain for protection. At the same time it induced Parliament to tax the colonies in order that they might carry a fair share of the financial burden of imperial defense. The colonists had not done much of the actual fighting against the French. English troops had carried the brunt of the war, and after its close it was English troops that had to put down an Indian uprising under Pontiac across the Alleghenies. The taxes paid by the average American colonist were less than one twenty-fifth of those paid by an Englishman. It seemed only fair to ask British Americans to carry some of the cost of maintaining English troops in North America.

In March 1765 Parliament imposed a stamp tax on paper of all sorts, including legal documents, commercial agreements, and newspapers.

Sensible and familiar to Europeans as such a tax was, it aroused furious opposition in America among lawyers, merchants, and editors—the most articulate groups. A congress of delegates from nine of the colonies urged "that no taxes be imposed on them but with their own consent," and went on to argue that there was no practical way for the British Parliament to get American "consent" to any taxation. A year after its passage, Parliament repealed the Stamp Act but at the same time declared that crown and Parliament had the right to tax the colonies if they wished to. In 1767 Parliament returned to the attack with an act imposing duties on imports into the colonies of tea, paper, paint, lead, and glass. This was met by a determined colonial boycott, and in 1770 all the duties but those on tea were withdrawn.

Up to this point the colonists had shown little appreciation of the financial and military problems of the Empire, and Parliament had shown little appreciation of the factors that made the colonists doubt or fear its authority. But so far there had been no irrevocable break. In 1774, however, matters came to a head. The year before, Parliament had taken over political responsibility in India from the East India Company and had set up a Governor General, thus founding British rule in India. In order to compensate the company for its loss of political power, it was allowed to sell its surplus tea directly to American retailers, a move that would presumably increase sales and thus the revenue from the tea duty. This action so infuriated a radical minority in Massachusetts that a party of Bostonians disguised as savages boarded three East Indiamen in Boston harbor in December 1773 and dumped thousands of pounds' worth of tea into the water. Parliament reacted with a violence out of all proportion to the incident. The port of Boston was closed and the Massachusetts legislature was deprived of much of its power (1774). This reaction drove the twelve other colonies to rally behind Massachusetts in fear for their own charters.

To make matters worse, an otherwise statesmanlike measure, the Quebec Act of 1774, was passed at a moment when it appeared to be a further attack on the English-speaking colonies by Parliament. The act guaranteed the preservation of the French language and the Catholic religion in Canada and defined Canada as including all territory north of the Ohio River and west of the Allegheny Mountains. By now the breach was irreparable. To George III, to a large majority in Parliament, and probably to a majority of Englishmen, the American colonists had proved to be thoroughly irresponsible rebels who must be taught a lesson. To a majority of the colonists, the policy of Parliament was leading directly to unbearable tyranny—the kind of tyranny that they now felt it had been their main purpose to escape when they had originally emigrated to America. Fighting broke out at Lexington and Concord in 1775. A Continental Congress was summoned to meet in Philadelphia, and on July 4, 1776, the colonies formally declared their independence of king and Parliament in a declaration whose words rang like a tocsin summoning the people to rebellion throughout the Old World.

The American War of Independence

The American War of Independence was in a certain sense a civil war within the British dominions on both sides of the Atlantic. The colonists had friends in England, and the Irish sympathized with American grievances. The Whig faction to which Edmund Burke belonged tried in vain to induce George III and his prime minister, Lord North (1770-82), to follow a more moderate policy. A group of true "radicals," inspired by a rather unlovable champion of freedom of speech and parliamentary reform named John Wilkes, attacked the king's influence in Parliament, urged the publication of Parliamentary debates, and agitated for more democracy in the election of members. These radicals were too small a minority to carry any weight, but their political faith was that of the Declaration of Independence: that government must be by consent of the governed. Conversely, there were "Tories" in the colonies who agreed with Parliament and deplored the breach with England. In all, 60,000 of them were to emigrate to Canada, never to return.

The War of Independence (1775–83) was won by the American colonists with French help. French supplies before the battle of Saratoga (1777) and French troops and ships after the battle were of inestimable help to General Washington in his struggle to wear down the British forces in the colonies. In the settlement in 1783 of the general European war in which Great Britain became involved, the thirteen colonies gained their independence and won title to all the land east of the Mississippi, north of Florida, and south of the Great Lakes.

During the war most of the colonies had summoned conventions and drafted written constitutions with bills of rights to form the basis of their new governments. In 1787 a constitutional convention of delegates from all the colonies met in Philadelphia and drafted a constitution that bound the colonies in a federal union. This union was so successful that in mid-twentieth century the government founded upon it could boast the longest continuous political tradition of any in the world except the British. In the same year, in the Northwest Ordinance, the colonists decided momentously to extend the principles for which they had fought to their still unsettled western territories.

When these territories became populated, they would become not colonies or dependencies but "states," equal in status to the thirteen original members of the union.

The Significance of
the American Revolution

The success of the American Revolution had profound effects on Europe and eventually on other parts of the world. As the liberals in Europe saw it, a people had taken its destiny into its own hands, had revolted against its established rulers, and had set up government and governors of its own choosing. It had gained its liberty without falling into license. John Locke's ideas—natural equality, unalienable rights, government by consent of the governed, and the ultimate right of revolution—had been vindicated. Montesquieu's theory of a separation of powers had been written into both state and federal constitutions across the Atlantic. The constitutional conventions of the former British colonies appeared to demonstrate that a people could create a society and a government by formal contract. Furthermore, events in America seemed to demonstrate that smaller political units could be federated into a larger union without recourse to despotism. In sum, the American Revolution dramatized and passed on to the western world two political ideas of great importance for the future: the idea of limited, or constitutional, government (which had a long history reaching far back into the ancient and medieval worlds), and the idea of popular sovereignty, or democracy (which was relatively new in an age still strongly aristocratic in its thinking).

The quarter-century between the Peace of Paris and the outbreak of revolution in France apparently opened to the western world three possible roads for future development: enlightened despotism, aristocratic reaction, and democratic revolution.

Suggestions for Further Reading

1. General

The best general account of the century in English will be found in the three relevant volumes of the *Rise of Modern Europe* series, each with excellent critical bibliographies: P. Roberts, *The Quest for Security, 1715–1740** (1947); W. L. Dorn, *Competition for Empire, 1740–1763** (1940); and L. Gershoy, *From Despotism to Revolution, 1763–1789** (1944). Volume VII of the *New Cambridge Modern History* (*The Old Régime, 1713–1763,* 1957) has good articles on every major aspect of the period, but is not for continuous reading. A. Sorel, *Europe under the Old Régime** (1947), is a translation of the introduction to a famous larger work of 1895–1904. R. R. Palmer, *The Age of the Democratic Revolution* (1959), is a major work of interpretation which sees the American and French Revolutions, together with the smaller disturbances of the period, as manifestations of a single great "democratic revolution." Another useful study is C. B. A. Behrens, *The Ancien Régime** (1967).

2. Economic and Social

See the works on mercantilism and economic history noted for Chapters 18 and 19. E. Williams, in *Capitalism and Slavery* (1944), argues that mercantilism was compatible with slavery, but that the new industrial capitalism undermined it. On the aristocracy, see *The European Nobility in the Eighteenth Century** (edited A. Goodwin, 1953), a collection of essays by various authors; and F. Ford, *The Robe and the Sword** (1953), a study of the French aristocracy. A. Young, *Tours in England and Wales* (1932), is a selection from the journals of a very keen observer of the eighteenth-century countryside. As

---

* Available in paperback edition.

brief introductions to the agricultural and industrial revolutions, the general economic histories of Europe by H. Heaton (rev. ed., 1948) and by S. B. Clough and C. W. Cole (1946) are useful.

3. Expansion Overseas

W. B. Willcox, *Star of Empire: A Study of Britain as a World Power, 1485–1945* (1950), and H. I. Priestley, *France Overseas Through the Old Régime: A Study of European Expansion* (1939), are good general works. J. R. Seeley, *The Expansion of England* (1883), is a very influential older account. C. G. Robertson, *Chatham and the British Empire* * (1948), is a good brief modern discussion. On India, see H. Dodwell, *Dupleix and Clive* (1920); E. Thompson and G. T. Garratt, *The Rise and Fulfillment of British Rule in India* (1934); and H. Furber, *John Company at Work: A Study of European Expansion in India in the Late Eighteenth Century* (1948). On America, in addition to the books cited for Chapters 19 and 20, see L. B. Wright, *The Atlantic Frontier: Colonial American Civilization, 1607–1763* (1947); and M. Kraus, *The Atlantic Civilization: Eighteenth-Century Origins* (1949). On the economic history of the British colonies, see C. P. Nettels, *The Roots of American Civilization* (1938). On social history see T. J. Wertenbaker, *The First Americans* (1927).

4. Political and Diplomatic

J. Lough, *Introduction to Eighteenth-Century France* (1960), is a very good starting point for study. The best brief introduction to England is J. H. Plumb, *England in the Eighteenth Century* * (1951). B. Williams, *The Whig Supremacy, 1714–1760* (1939), in the *Oxford History of England,* is a more extended topical treatment. Two other books by J. H. Plumb offer interesting reading: *Sir Robert Walpole* (1956), and *The First Four Georges* * (1957). The serious student of the English political system and how it operated should become acquainted with the various studies of L. B. Namier. On Prussia, there is excellent material in Dorn (Section 1, above); also a first-rate biography of Frederick William I, *The Potsdam Fuehrer,* by R. Ergang (1941); biographies of Frederick the Great by P. Gaxotte (1941) and G. P. Gooch (1947); and an expert general account by W. H. Bruford, *Germany in the Eighteenth Century* * (1952). C. L. Morris, *Maria Theresa: The Last Conservative* (1937), is probably the best of several biographies; and S. K. Padover, *The Revolutionary Emperor* (1934), the best of several accounts of Joseph II. On Joseph's most important reform, see E. M. Link, *The Emancipation of the Austrian Peasant, 1740–1798* (1949). There are many biographies of Catherine the Great, but G. S. Thomson, *Catherine the Great and the Expansion of Russia* (1947), is the most informing from the historian's point of view. On the enlightened despots as a group, G. Bruun, *The Enlightened Despots* * (1929), is brief but extremely good. The best accounts of the war and diplomacy of the age will be found in the *Rise of Modern Europe* series, but there is a very brief account in A. H. Buffinton, *The Second Hundred Years' War, 1689–1815* (1929); Sir Charles Petrie, *Diplomatic History, 1713–1933* (1946), helps provide the continuity lacking in separate volumes.

5. The American Revolution

Two volumes in the *New American Nation* series provide the best up-to-date introduction: L. H. Gipson, *The Coming of the Revolution, 1763–1775* * (1954); and J. R. Alden, *The American Revolution, 1775–1783* (1954). Another good account is J. C. Miller, *Origins of the American Revolution* * (1943), and the same author's *The Triumph of Freedom, 1775–1783* * (1948). L. Gottschalk, *The Place of the American Revolution in the Causal Pattern of the French Revolution* (1948), and E. S. Morgan, *The Birth of the Republic, 1763–1789* * (1956), offer a somewhat broader perspective. M. Beloff has selected an interesting set of contemporary sources in *The Debate on the American Revolution, 1761–1783* * (1949). On the side of ideas, C. L. Becker's study of the text of *The Declaration of Independence* * (1922, 1942) is consistently illuminating.

---

* Available in paperback edition.

8

The French Revolution and Napoleon

The French Revolution marked a turning point in European history. The events that began to unfold in 1787 and that terminated with the fall of Napoleon Bonaparte in 1815 unleashed forces that altered not only the political and social structure of states but the map of Europe. Many attempts were made, in France and in other European countries, to undo the work of the Revolution and to repress the ideas of liberty, equality, constitutionalism, democracy, and nationalism that the Revolution had inspired. But the Old Regime was dead, in France at least, and a Europe dominated by monarchy and aristocracy and by a hierarchical social order could never be fully restored. With the coming of the French Revolution, then, we enter into a more modern world—a world of class conflict, middle-class ascendancy, acute national consciousness, and popular democracy. Together with industrialization, the Revolution reshaped the institutions, the societies, and even the mentalities of European men.

Napoleon astride his charger Tauris. By the sculptor E. Frémiet.

The Origins of the French Revolution

By the last half of the eighteenth century, France appeared to have overcome the dismal cycle of famine, plague, and high mortality which, in the preceding century, had inhibited both demographic and economic growth. The vast majority of Frenchmen who lived in the villages and tilled the fields were better off than their counterparts in most of Europe. French peasants, for example, owned some 40 percent of the country's farm lands. The mild inflationary trend that characterized much of the eighteenth century increased the wealth of large landowners, and surplus wealth in agriculture served to stimulate the expansion of the French economy as a whole. Modest advances in the textile and metallurgical industries, the construction of new roads and canals, and urban growth were other indications of economic development.

Yet, despite evident signs of prosperity, there was great discontent and restlessness in France in the 1780's. Neither the institutions nor the social structure of the country had kept pace with the middle orders' rising desire for greater social mobility, equality, and political power. The economy, particularly in agriculture, remained unstable and subject to fluctuations that could drive the peasants and urban poor to starvation. An inefficient and inequitable tax-collecting system yielded too small an income to support the state and aggravated the tensions and divisions within French society. Thus on the eve of the Revolution, and in the aftermath of a depression that had set in toward the beginning of Louis XVI's reign, France faced a conjuncture of crises. Three of these crises—the agrarian distress, financial chaos, and the aristocratic reaction—were particularly acute.

The people of France support the clergy and the nobility in this 18th-century cartoon. The rabbits and doves eating the grain were protected by law for the sport of the upper classes, to the annoyance of the lower classes.

Agrarian Distress

In 1787 and 1788, rural France suffered a series of catastrophes that helped drive the peasants toward a radical solution of their ills. The wretched weather and poor harvests of these two years further weakened an already depressed agricultural economy. Grain shortages led to sharp price increases, particularly in the cost of bread. Moreover, from the late 1770's the long-term growth of the French economy had been interrupted in several important areas, such as the wine trade, and between 1776 and 1787, agricultural profits generally declined. At the same time, noblemen and other large landowners sought to save their own declining fortunes by demanding from their tenant farmers dues and obligations that had long been neglected. The countryside was ripe for revolution.

Financial Chaos

The finances of Louis XVI's government were a shambles. By 1787 one-half of the nation's tax revenues went to service the massive public debt that Louis XIV had left to his successors. France's involvement in the Seven Years' War and in the American War for Independence had driven the government further along the road to bankruptcy. Without a reform of the tax system the king could not meet his obligations. But such a reform would mean an attack on privilege, and this Louis could never quite summon the courage to do.

Three ministers in succession struggled with the problem. The first, the Swiss banker Necker, was dismissed by the king in 1781 after he had proposed some modest reforms. Necker's successor, Calonne, thought he could carry on without much change. But as the deficit mounted he grew alarmed, and in 1786 he proposed a much more radical reform program than Necker's. The most striking provision of Calonne's program was a direct tax on all landowners—noble and commoner, lay and clerical. To oversee the assessment of the new tax, Calonne suggested that the king create local and provincial assemblies in which all men of property would be represented regardless of social status. In addition, older taxes, such as the *taille,* which weighed upon the lower orders, were to be reduced. Calonne's reforms struck at the very heart of the system of privilege and the social hierarchy of the Old Regime.

Calonne, aware that there would be bitter opposition to his plans, persuaded Louis XVI to call a conference of notables in the hope that they could be induced to back his program. But the members of this assembly, which met in February 1787, were drawn largely from the privileged orders and refused to support Calonne.

The king now dismissed Calonne and put in his place one of Calonne's chief opponents, Lomenie de Brienne, Archbishop of Toulouse. This prelate, though a member of both the higher nobility and the higher clergy, soon came to the same conclusions as Calonne. He tried to enact a similar reform program, but the *Parlement* of Paris refused to register the royal edicts. It declared that only the Estates General, a symbol of aristocratic power, could approve such measures. When Brienne tried to break the opposition by exiling the magistrates of the *Parlement* and then by abolishing the high courts, he touched off a revolt of the provincial nobility. In face of attacks by the socially and politically powerful, the government backed away from its reform program. In July 1788, the king yielded to the opposition and ordered a meeting of the Estates General for May 1789.

The Aristocratic Reaction

During the 1780's, then, aristocratic demands on the peasantry were aggravating the distress of the countryside, and aristocratic resistance to tax reform was hampering the government in its attempts to revamp the nation's financial structure. These were two facets of the aristocratic reaction that was directly responsible for the coming of the French Revolution.

The tremendous strength of the French privileged classes had been built up steadily during the reigns of Louis XV and Louis XVI.

At every turn the poor, the aspiring middle class, and enlightened reformers in government confronted the fact of privilege. Some men of the Enlightenment, in particular Voltaire, and such royal ministers as Turgot and Calonne encouraged the king to rationalize state finance and to bring a measure of justice to French society at the expense of the privileged groups. Louis XVI, however, despite fitful support of reform, chose in the end to stand by his noblemen. By the 1780's it appeared that the French king was the prisoner of the nobility and that he would do nothing to displease them.

Moreover, the nobles were particularly skillful in confusing the issue. Certain privileges, such as those which protected the laws, institutions, and customs of the provinces from encroachments by the central government, limited the arbitrary power of the king. They could be called liberties rather than privileges. These liberties were compared to the restrictions on royal power in England, and the English were regarded as the freest people in Europe. Thus the nobles could resist royal attacks on any form of privilege by asserting that the king was going to attack all privileges and all liberties and that he was simply trying to get rid of all restrictions on his power. Through this device, the nobility and the *parlements* were able to gain wide support and considerable sympathy when they resisted the arbitrary orders of the king, even when those orders were directed toward desirable ends.

There were those, however, who were not deceived by the rhetoric of the privileged orders. The hesitations of the king and the intransigence of the aristocracy increased the bitterness of large sections of the population. They wanted to put an end to privilege, and they felt that the unreformed monarchy would not help them in this struggle. Thus the attack on privilege was the driving force in the Revolution from beginning to end. The aristocratic reaction against reform was merely the opening phase of a revolution that would soon be directed against both the aristocracy and the monarchy.

The French Revolution and the King

The Estates General, which had not met since 1614, was convened by the king at Versailles on May 5, 1789. The electoral process by which deputies were selected was a relatively generous one: All adult French males had the right to vote, indirectly, for representatives to the Third Estate, which served the interests of the commoners. The First (clerical) and Second (noble) Estates represented the privileged orders. The king had asked that all local electoral assemblies draw up *cahiers de doléances*—lists of grievances—to submit to the Estates General when it met. Thus in the months preceding the convening of the Estates General, a great political debate occurred. Almost all politically minded men agreed that the monarchy should yield some of its powers. By 1788 even some noblemen were willing to go part way in abolishing privileges and in equalizing taxation. But the early debates in the Estates General revealed that the lawyers and bourgeois who represented the Third Estate were bent on a much more drastic reform.

The Tennis Court Oath

June 20, 1789

The National Assembly, considering that it has been summoned to establish the constitution of the kingdom, to effect the regeneration of public order, and to maintain the true principles of monarchy; that nothing can prevent it from continuing its deliberations in whatever place it may be forced to establish itself; and finally, that wheresoever its members are assembled, *there* is the National Assembly:

Decrees that all members of this Assembly shall immediately take a solemn oath not to separate, and to reassemble wherever circumstances require, until the constitution of the kingdom is established and consolidated upon firm foundations. . . .

From *A Documentary Survey of the French Revolution*, ed. by John Hall Stewart (New York: Macmillan, 1951), p. 88.

The Estates General and the National Assembly

The mood of the Third Estate was best expressed by one of its deputies, the Abbé Sieyès. In a famous pamphlet, *What Is the Third Estate?*, Sieyès argued that the real French nation was made up of people who were neither clergymen nor noblemen, and that this majority should have the decisive voice in all political matters. This idea, which approached the doctrine of popular sovereignty, was translated into action during the opening debate on voting procedures in the Estates General. The Third Estate, which had as many representatives as the other two combined, wanted the three Estates to meet and vote together. Since a few liberal nobles and a somewhat larger number of the lower clergy were sure to support the Third Estate, joint meetings would give the Third Estate a clear majority. The king and the privileged orders, on the other hand, demanded that the Estates vote separately. This was traditional procedure in meetings of the Estates General, and it assured that the first two Estates would retain control.

The Third Estate not only rejected the king's plan for separate meetings; on June 17 it declared itself the National Assembly of France and invited the other Estates to sit with it. The National Assembly then assumed the right to approve all taxation as well as the right to withhold all taxation if its political demands were not met. In the face of this bold initiative, the king hesitated but finally resorted to a show of force. On June 20 Louis XVI had the Third Estate barred from its usual meeting place. The deputies then convened in a nearby indoor tennis court and took an oath not to disband until they had drafted a constitution. This Tennis Court Oath was the first great act of the bourgeois revolution.

In a dreary repetition of the political ineptitude he had shown in previous crises, Louis missed his chance to act as impartial mediator between the hostile Estates. On June 23 he went before the Estates General

The Oath at the Jeu de Paume, a painting by Jacques-Louis David. The deputies of the Third Estate swear not to disband until they have drafted a constitution.

and offered a program of reform that in no significant way met the demands of the Third Estate for a vote by head, for more equal taxation, or for the dismantling of the system of privilege. At about the same time, the king began to concentrate troops around Versailles and Paris. His aim was to put down any disturbances that might occur should he decide to dissolve the Assembly. By now, however, neither partial reform nor brute force was a sufficient answer to the political crisis. The revolution had already become a battle between the forces of democracy—those who desired a more equal and open society—and the forces of aristocracy.

The Popular Revolt

Most of the deputies in the Third Estate were lawyers, professional men, and lesser officeholders. Their aspirations were those of the French bourgeoisie. In the urban centers and the countryside resided yet another element of the Third Estate—the mass of Frenchmen who were poor. Their aspirations and needs were not identical with those of the deputies at Versailles. But in the summer of 1789 a series of spontaneous popular disturbances and revolts broke out that linked, for the moment at least, the bourgeoisie and the common people in an uneasy alliance against the aristocracy.

Notable among these uprisings was an attack on July 14 on the Bastille, a royal fortress and prison in Paris. By the end of June the city of Paris had grown tense. The economic depression of the 1780's and the poor harvests of 1788 and 1789 had reduced the urban poor to misery, and to misery was now added the fear that the king and the aristocrats were conspiring to dissolve the Estates General. When the king's troops appeared on the outskirts of the city, the Parisians well understood why they were there. The immediate reaction of the citizens was to arm themselves. It was their search for arms that brought the leaders of the Parisian electoral assembly and a crowd of journeymen and workers from the faubourg Saint-Antoine to the Bastille on July 14. When the commandant refused to surrender, the crowd, aided by members of the recently formed municipal guard, stormed the gates and slaughtered the garrison.

The fall of the Bastille was an event of small consequence in itself—the crowds had destroyed little more than a building—but its implications were immense. The attack was regarded as a blow against royal despotism. It demonstrated that the Revolution was not simply a debate over a constitution. Of greatest importance, it brought the city of Paris and the political leaders of Paris to the forefront. A new, insurrectionary municipal government was formed; henceforth Paris would shape the direction of the Revolution. Finally, the events in Paris set off revolts in the provinces.

About the same time that the Parisian crowds were taking the Revolution into their own hands, the French peasants, also disappointed with the slow pace of reform, began to take action of their own. Like the poor of the cities, the peasants had been heartened by the political promise of the winter of 1788–89. They had patiently drawn up their *cahiers* and they had chosen their electoral committees; then they had waited confidently for relief to follow. The Estates General met in May. Spring passed and summer came, but the peasants were still poor, they were still not allowed to till the unused land of the nobles, and they still had to pay their customary dues.

Then, during July 1789, the same month that saw the storming of the Bastille, rumors spread through rural France that there would be no reforms and that the aristocrats were coming with troops to impose reaction upon the countryside. The result was panic and rioting throughout the country. During the "Great Fear," as

it is called, frightened peasants gathered to defend themselves against the unnamed and unseen enemy. Once assembled and armed, however, they turned against the enemy they knew —the local lord. Though the lords themselves were rarely in residence, peasants all over France burned their chateaux, often tossing the first brand into the counting-house where the hated records of their payments were kept.

The Destruction of Privilege

The popular revolts and riots had a profound impact on the king, the aristocracy, and the deputies of the Third Estate alike. Louis XVI recognized the National Assembly and ordered the clergy and the nobles to sit with the Third Estate. He also recognized the revolutionary government of Paris and authorized the formation of a national guard composed largely of members of the bourgeoisie. But the king received no credit for his concessions from the revolutionary leaders, who felt, quite rightly, that his sympathies were still with the nobles. At the same time, Louis' indecision had discouraged many of the strongest supporters of the Old Regime. The most reactionary noblemen, headed by the king's brother, the Count of Artois, began to leave the country. Other members of the aristocracy sought to preserve their property by making dramatic concessions to the popular will for reform.

On the night of August 4, one nobleman, the Viscount de Noailles, stood before the Assembly and proposed that all feudal levies and obligations be abolished. In a performance at once impressive and bizarre, nobles, clerics, and provincial notables arose to renounce feudal privileges, clerical tithes, and provincial liberties. In effect, the Old Regime was dismantled in one night of heated oratory, and the way seemed clear for the Assembly's main business—to provide a constitution for France. The implementation of the concessions of August 4, however, was somewhat less tidy. The structure of aristocratic privilege was indeed abolished by decree, along with tax exemptions and hereditary officeholding, but feudal dues were to be levied until the peasants had paid them, thereby freeing themselves from feudal obligations.

The Declaration of the Rights of Man

On the whole, the National Assembly had succeeded in wiping out the remains of feudalism and the privileges of orders and provinces. Now it faced the task of creating new political, legal, and administrative structures for the country. The ideological framework for this task was set forth by the constitution-makers in the Declaration of the Rights of Man, which they adopted on August 27, 1789.

In this preamble to a constitution yet unformed, the members of the National Constituent Assembly (that is, the National Assembly in its constitution-making role) established a set of principles idealistic enough to sustain the enthusiasm of the mass of Frenchmen for the Revolution and sweeping enough to include all humanity. The basic ideas of this document were personal freedom, equality under the law, the sanctity of property rights, and national sovereignty. The first article declared that "men are born and remain free and equal in rights." There were to be no class privileges and no interference with freedom of thought and religion. Liberty, property, security, and resistance to oppression were declared inalienable and natural rights. Laws could be made and taxes levied only by the citizens or their representatives. The nation, not the king, was sovereign, and all power came from and was to be exercised in the name of the nation. Thus was established the framework for a system of liberty under law. The Declaration was a landmark in the fight against privilege and despotism, and it had a great appeal to revolutionary and democratic factions throughout Europe.

The October Days

The Declaration of the Rights of Man was not simply a page lifted from John Locke, the *philosophes,* and the Americans. It was a highly political document hammered out in an Assembly that was showing itself to be increasingly divided. There were those among the moderate

The Declaration of the Rights of Man

August 27, 1789

1. Men are born and remain free and equal in rights; social distinctions may be based only upon general usefulness.
2. The aim of every political association is the preservation of the natural and inalienable rights of man; these rights are liberty, property, security, and resistance to oppression.
3. The source of all sovereignty resides essentially in the nation; no group, no individual may exercise authority not emanating expressly therefrom.
6. Law is the expression of the general will; all citizens have the right to concur personally or through their representatives in its formation; it must be the same for all, whether it protects or punishes. All citizens, being equal before it, are equally admissible to all public offices, positions, and employments, according to their capacity, and without other distinction than that of virtues and talents.
10. No one is to be disquieted because of his opinions, even religious, provided their manifestation does not disturb the public order established by law.
11. Free communication of ideas and opinions is one of the most precious of the rights of man. Consequently every citizen may speak, write, and print freely, subject to responsibility for the abuse of such liberty in the cases determined by law. . . .

From *A Documentary Survey of the French Revolution,* ed. by John Hall Stewart (New York: Macmillan, 1951), p. 114.

leaders of the Assembly who found the Declaration too radical and sweeping. These men desired to reconcile Louis XVI with the Revolution and to construct a constitutional system on the English model with a relatively strong monarch. The issues that divided the crown and the country could not, however, be compromised. Louis simply refused to sanction the decrees and the Declaration that followed the night of August 4.

The king's recalcitrance, the divisions in the Assembly, and the food shortages combined to produce yet another popular explosion. On October 5, 1789, a crowd of some 20,000 armed Parisians marched on Versailles, demanding bread and insisting that the royal family return to Paris. The king considered flight, but he was persuaded by Necker, who had been recalled to the government, and by Lafayette, leader of the National Guard, to appease the crowd and leave Versailles. On October 6 the king, Queen Marie Antoinette, and the royal family drove into Paris in their carriage, surrounded by shouting crowds, and established themselves at their palace in the center of the city. A few days later, the National Constituent Assembly followed.

The Parisians seemed satisfied with the king's capitulation, and the Assembly, together with the king and his ministers, turned to the question of the constitution. Henceforth, however, the deliberations of the Assembly were to take place in the heated atmosphere of Parisian politics. Here in the capital many political clubs were formed to debate the issues. The most famous of these was the Jacobin Club, which included many of the radical members of the Assembly. Here too were political agitators, journalists of all opinions, and, above all, crowds that could be mobilized to bring pressure on the Assembly. From the autumn of 1789 on, the Revolution became more and more a Parisian affair.

The Achievements of the National Constituent Assembly, 1789–91

It took two years to make the constitution. By the end of that time the government had been reorganized, the Church had been dispossessed of its lands, and the rights of Frenchmen had been more clearly defined. Here are the main results of the Assembly's complex and lengthy deliberations:

The Monarchy. By acts passed in September 1789, Louis XVI was reduced from his position as a monarch by divine right to the role of a constitutional officer of the nation. He was given the right of suspensive veto over legislation, a right that allowed him to delay the passage of laws for two years. The monarchy remained a hereditary institution, and the king retained control of military and foreign affairs.

The Legislature. The Constitution of 1791 provided for a unicameral Legislative Assembly, elected for two years. The Assembly had the power to initiate and enact legislation and controlled the budget. It also had the exclusive right to declare war. Members of the Constituent Assembly were barred from serving in the new legislature.

The Electorate. The Constitution did not provide for universal manhood suffrage. It divided Frenchmen into active and passive citizens. Only the former, who met a property qualification, had the right to vote. The active category comprised some 4 million men in a total population of about 25 million. Active citizens voted for electors, who in turn elected the Legislative Assembly. These electors, as well as officeholders in the Assembly, were drawn from some 50,000 of the country's wealthiest men.

The Administration. The elimination of aristocratic privilege invalidated most of France's local administration, which had been controlled by the nobility. The Assembly completed the process of dismantling the administrative apparatus of the Old Regime by abolishing all former provinces, intendancies, and tax farms. On a clean administrative map they drew eighty-three departments, roughly equal in size, with uniform administrative and judicial systems. Administration was decentralized and put in the hands of some 40,000 local and departmental councils and assemblies.

The Church. The reorganization of the French Church was decreed by the Civil Constitution of the Clergy promulgated in August 1790. The Assembly confiscated the lands of the Church, and, to relieve the financial distress of the country, issued notes on the security of the confiscated lands. These notes, or *assignats,* circulated as money and temporarily relieved the financial crisis. In addition, clergymen became paid officials of the state, and priests and bishops were to be elected by property-owning citizens.

The Constitution of 1791, together with the Declaration of the Rights of Man, summed up the principles and politics of the men of 1789. In its emphasis on property rights, its restrictive franchise, and its fiscal policy, the Constitution had a distinctly bourgeois bias. To look upon the document simply as a product of selfish interest, however, would be to underestimate the achievement of the constituents. A new class of peasant proprietors had been created. The framework for a society open to talent had been established. Administrative decentralization, it was thought, had overcome the prevailing fear of despotism. Equality before the law, if not political equality, had been made a fact. These were impressive and revolutionary achievements. But to succeed and mature, the new order established by the Constituent Assembly needed peace, social stability, and the cooperation of the king. None of these was forthcoming. Within a year the Constitution of 1791 had become a dead letter, and the Revolution had entered a new phase.

The Failure of Constitutional Monarchy

The Constitution of 1791 was most certainly an imperfect instrument. The Civil Constitution of the Clergy, for example, offended the pope and, more important, forced a crisis of conscience upon French Catholics. Many bishops and priests refused to accept the Civil Constitution, and they found broad support in the country. Schism in the Church became a major factor in the eventual failure of the Assembly to create a stable government for France. Moreover, the restrictive franchise opened the constitution-makers to the charge that they wanted to substitute a wealthy oligarchy for an aristocracy. Such obvious defects, however, were not alone responsible for the failure of constitutional monarchy. The principal culprit was the monarch himself.

At the head of the government stood a king who was thoroughly discredited. In June 1791, Louis XVI tried to escape from France in order to join the forces of counterrevolution outside the country. He very nearly succeeded but was caught at Varennes, near the eastern frontier, and was brought back to Paris. This humiliating episode destroyed what little authority Louis still possessed. In order to keep himself from being completely displaced, he swore to obey the new constitution; but he was now no more than a figurehead. From the very beginning, the constitutional monarchy was flawed.

At this point the situation was complicated by outside pressures. Louis' fellow monarchs were unhappy over the way in which their royal colleague was being treated. The privileged orders in other countries feared that the leveling principles of the Revolution would spread. The English, many of whom had sympathized with the Revolution so long as it seemed to be following an English model, began to denounce the radicalism and violence of the French. Edmund Burke, in particular, saw clearly the radical nature of the Revolution. In his *Reflections on the Revolution in France,* he insisted on the importance of tradition in preserving an orderly society and declared that it was folly to abandon time-tested institutions in favor of new ones based on abstract ideas. And everywhere French refugees spread counter-revolutionary propaganda urging Europe's monarchs to intervene.

The Legislative Assembly, September 1791–September 1792

The Legislative Assembly met in an atmosphere of intrigue, fear, and factional strife. The Assembly, itself bitterly divided, was deprived of the hard-won political experience of the constituents.

The largest faction was composed of members of the Feuillant Club. These men were moderates who supported the constitution and were even willing to compromise some of the gains of the years 1789–91 in order to unify the country. Of the 745 members of the Assembly, 136 belonged to the radical Jacobin Club. They were republicans, with an extensive political organization throughout the country. The Jacobins, in turn, were divided into at least two factions. One of these was led by the Assembly's most powerful politician, Jacques Brissot. The other was composed of a small group of Parisian delegates and politicians who would find a leader in Maximilien Robespierre. No political group commanded a majority in the Assembly, and ambitious leaders like Brissot sought issues with which to win over the uncommitted center. One such issue was readily at hand: the question of war or peace.

The First Wars of the Revolution

In April 1792 the Legislative Assembly declared war on Austria. This act transformed the Revolution. With war came the end of the monarchy and the constitution. With it also came terror and dictatorship. France became not simply the home of the Revolution but the exporter of revolutionary ideals. Finally, under the stress and emotions of war, France became a nation.

The idea that a war of such momentous consequence was, at least in part, the product of intrigue and politics within the Legislative Assembly would have been abhorrent to those patriotic Frenchmen who rallied to the national defense and who formed the first mass national army in European history. In their view, the machinations of European monarchs, the treachery of the French court, and the threat of counterrevolution within the country had forced the conflict upon France. And there was some truth in this view. As early as August 1791, the Emperor of Austria and the King of Prussia, by the Declaration of Pillnitz, proclaimed that it was the common interest of the sovereigns of Europe to restore order and monarchy in France. Austria seemed bent on humiliating France, particularly after Emperor Francis II came to the throne in March 1792. In the French court, there were royal ministers who believed that a victorious war against Austria would strengthen the hand of the king and allow him to end the Revolution. Louis XVI and his Austrian queen, Marie Antoinette, apparently hoped not for victory but for a French defeat that would lead to the restoration of royal authority.

External threats and court plots played into the hands of Brissot's republican faction. Brissot believed that a crusade to unseat the monarchs of Europe would rekindle the revolutionary fervor of the French people and rally them around his plan to establish a republic in France. He was opposed in the Jacobin Club by Robespierre, who feared that a war would strengthen the conservatives and lead to dictatorship. But Brissot proved the stronger, and the powerful Jacobin Club passed a resolution advocating a declaration of war. Brissot took the issue before the Assembly and won approval for war from all but seven deputies.

The war began badly. The French army lacked leadership and discipline. The government was short of money and hampered by factional disputes. The royal family and their supporters encouraged the enemy. It is not surprising that the Austrians and their allies, the Prussians, were soon able to advance along the road to Paris.

Two things saved the Revolution at this moment of crisis. The Austrian and Prussian generals, who were at least as incompetent as the French, delayed and divided their forces. And there was a genuine outburst of patriotic and revolutionary enthusiasm in France. The French kept on fighting, despite their failures, and their army did not melt away as the refugee nobles had predicted. As a result, when the Austro-Prussian army was checked at Valmy in September 1792, its cautious commander decided to call off the invasion. The allies had lost their best chance to crush the Revolution before it gathered strength.

The French Republic

During these gloomy months, when everything seemed to be going wrong, the radical politicians of Paris gained a commanding position in the government. These Jacobins—Robespierre and Georges-Jacques Danton were the most important—based their power on national guards summoned to protect the capital, on the Parisian crowds, and, from August 9, 1792, on an insurrectionary Paris Commune that replaced the legal municipal government. In August the Jacobins touched off an uprising in Paris that forced the Legislative Assembly to suspend the king from office and to issue a call for a revision of the constitution. A National Convention, elected by universal manhood suffrage, was to determine the new form of the French government. The events of August triggered what is often called the Second French Revolution. This revolution began with the deposition of Louis XVI; it ended in a bloody terror that consumed its own leaders. In many ways it confirmed Edmund Burke's most hysterical prophecies. And yet the Second French Revolution did not follow inexorably upon the first. War created its own necessities, survival being the most pressing.

The Convention and the Jacobins

The National Convention met in Paris on September 21, 1792, in the wake of a fierce bloodletting earlier in the month—the so-called September massacres. These massacres, which took the lives of some 1,300 prisoners in Paris, were part of a pattern of fear, terror, and revolutionary justice that persisted throughout much of the Convention's three-year rule.

The delegates to the Convention were elected by a minority of Frenchmen, despite universal manhood suffrage. Many citizens were repelled by the deposition of the king and the violence of the summer of 1792. Others were intimidated. Some were excluded from the electorate by governmental decree. Thus the most radical elements of the French population had disproportionate strength in the elections. Not surprisingly, many of the delegates were Jacobins.

The Jacobins, however, were divided. The followers of Brissot, now called the Girondists, made up one faction. They dominated the Convention in its early months. In general, the

Girondists represented the interests of provincial republicans, and they were bitterly opposed to the Paris Commune. Their foreign policy was aggressive and expansionistic. It was they, for example, who issued a manifesto in November 1792 offering France's aid to all revolutionaries throughout Europe. In domestic affairs, the Girondists were relatively moderate—at least when compared to their Parisian enemies. On the prime issue of 1792, the fate of the king, the Girondists urged that Louis XVI be imprisoned for the duration of the war. But the evidence of Louis' treason was so overwhelming that he was condemned to death and guillotined on January 21, 1793. This victory for the so-called Mountain—Robespierre's and Danton's faction—was followed by a purge of the Girondists in June 1793. The architects of France's war policy were among the first victims of that policy.

The Jacobins and the War

The Girondists fell before their Jacobin opponents in the wake of crushing French defeats by an overwhelming new coalition of European powers. The death of Louis XVI, France's designs on Holland, and its annexation of Savoy and Nice prompted England, Spain, Portugal, and several lesser states to join Austria and Prussia in the war against France. In the face of such a formidable combination, the French armies suffered a series of reversals. The victor of Valmy, General Dumouriez, was badly defeated in Belgium, and, in the spring of 1793, he defected to the enemy.

Now the government, under the direction of a Committee of General Defense (later the Committee of Public Safety), undertook to organize the entire nation for war. It applied conscription on a nationwide scale for the first time in modern European history. It raised huge armies, far larger than those of Louis XIV, far larger than those that could be called up by the old-fashioned monarchies against which France was fighting. And it supported those armies by means of confiscation and heavy taxes. The armies were organized by a military genius, Lazare Carnot, an engineer who made a science out of the service of supply and established the division as a tactical unit.

The monarchies of Europe, which were used to fighting limited wars with limited resources for limited gains, were overcome by a French nation organized for war. They could not afford to arm all their people; they still depended on the old officer corps for their leaders. And, much as they despised the Revolution, they were still not prepared to sacrifice all their resources to put it down. Other questions distracted the crowned heads of Europe: England was seeking colonial conquests, and the eastern powers were still concerned with the Polish problem. So the French recovered from the blows of 1793 and by the late spring of 1794 had broken through into the Low Countries. When the Convention ended its work in 1795, France was stronger and held more territory than it had under Louis XIV at the height of his power.

The Instruments of Jacobin Rule

Military success was achieved only through the intensive and often brutal organization of the French people. The Constituent Assembly's program of administrative decentralization had left France without any effective chain of command linking the National Convention in Paris to the provinces. Moreover, the Convention was an ungainly body, incapable of swift action. Into this void moved the radical Jacobins. In the provinces, Jacobin clubs virtually replaced local governing bodies and through their committees of surveillance controlled public life. At the center, executive power was entrusted to two committees—the Committee of Public Safety and the Committee for General Security. The former wielded almost dictatorial power over France from July 1793 until July 1794. It had twelve members, of whom Robespierre was the most important.

The genuine achievement of the twelve capable men who composed the Committee

of Public Safety is often overlooked because of the "Reign of Terror" they imposed on France. The Terror, however, must be put into the context of the problems that confronted Robespierre, Carnot, and their colleagues. From early 1793 there had been a series of internal rebellions against the government. Conservative peasants of the Vendée, a region in the west of France, had revolted against the national conscription and in favor of their priests who opposed the Civil Constitution. Later in the year, the Girondists had stimulated local uprisings in several provinces. In the heat of war, such rebellions appeared treasonable, and the Terror was used as a political weapon to impose order. Also, during much of the Committee's tenure, Parisian politicians, both to the left and to the right of Robespierre, maneuvered to secure power. Terror, against Danton among others, was a weapon in these internecine conflicts. There was an economic terror directed against war profiteers and hoarders. Finally, there were local terrors, uncontrolled from the center, in which Jacobins and undisciplined representatives of the government took revenge on their enemies. In the end, the Terror gained a certain momentum of its own, and the list of suspects grew. Among the factors in Robespierre's fall was the fear of the Convention that its remaining members would soon become victims of revolutionary justice.

In all, some 40,000 people, many of them peasants, were killed by the government and its agents. Proper judicial procedures, such as the right of the accused to counsel, were undermined. Even the Committee of Public Safety finally divided over the excesses of the Terror. When military successes restored a measure of stability to France, the National Convention reasserted its authority. Among its first acts was the arrest and execution of Robespierre in July 1794.

Jacobinism and French Society

The militant phase of Jacobinism was of relatively short duration. The Committee of Public Safety ruled for a year, and Robespierre had complete authority for only four months.

Thus, beyond the brilliant organization of the national defense, the Jacobins made few permanent contributions to French institutions and society. Certain of their acts, however, have remained of symbolic significance to the French Left. Among these were the guarantees of the right to a public education for all and the right of public welfare for the poor; these guarantees were set forth in an abortive constitution drawn up in 1793. In addition, the Jacobins were responsible for decrees establishing price controls and providing for the division of confiscated property among the poor. These decrees, however, were not the product of a conscious social philosophy; rather, they were political acts designed to win over the disaffected crowds in the cities and the landless peasants at a time of national crisis. The Jacobins were radical democrats who believed deeply in political equality; they were not socialists. With their fall in the summer of 1794, the Revolution fell back into the hands of the propertied bourgeoisie. It was this class that in the end gained most from the Revolution.

The Directory, 1795–99

In 1795 the Convention finally presented France with a constitution. It provided for a five-man executive board, called the Directory, and a two-house legislature. Even the republican-oriented Convention had been sufficiently sobered by the Terror to abandon its promise of universal suffrage, and the franchise was weighted in favor of the propertied classes. Once in office, the Directory proved both corrupt and incompetent. It maintained a militantly aggressive foreign policy and allowed the French economy to deteriorate disastrously. It was beset by a royalist revival—elections in 1797 demonstrated an upsurge in royalist sentiment—and by Jacobin intrigue. The Directory's single source of strength was the army. With the economy foundering and popular unrest increasing, the Directory was ripe for the *coup d'état* which in 1799 brought one of its most successful generals, Napoleon Bonaparte, to power.

"Here lies all of France." An engraving of Robespierre guillotining the executioner after having guillotined everyone else in France.

Napoleon's Rise to Power

Napoleon Bonaparte was born on the island of Corsica in 1769, shortly after the island had been annexed by France. The Bonapartes were members of the minor nobility of Corsica, and at the age of nine Napoleon was admitted to a military school in France. From that time on, he knew no other life than the army. When most of the aristocratic officer corps left France

1789	1795	1799	Napoleon	1814
Revolutionary Governments	Directory	Consulate	First Empire	

1804

after the fall of the monarchy, Napoleon stayed on to serve the Republic. He rose to become a brigadier general in 1793 at the age of 24. By 1797, when the Directory felt its power slipping, Barras, one of the Directors, realized that Napoleon's support could be valuable. He sought Napoleon's friendship first by introducing the young general to one of his cast-off mistresses, Josephine Beauharnais (whom Napoleon married), and then by giving him command of an army that was preparing for an invasion of Lombardy, a province in north-

ern Italy that was then under the control of Austria.

The Italian campaign of 1797 was a success. It removed Austria from the war and established Napoleon's reputation as an outstanding general. After the defeat of the Austrians in Italy, only England was still at war with France. In 1798 Bonaparte took an army by sea to Egypt, where he hoped to sever England's lifeline to India. He easily defeated the Egyptians, but the English admiral, Horatio Nelson, sank the French fleet near the mouth of the Nile. Napoleon's army, trapped in Egypt, was soon decimated by disease and dysentery. In the midst of this crisis, Napoleon heard that the Directory was in danger of falling and that some of the Directors wanted to create a military dictatorship. Leaving his army in Egypt, he made his way secretly back to France to offer his services to the conspirators.

The most important Director was the Abbé Sieyès, and it was with this former leader of the First French Revolution that Napoleon conspired. On November 9, 1799, Bonaparte forced the legislators to abolish the Directory and substitute a new government in which a board of three consuls would have almost absolute power. The conspirators asked Napoleon to serve as one of the consuls. Apparently they hoped he would provide the personal popularity and military power needed to support a regime that would be dominated, behind the scenes, by the other two consuls. But when the new constitution was written—at Napoleon's orders—the general emerged as First Consul and virtual dictator of France. When the French people were invited to endorse the constitution in a plebiscite, they voted overwhelmingly to accept it. To Frenchmen exhausted by years of revolution, terror, and economic instability, Napoleon seemed to be the guarantor both of the gains of the Revolution and of order.

Bonaparte's Proclamation to the Army of Italy

April 26, 1796

This proclamation was issued after Piedmont had been overrun, but before a decisive victory had been won.

Soldiers! Until now you have fought for barren rocks. Lacking everything, you have accomplished everything. You have won battles without cannon, crossed rivers without bridges, made forced marches without boots, bivouacked without brandy and often without bread. Only the phalanx of the Republic, only the soldiers of Liberty, could endure the things that you have suffered.

But, soldiers, you have really done nothing if there still lies a task before you. As yet, neither Milan nor Turin is yours. Our country has the right to expect great things of you; will you be worthy of that trust? There are more battles before you, more cities to capture, more rivers to cross. You all burn to carry forward the glory of the French people; to dictate a glorious peace, and to be able, when you return to your villages, to exclaim with pride: "I belonged to the conquering army of Italy!"

As quoted in R. M. Johnston, *The Corsican* (Boston: Houghton Mifflin, 1921), p. 23.

Napoleon and Domestic Reform

Bonaparte was, above all, a military man, and his fortunes always hinged on military success or failure. Yet his domestic reforms were profound and enduring. If the French Revolution gave the country an ideology which, henceforth, would both inspire and divide Frenchmen, Napoleon gave France many of its characteristic institutions. Better than any eighteenth-century monarch, Bonaparte fulfilled the *philosophes'* dream of an enlightened despot.

Between 1799 and 1801 Napoleon led a series of successful campaigns against the coalition that England, Austria, and Prussia had formed to defeat him. He wanted to win a favorable peace so that he could devote himself to consolidating his position in France. Hostilities ended in 1801 and did not break out again on any major scale until 1805. Napoleon used those four years to restore domestic concord and economic stability and to establish a network of administrative institutions that gave coherence and uniformity to the work of his government.

Perhaps Napoleon's most characteristic contribution was the *Code Napoléon.* From the debris of the laws left by the several legal systems of the Old Regime and the succession of revolutionary governments, Napoleon's advisers compiled a uniform legal code that is still the basis of French law. The Code maintained in theory the revolutionary concept of the equality of all men before the law, but it was in fact far less egalitarian than the laws of the revolutionary era. It emphasized, for instance, the authority of the state over the people, of business corporations over their employees, and of male heads of families over their wives and children. Property rights received particularly strong protection under the Code.

Other Napoleonic reforms followed a similar pattern. They often upheld in principle the ideals of the Enlightenment and the Revolution but served in practice to strengthen France's new authoritarian state. Napoleon retained, for instance, the division of France into eighty-three uniformly administered departments. He used the departmental system, however, not to foster local responsibility, as had been intended, but to create a highly centralized administration controlled directly by the First Consul through field administrators called prefects. He also instituted a nationwide system of public schools that not only educated the young—an ideal of the *philosophes*—but imbued them with an exaggerated patriotism and devotion to their ruler.

In reforming France's finances Napoleon followed the British and American examples by chartering a privately owned national bank to provide both a depository for government funds and a source of credit for French businessmen. With government deposits as security, the bank issued paper money as legal tender. Increased currency, a stable franc, and improved credit helped to improve France's shaky economy. Napoleon also resolved that perennial problem of the Old Regime—tax-collecting—by creating a fiscal bureaucracy.

Although Napoleon himself was far from religious, he understood better than his republican predecessors that domestic peace could not be achieved until the religious question had been settled. Accordingly, he concluded an agreement with Pope Pius VII, the Concordat of 1801, which recognized that the majority of Frenchmen were Roman Catholics. The Catholic Church was not, however, to be the established church in France, nor were church properties confiscated during the Revolution to be restored. Moreover, the First Consul retained the right to appoint bishops. Through the Concordat of 1801, Napoleon regained the loyalty of French Catholics to the official government and at the same time won the gratitude of those who owned former church properties.

Although Napoleon brought a form of enlightened despotism to France, he did so at the expense of much of the individual liberty that had been the first principle of the Enlightenment. The legislative institutions created by the Constitution of 1799 were a sham. Political opposition was punished by police action, and the press was strictly censored. Napoleon's training was military, and too often his solution to political and even social problems was force. Nevertheless, his government in its early years was popular. He preserved the property of those who had gained from the Revolution. He satisfied the social ideal of the Revolution of 1789 by maintaining a society open to all men of talent. In his own administration, he incorporated royalists, constitutionalists, and Jacobins. With such accomplishments to his credit, he easily won popular approval when he declared himself First Consul for life in 1802. And two years later, on December 2, 1804, the nation rejoiced when, in the presence of the pope, he crowned himself Emperor of the French.

The Napoleonic Empire

Napoleon did not create French imperialism; he inherited, indeed he had been an agent of, a policy of aggressive expansion undertaken by the Convention and the Directory. A satellite republic had already been established in Holland in 1795, and during the victorious campaigns against Austria toward the end of the decade French armies had brought revolutionary ideals and French power to Switzerland and parts of Italy. This burst of French expansion had come to an end when Napoleon signed separate peace treaties with Austria, in 1801, and England, in 1802. Large-scale hostilities did not begin until 1805, but from that time until Napoleon's ultimate defeat ten years later, France was almost constantly at war.

If Napoleon could have avoided war he might have established his empire as the dominant state in Europe. But his own insatiable ambition and the continuing enmity of England made war almost inevitable. Napoleon could not resist the temptation to extend his sphere of influence by entering into intrigues in Germany and Italy. England was determined to keep France from becoming the dominant political and economic power in

Europe. French possessions in the Low Countries violated a basic rule of English foreign policy—namely, to keep these invasion bases and commercial centers out of the hands of a strong power. Moreover, the British and their ablest statesman of the period, William Pitt the Younger, were convinced that Napoleon was using the peace to ready France for yet another war. Pitt soon was able to persuade other continental states that they must join England to restore the balance of power and resist the spread of French influence in central Europe.

Napoleon was just as ready for war as was England. He felt that his empire could never be secure and that his plans for Europe could never be achieved until England had been thoroughly defeated. The two states drifted into war in 1803, and other continental powers—Austria, Russia, and finally Prussia—joined England.

It was a difficult war for the two major contestants. Napoleon could not gain control of the sea, and without this control he could not subdue England. He made his greatest effort in 1805 when he concentrated his army at Boulogne and tried to pull the English fleet out of the Channel by an elaborate set of naval feints in the Atlantic. But the English were not deceived. While one fleet guarded England against invasion, another, under Nelson, caught the French and their allies off Cape Trafalgar and annihilated them (October 21, 1805). Napoleon was never again able to threaten England with invasion. The English, on the other hand, could not defeat the French on the Continent and were dependent upon the armies of their allies.

By the fall of 1805 the armies of the Russian and Austrian emperors assembled in central Europe for a combined assault on Napoleon. Instead of waiting for the attack, Napoleon marched an army deep into central Europe and took the Austrian and Russian generals by surprise. He defeated the Austrian and Russian forces first at Ulm, and then again in the most spectacular of all his victories, at Austerlitz, on December 2, 1805.

With Austria defeated and Russia in retreat, Napoleon followed up his victory with a complete reorganization of the German states. He abolished the Holy Roman Empire and eliminated many of the small German principalities. Out of these petty states he created a satellite system composed of fourteen larger states which were united in a Confederation of the Rhine; Napoleon served as president of this German Confederation.

Prussia, which had not at first joined the coalition against Napoleon, entered the fray in 1806 and was soundly defeated at Jena in October of that year. King Frederick William III was forced to accept a humiliating peace and to become an ally of France. The following spring, Emperor Alexander I of Russia again sent an army against Napoleon, only to have it defeated at Friedland in June, 1807. In three campaigns in three successive years, Napoleon had defeated the three strongest powers on the Continent and established his position as master of Europe. Russia was too large to occupy, but Napoleon had taught Emperor Alexander the futility of opposition. A few weeks after Friedland, Napoleon and Alexander held a dramatic meeting near Tilsit. Alexander recognized Napoleon's supremacy in the West, and Napoleon agreed not to intervene in Russia's internal affairs or to prevent Alexander from extending Russian influence into the Ottoman-controlled Balkans.

Napoleonic Europe and the Continental System

Napoleon was now at the summit of his power. All Europe, save England, was to some degree under his rule. France, Belgium, Germany

One of a famous series of paintings by Goya on the miseries of the Spanish War. The French are executing a group of the Spaniards who rebelled in 1808 against the government of Joseph Bonaparte.

west of the Rhine, and parts of Italy and Illyria constituted a French Empire ruled directly by Napoleon as emperor. Holland, Westphalia (a Napoleonic creation in Germany), and southern Italy were theoretically independent kingdoms, over which Napoleon placed three of his brothers as kings. Northern Italy was also a kingdom, with Napoleon himself as king. The Grand Duchy of Warsaw was carved out of Prussia's Polish territories and given to France's ally, the King of Saxony. In 1808, the Bourbon monarch of Spain was overthrown and replaced by Joseph Bonaparte.

England alone resisted the tide of French expansion. From 1806 on, Napoleon tried to weaken England by wrecking English trade with the Continent. This so-called Continental System imposed heavy penalties on anyone trading with England and forbade the importation of English goods. Since England produced the cheapest manufactures and was a good market for food and raw materials, this ban put a heavy strain on the economies of the continental countries. England made the strain worse by blockading all countries that subscribed to the French system. The English blockade was harsh enough to drive Denmark into a close alliance with France and to help cause the War of 1812 with the United States. But on the whole it caused less ill will than Napoleon's decrees. It was simply impossible for the European economy to function properly without English trade.

Napoleon himself had to allow exceptions and grant special licenses, a procedure that irritated everyone who did not receive such favors. Smuggling became a highly organized and profitable business, and attempts to enforce French regulations strengthened the opposition to Napoleon everywhere. Most important of all, it led to a quarrel between Napoleon and Alexander of Russia.

Emperor Alexander had not been entirely happy with the results of his alliance with Napoleon. France had gained vast territories; Russia had acquired only Finland and Bessarabia. Napoleon's creation of the Grand Duchy of Warsaw menaced Russia's control of the Polish lands it had seized in the 1790's. But the great and overwhelming grievance of the Russians was the Continental System. Russia needed English markets for its grain, and Alexander would not and could not enforce the rules against trade with England. Napoleon, bent on the destruction of England, could not tolerate this breach in his system, which was already being weakened by the ill will of other rulers. He requested Alexander to stop the trade; when Alexander refused, Napoleon prepared to invade Russia.

The Weaknesses of the Napoleonic Empire

When Napoleon undertook his Russian campaign in June 1812, his hold on Europe and even on the French was weakening. Initially, French expansion had been greeted with some enthusiasm by parts of the conquered populations. In the wake of the French armies came French institutions and ideas that had a liberating effect on societies under the yoke of archaic political and social structures. Within the Empire, the *Code Napoléon* was established, the privileges of the Church and aristocracies were abolished, and fetters on local industry and commerce were removed. Napoleon saw himself, in other words, as the "revolution on horseback" and sought to impose a new order on Europe—a new order that was enlightened, rational, and French. This vision of Napoleon's was, at best, only partially achieved, and even those who had most enthusiastically received the invading French armies soon perceived that imperialism was a more important component of the Napoleonic system than was liberation. The Continental System contributed to a general economic crisis in Europe that alienated the commercial and industrial interests. High taxes and conscription were imposed on the tributary states. And the French system was enforced by tight police surveillance. Napoleonic tutelage, even at its most benevolent, appeared incompatible with the libertarian and nationalistic ideals of the French Revolution.

Increasingly, Napoleon was beset by the growth of nationalistic feelings and national resistance to his rule. In Germany, Italy, and Spain, national awakening was intimately linked to the opposition to French hegemony. This opposition took many forms. In Italy and Germany cultural movements arose that emphasized the common history, language, and literature shared by the fragmented parts of these countries. In Spain resistance was expressed in a more violent manner when rebellions broke out in 1808 against the regime of Joseph Bonaparte. It was in Spain that Napoleon first confronted guerrilla warfare and first encountered serious failure. A Spanish victory at Baylen in 1808 was the initial break in the emperor's record of invincibility. By 1812, the Spanish rebels, with the help of an English army under Wellington, had driven the French from Madrid and had organized a constitutional government that controlled more than half the country.

The appearance of a well-organized English army on the Continent was one indication that the balance of power in Europe was beginning to shift against Napoleon. There were other signs, the most important of which was the recovery of France's nominal ally and potential enemy, Prussia. After the humiliating defeat of the Prussians at Jena, the process of reconstructing the kingdom was begun. Under Generals Gneisenau and Scharnhorst, the Prussian army was modernized and a form of generalized military training for young men was introduced. To revitalize the country, another reformer, the Baron vom Stein, persuaded the king to abolish serfdom and to grant a large measure of liberty to Prussian municipalities. Stein's social legislation was limited in its effects, but the military reforms allowed Prussia to play a significant role in the final defeat of Napoleon.

At the same time that his enemies were strengthening themselves and challenging the French monopoly of force on the Continent, Napoleon began to lose his grip on the French people. French economic domination of Europe, which had been one of the goals of the Continental System, failed to materialize, and France, like the rest of the Continent, suffered from the economic crisis that marked the last years of Napoleon's reign. Internally, the regime grew more repressive, and Napoleon became increasingly intolerant of criticism and even of his ministers' advice. After his divorce from Josephine and his marriage to an Austrian princess, Maria Louisa, Napoleon more and more took on the airs of an Old Regime monarch. In the end, those Frenchmen who had provided him with his magnificent and spirited army were exhausted by the burdens of empire.

The Invasion of Russia and the Fall of Napoleon

In June 1812 Napoleon marched into Russia with 600,000 men, the largest army ever assembled up to that time. Only about a third were French. Most had been recruited in the German states or in other dependencies. Napoleon expected to deliver a fast and decisive blow, but the Russians, so greatly outnumbered, did not give battle. Instead

The Retreat from Moscow

The following is from a letter written by Napoleon to his Minister for Foreign Affairs, November 29, 1812.

The army is strong in numbers, but terribly disorganized. It would take a fortnight to reconstitute the regiments, and where is a fortnight to come from? The disorganization is due to cold and privations. We shall soon be at Vilna: shall we be able to hold out there? Yes, if we can do so for a week; but if we are attacked during the first week, it is doubtful whether we could stay there. Food, food, food! Without it, there is no limit to the horrors this undisciplined mass of men may bring upon the town. Perhaps the army will not rally until it is behind the Niemen. . . . I am particularly anxious that there should be no foreign agents at Vilna. The army is not for exhibition purposes at the moment.

As quoted in J. M. Thompson, *Napoleon Self-Revealed* (Boston: Houghton Mifflin, 1934), p. 319.

they retreated, drawing Napoleon behind them. After one costly but inconclusive engagement at Borodino, Napoleon occupied Moscow in September and waited for Alexander to offer peace terms. But no message came.

After five weeks Napoleon realized that he could not keep so large a force in Russia through the winter, and on October 19 he began the long march westward. Almost immediately he encountered difficulties. Since the land through which he passed had already been burned by both armies, he lost thousands of men to disease and starvation. When the cold weather came, the weakened soldiers were no match for the elements. As the remnants of Napoleon's army stumbled closer to the frontier, Polish and German soldiers deserted and headed homeward. When Napoleon reached the German border in December, he could not muster 100,000 men. If Austria or Prussia had chosen to launch an attack at this time, the war could have been ended. But the allies as yet had no clue to the enormity of the disaster.

"Every man for himself!" In this cartoon by Cruikshank, Napoleon flees from Waterloo on a crippled imperial eagle.

Once on German territory, Napoleon fled in disguise to Paris and organized a new army which he marched toward the Russian border in the spring of 1813. But defeat had deflated the Napoleonic image, and Napoleon was badly beaten at Leipzig in October by the combined armies of Austria, Prussia, and Russia. Napoleon lost about two-fifths of his men and retreated back across the Rhine. Meanwhile, the British general Wellington defeated another French army in Spain and crossed the border into southern France. On March 31, 1814, the combined armies entered Paris, and one week later Napoleon abdicated. After some debate, the allies restored the Bourbons to the throne of France and then called a peace conference in Vienna to settle the fate of the rest of Europe.

Napoleon was exiled to the island of Elba, off the Italian coast. But he still had one battle to fight. In March 1815 he escaped and landed in the south of France. The army proved loyal to the deposed leader and Napoleon was soon in control of France once again. But the allies were prepared. Napoleon was conclusively defeated at Waterloo on June 18, 1815, and three days later he abdicated for the second time. The allies now exiled him to St. Helena, a small and remote island off the Atlantic coast of Africa. The era of the Revolution and Napoleon had ended.

The era had ended, but it could not be effaced. The allies could restore a Bourbon to the throne of France, but the new king, Louis XVIII, could not restore the Old Regime. He had to keep many of Napoleon's officials. He had to preserve the Napoleonic administrative system and the Concordat with the Church. He had to accept both the revolutionary principle of equality under the law and the revolutionary land settlement. He had to grant a constitution to his people. It was a conservative constitution with a very limited electorate, but it meant that the king's rule was not absolute. And throughout Europe the great ideas of the Revolution—liberty, equality, and nationalism—lived on. These ideas were only partially recognized in some countries and totally suppressed in others, but they persisted everywhere—smoldering coals that were to burst into flame again and again during the nineteenth century.

The political balance of power in Europe had been permanently altered. No one could restore the petty states of Germany or the feeble republics of Italy. No one could ignore the claims of Russia to have, for the first time, a voice in the affairs of western Europe. No one could fail to recognize the tremendous strides that England had made in industry and commerce during the wars. Conversely, for the first time in two centuries, France was no longer the richest and strongest European state. These were some of the new political facts with which the diplomats at Vienna had to deal.

Suggestions for Further Reading

1. General

The best general work on the French Revolution is the authoritative study by G. Lefebvre, *The French Revolution* (1962–64). C. Brinton, *A Decade of Revolution, 1789–1799** (1934), in the *Rise of Modern Europe* series, is a fine introductory summary. Valuable source material may be found in J. H. Stewart, *A Documentary Survey of the French Revolution* (1951).

---

* Available in paperback edition.

J. M. Thompson, *The French Revolution** (1943), is a solid standard work. R. R. Palmer, *The Age of the Democratic Revolutions,* 2 vols. (1959–64), places the French Revolution in its broad European perspective. The same is done more briefly in N. Hampson, *The First European Revolution: 1776–1815** (1969), and, with a neo-Marxian approach, in E. J. Hobsbawm, *The Age of Revolution** (1962).

2. The Social History of the Revolution

An excellent introduction to the social history of the Revolution is N. Hampson, *Social History of the French Revolution* (1962). The essays in J. Kaplow, ed., *New Perspectives on the French Revolution** (1965), are indispensable for an understanding of the social movement. A. Cobban, *The Social Interpretation of the French Revolution* (1964), is an important revisionary statement. On the role of the masses, see G. Rudé, *The Crowd in the French Revolution** (1959), which breaks new ground. E. Barber, *The Bourgeoisie in XVIIth Century France** (1955), discusses the background of bourgeois discontent. Valuable material on the aristocracy may be found in F. L. Ford, *Robe and Sword: The Regrouping of the French Aristocracy after Louis XIV** (1953).

3. Major French Interpretations of the Revolution

Alexis de Tocqueville's *The Old Regime and the French Revolution** (1956) presents the classic view of the Revolution as the continuation of the centralizing tendencies of the Old Regime. G. Lefebvre, *The Coming of the French Revolution* (1947), gives an excellent picture of France in the first year of the Revolution and states precisely and clearly the nature and problem of the French Revolution as a whole. For a treatment from the republican side, see F. V. A. Aulard, *The French Revolution,* 4 vols. (1901, 1910). A. Mathiez, *The French Revolution** (1928), is a sympathetic leftist interpretation of the Revolution.

4. Special Topics

Perhaps the best introduction to the Convention and the Reign of Terror is the brief study by J. M. Thompson, *Robespierre and the French Revolution** (1953). R. R. Palmer, *Twelve Who Ruled** (1941), is a fascinating account of the Reign of Terror written from a biographical approach. D. M. Greer, *The Incidence of Terror During the French Revolution* (1935), is a grisly statistical account of who was actually executed and how. The role of Paris in the Revolution is the subject of A. Soboul, *The Parisian Sans-Culottes and the French Revolution* (1964). On party politics during the Legislative Assembly and the Convention, see M. J. Sydenham, *The Girondins* (1961). The fall of the Jacobins and the period of the Directory are dealt with authoritatively in G. Lefebvre's *The Thermidoriens** (1937) and in the same author's *The Directory** (1946).

5. Napoleon and the Napoleonic Empire

G. Bruun, *Europe and the French Imperium** (1938), in the *Rise of Modern Europe* series, is a good general introduction. Recent biographies of Napoleon include J. M. Thompson, *Napoleon Bonaparte* (1952), and F. Markham, *Napoleon** (1966). The best guide to interpretations of the period and perhaps the best book on Napoleon in English is P. Geyl, *Napoleon:*

---

* Available in paperback edition.

*For and Against** (1949). The best treatment in any language is the soon-to-be-translated volume by G. Lefebvre, *Napoléon* (rev. ed., 1953). On Napoleon's domestic policy, see R. Holtman, *The Napoleonic Revolution** (1967). Both R. B. Mowat, *The Diplomacy of Napoleon* (1924), and H. C. Deutsch, *The Genesis of Napoleonic Imperialism, 1801–1805* (1938), remain standard works on foreign policy. The best recent treatment of Napoleon's military career is D. Chandler, *The Campaigns of Napoleon* (1966). O. Connelly, *Napoleon's Satellite Kingdoms* (1965), deals with the rule of Napoleon and his relatives over most of Europe. G. H. Lovett, *Napoleon and the Birth of Modern Spain,* 2 vols. (1965), tells a dramatic story. Napoleon's relations with the two peripheral powers of Europe are treated in C. Oman, *Britain Against Napoleon* (1944), and in A. Palmer, *Napoleon in Russia* (1967).

---

* Available in paperback edition.

9

The Search for Stability, 1815–1850

The unrest that had prevailed in Europe since the French Revolution did not end with the defeat of Napoleon. Another half-century was to pass before the Continent once again reached a semblance of stability. Many of Europe's troubles, of course, stemmed from the long and costly series of recent wars. But there were other causes of unrest. Politically, Europe continued to feel the effects of the issues first raised by the French Revolution—notably liberalism and nationalism. Intellectually, the years after Napoleon were part of the Age of Romanticism, with its protest against the rationalism of the Enlightenment. Economically and socially, the Continent in the first half of the nineteenth century began to feel in earnest the effects of the "Industrial Revolution," which England had already experienced in the eighteenth century (see Chapter 10). We shall concentrate in this chapter mainly on political and intellectual developments. But we must keep in mind that political tension was often merely the manifestation of underlying economic and social unrest. The rapid increase of population alone—from 180 million in 1800 to 266 million in 1850—could not help but have unsettling economic and political results. And the fact that more and more people now lived in cities did much to change the everyday lives of many Europeans.

Le Ventre législatif, by Honoré Daumier (1809–79). The political ideal of the middle class in the early 19th century has been aptly characterized as "government of the wealthy, for the wealthy, by the wealthy." The result is shown with biting irony in this lithograph of the French legislature in 1834 by one of France's outstanding caricaturists. The title means "the legislative belly."

Europe's search for stability after 1815 was marked by a contest between the forces of the past and the forces of the future. For a while it seemed as though the traditional agencies of power—the monarchs, the landed aristocracy, and the Church—might once again resume full control. But potent new forces were ready to oppose this relapse into the past. With the quickening of industrialization, there was now not only a middle class of growing size and significance but a wholly new class, the urban proletariat. Each class had its own political and economic philosophy—liberalism and socialism, respectively—which stood opposed to each other as well as to the traditional conservatism of the old order. It was inevitable that these rival classes and ideologies should clash. The resulting revolutions did not end until 1850. By that time

the forces of the past were still not defeated, but they were everywhere on the defensive.

Economic growth and ideological unrest were not the only causes for revolution in the early nineteenth century. There was also the force of nationalism, which made itself increasingly felt among Europeans everywhere. Nationalism as an awareness of belonging to a particular nationality was nothing new. What was new was the intensity that this awareness now assumed. There were still some signs of eighteenth-century cosmopolitanism, especially among the aristocracy. But for the mass of the people, nationalism became their most ardent emotion, and national unification or independence their most cherished aim.

Generally speaking, the early nineteenth century was a major phase in the slow change

Prince Talleyrand, "the man with the six heads, knight of the order of the weather vane." A satire on the French statesman's shifting political allegiances.

from an essentially aristocratic and agrarian society into an essentially democratic and industrial society. The problem before political leaders everywhere was to give political expression to the economic and social changes resulting from the industrial transformation of Europe. In trying to do this, they hoped to bring some degree of stability to their deeply unsettled world.

The Restoration of the Old Order

The first task facing the allies after defeating Napoleon was to bring order to a continent that had been disrupted by two decades of war. Europe's statesmen in the main tried to restore conditions as they had been before the French Revolution. In domestic affairs they adopted the principle of "legitimacy"—that is, they brought back almost everywhere the rulers who had been ousted by revolution or war. In international affairs they tried to reconstruct the balance of power that had been upset by France. In retrospect this preoccupation with the past may seem shortsighted. But history shows that most peace settlements are made with a view to the past rather than a vision of the future.

The Congress of Vienna

Peace conferences are usually dominated by a few leading statesmen. In 1814–15 the decisive figures were Austria's chancellor Prince Metternich, Britain's foreign minister Lord Castlereagh, Tsar Alexander I of Russia, and the Prussian King Frederick William III. To this list we must add France's representative, Talleyrand. The fact that the vanquished were able to make their voice heard shows the moderation and common sense of the victors.

The final peace with France was concluded at Paris in November 1815. France was the first to experience the principle of legitimacy. The new French king, Louis XVIII, was the brother of Louis XVI and the uncle of the dauphin, Louis XVII, who had died. Considering the many hardships the French had inflicted upon Europe, the peace settlement was remarkably lenient.

Metternich

PRO

He was a statesman of unusual proportions: the greatest foreign minister that Austria ever had, and one of the greatest masters of international politics in the history of the modern European states. . . . He lifted Austria from its deepest downfall to a proud height. . . . He had the greatest part in bringing it about that for thirty years Europe enjoyed comparative international peace, and that during this time, in the center of the continent, learning and art could have a period of the most salutary, quiet cultivation, capital and the spirit of enterprise could undergo a strong increase, and religion and religious communities could experience intensification and consolidation.

CON

The question has often been raised whether he was not rather a good diplomat than a statesman. The question appears to be thoroughly justified: he lacked virtually all the characteristics necessary to a real and great statesman—courage, resolution, strength, seriousness, the gift of breadth of vision, the correct evaluation of the fruitful forces of the future, in brief, everything creative. . . . All revolutions, he held, came not from economic misery or dissatisfaction with bad political conditions, but arose from the secret societies, visionaries and doctrinaires. The new, world-moving force, the idea of national self-determination, counted for nothing with him. Peoples, in his eyes, were "children or nervous women," "simpletons." Liberalism to him was a "spectre" which must be banished by forceful action, a mere fog, which would disappear of its own accord.

From Heinrich von Srbik, *Metternich, der Staatsmann und der Mensch* (Munich, 1925); and Viktor Bibl, *Metternich, der Dämon Oesterreichs* (Vienna, 1936), as quoted in Henry F. Schwarz, ed., *Metternich, the "Coachman of Europe"* (Boston: D. C. Heath, 1962), pp. 15–16, 22–23.

France was reduced to her frontiers of 1790; she had to pay an indemnity; and she had to submit to an allied army of occupation.

The settlement with France, however, was only part of the work of restoration. A far more difficult task was to reorder the affairs of the

Europe in 1815

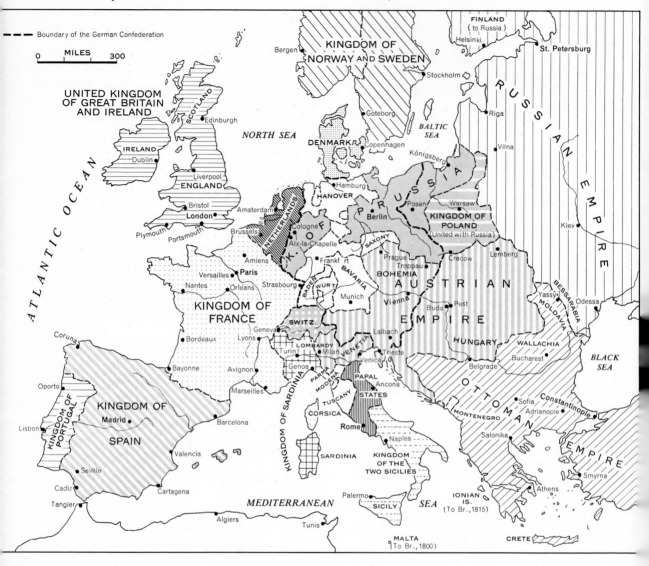

- - - Boundary of the German Confederation

MILES
0   300

FINLAND
(to Russia)
Helsinki

KINGDOM OF
NORWAY AND SWEDEN

Bergen

St. Petersburg

RUSSIAN EMPIRE

UNITED KINGDOM
OF GREAT BRITAIN
AND IRELAND

SCOTLAND
Edinburgh

NORTH SEA

Göteborg

Stockholm

BALTIC
SEA

Riga

Vilna

IRELAND
Dublin

DENMARK
Copenhagen

Königsberg

Liverpool
ENGLAND

Hamburg
HANOVER

PRUSSIA
Berlin
Posen
Warsaw

KINGDOM OF
POLAND
(United with Russia)

Kiev

Bristol
London

Plymouth
Portsmouth

Amsterdam
Brussels
Cologne
Aix-la-Chapelle

K
O
F

SAXONY

Frankfurt
Prague

Troppau
Cracow

Lemberg

ATLANTIC OCEAN

Amiens

Versailles Paris

Nantes Orleans Strasbourg

BADEN
WÜRT.
BAVARIA

Munich

BOHEMIA
AUSTRIAN
Vienna
Buda Pest

BESSARABIA
Yassy
Odessa
MOLDAVIA

KINGDOM OF
FRANCE

Bordeaux

Geneva
Lyons
SWITZ.

EMPIRE

HUNGARY
WALLACHIA
Bucharest

BLACK
SEA

Coruna

KINGDOM OF SARDINIA

Bayonne

Avignon

Marseilles

LOMBARDY
Turin
Milan
Genoa
VENETIA
Venice
Laibach
Trieste

Belgrade

MONTENEGRO

OTTOMAN
Sofia
Adrianople
Constantinople

Oporto

KINGDOM OF
PORTUGAL

Lisbon

KINGDOM OF
SPAIN
Madrid

Barcelona

Valencia

PARMA
MODENA
TUSCANY
CORSICA

PAPAL
STATES
Ancona
Rome

EMPIRE

Salonika

Smyrna

Seville

Cadiz

Cartagena

Tangier

SARDINIA

KINGDOM
OF THE
TWO SICILIES
Naples

Athens

IONIAN
IS.
(To Br.,1815)

MEDITERRANEAN

Algiers

Tunis

Palermo
SICILY

SEA

MALTA
(To Br.,1800)

CRETE

rest of Europe. This was done at a separate conference in Vienna. The Congress of Vienna aroused high hopes among those Europeans who desired a stronger voice in the government of their respective countries or who, like the Germans and the Italians, longed for national unification. Their hopes were to be disappointed. The statesmen at Vienna, notably Metternich, had been deeply disturbed by the excesses of revolution and war and thus were firmly opposed

to the forces of liberalism and nationalism in whose name these excesses had been committed.

Considering the conflicting aims of the powers, it is surprising how much agreement was actually reached at Vienna. Following the principle of legitimacy, the Bourbons were restored in Spain and Naples, and other legitimate rulers were put back on their thrones in the smaller Italian states. Yet the idea of legitimacy was frequently ignored, especially in the case of republics like Genoa and Venice, neither of which regained its independence. In the interests of maintaining the balance of power and of keeping France from repeating her recent acts of aggression, the countries along her eastern frontier were either enlarged or otherwise strengthened. In the North, the Republic of Holland was given a king and was joined with the former Austrian Netherlands (Belgium). In place of the defunct Holy Roman Empire, a loosely joined confederation of thirty-nine states was set up in Germany. This was a far cry from the united nation that many Germans had hoped for. To provide an effective barrier to French expansion in the southeast, Switzerland was re-established as an independent confederation and was declared perpetually neutral. The protective belt against France was completed by strengthening the Kingdom of Piedmont in northern Italy. To compensate Austria for relinquishing Belgium, she received the Italian provinces of Lombardy and Venetia as well as the Illyrian provinces and the Tyrol (some of which she had ruled before 1789). This made Austria the leading power in Italian affairs.

Most of these changes caused no major difficulties, chiefly because the great powers saw eye-to-eye on them. There was one issue, however, that caused much disagreement and at one point threatened to plunge the powers into war. That issue was Poland. One of the favorite schemes of Tsar Alexander I at Vienna was to pose as the "liberator" of Poland by setting up a Polish kingdom under Russian tutelage. The other powers objected to this, Prussia and Austria because they expected the return of those parts of Poland they had held before Napoleon, and England because she had no desire to see Russia grow too powerful. To gain his end, Alexander promised the Prussians compensations elsewhere if they would support his Polish scheme. The result was a deadlock at Vienna, with England and Austria facing Russia and Prussia. An armed conflict was narrowly avoided when Talleyrand threw the weight of France behind England and Austria. The compromise that was reached was more beneficial to Prussia than to Russia. Russia received part of Poland, though less than she

had hoped for, while Prussia got compensations in northern Germany which made her a powerful contender for leadership within the new German Confederation and the guardian of Germany's interests along the Rhine.

Until we learned through first-hand experience the difficulty of setting the world in order after a major war, the Congress of Vienna used to come in for considerable criticism. It is true that the Vienna settlement ignored the stirrings of nationalism and the hopes for democracy that had been awakened by the French Revolution. But more widespread than the middle-class dreams of nationalism and liberalism in 1815 was the hope for peace and order. It was in fulfilling this hope that the statesmen of Vienna scored their major success. There was no war among the great powers for forty years, and no war of world-wide dimensions for a whole century.

The "Holy Alliance" and the "Concert of Europe"

An indication of how sincerely the framers of the Vienna settlement were interested in peace may be seen in the arrangements they made to maintain it. The most famous of these, though the least important, was the "Holy Alliance" of Alexander I. The tsar had long shown signs that he thought of himself as a savior of the world. In this role he proposed to his fellow monarchs that they conduct their relations with each other and with their subjects in a spirit of Christian love. To humor the tsar, most European rulers signed his "Holy Alliance," though it never achieved any practical significance.

Of far greater importance than this "piece of sublime mysticism and nonsense" (as Castlereagh called it) was the Quadruple Alliance signed by England, Austria, Russia, and Prussia at the time of the peace treaty with France in 1815. Its primary purpose was to prevent any future French violation of the peace settlement. But the powers also agreed at the time to hold periodic conferences (ultimately to include France as well) to discuss matters of general European concern. This was an important innovation. For the first time statesmen seemed to realize that peace might be preserved by dealing with crises before they led to general war. The "Concert of Europe" was thus born.

As it turned out, however, the congress system was not a great success. At the very first meeting, at Aix-la-Chapelle in 1818, it became clear that the powers did not really see eye-to-eye on the fundamental purpose of their system of international government. To Castlereagh, the Quadruple Alliance was mainly an instrument for keeping France in her place and for maintaining international peace. To Alexander I, on the other hand, the Alliance seemed a convenient means of maintaining domestic peace as well. This difference was clearly revealed when Alexander proposed a new alliance that would guarantee not only the territorial *status quo* in Europe but the existing form of government in every European country. This latter proposal met with determined opposition from Castlereagh.

The problem of aiding legitimate governments against revolution became acute shortly after Aix-la-Chapelle when a whole series of revolutions suddenly broke out over most of southern Europe. Here was a welcome opportunity for Alexander to repeat his plea for joint intervention. But Britain again voiced her opposition. And to underline his determination not to meddle in the affairs of other nations, Castlereagh refused to attend the Congress of Troppau, at which such intervention was to be discussed.

With England absent, the other powers were able to adopt the "Troppau Protocol," which promised military aid to any government threatened by revolution at home. The effects of the Protocol became clear in 1821. In that year a third congress, at Laibach, commissioned Austria to send her forces into the Italian peninsula to put down the insurrections there. Britain protested, but in vain. Similar action was taken at the next and last congress, which met at Verona in 1822. Again the continental powers, against England's objections, sanctioned the dispatch of a French force to put down the Spanish revolution, which had flared up in 1820.

Government by congress, so promising at first, had thus failed. It had failed because of a fundamental divergence among the victors over the issue of political change, with Britain op-posing and the rest of the powers supporting intervention in the domestic affairs of other states to prevent liberal or national uprisings. There were other efforts to hold congresses, but England refused to attend.

A Wave of Reaction

The revolutions of the early 1820's, which we shall discuss below, were caused by the wave of reaction that followed the peace settlements of 1815. Wherever a legitimate monarch returned, he hastened to restore conditions exactly as they had been before he was ousted. In Spain and Naples the returning Bourbons abolished the liberal reforms that had been granted in 1812. In the Papal States, Pope Pius VII got rid of French legal reforms, re-established the Jesuits, put the Jews back into ghettos, and forbade vaccination against smallpox. In Piedmont, Victor Emmanuel I had the French botanical gardens torn up by the roots and the French furniture thrown out of the windows of his palace.

Elsewhere in Italy and over much of Europe the picture was the same. Both Frederick William III of Prussia and Francis I of Austria favored rigorous measures of repression in their respective countries. By tradition as well as actual power, Austria dominated the Diet of the new German Confederation at Frankfurt. Here it was Metternich who used his influence to suppress liberal or national stirrings wherever they appeared in Germany. As protests against this repressive "Metternich System" grew more vociferous, Austria and Prussia in 1819 pressured the Frankfurt Diet into adopting the so-called Carlsbad Decrees, which strictly limited intellectual freedom, especially at the universities.

There were very few exceptions to this general rule of reaction. It was felt even in England, whose foreign policy was so much more enlightened than that of the continental powers. There was much unrest in postwar Britain, created chiefly by economic causes. Overproduction during the war caused prices to fall, which in turn led to lower wages and growing unemployment. To remedy Britain's ills, a number of middle-class radicals advocated that the government be liberalized through parliamentary

The Peterloo Massacre.

reform. But any agitation for reform was met by stern repression. In 1819, after the so-called Peterloo Massacre—when the constabulary of Manchester charged into a peaceful public meeting on parliamentary reform, causing many casualties—Parliament passed the repressive "Six Acts" which did for England what the Carlsbad Decrees did for Germany.

The Romantic Protest

Before we deal with the several waves of revolution that swept over Europe between 1820 and 1850, we must consider the intellectual climate in which these events took place. Much of the political turmoil of the generation after Napoleon had its counterpart and its cause in the spiritual ferment that we associate with the "Age of Romanticism."

The Main Characteristics of Romanticism

The term *Romanticism* defies clear definition. It differed not only from country to country but from Romanticist to Romanticist. It inspired reactionaries as well as revolutionaries. It made conservatives look longingly to the past and liberals look hopefully to the future. It meant escapism for some and a call to action for others. But with all its contradictions, there were certain characteristics that most Romanticists shared.

Most prominent among these was their protest against the rationalism of the eighteenth century. The Enlightenment, with its emphasis on the rational nature of man and the rational order of the universe, had ignored irrational forces. It had been a brilliantly civilized but overly intellectual age. We have already seen some earlier reactions to this narrow rationalism. The French Revolution and the age of Napoleon had given further impetus to this protest. Reason, it seemed, was not the solution to man's problems that the *philosophes* had promised it to be. If reason had failed, what was there left to turn to but its opposite—faith? As the French writer, Madame de Staël, wrote in 1815: "I do not know exactly *what* we must believe, but I believe *that* we must believe! The eighteenth century did nothing but deny. The human spirit lives by its beliefs. Acquire faith through Christianity, or through German philosophy, or merely through enthusiasm, but believe in something!"

The desire "to believe in something" was the characteristic of Romanticists everywhere. The typical Romantic followed his heart rather than his head. As the hero of Goethe's romantic novel, *The Sorrows of Young Werther,* exclaimed: "What I know, anyone can know—but my heart is my own, peculiar to myself." The Romantic was an individualist. The Enlightenment had spoken of Man, as though he were the same everywhere. The Romanticist stressed the differences among men and felt that each should be a law unto himself. Much of Romantic writing was devoted to the strong personality, the hero, both in history and in fiction. One manifestation of Romanticism's interest in the individual was the growing vogue of autobiographies. One of the most revealing of these was Rousseau's famous *Confessions.* It was Rousseau also who stressed the importance of education as a means of realizing a person's individuality. The Enlightenment, with its belief in the essential sameness of human minds, had been interested in formal rather than individualized education. Rousseau held that the best education was practically no education at all. Each child should be left as free as possible to develop his own abilities and potentialities.

While many Romanticists took a lively interest in the world in which they lived, others used their imagination as a means of escape. To the eighteenth-century *philosophe* the world had appeared as a well-ordered mechanism. To the Romanticist, on the other hand, nature was a mysterious force whose moods expressed the innermost feelings of the Romantic poet. The Enlightenment had preferred landscapes that showed the civilizing influence of man. The Romanticist, by contrast, liked his nature wild—waterfalls, the roaring sea, majestic mountains—or dreamlike—veiled in mist or bathed in mellow moonlight, the kind of landscape painted by Constable and Turner in England or Caspar David Friedrich in Germany.

The Romantic love of the unusual or the unreal in nature contained a strong element of escapism. As factories began to disfigure the landscape of western Europe and cities began to encroach on their surrounding countryside, the Romanticist longed to return to an unspoiled and simple life. He abhorred the ugliness and artificiality of city life and extolled the virtues of country-folk, whose customs, tales, and songs he hoped to preserve. The escapism of the Romanticist took other forms as well. Some Romantic writers let their imagination roam in faraway, exotic places; others preferred to dwell in the realm of ghosts and the supernatural. A particularly important and effective way to escape reality was provided by religion.

Romanticism and Religion

The close relationship between Romanticism and religion is understandable, since both stressed the emotional, irrational side of man. Catholicism in particular answered the Romanticist's need to "believe in something." The mystery of Catholic theology and the splendor of its ritual provided just the kind of emotional experience the Romanticist craved. As a result, many Romanticists returned or were converted to Catholicism, and the Catholic Church, which had been on the defensive since the French Revolution, was able to reassert itself. In 1814, the Jesuit order was officially restored. In 1816, divorce, which had been permitted since the Revolution,

The Hay Wain, by John Constable (1776–1837). Landscape painting, previously considered a minor art form, came into its own with Romanticism. This scene, painted in 1821, reflects the artist's awareness of nature's beauty and conveys a mood of peace and tranquillity.

was once again abolished in France. In Spain and parts of Italy, the Inquisition returned. And almost everywhere on the Continent, education once again became a monopoly of the clergy.

Veneration of the Past

The revival of religious interest was closely allied to the general veneration the Romanticists showed for the past. The Enlightenment had derived much of its inspiration from the ancient Greeks and Romans. To the eighteenth century their civilizations had appeared particularly reasonable and attractive. The intervening period, from about 400 to 1200 A.D., had been merely "Dark Ages" of ignorance and superstition. It

was to these hitherto neglected centuries that the Romanticists now turned, attracted by the mystery, the glamor, and the grandeur that had survived in medieval castles and cathedrals.

The Romantic interest in the Middle Ages, by arousing an interest in the past, also awakened a general interest in the study of history. The eighteenth century had viewed the world as a well-ordered, static mechanism that had been set in motion at some specific time in the past. To the Romanticist, on the other hand, the world was an organism that had grown slowly, changed constantly, and was still growing and changing. In an effort to retrace this gradual change, historians in the early nineteenth century developed a careful method of inquiry, using historical sources—documents and other remains—to gain a truer understanding of the past. Historical scholarship, as we know it today, was thus originated in the Age of Romanticism.

Nationalism and Conservatism

One of the things a study of the past teaches us is that mankind has gradually come to be divided into separate groups, living in common geographic areas, usually speaking the same language, and sharing the same historic experiences. In time, all these elements together create a common feeling that may be called "national consciousness." Some such feeling had existed in countries like England, France, and even Germany since medieval or early modern times. To transform this national consciousness into nationalism, however, something more was needed—a sense not only of being different from,

What is Nationalism?

Nationalities are the products of the living forces of history and [are] therefore fluctuating and never rigid. They are groups of the utmost complexity and defy exact definition. Most of them possess certain objective factors distinguishing them from other nationalities, like common descent, language, territory, political entity, customs and traditions, or religion. But it is clear that none of these factors is essential to the existence or definition of nationality. Thus the people of the United States do not claim common descent to form a nationality, and the people of Switzerland speak three or four languages and yet form one well-defined nationality. Although objective factors are of great importance for the formation of nationalities, the most essential element is a living and active corporate will. It is this will which we call nationalism, a state of mind inspiring the large majority of a people and claiming to inspire all its members. It asserts that the nation state is the ideal and the only legitimate form of political organization and that the nationality is the source of all cultural creative energy and of economic well-being.

From Hans Kohn, *Nationalism: Its Meaning and History* (Princeton: Van Nostrand, 1955), pp. 9–10.

but of being superior to, other national groups. This pride in one's nationality is largely a state of mind. We saw its first modern manifestations during the French Revolution and the Napoleonic Wars. With its appeal to the emotions, this new nationalism fitted quite naturally into the climate of Romanticism. To the Romanticist, nationalism, like Catholicism, provided something in which he could believe. Unfortunately, however, with the memories of the recent wars still fresh in their minds, some Romanticists, notably in Germany, tended to express their nationalism in unpleasantly strident tones.

Nationalism in the early nineteenth century was a revolutionary creed. Since it aimed at the liberation of peoples from foreign domination or their unification into a common state, it posed a threat to the established order. In defense of that order, a new political philosophy had already appeared during the French Revolution, the philosophy of conservatism. Its leading proponent was the Englishman Edmund Burke. We have seen how Burke, in his *Reflections on the Revolution in France,* had warned against the ultimate consequences of that upheaval. He had in particular attacked the revolutionaries for their eighteenth-century belief that man was naturally good and endowed with certain natural rights. Far from having any natural rights, man, according to Burke, merely inherited the rights and duties that existed within his society. Since these rights and duties had developed over many centuries, they constituted an inheritance that no single generation had the right to destroy. Burke also turned against the eighteenth-century idea that government was the result of a contract among its citizens. Instead, he held that the state was an organism, a mystic community, to which the individual must submit.

Burke's conservatism, with its veneration for the past, its organic view of society, and its prediction of many of the dire consequences of the French Revolution, had great appeal to the generation after 1815. Like nationalism, conservatism greatly attracted the Romanticists, and Burke found ardent proponents and imitators on the Continent. Initially, conservatism and nationalism were often in conflict with each other. Nationalism, to achieve its ends, was not averse to revolution, the very thing most conservatives abhorred. Conservatism, on the other hand, in its opposition to radical change, often became indistinguishable from outright reaction, which opposed change of any kind. Only gradually during the nineteenth century did it become clear that nationalism, once it had reached its aims, tended to become conservative in order to defend its gains.

There was one point, however, on which conservatives and nationalists saw eye-to-eye from the beginning, and that was their admiration of the state as the highest social organism. The leading advocate of the supreme importance of the state was the German philosopher Georg Wilhelm Friedrich Hegel. Like the conservatives, Hegel viewed the state as an organism that had evolved historically. Only in submission to a powerful state, Hegel held, could the individual achieve his true freedom. To be strong, a state must be unified, preferably under the authority of a monarch. Each state, according to Hegel, had its own particular spirit, and by developing that spirit it contributed to the World-Spirit. "The State," Hegel wrote, "is the Divine Idea as it exists on earth." As such it is not bound by the usual laws of morality; its only judge is history. The course of history had evolved in three stages: the Oriental, in which only a despot was free; the Greek and the Roman, in which a few were free; and finally the Germanic, in which all would be free. It was his later stress on the unique position of Germany and of Prussia that endeared Hegel to German nationalists.

The Impact of Romanticism

Romanticism, as our brief survey shows, was a bundle of contradictions. It helps us understand the conservatives, who made the Vienna settlement, as well as the revolutionaries, who tried to overthrow it. It was a movement affecting all provinces of human life and thought. It was particularly strong in the arts, not only in literature but in all other forms of artistic expression, especially music. The influence of Romanticism was deep and widespread. All the

nations of Europe contributed to it, and it also was a vital force in the United States. Politically, America during the nineteenth century continued its emancipation from Europe. But culturally there were not two worlds—the New World continued to be influenced by, and continued to influence, the old.

The Romantic protest, or at least the Romantic attitude, did not, of course, end with the Romantic era. Its influence is felt to the present day. Romanticism has been criticized as a rebellion against reason, against measure, against discipline, and a surrender to the murky passions and emotions of the human heart. The old Goethe, himself a Romantic in his youth, looked back with nostalgia to the reasonableness and clarity of eighteenth-century classicism. "Classic," he said, "is that which is healthy; romantic that which is sick." Romanticism, it is true, did destroy the clear simplicity and unity of thought that had prevailed during the Enlightenment. There was no longer one dominant philosophy that expressed all the aims and ideals of western civilization as rationalism had done during the eighteenth century. But then rationalism had provided a narrow, one-sided view of the world, ignoring whole provinces of human experience. Romanticism did much to correct that unbalance. By insisting that the world was not the simple machine it had seemed since Newton, and that man was not a mere cog in that machine, Romanticism provided a more complex but also a truer view of the world. With its emphasis on evolution throughout the universe, and its stress on the creativity and uniqueness of the individual, Romanticism came as a breath of fresh air after the rigid formalism of the Enlightenment. This was its major and lasting contribution.

The First Wave of Revolutions, 1820–29

The restoration of the old order, though it saved Europe from major international wars, was also responsible for the almost unbroken series of domestic wars and revolutions that lasted for more than a generation. We have already noted the unrest in Germany and England shortly after 1815. In France, the assassination in 1820 of the Duke of Berri, who was in line to be Louis XVIII's successor, was the signal for abandoning the moderate course Louis had tried to steer. More serious, however, than these sporadic acts of violence was the whole wave of revolutions that swept through southern Europe in the 1820's.

Revolt in Southern Europe

The first of these revolutions broke out in Spain in 1820. From there revolution spread to Portugal and somewhat later to Italy. In every case it was the army that took the initiative, forcing reactionary monarchs to grant liberal constitutions. The situation in Italy was particularly complicated. The Italian peninsula was still divided into a number of sovereign states of varying size, the most important being the Kingdom of the Two Sicilies in the South, the Papal States in the center, and the Kingdom of Piedmont in the North. In addition, Austria ruled directly over the northern provinces of Lombardy and Venetia, and Austrian influence over the rest of Italy was exerted indirectly through Austrian or pro-Austrian rulers in some of the smaller Italian states. The revolutions in Italy, therefore, were directed not merely against the reactionary policy of the various local rulers but against the alien influence of Austria in Italian affairs; the motives of the Italian revolutionaries were national as well as liberal.

As a result of these upheavals, the old order over much of southern Europe seemed to be on the way out. But the initial success of the revolutions did not last. The revolutionaries everywhere constituted only a small minority, finding little support among the apathetic mass of illiterate peasants. In addition, there was much disagreement among the leaders when it came to establishing more liberal regimes. But more harmful than the lack of popular following and

the inexperience of the revolutionaries was the intervention of outside forces. We have seen how Austria, with the blessing of the three eastern powers, intervened in Italy in 1821, and how France intervened in Spain in 1823. Only in Portugal was a semblance of parliamentary government maintained, thanks to the support of Great Britain.

The Monroe Doctrine

With reaction thus triumphant, there was now a possibility that the powers might try to help Spain recover her colonies in Latin America. Largely under the impact of the French Revolution and the Napoleonic conquest of their mother country, the Spanish colonies, beginning in 1810, had followed the example of the United States and declared their independence. In this they had the sympathy of both the United States and Great Britain, whose commercial interests were eager to gain access to the South American market. In 1822, Britain's new foreign secretary, George Canning, proposed a joint statement by England and the United States to oppose any European intervention against the Spanish colonies.

But the United States was concerned not only over South America but over the possible extension of Russian influence southward from Alaska and over England's designs on Cuba. President Monroe, therefore, decided to act on his own. In a message to Congress in December 1823, he warned that any attempt by the powers of Europe to extend their influence over the Western Hemisphere would be considered a "manifestation of an unfriendly disposition toward the United States." The immediate effectiveness of the Monroe Doctrine, of course, depended on the backing of the British navy rather than on the insignificant power of the United States. For that reason, Canning was justified in his famous boast that he "called the New World into existence to redress the balance of the Old."

The Greek War of Independence

The revolutions in the Iberian and Italian peninsulas, in their aims as well as their failures, had all been quite similar. But the most important revolution of the 1820's, the Greek War of Independence, was quite a different matter. That war was almost entirely motivated by nationalism. And while the other revolutions failed largely because of outside intervention, the Greek revolt succeeded because the powers helped rather than hindered it. The Greek revolt against the Ottoman Empire was merely the latest chapter in the slow disintegration of the "Sick Man of Europe." The Serbs had already staged a successful revolt after 1815. Greek nationalism had been gathering force for some time, especially among the "Island" Greeks, whose far-flung commercial contacts had put them in touch with western ideas. The Island Greeks had founded a secret society, the *Hetàiria Philikĕ,* and it was this society that inspired the uprising in early 1821 that started the war against Turkey.

The Greeks, however, were no match for the Turks, especially after the sultan called in his Egyptian vassal, Mehemet Ali, to help him. The great powers, though they watched events in Greece closely, at first were kept from intervention through mutual jealousies. When the very existence of the Greeks seemed at stake, however, they realized that something had to be done.

Public opinion in the West had favored the Greek cause all along, and the pressure of this "Philhellenism" was partly responsible for the intervention of the powers. In 1827, British, French, and Russian squadrons destroyed the combined Turkish and Egyptian navies in the battle of Navarino. The following year, Russia declared war on Turkey. After brief fighting, the Turks had to submit to the Treaty of Adrianople (1829). Its terms were moderate, except that Russia was given a protectorate over the Danubian principalities of Moldavia and Wallachia, which later became Rumania. After some further negotiations, Greece was set up as an independent kingdom.

The Monroe Doctrine

In the wars of the European powers in matters relating to themselves we have never taken any part, nor does it comport with our policy so to do. It is only when our rights are invaded or seriously menaced that we resent injuries or make preparation for our defense. With the movements in this hemisphere we are of necessity more immediately connected, and by causes which must be obvious to all enlightened and impartial observers. The political system of the allied powers is essentially different in this respect from that of America. . . . We owe it, therefore, to candor and to the amicable relations existing between the United States and those powers to declare that we should consider any attempt on their part to extend their system to any portion of this hemisphere as dangerous to our peace and safety. With the existing colonies or dependencies of any European power we have not interfered and shall not interfere. But with the governments who have declared their independence and maintained it, and whose independence we have, on great consideration and on just principles, acknowledged, we could not view any interposition for the purpose of oppressing them, or controlling in any other manner their destiny, by any European power in any other light than as the manifestation of an unfriendly disposition toward the United States.

From President Monroe's Message to Congress, December 2, 1823.

The Decembrist Revolt

While the Greek uprising was still going on, there had been one other attempt at revolution, this time against the most powerful stronghold of reaction, the tsarist regime in Russia. Like the Spanish and Italian revolts, it failed. We have already encountered the enigmatic Alexander I, who liked to pose as a liberal while actually becoming more and more reactionary. He left the direction of Russian affairs largely in the hands of the efficient but equally reactionary Arakcheiev, who used Alexander's fear of revolution to introduce a regime of ruthless political oppression.

This policy of oppression naturally aroused the opposition of what liberal elements there were in Russia. Many members of the upper class had come in contact with western ideas during the wars against Napoleon and the subsequent allied occupation of France. These officers now founded several secret societies. An opportunity for the conspirators to act came in December 1825, when Alexander suddenly died and there was some doubt about which of his brothers would succeed him. The revolt failed, however, because its leaders were disunited and lacked popular following. Even so, this so-called Decembrist Revolt was significant. There had been earlier uprisings in Russia, but they had been entirely spontaneous. Here, for the first time, was a revolt that had been planned by a small minority with a definite program. The Decembrist uprising served as an inspiration to all later revolutionary movements in Russia. Meanwhile, the December events inspired in Alexander's successor, Nicholas I, an almost pathological fear of revolution. For thirty years he remained the leading proponent of reaction abroad and repression at home.

The Second Wave of Revolutions, 1830–33

The first wave of revolutions after 1815, far from upsetting the old order, merely seemed to have strengthened its hold. The uprisings had been too sporadic, the work of small army cliques with no following among the mass of the people. The second wave of revolutions was different. It started among the people of Paris, and from there it spread over most of Europe, leaving behind some important political changes.

The French Revolution of 1830

The first years of the restored Bourbon monarchy in France had, on the whole, been happy ones. Louis XVIII had tried sincerely to rally his deeply divided country. But he found it increasingly difficult to do so. To the Liberals, led by Lafayette, the new constitution, the Charter, with its limited franchise did not go far enough. To the Royalists, or "Ultras," led by the king's brother, the Count of Artois, the Charter was the source of all France's ills. Up to 1820, Louis had been able to maintain a moderate, middle-of-the-road course. But after the assassination of the Duke of Berri, the Royalist faction gained the upper hand and moderation came to an end.

Louis XVIII died in 1824 and was succeeded by the Count of Artois, as Charles X. Reaction now went into full force. While Liberal opposition became more outspoken, the government's policy became more repressive. In 1829 Charles appointed as his first minister one of the most notorious reactionaries, the Prince de Polignac. In the past the king had always been careful to enlist parliamentary backing. This situation now changed. In the spring of 1830, when the Chamber turned against the government, Charles simply dismissed it. And when new elections brought in another Liberal majority, Polignac had the king promulgate the Five Ordinances, which dissolved the Chamber, imposed strict censorship, and changed the electoral law so that the government in the future would be sure of a favorable majority.

Discontent with this arbitrary policy came to a head in the July revolution of 1830. The hope of the men who fought on the barricades—workers, students, some members of the middle class—was for a republic. But this was not what the more moderate Liberals wanted. Much as they hated the high-handed government of Charles X, they were equally opposed to a republic, which recalled the violent phase of the earlier French Revolution. It was due to the careful machinations of these moderates that France emerged from her July revolution as a constitutional monarchy rather than a republic.

The new king was Louis Philippe, Duke of Orléans. Though a relative of the Bourbons, he had stayed clear of the Royalists and had affected a thoroughly bourgeois mode of life. As Louis Philippe became King of the French People and took an oath to uphold the Charter, Charles X, disappointed in his hope that his fellow monarchs would intervene on his behalf, went into exile. The other powers had been taken too much by surprise and were too little united to take any action. Their attention, furthermore, was soon caught by events elsewhere, as the

French example set off a whole series of revolutions in other countries.

Revolution in Belgium

The first to follow the example of France was Belgium. Her union with Holland at Vienna had not proved very successful. The only area in which the two countries got along was in economic matters, and even here the Belgians in time developed grievances. Still, there had been hardly any agitation for Belgian independence prior to 1830. Seldom has nationalism arisen so suddenly and found such quick fulfillment. In August 1830, in part inspired by events in Paris, rioting broke out in Brussels. King William I tried to save the situation by granting a separate administration for Belgium, but he was too late. The Dutch troops sent to quell the uprising were quickly defeated; but the ultimate fate of Belgium depended on the attitude of the great powers. France and England looked favorably upon the new state, but the three eastern powers were hostile. Since Austria and Russia were preoccupied with disturbances in Italy and Poland, however, any aid to Holland was out of the question. In December 1830 the five powers agreed to recognize the independence of Belgium. The new state was to remain perpetually neutral.

Europe in Revolt

France and Belgium were the only nations in which the revolutions of 1830 achieved any lasting success. But there was hardly a country that did not feel the tremors of revolution. Across the Rhine the events in Paris caused wild excitement among German intellectuals, though there was little echo among the people. Some of the smaller states rid themselves of rulers who were particularly corrupt and vicious, and others won moderately liberal constitutions.

Southern Europe, which had been the scene of revolution a decade earlier, was also aroused by the news from Paris. In Spain and Portugal, struggles among rival claimants to the thrones of these two countries, together with disturbances fostered by liberals, created widespread confusion. Both nations finally emerged, at least

nominally, as constitutional monarchies. In Italy, where secret societies such as the *Carbonari,* or "charcoal burners," were flourishing, revolutions broke out in several states. The revolutionaries hoped to receive aid from France, and had they done so they might have won. But Louis Philippe could not afford to antagonize Austria, and Metternich had a free hand. Again Austrian troops restored the legitimate rulers, who then took revenge against the insurgents.

The Polish Insurrection of 1830

The bloodiest struggle of all in 1830 took place in Poland. The Kingdom of Poland already had been a source of constant trouble to Alexander I. Under Nicholas I tension mounted further. Like revolutionaries elsewhere, the Polish insurgents had founded a number of secret societies to propagate nationalism and to prepare for revolution. When rumors reached Poland in 1830 that Nicholas was planning to use Polish forces to help put down the revolutions in France and Belgium, the conspirators decided to act. Had the Polish people stood united, the revolt might have succeeded. But the revolutionaries were split into moderates and radicals, with neither faction having much following among the mass of the peasants. The hope, furthermore, that England and France would come to their aid proved vain. Even so, it took almost a year before Russia was able to subdue the rebellious Poles and impose a regime of severe repression. For two generations Russian Poland remained a sad and silent land.

Reform in Great Britain

There was one other country besides France and Belgium where unrest in 1830 and after led to major political changes. More than any other nation, Great Britain had been feeling the effects of rapid industrialization. The change from an agrarian to an industrial society could not help but have political repercussions. That England was able to make this adjustment without a revolution was due to her long parliamentary tradition and her able political leadership. We have already seen how Britain had shared in the initial wave of reaction after 1815. With George

Ceremonial meeting of the *Carbonari,* most active and best known of the early-19th-century secret societies conspiring against despotic governments. By 1820, most of the patriotic intelligentsia in Italy were members.

IV, the worst of George III's sons, succeeding his father in 1820, and with the Tories in control of Parliament, little relief was in sight.

Beginning in 1822, however, a new and more enlightened element within the Tory Party became aware of the political implications of economic change. The first sign that some relief from repression was imminent came with the reform of Britain's criminal code after 1822. In 1824 the Combination Acts, forbidding workers to organize, were repealed. In 1828 a new Corn Law modified the duties on foreign grain, thus lowering the price of bread. The most important reform of the 1820's, however, was the establishment of religious equality. In 1828 the Test and Corporations Acts, which barred Protestant Dissenters from holding state offices, were repealed; and in 1829 the Emancipation Bill permitted Catholics to sit in Parliament.

In most of these reforms the liberal element among the Tories had the support of the Whigs. The leaders of the Whig Party, in social background and behavior, differed little from their Tory rivals. But while the main backing of the Tory Party continued to come from the landed gentry and the established church, the Whigs were supported by the rising merchant and manufacturing class. For that reason they became the main advocates of parliamentary reform. To the Whigs, parliamentary reform meant giving a fairer share of representation in Parliament to the well-to-do middle class. This they were finally able to achieve in 1832.

The Great Reform Bill of 1832 was passed only after domestic unrest had at times brought England to the verge of revolution. Under the new bill, the franchise was extended to about half again as many voters and proper representation was given to the new industrial towns. The workers and the poor were still left without a vote, but this was no different from the situation that prevailed elsewhere in Europe. Even though there was no change in Britain's form of government in 1832, the Reform Bill was every bit as much a revolution as the overthrow of Charles X had been in France.

Because the revolutions in the early 1830's were successful only in western Europe, they helped widen the already existing gap between the powers of the East and the West. France and England, constitutional monarchies both, had seen to it that the revolution in Belgium succeeded. Austria, Russia, and Prussia, still essentially autocratic, had suppressed the uprisings in Germany, Italy, and Poland. The main reason for the success of revolutions in the West had been their popular support. The middle class everywhere had taken the lead, but it had been aided by the urban lower class. East of the Rhine, revolutions had found little popular backing, and hence they had failed. Industrialization, which had bolstered the ranks of the middle and lower classes in the West, had as yet made little headway in the East. But while the revolutions in western Europe had been successful, they had chiefly benefited the middle class. The workers, who had done much of the rioting and fighting, were left with empty hands. In the West as in the East, therefore, the revolutions of 1830 left much unfinished. Here we have the main cause for the third and largest wave of revolutions, which swept across Europe in 1848–49.

The Third Wave of Revolutions, 1848–49

The third wave of revolutions lasted for over a year and affected most of Europe. Among the major powers, only England and Russia were spared, though England came close to revolt. There were, of course, countless differences among all these upheavals, but there were also some notable similarities. Generally speaking, the revolutions of 1848 were a further attempt to undo the settlement of 1815. In Italy, Germany, Austria, and Hungary the fundamental grievance was still the lack of national freedom and unity. There was also hope for more liberal governments and for the abolition of the many vestiges of feudalism that still remained. But these were secondary aims. Nationalism was the dominant concern of the revolutionaries in central Europe. In western Europe, neither nationalism nor feudalism was any longer an issue. Here the chief aim of revolution was the extension of political

Revolutions: The Third Wave 1848–49

power beyond the upper middle class. The revolutionaries did not always agree on how far this democratization should go. While the middle class wanted merely to widen the franchise to include the more substantial citizens, the working class wanted political democracy for everyone and some measure of social and economic democracy as well. With the revolutions of 1848, socialism for the first time becomes an issue in modern politics.

Aside from these underlying tensions, there were also economic reasons for the outbreak of revolutions. Despite, or because of, the unprecedented economic growth of Europe since 1815, there had been several severe economic crises, the latest in 1846–47. These upsets particularly affected the lower classes. Everywhere the small artisan was fighting against the competition of large-scale industry, which threatened to deprive him of his livelihood. At the same time, the industrial workers in the new factories were eking out a miserable existence on a minimum wage. There were also periodic upheavals in agriculture, primarily as a result of crop failures. Economic hardship, then, in many cases preceded and helped precipitate political action.

There were other common features among the revolutions of 1848. They were all essentially urban. The leaders came from the middle class, with lawyers, journalists, and professors especially prominent. Much of the actual fighting was done by the urban lower classes, by artisans and workers. Students also played an important part. None of the revolutions had any agrarian program beyond the abolition of feudal dues and services. Once these had been abolished, the conservative peasants withdrew what little initial support they had provided.

Europe, in the spring of 1848, was discontented and restless. The causes of discontent differed from middle class to workers to peasants. But so long as these three groups stood united, it was easy for them to overthrow the old order. When it came to building something new, however, all the differences among the revolutionaries asserted themselves. The history of revolution in 1848 is thus a frustrating tale of missed opportunities.

The "July Monarchy" in France

The key nation in the events of 1848 was again France. The reasons for the failure of Louis Philippe's government are not too obvious. France under the "July Monarchy" was prosperous and progressive, with a liberal constitution, a free press, and a competent king. Louis Philippe had all the bourgeois virtues—he was thrifty, kindly, and industrious. He was served, furthermore, by capable ministers. Until about 1846 trade and industry flourished. France, which had fallen behind England economically as a result of the French Revolution, now started to regain some of her lost ground. Yet with all these advantages, the July Monarchy was far from popular. The French, it has been said, were bored. They were bored by a colorless king, bored by a dull domestic policy that favored the wealthy, and bored by a foreign policy of peace and compromise. Most Frenchmen still smarted from the defeat of Napoleon. Only a glorious foreign policy could wipe out that humiliation. But no sooner was there an opportunity for such a policy than the genuine pacifism of Louis Philippe spoiled it.

In time the opposition against Louis Philippe became crystallized in three groups: the Liberals, the Bonapartists, and the Republicans. The Liberals wanted a further extension of the franchise. The Bonapartists hoped to overthrow Louis Philippe in favor of Prince Louis Napoleon, the emperor's nephew, who promised to restore to France some of the glories associated with the great Bonaparte's name. As for Republicanism, it had its roots in the failure of the radicals to assert themselves in 1830. As the number of workers increased, Republican feeling became more widespread. And since the workers also began to make economic demands, Republicanism gradually became tinged with socialism.

Discontent in France mounted after 1846, primarily for economic reasons. In the fall of that year, Europe was hit by a serious depression. In France as elsewhere, rising prices and growing unemployment particularly affected the workers. Yet the government made no effort to help them, and the lower classes became more and more restive. To ease the situation, Liberals and Republicans joined forces in the summer of 1847 to hold a series of political meetings to discuss parliamentary reform. In February 1848 the government's ban against such a meeting brought on a peaceful popular demonstration. As a precaution, the king called out the army, and in the ensuing confusion several of the demonstrators were killed. Blood had been spilled and the revolution was on. Major bloodshed was avoided by Louis Philippe's decision to abdicate and go to England. On February 25 a republic was proclaimed.

The Second French Republic

In a very short time and with little loss of life, a tremendous change had thus been brought about. The people who had been cheated out of the fruits of revolution in 1830 now had reached their goal; the days of upper-middle-class predominance seemed to be over. But this radical phase of the revolution did not last. The new provisional government was faced with tremendous difficulties. Paris was in a constant state of excitement, with several political factions jockeying for position. Some wanted to concentrate all their efforts on domestic reforms; others were more concerned with carrying the revolution beyond the French borders. The socialists in the government proclaimed the right to work and introduced a system of "national workshops," which had been advocated by the socialist Louis Blanc (see p. 280).

In this period of confusion, the elections to the new National Assembly came as a severe shock to the radicals. Of some 900 delegates elected, fewer than 100 supported the radical Republicans. The main reason for this sudden shift lay with the French peasantry, whose aims had been largely met by the first French Revolution and who had subsequently become stanchly conservative.

But the radical element did not intend to give up without a fight. There now followed a series of clashes between the radicals in the provisional government and the moderate National Assembly. Tension came to a head in the bloody "June Days," when the Assembly dissolved the workshops, which it considered breeding-grounds of discontent. The workers again took to the barricades, and the resulting street

The February Days in Paris

I spent the whole afternoon in walking about Paris. Two things in particular struck me: the first was, I will not say the mainly, but the uniquely and exclusively popular character of the revolution that had just taken place; the omnipotence it had given to the people properly so-called—that is to say, the classes who work with their hands—over all others. . . . Although the working classes had often played the leading part in the events of the First Revolution, they had never been the sole leaders and masters of the State. . . . The Revolution of July [1830] was effected by the people, but the middle class had stirred it up and led it, and secured the principal fruits of it. The Revolution of February, on the contrary, seemed to be made entirely outside the bourgeoisie and against it. . . .

Throughout this day, I did not see in Paris a single one of the former agents of the public authority; not a soldier, not a gendarme, not a policeman; the National Guard itself had disappeared. The people alone bore arms, guarded the public buildings, watched, gave orders, punished; it was an extraordinary and terrible thing to see in the sole hands of those who possessed nothing, all this immense town, so full of riches, or rather this great nation: for, thanks to centralization, he who reigns in Paris governs France. Hence the terror of all the other classes was extreme; I doubt whether at any period of the revolution it had been so great, and I should say that it was only to be compared to that which the civilized cities of the Roman Empire must have experienced when they suddenly found themselves in the power of the Goths and Vandals.

The Recollections of Alexis de Tocqueville, trans. by Alexander Teixeira de Mattos, ed. by J. P. Mayer (New York: Columbia U. Press, 1949), pp. 72–75.

fighting was the most savage ever, causing thousands of casualties. By the end of June the back of lower-class resistance had been broken, and the middle class once again could make its wishes prevail. The Constitution of the Second French Republic set up a single legislative Chamber of Representatives, to be elected by universal male suffrage. Executive power was vested in a powerful president, to be elected by the people.

The first presidential election took place in December 1848. There were five candidates, among them Prince Louis Napoleon. The French middle class and the French peasants wanted a strong man as president, a man who would banish the "red peril" of socialism. Such a man, they felt, was Louis Napoleon. The first Napoleon had taken over the reins of government after a similar revolution fifty years ago, and he had brought order at home and glory abroad. Why should history not repeat itself? The victory of Louis Napoleon by an overwhelming majority was thus due chiefly to the glamor of his name. A sign that he was ready to live up to that name came four years later, in 1852, when he proclaimed himself Emperor Napoleon III. For better or worse, history seemed well on the way toward repeating itself.

The Italian Revolution of 1848

History seemed also to be repeating itself in Italy. Revolution had broken out in Sicily as early as January 1848. From there it had spread north. By the middle of March, most of the Italian states except Lombardy and Venetia had won liberal constitutions. Since the abortive risings of 1830, Italian intellectuals had been making plans for the future liberation and unification of their country. Out of the maze of their projects, three main schemes had emerged: Giuseppe Mazzini, a noted Liberal and an ardent Italian nationalist, advocated the formation of a free, united, and republican Italy. Vincenzo Gioberti, a moderate Liberal and a priest, objected to the republican and centralizing tendencies of Mazzini and instead proposed a federated monarchy with a liberal constitution, headed by the pope. The election of a reputedly liberal pope, Pius IX, in 1846 gave special emphasis to Gioberti's proposals. A third scheme for the future of Italy looked forward to Italian unification under the leadership of the house of Piedmont-Sardinia. Here, then, were three different schemes for the liberation and unification of Italy. Each was tried, and each failed. The fact that there were several plans, rather than one, in part accounts for that failure.

With Austria the main obstacle to Italian unification, the outbreak of revolution in Vienna (see p. 259) naturally aided the Italian cause. As insurrections broke out in the Austrian provinces of Lombardy and Venetia, Charles Albert of Piedmont, in March 1848, gave way to popular pressure and declared war on Austria. Contingents from other Italian states joined the Piedmontese. Pius IX, however, could ill afford to support a war against Austria, the leading Catholic power of Europe. His neutrality and subsequent flight from Rome dashed the hopes of those who had looked to the pope as the leader of Italian liberation.

The war of Piedmont against Austria likewise ended in failure. The forces of Charles Albert were no match for the seasoned troops of the Austrian general Radetzky, especially after the Austrian government had succeeded in putting down its revolution at home. The final defeat of Charles Albert at Novara in March 1849 ended, for the time being, the chance of uniting Italy under the leadership of Piedmont-Sardinia.

The third alternative for the unification of Italy, the creation of a republic, also was given a brief try. With Pius IX away from Rome, radicalism had a free hand. In February 1849 a constituent assembly proclaimed the Roman Republic, under the leadership of Mazzini and with an army led by another hero of Italian unification, Giuseppe Garibaldi. But as Austria regained her position in northern Italy and as the troops of Ferdinand II reconquered Sicily, the Roman Republic became an island in a sea of reaction. To make matters worse, Louis Napoleon, newly elected president of France, tried to ingratiate himself with his Catholic subjects by sending an expeditionary force against Rome. It defeated the forces of Garibaldi and thus ended the dream of a republican Italy.

The revolution in Italy thus had failed. It had done so chiefly because the Austrians had once again proved too strong and because the Italians had proved too little united. Piedmont had been the only state to put up any fight and had thus earned the leadership in Italian affairs. To rally the rest of Italy behind the national cause, the people had to be promised not only unification but political liberty as well. This the government of Piedmont, now under Victor Emmanuel II, realized. Alone among Italian states, Piedmont kept the liberal constitution that had been adopted during the revolution. She thus became the hope of Italian nationalists and liberals alike.

Revolutions in the Habsburg Empire

In Italy, revolution had erupted before it did in France. But the outbreaks in Austria were directly touched off by the events in Paris. The Habsburg Empire had long been ripe for revolution. Its government was cumbersome and corrupt, and Metternich's efforts at reform had been of no avail. The main problem facing the Austrian Empire was its conglomeration of nationalities. Besides the Germans in Austria proper, there were the Magyars in Hungary, the Czechs and Slovaks in Bohemia and Moravia, the Poles in Galicia, and the Italians in Lombardy and Venetia. None of these regions, moreover, was entirely inhabited by one nationality; almost everywhere the peoples just mentioned, together with Slovenes, Croats, Serbs, Ruthenians, and Rumanians, created a situation of utmost ethnic confusion. With the advent of nationalism, this situation endangered the very existence of the Habsburg Empire.

Besides the demands of these subject peoples for some measure of autonomy, there was also a growing demand for governmental reforms in Austria proper. Industrial progress had swelled the ranks of the middle class and had created an urban proletariat, both of which now added their voices to the liberal protests of university professors and other intellectuals. The news of the revolution in Paris, however, caused much more excitement among the subject nationalities than it did in Austria. There were some student demonstrations and some violence in Vienna, and a deputation of citizens asked for the resignation of Metternich. But he resigned under pressure from the imperial family rather than from the populace. With Metternich gone, events moved swiftly and smoothly. The emperor removed himself to Innsbruck, and the citizens of Vienna elected a National Assembly to draft a constitution. One of the Assembly's first acts was to remove the last feudal burdens from Austria's peasants, thus completing a process begun by Joseph II two generations earlier.

From Vienna, revolution spread to other parts of the Empire. We have already discussed the uprisings in Lombardy and Venetia. In Bohemia, except for some local unrest, things remained quiet until early in June. At that time, disturbances broke out in connection with the first Pan-Slav Congress in Prague, which proclaimed the solidarity of the Slavic peoples against the Germans. Popular demonstrations were quelled when Austria's military governor ordered the bombardment of Prague. This was a significant event, for it was the first major setback of revolution anywhere in Europe. In Hungary, meanwhile, the Austrian government had agreed to the March Laws, which guaranteed a large measure of self-government. Hungary also followed the Austrian example in abolishing the remains of feudalism. But while the Hungarians thus secured freedom for themselves, they refused to grant the same freedom to the Croats within their own borders. Austria could thus play one nationality against the other. In September 1848, Croatian forces with Austrian backing invaded Hungary.

With imperial armies thus scoring successes against the revolutionaries in Bohemia, Hungary, and Lombardy, the tide of revolution in the Austrian Empire was definitely turning. There was a second, more radical outbreak in Vienna in October 1848, but it was soon put down. The Austrian government was now entrusted to Prince Felix Schwarzenberg, a strong-willed reactionary who urged the emperor, Ferdinand I, to resign in favor of his nephew, Francis Joseph. In March 1849 Schwarzenberg dissolved the National Assembly and imposed his own centralized constitution on the whole Empire.

By early spring of 1849 the Austrian government was thus again in control everywhere except in Hungary. At this point Francis Joseph accepted the offer of Nicholas I of Russia to help put down the Hungarians. The tsar was motivated by feelings of monarchical solidarity and by the fear that revolution might spread to the Danubian principalities and Poland. Under the joint invasion of Russian and Austrian forces, and simultaneous uprisings among the Slavic peoples of southern Hungary, Hungarian resistance was finally crushed. By mid-August of 1849 Austria was once again in control of her own house.

The "Germanies" in Revolt

The victory of reaction in Austria, as we have seen, also affected the fate of revolution in Italy. It had a similar effect in Germany. There the chances for the success of revolution actually seemed most favorable. Unlike Austria, Germany did not suffer from ethnic disunity, nor was there any need to expel a foreign power, as there was in Italy. If revolution nevertheless failed, it was due to many causes, most important among them the division of the country into many separate states and the general apathy of the population. The majority of Germans seemed content to lead a life of modest comfort and to pursue cultural rather than political interests.

Still, there was enough ferment among German intellectuals to keep alive the agitation for a united and liberal Germany. These aims also found support among the growing industrial middle class. The formation of the German customs union, or *Zollverein,* under Prussian leadership, had been the only notable German achievement since 1815. By easing the movement of goods throughout Germany, it had aided both commerce and industry. But industrialization had also brought many hardships, especially to the artisans. Another discontented group were the peasants in eastern Germany, who, since their liberation from serfdom, were often unable to make a living on their small holdings and instead had to become agricultural or industrial laborers. This economic discontent, which became especially strong during the 1840's, added a new dimension to the liberal and national aims of the German intellectuals. Had the revolutionary leaders understood and utilized this discontent, the results of the revolutions might have been different.

The first German uprising occurred in Bavaria before the events in France. But only with the news from Paris did the revolutions become general. Because Prussia, next to Austria, played the leading role in the German Confederation, events in Berlin were watched with particular interest. Prussia, since 1840, had been ruled by the brilliant but unstable Frederick William IV. The new king started out with a series of liberal reforms, but his liberalism, like that of Alexander I, was largely a pose. When the revolution came to Berlin in March 1848, Frederick William was easily frightened into appointing a liberal ministry and agreeing to a constituent assembly. But the old regime in Prussia was not really beaten, especially since the Prussian army had remained intact. While middle-class delegates were drawing up a liberal constitution, the lower classes were agitating for more drastic changes—including universal suffrage, socialism, and even a republic. These radical demands drove the middle class, including the well-to-do peasants, back into the arms of reaction. As news reached Berlin in the fall of 1848 that the Austrian government was successfully moving against the revolution in Vienna, Frederick William dissolved the Constituent Assembly and imposed his own constitution. By the end of 1848, the revolution in Prussia had been defeated.

But German liberals did not give up hope. Since spring, another constituent assembly had been in session in Frankfurt. Its delegates had been elected from all over Germany. The majority were professional people, including many professors. The main task of these delegates was to draft a constitution for a unified Germany. Deliberations dragged on for almost a year. The main argument developed over the question of whether or not the new German state should be under the leadership of and include Austria. The *grossdeutsch* (greater-German) faction, which favored this solution, was opposed by the *kleindeutsch* (small-German) group, which advocated the exclusion of Austria and the leadership of Prussia. The issue resolved itself when the victory of reaction in Vienna disqualified Austria in the eyes of German liberals.

The Frankfurt Constitution, which was finally adopted in March 1849, called for a constitutional monarchy with a parliament elected by universal suffrage. As "Emperor of the Germans," the Frankfurt Parliament elected Frederick William IV. But the king of Prussia refused a crown that was offered him by the people. He would accept it only from his fellow princes. With reaction everywhere triumphant, Frederick William's refusal all but finished the revolution in Germany. There were some last flashes of violence in the smaller states, but Prussian troops soon restored order. The attempt of the German people to build a unified nation under a government of their own choosing had failed.

England in the Age of Reform

The one country in Europe where many people had expected revolution to strike first was England. And yet, thanks largely to a number of timely reforms, England proved the major exception to the rule of revolution in western Europe. The Reform Bill of 1832 had been merely the most prominent among a large series of reforms. Most important among these was the establishment of free trade. Britain's merchants and industrialists had long agitated against import duties, but tariffs had been defended on the grounds that the government needed the income. With the reintroduction of the income tax in 1842, however, that argument lost its point, and protective tariffs were gradually abolished. Only in agriculture did they survive. To fight for the abolition of agricultural tariffs, the Anti-Corn Law League had been formed in 1839. In 1846 its relentless pressure succeeded and the Corn Laws were repealed.

Along with this agitation for economic freedom, there also arose during the 1830's a movement for greater political freedom. The Reform Bill of 1832 had been a disappointment to the lower classes, and it was here that the so-called Chartist Movement gained its major support. The movement took its name from the "People's Charter" of 1838, drawn up by a group of radical reformers and calling for a further democratization of Parliament. But this radical program ran into heavy opposition, and Parliament repeatedly turned down petitions based on the Charter. By 1848 discontent had mounted to such a pitch that there seemed to be a real threat of revolution. The Chartists prepared a "monster petition" with some six million signatures (many of them false) and started a demonstration to present it to Parliament. When it began to rain, however, the demonstrators let themselves be dispersed peacefully. The truth of the matter is that there had been a good deal of economic discontent behind Chartism, which had disappeared with the repeal of the Corn Laws and a general increase in prosperity. Henceforth workers were turning more and more to trade unionism as a means of improving their status. England thus remained a quiet haven of refuge in the upheavals of 1848, giving asylum to refugees from revolution and from reaction alike. Many of the revolutionaries, however, preferred to leave Europe altogether, going to the United States, where they were received with open arms.

Why Did the Revolutions of 1848 Fail?

The revolutions of 1848 thus had failed everywhere. They had done so because of weaknesses in the revolutionary camp, especially the lack of widespread popular support, and because of the continued strength of the forces of reaction. A subsidiary cause of failure was the fact that the economic conditions that helped bring on the revolutions did not last. The economic picture in many countries improved, despite the unsettling effect of revolution. The weakness of the revolutionaries was also due to indecision among their leaders and to the lack of well-defined programs or the existence of too many different programs. This indecision led to the waste of valuable time, which the reactionaries used to prepare for counterrevolution. The middle class, in most countries, did not really want a revolution. It preferred to achieve its aims through reform, as had been done in England. But once revolution came, sometimes by spontaneous combustion, the middle class tried to reap its benefits. Much of the actual fighting in the revolutions was done by the workers, and the workers wanted more than limited democracy for the well-to-do. They wanted complete democracy, political and, in some cases, economic as well. To the middle class, these demands, especially the socialist ones, not only threatened its political predominance but its very existence. This bourgeois fear of a "red peril" was exaggerated. Despite the incendiary language of the *Communist Manifesto* (which appeared in 1848; see p. 281), the majority of the lower class were perfectly ready to follow the leadership of the middle class if that would improve their condition. But the middle class did not live up to these lower-class expectations; as a result the lower class more and more came to distrust the men it had helped gain power.

Not only was there disunity among the revolutionary forces within each country, there was no attempt to coordinate the revolutions in different countries. Although the forces of reaction worked together, there was little collaboration among the revolutionaries. On the contrary, almost everywhere their programs showed traces of a selfish nationalism. There was nationalism behind France's talk of spreading the blessings of revolution. The Germans wanted to unite all German-speaking peoples, but they also wanted to lord it over the Poles and they actually carried on a brief war against the Danes. The Poles wanted to be liberated and united, but they did not want to see the Ukrainians win the same benefits. And we have already seen that the Hungarians behaved every bit as selfishly toward the Croats as the Austrians did toward the Hungarians.

Yet, though reaction won a full victory in 1849, the revolutions of 1848 had not been entirely in vain. Some changes for the better were preserved. In France, political participation had been considerably broadened. In Italy some lead-

ers had learned useful lessons of how to go about achieving unification. In Austria the abolition of serfdom during the revolution could not be undone, and Metternich did not return to power. Even in Germany, where the failure of revolution probably had more tragic long-range consequences than anywhere else, a few lasting gains were made.

The mid-century revolutions came at a turning-point in European history. Up to this time, the economy of the Continent had still been largely agrarian. From now on, industrialization was really to take hold. Metternich, the dominant figure after 1815, in many ways had been a relic of the eighteenth century. The future was to belong to a different, more modern type of politician. Two forces emerged from the revolutions that henceforth were to dominate the history of Europe—nationalism and socialism. Neither was new, but both had lost much of their earlier idealism and utopianism. Nationalism and socialism respectively now became the main issues in the struggle of nation against nation and class against class.

Suggestions for Further Reading

1. General

The most stimulating introduction to the half-century following the French Revolution is E. J. Hobsbawm, *The Age of Revolution, 1789–1848** (1962). J. L. Talmon, *Romanticism and Revolt: Europe 1815–1848** (1967), is briefer; and F. A. Artz, *Reaction and Revolution, 1814–1832** (1934), and *The Zenith of European Power, 1830–1870* (1964) (Vol. X of *The Cambridge Modern History*), are more detailed. Among national histories, the following stand out: É. Halévy, *History of the English People in the Nineteenth Century**, Vols. II and III (1926); T. S. Hamerow, *Restoration, Revolution, Reaction: Economics and Politics in Germany, 1815–1871** (1958); A. J. P. Taylor, *The Hapsburg Monarchy, 1809–1918** (1948); A. Cobban, *A History of Modern France**, Vol. II (1957); A. J. Whyte, *The Evolution of Modern Italy, 1715–1920** (1944); and H. Seton-Watson, *The Russian Empire, 1801–1917* (1967). The emergence of liberalism is traced in G. Ruggiero, *History of European Liberalism** (1927), and H. J. Laski, *The Rise of European Liberalism* (1936). The standard works on nationalism are C. J. H. Hayes, *The Historical Evolution of Modern Nationalism* (1931), and H. Kohn, *The Idea of Nationalism: A Study in Its Origin and Background** (1944). More recent treatments are: B. C. Shafer, *Nationalism: Myth and Reality** (1955); E. Kedouri, *Nationalism** (1960); and K. R. Minogue, *Nationalism** (1967).

2. The Restoration of the Old Order

The standard works on the diplomatic settlements after Napoleon are C. K. Webster, *The Foreign Policy of Castlereagh, 1812–1815* (1931), and *The Congress of Vienna, 1814–1815* (1934).

---

* Available in paperback edition.

H. Nicolson, *The Congress of Vienna: A Study in Allied Unity, 1812–1822** (1946), is briefer and makes delightful reading. Good biographies of the leading statesmen at Vienna are: G. de Bertier de Sauvigny, *Metternich and His Times* (1962); C. Brinton, *The Lives of Talleyrand** (1936); L. I. Strakhovsky, *Alexander I of Russia* (1947); and J. C. Bartlett, *Castlereagh* (1967). The diplomatic aftermath of the Congress of Vienna is discussed in H. G. Schenk, *The Aftermath of the Napoleonic Wars: The Concert of Europe* (1947); P. W. Schroeder, *Metternich's Diplomacy at Its Zenith, 1820–1823* (1962); and H. A. Kissinger, *A World Restored** (1957). The situation arising from the revolutions in Latin America is summed up in D. Perkins, *Hands Off! A History of the Monroe Doctrine** (1941). See also B. Perkins, *Castlereagh and Adams: England and the United States, 1812–1823* (1964).

3. Romanticism

A good introduction to the complexities of Romanticism is H. E. Hugo, ed., *The Romantic Reader** (1957). Another useful collection is J. B. Halsted, ed., *Romanticism** (1965). I. Babbitt, *Rousseau and Romanticism** (1919), is a classic indictment. See also W. J. Bate, *From Classic to Romantic** (1946). The impact of Romanticism on political thought is treated in the works on nationalism cited above, as well as in H. S. Reiss, *The Political Thought of the German Romantics* (1955); C. Brinton, *The Political Ideas of the English Romanticists** (1926); and R. H. Soltau, *French Political Thought of the Nineteenth Century* (1931). On conservatism, see: P. Viereck, *Conservatism: From John Adams to Churchill** (1956); R. J. S. Hoffman and P. Levack, eds., *Burke's Politics* (1949); and E. L. Woodward, *Three Studies in European Conservatism* (1929).

4. Revolutions Before 1848

Good accounts of the countless upheavals in the 1820's and 1830's may be found in the general histories cited above. For events in France, see also J. Plamenatz, *The Revolutionary Movement in France, 1815–1871* (1952), and N. E. Hudson, *Ultraroyalism and the French Restoration* (1936). Recent biographies of leading figures include D. W. Johnson's *Guizot* (1963) and T. Howarth's *Citizen-King* (1961) on Louis Philippe. Russia's Decembrist revolt is treated in A. G. Mazour, *The First Russian Revolution, 1825** (1937). The general subject of the disintegrating Ottoman Empire is admirably summarized in M. S. Anderson, *The Eastern Question, 1774–1923* (1966). Much has been written on parliamentary and social reforms in Great Britain; especially recommended are: E. L. Woodward, *The Age of Reform, 1815–1870* (1938); N. Gash, *Politics in the Age of Peel* (1953); A. Briggs, ed., *Chartist Studies* (1960); M. Hovell, *The Chartist Movement* (1925); and D. Owen, *English Philanthropy, 1660–1960* (1964). On social unrest, see R. J. White, *Waterloo to Peterloo* (1957), and G. F. E. Rudé, *The Crowd in History, 1730–1848** (1964). The latter treats both England and France.

5. The Revolutions of 1848

Among several attempts to present a comprehensive picture of these confusing events, the most successful is P. Robertson, *Revolutions of 1848: A Social History** (1952). G. Bruun, *Revolution and Reaction, 1848–1852** (1952), provides a brief introduction, supplemented by documents. R. Postgate, *Story of a Year: 1848** (1955), describes entertainingly the revolutions as seen from England. A. Whitridge, *Men in Crisis: The Revolutions of 1848* (1949), concentrates on a few leading figures in various countries. V. Valentin, *1848: Chapters in German History* (1940), is stimulating but fragmentary. Among specialized works on various aspects of the revolution, the following deserve mention: D. C. McKay, *The National Workshops: A Study in the French Revolution of 1848* (1933); J. Blum, *Noble Landowners and Agriculture in Austria, 1814–1848** (1948); A. J. P. Taylor, *The Italian Problem in European Diplomacy, 1847–1849* (1939); and L. B. Namier, *1848: The Revolution of the Intellectuals** (1947).

---

* Available in paperback edition.

10

The Coming of the Industrial Age

Much of the political tension of Europe during the first half of the nineteenth century was a manifestation of underlying economic unrest caused by the gradual transformation of Europe's economy from agriculture to industry. This change is usually dated from the middle of the eighteenth century, but it did not really become pronounced until after 1815. From then on it gathered momentum, first in England and later on the Continent, until by the end of the nineteenth century most of western Europe had become industrialized.

This industrialization of society is often referred to as the "Industrial Revolution." But this term has come in for some criticism. The change from agriculture to industry, it seems, was much slower than the term *revolution* would imply. What used to be called a revolution now appears to have been a gradual process of evolution. When we consider the total effect of this transformation from agriculture to industry, however, the term *revolution* seems more than justified. Industrialization, by vastly improving the means of communication, has made the world seem much smaller; by enabling more people to make a living, it has made the world much more crowded; and by raising the standard of living, it has made life infinitely more com-

The Great Exhibition of 1851 in London's Crystal Palace was the first major international exposition of the industrial age. It showed a profusion of manufactured goods and gave proof of Britain's industrial leadership. The Crystal Palace, of which this illustration shows the Main Avenue, was built of iron and glass and was hailed as a major architectural achievement. It survived until 1941.

fortable. Industrialization has elevated some nations that heretofore were insignificant and has demoted others that did not have the manpower or the raw materials that industry requires. Industrialization has dissolved a rigid and hierarchical order of society and has substituted a fluid and egalitarian mass society. Not all these changes have necessarily been for the better. While industry created wealth for some, it merely emphasized the poverty of others. While it made nations and individuals more dependent on each other, it also increased their rivalry for a share of the riches industry has to offer. The preoccupation of modern industrial society with material well-being has diverted mankind from more spiritual concerns. But while one may wonder how beneficial the change to industry has been in some areas, about the magnitude of that change there can be no doubt.

The Roots of Modern Industrialism

Modern industrialism, quite simply, is the mass production of goods by means of machines driven by artificial power and set up in factories. There had been few mechanical inventions before the eighteenth century. During the Middle Ages, consumer goods had been produced by hand and for local consumption. With the Age of Discovery and the "Commercial Revolution" in the sixteenth century, the rate of production had increased to provide goods for export. Since the small artisan did not have the capital to buy large quantities of raw materials, to produce a large stock, and to sell it in a distant market, a class of wealthy capitalists and merchants began to inject themselves into the production process. They supplied the artisan with raw materials and sometimes with tools, and they took over the finished product to sell at a profit. This "domestic," or "putting-out," system had become quite common by the seventeenth century. There were even a few simple machines, but they still had to be operated by humans or animals, or by the natural power of wind or water. During the eighteenth century the trend toward large-scale production was accelerated by numerous

mechanical inventions that increased the speed and thus the volume of production. The most important step came with the application of steam power to these new machines. This step brought the decline of the domestic system and the gradual shift of production from home to factory. The beginnings of modern industrialism fall into the period after 1760.

It was no accident that modern industrialism should have got its start in the eighteenth century. The intellectual climate of the Enlightenment, its interest in science, and its emphasis on the good life on earth were particularly favorable to such a development. The acceleration of industrialism was most pronounced in England, for several reasons: England had an effective parliamentary government which gave some voice to the rising commercial and industrial classes; she had large colonial holdings and far-flung commercial interests; she had a sound financial system and sufficient surplus capital; and she had an ample supply of basic raw materials and manpower. The manpower had been made available in part by drastic changes in British agriculture—an "Agrarian Revolution"—which converted farmers into laborers and materially increased Britain's food supply.

The Agricultural Revolution

Most of the land in Britain before the eighteenth century was still worked under the open-field system, which meant that the holdings of individual owners were scattered about in many strips, separated from those of other landholders by a double furrow. In addition, each landholder shared in the common pastures and woodlands of his community. This arrangement was of particular advantage to the small farmers and cottagers, who participated in the grazing and fueling rights of the "commons." But the open-field system was both inefficient and wasteful. The prevailing method of cultivation was still the medieval system of three-field rotation, under which one-third of the land remained fallow each year. Any attempt to change this routine by experimenting with new crops was impossible, since all strips in a given field had to be cultivated at the same time and planted with the same crop.

The "Enclosure Movement"

Beginning at the time of the Tudors, an "enclosure movement" had started in England, under which the scattered strips of individual owners were consolidated into compact holdings surrounded by fences or hedges. Enclosure meant a gain of usable land because it did away with the double furrows, and it made for much easier cultivation. But since enclosure also involved a division of the commons, it worked to the detriment of the small farmer, who thus lost part of his livelihood. As the population of England increased, agricultural production for the general market rather than for local consumption became more profitable. The trend toward more efficient large-scale farming, and especially sheep-raising, through enclosures therefore gained momentum. It reached its climax in the eighteenth century. Between 1702 and 1797, Parliament passed some 1,776 enclosure acts affecting three million acres. In each case the larger landowner profited at the expense of the smaller farmer. The latter, left with too little land of his own and deprived of his share in the commons, had no choice but to become a tenant farmer or move to the cities. Many took the latter course, thus providing some of the manpower without which the rapid growth of Britain's industry could not have taken place.

The enclosure movement brought hardships to many people, but it brought a dramatic improvement in agriculture. Freed from the restrictions of collective cultivation, landowners were now able to try new methods and new crops. This enabled them to grow more food on the same amount of land. The improvement was such as to give substance to the term "Agricultural Revolution." Like its industrial counterpart, the Agricultural Revolution at first was almost entirely restricted to Britain. Only with the advent of industrialization did the larger landholders on the Continent seriously begin to experiment with British methods. The small peasants, on the other hand, continued in their backward ways. As new industrial centers developed, new markets for agricultural produce opened up. Improvements in transportation, furthermore, facilitated marketing; and new scientific discoveries brought larger crop yields. These and other developments brought renewed hope for western Europe's farmers, who were gradually being pushed to the wall by the rising industries and were beginning to feel the competition of the rich agrarian lands of eastern Europe and America.

The Beginnings of Industrialization

The Role of Inventions

The early history of industrialization is intimately related to the rise of mechanical inventions. There were few of these at first, but they multiplied as one discovery created the need for another. When John Kay invented his flying shuttle in 1733, enabling one weaver to do the work of two, the need arose for some new device that would speed up spinning. This demand was met in 1764 by James Hargreaves and his spinning jenny, which permitted the simultaneous spinning of eight or more threads. A few years later, Richard Arkwright devised the water frame, and in 1779 Samuel Crompton perfected the "mule," a hybrid that combined features of both Hargreaves' and Arkwright's inventions. These improvements in spinning in turn called for further improvements in weaving. In 1787 Edmund Cartwright patented a new power loom. After it had become perfected, the demand for cotton increased. Cotton production received a boost when an American, Eli Whitney, in 1793 developed the cotton "gin," which speeded up and cut the cost of removing the cotton fiber from its boll. Almost all of the early inventions were made in the cotton industry. The reasons were that it was a new industry, it had a large overseas market, and cotton lent itself particularly well to mechanical treatment.

The Rise of the Factory System

Since most of the earlier devices were small, relatively inexpensive, and hand-operated, they could be used as part of the domestic system in the workers' cottages. Arkwright's water frame, however, was large and expensive, and it needed water power to operate. Arkwright, therefore, moved into the heart of the English textile region of Nottingham, and there in 1771 he opened the first spinning mill. By 1779 he was employing some 300 workers who operated several thousand spindles. With this important innovation, the modern factory system had been born. Arkwright's example was soon followed by other manufacturers, especially as the steam engine became the major source of power for newer and larger machines.

The Steam Engine

Of all the inventions in the early years of industrialism, the steam engine was the most important. Until the advent of electricity it remained the chief source of power, and even in our atomic age its usefulness has not ended. The development of the steam engine is closely related to the two industries that ultimately proved basic to all modern economic progress—coal and iron. At the beginning of the eighteenth century the smelting of iron was still done by charcoal. The depletion of Britain's wood supply, however, and the discovery, shortly after 1700, of a process for smelting iron with coke, shifted the emphasis to coal. The mining of coal was made considerably easier with the aid of a primitive steam engine, developed by Thomas Newcomen, which was used to pump water from the coal mines. This early-eighteenth-century engine was a long way from the kind of steam engine that could be used to run other machines, however. The credit for developing such an engine belongs to the Scotsman James Watt, who patented his first steam engine in 1769. By 1800 some 300 steam engines were at work in England, mostly in the cotton industry. The use of steam engines, of course, further increased the need for coal and iron. Improvements in iron production, on the other hand, in turn led to improvements in the making of steam engines. The interaction of one discovery with another thus continued to be a major characteristic of industrial development.

Early Industry on the Continent

Prior to 1815 the "Industrial Revolution" was chiefly a British phenomenon. There had been an economic revival in France after 1763, to compensate for the loss of the French colonies to Britain, but it had been interrupted by the French Revolution. The "continental system" of Napoleon, on the other hand, by excluding British goods from the Continent had proved most beneficial to French industry.

In the rest of Europe there were not even the beginnings of modern industrialization. Economic development in Germany was retarded by political disunity. The rich coal fields of the Ruhr and Silesia were hardly worked before 1815, and what little industry there was, especially in textiles, still operated under the "putting-out" system. Russia, Italy, and Austria were almost wholly agrarian. Even after 1815, continental industries were slow to assert themselves against British competition. It was only after the advent of the railroad in the 1830's that the situation began to improve.

The Railway Age

Transportation in the Eighteenth Century

Industrial development was closely related to the improvement of transportation. Here England again had a special advantage in being able to use coastal shipping for the movement of bulky goods. But like any other country she depended on roads and canals for inland transportation. As industrialization made for increased transport and travel, the construction of toll roads and canals became a profitable business. England added thousands of miles to its system of roads and canals during the eighteenth century, and France before the Revolution had the finest highway system in Europe. Napoleon improved the situation further by pushing highways far into Germany and the Netherlands. In eastern Europe, however, paved roads were rare. Prussia's kings constructed canals and improved riverways, but the movement of goods was

The Stourbridge Lion, purchased in England for the Delaware and Hudson Company, introduced practical steam locomotives to America. Horatio Allen drove this engine three miles on August 8, 1829, at Honesdale, Pennsylvania.

hampered by innumerable tolls and tariffs. Farther east, dirt roads that regularly turned to mud, and rivers that ran shallow during the summer and froze during the winter, were the only arteries of communication.

The Advent of the Railroad

The railroad, which was to change all this, had its start in England. Well before 1800, horse-drawn carts, moving first on wooden and later on iron rails, had been used to haul coal and iron. During the 1820's there were several hundred miles of such "rail ways." The problem of providing a faster means of locomotion was solved by putting the steam engine on wheels. The first commercial steam railroad was opened between Liverpool and Manchester in 1830. By 1840 Britain had some 800 miles of track, and by 1850 she had more than 6,000. On the Continent, the railroad was somewhat slower in

taking hold. The first railroad in France was opened in 1837, and by the middle of the century she had 2,000 miles of track. Germany then had 3,000 miles, Austria 1,000 miles, and Italy and Russia had merely a few fragmentary lines.

The economic impact of the railroad, of course, was overwhelming. Here was an entirely new industry, answering a universal need, employing thousands of people, offering unprecedented opportunities for investment, and introducing greater speed into all industrial and commercial transactions. England, already far ahead of the Continent in economic development, took the Railway Age pretty much in her stride. She had been the workshop of the world for some time, and there seemed to be no prospect that she would cease to be. Railroad construction vastly increased the demand for coal and iron, and England continued to lead the world in the production of both.

She also maintained her lead in shipping. The shipping industry was slow to feel the impact of steam. Even though Robert Fulton's steamboat had made its first successful trip on the Hudson River in 1807, it was not until 1840 that Samuel Cunard established the first transatlantic steamer line. Even then the inefficiency of marine engines and the large amounts of coal needed for long voyages retarded the development of steamship service. Until well into the second half of the nineteenth century the fast clipper ship remained the chief means of ocean transport.

There were other important innovations and inventions in the early nineteenth century, with England again leading the way. The introduction of the penny post in 1840 helped business and private individuals alike. The telegraph, invented by the American Samuel Morse, was first used extensively by Julius Reuter's news agency, which was established in 1851, the same year in which the first submarine cable was laid under the English Channel. A reduction in the stamp tax in 1836 substantially lowered the price of newspapers, and by the middle of the century the circulation of the British press had risen more than threefold. The communication of news and ideas was thus keeping pace with the faster movements of goods and persons.

The Railway Age on the Continent

In May 1851 the "Great Exhibition of the Works of Industry of All Nations" was opened in London. This first "world's fair" was dramatic proof of Britain's industrial world leadership, but it also showed that other nations were beginning to profit from her example. The country in which industrialization made the most rapid progress was little Belgium. An ample supply of coal and a skilled labor force were the chief reasons, but technical aid by British engineers and investment of British capital also helped.

In France, economic development was much slower. The French had lost some of their best coal mines to Belgium in 1815; and while everywhere in Europe populations were increasing, the French birth rate, by the middle of the century, had actually begun to decline. Still, with

all the encouragement given to commerce and industry by the July Monarchy, the middle class could not help but prosper. Pig-iron production, generally considered an index of industrial development, increased fourfold in France during the thirty years after 1825; but it was still only one-quarter that of Great Britain. While England's population by the middle of the century was more than half urban, France remained predominantly rural. This made large imports of food unnecessary and accounted for a self-contained domestic market.

Both Italy and Germany were slowed down in their economic growth by political disunity. There was some industry in northern Italy, but it remained insignificant until later in the century. In Germany, the *Zollverein* did much to aid industrial development. Machines, imported from England, were being used more and more in the textile industry. With the sinking of the first deep pit in the Ruhr, in 1841, coal production began in earnest. Even so, France, despite much slimmer resources, still produced more coal than Germany. As for pig iron, the total German output in 1855 was only half that of France. Railroad construction in Germany made rapid progress during the 1840's. The absence of natural obstacles kept construction costs far below those of Great Britain. It was the progress in railroad building that gave some inkling of the tremendous economic vitality of the German people, which was merely awaiting political unification to assert itself.

Beyond western and central Europe, industrialization had made hardly any headway by 1850. Austria and Russia were still predominantly agrarian. Industrial development depended first and foremost on an abundant supply of free labor. This supply did not exist in Austria until after the last feudal restrictions were abolished in 1849, and in Russia it had to wait until the abolition of serfdom in 1861. Outside Europe only the United States was showing signs of industrialization. By 1850 New England had become largely industrialized, but the total output of American industry was still behind that of France and far behind that of Britain. Like Germany, the United States was to become a leading industrial power only toward the end of the century.

The Social Effects of Industrialization

The beginnings of modern industrialization in the eighteenth century appeared to bear out the belief of the Enlightenment that human reason and ingenuity had the power to make the world a better place. The invention of labor-saving machines promised to transform man from a beast of burden into a creature of leisure. But that promise soon began to fade. The "Industrial Revolution," in the beginning at least, benefited only a minority, the middle class, while it brought utmost misery and destitution to the growing proletariat. It was only after industrialization had outgrown its infancy that some of its blessings came to be shared by all classes alike.

Population Growth

Many of the early difficulties of industrialization were due to the unsettling effects that the tremendous population growth had on European society. Between 1815 and 1914, the population of Europe increased more than two-fold, from 200 million to 460 million. Another 40 million Europeans during this time emigrated to other parts of the world, especially the United States. The rate of growth differed from country to country. It was largest in Russia, less in England and Germany, and least in France. Population growth was probably due less to an

London Slums (1872), by Gustave Doré. Note the dismally overcrowded housing conditions caused by rapid industrialization and urbanization.

increase in the birth rate than to a decrease in the death rate. This decrease had many causes: improvements in medicine and public sanitation, absence of major wars, greater efficiency in government and administration, the revolution in agriculture, and, most important, the acceleration of industrial development. Industry pro-

Child Labor

PRO

I have visited many factories, both in Manchester and in the surrounding districts, during a period of several months, entering the spinning rooms unexpectedly, and often alone, at different times of the day, and I never saw a single instance of corporal chastisement inflicted on a child, nor indeed did I ever see children in ill-humor. They seemed to be always cheerful and alert, taking pleasure in the light play of their muscles—enjoying the mobility natural to their age. The scene of industry, so far from exciting sad emotions in my mind, was always exhilarating. . . . The work of these lively elves seemed to resemble a sport, in which habit gave them a pleasing dexterity. . . . As to exhaustion by the day's work, they evinced no trace of it on emerging from the mill in the evening; for they immediately began to skip about any neighboring playground, and to commence their little amusements with the same alacrity as boys issuing from a school.

CON

The report of the Central Commission relates that the manufacturers began to employ children rarely of five years, often of six, very often of seven, usually of eight to nine years; that the working-day often lasted fourteen to sixteen hours, exclusive of meals and intervals; that the manufacturers permitted overlookers to flog and maltreat children, and often took an active part in so doing themselves. One case is related of a Scotch manufacturer who rode after a sixteen years old runaway, forced him to return running before the employer as fast as the master's horse trotted, and beat him the whole way with a long whip.

From Andrew Ure, *The Philosophy of Manufactures* (3rd. ed.; London: H. G. Bohn, 1961), p. 301; and Friedrich Engels, *The Condition of the Working Class in England in 1844* (New York: J. W. Lovell, 1887), p. 101.

vided the means whereby more people could live, and the increase of population, in turn, supplied the necessary industrial labor force and swelled the ranks of consumers. The growth of population and the industrialization of society thus acted upon and stimulated each other.

Working-Class Misery

With the increase in population and the growth of industry there came a further important change in European society—the movement of people from the country to the city. Large-scale urbanization had been virtually unknown before the early nineteenth century. But as workers began to flock to the mills, small villages grew into crowded towns and quiet towns into noisy cities. This sudden influx of people brought on wretched housing conditions. Teeming slums, almost totally lacking in sanitation facilities, turned into breeding places of disease and vice. There was as yet no effective municipal administration to cope with these novel problems, and the workers themselves were too poor to improve their condition.

Poor housing was not the only hardship afflicting the early workingman. Since mechanized industry required little skill, there was always an abundance of manpower and wages were kept at a minimum. The average working day was between twelve and sixteen hours, but even this rarely yielded sufficient pay to support a worker's family; so women and children had to work as well. Women and children were much in demand, since they were more docile and received less pay. But they also suffered more than men did from the harsh conditions in factories and mines. No provisions were made for the workers' safety, and accidents resulting from machines to which they were not accustomed were frequent. There was no insurance against accidents, sickness, or old age. Furthermore, as more machines were added and as more efficient machines were invented, unemployment became another of the worker's hardships. As industrialization spread to the Continent, so did the abuses that accompanied it. Conditions in Belgium and France were almost as bad as those in England.

Middle-Class Indifference

The attitude of much of the middle class toward the misery of the working class was one of indifference. The pioneers of modern industrialization, the new "captains of industry," were tough and ruthless men. They had to be if they wanted to survive because competition was keen and risks were great. For every one of them who made good, there were several who fell by the wayside; the road of early industrialism was lined with bankruptcies. There were economic booms that burst; there were wars that closed markets; there was machinery that broke down or became obsolete; and there was the constant opposition by the agrarian supporters of the old order, who fought stubbornly against middle-class efforts to gain economic and political influence.

In order to understand the seemingly callous attitude of the middle class toward the hardships of the workers, we must consider briefly the middle-class philosophy of liberalism, which tried to justify such selfish behavior. It was the belief in economic liberalism, as we shall see, that prevented any drastic measures of social reform in the early part of the nineteenth century. The absence of such reform, in turn, led to various protests on behalf of the worker, of which Marxian socialism became the most effective.

Middle-Class Liberalism

The term *liberalism* in our own day has assumed so many different meanings that it defies clear definition. In the early nineteenth century, however, liberalism had a definite meaning and specific aims. A liberal was a person who believed in freedom—freedom of thought, freedom of religion, freedom from economic restrictions, freedom of trade, and freedom from the political injustices of the old regime. Most of these freedoms had already been demanded by the leaders of the Enlightenment. The *philosophes* had held that every man had certain natural rights—life, liberty, and property. These rights the middle class had already demanded before and during the French Revolution, and it continued to demand them. But as time went on, its claims

were made not on the basis of natural law, as they had been during the eighteenth century, but on the grounds that they were the most sensible and useful way of bringing about the "greatest happiness of the greatest number." This attitude of applying the principle of utility to political and social institutions is called "utilitarianism."

"Utilitarianism"

The key figure in the transformation of liberal thought from the Enlightenment to the nineteenth century was the English philosopher and reformer Jeremy Bentham (1748–1832), the founder of utilitarianism. Bentham was a rationalist, but the reasonableness of an institution for him did not depend on its conformity with natural law; it depended on its utility. How was this utility to be determined? Bentham wrote: "For everyone, his own pleasure and his own freedom from pain is the sole good, his own pain and his own unfreedom the sole evil. Man's happiness and welfare consist exclusively of pleasurable feelings and of freedom from pain." Translated into politics, this meant that the best government was the one that ensured the most pleasure and gave the least pain to the largest number of people. The type of government most likely to produce that effect, according to Bentham, was a democracy.

Bentham's philosophy found many disciples, especially in England. Many of the British reforms in the 1820's and 1830's were due to the agitation of the "Utilitarians," or "Philosophical Radicals." The most influential follower of Bentham was John Stuart Mill (1806–73). Mill was an active public servant, a leading reformer, and a prolific writer on a wide range of subjects. Among his most famous books was the essay *On Liberty* (1859). Its purpose, according to Mill, was to set forth the basic principle according to which relations between the individual and society, between the citizen and his government, should be regulated. That principle, Mill said, is "that the sole end for which mankind may interfere with the liberty of action of the individual is self-protection. The only purpose for which power can be rightfully exercised over any member of a civilized community, against his will, is to prevent harm to others." Here we have a categorical statement in favor of individual liberty. Mill based his plea not on natural law, as earlier advocates of individual freedom had done, but on utility. "I regard utility," he said, "as the ultimate appeal on all ethical questions."

Mill's emphasis on individual freedom, on the right of everyone to do as he saw fit as long as his actions did not conflict with society, had tremendous appeal to the middle-class industrialist and businessman of the nineteenth century. Here was a philosophy that frowned on any but the most necessary interference by the government in the affairs of the individual. "That government is best that governs least," that leaves the individual free to develop his own abilities. In another essay, *Considerations on Representative Government* (1861), Mill discussed the purpose of government in terms that sounded familiar to businessmen. "Government," he said, "is a problem to be worked like any other question of business. The first step is to define the purpose which governments are required to promote. The next is to inquire what form of government is best fitted to fulfill these purposes." In answer to the first question, what is the purpose of good government, Mill held that it was "to promote the virtue and intelligence of its people"; and in answer to the second question, what form of government is best, Mill, like Bentham, decided in favor of democracy.

Mill's belief in democracy was not shared by most members of the middle class. Nor were his proposals that the government should intervene to protect working children and improve housing and working conditions. Mill was highly critical of the economic injustices and inequities he found in his own society. He suggested as possible remedies the formation of trade unions and a share in the profits for workers. He even went so far as to question the sanctity of private property. These were definitely signs of the new type of liberalism that was ultimately to replace the dogmatic liberalism of the early nineteenth century (see p. 347). But even though Mill showed greater compassion for the fate of the lower classes, his demand that the government leave the individual alone as much as possible clearly expressed the sentiments held by the majority of the middle class throughout the nineteenth century.

Liberalism in Politics

The middle class was, of course, primarily concerned with economic matters. (We shall see presently how liberalism developed its own economic doctrine.) But the industrialists, merchants, and bankers also realized that economic freedom was of no value unless it was supplemented by political freedom, that economic rights, to be effective, must be guaranteed by political rights. The main guarantee of such rights in the early nineteenth century was thought to be a written constitution, like that of the United States. The first document of this kind in recent European history had been the French Constitution of 1791. There were many others, as we have seen, between 1812 and 1849. Most of these constitutions favored limited, constitutional monarchy, and none of them was truly democratic. To ensure the predominance of the middle class, property qualifications for voting and for holding government office were part of all liberal constitutions. Anyone who found this restriction unjust was told that he needed only to work hard and improve his economic status in order to gain a share in the government. Only in their guarantee of individual liberty did these constitutions make some concession to the masses as well as to the classes. Freedom of the press, freedom of conscience, freedom of association, and freedom from arbitrary arrest—these were shared by rich and poor alike, at least theoretically. Workers who organized in order to improve their condition through collective bargaining, or socialists who used the press to call attention to existing injustices, would soon find out that the individual liberties guaranteed in the constitutions of the early nineteenth century did not apply to them. The political ideal of early nineteenth-century liberalism was limited democracy. It has been aptly characterized as government of the wealthy, for the wealthy, by the wealthy. It was this ideal that motivated the middle class in the various revolutions discussed previously and that accounted for the widening rift between the middle and lower classes in these revolutions.

The "Classical Economists"

As for the economic philosophy of liberalism, its roots, too, went back to the eighteenth century. Its basic elements were already contained in the writings of Adam Smith (1723–90). We have seen how this Glasgow professor, in his *Wealth of Nations* (1776), had argued for a policy of individual self-interest, free from any government interference, as the surest road to economic prosperity for society as a whole. Smith had proposed this policy of laissez faire, of leaving things alone, in order to liberate the individual from the many governmental restrictions that had hampered economic progress under mercantilism. He was the first of several writers on economic subjects who are usually called the classical economists. These men, for the first time formulated certain general economic laws that seemed to apply at all times and in all societies. Besides Smith, the two most prominent members of the group were Robert Malthus (1766–1834) and David Ricardo (1772–1823).

Malthus wrote his famous *Essay on the Principles of Population* in 1798. The book grew out of an argument he had with his father. The elder Malthus, a typical product of the eighteenth century, believed that if the world was reformed along rational lines there would be no end to human progress. Young Malthus did not agree. He pointed to the rapidly increasing population of western Europe in the late eighteenth and early nineteenth centuries as an insurmountable obstacle to progress. "The power of population," he wrote, "is indefinitely greater than the power in earth to produce subsistence for man. Population, when unchecked, increases in a geometrical ratio. Subsistence only increases in an arithmetical ratio." Here was the basic hypothesis of Malthusianism: People multiplied much more rapidly than the supply of food that was needed to keep them alive. Human misery, it seemed, was unavoidable. Poverty rather than progress was the normal state of human society.

Adam Smith on the Limitations of Government

1776

According to the system of natural liberty, the sovereign has only three duties to attend to; three duties of great importance, indeed, but plain and intelligible to common understandings: first, the duty of protecting the society from the violence and invasion of other independent societies; secondly, the duty of protecting, as far as possible, every member of the society from the injustice or oppression of every other member of it, or the duty of establishing an exact administration of justice; and, thirdly, the duty of erecting and maintaining certain public works and certain public institutions, which it can never be for the interest of any individual, or small number of individuals, to erect and maintain; because the profit could never repay the expense to any individual or small number of individuals, though it may frequently do much more than repay it to a great society.

Adam Smith, *An Inquiry into the Nature and Causes of the Wealth of Nations,* ed. Edwin Cannan (New York: Random House, 1937), p. 651.

Many objections might be raised against the dire prophecies of Malthus. Even in his own day, improvements in agriculture and the opening to cultivation of vast new regions in America and elsewhere were increasing the world's food supply. Since then there have been further changes, especially the development of birth control as a check on population growth. But even though Malthus' predictions have proved false or exaggerated, the increase of population remains of major concern to the present day. Malthus deserves credit for having dramatized this issue by connecting it to economic productivity.

To the majority of people in the early nineteenth century, the warnings of Malthus came as a shock. The future, which only recently had held such promise, now suddenly looked bleak; no wonder the new science of political economy was soon called the "dismal science."

Yet it was not dismal to everyone—certainly not to the middle class. As industrialists were growing rich while workers were sinking into misery, some voices now favored a more equitable distribution of profits. Such proposals, however, could not stand up against Malthus' assertion that poverty was inevitable. The poor were already increasing much faster than the rich. Giving them more wages or charity, the middle class could argue, would only result in their having more children. The best solution was to keep the poor as poor as possible. Adam Smith had asked government to keep its hands off business; Malthus advocated a similar attitude of laissez faire in regard to social reform.

The pessimistic note that characterizes the teachings of Malthus is also found in the writings of David Ricardo. His basic work, *On the Principles of Political Economy and Taxation* (1817), was the first real textbook on economics. One of Ricardo's major contributions to the economic theory of early nineteenth-century liberalism was what his disciples called the "iron law of wages." Labor, to Ricardo, was very much like any other commodity. When it was plentiful, it was cheap; when it was scarce, it was expensive. As long as there is an ample supply of workers, wages will inevitably sink to the lowest possible level of subsistence, just above starvation. To try to remedy this situation by lowering profits and raising wages would be futile, since it would merely increase the number of workers' children and, by limiting the supply of capital, cut down production. "Like all other contracts," Ricardo said, "wages should be left to the fair and free competition of the market, and should never be controlled by the interference of the legislature."

Here was another economic law as dismal in its prospects for the lower classes as Malthus' predictions on the increase of population. If there were people living on the verge of starvation, if wages were low and children had to work sixteen hours a day, that was unfortunate; but it was also, as Malthus and Ricardo had shown, inevitable. Attempts to change the situation through charity or legislation designed to im-

prove wages and hours were opposed by middle-class liberals as an interference with the beneficent principle of laissez faire.

Liberalism on the Continent

All the intellectual figures we have mentioned so far in our discussion of liberalism were British. Since England had a larger and more influential middle class than most continental countries, this is not surprising. But the writings of these men had a deep effect on continental liberalism as well. Adam Smith's *Wealth of Nations* in particular supplied most of the ammunition for the attacks of continental liberals on the economic restrictions and regulations of their governments. There were some differences in the direction or emphasis of these attacks. French liberalism, for instance, was more concerned with economic matters than liberalism in Germany, where the problem of national unification overshadowed all other issues. Outside England, France, and Germany, the philosophy of liberalism had few contributors. Liberalism, after all, was the credo of a class that had as yet made little headway outside western Europe.

Social Reform

Given the laissez-faire attitude of liberalism, it is not surprising that efforts to solve social problems through government action found little support among the middle class. What social reforms were introduced owed much to the agitation of a few individuals, who were motivated either by humanitarianism or, as in the case of Britain's "Philosophical Radicals," by a desire to be utilitarian and efficient.

Factory Acts

Some of the most effective opposition to early nineteenth-century liberalism came from among the representatives of the old order. For political and economic but also humanitarian reasons, some Tories attacked the new industrial system in its most vulnerable spot, the terrible conditions in the mines and factories. As far back as 1802, Parliament had passed an act that cut down the working hours of apprentices. The first real factory act, passed in 1819, forbade the employment in cotton mills of children under nine years of age and limited the daily labor of older children to twelve hours. In 1831 night work was abolished for persons under twenty-one. In 1847 the maximum working day for women and children was set at ten hours. Two acts in 1842 and 1855 made it illegal to employ women and children in the mining industry.

Despite the best intentions on the part of their sponsors, however, these early factory acts were not very effective. They were not strictly enforced, and they applied chiefly to the cotton industry. Not until 1833 was their scope extended to include other industries, and only then was some system of inspection set up to enforce the new provisions.

Social Legislation

There were other reforms in England besides factory acts. The Municipal Corporations Act of 1835 enabled municipalities to cope more effectively with some of the local problems arising from rapid urbanization. To ensure some degree of uniformity in matters of public health, Parliament in 1848 set up a system of local boards of health. One of the most pressing social problems was the care of the poor. The New Poor Law of 1834 for the first time brought some order into the complicated system of poor relief. It was not, however, an unmixed blessing to the poor. The law abolished the traditional practice of "outdoor relief," under which the wages of the poorest workers had been supplemented from public funds. Henceforth, to be eligible for relief, the poor had to report to workhouses; and by making conditions in these establishments as unpleasant as possible, all but those who could not possibly make a living otherwise were discouraged from going on relief. Here was a measure, clearly utilitarian, that delighted the middle class. It discouraged idleness and cut the expense of poor relief.

An illustration from the Shaftesbury Report, showing the employment of women and children in the mining industry. The evidence presented in this report brought about the Coal Mines Act of 1842 and subsequent measures to alleviate industrial abuses.

On the Continent, little was done to reform the abuses of early industrialism. A French law in 1803 prohibited work in factories before 3:00 a.m. Under the reign of Louis Philippe, the employment of children under eight was prohibited and the work of children under twelve was limited to eight hours a day. But enforcement of these laws, in France as in England, was very lax. In Belgium, nothing at all was being done to improve the lot of the workers. In Germany, the only state with any industry was Prussia, and the Prussian government, in 1839, introduced a factory law that forbade the employment of children under nine and limited the working hours of older children to ten hours.

Liberalism and Education

The only field of social reform in which the Continent was ahead of Great Britain was education. Here, for once, liberalism was not a hindrance but a help. Like the *philosophe* of the eighteenth century, the nineteenth-century liberal was a firm believer in education as a means of improving the world and of helping children get ahead. Any governmental measure in favor of education, therefore, had liberal support. Both France and Prussia had a long tradition of public education, and this they maintained during the nineteenth century. There was a brief reaction in favor of religious education under the Bourbons, but the Education Act passed under Louis Philippe again asserted the state's role in education. In Britain the first provision of public funds for education was not made until 1833. It was increased in subsequent years, but even so the amount set aside for education in 1839 was still only half of what it cost to maintain Queen Victoria's horses. Not until 1870 was the first general education act adopted in England. In the meantime, education depended on private initiative, and here the middle class played a leading and beneficial role.

As our discussion has shown, some genuine attempts were made in the first half of the nineteenth century to cope with the ills of early industrialism through social reform. But such attempts ran counter to the laissez-faire philosophy of liberalism. Economic liberalism was, to some extent, a mere rationalization of selfish interests by the middle class. But there was also in it much of the eighteenth-century belief that the world operated according to certain basic laws which could not be altered and which ultimately made for the greatest happiness of the greatest number.

This passive acquiescence in things as they were, however, could not possibly satisfy the workers. They refused to believe that the only solution to their troubles was to do nothing, to let matters take their course. They demanded that some remedial action be taken on their behalf. Otherwise they were prepared to act for themselves.

Working-Class Protest

The protest of the working class took various forms. Some of the discontent expressed itself in political action, as in the revolutions of 1830 and 1848. In another form of protest, workers vented their anger and frustration on the very instruments that to their simple minds seemed primarily responsible for their plight—the machines. There were sporadic instances of such "machine-breaking" during the early phase of industrialization, both in England and on the Continent. But these acts of despair proved futile; they could not halt the advance of the machine age. Instead of waging war against mechanization, workers increasingly tried to escape industrialization altogether by emigrating to the United States, where industry was still in its infancy and virgin lands offered a chance for making a better living.

Early Labor Unions

There was another, more effective way in which the working class tried to fight the injustices of industrialism. As the workers grew in number, they became aware that they constituted a new and separate class whose interests conflicted with those of their employers. This growing class-consciousness among the workers led them to organize their forces in an effort to gain better treatment for themselves.

The first country in which this trend toward labor unions made any headway was again Great Britain. The British government, impressed by the radicalism of the French Revolution, watched with apprehension labor's early efforts to organize. In 1799 and 1800 Parliament passed the Combination Acts, which prohibited workers from organizing to improve their condition. Labor's continued activities, however, together with the agitation of some middle-class reformers, finally made the government relent. In 1824–25, as we have seen, the Combination Acts were repealed. Henceforth, trade unions in England were no longer illegal, though it was still impossible under the law of conspiracy to engage in strikes and other overt forms of protest. Even so, under the new dispensation local unions arose throughout Britain. The next logical step was the formation of a large labor organization. This step was taken in 1845, with the organization of the "National Association for the Protection of Labour." In 1859 the Association was instrumental in having Parliament permit peaceful picketing. In 1868 a Trades Union Congress representing more than 100,000 members met in Manchester. Finally, in 1871 trade unions in Britain were granted full legal status; the British labor movement had at last come into its own.

On the Continent, labor's efforts at self-help were much less successful. In Belgium, labor unions were forbidden until 1866, and in Germany there was no labor movement to speak of until after 1870. In France, the right of workers to organize had been forbidden even during the Revolution. This ban was reiterated in the Napoleonic Code of 1803. Some French workers organized secret societies that fomented strikes and local uprisings; but these only made the government more determined in its repressive policy. The French banker Casimir Périer expressed the feelings of the government and the middle class when he said, "The workers must realize that their only salvation lies in patient resignation to their lot." There were others in France, however, who took a less passive view of the worker's fate. If England was prominent in defining the middle-class philosophy of liberalism, France was equally prominent in producing its counterpart, the working-class philosophy of socialism.

The Beginnings of Modern Socialism

Socialism as a mode of life, of course, was nothing new. It had always existed, and still does, in primitive communities where people work together and share the proceeds of their common labor. Socialism as an economic and social philosophy, on the other hand, is a relatively recent development, closely connected with the rise of modern industrialism. The term *socialism* did not come into common use until the 1830's. Like liberalism, it has assumed a wide variety of meanings. Today almost any kind of government interference with the free play of economic forces is called socialism by someone, whether it be the communist system of Russia or the "Great Society" of the United States.

While there are many varieties of socialism, all share certain fundamental principles. All socialists think that the existing distribution of wealth is unjust, since it gives a few people far more than they possibly need and leaves large numbers of people with barely enough to exist. To close the gap between the haves and the have-nots, socialists advocate common ownership of the resources and means of production that constitute and create society's wealth. The fruits of production—that is, the profits of human labor—socialists propose to distribute in such a way that every member of society receives an equal or at least an equitable share. All schools of socialism agree that there should be far-reaching changes in society in the direction of economic and social as well as political equality.

The Utopian Socialists

Historically, modern socialism is usually divided into pre-Marxian and post-Marxian socialism, or, in terms introduced by the Marxists, into "Utopian" and "scientific" socialism. The Utopian socialists earned their epithet because of the unrealistic nature of their schemes. Most of the Utopians were French, and they all came from the middle or upper class. In view of the poverty and lack of education of the working class, this is hardly surprising.

The first Utopian socialist to achieve any prominence was a French nobleman, Count

Henri de Saint-Simon (1760–1825). Impressed with the social and economic injustices of a laissez-faire economy, Saint-Simon suggested that the state take a hand in organizing society in such a way that people, instead of exploiting one another, join forces to exploit nature. "The whole society," he held, "ought to strive toward the amelioration of the moral and physical existence of the most numerous and poorest class." The principle according to which this amelioration should operate was defined by Saint-Simon as: "From each according to his capacity, to each according to his work." In time this became one of the most popular slogans of socialism.

A more typical Utopian was Charles Fourier (1772–1837). Most of the ills of society, Fourier held, were due to the improper social and physical environment in which most people lived. To provide a more favorable environment, Fourier proposed the creation of so-called *phalanges,* or phalanxes. These were to be pleasant communities of some 1,600 to 1,800 people, living on 5,000 acres of land, and forming a self-sufficient economic community. Fourier's plans never got very far in Europe. But in the United States, where land was cheap and pioneering more common, a number of cooperative establishments were tried. None of them, however, was a lasting success.

The only one among the French Utopians to play an active role in politics was Louis Blanc (1811–82). His reform proposals were a good deal more realistic than those of the other Utopians. Blanc realized that economic reform, to be effective, must be preceded by political reform. Once true democracy had been achieved, the state could initiate the new type of industrial organizations that Blanc proposed. These consisted of social or national workshops—that is, self-supporting units of production, owned and operated by the workers on a cooperative, profit-sharing basis. Workshops of this sort were given a brief try by the revolutionary government of 1848, of which Louis Blanc was a member. The experiment failed, however, largely because the original purpose of the workshops was subordinated to the needs of the moment. Instead of self-supporting industrial enterprises, the workshops of 1848 were used for the temporary relief of unemployment.

The most prominent Utopian socialist outside France was the British industrialist Robert Owen (1771–1858). Appalled by conditions he found when he took over the cotton mills at New Lanark in Scotland, Owen gave his workers decent housing, increased their pay, and shortened their working-hours. In the model community he created, both productivity and profits increased, thus bearing out Owen's contention that satisfied workers were also better workers. Owen was less fortunate with a project he attempted on this side of the Atlantic. The community of New Harmony in Indiana, conceived along the lines of Fourier's phalanxes, turned out to be a fiasco.

Utopian socialism, in fact, had little to show for its manifold efforts. Like the *philosophes,* the Utopians believed in the natural goodness of man and the perfectibility of the world. They soon discovered that most men were not naturally good and reasonable. But even the failure of the Utopians contained a useful lesson. It showed that idealism and the best intentions are not sufficient to reform society. A more realistic and more militant type of socialism was needed that would use the worker's potential economic and political power to wrest concessions from the middle class. This new kind of socialism was first presented in the writings of Karl Marx (1818–83) and Friedrich Engels (1820–95).

Marxian Socialism

One of the reasons for the failure of the Utopian socialists was that they never sparked any substantial movement among the workers. There were some political working-class organizations during the 1830's and 1840's, but they had to operate as secret conspiracies rather than open political parties. In France, Auguste Blanqui founded the "Society of Families" and the "Society of Seasons," both of them socialistic or communistic. Another such society, founded by German exiles, was the "League of the Just."

Its program was originally supplied by Wilhelm Weitling, a German tailor who in 1842 published his *Guarantee of Harmony and Freedom.* These various underground organizations were all influenced by the writings of the Utopian socialists, but in their demands for complete economic equality, or communism, they went considerably beyond the demands of the middle-class Utopians.

Communism—that is, the abolition of all private property—ultimately became the basis of most socialist programs. We must bear in mind, however, that a century ago the term *communism* did not have the connotations it has assumed since the Bolshevik Revolution. The number of communist socialists in the first half of the nineteenth century was extremely small, and very few people realized the ultimate implications of their aims. In 1844 two young Germans, Karl Marx and Friedrich Engels, established contact with the "League of the Just." Soon thereafter its name was changed to the "Communist League," and from secret revolutionary conspiracy it now shifted to open propaganda. In 1847–48 Marx and Engels supplied the League with its new program, which they called the *Communist Manifesto.*

Karl Marx and Friedrich Engels

Both Marx and Engels came from the middle class which they spent most of their lives attacking. Even as a university student in Germany, Marx had shown a lively interest in social issues and socialism. His early writings brought him into disfavor with the police and in 1843 led to his first exile in Paris. There he met Engels, the son of a wealthy German industrialist with industrial holdings in England. Engels was already a communist, and there developed between the two men a close intellectual partnership. Engels is usually overshadowed by Marx, but his contributions to Marxian doctrine were considerable; besides, Engels through most of his life supported Marx financially.

The first result of the collaboration between Marx and Engels was the *Communist Manifesto,* which appeared during the revolutions of 1848. Marx and his fellow exiles welcomed the revolu-

Karl Marx in 1863, looking every bit a member of the bourgeoisie he so much despised.

tions, and Marx himself was present during the upheavals in Paris. When the revolutions failed, he went to England; there he remained until his death in 1883, leading a none-too-happy life, constantly beset by financial worries and ill health. It was during the years in England that Marx wrote most of his basic works, notably *Das Kapital,* the first volume of which appeared in 1867.

The Communist Manifesto

The basic elements of Marx's social philosophy were contained in the brief and persuasive *Communist Manifesto.* Its fundamental proposition, as restated by Engels in his introduction to a later edition of the *Manifesto,* was

> that in every historical epoch the prevailing mode of economic production and exchange, and the social organization necessarily following from it, form the basis upon which is built up, and from which alone can be explained, the political and intellectual history of that epoch; that consequently the whole history of mankind (since the dissolution of primitive tribal society, holding land in common ownership) has been a history of class struggles, contests between exploiting and exploited, ruling and oppressed classes; that the history of these struggles forms a series of evolutions in which, nowadays, a stage has been reached where the exploited and oppressed class—the proletariat—cannot attain its emancipation from the sway of the exploiting and ruling class—the bourgeoisie—without, at the same time and once and for all, emancipating society at large from all exploitation, oppression, class distinctions, and class struggles.

Here we have the two things for which Marx is most famous: his economic, or materialistic, interpretation of history, and his theory of the class struggle. Other thinkers before Marx had recognized the influence of material circumstances and of the environment upon history. But Marx focused his attention on one particular aspect of environment that he considered fundamental: the means of production, the way in which people make a living. It is the economic structure of society, according to Marx, that determines its social, political, legal, and even cultural aspects. All these things—politics, law, religion, the arts—are ultimately determined by economic factors. Historians before Marx, especially after the eighteenth century, had viewed history as an intellectually determined process. Here we have a diametrically opposite view, an emphasis on material, economic, nonintellectual forces as the sole determining factors.

To illustrate his economic interpretation of history as well as his theory of the class struggle, in the *Communist Manifesto* Marx gave a brief survey of the history of western civilization as he saw it:

> The history of all hitherto existing society is the history of class struggles. Freeman and slave, patrician and plebeian, lord and serf, guildmaster and journeyman, in a word, oppressor and oppressed, stood in constant opposition to one another, carried on an uninterrupted, now hidden, now open fight, a fight that each time ended either in a revolutionary reconstitution of society at large, or in the common ruin of the contending classes.

Marx then goes on to examine the history of western society more closely, beginning with the Middle Ages. At that time, the economy of Europe was predominantly agrarian, with a large class of serfs supporting a small class of feudal nobles. Upon this society, material changes begin to work: money, trade, the beginnings of a commercial, capitalist economy. As these changes take hold, a new class, a trading or bourgeois class, is formed. And between the old feudal nobility and the new middle class a struggle arises, which leads to some preliminary victories of the bourgeoisie in England and Holland and culminates in the American War of Independence and the French Revolution.

The final victory of the middle class came in the nineteenth century. But this did not end the struggle. Because now a new struggle began, this time between the bourgeoisie and the proletariat. It was brought about by another change in the mode of production, the introduction of the factory system and the rise of industrial capitalism. The workers in this new struggle, which Marx saw going on around him, were now herded together in large factories, under the eyes of their "oppressors." They were held down by the iron laws of capitalist economics to a bare subsistence level. But there was one thing these workers could do, according to Marx: they could organize themselves, they could become class-conscious.

Marx felt certain that the bourgeoisie and the workers were already locked in their death struggle. And the victory of the proletariat in this struggle, Marx held, could be predicted with the certainty of a scientific experiment—hence the term "scientific socialism." By the laws of capitalist competition there were bound to be periodic crises, caused by "epidemics of overproduction." As a result of these crises, the poor would get poorer and the rich would get richer. And there would finally come a time when "it becomes evident, that the bourgeoisie is unfit any longer to be the ruling class in society . . . because it is incompetent to assure an existence to its slave within his slavery. . . . Society can no longer live under this bourgeoisie. . . . Its fall and the victory of the proletariat are equally inevitable."

So much for the collapse of capitalism. What then? What will the world be like after the proletariat has won? On that subject Marx is rather vague. At one point he envisages a kind of transition period—the dictatorship of the proletariat, as he calls it—in which the proletariat by revolution will destroy the existing political machinery of the state, will convert the means of production into public property, and will gradually bring about a classless society. The state, as Engels put it, will gradually "wither away." Then what? "In place of the old bourgeois society, with its classes and class antagonisms," Marx concludes, "we shall have an association in which the free development of each is the condition for the free development of all." This is an idyllic, but also a rather vague, picture, not very different, moreover, from the kind of society certain eighteenth-century writers had envisaged. There was, in truth, a good deal of the eighteenth century in Marxism. It shared the later *philosophes'* belief in progress, in the good life here on earth, and in the natural goodness of man.

The Errors and Contributions of Marx

What about Marx's concept of classes, and of history as a series of class struggles? The concept of class certainly was a useful contribution; and if Marx did not make us class-conscious, he helped our understanding of past and present society by making us aware of classes. But his definition of classes entirely in economic terms is much too narrow; and by denying any influence to the individual, it runs counter to

On Understanding Marx

Rigorous examination is one thing Marx's ideas will not stand because they were not rigorously formulated. To do justice to his intent they must often be reinterpreted and qualified. They constitute a mixture of the true, the vague, and the false.

It should be apparent to any sensitive reader that Marx writes primarily as a critic of capitalism, as a man fired with a passionate ideal to eliminate the social inequalities, the poverty, and injustices of his time. Much of what he said makes sense and good sense considered as a description of the capitalist society of his time and as a prediction of the probable historical development of any capitalist system *on the assumption* that nothing outside that system, especially political influences, interferes with its development. Marx's fundamental errors arise from an uncritical extrapolation of what he observed in capitalist societies to all class societies, and from a disregard of the enormous influence which political, national, and moral forces have exerted on the development of capitalism as an economic system.

From Sidney Hook, *Marx and the Marxists: The Ambiguous Legacy* (Princeton: Van Nostrand, 1955), p. 35.

our widely held belief in individualism. As for Marx's view of the past as a series of class struggles, it does not really fit the facts of history, nor does his emphasis on merely two opposing classes. Marx recognized the existence of other classes, but he believed that they would ultimately be absorbed by one or the other of the two contending groups—the bourgeoisie and the proletariat. This prediction, like so many others Marx made, thus far has failed to materialize.

There were, then, a good many blind spots in Marx's socialist theories. While the rich were getting richer, the poor did not necessarily get poorer. The general standard of living in the world's industrial nations was to reach heights undreamed of by Marx. Man, furthermore, does not seem to be motivated exclusively, or even primarily, by economic concerns. Despite Marx's attacks on religion, the established churches have continued to play an important part even in the lives of the lower classes. Another force that increasingly came to command the allegiance of rich and poor alike was nationalism. The great wars of the last century have been fought not between the "oppressed" and their "oppressors," but between the workers of different nations for the defense or the greater glory of their own country.

Despite errors and shortcomings in his teachings, however, the contributions of Marx to modern thought have been most fruitful. By bridging the gap between politics and economics, he enriched our understanding of the past. We may not accept the dominant role he assigned to economic factors, but we have come to realize the importance of these factors. Prior to Marx, the division of society into rich and poor, haves and have-nots, was accepted as a natural, unchangeable fact. It was chiefly due to Marx that society was jolted out of such complacent acceptance of the *status quo*. By predicting far-reaching changes, he made people aware that changes were possible. The threat of revolutionary change conjured up in Marx's writings did much to hasten the peaceful evolution that has so markedly improved the condition of the lower classes in all industrial societies. Marxian socialism offered its followers a seemingly logical, scientifically certain answer to the many perplexities of modern society. This explains its appeal to simple workers and sophisticated intellectuals alike. The ultimate success of Marxism lay in the almost religious fervor it inspired among its disciples.

Other Forms of Social Criticism

Marxian socialism, in its ultimate effects on society, turned out to be the most important attack on the capitalist philosophy of laissez faire. There were other critics of this philosophy, however, who tried in various ways to awaken their contemporaries to the social problems created by the industrialization of society.

Humanitarianism

Writers like Honoré de Balzac in France and Charles Dickens in England, by dwelling in their novels on the more sordid aspects of the new industrialism, played on human sympathy in the hope of creating a climate favorable to reform. The historian Thomas Carlyle, in his *Past and Present* (1843), showed deep concern over the growing division between the working classes on the one hand and the wealthy classes on the other. He turned against the "mammonism" and the "mechanism" of his age and admonished the new captains of industry to be aware of their responsibilities as successors to the old aristocracy. Like Carlyle, Benjamin Disraeli, one of the rising young Tories, in his social novel *Sybil* (1845), deplored the wide gap that industrialization had opened between the rich and the poor. It was, he said, as though England had split into two nations "between whom there was no intercourse and no sympathy."

Christian Socialism

Another body of social criticism arose within the Christian churches, first in England and later on the Continent. For centuries past, organized Christianity had been the chief dispenser of charity to the poor and the aged. The beginnings of modern Christian socialism go back to a small group of English clergymen who felt that the best way to attack the evils of industrialism was to reaffirm the gospel of charity and brotherly love. The leader of the Christian Socialist movement was the Anglican theologian Frederick Denison Maurice. Its best-known propagandist was the English clergyman and novelist Charles Kingsley. In his famous tract, *Cheap Clothes and Nasty* (1850), written under the pseudonym of "Parson Lot," Kingsley attacked the condition of "ever-increasing darkness and despair" in the British clothing industry, whose sweatshops were "rank with human blood." To remedy a situation in which men were like "beasts of prey, eating one another up by competition, as in some confined pike-pond, where the great pike, having dispatched the little ones, begin to devour each other," Kingsley proposed the formation of cooperative enterprises in which everyone would be "working together for common profit in the spirit of mutual self-sacrifice." Christian Socialism, in appealing to the social consciousness of "every gentleman and every Christian," helped to modify the belief in laissez faire and to prepare the soil for the movement of social reform that gained momentum in the second half of the nineteenth century.

Anarchism

One other form of social protest of quite a different nature deserves mention here, even though its effects were not felt until later in the century. Anarchism, like socialism, hoped to overthrow capitalism. But while the socialists were ready to use the state as a stepping stone for the realization of their aims, the anarchists were deeply opposed to any kind of governmental authority and organization. One of the earliest theorists of anarchism was the French publicist Pierre-Joseph Proudhon (1809–65). In his pamphlet *First Memoir on Property* (1840) he asked the question, "What is property?" and replied with the well-known slogan, "Property is theft!" This seeming opposition to private property appeared to align Proudhon with communism and endeared him to Marx. The latter's admiration cooled, however, when he discovered that Proudhon was less interested in overthrowing the middle class than in raising the worker to the level of that class. Proudhon was against any kind of government, be it by one man, a party, or a democratic majority. "Society," he wrote, "finds its highest perfection in the union of order with anarchy."

The most famous proponent of anarchism was a Russian nobleman, Mikhail Bakunin (1814–76). A theorist of anarchism, he also practiced what he preached. Bakunin was involved in several revolutions, was three times condemned to death, and spent long years in prison and Siberian exile. Most of the evils of his day Bakunin attributed to two agencies—the state and the Church. His ideal society was a loose federation of local communities, each with a maximum of autonomy. In each of these communities the means of production were to be held in common. The way to achieve this governmentless state of affairs, Bakunin held, was not by waiting patiently for the state to wither away, as Marx had held, but by helping matters along, if necessary by means of terrorism, assassination, and insurrection. The last decade of the nineteenth century, as we shall see, witnessed a whole series of assassinations attributed to anarchists. But anarchism never developed into a well-defined movement, partly because of Bakunin's death in 1876, partly because of the impracticable nature of its doctrine. Traces of it, however, survived into the twentieth century and contributed to another type of social protest, syndicalism (see p. 335).

By the middle of the nineteenth century, the coming of the Industrial Age, with its revolutionary political, social, and economic effects, had made itself felt over most of Europe. As we shall see, it also extended to other parts of the world (see Chapter 12). For the next two decades, people's attention in Europe and the United States became absorbed by momentous political developments. A series of wars radically changed the existing order and overshadowed economic developments. Once the political situation had become stabilized, however, shortly after 1870, a second wave of economic development swept over Europe and the world, a wave of such magnitude that it is often referred to as a "Second Industrial Revolution."

Suggestions for Further Reading

1. General

Historians' views of the "Industrial Revolution" have changed over the years, as is shown in E. E. Lampard's perceptive essay, *Industrial Revolution: Interpretations and Perspectives* (1957). A good recent account of early industrialization is P. Deane, *The First Industrial Revolution** (1965). H. J. Habbakuk

---

* Available in paperback edition.

and M. Postan, eds., *The Industrial Revolutions and After* (1965) (Vol. VI of *The Cambridge Economic History of Europe*), contains essays by noted specialists. The widening scope of industrialization is stressed in W. O. Henderson, *The Industrial Revolution on the Continent* (1961). A. P. Usher, *A History of Mechanical Inventions* (1929), and G. Fussell, *The Farmer's Tools, 1500–1900* (1952), discuss the importance of technological change; and A. M. Carr-Saunders, *World Population: Past Growth and Present Trends* (1937), traces the beginnings of our current "population explosion." The impact of technology on man is viewed, with some alarm, by L. Mumford, *Technics and Civilization* (1934), and S. Chase, *Men and Machines* (1929).

2. Economic Changes in Britain

Because England was the first country to undergo the transition to modern industrialism, its agricultural and industrial revolutions have been studied most intensively. Both P. Mantoux, *The Industrial Revolution in the Eighteenth Century* (1929), and T. S. Ashton, *An Economic History of England: The Eighteenth Century* (1955), deal with the roots of these developments. A small volume by T. S. Ashton, *The Industrial Revolution, 1760–1830** (1948), helps to dispel many misconceptions about early modern industrialism. J. Clapham, *An Economic History of Modern Britain,* Vol. I (1926), covers the period between 1820 and 1850. Briefer treatments are W. H. B. Court, *A Concise Economic History of Britain from 1750 to Recent Times* (1954), and A. Redford, *An Economic History of England, 1760–1860* (1947). The changes in British agriculture are the subject of G. Slater, *The English Peasantry and the Enclosure of the Common Fields* (1907); Lord Ernle, *English Farming, Past and Present* (1936); J. L. Hammond and B. Hammond, *The Village Labourer, 1760–1832* (1918); and D. G. Barnes, *A History of the English Corn Laws, 1660–1846* (1930). The following are detailed studies on special aspects of the Industrial Revolution in England: T. S. Ashton, *Iron and Steel in the Industrial Revolution* (1951); W. H. B. Court, *The Rise of the Midland Industries, 1600–1838* (1938); A. Redford, *Manchester Merchants and Foreign Trade, 1794–1858* (1934); and E. P. Thompson, *The Making of the English Working Class** (1963). The most important single invention of early industrialism is the subject of H. W. Dickinson, *A Short History of the Steam Engine* (1939), and of J. Lord, *Capital and Steam Power, 1750–1800* (1923).

3. The Spread of Industrialism

Besides England, only France experienced any noticeable industrial development during the eighteenth century. These beginnings are discussed in H. E. Sée, *Economic and Social Conditions in France During the Eighteenth Century* (1927), and in S. T. McCloy, *French Inventions of the Eighteenth Century* (1954). Later developments in France are treated in A. L. Dunham, *The Industrial Revolution in France, 1815–1848* (1955), and R. E. Cameron, *France and the Economic Development of Europe, 1800–1914,* 2nd ed.* (1961). British influence on economic developments abroad is traced by W. O. Henderson, *Britain and Industrial Europe, 1750–1870* (1965), and L. C. A. Knowles, *Economic Development in the Nineteenth Century: France, Germany, Russia, and the United States* (1932). Other useful economic histories are: J. H. Clapham, *Economic Development of France and Germany, 1815–1914** (1936); S. B. Clough, *France: A History of Natural Economics* (1939); W. O. Henderson, *The Zollverein* (1939); and J. Blum, *Lord and Peasant in Russia** (1961).

4. The Social Effects of Industrialization

The traditional emphasis on the negative effects of early industrialism is evident in J. L. Hammond and B. Hammond, *The Town Labourer, 1760–1832* (1917), *The Skilled Labourer, 1760–1832* (1919), and *The Bleak Age** (1947). A Marxian view of the same subject may be found in J. Kuczynski, *A Short History of Labour Conditions under Industrial Capitalism,* 4 vols. (1944–46). A more balanced picture is drawn in A. Briggs, *The Age of Improvement, 1783–1867* (1959); S. G. Checkland, *The Rise of Industrial Society in England, 1815–1885* (1964); and R. W. Postgate, *The Common People, 1746–1946**

---

* Available in paperback edition.

(1949). On urban growth, see A. Redford, *Labour Migration in England, 1800–1850* (1929); and on landed interests, F. M. Thompson, *English Landed Society in the Nineteenth Century* (1963).

5. Economic Liberalism

The best way to study the utilitarians and classical economists is through their writings. The most important of these—J. S. Mill, *Autobiography** and *On Liberty**; T. R. Malthus, *An Essay on Population**; and D. Ricardo, *Principles of Political Economy and Taxation**—are available in several editions. The general development of modern economic thought is presented in C. Gide and C. Rist, *History of Economic Doctrines from the Physiocrats to the Present Day* (1913, 1948), and in E. Roll, *A History of Economic Thought* (1942). The standard work on Bentham and the utilitarians is É. Halévy, *The Growth of Philosophic Radicalism** (1955). More recent treatments are J. Hamburger, *Intellectuals in Politics: John Stuart Mill and the Philosophic Radicals* (1965), and S. H. Letwin, *The Pursuit of Certainty: David Hume; Jeremy Bentham; John Stuart Mill; Beatrice Webb* (1965). There are also pertinent chapters in C. Brinton, *English Political Thought in the Nineteenth Century** (1949).

6. Social Reform

Social reform in the first half of the nineteenth century was almost entirely restricted to Great Britain. M. W. Thomas, *The Early Factory Legislation* (1948), deals with the period between 1802 and 1853. Other notable reform efforts are dealt with in E. L. Woodward, *The Age of Reform, 1815–1870* (1938); L. Radzinowitz, *A History of English Criminal Law: The Movement for Reform, 1750–1833* (1948); and S. Webb and B. Webb, *English Local Government: English Poor Law History,* 3 vols. (1927–29). For early attempts of the working class to organize itself politically and economically, see G. D. H. Cole, *British Working Class Politics, 1832–1914* (1941); G. D. H. Cole and A. W. Filson, eds., *British Working Class Movements: Select Documents, 1789–1875** (1951); and S. Webb and B. Webb, *History of Trade Unionism* (1920). A good introduction to social reform is through the biographies of some of the leading reformers; G. D. H. Cole, *The Life of William Cobbett* (1942); G. Wallas, *Life of Francis Place* (1925); G. F. A. Best, *Shaftesbury* (1964); and G. M. Trevelyan, *Lord Grey of the Reform Bill* (1929).

7. Socialism

Good surveys of the subject are G. D. H. Cole, *A History of Socialist Thought,* 2 vols. (1953), and H. W. Laidler, *Social-Economic Movements* (1949). Less systematic but more readable is E. Wilson, *To the Finland Station** (1953). R. Owen, *The Life of Robert Owen, by Himself* (1920), gives insights into the thought of this leading utopian reformer. Of several books about Owen, F. Podmore, *Robert Owen* (1924), is one of the best. F. Manuel, *The Prophets of Paris** (1962), takes a fresh look at the French utopian socialists. The literature on Marxian socialism is vast. A convenient collection of basic sources is available in *Karl Marx and Frederick Engels; Selected Works,* 2 vols. (1951). Briefer selections are found in S. Hook, *Marx and the Marxists** (1955). The easiest way for the layman to become acquainted with Marx's basic concepts is still K. Marx and F. Engels, *The Communist Manifesto** (1848), available in countless editions. G. D. H. Cole, *The Meaning of Marxism** (1948), offers one of many keys to an understanding of Marxist theory. George Lichtheim, *Marxism** (1961), is an important contribution. There are numerous biographies of Marx, some favorable, like F. Mehring, *Karl Marx: The Story of his Life* (1936), and others hostile, like L. Schwarzschild, *The Red Prussian: The Life and Legend of Karl Marx** (1947). A balanced treatment is I. Berlin, *Karl Marx: His Life and Environment** (1948). The role of Engels in the genesis of Marxian socialism is emphasized by G. Mayer, *Friedrich Engels* (1935). For a discussion of anarchism, there are two excellent biographies of its founders: D. W. Brogan, *Proudhon* (1934), and E. H. Carr, *Michael Bakunin** (1937).

---

* Available in paperback edition.

EUROPE

CARTE DE L'Europe EN 1870

ILES BRITANNIQUES

MER DU NORD

OCEAN ATLANTIQUE

NORWÉGE SUÉDE

MER BALTIQUE

MER BLANCHE

RUSSIE

DANEMARK

HOLLANDE

HOLSTEIN

SUISSE

FRANCE

PORTUGAL

ESPAGNE

CORSE

SARDAIGNE

MER ADRIATIQUE

ITALIE

AUTRICHE

CRIMÉE

MER NOIRE

TURQUIE D'EUROPE

ARCHIPEL

Degrés de longitude

Ant.º E. Mockly, Paris

L'Angleterre, isolée, peste de rage et en oublie presque l'Irlande qu'elle tient en laisse. L'Espagne fume, appuyée sur le Portugal. La France repousse les envahissements de la Prusse, qui avance une main sur la Hollande l'autre sur L'Autriche. L'Italie, aussi, Bismarck. Ote donc tes pieds de la. La Corse et la Sardaigne... un vrai Gavroche qui rit de tout. Le Danemarck, qui a perdu ses jambes dans le Holstein, espère les reprendre. La Turquie d'Europe bâille et s'éveille. La Turquie d'Asie aspire la fumée de narguilhé. La Suède fait des bonds de panthère; et la Russie ressemble à un croquemitaine qui voudrait remplir sa hotte.

An animated French map of Europe in 1870. The caption explains what is going on: "England, isolated, swears with rage and almost forgets Ireland, whom she holds on a leash. Spain frets, propped up by Portugal. France repulses the invasion of Prussia, who reaches with one hand for Holland and the other for Austria. Italy also says to Bismarck: 'Take your feet away from there.' Corsica and Sardinia, a regular urchin who laughs at it all. Denmark, who has lost his legs in Holstein, hopes to regain them. European Turkey yawns and wakes up. Asiatic Turkey inhales the smoke of her water pipe. Sweden leaps like a panther, and Russia resembles a bugbear out to fill his basket."

288

11

A New Balance of Power, 1850–1871

The keynote of European history during the first half of the nineteenth century had been revolution. In a long series of upheavals that reached its climax in 1848, Europe had tried to find some adjustment between the traditional claims of the old monarchical and aristocratic order and the democratic demands of the rising middle and lower classes. By 1850 the middle class had won some notable victories, and parliamentary government had gained a hold in most of western Europe. East of the Rhine, however, the old regime had stood its ground, and the conflict between the claims of monarchical and popular sovereignty continued.

The nature of this conflict, however, changed during the next few decades. In the past, the issues dividing the defenders of the old order and the advocates of the new had been rigidly drawn along ideological lines. There had been little common ground between the conservatism of men like Metternich and Nicholas I and the liberal and national aspirations of the middle class. The men who rose to leadership after 1850 were less committed to ideology. They were realists, ready to forgo some of their principles in order to achieve some of their aims. It was in realistic appraisal of the new social and political forces brought to the fore by industrialization that Bismarck gave the German middle class

some of the concessions for which it had vainly fought several revolutions. By the same token, the middle class was ready to give up some of its political aims in order to protect and advance its economic interests. Demands for political reform continued. But the unprecedented economic growth of Europe, especially after 1870, helped to divert the attention of the middle class from politics to economics.

Besides economic growth, there was nationalism to preoccupy people's minds. Before 1850, domestic upheavals and international peace had been the order of the day; after 1850, the reverse was true. Five wars involving great powers were fought between 1854 and 1871, all of them prompted by nationalist aims and interests. In the past, whenever the *status quo* reached at Vienna had been threatened or actually changed, the "Concert of Europe" had collaborated to see that peace was speedily restored and that the balance of power was maintained. With the rise of nationalism, however, the European concert became more and more difficult to maintain. Even before 1850 the powers had failed to see eye-to-eye on certain international issues. But it was not until after 1850 that the first major showdown occurred. The Crimean War of 1854–55 was the first in a whole series of conflicts that put an end to the Concert of Europe. By

1871 a new balance of power had emerged on the Continent, significantly different from the balance that had existed twenty years earlier.

The Eastern Question

The Crimean War was the latest phase in the latent crisis caused by the slow disintegration of Turkish rule in the Balkans. The "Eastern Question" had already caused one brief war between Russia and Turkey in 1828–29. To ensure year-round navigation, Russia depended on free access to the Black Sea through the Turkish Straits. This she had gained for her merchant ships in the Treaty of Adrianople (1829). Attempts to gain exclusive passage for Russian warships, however, had run into opposition from the rest of the powers, since such an

arrangement would have guaranteed Russian predominance in the Black Sea. Instead, the Straits Convention of 1841 once more affirmed the closure of the Straits to *all* foreign warships.

The Straits were not the only issue involved in the Eastern Question. Both France and Great Britain had considerable commercial interests in the Near East, and the British regarded the eastern Mediterranean as the chief approach to India. These interests, the western powers felt, were threatened by Russia's gradual encroachment on Turkey, as evidenced in her occupation of the Danubian principalities of Moldavia and Wallachia after 1829. Another source of friction, which ultimately served as the immediate cause for the Crimean War, concerned the so-called Holy Places—that is, those sections of Jerusalem and Palestine that were closely associated with the life of Christ. Christians within the Ottoman

A Consultation about the State of Turkey, a contemporary cartoon. The "Sick Man of Europe" (Turkey) is threatened by Death (Russia), while the physicians (France and England) hold their consultation.

Empire had long been guaranteed certain rights by their Turkish masters, and foreign pilgrims had been granted access to the Holy Land. The interests of the western Christians were traditionally championed by France, while Russia considered herself the guardian of eastern, Greek Orthodox rights. Shortly after 1850, conflicts between the two religious groups led to a number of incidents. As a result, the tsar now tried to pressure Turkey into officially recognizing Russia's role as protector of Greek Orthodox rights in Turkey. In order to emphasize their interest in the negotiations taking place between Turkey and Russia, Britain and France sent naval contingents to the entrance of the Straits in 1853. Russia replied by reoccupying the Danubian principalities which she had evacuated two years earlier. The Concert of Europe, acting on Austrian initiative, vainly tried to keep tension from mounting. In October 1853 Turkey, trusting in British and French support, declared war on Russia. Pressure of public opinion and concern over the expansion of Russian influence later brought the western powers into the war on Turkey's side. For the first time in forty years, the great powers had become involved in war.

The Crimean War
and the Peace of Paris

The major action of the Crimean War was a year-long siege against the Russian stronghold of Sebastopol on the Crimean Peninsula. It was one of history's costliest operations, with most of the casualties caused by disease. One of its few positive effects was the creation of the first modern nursing and medical services under the direction of Florence Nightingale, from which ultimately arose the International Red Cross.

The Crimean War found most of the European powers lined up against the Russians. As the war progressed, Austria drew closer to the western powers and finally concluded an alliance with them. She never did any actual fighting, but even so the Russians resented her "ingratitude" for the aid Nicholas I had given the Austrians during the Hungarian uprising in 1849. Prussia outwardly followed Austria's lead but actually maintained a friendly neutrality and

secretly aided the Russian cause. The small kingdom of Piedmont-Sardinia also entered the war on the side of the western powers, contributing a small but welcome contingent of troops.

After eleven months of siege, the fortress of Sebastopol fell in September 1855. Nicholas I had died in March, and his successor, Alexander II, was now ready to talk peace. The Paris Peace Conference met in the spring of 1856. To curtail Russian influence over the area adjacent to the Ottoman Empire, the Black Sea was neutralized, which meant that Russia could not have any warships or fortifications there. In addition, navigation on the Danube River was declared free and open to all powers, and Russia had to surrender part of Bessarabia at the mouth of the Danube to the Turkish principality of Moldavia.

The Paris Conference also discussed the future of the Danubian principalities. Moldavia and Wallachia, it was decided, were to be under the temporary supervision of the great powers. Each principality was given a separate government. This, however, failed to satisfy the national aspirations of the Rumanians, who made up most of the population of the two regions. In 1858, therefore, both principalities elected the same man, Prince Alexander Cuza, as their ruler. After further consolidation of their common institutions, the principalities were finally recognized by the great powers in 1862 as the single and independent state of Rumania. The principle of nationality had triumphed once again.

Among the other decisions of the Paris Conference was the formal admission of Turkey to the family of powers, upon promise that she would introduce a number of much-needed reforms. The Paris Conference also issued a declaration against privateering and limited the rights of blockade by specifying that, to be effective, a blockade had to be backed by force. This principle of the "freedom of the seas" was intended to safeguard the rights of neutral countries in time of war. Finally, the Congress took notice, at least, of the "Italian Question" by permitting Cavour, the prime minister of Piedmont, to plead the cause of Italian unification before the assembled dignitaries. This was only a gesture, but it was a significant one.

The Congress of Paris, 1856. This first photograph of an international conference shows, left to right (seated): Baron Hübner (Austria), Ali Pasha (Turkey), Lord Clarendon (Britain), Count Walewski (France), Count Orlov (Russia), Baron de Bourqueney (France), and Lord Cowley (Britain). Standing, left to right, are: Count Cavour (Sardinia), De Villamarina (Sardinia), Count Hatzfeldt (Prussia), Count Vincent Benedetti (France), Mahommed Jemil Bey (Turkey), Baron Brunnov (Russia), Baron Manteuffel (Prussia), and Count Buol (Austria).

The Peace of Paris, like the Vienna settlement forty years earlier, was an effort by the great powers to remove the sources of tension that had led to war and to restore the balance of power that had been threatened by one of them. But while the Vienna settlement had succeeded in restoring international stability, the Paris settlement left a legacy of unresolved tensions. The Russians, in particular, felt humiliated and henceforth would try to recoup the losses they had suffered in the Crimean War. The French, having won an important victory, took pride in the fact that their emperor had emerged as the leading figure at the Paris Peace Conference. But Napoleon III's role as arbiter of Europe merely whetted his appetite for further foreign ventures, and he was soon to come up with new plans for revising the map of Europe. The fact, furthermore, that Cavour had been permitted to raise the question of Italy's future at the conference gave fresh hope to Italian nationalists, whose aspirations could be fulfilled only by war against Austria.

The country, other than Russia, to be most seriously affected by the Crimean War was Austria. Whether she realized it or not, Austria had been seriously weakened, not only by her estrangement from Russia but by the coolness that had developed between herself and Prussia. The latter, already restive under the domination that Austria had resumed in German affairs after 1850, was further alienated by Austria's attempts to involve the two leading German powers in the Crimean War. This isolation of Austria from her two traditional friends, Russia and Prussia, was perhaps the most significant result of the war. It was the more ominous because England, having learned a bitter lesson at Sebastopol, once more withdrew into her "splendid isolation." Austria was thus left entirely at the mercy of Italian and German nationalism. The stage had been set for one of the most dramatic periods in European history. The tragic hero of this drama was the French Emperor, Napoleon III.

The Second French Empire

We have already met the man who was to guide the destiny of France for the two fateful decades after 1850 (see p. 258). To this day, Louis Napoleon remains very much of an enigma. Was he a dictator, as some people have claimed, or was he a genuine democrat, as he himself claimed? After his fall from power in 1870, there was little doubt in anyone's mind that he was a fraud and a failure. More recently, however, historians have become somewhat more charitable in their judgment. In his domestic policy, Napoleon III gave France some of the happiest years in her history. And if in his foreign policy he showed an unerring instinct for doing the wrong thing, his motives were idealistic, and many of his reverses were due to forces over which he had no control.

Louis Napoleon became emperor by a cleverly managed *coup d'état*. Like most countries after 1848, the Second French Republic experienced a wave of reaction. Socialists were ejected from the legislature, the right to vote was curtailed, public meetings were restricted, and the freedom of the press was curbed. At the same time, however, France's new president, Louis Napoleon, was eager to gain the support of the French masses. In pursuit of this aim, he dissolved the Assembly in December 1851 and called for new presidential elections. There was some street fighting, but his *coup* succeeded. The French people once again endorsed the name Napoleon by a vast majority. A year later, the president finished his overthrow of the Republic by proclaiming himself Emperor of the French,

Napoleon III

Napoleon III was, to borrow Gamaliel Bradford's phrase, a "damaged soul"; and, after 1860, a damaged soul imprisoned in a damaged body. Grave, thoughtful, kind, devoted to noble causes, determined withal, fearless, and surprisingly practical, he had in him also the tortuousness of the eternal plotter, the vagueness of the Utopian, the weakened fiber of the sensualist, the fatalism of the gambler. Some characters in history are obvious in their greatness, mediocrity, or turpitude: even though our sympathies may widely differ, we feel we can focus Washington, Victoria, Gladstone, and even Napoleon I. Napoleon III is not one of these. His elusive physiognomy changes altogether with the light that is turned upon it. At one moment, he appears impressive: the only political leader in the nineteenth century whose thought could still be a guide for us today. At other times, the caricature drawn by Kinglake and Victor Hugo seems almost convincing: the middle-aged rake in imperial trappings, sinister even in his futility. The most searching, the most persistent light of all, the one in which he was seen by every one who approached him, reveals him as gentle, not merely in speech and smile, but to the very depths of his being.

From Albert Guérard, *Napoleon III* (Cambridge, Mass.: Harvard U. Press, 1943), p. 290.

thus pursuing further the historical parallel between himself and his uncle.

The parallel was carried still further in the Empire's political institutions, which closely followed those of the first Napoleon. There were two parliamentary bodies—an appointive senate and a legislature elected by universal male suffrage—both of which could merely discuss what the emperor saw fit to put before them. By carefully managing elections, furthermore, Napoleon was always in a position to command a parliamentary majority. Most major decisions were reached by the emperor himself in consultation with a Council of State made up of experts with purely advisory functions. The Second Empire, at least during its first ten years, was thus little more than a thinly disguised dictatorship.

The "Authoritarian Empire"

Despite the absence of political freedom, however, the authoritarian phase of Napoleon's rule was a happy period. The emperor gave his countrymen what they wanted most—prosperity at home and glory abroad. Like many a dictator since, Napoleon III tried to do something for everyone. The peasants, who had voted him into office and who continued to endorse his policy in numerous plebiscites, were helped by large-scale public works and improved credit facilities. The workers, who continued to remain cool to the new regime, were aided by far-reaching social legislation and public housing. But the class with which Napoleon's relations were most harmonious, at least in times of prosperity, was the industrial and commercial middle class.

More than any other statesman of his time, the Emperor of the French realized the importance and implications of modern industrialization, and he did his best to create conditions favorable to industrial growth. As a result, French railway mileage during the 1850's alone increased more than fivefold. A French law of 1863 permitted the formation of "limited liability" companies. By limiting the liability of stockholders to the stock they owned, investment was made less risky and the savings of the proverbially thrifty Frenchman were now attracted to industry. In a series of farsighted commercial agreements, notably the Cobden-Chevalier treaty (1860) with England, Napoleon abandoned the traditional protectionism of France in favor of moderate free trade. As a result, French exports soon exceeded imports. France in 1870 was still the chief industrial competitor of Great Britain. French industrial expansion had some negative aspects as well. There was an air of gaudiness and vulgarity about the newly enriched middle class. Speculation and overexpansion led to periodic crises and depressions. But on the whole the new prosperity was sound and was shared by all classes of the population.

As a symbol of the Empire's prosperity and splendor, Napoleon was instrumental in having the city of Paris transformed into the beautiful work of art it remains to the present day. The center of the city was completely rebuilt, with wide boulevards, stately squares, and lovely parks. Like so many of Napoleon's projects, this "urban renewal program" served a dual purpose. By providing employment and eradicating ugly slums, it aided the workers; but at the same time it did away with the breeding-grounds of radicalism and revolution. The wide avenues of the new city were unsuitable for erecting barricades, and they permitted the use of cavalry and artillery in case there should ever be another popular uprising.

The Second Empire came to an end on the battlefield in the war against Prussia in 1870. Before that time, however, domestic discontent had already forced Napoleon to abandon many of the authoritarian practices of his earlier years. Most of this discontent was provoked by his blundering foreign policy. The French people, still smarting from the defeat they had suffered forty years earlier, were not opposed to war, so long as they won. France's involvement in the Crimean War had been popular, and the same was true of a number of small colonial ventures. The occupation of Algeria was completed; new French settlements were established in West Africa; New Caledonia was occupied in 1853; and during the 1860's protectorates were secured over Cambodia and the region later called French Indochina. The French participation in the wars of Italian unification, on the other hand, while it brought some military glory and new territory, was deeply resented by French Catholics, since it deprived the papacy of its territorial holdings. Still more disastrous in French eyes were Napoleon's futile efforts, between 1862 and 1867, to establish a French protectorate over Mexico (see p. 322). The crowning blow to Napoleon's prestige, however, came when he failed to secure territorial compensations for France during Prussia's unification of Germany (see p. 303).

The "Liberal Empire"

To pacify the growing domestic opposition, Napoleon, during the 1860's, attempted a gradual liberalization of French political life. The "Liberal Empire" was initiated in 1860 when restrictions on debate in the legislative body were lifted and parliamentary proceedings were made public. Subsequent decrees extended the powers of the legislature and relaxed the restrictions on public meetings and the press that had existed since 1852. But these concessions only helped to swell the ranks of the opposition. By 1869 the government had so lost its grip that the parliamentary elections of that year returned ninety-three opposition candidates, thirty of whom were republicans. With labor unrest prompting a growing epidemic of strikes, and with the republican program of Léon Gambetta gaining more and more adherents, the government made some sweeping last-minute efforts to save its life. In their totality, these reforms amounted to the establishment of a parliamentary regime. In May 1870 the French electorate endorsed these constitutional changes with a rousing majority. But it was too late. Two months later the war with Prussia broke out, sweeping away the Empire and bringing in the Third Republic.

The Unification of Italy

The domestic events in France that we have just discussed must be viewed against the background of Napoleon's foreign policy. He had two main motives: to gain glory for France and to win freedom for suppressed nationalities. It was the conflict between the selfishness and the altruism, the realism and the idealism, inherent in these aims that accounts for much of the fateful vacillation in Napoleon's policy. The vacillation first manifested itself in his dealings with Italy.

Italy After 1848

Italy before 1848 had been an unhappy country, ridden by many factions, each hoping to bring about political unification according to its own plans. As a result of the abortive revolutions of 1848, however, unification under the leadership of the kingdom of Piedmont-Sardinia had emerged as the most feasible scheme. The king of Piedmont, Victor Emmanuel II, had been unique in not revoking the liberal constitution granted during the revolution. He did not relent, furthermore, in his hostile policy toward Austria. Turin, the capital of Piedmont, soon became a haven for Italian patriots from all over the peninsula trying to escape the persecutions of their reactionary, pro-Austrian rulers.

The man who realized the unique position of Piedmont and used it to bring about the unification of Italy was Count Camillo di Cavour. At the age of forty, in 1850, Cavour was appointed minister of agriculture and commerce, and in 1852 he became prime minister. Cavour at first was not so much interested in uniting the whole of Italy as he was in extending the power of Piedmont in the North. This, he realized, could be done only against the opposition and at the expense of Austria. To prepare for a showdown with Austria thus became one of his major concerns.

Before Austria could be tackled, however, several things were needed. The first was to create sympathy for the "Italian Question" outside Italy. This was done by having Piedmontese troops participate in the Crimean War and by having the Italian problem discussed by the powers at the Paris Peace Conference. A second prerequisite for a successful war against Austria was the military and economic strengthening of Piedmont. Cavour did his best to improve the armed forces and to further the building of railroads, of whose strategic importance he was very much aware. In a number of commercial treaties, Cavour integrated the economy of Piedmont with that of western Europe. He also fostered legislation improving the structure of business corporations, credit institutions, and cooperative societies. These economic measures alone entitle Cavour to a place of honor in his country's history.

Cavour and Napoleon III

The third requirement for Piedmont to be able to move against Austria was outside military aid. To get such aid, Cavour looked to France and Napoleon III. The French emperor had always held a lingering affection for Italy. To aid Italian unification not only appealed to his idealism but it also might strengthen the prestige of France and of himself. It was considerations like these that led to a super-secret meeting at Plombières in 1858 at which Napoleon promised Cavour his aid if Piedmont should become involved in a war with Austria. Once the war was won, Piedmont would form an enlarged kingdom of Upper Italy, and the whole peninsula was then to be united in a loose federation with the pope as president. France was to be rewarded for her help with the Piedmontese regions of Nice and Savoy. It is important to note that the Plombières agreement did not call for an Italy united under Piedmont.

The main difficulty was finding a pretext for war with Austria. While waiting for an opportunity, the two conspirators continued their preparations. As rumors of an impending war in Italy grew more persistent, the other powers began to show concern. Austria was the least worried. She was used to recurrent rumors of an Italian war and refused to take them seriously. England and Prussia, on the other hand, were less confident. The former, in the spring of 1859, came out with a plan for the evacuation of Austrian troops from the peninsula and the creation of an Italian federation. This was such an appealing scheme that Napoleon began to show signs of trying to back out of his agreement with Piedmont. At this point, when Cavour's carefully laid plans seemed about to fail, the Austrian emperor, Francis Joseph, forced a showdown by demanding that Piedmont refrain from any further preparations for war. When Piedmont turned down this ultimatum, Austrian troops, on April 29, 1859, invaded Piedmont. France thereupon joined her ally in the war against Austria.

The War of 1859

Had the Austrians moved quickly, they might have won the war. But by wasting time,

they allowed the French to pour their forces into Italy. After six weeks of bloody fighting, the French and Italian forces had won two indecisive victories at Magenta and Solferino and had driven the Austrians out of Lombardy. The next obvious step was the liberation of Venetia.

At this point, in July 1859, Napoleon surprised his ally and the world by concluding an armistice with Francis Joseph at Villafranca. There were several reasons for Napoleon's sudden defection: He apparently had been shocked by the bloodshed at Magenta and Solferino; the Austrian army was by no means beaten; there was dissatisfaction among many Frenchmen with a war against another Catholic power; and there was some fear that Prussia might come to Austria's aid. Under the terms of the Villafranca agreement, Napoleon broke his promise that Piedmont should get both Lombardy and Venetia. Austria merely surrendered Lombardy, which Napoleon then offered to Victor Emmanuel. The king, much to Cavour's consternation, accepted.

The First Phase of Italian Unification

Villafranca, however, turned out to be a blessing in disguise for the Italians. Up to this point the war had been waged chiefly for the enlargement of Piedmont. Now suddenly it became a war for Italian unification. At the start of the war, some of the small states in northern and central Italy had revolted and driven out their rulers. The prospect of their return now led the populace of these regions to raise an army and to proclaim their union with Piedmont. Cavour, in January 1860, asked Napoleon's consent to Piedmont's annexation of the central Italian states. Napoleon agreed, in return for the surrender of Nice and Savoy, which he had been promised at Plombières but which he had forfeited at Villafranca. In March 1860, plebiscites in Parma, Modena, Romagna, and Tuscany confirmed the union of central Italy with Piedmont.

The next act in the drama of unification was dominated not by Cavour but by a man who was his opposite in all respects—a romantic, a republican, an effective leader of men, but a complete political amateur—Giuseppe Garibaldi. We have already spoken of this colorful figure

Piedmont-Sardinia on the
eve of war in 1859

Acquired in 1859 through
war with Austria

Additions in 1860

Addition in 1866

Addition in 1870

and his role in the brief fiasco of the Roman republic in 1849. In May 1860, Garibaldi assembled an expeditionary force at Genoa. Its task was to help complete the liberation of the Kingdom of the Two Sicilies, where an uprising against the reactionary Bourbon regime had taken place. Garibaldi's expedition was a huge success. Aided by the local population, his small force of "Redshirts" defeated an army twenty times its size. By August Sicily was in Garibaldi's hands, and he was ready to cross to the mainland.

Garibaldi's success, however, raised a number of problems. His growing popularity threatened to displace Victor Emmanuel as the leader of a united Italy. Garibaldi might give in to the urgings of Mazzini and surrender the southern half of the peninsula to republicanism; or else he might move against Rome, to complete the unification of Italy. Such a move might lead

to a conflict with France, which still considered herself the protector of the papacy. To avert such a crisis, Cavour convinced Napoleon that the only way to stop Garibaldi was for Victor Emmanuel to meet him on the way. Promising to respect the independence of Rome itself, the Piedmontese army now invaded the Papal States, defeated the papal forces, and after bypassing Rome came face to face with Garibaldi's band not far from Naples. The situation was tense. But Garibaldi was too much of a patriot to let selfish ambitions interfere with his hope for a united Italy. Instead, he voluntarily submitted to Victor Emmanuel, thus completing the first phase of Italian unification.

The Kingdom of Italy

The Kingdom of Italy was proclaimed in March 1861. Two months later, Cavour suc-

Giuseppe Garibaldi, 1807–82.

interfered with the integration of the eight or more separate states. Tensions between the North and the South were especially marked. The poverty and illiteracy of the Italian masses, furthermore, made the extension of democracy a slow process, and Italy's parliamentary regime soon became known for its corruption. The wars of unification imposed staggering financial burdens, and taxes now were higher than ever before. At the same time, lack of coal and iron prevented large-scale industrialization, which might have relieved Italy's economic plight. Yet despite these shortcomings, the new Italy considered herself one of the great powers and tried to imitate the wealthier nations by maintaining an army and navy far beyond her means.

Much of the discontent and disillusionment in Italy after unification was blamed on Cavour's hurried policy. But we must remember that the unification of Italy had not really been his goal at the start. Much of his policy was determined by the other two makers of Italy, Napoleon III and Garibaldi. Where we may find fault with Cavour is in the ruthless methods he employed to achieve his aims. But such *Realpolitik*, as it came to be called, was not considered out of place by an age that gloried in nationalism and worshiped success. Much the same spirit that animated Cavour was to guide Bismarck in his German policy. And just as Cavour had started out in the hope of enlarging Piedmont but ended by creating the Kingdom of Italy, so Bismarck began working for a greater Prussia and wound up with a German Reich.

Austro-Prussian Rivalry

The most striking similarity between the unification of Italy and that of Germany was Austria's involvement in both. Austria's defeats in 1859 and 1866 were due in large measure to internal weakness caused by political disunity. Nationalism, which proved a boon to Cavour and Bismarck, was a source of infinite trouble to Francis Joseph and the many capable Austrian ministers who tried to find some way of keeping their empire from falling to pieces.

cumbed to an attack of typhoid fever and died, just as his country needed him most. The unification of Italy was by no means completed. Venetia did not become part of the kingdom until after another Austrian defeat, this time by Prussia in 1866; and Rome remained in papal hands until 1870. There were other difficulties besetting the new state. Not all Italians were happy with the results of unification. The followers of Mazzini would have preferred a republic to a monarchy, and even many monarchists would rather have seen a loosely federated union than the centralized monarchy that resulted from the "conquest" of the peninsula by Piedmont. Regionalism and particularism also

Nationalism in the Austrian Empire

Prince Schwarzenberg, who had succeeded Metternich in 1848, had given Austria a constitution early in 1849. While calling for a high degree of centralization, it had recognized at least some local and provincial privileges. These mild concessions in the spirit of nationalism, however, were only temporary. Beginning in 1850, all but the centralizing tendencies of the constitution were ignored. Schwarzenberg died in 1852, but his policies were continued. Petty officials, most of them German, directed the affairs of provinces whose language they did not speak and whose customs they ignored. Yet instead of counteracting the centrifugal tendencies of nationalism, this system merely increased the tension between the German ruling caste and the subject peoples.

Austria's defeat at the hands of France and Piedmont in 1859 once again brought home the need for reform. As a result, the excessive centralization of the preceding decade now gave way to some degree of provincial autonomy. In 1861 a new constitution established a central legislature, the *Reichsrat,* made up of delegates from the various regional diets. But the new system, like all earlier ones, had serious flaws. Since the German element was still guaranteed a majority, some of the other nationalities, especially the Hungarians, refused to attend the meetings of the *Reichsrat.* It soon became clear that another effort at solving the nationalities problem had failed. In September 1865 Francis Joseph suspended the constitution of 1861.

At this point the war with Prussia intervened (see below), leaving Austria still weaker and less able to resist the demands of the Hungarian nationalists. As a result of extended negotiations between Austrian and Hungarian leaders, a compromise, or *Ausgleich,* was finally reached in 1867. Under the new arrangement a Dual Monarchy was established, with Francis Joseph serving both as Emperor of Austria and King of Hungary. Except in such fields as finance, foreign affairs, and war, where joint ministries were set up, the two parts of the monarchy now were entirely autonomous. Yet since in neither half of the Dual Monarchy the Germans or the Hungarians held a majority, the *Ausgleich* did not solve the nationalities problem. Subsequent efforts to recognize the Slavic regions by establishing a Triple Monarchy were defeated by opposition from Germans and Magyars alike. This continued oppression of Slavic nationalism constituted a major threat to the existence of Austria-Hungary and to the peace of Europe.

Prussia After 1850

As we turn from Austria to the other major power in central Europe, Prussia, we find quite a different picture. In administrative efficiency, financial soundness, and military strength, Prussia after 1850 was far superior to her Austrian rival. Except for a small Polish minority in her eastern provinces, her population was homogeneous. And while in Austria industrialization had hardly begun, Prussia during the 1850's began to take her place among the leading industrial powers of the Continent.

Like Austria, Prussia had been granted a constitution in 1849. Since it provided for universal suffrage, it had a deceptively democratic appearance. But by dividing the electorate into three classes, according to the taxes each voter paid, the Prussian constitution made certain that the wealthiest citizens controlled a majority in the lower house of the *Landtag.* With this constitutional arrangement it was not surprising that Prussia continued to be one of the most reactionary states in Germany. In 1857 King Frederick William IV was succeeded by his brother, Prince William. William was sixty-two years old and an arch-conservative. Having spent most of his life in the army, he had little experience in government. It was due to William's concern over the shortcomings of Prussia's military establishment that Prussia, in 1860, entered upon one of the most serious domestic crises in her history.

Despite a considerable increase in population, Prussia's armed forces in 1860 were still essentially what they had been in 1814. When William tried to correct this situation, however, he ran into opposition from the liberal majority in the *Landtag* which, under the constitution, had to authorize the necessary funds and which objected to some of the details of the government's reform proposals. By 1862 king and parliament had become deadlocked over the issue. At this point William decided to recall his ambassador to Paris, Otto von Bismarck, and charge him with carrying on the fight with the *Landtag.*

Bismarck and the Constitutional Conflict

The man who was soon to direct the affairs of Germany as first chancellor of the German Reich was then forty-seven years old. He came from an old Prussian family of noble landowners, or *Junkers.* During the revolution of 1848 he had proved himself a devoted royalist. As a reward he had been appointed Prussia's representative to the Frankfurt Diet during the 1850's and later ambassador to St. Petersburg and Paris. In these various assignments he had shown outstanding ability as a diplomat and as a manipulator of men. But he was also known as a fighter. It was this combination that had recommended him to William I.

Bismarck first tried to mediate the conflict between king and parliament. When this proved impossible, however, he did not give in but carried out the proposed army reforms without parliamentary approval, using funds earmarked for other purposes. The conflict was never resolved but was ultimately overshadowed by more spectacular events. Two wars, in 1864 and 1866, not only gave proof of the excellence of Prussia's reformed army but so aroused the patriotism of the *Landtag* delegates that they were ready to forget their liberal principles. When, during the war with Austria in 1866, Bismarck asked parliament for retroactive assent to the unauthorized expenditures of the previous years, the majority of delegates supported him.

The Prussian constitutional conflict had thus been "solved," as Bismarck had predicted, "by blood and iron." But in the process, Prussian and German liberalism had suffered a serious defeat. Liberals in Germany henceforth were split in two factions—a larger one that continued to support Bismarck, putting nationalism above liberalism, and a smaller faction that stuck to its liberal principles. This split within German lib-

eralism was never healed. It was the most fateful legacy of the period of German unification.

Rivalry Between Austria and Prussia

Bismarck did not really plan the unification of Germany; it developed more or less accidentally out of Prussia's desire to assert herself against Austria's claims for supremacy in German affairs. The rivalry between Austria and Prussia was of long standing—it went back at least to the days of Frederick the Great and Maria Theresa in the eighteenth century. During most of the intervening period, Prussia had been quite ready to recognize Austria's traditional leadership. The most recent manifestation of Prussia's subjection to Austria had occurred in 1850, when Austria had prevented a scheme advanced by Frederick William IV for a union of German princes under Prussian leadership. Instead, Austria had insisted that the diet of the German Confederation under the presidency of Austria be reconstituted at Frankfurt.

Bismarck, as Prussia's delegate to the Frankfurt Diet, did not object to Austria's leadership in German affairs so long as Austria, in return, recognized Prussia's preeminence in northern Germany. Only after Bismarck realized Austria's unwillingness to cooperate did he decide that the interest of Prussia demanded that Austria be excluded from Germany. Before Prussia could assume leadership in Germany, however, she had to make sure of the good will, or at least the acquiescence, of the great powers. While the Italian national movement had enjoyed the sympathy of almost everyone outside Austria, few people in Europe wanted to see a Germany united under Prussian auspices. During the Crimean War, Austria had tried to induce Prussia to join her in aiding the western powers, but Prussia had remained friendly toward Russia. Here we have the basis for that close friendship between Prussia and Russia that was to remain a constant element in international affairs for the next few decades.

The first outward sign of Prussia's emancipation from Austrian tutelage came during the Italian war of 1859. Austria at the time fully expected Prussia to join her against Piedmont and France. Prussia was ready to comply, but asked to be put in charge of her own and whatever other German forces might be raised. Austria, however, still filled with her own importance, refused this understandable request. Prussia's neutrality during the war won her the gratitude of both France and Italy. Austria's defeat, on the other hand, clearly showed how much her claim to leadership was based on past prestige rather than present power.

By the end of the 1850's most German liberals were expecting Prussia to take the lead in unifying Germany. The constitutional struggle over the reform of the Prussian army, however, put a temporary damper on their enthusiasm. At the same time, the Austrian constitution of 1861 seemed to indicate more liberal tendencies in the Habsburg Empire. It thus encouraged the Catholic and traditionalist forces, especially in southern Germany, who hoped for a united Germany under Austrian leadership. To take advantage of this shift in opinion, Austria convened a congress in 1863 to consider the reform of the German Confederation in the direction of greater national unity. But Bismarck urged his king to boycott the Austrian project. With Prussia absent, the Frankfurt meeting was doomed to failure.

The Schleswig-Holstein Question and the War with Denmark

The final showdown between Austria and Prussia grew out of their involvement in the affairs of the two northern German duchies of Schleswig and Holstein. The Schleswig-Holstein question is famous for its intricacy, and its details need not concern us here. The duchies, largely German but partly Danish, had long been held in personal union by the king of Denmark. In an age of rising nationalism, however, this indeterminate status became increasingly difficult to maintain. The issue had already led to a brief war between Danes and Germans in 1848, in which Denmark had been defeated. The future of the duchies became acute again in 1863, when Denmark tried to annex Schleswig. This time both Austria and Prussia rushed to the defense. Their motives for intervention were complex.

Both wanted to pose as defenders of German unity, but Prussia also wanted to expand her power in northern Germany.

The war itself was brief. The Danes, as was to be expected, suffered a crushing defeat. Under the Peace of Vienna in 1864 Denmark surrendered Schleswig and Holstein to Austria and Prussia. In this joint possession of the duchies lay the seeds of the war that broke out between Austria and Prussia two years later. Although Austria and most of the German states wanted the duchies to go to a German claimant, the Duke of Augustenburg, Bismarck wanted the duchies for Prussia. The question was how to bring about such annexation. In 1865 the victors reached a temporary compromise in the Convention of Gastein, under which Prussia was to administer Schleswig and Austria Holstein, while the future of the duchies was to remain a joint responsibility. But this arrangement solved nothing. As Austria continued to encourage the aspirations of the Duke of Augustenburg, and as Prussia proceeded to make herself at home in Schleswig, it became clear that force might be needed to decide the fate of both duchies.

The War of 1866

In the fall of 1865, Bismarck met Napoleon III at Biarritz to sound him out on France's attitude toward a possible war between Prussia and Austria. The meeting suggests a certain parallel to the Plombières meeting of Cavour and Napoleon, except that Bismarck was not asking for French aid; all he wanted was a promise of neutrality. This Napoleon gave him, hinting at some unspecified compensations for France. Bismarck agreed. In the spring of 1866, Prussia concluded an alliance with Italy, to which Napoleon also gave his blessing. The remaining great powers did not present much of a problem. Since England had stood by while Denmark was defeated, Bismarck felt that she would not intervene to save Austria. So far as Russia was concerned, her friendship for Prussia and her antagonism toward Austria left little doubt where she would stand.

With the diplomatic spadework done, Bismarck's next task was to find a cause for war with Austria that would rally the rest of Germany to Prussia's side. This was not easy, since most of the German princes sided with Austria on the future of Schleswig-Holstein. Bismarck finally used Prussia's differences with Austria over the duchies as an excuse to order Prussian troops into Holstein. But this in turn made the remaining members of the German Confederation join the Austrian side. The war of 1866 was thus not only a war of Prussia against Austria but against most of the rest of Germany as well.

There was little enthusiasm in either camp at the start of the war. Austria was deeply divided and poorly prepared. She was further handicapped by having to fight on two fronts. The Prussians, on the other hand, were in excellent military form, equipped with the latest weapons and led by a master-strategist, Count Helmuth von Moltke. As the first news of victory arrived, moreover, the attitude of the Prussian people changed from apathy to enthusiasm. The war was over in a few weeks. It was decided almost entirely by one major battle, near Königgrätz (Sadowa), in which the Austrians were defeated, though not annihilated.

The final peace treaty was signed at Prague in August 1866. Chiefly because of Bismarck's insistence, the settlement was remarkably lenient. Bismarck realized that the rest of the powers, especially France, would not stand for a punitive peace. Austria consented to the dissolution of the German Confederation and recognized the various territorial gains Prussia had made in the North, including Schleswig-Holstein. In a separate settlement Austria surrendered Venetia, which went to Italy. As for Austria's German allies, most of the northern ones were annexed by Prussia, while the southern ones had to pay indemnities and conclude military alliances with Prussia. Prussia thus consolidated her holdings in the North and assumed indirect control over the rest of Germany. As far as she was concerned, the war of 1866 had been a rousing success.

The Unification of Germany

The war of 1866 had been waged for the aggrandizement of Prussia. But in the minds of most Germans it soon appeared as a deliberate stage in the unification of Germany. During the winter of 1866–67, delegates from the states that were left in northern Germany after the peace settlement met in Berlin to form a North German Confederation. The plan had originated with Bismarck, whose aim was to establish Prussia's preponderance over the whole region north of the Main River.

The North German Confederation

The constitution of the North German Confederation established a federal system under which the central government controlled foreign and military affairs. The executive was vested in the king of Prussia as president, assisted by a chancellor—Bismarck. An upper house, or *Bundesrat,* consisted of delegates from the various member states. The lower house, or *Reichstag,* was made up of deputies elected by universal suffrage. Most of the power was vested in the upper house, in which Prussian influence prevailed. There was no ministerial responsibility, since the only minister was the chancellor, and he was responsible only to the president.

The main significance of the North German Confederation's constitution was that it served as a basis for the constitution of the German Empire after 1871. Just as it assured the domination of Prussia in northern Germany after 1867, so after 1871 it perpetuated Prussia's domination over the rest of Germany. How far Bismarck actually foresaw developments beyond 1867 is difficult to say. He never was a German nationalist—his major concern was with the power and security of Prussia. Nor was there much desire among the rulers of South Germany to submit to the king of Prussia. The state of affairs that existed in 1867, therefore, could have lasted for a long time had it not been for the unfortunate machinations of Napoleon III. Like his uncle, Napoleon thus served as the involuntary agent of German nationalism.

Bismarck and Napoleon III

Napoleon's readiness at Biarritz to let Prussia settle accounts with Austria had been due to his underestimation of Prussian strength. Thinking Prussia and Austria pretty evenly matched,

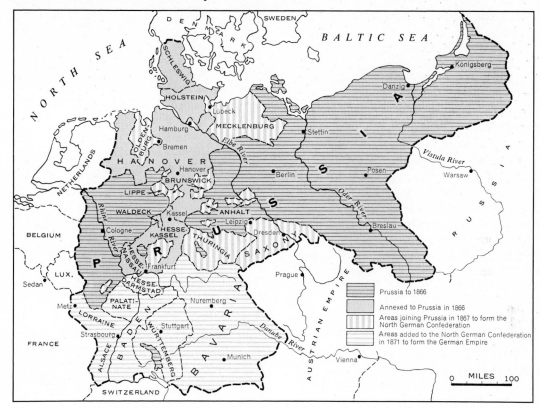

Legend:
- Prussia to 1866
- Annexed to Prussia in 1866
- Areas joining Prussia in 1867 to form the North German Confederation
- Areas added to the North German Confederation in 1871 to form the German Empire

0   MILES   100

he had expected to throw French power into the balance at the crucial moment. Austria's defeat at Sadowa, therefore, had come as a shock. Together with France's fiasco in Mexico, the defeat of Austria was built up by Napoleon's domestic opponents as a major French defeat. The only way to save French prestige was through some kind of territorial compensations such as she had received during the unification of Italy.

Napoleon should have pressed his demands for compensations while the fate of Austria still hung in the balance. Once Prussia had won the war, Bismarck was no longer in any mood to make concessions. On the contrary, Napoleon's demands served him to good effect in furthering his own policy. He used Napoleon's bid for territories in the west or south of Germany to cement ties with the southern German states as the best possible protection against French designs; and he later used Napoleon's request for

Prussian support in the acquisition of Belgium to incriminate France in the eyes of Great Britain. In a third attempt to gain territorial compensation, Napoleon tried to buy the Duchy of Luxembourg. Bismarck at first approved of the deal but later changed his mind.

Napoleon III, faced with mounting criticism at home and frustrated in his efforts to gather laurels abroad, gradually realized that an armed showdown with Prussia might be inevitable. To prepare himself, he began casting about for allies. But neither Austria nor Italy, whom he approached, had any desire to become involved in a war between France and Prussia. Even so, Napoleon assumed that in case of a war with Prussia he could count on the aid of one or both of the Catholic powers.

The War of 1870

The immediate cause of the war between France and Prussia was the offer of the vacant

Franco-German Agreement on Causes of the War of 1870

1951

A fair judgment on the outbreak of war in 1870 must admit that both sides contributed to an increase of existing tensions:

1. Bismarck by his secret support of the Hohenzollern candidacy for the Spanish throne. He thus hoped to outwit Napoleon and to press him diplomatically so that the fall of the imperial regime might result. He may also have intended to weaken France militarily in case of war by creating a front in the Pyrenees.

2. Napoleon and his cabinet by their exaggerated diplomatic and political counter-offensive since July 6, especially by their demand of a guarantee from King William [that the candidacy would not be renewed]. This put France in the wrong with the rest of Europe, although Napoleon and most of his ministers feared war more than they desired it.

3. Finally Bismarck by the well-known editing of the Ems dispatch, which was not a "falsification" but a conscious aggravation with the aim of forcing France into a serious diplomatic defeat or a declaration of war.

It must be recognized that the German as well as the French peoples went to war in the honest conviction that they were challenged by the other side. Neither of them knew the diplomatic details, which were cleared up only much later.

From "Deutsch-französische Vereinbarung über strittige Fragen europäischer Geschichte," *Internationales Jahrbuch für Geschichtsunterricht,* Vol. II (1951), pp. 81–82.

throne of Spain in 1870 to a Hohenzollern prince, distantly related to the king of Prussia. Bismarck was instrumental in having the prince accept the Spanish offer; yet there is no clear evidence that he intended to use the affair to provoke a war with France. Moreover, when France protested the Spanish candidacy, the Prussian government urged the prince to abandon the project. But this did not satisfy the French, who demanded an apology from King William and a promise that the candidacy would not be renewed. This unreasonable demand was made in a famous interview between the French ambassador and the king at the watering-place of Ems, an interview that William cut short. When news of this incident reached Berlin, Bismarck edited the report in such a way to make it look as though France had suffered a major diplomatic defeat. It was this edited "Ems dispatch" that led France to declare war on Prussia. In this case Bismarck had foreseen the results, and to that extent he may be held responsible for the war of 1870. Yet his action was merely the latest in a whole series of mutual recriminations, and most historians now agree that responsibility for the war must be shared by both sides.

Events in the early summer of 1870 had moved so quickly that all of Europe was taken by surprise. France's precipitate action lost her whatever sympathy she had enjoyed among the other powers. England maintained the aloofness she had shown ever since the Crimean War. Russia continued her policy of benevolent neutrality toward Prussia. Italy was preoccupied with completing her unification by taking the city of Rome. And Austria would prove dangerous only if Prussia ran into difficulties. But there was little chance of that. In numbers, leadership, and morale Prussia's forces were far superior to those of France. The participation of southern German contingents made this a national German war. The French army was to fight valiantly, but its leadership was poor and its morale was low. The fact that Napoleon III, worn out by a lingering illness, assumed personal command did not help matters.

The war itself was decided in a series of bloody battles. The climax came on September 2, with Napoleon's capitulation at Sedan. But the fighting continued for several more months and the city of Paris, where a republic had been proclaimed, did not surrender until the end of January 1871. A temporary armistice was concluded on January 28, pending the election of a representative assembly. The National Assembly chose the liberal monarchist Adolphe Thiers as chief executive. The first task of the new government was to negotiate a final settlement with Bismarck.

The Results of the War

The peace signed at Frankfurt on May 10, 1871, was a harsh one. France had to pay an indemnity of 5 billion francs, and the country was to remain occupied until the indemnity had been paid. In addition, France had to cede Alsace and part of Lorraine, which, for the most part, she had taken from the Holy Roman Empire in the seventeenth century. The inhabitants of Alsace spoke German, but they were pro-French and anti-Prussian in feeling. To take so large a slice of territory in an age of ardent nationalism was a dangerous move. The issue of France's "lost provinces" remained an insuperable obstacle to closer Franco-German relations.

The signing of the peace did not end France's troubles. The new National Assembly had a majority of monarchists, and the survival of the republic thus depended on the continued split among the three monarchist factions—Bourbon, Orléanist, and Bonapartist. The republican mi-

nority had its main support in the city of Paris. It was here, in March 1871, that fear of a monarchist revival, indignation over a humiliating peace, and general misery resulting from the recent siege of the city led to a violent uprising. The Paris Commune, as the government of the insurgents was called, lasted until the end of May. Its aims, on the whole, were moderate. But the Commune also included a few socialists. This fact, plus some of the excesses committed during the fighting against the troops of the National Assembly, did much to reawaken middle-class fear of a "red peril." After their defeat in the final "Bloody Week" of May, thousands of Communards were executed, imprisoned, or deported. The issue of republic against monarchy continued in the balance for some time.

While the siege of Paris was still under way, another important event had taken place. On January 18, 1871, in the Hall of Mirrors in the

Europe in 1871

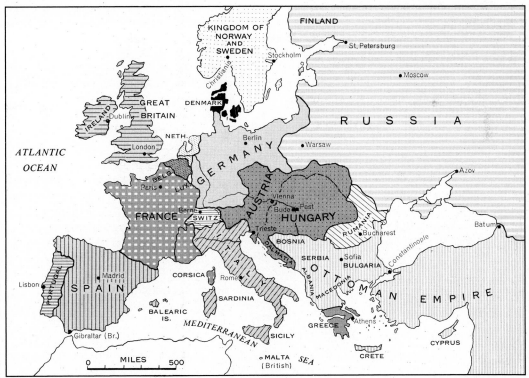

Proclamation of King William I of Prussia as German Emperor, Versailles, January 18, 1871. On the platform behind William stands the crown prince, who briefly became emperor as Frederick III in 1888. Bismarck (in the white uniform), the architect of German unification, occupies the center of the stage.

palace at Versailles, King William of Prussia was proclaimed German emperor. This ceremony was the climax of long negotiations between Bismarck and the rulers of southern Germany. There had been much hesitation among these Catholic and more liberal states to submit to a confederation dominated by Protestant and reactionary Prussia. Many conservative Prussians were equally hesitant, fearing that Prussia might lose her identity in the larger empire. Even Bismarck, the architect of unification, was not motivated by national enthusiasm. But by fulfilling the German people's dream for unity, he hoped further to increase the power and prestige of his beloved Prussia.

The Franco-German War not only completed the unification of Germany; it ended the long struggle for Italian unity. After a plebiscite in October 1870, Rome was annexed to Italy

and became Italy's capital. A subsequent effort to mollify the papacy by a generous Law of Papal Guarantees was turned down by the pope, who henceforth considered himself "the prisoner of the Vatican." This state of affairs remained unchanged until 1929.

The year 1871, like the year 1815, was a landmark in European history. Both years saw the end of a major war, and both initiated a long period of peace among the major powers. But this is about as far as the parallel goes. Relations among states in 1815 and after had still been conducted according to certain general rules. But the cynical diplomacy of Cavour, Napoleon III, and Bismarck had changed this. From now on, suspicion rather than trust characterized international dealings, and, though there was to be no major war for forty-three years, the threat of war was almost always present.

Moreover, in 1815 the balance of power had been revived along traditional lines, but by 1871 an entirely new balance had emerged. Austria, Russia, Great Britain, and France had been the leading powers at Vienna, with Prussia lagging far behind, and with Italy a mere "geographical expression." By 1871 that order had been thoroughly revised. Both Austria and France now were overshadowed by a Prussianized Germany, and even Italy demanded recognition as a great power. England and Russia continued in their former status, but while at Vienna they had taken an active part in shaping the affairs of the Continent, the balance of 1871 had been brought about without their participation. Here, perhaps, lies the major difference between 1815 and 1871. When Napoleon I had upset the balance of power, the Concert of Europe met at the Congress of Vienna to restore it. There was no such concert in 1871, and hence there was no congress. The Concert of Europe had gone to pieces over the Crimean War. Both Great Britain and Russia had kept out of the subsequent wars of Italian and German unification. It was the passivity of these peripheral powers, as much as the activities of Cavour, Bismarck, and Napoleon III, that helped to bring about the changed European balance of 1871.

England's "Victorian Compromise"

England had always maintained a certain isolation from the Continent, and she had added reason to do so after the middle of the nineteenth century. The British people did not remain immune from the virus of nationalism. But the Crimean War had brought home the futility of military involvement. And besides, it had brought defeat to Russia, whose advances in the eastern Mediterranean had presented the only real threat to British commerce.

The "Workshop of the World"

The twenty years after 1850 were the most prosperous in British history. While wars elsewhere helped retard economic development, Britain's industry and commerce experienced an unprecedented boom. This was the heyday of free trade, a policy from which Britain, as the most advanced industrial nation, profited most. The change in shipbuilding from wood to iron, furthermore, opened up a wholly new field for expansion. By 1870, Britain's carrying trade enjoyed a virtual monopoly. While British engineers were building railroads the world over, Britain's surplus capital sought outlets for investment on the Continent and overseas. Between 1854 and 1870, England's foreign holdings more than doubled.

Though Britain was reluctant to become involved in European politics, she showed no such hesitation overseas. We shall have more to say about British colonial policy in the next chapter. While in some parts of the British Empire, such as Canada and Australia, the basis for self-government was being laid, elsewhere, notably in India, Britain tightened her reins. In 1859 the rule of the East India Company was taken over by the British government. Commercial expansion in China, begun in the 1840's, made rapid advances in the late 1850's. The new Suez Canal, built by French interests, soon became a major link in England's communications network.

The Second Reform Bill

Britain's prosperity, however, did not do away with political discontent. There had been no major political reforms since 1832. The Tories, now called Conservatives, had acquiesced in the new conditions created by the Great Reform Bill; and the Whigs, now called Liberals, while favoring reforms in other fields, also considered the Reform Bill final. The aims of the two parties had thus become almost indistinguishable. Neither the aristocracy nor the middle class enjoyed undisputed supremacy. Government proceeded by compromise.

Meanwhile, as a result of advancing industrialization, Britain's middle and working classes were growing rapidly. This growth could not help but create a demand for further extension of the franchise. By the 1860's the need for reform could no longer be ignored. Both parties at the time had leaders ready to take charge of the contest over parliamentary reform. Since 1852 the Conservative Benjamin Disraeli and the Liberal William Gladstone had played important roles in cabinets of their respective parties. In 1866 Gladstone introduced a moderate reform bill that was promptly defeated by the Conservatives. An even more radical bill introduced the next year by Disraeli was passed, largely with Liberal support. The Second Reform Bill of 1867, by giving the vote to urban workers, doubled the number of voters. It did not introduce universal suffrage, but it did give the majority of the British people a voice in their government.

Gladstone's First "Great Ministry"

The agitation surrounding the Second Reform Bill had ended the Victorian Compromise. Both Conservatives and Liberals now tightened their organizations and became parties in the modern sense. When the elections of 1868 returned a Liberal majority, Gladstone formed his first "great ministry." Just as the Bill of 1832 had been followed by a long series of domestic reforms, so the years after 1867 saw many overdue measures enacted. Notable among them was the Education Act of 1870, which, at long last, relieved a situation in which almost half of Britain's children had received no schooling.

There was one problem that concerned Gladstone above all others—the problem of Ireland. That unhappy country, vastly overpopulated, had long been on the verge of starvation. Migration to the United States relieved some of the pressure but also added to unrest. The Fenian Brotherhood, founded in New York in 1858, was responsible for many acts of violence in England and Ireland. Gladstone considered the solution of the Irish problem his major mission. Its roots were partly religious, partly economic. To solve Ireland's religious grievances, the Disestablishment Act of 1869 freed Irish Catholics from having to support the Anglican Church. To improve land tenure, the Land Act of 1870 curtailed the power of absentee landlords to evict their tenants without compensation. But since the Land Act did not heed Ireland's demands for the "three F's"—fair rent, fixity of tenure, and free sale—it was only a half-measure.

Like most of Gladstone's reforms, his Irish policy violated many vested interests and contributed to his defeat in 1874. There were other causes of discontent. Though elected by working-class votes, Gladstone had done little to improve the status of the laborer. Prosperity, meanwhile, had begun to level off, and from 1873 on depression elsewhere made itself felt in Britain as well. Finally, Gladstone's foreign policy—peaceful, sensible, but unexciting—lacked popular support. With Disraeli, who succeeded him in 1874 and who combined social legislation at home with an active imperial policy abroad, a new chapter in British history began.

Russia: Reaction and Reform

The second great power on the periphery of Europe, tsarist Russia, pursued her own peculiar course through most of the nineteenth century. The westernization of Russia that had begun during the eighteenth century continued, but very slowly. Because of her vast size and the multiplicity of her backward peoples, Russia faced a number of problems not shared by any of the other great powers. To establish political control against such obstacles required a regime of strict autocracy. The will of the tsar was law. His decrees were translated into action by a huge bureaucracy whose openness to bribery helped somewhat to soften the harshness of tsarist rule. Russia's government has been aptly described as "despotism tempered by corruption."

Aside from autocracy, there were other institutions peculiar to the tsarist empire. While in western Europe the nobility had lost much of its power, Russia's aristocracy continued to enjoy its traditional privileges. Besides owning almost all the land, the nobles were exempt from taxation and from military service. There was as yet no middle class to speak of, except in the few larger towns. The majority of the tsar's subjects, more than 95 percent, were peasants, and most of them were still serfs. Serfdom in Russia was much more burdensome than it had been in western Europe. Even the legally free peasants, who by 1833 constituted about a third of the population, were kept in a decidedly inferior position. Occasionally, when the misery of the Russian masses became too much to bear, they sought relief in local uprisings. There had been more than 500 such mutinies during the rule of Nicholas I (1825–55). Nicholas actually had introduced some measures aimed at alleviating the worst abuses of serfdom, but to go to the root of the evil and to liberate the serfs would have meant taking land away from the nobility; that even the autocratic tsars did not dare do. Instead, Nicholas continued to preach the principles dearest to his reactionary heart—obedience to autocracy, adherence to the traditional Orthodox religion, and patriotic faith in the virtues of Russian nationality.

"Westerners" Versus "Slavophils"

The obstacles that the tsarist government put in the way of education and the restriction it imposed on western ideas helped to keep down the numbers of the Russian "intelligentsia"— that is, those few people whose intellectual interests set them apart from the illiterate masses. Still, by the middle of the nineteenth century this group had grown numerous enough to make its influence felt. There were two clearly defined factions among Russian intellectuals—the "Westerners" and the "Slavophils." The Westerners saw their country as essentially a part of western civilization, merely lagging behind but able eventually to catch up. The Slavophils, on the other hand, held that the difference between Russia and the West was not one of degree but of kind. They pointed to the peculiar foundations of Russian civilization—Byzantine, Slavic, and Greek-Orthodox as compared to the Roman,

Germanic, and Catholic roots of western civilization. And they believed that each nation should live according to its own traditions rather than trying to imitate the institutions and practices of other countries. These theoretical differences between Westerners and Slavophils also determined their attitudes toward current problems. While the Westerners favored constitutional government, rationalism, and industrial progress, the Slavophils saw the salvation of Russia in benevolent autocracy, Orthodox Christianity, and the reform of Russia's predominantly agrarian society. This eastern-versus-western orientation henceforth remained a permanent characteristic of Russian political and social philosophy.

The most important political developments during the regime of Nicholas I were in foreign affairs. One of the main aims of Russian policy continued to be the domination, direct or indirect, over the disintegrating Ottoman Empire. Western opposition to Russia's Turkish aspirations had finally led to the Crimean War. More than any previous event, this conflict had shown the inefficiency, corruption, and poor leadership of the tsarist regime. Nicholas had died during the war. His successor, Alexander II (1855–81), was far less reactionary. Though he had little understanding of social and economic problems, he was impressed by the clamor for reform that had set in after the Crimean defeat. The most widespread demand was for the emancipation of the serfs.

The Emancipation of the Serfs

Alexander II realized that the alternative to abolishing serfdom from above might ultimately be revolution from below. He therefore initiated a careful study of the situation which finally, in March 1861, led to the Emancipation Edict. Its immediate effects, however, were far from happy. It was of little use for the Russian serf to gain his freedom without at the same time obtaining sufficient land to make a living. Yet to deprive the nobility of its labor force and most of its land would have placed the burden of emancipation entirely upon that class. The solution finally arrived at was a compromise that satisfied no one. The peasants were given almost half the land,

Serfdom

Few realize what serfdom was in reality. There is a dim conception that the conditions which it created were very bad; but those conditions, as they affected human beings bodily and mentally, are not generally understood. It is amazing, indeed, to see how quickly an institution and its social consequences are forgotten when the institution has ceased to exist, and with what rapidity men and things change. I will try to recall the conditions of serfdom by telling, not what I heard, but what I saw . . . :

Father . . . calls in Makár, the piano-tuner and sub-butler, and reminds him of all his recent sins. . . . Of a sudden there is a lull in the storm. My father takes a seat at the table and writes a note. "Take Makár with this note to the police station, and let a hundred lashes with the birch rod be given him."

Terror and absolute muteness reign in the house. The clock strikes four, and we all go down to dinner. . . . "Where is Makár?" our stepmother asks. "Call him in." Makár does not appear, and the order is repeated. He enters at last, pale, with a distorted face, ashamed, his eyes cast down. . . . Tears suffocate me, and immediately after dinner is over I run out, catch Makár in the dark passage, and try to kiss his hand; but he tears it away, and says, either as a reproach or as a question, "Let me alone; you, too, when you are grown up, will you not be just the same?"

From Prince Peter Kropotkin, *Memoirs of a Revolutionist* (Boston: Houghton Mifflin, 1899), pp. 49–51.

not in direct ownership but in large holdings administered by the village community, the *mir*. The *mir* in turn apportioned land use among the village households. The landowners were compensated by the government; but the redemption money that the government paid to the nobles had to be repaid over a period of forty-nine years by each village community.

Emancipation thus freed the individual peasant from servitude to his noble master but subjected him to the communal control of his village. It substituted a new "peasant problem" for the old problem of serfdom. To be freed from the redemption payments and the tutelage of the *mir*, and to get hold of the land still in the hands of the nobility—these remained burning issues for the Russian peasantry into the twentieth century.

Reform, Radicalism, and Reaction

The liberation of the serfs, while the most spectacular of Alexander's acts, was not the only effort he made to strengthen his regime through timely reforms. In 1863 he granted universities a greater degree of academic freedom. In 1864 he reformed the Russian judicial system along western lines. The same year Alexander introduced a measure of local and regional self-government through elected assemblies, or *zemstvos*. The hope of the reformers that this development might eventually culminate in a national assembly was disappointed. But even so, the *zemstvos* provided some opportunity for public discussion and the development of civic responsibility, both hitherto unknown in Russia.

The more changes Alexander introduced, the more hopes he aroused. One of the results of his policy had been to give an impetus to various reform movements among the intelligentsia, whose aims and agitation became ever more radical. Western socialism had been slow to gain a hold in Russia, where industry was still in its infancy. Consequently, Russian socialists like Alexander Herzen tried to appeal to the Russian peasant, whose village community already exhibited many of the collective features cherished by socialists. In the 1860's it became the fashion for members of the intelligentsia to go out and live among the peasants in the hope of arousing them from their apathy and urging them into starting a revolution. This "go-to-the-people" movement (*Narodniki*), however, failed because the peasants were too backward and the authorities too vigilant. In their opposition to everything their government stood for, the younger members of the intelligentsia now began to refer to themselves as "nihilists," believers in nothing. Most of them vented their anger over the existing system merely by expounding radical ideas and by disregarding conventional manners and mores.

During the 1870's, however, some of the nihilists fell under the influence of Mikhail Bakunin and his philosophy of anarchism. In 1879 this terrorist faction formed a secret society, "The Will of the People," whose aim was to overthrow the government by direct action and assassination.

Frightened by these manifestations of radicalism, Alexander II reverted to a policy of renewed reaction. Yet by reverting to repression, he merely helped to strengthen the revolutionary forces he hoped to combat. This fact was brought home to him in several attempts on his life, and in 1880 he tried once again to return to his initial policy of reform. But by then it was too late. Alexander II was killed by a terrorist bomb in 1881.

The Primacy of Foreign Policy

Our discussion of Alexander II has taken us somewhat beyond 1871. We shall have more to say on the domestic affairs of the major powers later. In this chapter we have been chiefly concerned with international affairs. During the two decades after 1850 foreign policy in most of Europe overshadowed domestic policy. There were few discernible trends in domestic affairs. Industrialization continued, but its progress was still uneven. Democracy made gains in some countries (notably England), but it suffered reversals in others (notably Germany). Some important reforms helped ease tension—the Emancipation Edict in Russia, the *Ausgleich* between Austria and Hungary, the Second Reform Bill in England. But for each of these issues resolved, others arose elsewhere—the conflict between monarchism and republicanism in France, the defeat of liberalism in Germany, the tension between North and South in Italy—to mention but a few.

The most significant event in the "era of unification" was the emergence of Germany as a great power. From 1871 to 1945 the influence of that belatedly unified nation made itself felt in every major international crisis and in the history of every country. Compared to German unification, the unification of Italy today seems of minor importance, though it did not appear so at the time. Of much greater consequence was the tragic fate of the Second French Empire. Its defeat at the hands of Prussia sowed some of the seeds that brought forth the great wars of our century. But these events were far off in 1871. At the time it seemed as though the Continent at long last had found the stability that statesmen before 1850 had tried so hard to achieve. The future was to show the precariousness of the new balance of power.

Suggestions for Further Reading

1. General

Most of the general works cited after Chapter 24 also cover this later period. An admirably comprehensive view may be gained from R. C. Binkley, *Realism and Nationalism, 1852–1871* * (1935), a volume in the *Rise of Modern Europe* series. The international affairs of Europe are covered in A. J. P. Taylor, *The Struggle for Mastery in Europe, 1848–1918* (1954).

2. The Eastern Question

The disintegration of the Ottoman Empire is treated authoritatively in J. A. R. Marriott, *The Eastern Question in European Diplomacy* (1926), and more briefly in M. S. Anderson, *The Eastern Question* (1966). On the background of the Crimean War, see: E. Horvath, *Origins of the Crimean War*

---

* Available in paperback edition.

(1937); H. W. V. Temperley, *England and the Near East: The Crimea* (1936); and G. B. Henderson, *Crimean War Diplomacy and Other Historical Essays* (1947). B. D. Gooch, ed., *Origins of the Crimean War** (1969), presents various interpretations by different historians. W. E. Mosse, *The Rise and Fall of the Crimean System, 1855–1871* (1967), takes a new look at the larger issues connected with the war. The war itself is vividly portrayed in N. Bentley, ed., *William H. Russell's Despatches from the Crimea, 1854–1856* (1967). The Crimean War also provides a somber background for two fine books by C. Woodham-Smith: *Florence Nightingale, 1820–1919** (1951), and *The Reason Why** (1953).

3. The Second French Empire

The most thorough studies of Napoleon III's early career are F. A. Simpson, *The Rise of Louis Napoleon* (1950), and *Louis Napoleon and the Recovery of France, 1848–1856,* 3rd ed. (1951). The political history of the Empire is covered in O. Aubry, *The Second Empire* (1940), and in J. M. Thompson, *Louis Napoleon and the Second Empire* (1955). A. Guérard, *Reflections on the Napoleonic Legend* (1924), traces the Napoleonic heritage of the emperor. The same author, in his *Napoleon III** (1943), draws a sympathetic picture of a man whom others have called a "herald of fascism." A collection of contrasting interpretations of Napoleon III may be found in B. D. Gooch, *Napoleon III: Man of Destiny—Enlightened Statesman or Proto-Fascist?** (1963). Among more specialized studies on the Empire, the following are of special interest: T. Zeldin, *The Political System of Napoleon II* (1958); F. C. Palm, *England and Napoleon III: A Study in the Rise of a Utopian Dictator* (1948); L. M. Case, *French Opinion on War and Diplomacy During the Second Empire* (1953); A. L. Dunham, *The Anglo-French Treaty of Commerce of 1860 and the Progress of the Industrial Revolution in France (1930);* and D. S. Pinckney, *Napoleon III and the Reconstruction of Paris* (1958). R. L. Williams, *Gaslight and Shadow: The World of Napoleon III** (1957), conveys some of the glamour and excitement of one of the most brilliant periods in French history.

4. The Unification of Italy

The dramatic events of these crucial years are best studied through the lives of the main architects of unification, including Napoleon III. A. J. Whyte, *The Political Life and Letters of Cavour, 1848–1861* (1930), and W. R. Thayer, *The Life and Times of Cavour,* 2 vols. (1914), are standard works. The same holds true for the classic accounts of Garibaldi's colorful exploits in G. M. Trevelyan, *Garibaldi and the Thousand* (1911), and *Garibaldi and the Making of Italy* (1911). More recent are the studies by D. Mack Smith, *Cavour and Garibaldi, 1860: A Study in Political Conflict* (1954), and *Garibaldi* (1956). Ch. Hibbert, *Garibaldi and His Enemies: The Clash of Arms and Personalities in the Making of Italy* (1966), is lively and readable. The best biographies of Mazzini are B. King, *The Life of Mazzini* (1902), and G. O. Griffith, *Mazzini: Prophet of Modern Europe* (1932). The role of Napoleon III in the unification of Italy is treated in most of the works on the Second Empire cited above, as well as in L. M. Case, *Franco-Italian Relations, 1860–1865* (1932).

5. The Unification of Germany

The most recent comprehensive account of the events culminating in 1871 is O. Pflanze, *Bismarck and the Development of Germany: The Period of Unification, 1815–1871 (1963).* On the war with Denmark, L. D. Steefel, *The Schleswig-Holstein Question* (1932), remains standard. For an understanding of Austro-Prussian rivalry, H. Friedjung, *The Struggle for Supremacy in Germany, 1859–1866* (1897, 1935), is still important. See also C. W. Clark, *Franz Joseph and Bismarck: The Diplomacy of Austria Before the War of 1866* (1934). Subsequent Austrian developments are covered in A. J. May, *The*

---

* Available in paperback edition.

Hapsburg Monarchy, 1867–1914 (1951), and in R. A. Kann, *The Habsburg Empire* (1957). On the war of 1866, see G. Craig, *The Battle of Koniggratz: Prussia's Victory over Austria, 1866* (1964). Opposing interpretations on the background of the Franco-Prussian War are offered in R. H. Lord, *The Origins of the War of 1870;* H. Oncken, *Napoleon III and the Rhine: The Origins of the War of 1870–71* (1928); and L. D. Steefel, *Bismarck, the Hohenzollern Candidacy, and the Origins of the Franco-Prussian War* (1962). There are several biographies of Bismarck, none of them wholly satisfactory. E. Eyck, *Bismarck and the German Empire** (1950), is an abbreviation of a much longer work in German; A. J. P. Taylor, *Bismarck: The Man and the Statesman* (1955), is more readable but less sound. The international ramifications of German unification are admirably clarified in W. E. Mosse, *The European Powers and the German Question, 1848–1871* (1958). On the war between France and Prussia, see M. E. Howard, *The Franco-Prussian War** (1961).

6. England

Both A. Briggs, *The Age of Improvement, 1783–1867* (1959), and G. Kitson-Clark, *The Making of Victorian England* (1962), contain stimulating accounts of the mid-Victorian era. E. Longford, *Queen Victoria* (1965), is based on the queen's personal archives. British foreign policy and its chief maker are ably presented in D. Southgate, *Most English Minister: Politics and Policies of Palmerston* (1966). For a brilliant survey of social and intellectual life, see G. M. Young, *Victorian England: Portrait of an Age** (1936).

7. Russia

The political history of Russia is covered in M. T. Florinsky, *Russia: A History and an Interpretation,* Vol. 2 (1953); and in H. Seton-Watson, *The Russian Empire, 1801–1917* (1967). J. H. Billington, *The Icon and the Axe* (1966), is a comprehensive synthesis of Russian culture. A. Herzen, *My Past and Thoughts,* 6 vols. (1924–27), is a graphic contemporary account by one of Russia's leading intellectuals. On the crucial problem of serfdom, see G. T. Robinson, *Rural Russia under the Old Regime* (1949). D. M. Wallace, *Russia** (1912), is still valuable for an understanding of the Russian people. The following discuss two basic trends of Russian life and thought: H. Kohn, *Pan-Slavism: Its History and Ideology** (1953); and N. V. Riasinovsky, *Russia and the West in the Teaching of the Slavophiles* (1953). S. Graham, *Tsar of Freedom: The Life and Reign of Alexander II* (1935), deals sympathetically with a tragic figure. W. E. Mosse, *Alexander II and the Modernization of Russia** (1958), is a brief survey. A useful introduction to Russian foreign policy is presented in B. Jelavich, *A Century of Russian Foreign Policy, 1814–1914** (1964).

---

* Available in paperback edition.

12

Europe and the World
in the Nineteenth Century

From the "Age of Discovery" until the nineteenth century the world leadership of Europe had remained virtually unchallenged. As European nations established overseas commercial or colonial contacts, the ultimate conquest of the globe by western civilization appeared inevitable. But there had also been signs of a reverse trend, as some regions seemed to grow restive under European tutelage. The United States had been the first colony to gain independence, and there were soon to be similar movements for independence in the other British possessions where Europeans had settled. In time this unrest also affected some of the native peoples. Only one of them, the Japanese, managed to become sufficiently westernized to escape foreign control. But there were other potentially great powers, notably India and China, who wanted to emulate the Japanese. Despite the continued ascendancy of Europe during the nineteenth century, therefore, there were indications that the day of European supremacy was drawing to a close.

In this chapter we will deal only with the major spheres of European expansion—North and South America, the British Empire, and Asia. The African continent was not opened up to European penetration until the end of the nineteenth century, and the resulting rivalry among the powers there will be more profitably discussed in a later chapter. The United States will command far more of our attention than any of the other regions, mainly because America remains to this day the most important overseas extension of European civilization.

The United States
Becomes a Great Power

In 1815 America was of little concern to most Europeans. A century later, she had emerged as the decisive arbiter in the greatest war Europe had ever fought. The advent of this newcomer on the international stage was long delayed. Through most of the nineteenth century, America remained quite isolated from the rest of the world, so much so that "isolationism" has remained a strong trend in American foreign policy to the present day.

America and Europe

We have already seen how, in the "Monroe Doctrine" of 1823, America had warned Europe to desist from any further colonization in the

Her majesty Alexandrina Victoria, of the United Kingdom of Great Britain and Ireland, Queen, and of the Colonies and Dependencies thereof, Empress of India, Defender of the Faith.

Western Hemisphere. On several occasions during the nineteenth century, notably during the 1830's and 1840's, the United States became involved with her neighbors to the north and south over territorial issues. But these localized conflicts had no effect on the European balance of power. Even the international repercussions of the American Civil War did not lead to European interference. It was only at the close of the nineteenth century, in the war with Spain, that America once again went to war with a European power.

Despite the political isolation in which the United States thus shaped her destiny, cultural relations between the new republic and the old continent remained close, though America at first was a recipient rather than a contributor in this cultural exchange. In the 1830's and 1840's, foreign travelers still commented on the backwardness and boorishness of American manners and customs. But there were also some friendlier critics, like the young Frenchman Alexis de Tocqueville, whose *Democracy in America* (1835–40) predicted correctly the leading role that the United States would some day play in world affairs.

America had shared the European vogue of Romanticism, and some of Europe's early socialists had tried out their utopian experiments on American soil. By the middle of the nineteenth century American writers like Irving, Cooper, Longfellow, and Poe drew foreign attention to American literature, and the monumental works of the historians Prescott, Parkman, Bancroft, and Motley did the same for American historiography. There were other fields in which American influence made itself felt. The pioneering efforts of American reformers in advocating women's rights, pacifism, and temperance evoked responses overseas; and the gradual adoption in Europe of universal male suffrage and free public education profited greatly from the American example. In technical inventions America already showed signs of the genius that was ultimately to make her the leading industrial nation of the world. The cultural exchange between Europe and the United States thus became less one-sided as time went on. Better means of communication also played their part. By the 1860's, the steamship had begun to compete successfully with the sailing vessel, and the laying of a transatlantic cable in 1858 speeded the exchange of news and ideas.

The Westward Movement

In her domestic development the United States faced many of the same social and economic problems that confronted the nations of Europe. Since America was a new nation, however, unencumbered by traditions and endowed with a rich and virtually empty continent, she grew into something radically different from Europe. Within one century the territory of the United States increased more than fourfold. To assimilate and integrate these new lands proved

---

De Tocqueville on Russia and America

1835

There are at the present time two great nations in the world, which started from different points, but seem to tend towards the same end. I allude to the Russians and the Americans. . . . All other nations seem to have nearly reached their natural limits, and they have only to maintain their power; but these are still in the act of growth. . . . these alone are proceeding with ease and celerity along a path to which no limit can be perceived. The American struggles against the obstacles that nature opposes to him; the adversaries of the Russian are men. The former combats the wilderness and savage life; the latter, civilization with all its arms. The conquests of the American are therefore gained by the plowshare; those of the Russian by the sword. The Anglo-American relies upon personal interest to accomplish his ends and gives free scope to the unguided strength and common sense of the people; the Russian centers all the authority of society in a single arm. The principal instrument of the former is freedom; of the latter, servitude. Their starting-point is different and their courses are not the same; yet each of them seems marked out by the will of Heaven to sway the destinies of half the globe.

From Alexis de Tocqueville, *Democracy in America* (New York: Knopf, 1953), Vol. I, p. 434.

From the Old to the New World: German emigrants for New York embarking on a Hamburg steamer.

to be America's foremost political problem, and its final solution contributed to the origins of a bloody civil war. Yet the abundance of fertile lands also helped to relieve economic and social pressures that might have had similarly violent repercussions. The result of America's territorial expansion was a superpower marked by vast size, advantageous location, wide variety of climate, and great wealth of natural resources.

Immigration

The territorial growth of the United States was closely related to the phenomenal growth of its population. From less than 4 million in 1790, the population shot up to over 60 million in the course of a hundred years. Much of this increase was due to the ceaseless stream of European immigrants, totaling more than 35 million between 1815 and 1914. Many of them still came to escape political or religious persecution, but there was also the attraction of the seemingly unlimited economic opportunities of the New World. The constant supply of cheap labor provided by immigration was a boon to America's growing economy. The rapid Americanization of these new citizens was aided by the fact that the United States had no privileged classes, no established church, and no military caste. American society had its sectional and occupational groupings, but they lacked the rigidity of the European hierarchies. Economic opportunity for all, an open society in which ability and hard work determined success—these were the ingredients of the "American dream."

Early Industrialization

Like most European countries, the United States in the first part of the nineteenth century remained predominantly agrarian. It was the abundance of land that attracted land-hungry Europeans. But as in Europe, the vast increase of population required additional economic outlets, and these were provided by industry. By the middle of the nineteenth century the eastern states had thriving industries. At the same time, the opening up of western territories provided an ever-expanding market. Full-scale industrialization did not take hold until after the Civil War. Prior to 1860, however, many of the social effects of industrialization which we have seen at work in Europe had already made themselves felt. Labor conditions in American factories on the whole were better than those in Europe. We also find during the first half of the nineteenth century the beginnings of American labor unions, although a labor movement in the modern sense, in America as in Europe, did not develop until later.

In its economic philosophy, America shared the faith of European liberals in freedom from state control. The American Revolution, as we have seen, had been fought against the mercantilist restrictions imposed by the mother country. Once these restrictions had been removed, there remained few obstacles to free enterprise. A philosophy of laissez faire thus permeated the economic life of the United States from the start. There was only one field in which American industry not only tolerated but demanded government control, and that was tariff legislation. With the world's largest free-trade area within their own borders, American manufacturers were eager to keep foreign competitors out.

America After 1815

The revolutionary turmoil in Europe after 1815 had its parallel in the unrest that prevailed in the United States during the 1820's. The source of this unrest was economic and social. As America's population increased, and as the new territories acquired with the purchase of Louisiana (1803) and Florida (1819) filled up with new settlers, there arose a number of differences between the established interests in the East and the new forces on the frontier.

Another source of unrest arose among the new workers of the East, most of them recent immigrants with little bargaining power and no social standing. Thanks to the growth of the democratic process after the Revolution, this discontent was able to express itself at the ballot box.

Democracy in the United States had been slow to reach all levels of society, and it was not until the late 1820's that male suffrage had been adopted in the majority of states. It was as a result of this increased democratization that Andrew Jackson was elected president in 1828. More than any of his predecessors, Jackson could claim to be the people's choice. He was the first westerner to win the highest office, a popular hero of the War of 1812, and, most important, a man who had risen from poverty by his own efforts. The road from log cabin to White House henceforth became part of the American dream.

The "Age of Jackson"

The "Age of Jackson" was a period of major change in American life, more so even than the 1830's were in western Europe. The democratization of political life was carried further with the adoption of the patronage or "spoils system," and with the practice of having presidential candidates nominated by national conventions rather than by a handful of party leaders. Closest to Jackson's heart was the further development of the West. In a number of treaties concluded with Indian tribes, the federal government won title to millions of acres of virgin land. These were sold at auction at low cost, after free land for schools, roads, a state university, and other public purposes had been set aside. Jackson's opposition to eastern financial interests, furthermore, made him the advocate of state banks, whose lavish granting of credit helped the development of the West.

With the opening of the West sectional rivalry became one of the major issues in American politics. Not only the West, but the South as well, found itself at odds with the North, especially over tariffs. While the South, depending on cotton exports, favored free trade, the North demanded high tariffs to protect its infant industries. Finding itself more and more overshadowed by the North, the South used the proposal of a high tariff in 1828 as an occasion for raising the vital question of "states' rights." The relationship between state and federal governments had been an issue in American politics since the early days of the Republic. The Constitution of 1787 had considerably widened the power of the central government over what it had been under the Articles of Confederation, and the policy since then had been to carry this centralization further.

But there was also strong sentiment against this tendency. Critics of centralization took the view that the Constitution was primarily a compact among sovereign states, and that the states had the right to nullify an act of Congress if it violated the terms of that compact. It was this idea of nullification that was used by Jackson's vice president, John C. Calhoun, to fight the "tariff of abominations." In the ensuing crisis Jackson broke with Calhoun and defended the sovereignty of the Union against the advocates of states' rights. A final showdown was averted by the compromise tariff of 1833. But this did not remove the underlying conflict between federal power and state sovereignty.

Expansionism of the 1840's

In foreign affairs the Jacksonian period was uneventful. As more and more settlers began moving westward, however, it was inevitable that tensions would develop with the Canadians and Mexicans who held rival claims to western territories. These intermittent conflicts came to a head and were settled during the 1840's. American-British economic relations were so advantageous that it was in the interest of both to avoid a major crisis over the American-Canadian frontier. By the Webster-Ashburton Treaty (1842), therefore, the northeastern boundary was adjusted to mutual satisfaction. A similar compromise was reached for the Northwest in the Oregon Treaty (1846), which fixed Oregon's northern boundary along the forty-ninth parallel.

Relations with America's southern neighbor, Mexico, were considerably more stormy. The main controversy here arose over Texas. The influx of American settlers into this Mexican border region had begun in 1821. Because of constant difficulties with Mexican authorities, the American settlers first demanded autonomy and then, in 1836, proclaimed their independence. The next logical step, admission of Texas to the Union in 1845, led to war with Mexico. As a result of the Mexican War (1846–48), Mexico relinquished her claims to Texas. She also ceded California and New Mexico in return for $15 million. Eight years later, with the Gadsden Purchase, America acquired another slice of Mexican territory.

The settlement with Mexico, together with the Oregon Treaty, now gave the United States an extended frontage on the Pacific. The implications of this development for American foreign policy were to become evident only gradually. For the time being, the most pressing need of the vast regions of the new West was for settlers to substantiate America's claims. In a fitting climax to a decade of expansion, gold was discovered in the Sacramento Valley in 1848. The resulting gold rush profited only a few of the many thousands who streamed to California from all over the world. But these "forty-niners" helped to increase the population of California more than fourfold in a single decade.

The Slavery Issue

The expansionism of the 1840's also aggravated the long-standing sectional conflict between proslavery and antislavery forces. What we have said about the democratic nature of American society did not apply to the large number of Negro slaves in the South. While almost everywhere in the world slavery was being abolished, it was gaining a new lease on life in the American South. In a nation dedicated to the belief in the equality of man, there now arose an aristocracy of wealthy plantation-owners whose belief in their own superiority and the inferiority of the Negro race foreshadowed the racist ideologies that were to arise in Europe during the later nineteenth century.

The main concern of southern politicians in the first half of the nineteenth century was to prevent antislavery legislation. This could be

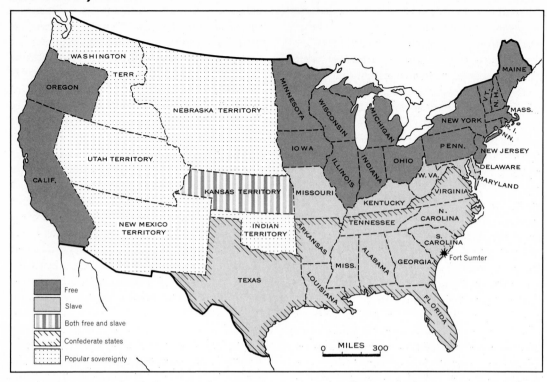

Free

Slave

Both free and slave

Confederate states

Popular sovereignty

done only if an even balance between slave and free states was maintained. Such a balance in the past had been maintained by compromise. But compromise became increasingly difficult as more and more territories were added to the Union. With the petition of California in 1849 for admission as a free state, the issue reached a critical stage. If granted, the admission would upset the existing balance between slave and free states. After prolonged debates, differences were once more patched up. The Compromise of 1850 called for the admission of California as a free state, but it left the question of whether the two new territories of New Mexico and Utah were ultimately to be admitted as free or slave states up to their own decisions. It was this introduction of state option, or popular sovereignty, which injected a new and disturbing element into the slavery controversy.

Beginning in the mid-1850's a series of tragic events and incidents made a compromise between the opposing factions on the slavery issue in-

creasingly difficult. The rivalry between pro-slavery and antislavery forces over whether Kansas was to be a free or slave state soon plunged that territory into a miniature civil war. The Supreme Court's Dred Scott decision (1857), which ruled that slaves were property and thus could not become free by moving to a free state, deeply antagonized the North. John Brown's futile raid on Harper's Ferry (1859), on the other hand, aroused the specter of a slave revolt in the South. The presidential campaign of 1860 was dominated by the slavery issue. The Democrats were divided into a southern, proslavery wing and a northern faction holding to the compromising policy of popular sovereignty. The Republicans, on the other hand, stood united against any further extension of slavery.

The Republican candidate, Abraham Lincoln, was chosen by an electorate divided along sectional lines. Repeatedly in previous years the South had talked of secession as a last resort in defending its way of life. Calhoun, the defender of states' rights, had suggested that if compromise proved impossible the states should "agree to separate and part in peace." It was South Carolina, the home of the "great nullifier," that now replied to Lincoln's election by passing its Ordinance of Secession. One after another, most of the slave states seceded from the Union and formed the Confederate States of America. In his inaugural address Lincoln strongly rejected the right of secession and vowed to maintain the Union. But he also left the door open for possible reconciliation. The issue of peace or war hung in the balance for a while longer. It was decided on April 12, 1861, when Confederate forces opened fire on the federal garrison at Fort Sumter in Charleston Harbor.

The American Civil War

The American Civil War was fought initially to preserve and protect the Union. To that extent it belongs among the great wars of national unification that were being waged in Europe at the same time. The Civil War was expected to be a brief conflict in which the immense advantages of the North would prove decisive. But the South put up a valiant fight, and in the early part of the war won some brilliant victories. Nobody would have predicted that the war would last four years and would turn into one of the most costly military ventures known up to that time.

Among the political developments of the war the most important was Lincoln's Emancipation Proclamation, to take effect on January 1, 1863. The extension of northern war aims to include the abolition of slavery changed the war from a mere political struggle into an ideological crusade. This change was brought about more by the pressure of circumstances than by actual design. Lincoln himself would have

"COME AND JOIN US BROTHERS." A poster for the recruitment of black regiments.

preferred a more gradual and voluntary process of emancipation.

The granting of freedom to the American Negro inevitably raised the closely related question of granting him equality as well. The abolitionist minority had never made any distinction between the two. But it took endless debates and several years before the country as a whole was ready to implement the gift of freedom with the guarantee of equality. This was done in several constitutional amendments and civil-rights acts. Beginning in the 1870's, however, the United States Supreme Court interpreted this postwar legislation in a way that violated its spirit, if not its letter, and that kept the American Negro in a state of inferiority for decades to come.

Europe and the Civil War

The Emancipation Proclamation made a very strong impression in Europe. The European powers had watched America's westward movement in the early part of the century with disapproval. During the Mexican War Great Britain actually considered joint intervention with France on behalf of Mexico, and during the 1850's these two powers tried to discourage American plans for the acquisition of Cuba from Spain. The outbreak of the Civil War led official European circles to hope that America would be permanently weakened by the secession of the southern states. Both the British and the French governments were decidedly cool toward the North, and on several occasions diplomatic rupture seemed imminent. When a northern warship removed two Confederate commissioners from the British steamer "Trent" in 1861, a major crisis was averted only by America's readiness to give in to British protests, and to release the commissioners. Great Britain, on the other hand, had to heed the protests of the North against permitting southern privateers to be outfitted and to operate from British ports.

American relations with France became strained when Napoleon III tried to bolster his position at home by establishing a puppet regime in Mexico. In 1863 French troops occupied Mexico City, and the following year Archduke Maximilian of Austria was proclaimed Emperor of Mexico. This was in open violation of the Monroe Doctrine, but the United States was too preoccupied to make any protest. Once the Civil War was over, however, she demanded the withdrawal of French troops (1866). Left without support, Maximilian could not last long. He was executed by a Mexican firing squad in 1867.

Not all the governments of Europe hoped to profit from America's domestic tragedy. The Prussian government was favorably disposed toward the North and wished to see the Union preserved as a counterweight to Britain's maritime supremacy. Russia took a similar attitude. The Russians had given up their settlements in California in 1844, and American fears that the tsarist government would take advantage of the Civil War to extend its sphere of influence southward from Alaska proved groundless. Alaska, the last remaining Russian colony in North America, was sold to the United States in 1867, for a mere $7.2 million. The same year America also occupied the Midway Islands, thus signifying her new interest in the Pacific area.

The most wholehearted support of the northern cause during the Civil War came from the rank and file of Europe's population. To the Germans and Italians the war appeared as a struggle for national unity, and to people everywhere the Civil War was another phase in the universal fight for freedom and independence that had been waged in Europe ever since the French Revolution. Even before Lincoln's Emancipation Proclamation, most Europeans saw the American war entirely in terms of liberating the southern slaves. The victory of the North was widely hailed as a triumph of democracy, and some historians feel that it contributed to the liberalization of the British and French governments after 1865.

Reconstruction in the South

America's reputation for liberalism and tolerance, however, was considerably tarnished by the Reconstruction period following the Civil War. The death of Lincoln had aroused worldwide indignation and sorrow, and the absence of his moderating influence was keenly felt in the American government's efforts to deal with the problems of the defeated South. In an attempt to enforce the political and social emancipation of the southern Negro, the Reconstruction Acts of 1867 and 1868 placed the South under military rule, from which it could escape only after drafting new constitutions that accepted the constitutional amendments and civil-rights legislation passed since the end of the war.

To the political tension thus generated, economic problems were added. The South emerged from the war with many of its cities destroyed, its economy disrupted, and one of its major economic assets, slavery, gone. The influx of northern "carpetbaggers," intent on making personal or political profit out of southern misfortune, kept alive the bitterness generated by war. The distinctive way of life on which southerners had prided themselves was gone forever; but the ideals on which it had rested remained alive. The slow process by which the southern Negro was once again disenfranchised and, by a series of "Jim Crow" laws, segregated as well, did not really gain momentum until the 1890's. Its cumulative effect was to perpetuate sectionalism by creating a "solid South" dominated by the Democratic Party and dedicated to keeping the Negro "in his place."

Economic Growth

Besides trying to heal the wounds of war, America, during the last decades of the nineteenth century, tried to fill in its remaining "open spaces" and to realize its great industrial potentialities. Both these developments were aided by the continued influx of millions of immigrants. Of considerable help in attracting new citizens and in aiding American farmers were the Homestead Act of 1862 and the easy access provided to the West by the construction of transcontinental railroads. The first such line was completed in 1869. American agriculture already had profited from mechanization. The invention of barbed wire in 1876 made possible the fencing-in of vast areas for cattle-raising, and the introduction of the refrigerator car proved a boon to the meat-packing industry. As a result of these

and other improvements, western farming took on some of the characteristics of an industry, producing on a large scale for sale in distant markets.

Even more important than the growth of America's agriculture after the Civil War was the expansion of her industries. The Civil War had created an industrial boom which continued once the war was over. Between 1860 and 1900 the amount of capital invested in American industry increased more than tenfold, and the export of manufactured articles by 1900 was four times what it had had been in 1860. By 1890 the United States had emerged as the world's leader in the production of steel and pig iron, and with close to 200,000 miles of railroads America in 1900 had more mileage than the whole of Europe. America also excelled in mass-production methods based on standardization, interchangeable parts, and ultimately the assembly line.

Government Regulation of Business

As happens in any rapidly expanding economy, America suffered a series of economic crises, of which the Panics of 1873 and 1893 were the most significant. Both had their parallels overseas, and the withdrawal of European capital from American industry in each case precipitated matters. To modify the effects of competition, American industry after 1873 began to combine its resources in order to fix prices and control markets. The first of these "trusts" was the Standard Oil Company of John D. Rockefeller (1879). But since these large organizations posed a serious threat to free enterprise, Congress in 1890 enacted the Sherman Antitrust Law. Its enforcement was sufficiently lax, however, to permit the continued concentration of control in business and banking.

There were other occasions when the federal government had to intervene in order to curb the excesses of laissez faire. Contrary to the practice in Europe, where governments had taken an active hand in the construction and operation of railroads, American lines were built through private initiative, aided by lavish grants of public lands. To realize maximum profits, American railroads charged exorbitant rates. There had been various earlier proposals for federal regulation of the railroads, but not until 1887 was the Interstate Commerce Act passed. The new law was chiefly concerned with rates, and it created an Interstate Commerce Commission to enforce its provisions.

There was one field in which American business did not mind governmental regulation. Protective tariffs had been a major concern of industrialists during the early nineteenth century. Southern opposition to protectionism, together with Britain's abolition of the Corn Laws in 1846, had brought a brief interval of free trade. But the economic and financial demands of the Civil War had reversed the trend. Beginning in 1861 America entered upon a new era of protectionism. Its high point came with the McKinley Tariff Act of 1890, which made the United States the most protectionist country in the world.

The unprecedented industrial expansion of the years after the Civil War gave an air of opulence and optimism to the "Gilded Age." Not all Americans, however, shared in the rise from rags to riches. The South in particular was slow to recover from its defeat and adjust to a world in which cotton was no longer king. The Panic of 1873, moreover, by causing price cuts among farmers and wage cuts among workers, bred widespread discontent. As a result, the 1870's saw the first serious efforts among these potentially powerful groups to assert their influence in national affairs.

Labor and Farm Unrest

There had been a growing awareness among American workers that they might improve their status by combining their small local unions into a more powerful national organization. The first such body to wield any real influence, the Knights of Labor, was founded in 1869. At its height, it had more than 700,000 members. In 1886 a wave of strikes culminated in the Haymarket Square riot in Chicago, in which several policemen were killed. The Knights of Labor, though not directly involved, were nevertheless blamed and as a result lost most of their following. Workers now joined a new national movement, the American Federation of Labor. It was to be the spearhead of the American labor movement for the next half-century.

Workers' attempts at organization, however, did not at first improve their condition very much. With large numbers of impoverished immigrants swelling the labor market, working conditions continued to be harsh, hours long, and wages low. Repeated strikes, in which hired strikebreakers fought vicious battles with strikers, further widened the gap between capital and labor. After the Pullman strike of 1894, the Supreme Court ruled that the Sherman Antitrust Act applied to labor unions if they obstructed interstate commerce. It was only after the turn of the century that American workers began to get a "square deal," but less because of the efforts of their own unions than through the intervention of a more sympathetic government.

Another large body of Americans who felt their interests neglected in a nation that was becoming rapidly industrialized were the farmers. In 1867 the National Grange of the Patrons of Husbandry had been formed, chiefly as a social organization, but also as a platform for agrarian discontent. The main grievance of farmers was the unfair practices of railways. The Interstate Commerce Act (1887) sought to improve the situation, but its initial effectiveness was limited. Suffering increasingly from protectionism abroad and falling prices at home, America's farmers during the 1880's formed regional groupings which ultimately grew into the National Farmers' Alliance and Industrial Union. Its purpose was to aid farmers by cooperative ventures and by bringing pressure against eastern industrial and banking interests who were held responsible for much of the farmer's plight. The climax of the farmers' discontent came with the formation of the People's Party in 1891. The Populists, profiting from the unrest among workers as well, soon emerged as a powerful third force in national politics. Their demands included currency reform, a graduated income tax, and government ownership of the railroads. A particular issue long close to farmers' hearts was the free and unlimited coinage of silver, from which they expected an upturn of farm prices. When the Democratic Party in 1896 adopted some of the Populist platform, including "free silver," the new party joined forces with the Democrats, thus making the latter more than before the spokesmen of agrarian and labor interests.

Foreign Policy After the Civil War

There were few noteworthy events in American foreign policy between the Civil War and the end of the century. In 1889 America signed a treaty with Germany and Great Britain that established tripartite control over the island of Samoa. The following year Congress adopted a sweeping naval program, calling for a fleet that would place the United States among the world's leading naval powers. Various plans during the 1890's for an American-controlled canal across Central America failed to materialize, as did attempts to annex Hawaii. The islands did not become American until the Spanish-American War in 1898.

Closer to home, the United States improved relations with the nations of the Western Hemisphere. In 1889 the first Pan-American Conference was held in Washington. In 1895, during a border dispute between Venezuela and British Guiana, Secretary of State Olney reaffirmed the principles of the Monroe Doctrine in strong and belligerent tones. A few years later, in 1898, the United States caught the expansionist fever that was driving the European powers into imperialist ventures. From now on American foreign policy became more and more involved with the rivalries of the other great powers. The days of American isolation were drawing to a close.

American Culture

In cultural matters the United States during the second half of the nineteenth century continued to share in the leading trends of Europe. American painters still went to study in Paris, American scholars were trained at foreign universities, and America's symphony orchestras and opera companies depended almost entirely on European talent. But there was some evidence of a native American culture, making up in freshness and originality for what it lacked in refinement. The writings of Walt Whitman and Mark Twain, the paintings of Winslow Homer and Thomas Eakins, the compositions of Edward MacDowell, and the functional architecture of Louis Sullivan all had an unmistakably American flavor. The most original and influential of America's intellectual contributions during the late nineteenth century was the philosophy of pragmatism. Its beginnings went back to the early 1870's, but it only attracted general attention with the writing of William James at the turn of the century. In the popular mind pragmatism justified America's preoccupation with practical pursuits and gave moral sanction to the fierce struggle for material success.

Most Americans were proud of this success. Yet there were some critical voices. In a period of progress and prosperity, both seemingly the result of laissez faire, the American journalist Henry George wrote his *Progress and Poverty* (1879), which challenged the free-enterprise system. Thorstein Veblen, in *The Theory of the Leisure Class* (1899), examined the role of the consumer in the economy of his day and found that such materialistic considerations as "conspicuous consumption" and "conspicuous waste" were exerting an unhealthy influence on the existing price structure. Social criticism also found expression in the novels of Edward Bellamy, Theodore Dreiser, and Frank Norris. All these writers had considerable influence in Europe, where concern over the effects of unrestrained economic liberalism had long agitated socialists and social critics alike.

In the realm of ideas, as in politics and economics, America at the end of the nineteenth century was thus making her influence felt far beyond her frontiers. Viewed with a mixture of awe and envy, hope and uneasiness, admiration and condescension, the United States appeared to most Europeans as the black sheep of their family that had struck out on its own and had made good.

Latin America:
An Age of Dictators

When Latin America won its independence from Spain and Portugal in the early nineteenth century, the region comprised nine sovereign states, most important among them Argentina, Brazil, Chile, Mexico, and Peru. By 1850 several of these states had split and their number had grown to seventeen; on the eve of the First World War there were twenty independent Latin-American nations. All these countries had certain things in common. With the exception of Brazil (where Portuguese was spoken), they were Spanish in culture and language; they were all predominantly Catholic; and the majority of their people were Indians, with white minorities that grew larger as more and more immigrants arrived from the Latin countries of Europe. Economically, Latin America throughout the nineteenth century remained predominantly agrarian and backward. Industrialization did not take hold until after the turn of the century, and then only slowly.

One other characteristic all Latin-American countries shared was extreme political instability. Lack of political experience, together with economic difficulties and sectional conflicts, brought an endless succession of dictators. Few countries produced any outstanding leaders. Mexico was an exception, with Santa Anna (1828–55), Benito Juárez (1855–72), and Porfirio Diaz (1877–1911) all gaining fame chiefly through their efforts to resist foreign encroachment.

The weakness and confusion of Latin America seemed to invite such encroachment. The United States, through its Monroe Doctrine, tried to forestall outside intervention. But it was chiefly Britain's support of American policy, combined with a temporary lull in overseas expansion, that kept Europe from challenging the Monroe Doctrine during the first half of the nineteenth century. By the time the first such challenge was delivered, during the Mexican venture of Napoleon III, the United States was strong enough to take a firm stand. Meanwhile Washington had embarked on its own course

of expansion at the expense of Mexico in the 1840's. This first phase of American imperialism was followed by a second round fifty years later (see p. 380). Except for this transitory intervention on the part of the United States, however, Latin America remained free from outside interference. This isolation had its political advantages, but it retarded the economic development of a potentially prosperous region.

The British Empire:
From Colonies to Dominions

Prior to 1800 only the American continents had attracted any substantial number of European settlers. Elsewhere, European influence had remained chiefly commercial. It was only during the course of the nineteenth century that Asia, Africa, Australia, and New Zealand were penetrated by Europeans. In this process of Europeanization, Great Britain led the way. As the nineteenth century opened, she still had vast holdings on the North American continent and in India. In addition, she had taken the first steps toward opening up Australia and had established claims to New Zealand.

The Empire After 1815

Despite these large possessions, however, England's colonial enthusiasm after 1815 was at a low ebb. The loss of the American colonies was partly responsible. With the decline of mercantilism, furthermore, the possession of colonies as sources of raw materials and possible markets had lost much of its meaning, since free trade enabled every nation to trade wherever it chose. By 1830 a number of British people were advocating the release of most of the remaining colonies from the control of the mother country. These proposals never got very far, however, mainly because of the agitation of a handful of men usually called the Colonial Reformers. Chief among them were Edward Gibbon Wakefield and the Earl of Durham. Wakefield, in his *Letter from Sidney* (1829), had laid down a plan for the systematic colonization of regions suitable for white settlement. Many of his ideas were subsequently carried out in Australia and New Zealand.

Canada: The First Dominion

Of still greater significance than Wakefield's activities were the proposals made by Lord Durham in his *Report on the Affairs of British North America* in 1839. Canada had been a source of trouble ever since it was taken over from the French in 1763. Its original French settlers resented the influx of large numbers of Britishers, especially after the American Revolution, and efforts to separate the two nationalities by the Canada Act of 1791 had not eased tensions. Discontent with British rule in both Upper and Lower Canada after 1815 had culminated in a brief uprising in 1837. To restore order, Lord Durham was made governor of Canada, and it was on the basis of his first-hand experience that he wrote his famous *Report*. In it he suggested that Upper Canada (Ontario) and Lower Canada (Quebec) be reunited and given responsible self-government. Durham's proposals were incorporated in the Union Act of 1840.

This new arrangement, noted for its granting of self-government, still did not solve the differences between French and British settlers. After long debates among the provincial leaders of Canada, a new federal constitution, the British North America Act, was finally adopted by Britain's Parliament in 1867. Ontario and Quebec were once more separated, and together with the provinces of New Brunswick and Nova Scotia were united in the Dominion of Canada. From the start the Dominion had complete control over its internal affairs, and as time went on it became more and more independent in external matters as well.

Australia, New Zealand, and the Union of South Africa

The evolution of dominion status for Canada was a landmark in the history of the British Empire. A former colony had been set free yet had remained loyal to the mother country. The first step had thus been taken on the road toward what later came to be known as the British Commonwealth. The practice followed in

Walter Bagehot on the Superiority of Englishmen

1869

Let us consider in what a village of English colonists is superior to a tribe of Australian natives who roam about them. Indisputably in one, and that a main sense, they are superior. They can beat the Australians in war when they like; they can take from them anything they like, and kill any of them they choose. . . . Nor is this all. Indisputably in the English village there are more means of happiness, a greater accumulation of the instruments of enjoyment, than in the Australian tribe. The English have all manner of books, utensils, and machines which the others do not use, value, or understand. . . . I think that the plainer and agreed-on superiorities of the Englishmen are these: first, that they have a greater command over the powers of nature upon the whole. . . . Secondly, that this power is not external only; it is also internal. The English not only possess better machines for moving nature, but are themselves better machines. . . . Thirdly, civilized man not only has greater powers over nature, but knows better how to use them, and by better I here mean better for the health and comfort of his present body and mind. . . . No doubt there will remain people like the aged savage who in his old age went back to his savage tribe and said that he had "tried civilization for forty years, and it was not worth the trouble." But we need not take account of the mistaken ideas of unfit men and beaten races.

Walter Bagehot, *Physics and Politics* (New York: Knopf, 1948), pp. 214–16.

Canada was in time also applied to other British settlements overseas. Australia's various states were granted self-government beginning in 1850 and were given dominion status as the Commonwealth of Australia in 1901. In New Zealand, self-government began in 1876 and dominion status was achieved in 1907. Finally, in South Africa various of the smaller territories were joined together in the Union of South Africa in 1910. This completed the list of Britain's original dominions.

The four self-governing dominions thus established were not by any means fully sovereign and independent states. In their foreign affairs in particular, they were still under the control of Great Britain. But such dependence was not felt as a burden. When war broke out in 1914, England did not have to bring pressure to bear on her dominions to join the fight against Germany. The bond of common ideals and institutions had created a community of interest that stood the test of war.

India Under the East India Company

The change from colonies to dominions happened only in those regions that had substantial numbers of white settlers. Elsewhere traditional colonialism continued. This was particularly true in the most valuable of England's possessions, India. We have already seen how, as a result of the Seven Years' War, England in 1763 had become the dominant European power in that part of the world. Britain's interests in India, since 1600, had been represented by the East India Company. This was a joint-stock company that enjoyed a monopoly of trade and operated with little interference from the British government. Primarily concerned with making profits for its investors, the company followed a system of exploitation that imposed great hardships on the natives.

In time the East India Company's policy began to run into criticism at home, forcing the government to impose restrictions on the company's activities. The Regulation Act of 1773 provided for a governor general appointed by the crown, and the India Act of 1784 placed the company's political activities under the supervision of a Board of Control in London. Later measures restricted and ultimately abolished the East India Company's trade monopoly. The general tendency before the middle of the nineteenth century was thus toward transferring more and

The British Empire   19th century

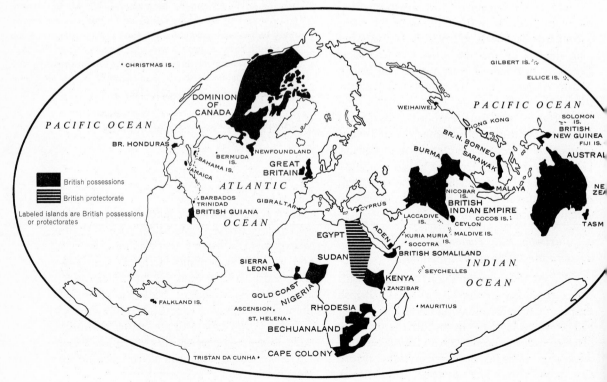

more of the company's functions and powers to the British government.

The event that brought the company's rule in India to an end was the Indian Mutiny of 1857. Britain's policy in India during the first half of the nineteenth century, especially under such able governor generals as Lord William Bentinck and the Earl of Dalhousie, had begun to be much more beneficial. India's finances had been overhauled, a system of western education had been introduced, and Indians had been given some participation in their government. Despite these and other improvements, however, there remained a great deal of discontent and unrest. Princes and landlords who had lost their former influence, orthodox Moslems and Hindus who feared the spread of Christianity, intellectuals who objected to the westernization of Indian culture, and the people at large who lived in acute misery—all these elements combined to bring about the "Great Mutiny" in 1857.

The revolt started over a minor incident among the sepoys—the native soldiers who made up the bulk of England's armed forces in India. The mutiny was poorly organized and short-lived, but its violence cast a long shadow on Anglo-Indian relations. The British public blamed the East India Company for most of the conditions that helped bring on the rebellion. In 1858, therefore, Parliament took over all the company's duties and obligations. The governor general now became a viceroy, and the place of the old Board of Control was taken by a secretary of state for India within the British cabinet.

British Rule in India

With the assumption of full control by the British government, the history of India entered a new phase. Under the Indian Councils Act of 1861, the viceroy was assisted by legislative and executive councils that included some Indian representation. But the viceroy retained the veto power. It was thus native participation rather than self-government that prevailed in India. Britain's efforts, moreover, to cope with the major problems of a rapidly growing population living in dismal poverty were only partly successful. The Indian farmer, paying exorbitant rents to his landlord and working small plots of exhausted soil, was subject to periodic famines. Industrialization, which might have absorbed much of the surplus population, was discouraged for fear that it might compete with industry back home.

Despite these shortcomings, however, British rule of India proved a vast improvement over what had existed under the East India Company. With the growth of a native middle class, demands for political and social reforms became more vociferous. In 1886 the most important native political party, the National Congress, held its first meeting. At the start the Congress demanded only moderate reforms. But as time went on it became more radical, and by 1907 there was a faction asking for complete independence. To encourage the moderates within the Congress, the British in 1909 made further concessions toward representative government. For the time being these improvements seemed to satisfy India's demands. When war broke out in 1914, India, like the dominions, rallied to the side of the mother country.

The "New Imperialism"

The lack of interest in colonial expansion, which had prevailed in England during the first half of the nineteenth century, came to an end after 1870. The man who helped rekindle the interest of his countrymen in the far-flung possessions of their empire was Benjamin Disraeli. In 1875 he quietly bought a controlling interest in the Suez Canal Company, thus starting Britain's involvement in Egypt. The following year Disraeli had Parliament confer the title of Empress of India upon Queen Victoria, an honor that pleased most of her subjects.

The revival of imperialist sentiment was not confined to England. Almost all the major and some of the minor powers of Europe now started competing for the still available regions of the world. The reasons for this sudden wave of "new imperialism" were partly political and largely economic. The rivalries resulting from this scramble for overseas possessions were a major factor in the mounting international tension leading up to the First World War. The main spheres of expansion were the newly explored continent of Africa and the ancient empire of China.

China and the Great Powers

Contacts between China and the western world in the past had been limited. Some commercial relations had developed with Dutch, Portuguese, and British traders, and in the eighteenth century Jesuit missionaries had been welcomed at the court of the Manchu dynasty. Beginning in 1757, however, the Chinese government, antagonized by the conduct of some of the European traders, had closed all its ports except Canton. Henceforth all business had to be transacted here and under narrowly prescribed rules. It was these irksome restrictions that generated most of the tension which ultimately led to the Opium War of 1839.

The Opium War

Various efforts in the early nineteenth century, especially on the part of the British government, to have additional ports opened to foreign trade remained unsuccessful. An added source of trouble between Britain and China was the flourishing trade in opium that had developed during the eighteenth century. There were few commodities China was ready to buy from the outside world, and opium was one of them. The Chinese government had long been alarmed

by the flourishing trade in opium and had vainly tried to stop it. In 1839 it moved to confiscate and destroy the vast quantities of the drug stored in Canton. It was this action that started the Opium War with Great Britain.

After three years of intermittent fighting, the Chinese were forced to agree to Britain's terms as laid down in the Treaty of Nanking (1842). Under its provisions, four ports in addition to Canton were opened to British traders and Britain was given the island of Hong Kong as a base. In subsequent treaties, France and the United States received additional concessions which came to be shared by all powers alike. Most important among these was the principle of "extraterritoriality," which placed all foreigners in China under the jurisdiction of their own consular courts.

The "first treaty settlement," as these various Chinese concessions came to be called, was a landmark in that country's history. As more and more "treaty ports" were added in the course of the century, many of them inland cities, the Chinese Empire was gradually opened up by foreign traders and missionaries, with far-reaching effects on China's economy and society. The first effects of this sudden contact between two very different civilizations were felt in one of the most violent crises in China's history, the Taiping Rebellion (1850–64).

The Taiping Rebellion

The underlying cause of the rebellion was the inefficiency and corruption of the Manchu government and the weakness it had shown in its dealings with the western powers. There had been mounting discontent with a system that exploited the masses of the people for the good of a small ruling clique. With the death of the emperor in 1850, various local manifestations of unrest came together in a general rebellion. In its ideology, the Taiping Rebellion was influenced by Christianity. Its leader was a religious mystic, Hung Hsiu-ch'üan. Its main appeal to the Chinese peasant lay in its abolition of the high land rent.

The Taiping rebels, though antiforeign, nevertheless hoped to gain the support of the European powers in their struggle against the Manchu regime. Tensions between China and the western powers had continued into the 1850's; and as the British and French continued to insist on their treaty rights, a new series of conflicts broke out. The Chinese government thus found itself at war with domestic as well as foreign elements. Had these two opponents joined forces, they could easily have overthrown the Manchu dynasty. As it turned out, however, the European powers, aided by the Taiping rebels, first defeated the Chinese government and then helped the government defeat the Taiping rebels.

After the fall of Canton and the occupation of Tientsin in 1858, Peking was once more ready to come to terms with the powers. Under the Treaties of Tientsin, China opened several more treaty ports, agreed to the establishment of

Imperialism in China 1842–1901

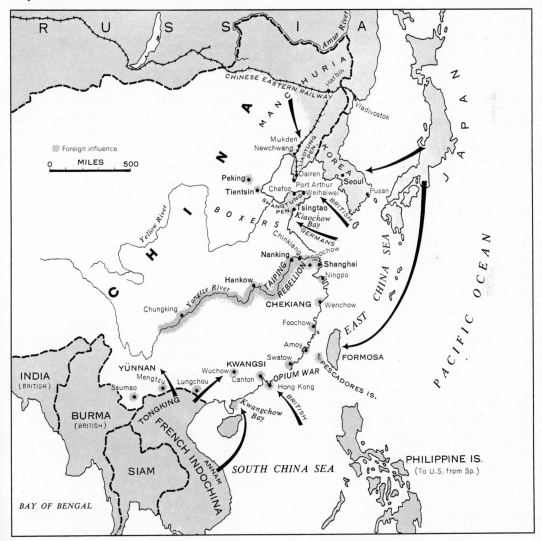

foreign legations at Peking, and permitted foreigners to move freely throughout the country. In addition, the Yangtze River was opened to foreign navigation and the opium trade was legalized. When the Chinese failed to honor these obligations, the French and British briefly resumed hostilities. The climax came with the storming of Peking and the burning of the emperor's summer palace. Under a new convention signed in 1860, China had to make further concessions. Simultaneously the Russians, taking advantage of China's embarrassment, secured for themselves a large slice of territory north of the Amur River, where they founded the port of Vladivostok. This gave them a long-desired outlet to the Pacific.

Once peace had been made, the Manchu government could turn its full force against the Taiping rebels. In this it had the support of the foreign powers. This western attitude has been rightly criticized. The Taiping rebels certainly were far more enlightened and progressive than the reactionary clique that surrounded the Manchu court. Yet the powers were mainly concerned with the preservation of their privileges, which the rebels had promised to abolish. Western policy was thus motivated by self-interest rather than a desire to reform China.

The suppression of the Taiping Rebellion ushered in a period of comparative peace in Chinese affairs. Some efforts were made to modernize China while maintaining her Confucian tradition, but these were not very successful. Beginning in 1877 China established her first diplomatic missions abroad. The telegraph meanwhile helped to bridge the country's vast distances, but the first railroad was not opened until 1888. The great powers did little to further China's reforming efforts. Some Chinese students studied abroad, and Protestant missionaries continued to bring western ideas to China. But frequent incidents in which Chinese crowds attacked foreigners served as convenient excuses for further foreign encroachment. France strengthered her influence over Indochina in 1884, and Britain's protectorate in Burma was recognized by China in 1886. These regions in the past had been tributaries of China.

The Sino-Japanese War

China's first major international conflict after 1860, however, was not with a western power but with an eastern rival, the empire of Japan. Japan, as we shall see presently, had been far more successful than China in adapting herself to western ways. The revelation of China's weakness in her dealings with the European powers had not been overlooked by the Japanese. The area over which the two came to blows in 1894 was Korea, the section of the mainland closest to Japan. Korea had long been a tributary of China, but it had also seen gradual encroachment by Japan. It was this encroachment that finally led to war.

The Sino-Japanese War (1894–95) was won by Japan, despite Chinese superiority in manpower and naval strength. Under the Treaty of Shimonoseki (1895), China had to recognize the independence of Korea and had to cede to Japan the island of Formosa, the Pescadores Islands, and the Liaotung Peninsula. The western powers, with the exception of England, were much alarmed by Japan's thus gaining a foothold on the Chinese mainland. Russia in particular did not want the Japanese in the Liaotung Peninsula. She was joined by France, with whom she had recently concluded an alliance, and by Germany, who was eager to get on better terms with Russia, in bringing pressure to bear upon Japan to forgo annexation of the peninsula. Japan had little choice but to give in. She got even with Russia ten years later (see p. 335).

The Scramble for Foreign Concessions

China's defeat by Japan came just when the rivalry among the great powers for overseas territory had reached a new height. The weakness of China now served as the occasion for an imperialist feast the likes of which the world had rarely seen. Between 1896 and 1898, all the major European powers received from China spheres of influence, trading rights, railway concessions, naval stations, mining rights, and whatever other forms of direct and indirect control western imperialists could devise. Russia got Port Arthur on the very same Liaotung Peninsula from which she had just ousted Japan; Germany acquired special rights on the Shantung Peninsula; the British secured a naval base at Weihaiwei; and the French obtained a lease of Kwangchow Bay. The United States, preoccupied with its own venture into imperialism during the Spanish-American War, merely issued a warning to the powers not to interfere with existing treaty ports and other interests in China. This "Open Door" note of 1899 had little immediate effect, but it expressed an important principle of American foreign policy for the Far East.

Reform and Reaction

At the height of the foreign encroachments in 1898, the imperial government made a belated attempt at reform. The short-lived "hundred days of reform," as this effort was called, was inspired and directed by K'ang Yu-wei, China's last great Confucian scholar. He hoped to create a constitutional monarchy, improve the civil service, reform the educational system, and introduce some western technology. The reformers had the support of the emperor, Kuang-hsü, but they were opposed by the established political and military hierarchy, which looked for leadership to the dowager empress Ts'ŭ Hsi. This remarkable lady had long been the center of resistance to all reforms. Discovering in the fall of 1898 that she was about to be arrested, she decided to strike first. She imprisoned the emperor and suppressed the reform movement. Until her death in 1908, the empress dowager ruled supreme.

The victory of reaction in China was aided by a military uprising at the turn of the century, directed primarily against foreigners. The "Fists of Righteous Harmony," or "Boxers," as these antiforeign elements were called, were chiefly active in the North of China. As more and more foreigners were attacked and the foreign legations in Peking put under siege, the great powers decided to strike back. An international expeditionary force descended on China, took Tientsin, and sacked Peking. Only the rivalry among the powers prevented the outright partitioning of the country. Instead, China had to pay a huge indemnity.

China's repeated defeats at the hands of the West had given ample proof that western civiliza-

Tz'ŭ Hsi (1834–1908), the dowager empress of China, who resisted foreign encroachment by encouraging the abortive Boxer Rebellion. Shortly after her death, the Manchu dynasty came to an end.

tion, at least in its technical aspects, was superior to that of the East. As demands for reform within China became stronger, the Manchu dynasty was forced into some half-hearted attempts to liberalize the government. In 1908 a draft constitution was published, calling for the election of a national parliament after nine years. Before it could go into effect, however, the Manchu regime was overthrown.

The Revolution of 1911

The leader of the revolution was a Chinese doctor, Sun Yat-sen, generally considered the founder of modern China. His movement—the Kuomintang, or National People's Party, as it was ultimately called—aimed to reform China and to save it from foreign encroachment. Its program consisted of three main points: national independence, democracy, and social justice. Prior to 1911 Sun's organization engineered some abortive local risings. To overthrow the Manchu dynasty, however, added support was needed. This was supplied by some of the provincial governors and military leaders who had long been at odds with the central government. Outstanding among these military figures was Yüan Shih-k'ai, a follower of the empress dowager, who had lost his position when the empress died in 1908. In 1911 the government asked Yüan to help put down a local uprising of Sun Yat-sen's followers at Hankow. Instead, Yüan helped depose the last Manchu emperor. It was this combination of forces that brought about the initial victory of the Revolution. In return for his support, Yüan was made president of the new Chinese Republic.

The main problem facing China after 1911 was how to reconcile the diverse elements in its government. In 1912 a provisional constitution called for a parliamentary government. But meanwhile Yüan Shih-k'ai was trying to extend his own power in the hope of ultimately founding a new dynasty. In 1914 Yüan embarked on a brief period of personal government. He died in 1916. With him China lost a leader who might have prevented the general anarchy and civil war that prevailed throughout China for the next ten years. China's efforts to set her own house in order had failed.

The Emergence of Modern Japan

China's contacts with the West had proved disastrous; Japan's experience was far more fortunate. In the first half of the seventeenth century, Japan had been virtually closed to western influence. It was not until the middle of the nineteenth century that internal weakness and outside pressure brought about the reopening of the island empire. Japan at the time was still being ruled as she had been for centuries—by the emperor's commander in chief, or shogun. This essentially feudal system, however, was

proving increasingly inefficient, and there was fear that unless Japan modernized her ways, she might suffer the fate of China and become a victim of western exploitation.

The Opening Up of Japan

Japan was reopened to the outside world, suddenly and dramatically, through the efforts of the American commodore Matthew Perry. His request in 1853 that commercial relations be established between the United States and Japan could not be refused, given Japan's military backwardness. In the resulting Treaty of Kanagawa (1854) the first Japanese ports were opened to foreign trade. Commercial and other agreements followed, not only with America but with other nations as well. The days of Japan's seclusion, thanks to American initiative, had been ended.

Japan did not become a victim but rather a competitor of the western powers in the colonization of the Far East. This she did by a policy of determined modernization and westernization. Japan's rapid transition from feudalism to industrialism did not come about without a major domestic upheaval. The sudden influx of foreigners caused deep resentment among many Japanese. While the shogun had been forced by circumstances to collaborate with the western powers, the emperor and his advisers had advocated resistance. The struggle between these two factions was decided in 1876, with the victory of the imperial supporters and the resignation of the last shogun. In 1868 the Meiji emperor assumed direct control over the nation, moving his capital from Kyoto to Edo, now renamed Tokyo.

The Meiji Period

The Meiji period (1868–1912) saw the emergence of Japan as a modern great power. The outstanding developments during the last decades of the nineteenth century were the abolition of feudalism and the industrialization of Japan. In 1871 an imperial decree abolished the large feudal fiefs and inaugurated a more highly centralized government along western lines. As the power of the old privileged families declined, so did the importance of their retainers, the samurai. When in 1876, the members of this traditional warrior class were forbidden to wear their two swords, the sign of their privileged status, they revolted. The Satsuma Rebellion (1877), involving some 200,000 men, was crushed by troops armed with modern weapons. With it the last resistance of feudal forces came to an end.

The modernization of Japan was most rapid and thorough in the industrial field. Industrialization had to start virtually from scratch, but the imperial government from the beginning took a hand in founding and running essential industries. When financial difficulties after 1880 forced the government to sell its enterprises, they were bought by a few wealthy families, the *zaibatsu*, who from then on dominated the economic life of Japan. The influence of the state over economic affairs, however, continued to be close, and the spirit of laissez faire, so prominent in the West, never gained a comparable hold in Japan.

The modernization of Japan affected every aspect of her life. Together with universal military service, universal education helped to transform illiterate peasants into trained and obedient workers. Buddhism was de-emphasized and Christianity was tolerated. There was also renewed interest in the ancient native religion of Japan, the cult of Shinto. With its veneration of the emperor as the Son of Heaven, Shintoism provided a religious basis for Japan's new nationalism. Japan's legal system was modernized along French lines, and its financial organization was borrowed from the United States. British officers helped build a new navy, and the new Japanese constitution followed the German model. In her efforts to catch up with the West, Japan thus borrowed freely wherever she could find the institutions best suited to her needs.

One of the main concerns of the Meiji period was the creation of some form of representative government. The emperor had promised a deliberative assembly in his "Charter Oath" of 1868.

But it was not until 1884 that the drafting of a Japanese constitution was begun. As promulgated in 1889, the constitution established an Imperial Diet of two houses. The lower house was elected under a restricted franchise which gave the vote to less than half a million Japanese. There was no ministerial responsibility. The emperor could issue decrees with the force of laws, and he could declare war. The Japanese constitution thus did not really affect the traditional power structure. Still, the introduction of parliamentary practices gave some voice and experience to the rising middle class, and the Japanese people gained more political influence than they had ever had before.

Despite her preoccupation with domestic reform, Japan also was able to carry on an active and successful foreign policy. Industrialization called for raw materials and markets, and a growing population called for living space. As early as 1874 Japan sent an expedition to Formosa. In 1876 she started the long rivalry with China over Korea which led to the Sino-Japanese War (1894–95). Japan's victory in that war, as we have seen, caused the tension with Russia that in turn led to a still more important war ten years later.

The Russo-Japanese War

The rivalry between Japan and Russia in the Far East went back to the middle of the nineteenth century. At that time Russia began extending her influence over the portion of China facing the Sea of Japan. By the end of the century, the only region opposite Japan still free from Russian domination was Korea. Japan continued to assert her interests in Korea after her victory over China in 1895. At the same time, however, the tsarist empire was stepping up its activities there. In 1902 Japan concluded an alliance with Great Britain, which had long opposed Russia's expansion in Asia. Japan thus was assured of the friendship of another major power with interests in the Far East.

Theodore Roosevelt with the Russian and Japanese representatives at the peace negotiations in Portsmouth, N.H., ending the Russo-Japanese War (1905). *Left to right:* Sergius Witte, Baron Rosen, Roosevelt, Baron Komura, and Baron Takahira.

The Russo-Japanese War, so long in the making, broke out in 1904. Japan had definite strategic advantages, but even so the world was little prepared for the resounding defeat she inflicted upon the Russians. After eighteen months of fighting, the war was ended by the mediation of President Theodore Roosevelt. The treaty of peace signed at Portsmouth, New Hampshire (1905), completed the emergence of Japan as a major power. Her interests in Korea were now recognized. In addition, she received control over the Liaotung Peninsula, together with some Russian railroad concessions in southern Manchuria. Russia also ceded to Japan the southern half of the island of Sakhalin.

Japan's victory over Russia marked a turning-point in relations between Europe and Asia. For the first time in modern history, one of the so-called backward nations had defeated one of the major powers of the West. The effects of this event were felt in an upsurge of nationalism among the nations of Asia, the ultimate repercussions of which have lasted into our own day.

An Evaluation of Western Imperialism

The growth of the United States into a major power, the transformation of the British Empire into a worldwide Commonwealth, the opening up of China, and the westernization of Japan —all these were manifestations of the vast influence that western civilization had gained in the course of a single century. There was one further region that became almost wholly subjected to western domination during the latter part of the nineteenth century—the continent of Africa.

Much of this expansion of western civilization had taken place in the last decades of the nineteenth century. In an age of ardent nationalism, it was considered a point of honor for any great power to raise its flag over as large an area of the globe as possible. At a time, furthermore, when unprecedented industrial growth created an urgent need for raw materials, markets, and outlets for surplus capital and population, colonies and foreign concessions seemed to provide a ready solution to economic problems. Finally, a civilization that considered itself superior to all others could easily convince itself that its members had a civilizing mission and should assume what Rudyard Kipling called "the white man's burden."

The various motives for imperialist expansion have come in for a good deal of criticism. There can be no doubt about the sincerity with which most western imperialists believed in the advantages that the spread of their civilization would bring to the rest of the world. It was only after the bitter experiences of the twentieth century, when the cause of western imperialism suffered one reversal after another, that this belief began to be shaken. Politically, western domination of colonial regions merely seemed to awaken among the subjected peoples a consciousness of their own national interests and a desire for independence. While this in itself may be a positive achievement, it certainly was not what the imperialists of the last century had envisaged. Economically, the advantages derived from imperialism were limited to small groups within the mother countries. As time went on it became clear that the most advantageous policy in the long run was the economic development rather than the exploitation of backward areas. Such development, however, was slow and expensive, and its ultimate effect was to emancipate rather than subdue colonial areas.

About the civilizing effects of the spread of western civilization, there are divided opinions. There is no need to point out the many advantages that have come to the rest of the world from its contacts with the West. In the field of medicine alone, the lives of millions of people have been saved by western scientists, and the slow but steady rise in the living standards of even the most backward regions would have been impossible without western aid and examples. The fault that has been found with the Europeanization of the world has been chiefly in the methods employed by western imperialists. Until quite recently the advantages that western civilization brought to many parts of the world were largely incidental to the primarily selfish

J. A. Hobson on Imperialism

1902

Thus do the industrial and financial forces of Imperialism, operating through the party, the press, the church, the school, mould public opinion and public policy by the false idealization of those primitive lusts of struggle, domination and acquisitiveness, which have survived throughout the eras of peaceful industrial order, and whose stimulation is needed once again for the work of imperial aggression, expansion, and the forceful exploitation of lower races. For these business politicians biology and sociology weave thin convenient theories of a race struggle for the subjugation of the inferior peoples, in order that we, the Anglo-Saxon, may take their lands and live upon their labours; while economics buttresses the argument by representing our work in conquering and ruling them as our share in the division of labour among nations, and history devises reasons why the lessons of past empire do not apply to ours, while social ethics paints the motive of "imperialism" as the desire to bear the "burden" of educating and elevating races of "children." Thus are the "cultured" or semi-cultured classes indoctrinated with the intellectual and moral grandeur of Imperialism. For the masses there is a cruder appeal to hero-worship and sensational glory, adventure and the sporting spirit: current history falsified in coarse flaring colours, for the direct stimulation of the combative instincts. . . . Imperialism is a depraved choice of national life, imposed by self-seeking interests which appeal to the lusts of quantitative acquisitiveness and of forceful domination surviving in a nation from early centuries of animal struggle for existence.

J. A. Hobson, *Imperialism: A Study* (Ann Arbor Paperbacks, 1965), pp. 221–22, 368.

aims and ambitions of the more advanced nations. The white man's burden, it has been said, has rested heavily on the shoulders of the black, brown, and yellow men who were subjugated by him. It is only in our own day that we have come to recognize and to correct some of the mistakes made by western imperialism in the past.

Suggestions for Further Reading

1. General

Because of the wide range of material, there are no general works covering the whole subject matter of this chapter. D. K. Fieldhouse, *The Colonial Empires* (1966), is a useful survey, as is also a small book by G. A. Lensen, *The World Beyond Europe** (1960). P. T. Moon, *Imperialism and World Politics* (1926), is a standard work on the expansion of Europe. K. S. Latourette, *A History of the Expansion of Christianity,* Vols. V and VI (1945), deals with one major aspect of Europe's spreading influence. Good general works on the Far East are E. O. Reischauer and A. M. Craig, *A History of East Asian Civilization,* Vol. II: *East Asia: The Modern Transformation* (1965); and G. M. Beckmann, *The Modernization of China and Japan* (1962). C. E. Carrington, *The British Overseas* (1950), deals with British colonization. The motives of modern imperialism are treated in numerous books, among them the classics by J. A. Hobson, *Imperialism: A Study** (1902), and N. Lenin, *Imperialism: The Highest State of Capitalism** (1916). More recent studies and critiques of imperialism are J. A. Schumpeter, *Imperialism and Social Classes** (1955), and E. M. Winslow, *The Pattern of Imperialism* (1948). See also A. P. Thornton, *Doctrines of Imperialism** (1965). On the spread of Europe's economic influence, see W. Woodruff, *Impact of Western Man: A Study of Europe's Role in the World Economy, 1750–1960* (1967).

2. The United States

The vast literature on American history during the nineteenth century makes any selection of representative titles difficult. An excellent introduction to the subject are the relevant chapters in J. M. Blum, *et al., The National Experience: A History of the United States,* 2nd ed. (1968), written by foremost scholars and containing comprehensive bibliographies. S. E. Morison, *History of the United States* (1965), is considered the great historian's masterpiece. On the pre-Jacksonian period, see G. Dangerfield, *The Era of Good Feelings** (1952), and *The Awakening of American Nationalism** (1965). The westward movement is discussed in R. G. Athearn, *America Moves West* (1964), and R. A. Billington, *Westward Expansion* (1967). Among studies on slavery, K. M. Stampp, *The Peculiar Institution** (1956), and E. D. Genovese, *The Political Economy of Slavery* (1965), stand out. Industrial development is treated in D. C. North, *The Economic Growth of the United States, 1790–1860** (1961). On the Age of Jackson, see G. G. Van Deusen, *The Jacksonian Era** (1959), and C. M. Wiltse, *The New Nation, 1800–1845** (1961). A. Nevins, *Ordeal of the Union,* 2 vols. (1947), and J. G. Randall and D. Donald, *The Civil War and Reconstruction* (1961), are representative works on the Civil War and its background. The aftermath of the war is treated in K. M. Stampp, *The Era of Reconstruction* (1965), and in C. V. Woodward, *Origins of the New South, 1877–1913,** (1951). The following are recommended for their insights into various phases of American thought and society: R. Hofstadter, *The American Political Tradition** (1955); L. Hartz, *The Liberal Tradition in America** (1955); and C. Rossiter, *Conservatism in America** (1955). On relations between the United States and Europe, see J. B. Brebner, *North Atlantic Triangle: The Interplay of Canada, the United States, and Great Britain* (1945), and H. Koht, *The American Spirit in Europe: A Survey of Transatlantic Influences* (1949).

3. Latin America

One of the best recent histories of Latin America is J. F. Rippy, *Latin America: A Modern History* (1958). Other good standard works are D. G. Munro, *The Latin American Republics* (1950); H. Herring, *A History of Latin America* (1955); and W. L. Schurz, *This New World: The Civilization of Latin America* (1954). The following deal with specific subjects: J. L. Mecham, *Church and State*

---

* Available in paperback edition.

in Latin America (1934); G. Plaza, *Problems of Democracy in Latin America* (1950); W. C. Gordon, *The Economy of Latin America* (1950); and R. Crawford, *A Century of Latin American Thought* (1944). On hemispheric relations, see A. P. Whitaker, *The Western Hemisphere Idea: Its Rise and Decline* (1954), and S. F. Bemis, *The Latin American Policy of the United States* (1943).

4. The British Empire

The most comprehensive work on the subject is J. H. Rose *et al.,* eds., *The Cambridge History of the British Empire,* 7 vols. (1929–40). For additional suggestions, see C. F. Mullett, *The British Empire-Commonwealth: Its Themes and Character* (1961). The four original dominions are treated individually in: J. M. S. Careless, *Canada: A Story of Challenge* (1953); G. Greenwood, ed., *Australia: A Social and Political History* (1955); J. B. Conliffe and W. T. G. Airey, *Short History of New Zealand* (1938); and C. W. de Kiewiet, *A History of South Africa: Social and Economic* (1941). Good brief histories of India are W. H. Moreland and A. C. Chatterjee, *A Short History of India* (1957), and P. Spear, *India: A Modern History* (1961). Britain's role in India is evaluated in: P. Woodruff, *The Men Who Ruled India,* 2 vols. (1954); R. P. Masani, *Britain in India* (1961); and M. Bearce, *British Attitudes Towards India* (1961). A key event in Indian history is the subject of T. R. Metcalf, *The Aftermath of Revolt: India 1857–1870* (1964).

5. China

Good histories of China are K. S. Latourette, *The Chinese: Their History and Culture;* W. Eberhard, *A History of China* (1950); and J. A. Harrison, *China Since 1800** (1968). R. Grousset, *The Rise and Splendour of the Chinese Empire** (1958), is more colorful. Recent developments are summarized in K. S. Latourette, *A History of Modern China** (1954). For a Chinese view of China's history, see Li Chien-nung, *The Political History of China, 1840–1928* (1956). A useful introduction to Chinese philosophy is H. G. Creel, *Chinese Thought from Confucius to Mao Tse-tung** (1953). F. Michael, *The Taiping Rebellion* (1966), is a pioneering work. The impact of the West on China is discussed in: Ssu-yu Teng and J. K. Fairbank, *China's Response to the West: A Documentary Survey, 1839–1923* (1954); R. Dawson, *The Chinese Chameleon: An Analysis of European Conceptions of Chinese Civilization* (1967); A. Iriye, *Across the Pacific: An Inner History of American-East Asian Relations* (1967); and J. K. Fairbank, *The United States and China** (1963).

6. Japan

E. O. Reischauer, *Japan: Past and Present* (1956), is a good introduction. One of the best brief histories of the last hundred years is H. Borton, *Japan's Modern Century* (1955). See also A. Tiedemann, *Modern Japan: A Brief History** (1955). Special aspects of Japanese history and culture are treated in: W. W. Lockwood, *The Economic Development of Japan* (1954); M. B. Jansen, ed., *Changing Japanese Attitudes Toward Modernization* (1965); H. Passin, *Society and Education in Japan* (1965); D. M. Brown, *Nationalism in Japan: An Introductory Historical Analysis* (1955); N. Ike, *The Beginnings of Political Democracy in Japan* (1950); and W. T. De Bary, ed., *Sources of the Japanese Tradition* (1958). G. B. Sansom, *The Western World and Japan: A Study in the Interaction of European and Asiatic Cultures* (1950), discusses the rest of Asia as well as Japan. Japanese relations with the United States are treated in E. O. Reischauer, *The United States and Japan* (1957), and in F. R. Dulles, *Yankees and Samurai: America's Role in the Emergence of Modern Japan* (1965). Important, though not always accurate, is R. Benedict, *The Chrysanthemum and the Sword: Patterns of Japanese Culture* (1946).

---

* Available in paperback edition.

13

The Period of Promise, 1870–1914

The last decades of the nineteenth century in Europe were optimistic years. With economic prosperity at home, with peace abroad, and with rapid advances in all fields of scientific research, the belief in unlimited progress that had prevailed since the Enlightenment seemed happily confirmed. Looking back from a later vantage point and with the knowledge of what happened in 1914, we can no longer share that belief. We now realize that despite rising prosperity many Europeans continued to live in poverty. Peace on the European continent was bought at the price of subjugating colonial peoples overseas and suppressing national minorities at home. The pre-eminence of science, finally, with its stress on material values, makes the pre-1914 period appear a crass and materialistic age in retrospect.

In this chapter we are primarily concerned with domestic affairs. Developments in various parts of Europe differed in many respects, but there were certain political, economic, and social trends common to most countries. In politics, Europe after 1870 witnessed the gradual spread of constitutional and democratic government. In economics, most countries shared in the unprecedented industrial growth that is sometimes referred to as the "Second Industrial Revolution." In the social sphere, the labor movement and its doctrine of socialism came to play an

increasingly important role in the affairs of almost all nations.

The Growth of Democracy

Before 1870 only Switzerland could be called a true democracy. By 1914 almost all the countries of western Europe had become democracies, and universal manhood suffrage, though not as yet parliamentary government, had been introduced even in central Europe. No country had truly universal suffrage. The efforts of a handful of determined "suffragettes" to gain political rights for women were met by the stanch opposition of the "stronger sex." But in many other respects women by 1914 had been freed from the legal inferiority and the economic and social disadvantages from which they had suffered in the past.

This extension of power from the aristocracy and the upper middle class to the mass of the people was most significant. The eradication of illiteracy, except in Russia and Italy, together with a popular press that profited from the many technical advances of the period, gave public opinion everywhere an increasing influence in the formation of policy. The "Age of the Masses" had arrived.

Varying Degrees of Democracy

The degree of democracy varied in different countries. In England some 20 percent of the

The Eiffel Tower (1889), proud monument to an age of progress.

Mrs. Sylvia Pankhurst, leader of America's "suffragettes," who demanded votes for women, being arrested in 1914.

male electorate still could not vote in 1914. In France and Italy universal manhood suffrage existed, but the smooth functioning of democracy was prevented by weaknesses in their respective parliamentary systems. Germany, too, had universal manhood suffrage. But since here the chancellor was not responsible to parliament, democracy hardly existed. In Austria-Hungary the main obstacle to democratic government was the perennial problem of nationalities. In Russia, finally, the franchise in 1914 was still limited and the National Assembly, or *Duma,* had merely advisory functions.

Democracy and Education

The success of democracy depended to no small extent on the existence of an informed electorate. Consequently the spread of democracy was accompanied almost everywhere by determined efforts to improve education. In England the Education Act of 1870, which introduced general education, was implemented by subsequent acts that made instruction free and compulsory. In Germany, already known for its

advanced school system, further progress was made, especially in technical training. The main concern of the French Third Republic was to make instruction compulsory and to exclude the Catholic Church from public education. Both aims were accomplished by the so-called "Ferry Laws" in the early 1880's.

The need for popular education was especially acute in countries with high illiteracy rates. To improve the status of some 68 percent of its population who could not read or write, the Italian government passed an act in 1877 making education compulsory. But this act became effective only after 1911, when the central government took over the financial support of local schools. While all other countries, including the smaller ones, made deliberate efforts to stamp out ignorance, the tsarist government of Russia tried to discourage lower-class education on the grounds that it would "draw people away from the environment to which they belong."

The growth of democracy and general education between 1870 and 1914 did not necessarily create the many blessings that liberals like

Mazzini had expected. Some earlier critics of democracy, like De Tocqueville and Mill, had already warned against imposing the standards of the majority upon society as a whole. This criticism continued in the late nineteenth century. To Henry Adams, democracy was one of the lower forms of government. The Englishman Walter Bagehot warned that the voice of the people might easily turn out to be the voice of the devil. And the German philosopher Friedrich Nietzsche criticized parliamentary government as a means "whereby cattle become masters." How justified these warnings would turn out to be in some countries was not realized until after the First World War.

The "Second Industrial Revolution"

The second general trend shared by most of Europe in the late nineteenth century was an unparalleled increase in the rate of industrial growth. In some respects this "Second Industrial Revolution" was merely a continuation of the first, but it had certain unique characteristics. New sources of power—electricity and oil—now competed with steam in driving more intricate machinery. Refined techniques of steel production, and the discovery of methods to use lower-grade ores made steel available in greater quantities and at a much lower price. Synthetic products, notably dyes produced from coal tars, became the foundation of whole new industries, and the introduction of dynamite by the Swedish chemist Alfred Nobel in 1867 had repercussions in the military as well as the industrial field.

There were many other novel features of industrialism at the end of the century: new means of communication and transportation helped to speed up business transactions; new methods of promotion boosted sales; a vast increase in the supply of liquid capital aided economic growth; and the rapid expansion of many enterprises led to new forms of industrial organization. All these innovations had one thing in common: They helped to increase the industrial output of Europe beyond anything ever known. The Second Industrial Revolution was mainly a quantitative phenomenon. The total production of the western world, including the United States, more than tripled between 1870 and 1914.

Social Effects

This increased industrialization accentuated earlier trends in society. The population of Europe continued to grow by leaps and bounds. With this growth of population, the shift from rural to urban life continued. While in 1800 most Europeans were still living in the country or in small towns, by 1900 from one-third to one-half of the population in the more highly industrialized countries lived in large cities. As industries expanded, agriculture declined. Through mechanization and chemical fertilizers, European farmers were able to achieve remarkable increases in crop yields. But even so, western Europe would have gone hungry had it not been for the expanding agricultural economies of Russia, the Americas, and Australia.

Industrialization continued to affect people's lives in many other ways. The invention of labor-saving devices and the mass production of consumer goods helped to make life easier and more comfortable. Central heating, the use of gas and electricity, the low-cost production of ready-made clothing, and the perfection of canning and refrigeration are only a few of the conveniences now enjoyed by rich and poor alike.

But mechanization and mass production also had their negative sides. Sociologists began to worry that the influence which machines gained over man might in time make him the slave rather than the master of his inventions. Mass production tended to standardize and cheapen public taste. Closely related to mass production was the problem of overproduction. To remedy this situation, advertising steadily gained in importance. The production of cheap paper from wood pulp in the 1880's and the resulting growth of popular journalism proved a boon to advertisers. Yet some people deplored the money spent by manufacturers to make people buy what they did not really need or want.

"Big Business"

One of the characteristics of industrial development since 1870 has been the substitution of "big business" for the smaller factories that had prevailed earlier. As enterprises became fewer, larger, and more competitive, producers found it desirable to form combinations to control production and price levels. The "trusts" of the United States, the "amalgamations" of Great Britain, the "cartels" of Germany, and the "syndicates" of Russia differed in detail but were alike in their efforts to establish some control over the production and distribution of goods. Opponents of this industrial concentration claimed that it tends to create monopolies that keep prices at artificially high levels. In response to such criticism, the United States in 1890 prohibited the formation of trusts, but it was the only major country to do so.

The period of "monopolistic capitalism" as the decades after 1870 are called, was also the heyday of the great industrialists—the Carnegies, Rockefellers, Krupps, Nobels, and others. The huge economic power of these "tycoons" could not help but give them political influence as well. But business leaders did not use their wealth only for their own ends. The ruthlessness that had characterized business during the early days of industrialization was gradually mitigated by signs of social consciousness on the part of some leading capitalists. One of the best examples of this humanitarian attitude was the steel magnate Andrew Carnegie. In his book *The Gospel of Wealth* (1900), Carnegie insisted that wealth was a public trust, not to be handed on within a single family but to be returned to the community from which it had been derived. To practice what he preached, Carnegie gave more than 300 million dollars to worthy causes in the United States and Great Britain. There were other humanitarian capitalists, not only in America but in Europe, where the "Nobel prizes" and the "Rhodes scholarships" commemorate two highly successful businessmen.

The Rise of the Working Class

A third general trend prevalent in Europe during the period after 1870 was the increasing influence of the working class and its socialist philosophy.

Much of the improvement in the worker's condition was due to the political power he came to wield through various socialist parties and to the economic power of his labor unions. As a result of the many efforts on his behalf, the status of the European worker by 1914 had been raised far above what it had been in 1870.

New Varieties of Socialism

We have already discussed the basic aims and ideas of modern socialism as derived from Karl Marx and Friedrich Engels. Marx had predicted an increasing concentration of capital, balanced by a growing impoverishment of the masses, leading eventually to the collapse of capitalism. Events during the late nineteenth century, however, failed to bear out Marx's predictions. While much capital was concentrated in a few hands, there was a corresponding diffusion of ownership by means of joint stock companies. And while in recently industrialized countries workers suffered from many of the hardships that had marked the First Industrial Revolution, once industrialization had taken hold their condition improved. By the end of the century, therefore, it became clear that Marx's prediction had to be adjusted to changed circumstances. The result of this adjustment in Marxian doctrine is called "revisionist," or "evolutionary," socialism.

The leading theorist of revisionism was the German socialist Eduard Bernstein. Bernstein had spent some time in England, where he came in contact with a non-Marxian brand of socialism advocated by a group of intellectuals, among them Sidney and Beatrice Webb, H. G. Wells, and George Bernard Shaw. Their socialism was called "Fabianism" after the Roman general Fabius, who preferred to defeat his enemies by gradually wearing them down rather than by direct attack. In this same manner the Fabian Socialists opposed violent revolution and sought instead to achieve socialization by way of gradual reform. Bernstein, on his return to Germany in the 1890's, began to expound his own revised version of Marxian socialism. One of its chief characteristics was the denial of Marx's concept of the class struggle. In his *Evolutionary Socialism* (1899), Bernstein advocated that instead of waging a revolutionary struggle against the middle class, the working class should collaborate with any group, proletarian or bourgeois, that would help to bring about a gradual improvement in the condition of the workers.

The revisionist ideas of Bernstein caused a major stir in Marxist circles. Orthodox Marxists denounced revisionism and reaffirmed their faith in the validity of all Marx's teachings. One of the most determined defenders of pure Marxism, the Russian Vladimir Ilyich Ulyanov, better known by his pseudonym Nikolai Lenin, held that collaboration with capitalism would help to perpetuate a system that would become more and more oppressive to the working class. Only a revolution could overthrow this system, and it was up to a minority within the proletariat, organized into a well-disciplined workers' party, to prepare the way for revolution by keeping alive the idea of class struggle. Except in eastern Europe, this revolutionary brand of "Leninism" found few followers before the First World War.

Marxism as a political movement had its international as well as its national aspects. Marx had believed that the best way to combat capitalism was for the workers of the world to unite their efforts. He had been instrumental, therefore, in founding the International Workingmen's Association in 1864. But the First International, as it was called, was not very successful. Marx's domineering manner, his controversy with Bakunin, who was among the leaders of the International, and the excesses of the Paris Commune in 1871, which were falsely blamed on the socialists, combined to bring about the gradual decline of the First International and its demise in 1876.

With the rise of socialist parties in most major countries during the next decade, however, the need for some kind of international organization was felt once again, and a Second International was formed in 1889. From the start it was beset by grave internal differences, especially on the issue of revisionism. As time went on, moreover, it became obvious that the national loyalties of most socialists were stronger than their feelings of international solidarity. The Second International opposed war as a means of settling international disputes; but when the test came in 1914

Leninism

I assert: [(1)] That no movement can be durable without a stable organization of leaders to maintain continuity; (2) that the more widely the masses are spontaneously drawn into the struggle and form the basis of the movement, the more necessary it is to have such an organization and the more stable must it be (for it is much easier then for demagogues to sidetrack the more backward sections of the masses); (3) that the organization must consist chiefly of persons engaged in revolutionary activities as a profession; (4) that in a country with an autocratic government, the more we *restrict* the membership of this organization to persons who are engaged in revolution as a profession and who have been professionally trained in the art of combating the political police, the more difficult will it be to catch the organization; and (5) the *wider* will be the circle of men and women of the working class or of other classes of society able to join the movement and perform active work in it.

From Nikolai Lenin, ''What Is to Be Done?'' 1902, *Selected Works* (London: Lawrence and Wishart, 1936), Vol. II, pp. 138–39.

the ideas of international socialism quickly gave way to the stronger appeal of national patriotism.

The Growth of Labor Unions

In addition to setting up their own political parties, workers tried to improve their lot through the formation of labor unions. In the early part of the nineteenth century, unions had made little progress anywhere except in Great Britain, and even here their activities remained restricted. This situation improved markedly after 1870. In England, in a series of legislative acts in 1874–75, unions were given permission to strike and to engage in peaceful picketing. The most important advance in the history of British organized labor came as a result of the famous London dock strike of 1889. The first major strike among unskilled workers, this event marked the extension of union activity beyond the skilled groups that in the past had made up union membership.

On the Continent the labor movement was slower in gaining momentum. In France labor

unions had made little headway by 1870. The Paris Commune of 1871 cast a shadow on any kind of labor activity, and it was not until 1884 that the Waldeck-Rousseau Law granted full legal status to unions and allowed them to form larger federations. The decisive step in this direction was taken in 1895, when the General Confederation of Labor (CGT) was organized. It advocated a program of direct action to destroy capitalism by means of general strikes and sabotage.

Germany, too, had seen little union activity before 1870. Since the German labor movement was closely allied with socialism from the start, it was adversely affected by the antisocialist measures of Bismarck. It thus did not really gain momentum until after 1890. Under the Imperial Industrial Code, German workers were permitted to strike, but an unfriendly government and hostile courts restricted the activities of organized labor wherever possible. Even so, the labor movement in Germany, by exerting pressure on government and employers, helped to improve the condition of German workers.

In the less industrialized countries of Italy, Austria-Hungary, and Russia, trade unionism played a minor role. In Italy the labor movement

Headquarters of the First International, in a Paris back street.

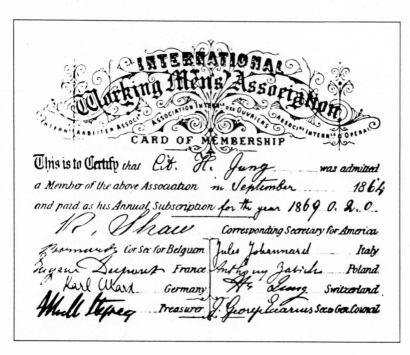

Membership card of the International Working Men's Association, 1869. Note the signature of Karl Marx as Corresponding Secretary for Germany.

was split into several factions, the largest of which, the socialist General Italian Federation of Labor, was founded in 1907. Socialist unions also held the lead in Austria, though there was hardly any organized labor in agrarian Hungary. Russia did not have any real labor unions until after 1905, and even then they did not gain much influence.

The "Welfare State"

The agitation of European workers for political, economic, and social reforms did much to make their governments adopt programs of social legislation designed to help the lower classes. Such intervention by the state in the affairs of the individual was a radical departure from the laissez-faire philosophy of early nineteenth-century liberalism. The idea that the state should concern itself with the welfare of its citizens and become, as we would say today, a "welfare state," found acceptance among politicians both in England and on the Continent. The social legislation resulting from this new attitude was so far-reaching that it has been referred to as "state socialism." Its chief purpose was to satisfy the reasonable grievances of the working class and by so doing to preserve the capitalist system.

Similar motives were behind various appeals of the Christian churches, notably the Catholic Church, for collaboration rather than conflict between employers and workers. "Christian Socialism" was nothing new, but it gained significance as the teachings of Marx began to compete with and to undermine the influence of Christianity among workers. The leading pronouncement on Christian social policy was made by Pope Leo XIII in his encyclical *Rerum novarum* in 1891, in which he condemned socialist attacks on private property and the Marxian concept of class struggle and suggested that the state aid its poorer citizens and that employers and workers settle their differences in a spirit of Christian brotherhood.

So much for the general trends—political, economic, and social—that prevailed in Europe between 1870 and 1914. As we now turn to a discussion of the domestic affairs of the major powers, we shall find these trends much in evidence.

England: "Mother of Democracy"

England after 1870 continued along the road of gradual political and social reform that she had followed since the early nineteenth century. The long reign of Queen Victoria reached its halfway mark in 1869. Gladstone's "great ministry" came to an end in 1874. For the next six years Disraeli, Earl of Beaconsfield since 1876, conducted a policy noted chiefly for its successes abroad. Between 1880 and 1895, Liberal and Conservative governments alternated, with Gladstone heading three more ministries and Lord Salisbury serving as his Conservative counterpart. The last two decades before 1914 were equally divided between the two major parties, the Conservatives remaining in power until 1905 and the Liberals leading thereafter. Generally speaking, the Liberals were more active in domestic affairs, where Gladstone's reforming zeal found its successor after the turn of the century in the dynamic David Lloyd George. The Conservatives, on the other hand, were more concerned with foreign affairs, especially England's overseas interests. Lord Salisbury personally assumed the post of foreign minister in his three cabinets, and he was ably seconded by Joseph Chamberlain as colonial secretary.

One British problem that overshadowed all others was the question of Ireland. Gladstone, who had long been working to improve that country's unhappy condition, sought once again to remedy some of the worst abuses of Irish land tenure in the Land Act of 1881. He failed, however, chiefly because of resistance from Ireland's Nationalists. Under the leadership of Stewart Parnell, the Nationalists demanded political rather than economic reforms. Gladstone hoped to satisfy Irish demands by two Home Rule Bills, but he was defeated both times by a coalition of Conservatives and dissident Liberals. Subsequent Land Purchase Acts, under Conservative sponsorship and aimed at helping Irish tenants buy their land, somewhat counteracted the agitation of Irish nationalism. The Irish question became acute once more in 1912 when the Liberals introduced a third Home Rule Bill, which did not become law until September 1914. By that time war had broken out and home rule had to be postponed.

If England, except for the perennial Irish question, was spared any really serious crises, one of the main reasons lay in the peaceful adjustments she continued to make to the demands of an increasingly democratic age. The franchise which had been granted to urban workers in the Reform Act of 1867 was extended to rural laborers under the Franchise Act of 1884. A Redistribution Bill in 1885 established uniform electoral districts, and the Parliament Bill of 1911 abolished the veto power of the House of Lords over money bills. Democracy had thus made considerable progress in Britain by 1914, leaving only some 20 percent of the male population— domestic servants, bachelors living with their parents, and men with no fixed abode—without a vote.

Economic Developments

As we turn from politics to economics, the picture in England looks somewhat less bright. Prior to 1870, British industry had enjoyed undisputed leadership, and despite the repeal of the Corn Laws in 1846 British agriculture had been able to hold its own. This situation gradually changed as Germany and the United States became England's chief industrial rivals, and as the influx of cheap agricultural products from overseas caused a rapid decline in British farming. In the basic iron and steel industries, England by 1914 had been overtaken by Germany and America, and her share of the world's total trade had fallen from 23 percent in 1876 to 15 percent in 1913.

Much of this relative decline in England's economic leadership was inevitable, of course, as nations that had once been Britain's customers began to supply their own needs and claim their own share of world trade. But there were other causes for the slowdown in England's economic growth. Her scientific and technical education lagged behind that of other nations, notably Germany. England was slow in modernizing her industrial equipment and adopting new methods, and she failed to realize the importance of effective salesmanship. Furthermore, while tariff walls were being erected everywhere else to protect industry and agriculture, Britain clung to her policy of free trade, despite efforts, notably by Joseph Chamberlain at the turn of the century, to change to protectionism.

Labor and Social Reform

Even though her economic leadership was declining, Britain was still the most prosperous nation of the world. This prosperity was shared by the British worker, who was far better off than the workers in most continental countries. Great Britain was the only major European country in which Marxian socialism did not gain any large following. In 1881 an organization advocating Marxist principles was founded, but its advocacy of violence had little attraction for the British workingman. The Fabian Society, founded in 1883, appealed chiefly to middle-class intellectuals. What political influence the British working class exerted before 1914 came chiefly from the British Labor Party. Its origins went back to the early 1890's, but its official beginning dates from 1900, when several groups, including trade unions and Fabians, joined forces behind the Labor Representation Committee. In the general election of 1906, the Labor Party won twenty-nine seats in Parliament. Its program called for the gradual socialization of key industries and utilities, very much along Fabian lines.

Another avenue through which British labor improved its status was union activity. We have already mentioned the victory of organized labor in the London dock strike of 1889. There were occasional reverses, such as the Taff Vale decision of 1901 and the Osborne Judgment of 1909, both handed down by the House of Lords. Under the Taff Vale decision, labor unions were to be liable for damages resulting from strikes, while the Osborne Judgment made it illegal for unions to pay stipends to Labor members of Parliament. Both restrictions were subsequently removed under the influence of the Labor Party.

While the worker was thus helping himself, the government also did its share to help him through welfare legislation. There had already been examples of such legislation earlier in the century, especially the several factory acts. Factory legislation was now extended by several acts—in 1878, 1901, and 1908—and a minimum-wage law was passed in 1912. In 1880, social insurance was initiated, first against accidents, then against old age (1909), and finally against sickness and unemployment (1911). To finance these expensive measures, which Conservatives and some old-time Liberals termed "socialist," the Liberal government of Lloyd George in 1909 introduced a "People's Budget," which shifted the main tax burden to the rich. It was passed only over the stiff opposition of the House of Lords, whose powers, as we have seen, were subsequently curtailed.

As the result of an enlightened policy at home and a strong position abroad, England in 1914 was at the height of her power. There were some danger signals—in Ireland and, farther away, India. Britain's economy was going "soft," and her political system needed further reforms. But there was no reason to assume that she would not be able to cope with these issues in the future as she had in the past. Britain, on the eve of the First World War, was contented and confident.

France: Republic in Crisis

Britain's steady progress toward political and social democracy had no parallel on the Continent. The French Third Republic, after stormy beginnings, developed a system of government which in some ways was more democratic, though it was far less stable, than that of Great Britain. The French presidency was largely a ceremonial office. The cabinet was responsible to a bicameral legislature, the lower body of which, the Chamber of Deputies, was elected by universal male suffrage. Instead of clearly defined political parties, France had a large number of loosely organized factions, each headed by some outstanding political figure. This feature made the formation of workable majorities in the Chamber of Deputies extremely difficult and led to a long series of coalition cabinets, more than fifty during the forty years before the First World War.

Republicans Versus Monarchists

One of the main reasons for the erratic course of French politics after 1870 was the antirepublican sentiment of many Frenchmen. On several occasions in the early years of the Republic, the various royalist factions had come dangerously close to resurrecting the monarchy. But the Third Republic survived, partly because of the lack of unity among its enemies. It was not until 1879 that the French government in its legislative and executive branches became wholly republican.

But the republican elements were no more united than their enemies. A radical faction, led since Gambetta's death in 1882 by Georges Clemenceau, was deeply anticlerical and interested chiefly in revenge against Germany. The moderate republicans, on the other hand, were willing to compromise on domestic and foreign issues. Their chief figure, Jules Ferry, emerged as France's leading statesman during the last decades of the century. During most of the 1880's, radicals and moderates managed to cooperate in launching the Republic on a successful course at home and abroad. Despite their many achievements, however, widespread opposition persisted. Beginning in 1886 this opposition rallied around the recently appointed minister of war, General Georges Boulanger. By early 1889 the popularity of the dashing general was such that he might easily have led a successful *coup* against the Republic, had not his courage failed him at the crucial moment. Nevertheless, the Republic had come dangerously close to being overthrown.

As it turned out, the Boulanger affair, by drawing the radical and moderate republicans more closely together, helped to strengthen the Republic. But this gain was soon lost again in the so-called Panama Scandal, in which a number of radical republican deputies were found to have accepted large bribes from the corrupt and bankrupt Panama Canal Company. The dust of this affair had still not quite settled when the Third Republic was shaken by an even more serious crisis, the Dreyfus case.

In the fall of 1894, Captain Alfred Dreyfus, a Jew, was accused of having betrayed military secrets to the Germans and was condemned to life imprisonment on Devil's Island. Despite clear evidence of his innocence, it took five years before he was fully vindicated. During this time, the reactionary right—monarchists, Catholics, and the army, together with a handful of anti-Semites—denounced any attempt to clear Dreyfus as an attack on the honor of the nation and the discipline of the army. The radical left, spearheading the defense of Dreyfus, cleared its reputation of the blemish incurred in the Panama Scandal. The Dreyfus case was an extended duel between the two factions that had fought each other since the founding of the Third Republic. While its outcome was a victory of republicanism, the struggle itself testified to the continued strength of the forces of reaction.

The most immediate result of the Dreyfus affair was a shift from moderate to radical republicanism. After winning the elections of 1902, the Radicals formed their first ministry and at long last were able to carry out their own program. Their most drastic measures were directed against the Catholic Church. A bill for the separation of church and state brought to an end the Concordat of 1801, whereby the state had paid the salaries of the clergy and had participated in the selection of priests. The Church, henceforth, was to be entirely on its own. In social reform the Radicals were less successful. With the emergence of socialism in France at the turn of the century, radicalism found a powerful rival with far more sweeping social and economic aims.

Economic Developments

France, which had enjoyed considerable prosperity before 1870, was set back by the Franco-Prussian War and was slow to profit from the Second Industrial Revolution. The losses in manpower and material, Germany's demand for a heavy indemnity, and especially the surrender of the valuable industrial region of Alsace-Lorraine, severely retarded French industrial growth. The majority of the French, moreover, were still engaged in agriculture, and protective tariffs, such as the Méline Tariff of 1892, mainly aided the farmers. What industry there was consisted largely of small establishments, and only a few industries were affected by the trend toward industrial concentration. French foreign trade almost doubled between 1870 and 1914. But since the commerce of her competitors increased at a much greater rate, France found herself demoted from second to fourth place in world trade. There was one activity in which France led the rest of the world: The amount of French money invested abroad during the thirty years before 1914 rose from 13 to 44 billion francs. These foreign loans were a valuable source of national income, and they were used as an effective instrument to facilitate French foreign policy.

Socialism and Social Reform

Since France was less industrialized than some other nations, its working class was smaller and French socialism never gained quite the influence it did elsewhere, especially in Germany. Socialism in France, furthermore, had received a serious setback in the disastrous Paris Commune, a setback from which it did not recover until the late 1870's. Like socialists in some other countries, the French were split into moderate and radical factions. The revolutionary group, led by Jules Guesde, and the moderates, led by Jean Jaurès, did not join forces until 1905, when they formed the United Socialist Party. Again like most other socialist parties, the French socialist party was revolutionary in theory but evolutionary in practice. Between 1906 and 1914, its membership in the Chamber of Deputies increased from 54 to 101.

In the realm of social reform, France lagged behind England. A factory law of 1874, amended by subsequent acts, fixed the minimum working age for children at thirteen, restricted working hours for adults to twelve hours, and introduced various other health and sanitation measures. Social insurance did not begin until the end of the century. Accident insurance was introduced in 1898, and old-age pensions were started in 1910. There was no protection against unemployment, and health insurance was left to private initiative under state supervision.

Even though the French working class was not as numerous as its counterparts in England and Germany, the government's failure to solve some of the economic and social problems of the worker caused continued domestic unrest during the years just before 1914. At the same time, the Third Republic continued to be attacked from the right. Royalism and a violent brand of "integral nationalism" were kept alive by a few wealthy reactionaries in the *Action Française* of Charles Maurras and Léon Daudet. Yet the majority of the French seemed to approve the programs of reforms at home and peace abroad, which brought resounding victory for the Radicals and Socialists in the elections of 1914. French pacifism, while admirable, came at a most inopportune time, just when Europe was getting ready for a major war. France, on the eve of the First World War, was still a nation divided on many vital issues.

Germany: Empire Triumphant

The new German *Reich* presented a spectacle of wealth, success, and supreme self-confidence. Had its unprecedented industrial growth been paralleled by political changes in the direction of a more liberal parliamentary government, Germany might easily have rivaled England as the happiest nation in Europe.

We have already discussed the constitutional framework of Germany and of its largest member state, Prussia. Repeated demands of liberals and socialists for the reform of the Prussian three-class franchise and for the introduction of parliamentary government in the Empire were of no avail. The *Reichstag,* to be sure, was elected by manhood suffrage. But the main direction of policy continued to rest with the chancellor (who was appointed by and responsible to the emperor) and the Federal Council, or *Bundesrat,* in which Prussia held a controlling position. Even so, the German electorate might have made its influence felt more decisively had it not been split into five or six major parties, each of which differed in political and economic aims and none of which ever won a majority.

Imperial Germany— A German Reappraisal

The integral unification of the nation had not been brought about; the Gordian knot was uncut. What had been achieved was paid for through losses to the nation's fabric and damage to the nation's psychology. Revitalized, the hard, Old Prussian character could be superimposed on the soft, amorphous German spirit, and Prussia's militaristic-*cum*-political civilization could form the grand alliance, foreshadowed in the *Zollverein,* with a civilization inspired by economics and technology. The middle classes, caught, as they had been since 1848, between the authoritarianism of the state and the demands of the Fourth Estate, completely lost their self-confidence. The spirit of culture, withering throughout the Occident, could put down no deep roots in the stony landscape of the new structure; and in the unsettled atmosphere, the cultural decline was bound to have more grievous effects than in the long-established countries of the West. The national character coarsened. In 1866, the nation's sense of right and wrong having been thrown into confusion, the success of a daemonic, charismatic statesman remolded that character; in the *Kulturkampf,* it was thrust back from the deep wells of religion, to which the schism had long blocked proper access, and the anti-Socialist law added an element of callousness. The unscrupulous vitality of *Realpolitik* took the place of vanished character traits. Bent on the acquisition of power and wealth, the Germans were at the same time incapable of recognizing the limits of the possible within their policy of realism. Indeed, they were dazzled by sudden good fortune which they failed to understand.

Ludwig Dehio, *The Precarious Balance,* trans. by Charles Fullman (New York: Random House, 1965), p. 221.

Repression at Home—Aggression Abroad

During its first twenty years, the German Empire was ruled by the strong hand of Bismarck. The "iron chancellor's" claim to fame rests on his foreign rather than his domestic policy. During the 1870's Bismarck antagonized large sections of the German people by his fierce struggle against the Catholic Church. The so-called *Kulturkampf,* while appealing to liberal anticlericalism, failed in its major objective—to prevent the rise of political Catholicism. The Catholic Center Party emerged from its persecution as a potent factor in German politics. Bismarck's attempt, during the 1880's, to prevent the rise of a strong Socialist Party was equally unsuccessful. By enlisting liberal support in his fight against Catholics and socialists, Bismarck perpetuated the political disunity of the German people and contributed further to the decline of German liberalism.

Bismarck had no worthy successor. The unceremonious manner in which the great chancellor was dismissed by William II in 1890 was indicative of the young emperor's desire to be his own chancellor. But William II was utterly unsuited for such a role. Erratic, unstable, and given to rash utterances, especially on matters of foreign policy, the kaiser launched Germany on an expansionist *Weltpolitik* (world policy) that soon lost her the international trust she had gained under Bismarck. More than in any other country, issues of foreign policy played a dominant role in Germany. The army, long powerful in Prussian affairs, remained one of the cornerstones of the empire. Except for its budget, which the *Reichstag* had to grant for several years in advance, it remained entirely free from civilian control.

Within the *Reichstag* there was very little chance for any effective opposition to the government's aggressive policy abroad and its repressive measures at home. The alliance between prominent industrialists and landowners, initiated under Bismarck, assured the government of a workable parliamentary majority. Both groups profited from tariff protectionism and both were united in their opposition to lower-class demands for political and social democracy. Against this coalition between the industrialist National Liberals and the agrarian Conservatives, the Socialist opposition and the occasionally critical Center and Progressive parties could do very little, especially as they were rarely united among themselves. On a few occasions, notably during the "Daily Telegraph Affair" in 1908, when William II, in an interview to the British press, made some irresponsible statements on Anglo-German relations, it seemed as though public indignation might enforce some check upon the kaiser's erratic rule. But the discipline so deeply instilled in every German, and the economic prosperity the nation enjoyed, kept the public from taking any drastic steps.

Economic Developments

The immediate effect of Germany's unification in 1871 had been a short-lived economic boom, which had come to a sudden halt in the worldwide depression of 1873. It was only during the last two decades of the century that Germany began to show her great economic power, a power based on ample resources of coal and iron and a well-trained and disciplined labor force. Much of Germany's economic success can be attributed to the protective policy that Bismarck initiated in 1879. Germany was not the first nation to abandon free trade, but it was Germany's step that ushered in a period of tariff rivalry among the major powers and thus injected a strong element of nationalism into economic relations.

While Germany's rapid economic growth was due in large measure to the development of her domestic market—her population increased from 41 million to 67 million between 1871 and 1914—German competition was also felt abroad. The main pillars of German prosperity were coal and iron, concentrated in Alsace-Lorraine, the Saar, Upper Silesia, and particularly the Ruhr area, where the firms of Krupp, Thyssen, and Stinnes built their huge industrial empires. Germans took the lead in other pursuits as well, especially the electrical and chemical industries. By 1914 Germany's merchant marine was second only to that of Great Britain, although the British commercial fleet was still more than three times as large as that of Germany.

Socialism and Social Reform

The main critics of German domestic and foreign policy were the Social Democrats. Theirs was the largest and most influential socialist party in Europe. The origins of the party went back to the 1860's, but it did not become a political force until 1875. At that time a non-Marxian faction, organized by Ferdinand Lassalle in 1864, and a Marxian faction, led by Wilhelm Liebknecht and August Bebel, united to form the Social Democratic Party (SPD). Despite severe restrictions and the persecution of its members by the Bismarckian government, the numbers of the SPD steadily increased until by 1912 it had become the largest party in the *Reichstag*. Its program, first formulated at Gotha in 1875 and revised at Erfurt in 1891, while strictly "orthodox" in tone, nevertheless included a number of "revisionist" demands for specific reforms.

The agitation of the SPD was directed against the political and social rather than the economic inequities of the empire. The phenomenal economic growth of the country could not help but be reflected in a rising standard of living for the workers. The German government, furthermore, through extensive programs of social reform, tried to alleviate the hardships inherent in massive industrialization. In 1878 factory inspection was made compulsory, and in 1891 an Imperial Industrial Code introduced the usual sanitary and safety provisions and regulated working hours for women and children. Germany's pioneering efforts were in the field of social legislation. In an effort to divert German workers from socialism, Bismarck, between 1883 and 1889, introduced far-reaching measures for health, accident, and old-age insurance. These served as models for similar measures in other countries, notably England.

The German Empire in 1914 was an anomaly among European powers—economically one of the most advanced yet politically one of the most backward. The majority of Germans, though not happy about their political impotence, took comfort in their economic achievements. They might criticize their government's domestic policy, but they saw little wrong with a foreign policy that demanded "a place in the sun" for Germany. Germany in 1914 was rich, powerful, and self-assertive.

Austria-Hungary: The "Ramshackle Empire"

The Austro-Hungarian Empire, ever since the *Ausgleich* of 1867, had been virtually divided into two separate states. Both Austria and Hungary were constitutional monarchies, but their governments were far from democratic. Various attempts before 1914 to improve this situation were complicated by the perennial problem of nationalities. After 1873 the Austrian lower house, or *Reichsrat,* was elected by a complicated four-class franchise, which gave disproportionate influence to the upper classes and the German minority among the population. This system, with some minor changes, lasted until 1907. By that time agitation among the various subject nationalities had become so strong that electoral reform could no longer be put off. The electoral law of 1907 at long last granted universal manhood suffrage. But the return in subsequent elections of a large majority of non-German delegates led to such constant wrangling in the *Reichsrat* that the orderly conduct of democratic government became impossible and rule by decree remained the order of the day. In Hungary the situation was still more hopeless. Here the upper crust of Magyar landowners completely dominated both houses of parliament. The rising protest of Hungary's subject nationalities brought some slight electoral reforms, but Hungary in 1914 remained essentially a feudal state dominated by a Magyar aristocracy.

Conflict of Nationalities

The overriding problem of Austria-Hungary continued to be the conflicts among its many nationalities. In Austria the Czechs were the main problem. The Poles of Galicia formed a compact group that was relatively well treated and enjoyed cultural autonomy. The Czechs, on the other hand, were closely intermingled with Germans. Attempts to introduce Czech, together with

German, as the official languages of Bohemia were met by German opposition. German nationalism found a mouthpiece in the German *Schulverein* of Georg von Schoenerer. Meanwhile, the "Young Czechs," led by Thomas Masaryk, fought for the rights of their own people.

While Austria made at least some concessions to her minorities, Hungary followed a strict policy of Magyarization, trying to eradicate rather than appease opposition. The major problem in Hungary was created by the Croats, who looked to Serbia for the lead in forming a Yugoslav—that is, South Slav—federation. The situation was complicated by the fact that the region of Bosnia-Herzegovina, since 1878 under Austrian administration, was also inhabited by Southern Slavs. The heir to the Austro-Hungarian crowns, Archduke Francis Ferdinand, was known to favor reforms that would give the Slavic element within the Dual Monarchy equal rights with Germans and Magyars. Such schemes were liked neither by Hungary nor by Serbia.

The existing state of affairs in Austria-Hungary thus had few real supporters. Emperor Francis Joseph, eighty years old in 1910 and the most respected monarch in Europe, tried his best to meet the rising tide of nationalism by appealing to the traditional loyalty to the House of Habsburg. But his efforts were in vain.

Economic Developments

Even though there was considerable industrialization in the Austrian half of the empire, the country as a whole remained predominantly agrarian. As such it suffered increasingly from the competition of the larger agrarian economies of Russia, the United States, and Australia. A high tariff policy, though it protected agriculture, kept living costs high, which in turn made for high wages and prevented Austrian industries from successfully competing abroad. Even so, there was some industrial progress. It would have been greater had the economic interdependence between Austria and Hungary been better utilized. As it was, industrial Austria and agrarian Hungary pursued separate and often contradictory economic policies.

Socialism and Social Reforms

Socialism in Austria did not become a factor to be reckoned with until the end of the century. In 1889, Victor Adler, the most prominent Austrian socialist, unified various socialist factions behind the Austrian Social Democratic party. Socialist agitation, in part, was responsible for the introduction of universal male suffrage in Austria in 1907. This development, in turn, helped the party to grow, so that by 1914 it had eighty-two members in the Austrian parliament. The program of the Austrian socialists was revisionist, and their main support came from the working-class population of Vienna. Their major weakness was national diversity: By 1911 the party had split into German, Czech, and Polish factions. There was no socialist movement to speak of in Hungary.

The Austrian government, like governments elsewhere, took a hand in improving the workers' lot. A system of factory inspection was set up in 1883, and an Industrial Code in 1907 set the minimum working age at twelve, provided for an eleven-hour working day, and introduced safety and sanitation standards for factories.

The economic and social problems of the Austro-Hungarian Empire in 1914 were still overshadowed by its nationalities problem. Every possible solution for this problem had been proposed and a few had been tried. Since each proposal left one or the other of the many nationality groups dissatisfied, a policy of repression always prevailed. The result of this negative policy was the assassination of Francis Ferdinand at Sarajevo on June 28, 1914.

Italy: "Great Power by Courtesy"

In Italy, economic backwardness and widespread illiteracy retarded the growth of democracy, although some superficial progress was made. The Italian constitution, the *Statuto,* which Piedmont had adopted in 1848, still limited the franchise in 1870 to a mere 2.5 percent of the population. Property qualifications and the voting age were gradually lowered, however, and virtually all adult males were permitted to vote by 1914. But this extension of the franchise was not an unmixed blessing. By giving the vote to the illiterate poor, it enabled a handful of ambitious politicians to manipulate elections and to make Italy's parliament a pliable instrument of their policy. The practice of "transformism"— that is, of avoiding parliamentary opposition by giving the most powerful critics a share in the government—avoided difficulties, but in the long run it proved a serious obstacle to the growth of democracy in Italy.

Poverty and Conflict

Despite marked economic improvements, Italy remained a poor and struggling country. A great power by courtesy more than through actual strength, Italy's frantic efforts to live up to a glorious past led her into military ventures she could hardly afford. The conservative forces that had brought about the country's unification remained in power until 1876. Regional opposition to extreme centralization, and widespread discontent with heavy taxation, then shifted the power to the liberal factions. From 1886 until the end of the century, Francesco Crispi provided firm dictatorial leadership. His attempts to divert the people's attention from discontent at home through colonial ventures abroad suffered a dismal defeat at the hands of Ethiopia in the battle of Adua (1896). The end of the century saw a rising tide of labor unrest, bread riots, and street fighting. In 1900 King Humbert fell victim to an anarchist assassin and was succeeded by the more liberal Victor Emmanuel III. During the last years before the war, Italy, under the capable but unprincipled Giovanni Giolitti, at long last made some headway in the solution of her worst economic difficulties. Giolitti also managed to effect a partial reconciliation between the Italian government and the Catholic Church. The pope continued to consider himself "the prisoner of the Vatican," but in 1905 he did lift the ban against the participation of Catholics in political affairs.

Economic Developments

Most of Italy's troubles were due to her poverty. Even more so than France, Italy was still primarily an agrarian nation. But while France was able to produce the bulk of her own food, Italy's soil was too poor and her agricultural methods too backward to support her rapidly growing population. The mounting population pressure could be relieved only through large-scale emigration and increased industrialization. The latter was hampered, however, by lack of essential raw materials and shortage of capital. Attempts at protectionism, furthermore, tended to affect Italy's own exports, and it was only with the conclusion of a series of commercial treaties in the 1890's that Italian exports picked up. With the help of hydroelectric power to make up for her coal shortage, Italy gradually developed her own textile industry, and in the production of silk she gained world leadership. But despite these improvements, and despite almost a doubling of her foreign commerce between 1900 and 1910, Italy's balance of trade continued to be unfavorable and she depended heavily on foreign loans.

Socialism and Social Reform

As it did almost everywhere else in Europe, industrialization in Italy brought in its wake the rise of socialism. The first socialist party in Italy was organized in 1891. It, too, had its initial difficulties over revisionism, and it was not until 1911 that the radical, "orthodox" element won the upper hand. The Italian socialist party did not gain any mass following until after 1900. Large numbers of Italian workers were attracted by the more violent programs of anarchism and syndicalism. Syndicalism applied the anarchist principle of direct action to economic affairs. The syndicalists hoped to overthrow capitalism by means of industrial sabotage and strikes, culminating in a general strike that would cripple the nation's economy and bring about the political victory of the working class. The first major general strike in Italy took place in 1904.

The Italian government tried to cope with the social effects of industrialization by factory acts and social legislation. Accident and old-age insurance were introduced in 1898. But the basic causes of trouble—poverty and illiteracy—could not be erased overnight. Meanwhile the Italian people, inexperienced in the ways of democracy, fell more and more under the influence of extremists of the right or left—the right calling for glorious ventures abroad, the left opposing war and demanding reforms at home. Thus divided, Italy was in no condition to enter a major war in 1914.

Russia: Stronghold of Autocracy

Tsarist Russia, to the bitter end in 1917, remained the most autocratic among European states. We have seen how the brief flurry of reforms under Alexander II during the 1860's had soon given way again to Russia's traditional policy of repression. The reign of Alexander II came to a violent end in 1881, when he was assassinated by members of the terrorist "Will of the People." His son, Alexander III (1881–94), was a reactionary and a Slavophil, not unlike Nicholas I. For well over a quarter-century Alexander III and his son and successor, Nicholas II (1894–1917), followed a policy of darkest reaction. Aided by Vyacheslav Plehve, director of the state police and later minister of the interior, and by Constantine Pobedonostsev, who as "Procurator of the Holy Synod" was the highest official in the Russian Orthodox Church and one of the most powerful men in Russia, the principles of orthodoxy, autocracy, and nationality once again became the watchwords of Russian policy. Catholics in Poland and Protestants in the Baltic provinces were persecuted; the powers of local and provincial councils, established under Alexander II, were curtailed; popular education was discouraged; and nationalism in Finland, Poland, the Ukraine, and elsewhere was suppressed. A particularly shocking feature of Russian policy was its persecution of the Jews. There were hardly any positive achievements during this period of unrelieved repression, except the economic reforms of Count Witte.

Economic Developments

Russia was the last major European power to feel the impact of industrialization. The government's main concern prior to 1890 had been the improvement of farming methods and the cultivation of new lands. Russia's agricultural exports between 1860 and 1900 increased almost fourfold, despite rising tariff barriers. Beginning in the 1890's, Russia also embarked on a program of industrialization, chiefly under the direction of her minister of finance and commerce, Count Sergei Witte. By introducing the gold standard in 1897, Witte stimulated economic activity and made investment in Russian industry more attractive to outsiders. The construction of the Trans-Siberian Railway helped open up the country's rich mineral resources and furthered the iron industry in the Ural Mountains. As a result Russia by 1900 held fourth place among the world's iron producers and second place in the production of oil. The opposition of agrarian interests to Witte's industrial policy, however, led to his retirement in 1903. Together with an economic depression and the Russian defeat in the war with Japan, Witte's departure helped to slow down Russia's industrial development. Lack of capital, the educational backwardness of the Russian worker, and his continued subjection to the village community were chiefly responsible for Russia's failure to realize her tremendous economic potentialities.

Socialism and Social Reform

Because of the government's vigilance toward all manifestations of social and political protest, socialism in Russia was slow to take hold. It was not until 1891 that the first Marxian socialist party was organized by Georgi V. Plekhanov. The activity of the Social Democratic Party was largely confined to underground agitation. At a party congress in London in 1903, Russia's socialists split into two groups. The Mensheviks (or minority), under Plekhanov, advocated a gradual evolution to democracy and socialism, while the Bolsheviks (or majority), under Lenin, followed the more radical, "Leninist" line. Besides Marxian socialism, which appealed to the rising industrial proletariat, there was also an organization of agrarian socialists in Russia, the Socialist Revolutionaries. Their program harked back to the socialist ideas of Alexander Herzen and to the populist "go-to-

"Bloody Sunday" (January 22, 1905). A procession of workers, led by the priest Father Gapon, is fired on by tsarist troops on its way to the winter palace; 70 people were killed and 240 wounded.

the-people" movement. To achieve their goals, the Socialist Revolutionaries advocated terrorism and assassination.

Increased industrialization in Russia brought the usual hardships for the working class. With an ample supply of manpower from landless peasants, wages remained low and the Russian worker had to slave long hours to eke out a meager existence. The government, in time, did regulate the employment of women and children and introduced maximum working-hours. But without a corresponding increase in wages, these restrictions merely tended to lower the total income of workers' families. Moreover, to voice discontent through labor unions was prohibited by law. Even so, unrest among the workers gave rise to frequent strikes of increasing violence.

The Revolution of 1905

The workers were not the only class that was restless at the turn of the century. There were the masses of landless peasants, whose grievances were kept alive by the Socialist Revolutionaries. And there was growing agitation among liberal members of the middle class, who demanded a change to constitutional government. As economic depression was worsening the lot of the workers, the Russo-Japanese war, by requiring that peasants be drafted, upset the rural economy. With the tide of war turning against Russia, tension mounted and finally erupted in revolution. The Revolution of 1905 began on January 22, "Bloody Sunday," when a peaceful protest march led by an Orthodox priest, Father Gapon, was fired upon by tsarist troops. A general strike soon crippled the major industrial centers, peasants rose against their landlords, and mutinies broke out in the army and navy. In October the Social Democrats and the Socialist Revolutionaries set up a Soviet of Workers' Delegates in St. Petersburg.

By that time, however, the revolution had run its course. Tsar Nicholas, after first intending to meet force by force, finally gave in and made a number of political concessions. The "October Manifesto" of 1905 guaranteed individual freedoms and called for the election of a National Assembly, or *Duma,* by almost universal male suffrage. But the promises made by Nicholas under duress were soon forgotten. It took three elections, each under a more restrictive franchise, before a *Duma* was finally elected which satisfied the tsar's wish for an advisory rather than a legislative body. Meanwhile the government had taken savage reprisals against the rank and file of the revolutionaries, killing an estimated fifteen thousand and arresting many times that number. Even so, Russia for the first time in her history now had an elected national assembly that could at least serve as a training-ground in parliamentary procedures. The democratic spirit thus penetrated, if ever so slightly, the last stronghold of autocracy.

Repression and Reform

The outstanding figure of the last decade before the war was Peter Stolypin, chief minister until 1911. A conservative monarchist, he nevertheless believed in a limited degree of representative government. He worked harmoniously with the moderate faction within the third *Duma,* the "Octobrists," who in contrast to the more liberal "Cadets" were satisfied with a mere consultative role. Stolypin's policy combined repression with reform. On the one hand he bore down hard on all revolutionary activities by Social Democrats and Socialist Revolutionaries. Their leaders were arrested, driven into exile (as were Lenin and Trotsky), or sent to Siberia (as was Stalin). These negative measures, however, were supplemented by far-reaching reforms. Realizing the desire of Russia's peasants for land of their own, and aware of the support that could

be gained from a large class of small farmers, Stolypin started to divide the communal holdings of the villages, distributing the land among the individual members of the *mir.* This was a slow and complicated process, and by 1917 only about one-tenth of Russia's peasants had become independent farmers. Nevertheless, it was a farsighted move, and it might have saved the tsarist regime if it had been completed in time.

Stolypin's reformist policy was opposed not only by the advocates of revolution, for whom it did not go far and fast enough, but also by the forces of reaction. The latter again gained the upper hand when Stolypin was assassinated in 1911. Nicholas II was a weak and vacillating monarch, firmly committed to the autocratic beliefs of his father and deeply under the influence of his German wife. The Tsarina Alexandra had fallen under the spell of an evil and ignorant "holy man," Gregory Rasputin. This power-hungry Siberian peasant gained such influence over the imperial family that he became the real power in Russia. Reaction coupled with corruption and inefficiency led to a gradual paralysis of Russia's government, making it doubly vulnerable to any major crisis. Such a crisis arose with the First World War.

The "Cult of Science"

Our discussion of the domestic affairs of the major powers between 1870 and 1914 thus far has dealt entirely with political, social, and economic events. Now we must sketch the intellectual climate in which these developments took place. The title of this chapter—"The Period of Promise"—fits particularly well the intellectual and cultural trends of these years. Their outstanding characteristic may be described as an overriding interest and a deep belief in science. Man had been interested in science before. But it was only in the second half of the nineteenth century that a veritable "cult of science" developed. Science offered a positive alternative to the seemingly futile idealism and Romanticism of the early nineteenth century.

Scientific research, in the past the domain of a few scientists and gentleman scholars, now became the concern of large numbers of people, especially as the application of science to industry gave an incentive for new inventions. "Pure" science continued to be of fundamental importance. But "applied" science—the "marriage of science and technology" so characteristic of the Second Industrial Revolution—now took precedence in the minds of most people. A virtually endless series of scientific inventions seemed to provide tangible evidence of man's ability to unlock the secrets of nature. If support was needed for the optimistic belief in unlimited progress, science provided it.

Materialism and Positivism

The growing concern of modern man with the material aspects of his civilization was also reflected in late nineteenth-century thought. A few basic scientific discoveries served as a foundation for an essentially materialistic philosophy that appealed to the educated middle class. Chemists and physicists earlier in the century had declared matter and energy to be constant and indestructible. These scientific findings were translated by certain "popularizers of science"—writers who interpreted the discoveries of scientists to the average layman—into a philosophy of materialism. An early exponent of this philosophy was the German philosopher Ludwig Feuerbach. More influential, however, was the German physician Ludwig Büchner, whose book *Force and Matter* (1855) went through twenty-one editions and was translated into all major languages. Proclaiming the eternity of force (i.e., energy) and matter, Büchner concluded that it was "impossible that the world can have been created. How could anything be created that cannot be annihilated?" Another influential scientific writer was Ernst Haeckel, a professor at the University of Jena, whose most famous book, *The Riddle of the Universe at the Close of the Nineteenth Century* (1899), became an international best-seller. Haeckel's "monistic philosophy" was entirely concerned with the material world, emphasizing not merely the eternity of matter and energy but insisting that even the human mind and soul had their material, physical substance. As for the riddles of the universe, Haeckel declared with the optimism typical of his age that all but one of them had been solved; and the remaining one, "what the pious believer calls Creator or God," was not worth troubling with, since there was no means of investigating it.

More lasting in its effect on western thought than materialism was another philosophy concerned with the impact of modern science on society—positivism. This philosophy had been worked out in the first half of the nineteenth century by the Frenchman Auguste Comte, but its influence was not felt until later. According to Comte, man in his development had passed through two well-defined phases, the theological and the metaphysical, and had now entered a third, the scientific or positive, phase. In this last phase man no longer concerned himself with ultimate causes, as he had during the metaphysical stage, but was satisfied with the material world and with whatever he might learn from observing it. Here was a philosophy that accepted science as its only guide and authority and which for that reason was eminently suited to the late nineteenth century.

The Darwinian Revolution

The scientific development that had the most revolutionary impact on almost every facet of western thought and society in the second half of the nineteenth century occurred in biology. It is concerned with the theory of evolution, and its major exponent was the British scientist Charles Darwin.

The idea of evolution was nothing new. Both in the general sense of a gradual development of human society from simple to more complex institutions, and in the more narrow biological sense that all organisms had evolved out of more elementary forms, the concept of evolution had deep roots in western thought. Darwin's major contribution was to provide a scientific basis for what had previously been a mere hypothesis.

Darwinism

Darwin was influenced in the formulation of his theory by the writings of the geologist Charles Lyell, and Robert Malthus' *Essay on Population*. Lyell, in his *Principles of Geology* (1830), had restated the thesis, already advanced some fifty years earlier by James Hutton, that the earth's physical appearance was the result of the same geological processes that are still active at the present time. This idea of vast changes brought about by natural causes, which Lyell had applied to the inorganic world, Darwin applied to the world of organisms. In searching for an explanation of organic evolution, Darwin was impressed by Malthus' account of the intense competition among mankind for the means of subsistence. The essence of Darwinism is stated in the full title of his basic work: *On the Origin of Species by Means of Natural Selection, or the Preservation of Favored Races in the Struggle for Life* (1859). His theory was subsequently elaborated and applied to the human species in *The Descent of Man* (1871). According to Darwin, life among all organisms is a constant "struggle for existence." In this struggle only the fittest survive. This survival of the fittest, Darwin held, was due to certain favorable variations within the given organism that proved of particular advantage in its competitive struggle with other organisms. These lucky variations, handed on to subsequent generations and enhanced by further variations, would in time evolve an entirely new organism, so radically different from its ancestor as to be considered a new species. This "natural selection," Darwin suggested, was further aided by "sexual selection"—that is, the mutual attraction and consequent mating of the fittest members of a species to bring forth the fittest offspring. Darwin also accepted the notion that certain "acquired characteristics"—the long neck of the giraffe, for example—may be inherited.

Many contemporary scientists accepted Darwin's theories only reluctantly. Yet his main idea —that all existing forms of life have evolved out of earlier and simpler forms—remains valid to this day. Only his account of the actual process of evolution has been challenged. The idea of the inheritance of acquired characteristics had been pretty well shaken by the end of the nineteenth century. Darwin's concept of evolution as a cumulative result of many minute changes, furthermore, has gradually given way to the view that evolution proceeds by way of larger and more sudden changes, or "mutations." These modifications, however, did not in any way lessen the revolutionary impact of Darwin's theories when they were first announced. More than any other single idea of the nineteenth century, the concept of evolution has left its mark on modern thought and society.

George Bernard Shaw on Darwin and Marx

The Socialists had an evolutionary prophet of their own, who had discredited Manchester as Darwin discredited the Garden of Eden. Karl Marx had proclaimed in his Communist Manifesto of 1848 (now enjoying Scriptural authority in Russia) that civilization is an organism evolving irresistibly by circumstantial selection; and he published the first volume of Das Kapital in 1867. The revolt against anthropomorphic idolatry, which was, as we have seen, the secret of Darwin's success, had been accompanied by a revolt against the conventional respectability which covered . . . the hypocrisy, inhumanity, snobbery, and greed of the bourgeoisie. . . . The moment Marx shewed that the relation of the bourgeoisie to society was grossly immoral and disastrous, and that the whited wall of starched shirt fronts concealed and defended the most infamous of all tyrannies and the basest of all robberies, he became an inspired prophet in the mind of every generous soul whom his book reached. . . . Now Marx was by no means infallible: his economics, half borrowed, and half home-made by a literary amateur, were not, when strictly followed up, even favorable to Socialism. . . . Compared to Darwin, he seemed to have no power of observation: there was not a fact in Das Kapital that had not been taken out of a book. . . . No matter: he exposed the bourgeoisie and made an end of its moral prestige. That was enough: like Darwin he had for the moment the World Will by the ear. . . . Thus Marx and Darwin between them toppled over two closely related idols, and became the prophets of two new creeds.

George Bernard Shaw, Preface to *Back to Methuselah* (New York: Brentano's, 1921), pp. lxvii–lxix.

The Impact of Darwinism

By applying the idea of evolution to all living organisms, including man, Darwin destroyed many of the most cherished beliefs of his contemporaries. Yet to an age that worshiped science, the thought that man was just as much subject to the logic of science as was everything else in nature also held a great fascination. Underlying much of Darwin's work was the idea of progress, an idea dear to the nineteenth century. History, the study of man's past, suddenly appeared in a new light—as a march toward some far-off, lofty goal. The gentle and retiring scientist himself took little part in the excitement and controversy stirred up by the doctrine that bore his name. The popularization of Darwin's thought was due chiefly to the efforts of other men, especially his friend Thomas Huxley. The application of the evolutionary concept to every aspect of human society, from physics to ethics, was carried out by another admirer of Darwin, Herbert Spencer. Spencer's ten-volume *Synthetic Philosophy* was hailed at the time as a brilliant synthesis of all existing scientific knowledge. Today it has been practically forgotten.

Of all Darwin's new ideas, the concept of life as a struggle for existence in which the fittest would survive had particular appeal to his contemporaries. The philosophy of laissez faire, with its emphasis on competition, had long been hailed as the root of economic success. With the advent of Darwinism, this belief in laissez faire seemed to have been given scientific sanction. Big business, according to John D. Rockefeller, was "merely a survival of the fittest . . . the working out of a law of nature and a law of God." But not only the capitalists derived great comfort from Darwin. His emphasis on the importance of environment for the improvement of man also gave hope to the socialists in their demands for social and economic reform. More than ten years before Darwin published his *Origin of Species,* Karl Marx, the "Darwin of the social sciences," had already sketched the evolution of society through a series of struggles among social classes.

The emphasis on struggle as a necessary condition for progress, however, was a narrow

Charles Darwin (1809–82) at the time he published his *Origin of Species.*

and one-sided interpretation of Darwinism, not shared by its author. In his *Descent of Man,* Darwin had emphasized that a feeling of sympathy and coherence, social and moral qualities, were needed for the advancement of society. But to the majority of people the struggle for existence assumed the validity of a natural law, a law, moreover, that applied not only to relations among individuals but also to relations among groups.

"Social Darwinism"

Herbert Spencer was one of the first to apply the theory of evolution to groups and states. History to Spencer was a struggle for existence among social organisms leading, as in the case of the struggle among individuals, to the "survival of the fittest." The classical statement of what came to be called "Social Darwinism" was made by the English banker and political scientist, Walter Bagehot, in his book *Physics and Politics: Thoughts on the Application of the Principles of Natural Selection and Inheritance to Political Science* (1872). According to Bagehot, the struggle for existence had always applied to groups as well as individuals, and in this struggle "the majority of the groups which win and conquer are better than the majority of those which fail and perish." In other words, among nations as among individuals, the strongest survive and the strongest, for that reason, are the best. Needless to say, this restatement of the well-known maxim that "might makes right" had little to do with Darwin's original theory.

Social Darwinism has been described as a blending of evolutionary and nationalist elements. To a generation that had recently experienced several major wars and that was actively engaged in numerous expeditions against colonial peoples overseas, Social Darwinism with its glorification of war came as a welcome rationalization. "The grandeur of war," Heinrich von Treitschke, one of Germany's most popular historians, told his students, "lies in the utter annihilation of puny man in the great conception of the state . . . In war the chaff is winnowed from the wheat." It is not surprising to find such views in a country that owed so much to war. But war also found advocates elsewhere. The Frenchman Ernest Renan praised it as "one of the conditions of progress, the sting which prevents a country from going to sleep"; and President Theodore Roosevelt held that war alone enabled man to "acquire those virile qualities necessary to win in the stern strife of actual life."

The influence of Social Darwinism may also be seen in the injection of racialism into nationalism. If being victorious meant being better, what was more natural than to view the triumph of one nation or race over another as a sign of the victor's inherent superiority? Among the earliest writers on racialism was the French count Arthur de Gobineau. His *Essay on the Inequality of the Human Races* (1853–55) proclaimed the superiority of the white race and distinguished within that race between the superior Germanic "Aryans" and the inferior Slavs and Jews.

Gobineau's racial doctrine, wholly unscientific, found its main echo in Germany. The idea of white, specifically Anglo-Saxon, superiority was also popular in England and America. It provided a welcome ideological justification for the imperialist expansion of the late nineteenth century.

The "Warfare of Science with Theology"

The most violent repercussions of Darwinism were felt in the religious field. The controversy between Darwinism and religion was part of a larger conflict that has been described as "the warfare of science with theology." The religious revival that we noted during the Age of Romanticism had soon given way to a noticeable decline in religious interest. As the state took over the functions of the churches in social welfare and education, and as some of the material benefits of industrialization spread among the lower classes, the need for the aid and comfort that religion had given in the past was no longer so acute. The tendency of the churches, furthermore, to favor the political *status quo* antagonized many liberals, and political anticlericalism became an important issue in most countries. Finally, there was the appeal that nationalism, socialism, and materialism came to have for many people. Both socialism and materialism were avowed enemies of religion.

Although these causes go far to explain the decline in religious interest in the second half of the nineteenth century, the most important reason was the effect modern science had on Christianity. Many scientific discoveries, especially in geology and biology, contradicted Christian beliefs, and the methods of scientific inquiry, when applied to Christianity itself, produced some disturbing results. In biblical or "higher" criticism, for instance, scholars studying the origins of the Bible discovered that most of its books had been written long after the events they described, and that few biblical writings existed exactly as they had originally been written. Another group of scholars, concerned with the study of comparative religion, detected striking similarities between Christianity and other religions. They found that there were few differences in dogma and ritual between early Christianity and some of the many mystery cults that had flourished in the eastern Mediterranean at the time of Christ. Christianity, it seemed, was merely the one among many similar religions that had survived.

These discoveries concerning the origins of Christianity became more widely known when they were used in up-to-date accounts of the life of Christ. A German scholar, David Friedrich Strauss, as early as 1835 had written a *Life of Jesus* that denied the divinity of Christ. Less scholarly and more popular was the *Life of Jesus* by the French writer Ernest Renan, published in 1863. Both works recognized Christ as a superior human being, but they denied that He had performed miracles or had risen from the dead.

Darwinism and Religion

Far more drastic in their effect on the faithful than these attempts to humanize Christ were the findings of Darwin. Not only did Darwin and Lyell challenge the biblical view of creation, but by making man a part of the general process of evolution Darwin dethroned the lords of creation from the unique position they had hitherto occupied. Why, one might now ask, should man alone of all creatures possess an immortal soul, and at what stage of his evolution was he endowed with it?

The Catholic Church, because it was more tightly organized and in its doctrine placed less exclusive emphasis on the Bible, was able to take a firmer and more consistent stand in this controversy than the various Protestant churches. In 1864 Pope Pius IX issued "A Syllabus of the Principal Errors of our Times," which condemned most of the new political, economic, and scientific tendencies. Six years later a general church council, in an effort to strengthen the pope's position, proclaimed the dogma of papal infallibility. The pope henceforth was to be infallible in all statements he made *ex cathedra*—that is, officially—on matters of faith and morals. The new dogma ran into some opposition among Catholics and it also contributed to the struggle between Church and state in Germany, Italy, and France.

The succession of the more conciliatory Leo XIII to the papacy in 1878 helped pacify matters somewhat. Leo was able to make peace with the German and, to a lesser extent, the French governments, and in the social and economic sphere, as we have seen, he tried to steer a middle course between capitalism and socialism. In science, Leo did not oppose any discoveries that did not affect Catholic doctrine. Only on the subject of evolution did the papacy persist in its rigid opposition. Some Catholics had begun searching for ways to reconcile the contradictions between science and theology. This "modernism," as such attempted compromise was called, was considered a heresy by the Church. Only after the First World War did the Church gradually take a more tolerant view.

In contrast to Catholicism, Protestant (and to some extent also Jewish) doctrine and ritual were almost entirely based on the Bible. The effect of scientific discoveries at variance with biblical statements, therefore, was felt more deeply. The fact, furthermore, that Protestantism was split into almost three hundred sects made any uniform stand in the warfare between science and theology very difficult. At the same time, however, Protestant emphasis on the freedom of the individual to work out his own relations with God made it possible for many Protestants to reach their own compromise between faith and reason. A minority of Protestant "Fundamentalists," less influential in Europe than in the United States, continued to cling to a literal interpretation of the Bible and insisted on the validity of the account of creation as given in the Book of Genesis.

Despite the confusion it caused not only among Christians but among Jews, the conflict between science and theology did not seriously interfere with the progress of science. The world in 1914 was still viewed as the intricate mechanism that Newton had supposedly shown it to be, a mechanism whose secrets would gradually yield to scientific inquiry. Only a handful of scientists realized that new developments—the discovery of X rays (1895), the isolation of radium (1898), and, most important, the formulation of the theory of relativity (1905)—had opened up an infinite number of new mysteries and had brought the world to the threshold of another scientific revolution.

Art in the Age of Science

The cult of science that dominated the intellectual climate at the end of the nineteenth century also had its devotees in art and literature. It is difficult in dealing with any period, especially one as complex as the one we are dealing with in this chapter, to single out those artistic trends that most clearly reflect the spirit of the age. To call the early nineteenth century an Age of Romanticism and the late nineteenth century an Age of Realism is, at best, an oversimplification. There were Realists and Romanticists in both these "ages," and some artists combined the characteristics of both periods in their work.

The Romantic artist, as we have seen, had preferred an ideal world of his imagination to the real world in which he lived. He had set his concept of natural beauty against the ugliness of early industrialism. And he had escaped from a harsh present to a more glamorous past. Even before the middle of the nineteenth century, however, some artists had begun to be interested in the world as it was, not as they felt it ought to be. This shift from Romanticism to Realism was most evident in literature; it was less pronounced in painting; and there were hardly any signs of it in music.

Realism and Naturalism

In literature the novel, hitherto a neglected literary form, now became the favorite mode of expression. And while the Romantic writer had been primarily interested in the unusual individual, the realistic novel was concerned with typical everyday society. Most of the great novels of the nineteenth century—from Dickens and Thackeray in England to Balzac and Flaubert in France and Turgenev and Tolstoy in Russia—fall into the category of social novels. Not only did these authors describe the society in which they lived; they dwelled on the problems of that society. Literature increasingly became a form of social criticism.

The trend toward Realism reached its climax in the late nineteenth century in a literary movement called Naturalism. Naturalism is of particular interest to us here, since it represented a conscious effort on the artist's part to apply scientific principles to art. The naturalistic writers —men like Emile Zola in France, Henrik Ibsen in Norway, and Gerhart Hauptmann in Germany—were not interested in the creation of beauty but, like the scientist, they were interested in truth. To get at truth they discarded subjectivity and intuition and strove to describe objectively what they had learned from study and observation. The Naturalist was much impressed with the findings of modern science, especially in biology and such new fields as sociology and psychology, and he made use of the new knowledge in his writing. It was one of his chief functions, the Naturalist felt, to call attention to existing evils and abuses. If this meant focusing his artistic efforts on the seamy side of life, he did so, hoping that by serving as diagnostician of society's illness he might help cure it.

Impressionism

The change from Romanticism to Realism, as we have said, was far less pronounced in painting than in literature, though even here some new trends appeared. While in the past artists had been concerned with the beautiful and unusual, they now turned more to ordinary everyday subjects heretofore considered unworthy of their attention—farmers, laborers, urban and even industrial scenes.

The real innovation in nineteenth-century painting, however, was not so much in its subject matter as in its technique. As in the case of Naturalism, it was the application of scientific principles to painting that characterized the school of Impressionism. Influenced by scientific discoveries about the composition of light, painters like Camille Pissaro, Claude Monet, Auguste Renoir, and others, used small dabs of color to depict nature in its ever-changing moods, not as it appeared to the logical mind but as it "impressed" the eye in viewing a whole scene rather than a series of specific objects. An Impressionist painting, examined at close range, thus appears as a maze of colored dots which, if seen from a distance, merge into recognizable objects with the vibrant quality imparted by light.

In trying to find the scientific temper of the late nineteenth century reflected in literature and art, however, we must guard against exaggeration. The relationship between art and science that we have noted certainly existed, and as such it testified to the predominantly realistic spirit of the age. But it would be wrong to assume that the majority of people at the time were aware of this relationship. The average European probably had little use for social novels or Impressionist paintings. He liked pictures that "told a story," preferably a sentimental one. And he liked second-rate novels of love and adventure by authors long since forgotten.

Symbolism

If these cultural interests of the average man expressed an unconscious desire to escape the realities of the present, a similar tendency may be noted among a few highly sensitive writers. No matter how critical the Naturalists were of their age, they still shared the faith of their contemporaries in the unlimited promise of science. But there were some intellectuals who did not share this general optimism. They deplored their generation's preoccupation with material values, and far from singing the praises of the industrial age they spoke out against its dirt and vulgarity. Earlier in the century, the Englishmen Matthew Arnold and John Ruskin had lamented the materialism and the loss of esthetic values resulting from industrialization. Their complaints were echoed later by their compatriot William Morris, who would have preferred to return from the machine age with its cheapening of taste to the simplicity and dignity of the Middle Ages.

There was a note of romanticism and escapism in this longing for beauty in an age of slums and soot. Yet the prevailing school of Naturalism had little use for beauty. To the Naturalist, art had to serve a purpose and preach a message. In opposition to this arid view of art, a group of French writers at the end of the century claimed that art was sufficient unto itself—"art for art's sake." Art to these neo-Romantic, or Symbolist, poets—Mallarmé, Paul Verlaine, and others—was not for the masses but only for the few to whom it spoke in "symbols," using words not merely for their meaning but for the images and analogies they conveyed, often by sound alone. Symbolism, like Romanticism before it, was deeply subjective and thus difficult to define. It is significant as a sign that there were people before 1914 who did not find all things perfect in a society that gloried in its material achievements and accepted the struggle for wealth as a sign of progress.

The Symbolists were not alone in their criticism. The most outspoken critic of the generation before 1914 was the German philosopher Friedrich Nietzsche. In a series of beautifully written books in the 1880's, Nietzsche attacked almost everything his age held sacred—democracy, socialism, nationalism, racialism, imperialism, militarism, materialism, intellectualism, and especially Christianity. Little understood by his contemporaries and much misunderstood since, Nietzsche's influence was felt more after than before the First World War. Few people today would agree with his wholesale condemnation of his society. Yet in striking out blindly, Nietzsche could not help but hit on many of the weaknesses we have since come to recognize in an age characterized above all by smugness and misplaced self-confidence.

Suggestions for Further Reading

1. General

The only work in this period that treats European civilization as an entity is C. J. H. Hayes, *A Generation of Materialism, 1871–1900** (1941), in the *Rise of Modern Europe* series. There are several general histories of Europe—such as D. C. Somerwell, *Modern Europe, 1871–1939* (1940), and M. Bruce, *The Shaping of the Modern World, 1870–1940* (1958)—but they treat developments in each country

---

* Available in paperback edition.

separately. National events are well covered in: R. C. K. Ensor, *England, 1870–1914* (1936); D. W. Brogan, *France under the Republic* (1940); K. S. Pinson, *Modern Germany, Its History and Civilization*, 2nd ed. (1966); D. Mack Smith, *Italy: A Modern History* (1959); A. J. May, *The Hapsburg Monarchy, 1867–1914* (1951); and H. Seton-Watson, *The Decline of Imperial Russia, 1855–1914** (1952).

2. The Growth of Democracy

The progress of political democracy in relation to rival ideologies is treated in A. Rosenberg, *Democracy and Socialism* (1939), and in J. S. Schapiro, *The World in Crisis: Political and Social Movements in the Twentieth Century* (1950). Other relevant works are J. Bowle, *Politics and Opinion in the Nineteenth Century** (1954), and C. Moraze, *The Triumph of the Middle Classes* (1966). Problems of parliamentary government in western Europe are discussed in É. Halévy, *History of the English People in the Nineteenth Century*, Vols. V and VI* (1926), and D. Thomson, *Democracy in France Since 1870,* 4th ed.* (1964). The peculiar situation in Germany is analyzed in two valuable studies by A. Rosenberg, *The Birth of the German Republic, 1871–1918** (1931), and A. Gerschenkron, *Bread and Democracy in Germany* (1943). Habsburg attempts to cope with the nationalities problem are disentangled in O. Jászi, *The Dissolution of the Habsburg Monarchy** (1929), and with emphasis on individual national groups in R. A. Kann, *The Multinational Empire,* 2 vols. (1950). The halfhearted efforts at political reform in Russia are discussed in G. Fischer, *Russian Liberalism from Gentry to Intelligentsia* (1958), and in B. Pares, *The Fall of the Russian Monarchy* (1939).

3. The "Second Industrial Revolution"

Several of the books mentioned for Chapter 25 also extend into this later period. Additional treatments for the major industrial countries are: A. L. Levine, *Industrial Retardation in Britain, 1880–1914* (1967); S. B. Clough, *France: A History of National Economics, 1789–1939* (1939); and G. Stolper, K. Häuser, and K. Borchardt, *The German Economy–1870 to the Present* (1967). M. S. Miller, *The Economic Development of Russia, 1905–1914* (1926), is more detailed, as is the distorted but informative account by P. I. Lyashchenko, *History of the National Economy of Russia to the 1917 Revolution* (1949). On European economic expansion overseas, see H. Feis, *Europe the World's Banker, 1870–1914** (1930).

4. The Rise of the Working Class

A good introduction to European radicalism is D. Caute, *The Left in Europe Since 1789** (1966). On evolutionary socialism, see P. Gay, *The Dilemma of Democratic Socialism: Eduard Bernstein's Challenge to Marx** (1952), and A. M. McBriar, *Fabian Socialism and English Politics, 1884–1918** (1962). Good surveys of international socialism are J. Joll, *The Second International, 1889–1914** (1955), and M. Beer, *Fifty Years of International Socialism* (1937). On the growth of organized labor, see W. A. McConagha, *The Development of the Labor Movement in Great Britain, France, and Germany* (1942), and H. Pelling, *The Origins of the Labour Party, 1880–1900,* 2nd ed. (1965). Social legislation before 1914 is covered in K. de Schweinitz, *England's Road to Social Security* (1943), and W. H. Dawson, *Social Insurance in Germany, 1883–1911* (1912). The influence of individual reformers in England is discussed in H. Ausubel, *In Hard Times: Reformers Among the Late Victorians* (1960), and in M. Richter, *The Politics of Conscience: T. H. Green and His Age* (1964). On the role of the churches in the field of social reform, see D. O. W. Wagner, *Church of England and Social Reform Since 1854* (1930), and J. N. Moody, ed., *Church and Society: Catholic Social and Political Thought and Movements, 1789–1950* (1953).

5. Domestic Affairs of the Major Powers

Much of this subject is covered in the works already cited. A pleasant way of supplementing the more formal accounts is by way of biographies. Among the standard lives of the great, L. Strachey,

---

* Available in paperback edition.

Queen Victoria* (1921), is a classic, though E. Longford, Queen Victoria (1965), is more reliable. R. Blake, Disraeli (1967), and P. Magnus, Gladstone (1955), are more readable than earlier standard accounts. Two great French leaders are commemorated in G. Bruun, Clemenceau (1943), and J. H. Jackson, Jean Jaurès: His Life and Work (1943). There are no comparable studies of the continental monarchs. M. Balfour, The Kaiser and his Times (1964), is entertaining, but far from definitive. J. Redlich, Emperor Francis Joseph (1929), is far too academic, and neither Nicholas II of Russia nor the kings of Italy have been found worthy of definitive biographies.

B. D. Wolfe, Three Who Made a Revolution* (1955), tells about the future rulers of Russia— Lenin, Trotsky, and Stalin—before their rise to power. The nineteenth-century background of Russia's revolutionary movement is described in E. Lampert, Studies in Rebellion (1957), and Sons Against Fathers (1965). See also A. Yarmolinsky, Road to Revolution (1957). T. H. von Laue, Sergei Witte and the Industrialization of Russia (1963), is an important contribution to Russian economic history.

Significant monographs in German history include P. G. J. Pulzer, The Rise of Political Anti-Semitism in Germany and Austria* (1964); J. C. G. Röhl, Germany Without Bismarck (1967); M. Kitchen, The German Officer Corps, 1890–1914 (1968); and G. Roth, Social Democrats in Imperial Germany (1963). For a balanced view of the most crucial event in French politics, see D. Johnson, France and the Dreyfus Affair (1967). Another phase of French politics is treated in W. C. Buthman, The Rise of Integral Nationalism in France (1939), and in M. Curtis, Three Against the Third Republic (1959), which deals with Sorel, Barrès, and Maurras. Britain on the eve of World War I is the subject of C. Cross, The Liberals in Power, 1905–1914 (1963), and S. H. Nowell-Smith, ed., Edwardian England (1964). The Italian scene is described in J. A. Thayer, Italy and the Great War: Politics and Culture, 1890–1915 (1964).

6. Intellectual History

The general works by J. H. Randall, The Making of the Modern Mind (1940), and C. Brinton, Ideas and Men (1950), have very good chapters on the intellectual life of the late nineteenth century. E. Weber, Paths to the Present: Aspects of European Thought from Romanticism to Existentialism* (1960), contains unusual selections of readings. On the history of science, see A. E. E. McKenzie, The Major Achievements of Science, 2 vols. (1960), and W. C. Dampier, A Shorter History of Science* (1957). The all-pervasive influence of Darwin is shown in P. B. Sears, Charles Darwin: The Naturalist as a Cultural Force (1950). On the contemporary impact of Darwinism, see W. Irvine, Apes, Angels, and Victorians (1955). J. Barzun, Darwin, Marx, Wagner* (1958), points out similarities in three outwardly different contemporaries. W. Bagehot, Physics and Politics* (1956), the work of a leading Social Darwinist, still makes interesting reading. The wide appeal of Social Darwinism is shown in R. Hofstadter, Social Darwinism in American Thought* (1955). H. D. Aiken, ed., The Age of Ideology* (1957), and M. White, The Age of Analysis* (1955), offer selections from leading philosophers of the nineteenth and twentieth centuries. W. Kaufmann, Nietzsche: Philosopher, Psychologist, Antichrist* (1956), is the best book on the most influential of these philosophers.

The classic study on the literature of the period is G. Brandes, Main Currents in Nineteenth-Century Literature, 6 vols. (1923). Briefer and more pertinent is E. Wilson, Axel's Castle: A Study in the Imaginative Literature of 1870–1930* (1958). For the impact of science on literature, see M. Nicolson, Science and Imagination (1956). The beautifully illustrated volume by M. Raynal, The Nineteenth Century: New Sources of Emotion from Goya to Gauguin (1951), shows the transition from traditional to modern art. H. Leichtentritt, Music, History, and Ideas (1938), and C. Gray, History of Music (1947), discuss new trends in music.

---

* Available in paperback edition.

14

The Struggle for a European Equilibrium, 1871–1914

In reviewing the diplomatic history of Europe and the world between 1871 and 1914, we must remember the political, economic, and cultural trends that we noted in the preceding chapter. The spirit of competition that pervaded relations among individuals and classes had its parallel in the political and economic rivalry among nations. Many international crises arose directly out of domestic tensions. Had the internal affairs of the powers before 1914 been more harmonious, international affairs might have been more peaceful.

Our view of international relations after 1870 is conditioned by our knowledge of what happened in 1914. Most historians today agree that, while some of the immediate causes that brought about war in 1914 could have been avoided, its real causes lay far deeper and defy any clear apportionment of responsibility among nations and individuals. To understand how deep the roots of the war went, we must remember the far-reaching effects that the unification of Italy and Germany had had on the European balance of power. Two regions that heretofore had been mere pawns in international affairs now had suddenly emerged as great powers. The

political and territorial framework of the Continent thus had lost much of its former elasticity. The only region in Europe where major changes were still possible was the Balkan Peninsula. Austria-Hungary, now excluded from German and Italian affairs, claimed the Balkans as her natural sphere of influence. Since Russia and to a lesser extent Italy made the same claim, the Balkans became the scene of recurrent international crises.

Another source of international tension was the growing colonial rivalry among the powers. With chances for territorial expansion on the Continent restricted, and with expanding economies clamoring for markets and raw materials, colonial conflicts injected an element of constant friction into international affairs. An added cause for tension was nationalism. As long as members of one nationality were subjected to domination by another, as was especially the case in the multinational empires of Austria-Hungary and Turkey, the peace of Europe remained precarious at best.

The Age of Bismarck, 1871–90

Despite the unsettling effects of Italian and German unification, Europe at first managed to adjust peacefully to the changed situation. The

Bismarck, the "European Equilibrist," posed on a seesaw between War and Peace, juggles the great powers in his "League of Peace."

Bismarck

PRO

Bismarck is generally described in the textbooks as the first *Realpolitiker*; but unfortunately so much has been written about *Realpolitik* that its meaning has become obscure and mixed up with blood and iron and incitement to war by the malicious revision of royal telegrams. . . . It may be permissible to suggest that the essence of Bismarck's realism was his recognition of the limitations of his craft, and that it was this, coupled with the passion and the responsibility that he brought to his vocation, that made him a great statesman.

CON

Himself always plotting combinations against others, Bismarck was convinced that all the world was plotting combinations against him and lived in a half-mad imaginary world in which every statesman was as subtle and calculating, as ruthless and assiduous as he was himself. . . . At bottom he was a barbarian of genius, mastering in the highest degree the mechanical and intellectual side of civilization, altogether untouched by its spirit.

From Gordon A. Craig, *From Bismarck to Adenauer* (Baltimore: Johns Hopkins, 1958), p. 28; A. J. P. Taylor, *The Course of German History* (New York: Coward-McCann, 1946), pp. 95–96.

chief credit for the relative stability that prevailed for the two decades after 1871 belongs to Count Bismarck. The fundamental aim of the German chancellor was the consolidation of the new German *Reich*. For this he needed peace. Bismarck considered Germany a "satiated" power, with no further territorial ambitions. The main threat to her security was France's desire for revenge. To keep France isolated, therefore, became the guiding principle of Bismarck's foreign policy.

The basic moderation of the German chancellor's aims and the consummate skill of his diplomacy rightly command admiration. They show that *Realpolitik* need not necessarily rely on "blood and iron" but can use with equal effect peaceful pressure and persuasion. Yet in merely trying to maintain existing conditions and ignoring those forces that were straining against the *status quo*—notably nationalism and imperialism—Bismarck showed the same blindness that had characterized Metternich before him. Admirable as the Bismarckian system was, it was to fall to pieces as soon as the masterful guidance of its creator was removed.

The "Three Emperors' League"

The first of Bismarck's many international agreements was concluded in 1872 among Germany, Austria, and Russia. The *Dreikaiserbund* tried to revive the collaboration that had existed in the days of the "Holy Alliance." But the feeling of solidarity that had animated the three conservative powers in the days of Metternich had since given way to mutual rivalries. Russia, in particular, had never forgiven Austria her "ingratitude" during the Crimean War, and she now resented the leadership that Germany assumed within the new Three Emperors' League. A first sign of disagreement between Germany and Russia appeared during the so-called war-in-sight crisis of 1875, when rumors that Germany was planning a preventive war against France brought heavy protests from England and Russia. Bismarck's role in fomenting the crisis is not quite clear, though there is no evidence that he was seriously considering war against France. Russia's policy, therefore, seemed unnecessarily meddlesome, especially in view of her traditional friendship with Prussia. The monarchical front had shown itself far from solid.

The Russo-Turkish War and the Congress of Berlin

A far more serious rift within the Three Emperors' League developed out of Russia's ambitions in the Balkans. The inefficiency and corruption of the disintegrating Ottoman Empire had invited intervention several times before, most recently during the Crimean War. In 1875 new revolts against Turkish misrule broke out in the Balkans. The Turks acted with their usual ferocity in putting down these nationalist uprisings and would have held the upper hand if Russia, in the spring of 1877, had not joined

The Treaty of San Stefano   1878

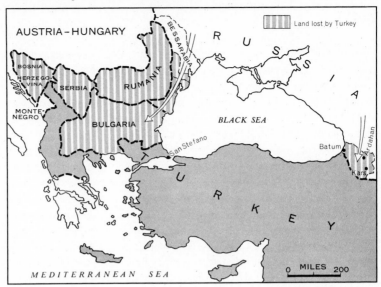

The Congress of Berlin   1878

the insurgents. She did so after making sure of Austrian neutrality and recognizing in return Austria's right to occupy the Turkish provinces of Bosnia and Herzegovina. In addition, Russia promised not to support the formation of any large Balkan state.

The Russo-Turkish War, after some reversals, ended in Russian victory. In a treaty signed at

San Stefano in March 1878, several of Turkey's subject nationalities were granted independence. Among them was to be a large Bulgarian state, which Russia was to occupy for several years. In addition, Russia was to get some territorial compensations. This startling increase of Russian influence in the Balkans deeply alarmed the other great powers. It was due to their pressure that

Russia finally agreed to submit the settlement to an international conference at Berlin in June 1878.

Most of the important decisions of the Congress of Berlin were actually reached in preliminary agreements, which the Congress then confirmed. The proposed Greater Bulgaria was divided into three parts, leaving only a small Bulgarian state; Serbia, Montenegro, and Rumania were granted full independence; Austria was given the right to occupy and administer Bosnia and Herzegovina; and England was given control over the island of Cyprus. Russia rightly felt that she had been cheated out of her victory. While England and Austria made substantial gains, Russia had to be satisfied with Bessarabia and some gains in the Caucasus. The Russians blamed their defeat on Bismarck, who, they held, had violated his self-styled role as "honest broker" by favoring the interests of Russia's adversaries. The Congress of Berlin thus provoked a serious crisis in the relations between Germany and Russia and ended the Three Emperors' League.

The Austro-German Alliance

The break-up of the Three Emperors' League forced Bismarck to find a substitute. This he did in a secret alliance with Austria. The Dual Alliance of 1879 was the climax of Germany's *rapprochement* with Austria that had been Bismarck's concern since 1866. The alliance was renewed periodically and remained in force until 1918. Its provisions were purely defensive, calling for mutual aid if either member was attacked by Russia. Bismarck has been criticized for thus tying Germany's fate to the ramshackle Dual Monarchy. But he did not necessarily envisage the alliance as permanent, and he thought Germany strong enough to keep Austria's ambitions in the Balkans in check so as to avoid a showdown with Russia. Nor did the union with Austria mean that Germany was ready to sever relations with Russia altogether. Bismarck expected that Russia, unable for ideological reasons to draw closer to republican France, and separated from England by rivalries in Asia, would feel sufficiently isolated to desire a renewal of her former ties with Germany. Bismarck's assumption proved correct.

The Second "Three Emperors' League"

Russia would have preferred a treaty with Germany alone, but Bismarck insisted that Austria be included as well. A new Three Emperors' League was finally concluded in 1881. It provided that in case one of the members became involved in war with a fourth power, the other two would remain neutral. Bismarck's fear that Russia might join France in a war against Germany was thus relieved. The most important provisions of the treaty dealt with the Balkans: Any territorial changes in that region henceforth were to require the consent of all three powers; Austria was given the right to annex Bosnia and Herzegovina at a time of her own choosing; and Russia's wish for the eventual union of Bulgaria and Eastern Roumelia (one of the regions separated from Greater Bulgaria at Berlin) was recognized. By thus dividing the Balkans into spheres of influence, the Balkan problem seemed finally to have been brought under control. The new arrangement, however, overlooked the national aspirations of the Balkan peoples themselves.

The Triple Alliance

Before the Balkan question became acute once more in 1885, Bismarck had further extended his diplomatic structure with the Triple Alliance between Germany, Austria, and Italy in 1882. The initiative this time came from the Italians. Italy for some time had hoped to enhance her status as a great power by occupying the Turkish region of Tunis in North Africa. She was deeply distressed, therefore, when the French took Tunis in 1881. To strengthen her diplomatic position for the future, Italy now sought closer ties with Austria and Germany. Like the rest of Bismarck's treaties, the Triple Alliance was primarily defensive. Bismarck never took it very seriously, except for the fact that it further contributed to the diplomatic isolation of France.

The years immediately after 1882 mark the high point of Bismarck's influence in Europe.

Bismarck, after his retirement, approaches the imperial castle in Berlin on the arm of the Kaiser's brother for reconciliation with William II.

French nationalism appeared to have been successfully diverted into colonial channels in North Africa; the situation in the Balkans appeared under control; and Austria's position had been strengthened by a secret treaty with Serbia in 1881 which made Austria the protector of her small neighbor. In 1883 Rumania concluded an alliance with Austria, to which Germany adhered later. The treaty was chiefly directed against Russian ambitions in the Balkans, where a new crisis flared up in 1885.

The Reinsurance Treaty

The details of this latest Balkan crisis need not concern us here. It was touched off by an upsurge of Bulgarian nationalism in Eastern Roumelia, leading to the reunion of that region with Bulgaria. During the ensuing wrangle the Three Emperors' League met its final fate. For some time Russian nationalists, resenting German support of Austria in the Balkans, had demanded that Russia seek the friendship of France. Bismarck's worst fears thus seemed about

to come true. But the tsarist government was reluctant to cut its connections with Berlin. Russia, therefore, proposed to the Germans that they enter into an agreement without Austria. The upshot was the so-called Reinsurance Treaty of 1887, which provided for benevolent neutrality in case either partner became involved in war, unless Germany attacked France or Russia attacked Austria. The Reinsurance Treaty also recognized Russia's interests in Bulgaria and the Turkish Straits.

This last of Bismarck's major treaties has been both hailed as a diplomatic masterpiece and condemned as an act of duplicity. It certainly did run counter to the spirit, if not the letter, of the Dual Alliance. But while Bismarck encouraged Russia's Balkan ambitions, he at the same time put an obstacle in the way of these ambitions by sponsoring the so-called Mediterranean Agreements between England, Italy, and Austria. Signed also in 1887, these agreements called for the maintenance of the *status quo* in the Mediterranean, including the Balkans. Any promises Bismarck had made to Russia concerning Bulgaria and the Straits were thus successfully neutralized.

In making a fair appraisal of Bismarck's diplomacy, we must go beyond a mere comparison of treaty texts and consider the motives behind his treaties. These invariably were to maintain peace. Bismarck hoped to achieve this aim by isolating France and balancing the rest of the powers so that any unilateral disturbance of the peace would automatically result in a hostile coalition against the aggressor. Seen in this light, Bismarck's policy was less crafty than it appeared when the world first learned about the Reinsurance Treaty after the chancellor's retirement. A more valid criticism one can make of Bismarck's policy is that it was far too complicated to be successful in the long run and that it rested too narrowly on the attitudes of Europe's statesmen rather than on the sentiments of their peoples. In an age of democracy and nationalism, such disregard of public opinion became increasingly difficult.

From European to World Politics

One of the most important trends in international affairs since Bismarck's time has been the growing involvement of Europe in world affairs. This development had started much earlier, of course; but it was only at the end of the nineteenth century that events in Europe and overseas became so intricately interwoven that the histories of Europe and the world could no longer be treated separately.

The "New Imperialism"

The expansion of European influence in the late nineteenth century is often called the "new imperialism," to distinguish it from earlier phases of overseas expansion. Its motives were similar to those we found earlier in the century, although they now operated with far greater intensity. Imperialism in the past had been chiefly limited in its appeal to the upper classes. Now suddenly it became of vital concern to everyone. More than any other movement, the new imperialism

expressed the most characteristic elements of the period before 1914. Aggressive nationalism, ruthless economic competition, the restless struggle for success, all found an outlet in the scramble for overseas colonies and concessions, protectorates and spheres of influence. Here was an opportunity for men of daring and initiative to suffer hardships in distant lands not merely to advance their own fortunes but also, as they never tired telling the world, to undertake a "civilizing mission" for the good of mankind. Among the many driving forces behind the new imperialism, this "aggressive altruism" was one of the most potent.

England continued to lead in the new imperialism as she had in the old. After a period of declining interest in overseas expansion, Britain resumed her imperialist course after 1870. By 1914 she controlled one-fifth of the world's land and one-fourth of its population. The second largest colonial empire in 1914, that of France, had been acquired almost entirely during the nineteenth century. In her expansion into North Africa, France became involved first with England over Egypt and the Sudan, and then, after the turn of the century, with Germany over Morocco. Germany, prior to 1880, had no overseas possessions, and Bismarck was slow to enter the colonial race. When he finally did, beginning in 1884, it was chiefly to enhance Germany's bargaining position in Europe. It was under William II that Germany was launched in earnest on a course of *Weltpolitik,* in pursuit of which she provoked several international crises. Similar friction was caused by Italy's belated claims to colonies. Russia, as in the past, confined her expansion to adjacent areas in Asia. The only major power refraining from colonial expansion was Austria.

The Conquest of Africa

The most spectacular expansion of European influence after 1870 took place in Africa. To simplify the complicated story of the scramble for African territory, we will discuss events in the northern, central, and southern regions

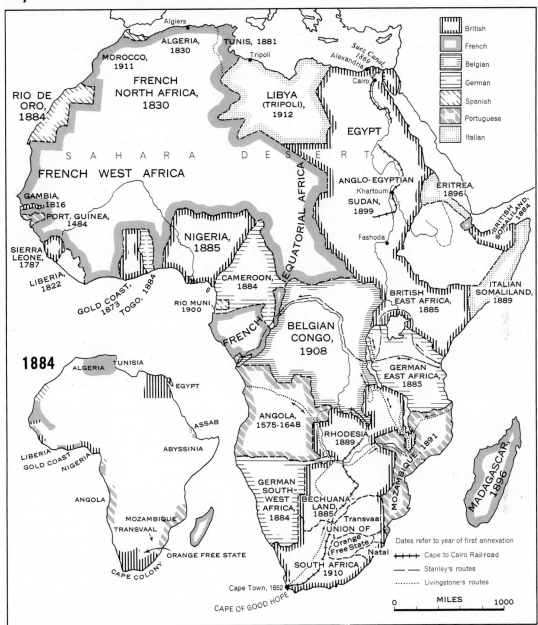

The map shows European colonial claims in Africa. Legend: British, French, Belgian, German, Spanish, Portuguese, Italian.

ALGERIA, 1830
TUNIS, 1881
MOROCCO, 1911
FRENCH NORTH AFRICA, 1830
RIO DE ORO, 1884
LIBYA (TRIPOLI), 1912
Suez Canal, 1869
Algiers
Tripoli
Alexandria
Cairo
EGYPT
SAHARA DESERT
FRENCH WEST AFRICA
ANGLO-EGYPTIAN SUDAN, 1899
Khartoum
ERITREA, 1896
BRITISH SOMALILAND, 1884
GAMBIA, 1816
PORT. GUINEA, 1484
NIGERIA, 1885
Fashoda
SIERRA LEONE, 1787
LIBERIA, 1822
GOLD COAST, 1873
TOGO, 1884
CAMEROON, 1884
RIO MUNI, 1900
FRENCH EQUATORIAL AFRICA
BRITISH EAST AFRICA, 1885
ITALIAN SOMALILAND, 1889
BELGIAN CONGO, 1908
GERMAN EAST AFRICA, 1885
ANGOLA, 1575-1648
RHODESIA, 1889
MOZAMBIQUE, 1891
MADAGASCAR, 1896
GERMAN SOUTH-WEST AFRICA, 1884
BECHUANA-LAND, 1885
Transvaal
UNION OF SOUTH AFRICA, 1910
Orange Free State
Natal
Cape Town, 1652
CAPE OF GOOD HOPE

1884
ALGERIA
TUNISIA
EGYPT
ASSAB
ABYSSINIA
LIBERIA
GOLD COAST
NIGERIA
ANGOLA
MOZAMBIQUE
TRANSVAAL
ORANGE FREE STATE
CAPE COLONY

Dates refer to year of first annexation
+++ Cape to Cairo Railroad
— — — Stanley's routes
········· Livingstone's routes

0   MILES   1000

separately. But we must remember that many of these developments actually happened simultaneously.

North Africa

The Mediterranean coast of Africa, since the seventh century, had been under the influence of Moslem civilization; since the early sixteenth century, it had been under the direct or indirect rule of the Ottoman Empire. France gained her first foothold in North Africa with the acquisition of Algiers in 1830. In the course of the century she extended her sphere of influence inland and in time Algeria became an integral part of France. The next major move came with the establishment of a French protectorate over Algeria's eastern neighbor, Tunis, in 1881. Subsequently France began extending her influence westward over the sultanate of Morocco. The situation here was complicated by the fact that several other powers, notably Germany, also had economic interests in that region. A French protectorate over Morocco was thus not won until 1911, and then only after two major international crises.

Egypt and the Sudan

While France was establishing herself in the western half of North Africa, the British were doing the same in Egypt and the Sudan. Egypt in 1870 was still nominally part of the Turkish Empire. Its gradual subjugation to foreign control was due to reckless borrowing of foreign money at prohibitive interest rates. When the Egyptian government, in 1876, suspended interest payments on some of its foreign obligations, Britain and France, the leading creditors, established a dual control over Egypt's finances. The subsequent rise in taxes infuriated the Egyptian taxpayer. To counteract a rising tide of Egyptian nationalism, Britain, in 1882, occupied Egypt. As a result, Anglo-French dual control over Egypt came to an end.

France, needless to say, resented her exclusion from Egypt and on every occasion tried to put obstacles in England's way. Tension between the two powers was aggravated by their rivalry over the Sudan. This Egyptian dependency had won temporary independence in 1885. But when France and Belgium began advancing toward the Sudan from central Africa, British and Egyptian forces in 1896 started to retake the region. The climax of their expedition came in 1898 when British and French forces met at Fashoda on the Upper Nile. As both Britain and France now laid claim to the Sudan, war seemed imminent. But the French government, troubled by the Dreyfus affair at home and inferior in naval strength, finally had to give in and leave England in control. In 1899 Egypt and England established joint control over what came to be known as the Anglo-Egyptian Sudan.

There remained one stretch of land along the Mediterranean that had not as yet come under foreign control—the region of Tripoli between Egypt and Tunis. It was of little value, consisting largely of desert. But in an age when overseas expansion was a matter of prestige, even so poor a prize seemed worth taking. After making certain of French support by recognizing France's claims in Morocco, Italy in 1911–12 waged war against Turkey and annexed Tripoli. The Italian colony of Libya, as it was called, was one of the least lucrative of imperialist ventures. But it was a source of great pride to the Italians.

Central Africa

As we turn to central Africa, we must realize that very little of it had been explored before the second half of the nineteenth century. Among the most famous explorers of the region were David Livingstone and Henry Morton Stanley. Livingstone, a Scottish missionary, spent almost thirty years in Africa. When he failed to return from his third and last major expedition in 1871, Stanley, a British-born American journalist, was sent to find him. Stanley's successful search for Livingstone gave him a taste for exploration that made him the leading explorer of the Congo region. After vainly seeking to interest the British in his plans for opening up the Congo, Stanley found a sponsor in King Leopold II of Belgium. Leopold's claims to the Congo Free State were recognized by an international conference at Berlin in 1885. For the next twenty years a policy of the most ruthless colonial exploitation made a vast fortune for Leopold's various enterprises. Only after these brutal methods were revealed was control over the Congo transferred to the Belgian state in 1908.

The practice whereby enterprising individuals staked out claims that were later protected by their governments was also used to great advantage by the Germans. Beginning in 1884 the German government took over the rights that various German merchants and explorers had staked out over large parts of southwest, central, and east Africa. The British tried to discourage these German moves. When this attempt proved fruitless, they moved quickly to stake out their own claims for the interior of the continent. France, in return for relinquishing some rights on the mainland, was given a free hand on the island of Madagascar. Italy acquired Eritrea and Somaliland at the southern end of the Red Sea in 1890. Attempts to extend Italy's holdings inland into Abyssinia were stopped by Ethiopian forces in the Battle of Adua (1896).

South Africa

Some of the events just described actually took place in the southern part of the continent. Here Britain had acquired the Dutch Cape Colony in 1806. As a result of tension between the new British immigrants and the original Dutch settlers, or Boers, the latter, beginning in the 1830's, had moved northward, founding two new Dutch colonies, the Orange Free State and the Transvaal. Britain recognized the independence of these republics in 1852. With the subsequent discovery of diamonds and gold in these regions, however, the inhabitants of the Cape Colony began to call for an extension of British sovereignty over the Boer republics.

The leading advocate of Britain's South African interests in the late nineteenth century was Cecil Rhodes. A typical "empire builder," Rhodes owned extensive interests in South Africa's diamond and gold fields. He became prime minister of the Cape Colony in 1890. Meanwhile the new discovery of gold in the Transvaal in 1886 had touched off a veritable British invasion into the region. To discourage this foreign influx, the president of the Transvaal, Paul Krüger, placed heavy restrictions on British immigrants. One of the more spectacular incidents in the growing tension between Britons and Boers was the abortive Jameson Raid at the turn of the year 1895–96, an attempt by one of Rhodes' associates to start a revolution among the British minority in the Transvaal. An ill-advised telegram from the German kaiser congratulating Krüger on his defeat of the plot cast a deep shadow on Anglo-German relations at the time.

Finally, in 1899 tension between the Boers and the British led to war. It took Britain two and a half years to defeat the tenacious Boers.

Sir Henry Morton Stanley (1841–1904), the Welsh-American journalist and explorer who was responsible for opening up much of the interior of the "Dark Continent."

Not until 1902 did the Boers lay down their arms, and then only on the promise of very lenient peace terms. As a result of this leniency, the issues of the past were quickly forgotten. When the Union of South Africa was formed in 1910, a former Boer general became the first prime minister of this newest self-governing dominion.

The New Imperialism in Asia and the Pacific

The sudden outburst of imperialism after 1880 also affected Asia and the Pacific. In contrast to Africa, large parts of this region had been under European domination for some tine. We have already discussed developments in India and China (see pp. 328–34); we shall now turn to the rest of the continent and to the Pacific islands.

Russia in Asia

One of the principal powers with interests in Asia was Russia. Her advances there took three main directions: to the southwest into the Near East—the Ottoman Empire and especially the region around the entrance to the Black Sea; to the Far East—Siberia and the adjacent coastal regions of China; and to the Middle East —Afghanistan and Persia. Foremost among Russia's aims in the Near and Far East was to find outlets to the sea that would enable her to escape her land-locked position. Attempts to do so in the Near East, as we have seen, were met by resistance from the other great powers, notably England. Whenever she met with a setback, as in 1878, Russia shifted her attention from west to east, from Europe to Asia.

Russian expansion into Siberia had proceeded slowly but steadily for more than three centuries. It was greatly facilitated by the acquisition of a section of China's coast along the Sea of Japan in 1860 and the founding of the Pacific port of Vladivostok. Russia's aim was to expand southward across the Amur River into Manchuria and then into Korea. But as we have seen, her plans were foiled by the conflicting interests of Japan. As a result of the Russo-Japanese War, Russia's territorial position in the Far East in 1905 was substantially what it had been fifty years earlier. Her failures in the Far East in part explain her renewed interest in the affairs of Europe and the Near East during the last decade before the First World War.

Anglo-Russian Rivalry

In the third sphere of Russian expansion, the Middle East and central Asia, Russia made considerable progress during the nineteenth century. By 1880 the whole region north of Persia and Afghanistan had become Russian. This extension of Russian power was watched with growing apprehension by Great Britain, who feared that Russia's advance was ultimately directed at India. The mountainous country of Afghanistan served as a buffer against a possible invasion of India from the northwest. In 1879 England had overthrown the pro-Russian ruler of Afghanistan and had occupied most of the country. But British-Russian rivalry continued. It was not resolved until 1907, when Russia finally recognized England's predominant position in Afghanistan.

Another scene of Anglo-Russian rivalry was Persia. The contest here was primarily economic, with both Russian and British interests seeking concessions. But England also feared that Persia might serve as another approach to India. The details of the drawn-out struggle over Persia need not concern us here. Differences in Persia, as in Afghanistan, were settled by the Anglo-Russian Entente in 1907.

This encroachment of the great powers on hitherto sovereign states was typical of much of European imperialism in Asia. We have already seen examples of it in the gradual subjection of China to foreign tutelage during the second half of the nineteenth century. Another example was Siam. The French, after extending their protectorate over Indochina during the 1880's, turned their attention westward. Here they came in conflict with the English, who were interested in Siam because it bordered on Burma, which Britain had taken in 1852. After a certain amount of controversy, Siam in 1896 was made into a neutral buffer state between Burma and Indochina.

The Pacific

The most valuable islands of the Pacific had already been taken long before 1870. The rivalry of the powers over the few remaining little islands was a sign of how intense the imperialist urge had become. The main contestants in the Pacific were England and Germany, with the United States and France intervening occasionally. It is unnecessary to enumerate all the bits and pieces of land picked up by these powers. The most important, besides America's annexation of the Philippines, was the acquisition of eastern New Guinea by England and Germany in 1884. The most serious crisis arose over the Samoan Islands, which were claimed by Britain, Germany, and the United States. After ten years of intermittent dispute, the islands were divided in 1899 between the United States and Germany, with England receiving compensations in the Solomons.

The United States as a World Power

America's role in the controversy over Samoa was part of her involvement in the imperialist rivalries of the great powers. Developments in the United States during the period before 1914 were remarkably similar to developments in Europe. In the political sphere, there was less need for further democratization than there was in some European countries, although the success of the Populists in the 1890's and of the Progressive Party in 1912 showed that there were many Americans who felt their interests neglected under the two-party system. In the economic sphere, the United States shared fully in the industrial expansion that took place in Europe, and by 1914 America led the world in the production of coal, iron, and petroleum. In trying to cope with the social and economic problems resulting from rapid industrialization, the activities of both the labor unions and the government, in America as in Europe, brought a marked improvement of the worker's status. The efforts of Theodore Roosevelt, after the turn of the century, to secure a "square deal" for the workingman, and his attempts at "trust busting," helped to bridge the gap between capital and labor. Despite the opposition of many Americans to governmental intervention in economic affairs, the United States showed the same tendency toward becoming a "welfare state" that we found in most European countries. In the one field in which American business had welcomed government interference—tariff legislation—the trend by 1914 was in the direction of lower tariffs. This was a sign that American industry had come of age and that it was ready to compete with foreign imports on the home market.

The Spanish-American War

America at the end of the nineteenth century thus shared most of the major tendencies of Europe. This was nowhere more evident than in foreign affairs. Agitation during the 1890's to annex Hawaii and to construct a canal across Central America ran parallel to European expansionism during the same period. Under the administration of Grover Cleveland, such expansionist sentiments were kept under control. His successor, William McKinley, however, was less able to resist the pressures of American nationalism. One of the main subjects of agitation at the time was Cuba, where a revolt against Spanish rule had started in 1895. American sentiment sided with the Cuban rebels and demanded that the United States go to their aid. When the

President McKinley and the Philippines

I have been criticized a good deal about the Philippines, but I don't deserve it. The truth is, I didn't want the Philippines, and when they came to us, as a gift from the gods, I did not know what to do with them. . . . I walked the floor of the White House night after night until midnight; and I am not ashamed to tell you, gentlemen, that I went down on my knees and prayed Almighty God for light and guidance. And one night late it came to me this way—I don't know how it was, but it came: (1) That we could not give them back to Spain—that would be cowardly and dishonorable; (2) that we could not turn them over to France or Germany— that would be bad business and discreditable; (3) that we could not leave them to govern themselves—they were unfit for self-government . . . and (4) that there was nothing left for us to do but to take them all, and to educate the Philippinos, and uplift and civilize and Christianize them, and, by God's grace, do the very best we could by them, as our fellow men for whom Christ also died. And then I went to bed, and went to sleep, and slept soundly, and next morning I sent for the chief engineer of the War Department (our map-maker), and told him to put the Philippines on the map of the United States.

From William McKinley as quoted in G. A. Malcolm and M. M. Kalaw, *Philippine Government* (Manila: Associated Publishers, 1923), pp. 65–66.

American forces landing at a Cuban port during the Spanish-American War.

U.S.S. "Maine" mysteriously exploded in Havana harbor in early 1898, the clamor for war became too strong to be resisted any longer.

The Spanish-American War was the first war between the United States and a European power since 1814. The United States had little difficulty in winning the "splendid little war" against Spain. In the peace treaty signed at Paris in December 1898, the United States obtained Puerto Rico, the Philippines, and Guam. Cuba received her independence, though the Platt Amendment, adopted by Congress in 1901, made her a virtual American protectorate.

America made her influence felt in the Far East and elsewhere in other ways as well. In 1898 the United States finally annexed Hawaii, and in the following year she divided the Samoan Islands with Germany. Also in 1899, Secretary of State John Hay proclaimed the "open door" policy in regard to China, and in 1900 an American contingent participated in a joint expedition of the powers to put down the Boxer Rebellion in that country. The United States also sent delegates to the First Hague Peace Conference in 1899, at which a Permanent Court of International Arbitration was created; and in 1905 President Roosevelt helped settle the Russo-Japanese War in the Treaty of Portsmouth.

The United States and Latin America

America's first and foremost concern, however, was with affairs closer to home. Theodore Roosevelt in particular had long favored an active American policy in Central America. The Hay-Pauncefote Treaty of 1901 secured British consent for the construction of an American canal across the isthmus. In 1903 Panama, in a revolt supported by American interests, seceded from Colombia and the United States was able to acquire the necessary land for its canal. The Panama Canal was opened shortly after the outbreak of war in 1914.

One of the chief dangers to peace in Latin America came from the loans that European investors in search of large profits had granted to the dictators of that region. Failures to meet payments invariably led to foreign intervention and threatened violations of the Monroe Doctrine. In 1902, Germany, Italy, and Great Britain sent warships to force Venezuela to pay her debts. Two years later another group of powers moved against the Dominican Republic. As a warning, and to forestall European intervention, the United States, in 1904, proclaimed the Roosevelt Corollary to the Monroe Doctrine. It reserved the right to exercise international police power in the Western Hemisphere exclusively to the United States. In line with her new policy, America sent marines to Cuba in 1906 and to Nicaragua in 1912.

The motive for America's intervention on these occasions was not merely to maintain order but to protect her own financial interests. This "dollar diplomacy," as its opponents called it, caused much resentment in the countries concerned and among the other great powers. America's policy, her Latin American neighbors charged, despite idealistic pronouncements, was every bit as imperialistic as that of the rest of the powers.

The Formation of the Triple Entente, 1890–1907

The events outside Europe that we have discussed in the preceding pages provide the background for the diplomatic realignment of Europe after 1890 and the succession of international crises that culminated in the First World War.

The Franco-Russian Alliance

When Bismarck was dismissed in 1890, his complicated diplomatic system did not long survive. To start with, William II followed the advice of some of Bismarck's more timid underlings and refused to renew the Reinsurance Treaty with Russia. The cutting of Bismarck's "wire to St. Petersburg" did not by itself make the subsequent *rapprochement* between Russia and France inevitable. Only when Germany continued to show deliberate coolness toward her former friend while drawing closer to England did Russia begin to listen to French suggestions for a better understanding. The Anglo-German Heligoland Treaty of 1890, by which Germany surrendered large claims in East Africa to England in return for the small strategic island of Heligoland in the North Sea, was generally

interpreted as a sign of German eagerness to oblige England. At the same time, a tariff war was impairing Russo-German commercial relations, and an increase in Germany's armed forces was seen as preparation for a possible war on two fronts. Germany's policy toward Russia, it seemed, was undergoing a complete reorientation.

Even so, Russia was slow to respond to France's overtures. The main obstacle was the differences between their autocratic and republican systems of government. It took four years of deliberations before a final agreement was reached. On January 4, 1894, France and Russia signed a secret military convention that amounted to an alliance. It was designed as a counterpart to the Triple Alliance. Like the latter, the Franco-Russian alliance was defensive in intent. It protected France against an attack by Germany, or by Italy supported by Germany; and it protected Russia against an attack by Germany, or by Austria supported by Germany.

By the middle of the 1890's, therefore, we find two sets of European alliances side by side. This did not mean, however, that the Continent had been split in two. There were many subsequent occasions when Russia cooperated with Germany and Austria, or when Germany cooperated with Russia and France. International rivalries for the next decade shifted almost entirely to regions outside Europe. Both French and Russian interests in many parts of the world conflicted with those of Great Britain; and Germany, unable to tie England as closely to her side as she wished, now frequently joined the two in opposing British aims. Faced by the discomforting possibility of a continental alliance against her, it was Britain rather than Germany who had cause to be alarmed by the new alignment of powers.

Britain's Colonial Rivalries

The regions over which Britain came into conflict with one or several of the continental powers during the 1890's were chiefly the Near and Far East, the Sudan, and South Africa. In the Near East the source of trouble, as usual, was the disintegrating Ottoman Empire. Beginning in 1894 a series of Armenian uprisings against Turkish repression were put down with the massacre of thousands of Armenians. England tried repeatedly to intervene, and Lord Salisbury on two occasions suggested plans for partitioning the Ottoman Empire. But rival interests among the powers and suspicion of British motives prevented what might well have been a final solution of the troubles of the Near East. The situation was further complicated by an insurrection on the island of Crete in 1897 in favor of union with Greece. In the resulting war between Greece and Turkey, the British supported the Greeks, but the rest of the powers prevented any aid from reaching Greece. The Turks remained victorious, though the powers succeeded in obtaining autonomy for Crete.

While Britain thus found herself at cross-purposes with the rest of Europe in the Near East, Germany took advantage of the various crises in that region to advance her own economic interests. The main instrument of her push to the southeast was to be a Berlin-to-Baghdad railway, for which the sultan granted a concession in 1899. In 1898, Emperor William, on a visit to Damascus, proclaimed himself the friend of the world's 300 million Moslems. Germany appeared well on the way toward replacing England as the protector of Turkey.

In the Far East the first serious differences between England and the three continental powers came as a result of the Sino-Japanese War in 1895. When Russia, Germany, and France asked British participation in forcing Japan to give up most of the territory she had taken from China, Britain refused, thus allowing the rest of the powers, notably Russia, to strengthen their hold over China. In the subsequent scramble for concessions, Russia, France, and Germany gained at the expense of England's hitherto unchallenged dominance in China.

To understand the full extent of Britain's troubles we must realize that all the time she was losing ground in the Near and Far East the situation in Africa was even more serious. First there was the trouble with Germany over the kaiser's "Krüger telegram"; then came the showdown with France over the Sudan; and finally,

in 1899 the Boer War broke out. During that war Britain was without a single friend, and it is surprising that Russian proposals for a continental coalition in favor of the Boers did not materialize. The plan failed because of Germany's insistence that the three powers first guarantee each other's own territories in Europe. This would have meant French renunciation of Alsace-Lorraine.

In view of England's many predicaments, it is understandable that she should look for some way out of her no longer splendid isolation. The obvious choice for a possible ally, considering Britain's many points of friction with France and Russia, was Germany. So in 1898, England began to sound out Germany on a closer understanding.

Britain Abandons Isolation

The main reason for the failure of the Anglo-German negotiations was the reluctance of the Germans to abandon what they considered an unusually favorable position between the Franco-Russian and British camps. Overestimating Britain's eagerness to come to an understanding and underestimating Britain's ability to find friends elsewhere, Germany's foreign secretary Bernhard von Bülow, and his chief adviser, Baron Holstein, made demands on England that she was unwilling to meet. Britain was primarily interested in enlisting German support against further Russian encroachment in the Far East. Germany, on the other hand, was chiefly worried about a war between Russia and Austria in which Germany might become involved and for which she wanted British aid. Britain, however, refused to extend her commitments to eastern Europe where, as a naval power, she could not be of much use anyway.

When Anglo-German negotiations finally broke down in 1901, England turned elsewhere. In 1902 she concluded an alliance with Japan. This did not end England's isolation in Europe, but it fulfilled its main purpose—to stop Russia's advance in the Far East. Two years later Japan took advantage of this situation and in the Russo-Japanese War destroyed Russian sea power in the Pacific (see p. 335). Japan thus emerged as the dominant power in the Far East.

Before the showdown between Russia and Japan, England had already taken another step, this time in Europe, to escape her isolation. The *rapprochement* between England and France had several causes. As far as England was concerned, she had long been irked by her dependence on Germany, which the latter used on every possible occasion to wring concessions from the British. By settling her long-standing differences with France, Britain not only hoped to find support against Germany but also to allay once and for all her fear of a continental alliance against her. France for her part also felt a need for new friends. Her alliance with Russia had proved disappointing, especially during the Fashoda crisis, when the Russians had refused to back up their ally. After Fashoda, France had turned her attention once more to the Continent. The aim of her nationalistic foreign minister, Théophile Delcassé, was to strengthen France's position by improving her relations with powers other than Germany. He had taken a first step in this direction in 1902 by concluding a secret agreement with Italy. In return for French support of Italian ambitions in North Africa, the Italians promised to remain neutral in case France became involved in a defensive war, even if France "as the result of a direct provocation" should find it necessary to declare such a war herself. France had thus found a new friend and the Triple Alliance had been seriously weakened.

A far greater achievement of Delcassé, however, was the Entente Cordiale between France and England. The Anglo-French agreement of 1904 settled the main colonial differences that had hitherto disturbed relations between the two countries, especially in Africa. Most important was France's recognition of England's interests in Egypt and Britain's recognition of French interests in Morocco. The agreement was merely a "friendly understanding." It was not an alliance, and it need never have assumed the character of one had it not been for the careless actions of Germany.

The First Moroccan Crisis

The Germans, understandably alarmed by the agreement between France and Britain, de-cided to test the strength of the Entente. In March 1905 William II, on a visit to Tangier in Spanish Morocco, proclaimed Germany's continued support of Moroccan independence and served notice that Germany, too, had an interest in Morocco. In the ensuing crisis, Germany forced the resignation of Delcassé and seemed ready to go to war. Franco-German differences were finally brought before an international conference at Algeciras (1906). Here the independence of Morocco was reaffirmed; but in settling specific questions of Moroccan internal administration, the majority of the powers supported the French. Only Austria-Hungary stood by her German ally. Germany's attempt to split the Anglo-French Entente had thus backfired.

Actually, the first Moroccan crisis brought the French and British still closer together by inaugurating conversations between French and British military and naval authorities concerning possible cooperation in case of war. These conversations continued intermittently until 1914. Beginning in 1912, furthermore, the British navy concentrated its forces in the North Sea, permitting the French to shift their own warships to the Mediterranean. England thus assumed at least a moral responsibility for protecting France's northern coast in case of war. The Entente Cordiale, in spirit if not in fact, had been transformed into a virtual alliance.

The Triple Entente

England's close affiliation with France quite naturally raised the question of her relations with France's ally Russia. As a result of Russia's war with Japan, the threat of Russian predominance in China had been removed and there was now no reason why England should not try to settle her colonial differences with Russia as she had with France. This was done in the Anglo-Russian Entente of 1907, which settled the long-standing rivalries of the powers in Afghanistan, Persia, and Tibet.

The formation of the Triple Entente, as the agreements of 1904 and 1907 together are called, amounted to a diplomatic revolution. A situation that only a few years earlier Germany had considered impossible had now come to pass: England had settled her differences with France and Russia, and the Triple Alliance had found its match in the Triple Entente. The latter was no more aggressive in its initial intent than the Triple Alliance had originally been. But as areas for compromise outside Europe became fewer with the annexation of the remaining colonial spoils, the scene of international rivalries once more shifted to Europe and especially to the Balkans. In the past, Russia's ambitions in this area had been held in check by the rest of the powers. Now she could count on French and British support against Germany and Austria. Germany, on the other hand, left with only Austria as a reliable friend, could no longer restrain Austria's Balkan policy as she had in the past. Any change in the *status quo* of the Balkans, therefore, was sure to lead to a major crisis.

The Mounting Crisis, 1908–13

This brings us to the last fateful years before 1914, when growing international tension, at least in retrospect, appears as a fitting prelude to an inevitable showdown.

Revolution in Turkey and the Bosnian Crisis

The Balkans became the scene of international complications in 1908 when a revolution broke out in the Ottoman Empire. Turkey's ruler since 1876, Abdul-Hamid II, had never lived up to his repeated promises of reform. Opposition to the sultan's corrupt and decadent regime centered in a group of liberal patriots, the "Young Turks." Their aim was to reform Turkey along the lines of a liberal constitution that had been granted in 1876 but had been completely disregarded afterward. The revolutionaries had a large following among the Turkish army, and the government's resistance to the uprising in 1908 soon collapsed. The Young Turks, however, though liberal in some respects, were extremely nationalistic in their dealings with Turkey's many national and religious minorities. Persecution of Greek Orthodox Christians and efforts to assimilate Turkey's subject peoples soon led to further disruption of the empire: Bulgaria proclaimed her independence in 1908; Crete completed her union with Greece in 1912; and Albania, after a series of bloody uprisings, finally became independent in 1913.

The Dissolution of the Ottoman Empire to 1914

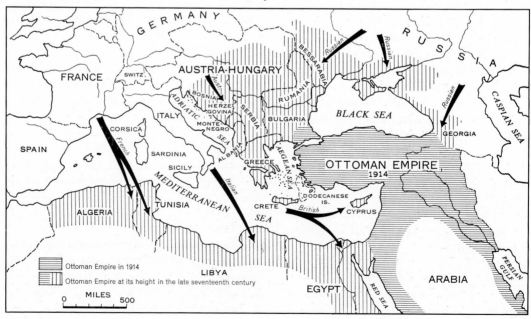

The most important event connected with the Turkish revolution, in its effects upon relations among the great powers, was Austria's annexation of Bosnia and Herzegovina in 1908. There had been no serious tension between Austria and Russia over the Balkans for some twenty years. But this peaceful situation changed after 1905, as Russia once again turned her attention from the Far to the Near East. Russia's foreign minister, Alexander Izvolsky, was an unusually ambitious man, and he found a kindred spirit in his Austrian colleague, Count Aehrenthal. Russia had long hoped to lift the closure of the Turkish Straits to Russian warships; Austria, for her part, had been looking forward to annexing Bosnia and Herzegovina, which she had been administering since 1878. Encouraged by the Turkish revolution, Izvolsky and Aehrenthal met at the latter's castle of Buchlau in September 1908 and there pledged mutual support for their respective aims.

The Bosnian crisis was precipitated when shortly after the Buchlau Agreement Austria went ahead and proclaimed the annexation of Bosnia and Herzegovina without waiting for Russia to act in the Straits. Russia, thereupon, backed by France and England, demanded that Austria's action be brought before an international conference. Germany, on the other hand, supported Austria in opposing a conference unless the annexation of Bosnia-Herzegovina was recognized beforehand. The situation was made more serious because Serbia also had hoped one day to take Bosnia-Herzegovina. Encouraged by Pan-Slav propaganda emanating from Russia, Serbia now demanded compensation from Austria. Since Russia, however, was in no position to fight a war at this time, she finally had to bring pressure on Serbia to recognize the *fait accompli* in Bosnia and Herzegovina. This the Serbs did under protest.

The Bosnian crisis left a legacy of tension that lasted until the First World War. Both Russia and Serbia had been humiliated. To prevent the recurrence of such a defeat, Russia now began to prepare in earnest for the showdown that seemed inevitable, while Serbia stepped up her agitation among Austria's southern Slavs.

Austria had been the real culprit in the affair. She would have had to back down, however, had it not been for the support of Germany. The fact that such support had been given only reluctantly was not known to the rest of the world. Italy, finally, was hurt not to have been consulted by Austria about the annexation of Bosnia and Herzegovina and not to have received compensations, both of which she felt entitled to under the Triple Alliance. In October 1909 she entered into a secret understanding with Russia, the Racconigi Agreement, in which she promised to support Russia's interests in the Straits while Russia agreed to back Italy's designs in Tripoli. Italy thus had taken another step away from the Triple Alliance.

The Second Moroccan Crisis

Europe had barely recovered from the Bosnian affair when another crisis arose, this time in North Africa. Despite the Act of Algeciras of 1906, friction in Morocco between French and German interests had continued. When native disturbances in Morocco in 1911 forced French troops to intervene, Germany protested against what she considered a violation of Moroccan independence. To make up for France's increased influence in Morocco, Germany now claimed compensations elsewhere. And to give weight to her demands, she sent a German gunboat, the "Panther," to the Moroccan port of Agadir, ostensibly to protect German lives and interests. It was due chiefly to British intervention that Germany was finally forced to modify her claims and that the crisis was settled. But meanwhile Europe had once again been brought to the brink of war.

Anglo-German Naval Rivalry

England, throughout the crisis, suspected that Germany's real aim was to secure a naval base in Morocco, which would have posed a threat to Britain's base at Gibraltar. Anglo-German naval rivalry had by now become a matter of deep concern to the British. Naval expansion was closely related to imperialism. A powerful fleet was considered necessary to protect overseas possessions, and overseas possessions in turn were needed as naval bases and coaling stations. As a precaution against the naval increases of the rest of the world, England in 1889 had adopted a "two-power standard," which called for a British fleet 10 percent stronger than the combined naval forces of the two next-strongest powers.

The most serious challenge to Britain's naval power came from Germany. Beginning in 1898, Germany entered upon a course of naval expansion that, by 1914, had made her the second-strongest naval power in the world. Germany's secretary of the navy, Admiral Alfred von Tirpitz, knew that he could not possibly expect to catch up with the British. What he tried to do was to build a navy strong enough so that no other country would dare risk getting into a fight with Germany. The German navy was thus built not so much for a possible showdown with England as for reasons of prestige.

Yet it was difficult for England to see matters in quite the same light. The British felt that Germany, primarily a land power, did not really need a navy, especially since she already had a powerful army. If, nevertheless, the Germans went to the great expense of building a navy, this could only mean that they expected some day to challenge Britain's naval supremacy. Again and again, notably in 1908 and 1912, Great Britain urged Germany to slow down her naval construction, offering in return to support German colonial aspirations. But William II and Tirpitz saw these efforts merely as a confirmation of their "risk theory" and looked forward to the day when England would be forced to seek an agreement on Germany's terms. More than any other issue, this naval race was responsible for the growing tension between Germany and England during the last decade before the war.

The Balkan Wars

The Moroccan crisis of 1911—besides further strengthening the Anglo-French Entente—also helped to start a series of small wars aimed at the further disruption of the Ottoman Empire. The first of these broke out in the fall of 1911 when Italy, encouraged by France's success in Morocco, decided to embark on the annexation of Tripoli. Since she had carefully secured the prior consent of all the great powers, Italy's war with Turkey in 1911–12 did not by itself cause any major crisis. As we have seen, it brought Italy her long-coveted North African colony. The Tripolitanian War, however, encouraged several small Balkan states to move against Turkey and thus to reopen the Balkan question with all its inherent dangers.

The chief motive behind the First Balkan War (1912) was the desire of Bulgaria, Serbia, and Greece to gain further concessions at the expense of Turkey. Together with Montenegro, these countries had formed a Balkan League in early 1912. Taking advantage of the war over Tripoli, they invaded the Ottoman Empire in October of that year. The Turks were decisively defeated, and under the Treaty of London (May 1913) Turkey lost all her European possessions except the region adjacent to the Straits. The peace was less than a month old when a Second Balkan War broke out, this time among the victors over the distribution of the spoils. Under arrangements made before the first war, Serbia was to receive an outlet to the Adriatic in Albania. This met with Austrian and Italian protests, however. As compensation for her loss, Serbia now demanded some of the territory that Bulgaria had received in Macedonia; and when the Bulgarians refused, war ensued between Bulgaria on the one hand and Serbia, Greece, Montenegro, Rumania, and Turkey on the other. Against such an overwhelming coalition, the Bulgarians proved powerless. In the Treaty of Bucharest (August 1913), Bulgaria kept only a small part of Macedonia, the Greeks and Serbs taking the rest.

The Balkan Wars caused deep anxiety among the great powers. A Conference of Ambassadors was convened in London to deal with the Balkan problem, notably the controversy between Austria and Serbia over the latter's aspirations in Albania. As in the past, Russia backed Serbia. Germany, on the other hand, served as a brake on Austria's desire to intervene against Serbia. Since England and Italy also favored the independence of Albania, Russia finally withdrew her support from Serbia and peace was preserved. In the course of events, however, Austria and

Russia, together with their allies, had again come close to war. Serbia had suffered another defeat, for which she blamed Austria and for which even her gains in Macedonia could not console her. Serbia's outraged nationalism sought revenge a year later in the assassination of the Austrian Archduke Francis Ferdinand at Sarajevo.

The Outbreak of the Great War

In discussing the origins of the First World War, historians distinguish between underlying and immediate causes. In the first category belong all those factors that contributed to the acute state of international tension before 1914: nationalism, territorial disputes, economic competition, and imperialist rivalries. Some of the tension has also been blamed on the secret diplomacy of the powers, which led to secret alliances that involved nations in conflicts not of their making. But it has been held that there was not enough secret diplomacy, that a "summit" meeting of Europe's leading statesmen in the summer of 1914, away from the clamor of their nationalistic press, might have resolved the differences that

instead led to war. There had been many instances in the past when such joint action on the part of the Concert of Europe had proved effective. By 1914, however, the feeling of European solidarity that had animated the great powers in the days of Metternich and even Bismarck had everywhere given way to the powerful and divisive force of nationalism. It was the absence of any effective international agency to preserve peace that, more than anything else, caused the catastrophe of 1914.

Sarajevo

As we turn from the underlying to the immediate causes of the war, the most important was the assassination of the Austrian archduke at the Bosnian town of Sarajevo, on June 28, 1914. The story of why and how the war came about has been told many times and in great detail. But there are to this day some important points on which information is missing; and there are still wide differences among historians in the evaluation of the available evidence. It is quite possible that a different action by one or another of the statesmen in the summer of 1914 might have once more prevented a general

Archduke Francis Ferdinand of Austria and his wife at Sarajevo on June 28, 1914, about to enter the automobile that carried them to their deaths.

The Origins
of the First World War

The origins of this war were complex in the extreme. . . .
Some were of a long-term nature: the still-unsolved problem
of the breakup of the old Turkish Empire, the restlessness
of subject peoples in the Danubian basin, the loss of what
the French call the *élan vital* in Austria-Hungary, the relative
growth of German power, the rivalry between Germany and
England. Others were of a short-term nature: the stupidities
and timidities of statesmen, the pressures of public opinion,
the vagaries of coincidence. If you tried to compute the
various degrees of guilt, you got a rather fuzzy pattern: the
Austrians and the Russians no doubt in first place, the Germans with less but certainly with a goodly share, and no
one with none at all. Above all, you could not say that
anyone had deliberately started the war or schemed it. It
was a tragic, helpless sort of war from the beginning. Poor
old Europe had got herself into a box. The structure of her
international life had a weak spot. The shot at Sarajevo
struck into that weak spot—and suddenly no one knew how
not to go to war.

From George F. Kennan, *American Diplomacy 1900–1950*
(New York: New American Library, 1952), pp. 58–59.

war. Yet it seems unlikely that such a war could
have been postponed much longer. If ever there
was a time that seemed ripe for war, it was the
summer of 1914.

The assassination of Archduke Francis Ferdinand and his wife was carried out by an
Austro-Bosnian citizen of Serb nationality,
Gavrilo Princip. The crime had been planned
and its execution aided by a secret society of
Serb nationalists, the "Black Hand." The archduke had been chosen as victim because he was
known to favor reconciling the southern Slav
element in the Dual Monarchy, a policy that
interfered with the aspirations of Serb nationalism, which hoped for the ultimate union of all
southern Slavs under Serbian rule. There is no
evidence that the Serbian government had any
hand in the plot itself; but Serbia's prime minister, Nicholas Pashitch, had general knowledge
of it. Austria, taking for granted that the Serbian

government was involved, now decided once and
for all to settle accounts with Serbia. This she
hoped to do in a localized war. But Austria's
foreign minister, Count Berchtold, seemed not
averse to a larger war if it was necessary to achieve
his aim.

European reaction to the assassination at first
was one of deep shock and of genuine sympathy
for Austria. It was in indignation over the
horrible crime that Germany gave Austria that
fateful promise to "stand behind her as an ally
and friend" in anything the Austrian government
should decide to do. As it became clear, however,
that Austria intended to use the Sarajevo incident
to punish Serbia, the powers became alarmed.
Russia warned the Austrians that she "would
not be indifferent to any effort to humiliate
Serbia." At the same time, France's President
Raymond Poincaré assured the Russians of
French support in any action they took on behalf
of Serbia. By the middle of July, therefore, it
was clear that Austria, backed by Germany, was
ready to move against Serbia, and that Russia,
backed by France, was equally ready to protect
Serbia.

The Eve of War

The situation thus far was serious, but it
was not as yet critical. It became so when Austria,
on July 23, presented a stiff ultimatum to Serbia.
The latter's reply, while evasive, nevertheless was
favorable enough to justify further negotiations.
Instead, Austria broke off diplomatic relations
and on July 28 declared war on Serbia. Germany
had little choice but to live up to her earlier
"blank check" and to support Austria. By doing
so, the Germans hoped to discourage Russia from
helping Serbia and thus to localize the Austro-
Serbian conflict. But the Germans were also ready
to stand by Austria if the conflict should develop
into a general war.

The decision whether the war was to be a
local or a general one rested primarily with
Russia. Germany's action throughout the crisis
had given the impression that far from trying
to discourage Austria, the German government
was actually urging her on into the showdown
with Serbia. Since an Austrian victory over Serbia
would be tantamount to a Russian defeat, Rus-

sian military authorities now began calling for mobilization. The question was, should such mobilization be partial, against Austria-Hungary only, or should it be general, against Germany as well? A partial mobilization had never been envisaged and would have entailed considerable disadvantages in case general mobilization should become necessary later on. But a general mobilization, it was understood, would make a European war inevitable. The internal debate over this issue went on for several days. Only when the tsar finally became convinced, on July 30, that efforts to restrain Austria were futile, was general mobilization decided upon.

The Outbreak of War

Germany's chief of staff, General Helmuth von Moltke, nephew of the great Moltke of Bismarckian times, was worried by reports from Russia. He therefore urged Austria, behind his government's back, to mobilize against Russia, promising unconditional German support. Austria ordered general mobilization on July 31, thus killing any chance for last-minute peace efforts. The same day Germany sent an ultimatum to Russia, demanding that the latter cease her preparations for war. When the tsar's government replied that this was impossible, Germany, on August 1, mobilized her own forces and a few hours later declared war on Russia. France, in the meantime, had also begun military preparations. To a German inquiry about her attitude in a Russo-German war, France replied that she would "act in accordance with her interests." On August 3, Germany declared war on France.

The reason for Germany's haste in declaring war lay in the plans that her general staff had worked out for a war on two fronts. The basic idea of the "Schlieffen Plan"—named after its originator, Count Schlieffen, who had been chief of the general staff from 1891 to 1906—was for Germany's main forces to turn west, deliver an annihilating blow against France, and then turn east against the slowly mobilizing Russians. To succeed with her plan, Germany not only needed to mobilize as quickly as possible, but she also had to invade France at her most vulnerable spot, the northeastern frontier between France and Belgium. The "Schlieffen Plan," in other words,

called for German violation of Belgian neutrality, which, together with the rest of Europe, the Germans had guaranteed in 1830.

Germany's invasion of Belgium on August 3 brought England into the war the next day. Great Britain has been reproached for not making her position in the crisis clear enough from the start, the argument being that if she had come off the fence earlier she would have deterred the Austrians from going to war against Serbia. Through the Entente Cordiale, especially its secret military and naval understandings, England was deeply committed to France. On the other hand, there had been a marked improvement in Anglo-German relations in the early months of 1914; and England's Entente with Russia had never been very popular. For reasons of her own security, Britain could not possibly afford to stand idly by while Germany won victories over France and Russia that would make her the dominant power on the Continent. But to get the British public to approve involvement in the war, some event was needed to dramatize the German danger. Such an event was Germany's violation of Belgian neutrality. Almost overnight it helped to convert Britain's indecisive neutrality into determined belligerency.

"War Guilt"

A word remains to be said about the question of "war guilt," which remains a subject of controversy to the present day. Most historians agree that Germany, Austria, and Russia bear a major share of the responsibility; England clearly belongs at the other extreme, her errors being chiefly of omission; and France stands somewhere in between. This much is certain: no one power alone was responsible for the war and none of the great powers was entirely free from responsibility. Many Europeans actually welcomed the war as a relief from the almost unbearable tension that had preceded it. Yet most of the leading statesmen, when faced with the certainty of war, were overcome by fear and desperation. It was as though they had a foreboding that the war they had failed to avert would be far more terrible than they could imagine, and that the world they had known would never be the same again.

Suggestions for Further Reading

1. General

Among the major studies on the diplomatic background of the First World War, L. Albertini, *The Origins of the War of 1914,* 3 vols. (1952–57), is generally considered the best. A. J. P. Taylor, *The Struggle for Mastery in Europe, 1848–1918* (1954), is shorter and less judicious. L. C. B. Seaman, *From Vienna to Versailles** (1956), is the briefest and most readable account. L. Lafore, *The Long Fuse** (1965), emphasizes the disintegration of Austria-Hungary as a cause of war.

2. The Age of Bismarck

The outstanding book is W. L. Langer, *European Alliances and Alignments** (1950), which includes an exhaustive bibliography. The Near Eastern crisis of the seventies is brilliantly discussed in B. H. Sumner, *Russia and the Balkans, 1870–1880* (1937), and its outcome is treated in W. N. Medlicott, *The Congress of Berlin and After* (1938). For the formation of Bismarck's system of alliances, see A. C. Coolidge, *The Origins of the Triple Alliance* (1926). P. B. Mitchell, *The Bismarckian Policy of Conciliation with France* (1935), rounds out the picture in the West. Germany's first colonial ventures are described in M. E. Townsend, *The Origins of Modern German Colonization, 1871–1885* (1921), and in A. J. P. Taylor, *Germany's First Bid for Colonies* (1938). The closing years of Bismarck's career are studied critically by J. V. Fuller, *Bismarck's Diplomacy at Its Zenith* (1922). The chancellor's dismissal is covered in K. F. Nowak, *Kaiser and Chancellor* (1930). G. A. Craig, *From Bismarck to Adenauer: Aspects of German Statecraft** (1958), offers a sympathetic appraisal of Bismarck the diplomat.

3. Imperialism in Africa and Asia

The definitive work on the imperialist rivalries of the great powers is W. L. Langer, *The Diplomacy of Imperialism, 1890–1902,* 2 vols. (1951). The colonization of Africa is covered in: R. Robinson and J. Gallagher, *Africa and the Victorians** (1961); E. A. Walker, *A History of Southern Africa* (1957); R. L. Tignor, *Modernization and British Colonial Rule in Egypt, 1882–1914* (1966); and P. Gifford and W. R. Louis, eds., *Britain and Germany in Africa: Imperial Rivalry and Colonial Rule* (1967). See also N. Ascherson, *The King Incorporated: Leopold II of the Belgians* (1963), and J. Duffy, *Portuguese Africa* (1959). The best brief book on the Far East is G. F. Hudson, *The Far East in World Politics* (1939). More specialized are P. Joseph, *Foreign Diplomacy in China, 1894–1900* (1928), and B. H. Sumner, *Tsardom and Imperialism in the Far East and Middle East* (1942). For the economic penetration of the Middle East, see S. N. Fisher, *The Middle East* (1959), and J. B. Wolf, *The Diplomatic History of the Baghdad Railway* (1936). Financial imperialism is given its due in H. Feis, *Europe the World's Banker, 1870–1914** (1930), and in E. Staley, *War and the Private Investor* (1935). Recent monographs on various aspects of the diplomacy of imperialism include: A. White, *The Diplomacy of the Russo-Japanese War* (1964); G. N. Sanderson, *England, Europe and the Upper Nile, 1882–1899* (1965); and I. H. Nish, *The Anglo-Japanese Alliance: The Diplomacy of Two Island Empires, 1894–1907* (1966).

4. The United States as a World Power

America's share in the scramble for overseas possessions is treated in: A. K. Weinberg, *Manifest Destiny* (1935); J. W. Pratt, *America's Colonial Experiment* (1950); and H. K. Beale, *Theodore Roosevelt and the Rise of America to World Power** (1956). The best books on the Spanish-American War are: J. W. Pratt, *Expansionists of 1898** (1936); F. B. Freidel, *Splendid Little War** (1958); and H. W. Morgan, *America's Road to Empire: The War with Spain and Overseas Expansion** (1965). Other phases of American

---

* Available in paperback edition.

foreign policy are dealt with in E. H. Zabriskie, *American-Russian Rivalry in the Far East* (1946); H. Sprout and M. Sprout, *The Rise of American Naval Power, 1776–1918* (1939); and R. H. Heindel, *The American Impact on Great Britain, 1898–1914* (1940). For a keen analysis of America's involvement in world affairs since 1898, see G. F. Kennan, *American Diplomacy, 1900–1950** (1951).

5. The Formation of the Triple Entente

W. L. Langer, *The Franco-Russian Alliance, 1890–1894* (1929), is another authoritative study by this distinguished diplomatic historian. On the formation of the Entente, see J. J. Mathews, *Egypt and the Formation of the Anglo-French Entente of 1904* (1939), and R. P. Churchill, *The Anglo-Russian Convention of 1907* (1939). Also relevant is E. N. Anderson, *The First Moroccan Crisis* (1930). There is no comprehensive work in English on Anglo-German relations during this period, but the following discuss various aspects of the problem: R. J. Sontag, *Germany and England: Background of Conflict, 1848–1894* (1938); R. J. S. Hoffman, *Great Britain and the German Trade Rivalry, 1875–1914* (1933); and P. R. Anderson, *The Background of Anti-English Feeling in Germany, 1890–1902* (1939). The influence of sea power on diplomacy is treated in: E. L. Woodward, *Great Britain and the German Navy* (1935); A. J. Marder, *The Anatomy of British Sea Power* (1940); and *From the Dreadnought to Scapa Flow: The Royal Navy in the Fisher Era, 1904–1919,* 3 vols. (1961–66). A good deal of diplomatic history is contained in N. Rich, *Friedrich von Holstein: Politics and Diplomacy in the Era of Bismarck and Wilhelm II,* 2 vols. (1965).

6. The Mounting Crisis

The events of the last decade before the war are summarized in G. L. Dickinson, *The International Anarchy, 1904–1914* (1926). On individual phases of the mounting crisis, see: B. E. Schmitt, *The Annexation of Bosnia* (1937); I. Barlow, *The Agadir Crisis* (1940); W. C. Askew, *Europe and Italy's Acquisition of Libya, 1911–1912* (1942); E. C. Helmreich, *The Diplomacy of the Balkan Wars* (1938); and E. C. Thaden, *Russia and the Balkan Alliance of 1912* (1965). The influence of public opinion on foreign policy during the prewar era is explored by O. J. Hale, *Publicity and Diplomacy* (1940), and by E. M. Carroll, *Germany and the Great Powers, 1866–1914: A Study in Public Opinion and Foreign Policy* (1939), and *French Public Opinion and Foreign Affairs, 1870–1914* (1930).

7. The Outbreak of War

V. Dedijer, *The Road to Sarajevo* (1966), is comprehensive and dispassionate. The assassination of the Austrian archduke is dramatically told in J. Remak, *Sarajevo* (1959). Although the crisis thus set in motion has been more carefully studied than any comparable event in history, historians still do not agree on the question of who was responsible for the war. S. B. Fay, *The Origins of the World War** (1932), puts the major blame on Serbia and Russia. B. E. Schmitt, *The Coming of the War, 1914,* 2 vols. (1930), is more severe toward Germany and Austria. The German case is presented in E. Brandenburg, *From Bismarck to the World War: A History of German Foreign Policy, 1870–1914* (1927), and the French position is stated in P. Renouvin, *The Immediate Origins of the War* (1928). More recently, two German historians have placed the major blame on their own nation: F. Fischer, *Germany's Aims in the First World War* (1967); and I. Geiss, ed., *July 1914: The Outbreak of the First World War* (1968). Their works have touched off a major historical controversy.

---

* Available in paperback edition.

War propaganda. Germany's ambassador to Washington, Count Bernstorff, and his famed announcement of U-boat danger that led to the sinking of the *Lusitania*.

15

War, Revolution, and Peace, 1914–1929

The "Great War," as it was called at the time, only gradually turned into a "World War." It was not the first world-wide conflict, but it was the largest. Before the war ended in November 1918, 49 million men had been mobilized in the "Allied" camp, against 25 million among the "Central Powers." It was truly war on an unprecedented scale. Also, more than any previous conflict, this war involved everyone, not only soldiers. The concept of "total war" was born in the First World War. The war lasted much longer than anyone had thought a modern war could, and it brought far more sweeping changes than anyone would have thought possible. Traditional empires collapsed and new nations arose from the wreckage. The "New World," hitherto of little significance in European affairs, suddenly emerged as the decisive factor. Europe, which in the past had always settled its own affairs, apparently was able to do so no longer.

The Great War was a transitional phase in modern history, and that is how we shall treat it here. There was no clear-cut end to the war—certainly not the peace settlements of 1919-20. The problems that the statesmen at Paris wrestled with then continued to plague Europe and the world for at least a decade thereafter. The ways in which these problems were tackled were still very much reminiscent

of the nineteenth century. It took a new series of crises, touched off by the Great Depression of 1929 and culminating in another World War, before the transition from nineteenth to twentieth century was completed.

The Comparative Strength of the Powers

Despite differences in numbers, the actual military strength of the Allies and the Central Powers at the start of the war was quite evenly balanced. The impressive size of the Allied armies was due chiefly to the ill-trained and poorly equipped Russian army. Germany's forces, on the other hand, were the best in the world. France and Britain matched the Germans in numbers, but the Germans excelled in the quality and quantity of their equipment. The Austrian army was inferior to that of Germany and was weakened by its large Slav contingent. But since the main showdown was expected in the West, this handicap did not seem serious.

Aside from their superior strength on land, the Central Powers had other advantages. Command of the interior lines of communication enabled them to shift their forces rapidly from one theater of war to another. The Allies, on the other hand, were widely separated; Russia

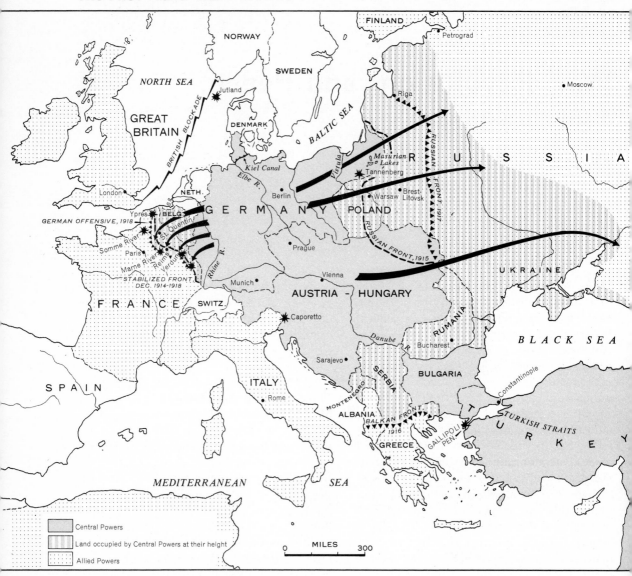

The First World War 1914–18

Central Powers

Land occupied by Central Powers at their height

Allied Powers

MILES   0   300

in particular, with the closing of the Baltic and Black Seas, was cut off from much-needed aid. German industry, furthermore, was more readily converted to war production than the industries of her opponents. The Central Powers had more than enough coal and iron, and territories seized on the western front increased their resources. Only in their supplies of foodstuffs did Austria and Germany fall seriously short of their needs.

Had the war been as brief as most wars of the nineteenth century, Germany and Austria might have won it. But as the fighting dragged on, Allied inherent superiority made itself felt. Their manpower was greater; their industrial potential was superior; and, thanks to Great Britain, the Allies enjoyed naval supremacy. By keeping the sea lanes open, the British navy assured the uninterrupted flow of men and material; and by clamping a tight blockade upon Central Europe, Britain enhanced Germany's and Austria's food problems.

One way in which each side tried to strengthen its position further was by seeking additional partners. Since the Allies usually had more to offer, they were more successful in this contest. At the end of the war, more than twenty-five "Allied and Associated Powers" were ranged against the Central Powers—Germany, Austria-Hungary, Turkey, and Bulgaria.

The most important additions to the Allied camp, aside from the United States, were Japan, Italy, Rumania, and Greece. Japan's entry into the war in August 1914 proved to be a most profitable move. Without delay the Japanese seized Germany's holdings in China's Shantung Province and occupied Germany's Pacific islands north of the equator. Italy did not join the war until 1915. She had refused to honor her obligations under the Triple Alliance, claiming that its terms did not apply. To balance possible Austrian gains in the Balkans, moreover, the Italians had demanded territorial concessions from Austria. The Austrians agreed to some of Italy's demands, but the Allies were able to offer more. By the secret Treaty of London in April 1915, England, France, and Russia promised Italy not only the Austrian regions inhabited by Italians but also considerable territory along the eastern Adriatic and in Asia Minor and Africa. Having received these generous promises, the Italians, in May 1915, declared war against Austria-Hungary. Rumania joined the Allies in August 1916, and Greece followed in June 1917. In both cases the pressure of military events and the hope for territorial gains were decisive.

The only two countries that joined the Central Powers were Turkey and Bulgaria. The Ottoman Empire had long maintained close economic ties with Germany and its army had been trained by German officers. In August 1914 Turkey concluded an alliance with Germany; three months later a Turkish naval squadron bombarded Russia's Black Sea ports; and in early November 1914 the Allies declared war on the Ottoman Empire. Bulgaria, finally, had been wooed by both sides. In this case, however, the Central Powers were able to promise more, and in October 1915 Bulgaria joined the Germans and Austrians in a major drive against Serbia.

The Great Stalemate, 1914–16

Both sides had prepared themselves for a brief offensive war. In its grand simplicity, however, the German Schlieffen Plan was far superior to France's Plan XVII, which called for an invasion of Alsace-Lorraine.

1914: The Allies Ahead

From the start of hostilities on the western front, Germany held the initiative. After one month of fighting, German forces had advanced to within twenty-five miles of Paris. In early September 1914, however, the German drive was halted at the river Marne. The battle of the Marne was one of the decisive events of the war, since it ended Germany's hope for an early victory. There were many reasons for Germany's disappointment. Belgium had put up more resistance than had been expected. Germany, furthermore, had failed to concentrate sufficient forces on the right wing of her invading armies to make possible the gigantic enveloping move that was to strike at the rear of France's forces southeast of Paris. The Schlieffen Plan depended on the closest possible communications between field commanders and the high command, and on rapid lines of supply; neither of these had been provided for.

The battle of the Marne was followed by a series of engagements in which each side hoped to outflank the other, and in the course of which the front was gradually extended to the sea. By November 1914 the fighting in the West had changed from a war of movement to a war of position. Until the spring of 1918 the western front, except for an occasional thrust of a few miles in one direction or the other, remained unchanged.

With the bulk of Germany's forces tied down in the West, Russia was able to score some unexpected successes in the East. In mid-August 1914 two Russian armies invaded East Prussia

Scene in a German trench (1915).

and within a few days overran almost half of Germany's easternmost province. At the height of danger, the kaiser recalled from retirement General Paul von Hindenburg, a specialist on conditions in the East, and appointed as Hindenburg's chief of staff the younger and more capable Erich von Ludendorff. These men soon reversed the situation on the eastern front. In two major battles, at Tannenberg and the Masurian Lakes, Russia lost close to 250,000 men. Russia's reversals in the north were balanced by successes in the southeast against Austria. In a sweeping campaign under Russia's commander in chief, Grand Duke Nicholas, Russian forces in September took most of Galicia and advanced to the Carpathian frontier of Hungary.

In the East, as in the West, the end of 1914 thus found the Allied and Central Powers locked in a stalemate. Since Germany had failed to

deliver a knock-out blow in the West, however, and appeared to be stalled in the East, the advantage was felt to lie with the Allies. In addition, British naval superiority had been responsible for the sinking of a German naval squadron off the coast of South America and for the seizure of most of the colonies that had belonged to Germany.

1915: Allied Reverses

But Allied dreams of victory proved premature. The new Italian ally they gained in the spring of 1915 proved to be of little use. A British attack against the Gallipoli peninsula and the Turkish Straits, furthermore, failed. Had it succeeded, Turkey would have been seriously weakened and the Black Sea opened to Allied shipping. Instead, the Straits remained closed for the rest of the war.

The most serious Allied reverses during 1915 were on the eastern front and in the Balkans. In the spring and summer, German forces in the North and combined Austro-German forces in the South advanced in a series of offensives that cost the Russians Poland, Lithuania, and Courland, drove them out of Galicia, and lost them almost a million men. All of central and eastern Europe was now in German and Austrian hands. In October the Central Powers turned against Serbia; and in November they moved into Montenegro and Albania.

By the beginning of 1916 the tide of war on land seemed definitely to have turned against the Allies. Even on the high seas the Germans were able to make some gains. To counteract Britain's blockade, the German government, in early 1915, imposed its own submarine blockade against the British Isles. The first phase of German submarine warfare came to a head with the sinking of the British liner *Lusitania* in May 1915. The loss of its 139 American passengers caused a serious crisis in American-German relations. It was settled only after Germany promised to restrict her submarine tactics in the future.

1916: Stalemate

Since time was clearly on the side of the Allies, it seemed imperative to the Germans to force a major showdown. In February 1916, therefore, they launched an all-out offensive against the French stronghold of Verdun. The battle of Verdun was the most famous battle of the war. It lasted more than four months and caused more than 700,000 casualties; yet it ended undecided. Its chief hero on the French side was General Henri Philippe Pétain. Like Hindenburg after the battle of Tannenberg, Pétain became the idol of his people. Both men were to play fateful roles in later years. The battle of Verdun led to an Allied counteroffensive along the Somme River. But the battle of the Somme, like that of Verdun, failed to force a final decision in the West.

Events elsewhere during 1916 were equally indecisive. In June, Russian forces under General Brusilov started a major drive against the Aus-

The Sinking of the Lusitania

The full horror of the sinking of the *Lusitania* has now been revealed; and it has stirred the people of this country more deeply than even the poison clouds, or any other of the wanton and murderous acts committed by the Germans. . . . By thousands of dastardly crimes the Germans have demonstrated that they are determined to wage this war under conditions of cold-blooded and deliberate murder and outrage, of destruction and brutality, such as the world has never known. . . . Never before, since the world began, has there been witnessed the spectacle of a whole race, numbering many millions, scientifically organised for the objects of wholesale murder and devastation. . . . It is universally seen now that the Germans are a nation apart, that their civilisation is a mere veneer, that they have fallen immeasurably lower than their tribal forbears, and that their calculated and organised barbarity is without precedent in history. Nations, we perceive, can sink to unprecedented depths. No nation has ever fallen so low in infamy. . . .

From an editorial in *The Times* (London), May 10, 1915.

trian lines and within a few weeks had taken most of eastern Galicia. These successes brought Rumania into the war. But her participation only made matters worse. In late September, Austro-German forces invaded Rumania, and by January 1917 most of that country's rich resources were in the hands of the Central Powers. In the East as in the West, the outcome of the war continued to hang in balance.

The year 1916 also saw the one great naval battle of the war between Germany and Britain. The German navy, to have a chance of success, had to fight in its home waters. But the British refused to venture forth that far. On several occasions the Germans went out into the North Sea, hoping to entice the British into battle. It was on one of these sallies that the two fleets made contact off the coast of Jutland in May 1916. The battle of Jutland was costly and indecisive. The British lost more naval tonnage than the Germans, but they could better afford to. The German fleet henceforth remained safely at home.

By the end of 1916 a stalemate had been reached on all fronts, and victory for either side seemed far away. Meanwhile losses and material costs of the war had been staggering, and the strain of war had begun to tell on the home fronts as well as on the battlefields.

The Home Fronts

The outbreak of war had been greeted everywhere with enthusiastic demonstrations of national unity. Each side believed that it was fighting a "just war." In addition, the war was expected to be short. The Germans hoped to be in Paris before the summer was out, and the French were looking forward to Christmas in Berlin. When instead the war dragged on for two years, with no end in sight, enthusiasm gave way to deep depression.

One of the important conditions for victory was effective leadership. Both France and England found outstanding civilian leaders—the British in David Lloyd George, and the French in Georges Clemenceau. In Germany, Austria, and Russia, on the other hand, where the monarch was both chief executive and symbol of national unity, much depended on the leadership he provided. In none of the three countries did the ruler measure up to expectations. William II had neither the ability nor the energy to cope with the problems of a total war. As he gradually faded into the background, his role was taken over by Hindenburg and Ludendorff. In Austria, Francis Joseph was too old, and his grand-nephew Charles, who succeeded him in 1916, was too inexperienced to keep the crumbling empire together. The saddest figure among Europe's conservative monarchs was Nicholas II of Russia. In 1915 he assumed personal command of his armed forces, leaving the government in the hands of his wife and her sinister adviser, Rasputin.

Total War

The demands of total war presented many new and difficult problems. All the powers experienced periodic munitions shortages. Scar-city of labor was another burning issue. Women were employed in growing numbers and Germany imported workers from Belgium and France. Except for the Russians, who were almost completely isolated, the Allies were able to supplement their domestic production of food and war materials with imports from abroad. The Central Powers, on the other hand, cut off by the blockade, were chiefly dependent on their own resources. The Germans tackled the problem with customary efficiency, devising scores of ersatz, or substitute, products and perfecting new processes to obtain scarce materials. Austria-Hungary was far less successful in these respects. The difficulties were made worse by continuous economic feuds between Austria and Hungary.

The most serious shortages of the Central Powers were in food and clothing. Germany began rationing in 1915, but rationing did not increase available supplies. Shortages of labor and transportation cut down the coal supply, adding the misery of cold to hunger. Faced with these hardships, many Germans, especially among the working class, hoped for a speedy end to the war, even without victory.

War Aims and Peace Proposals

Neither side ever stated its war aims openly, except in the most general terms. Secretly, however, the Allies had agreed on the following distribution of spoils: Russia was to get most of the Polish regions under German and Austrian rule, as well as control over the Turkish Straits; France was promised the whole left bank of the Rhine; England was allotted the German colonies; and Italy was to have parts of Austria and territories elsewhere. In supplementary agreements most of the Ottoman Empire was divided into Russian, French, and British spheres.

The war aims of the Central Powers called for the "liberation" of the Poles and the Baltic peoples from Russian domination, the setting up of small satellite states under German and Austrian control, and the annexation of some regions outright. In the West, Germany hoped for additional regions rich in iron ore from France and political and economic control over Belgium. There were also ambitious schemes for a central European federation under German leadership, a *Mitteleuropa,* and for a compact central African colony.

In view of these far-reaching Allied and German war aims, it is not surprising that efforts to reach a compromise peace proved fruitless. The Central Powers took the first official step in December 1916, informing President Wilson that they were ready to enter into peace negotiations. Wilson thereupon asked both sides to state their terms. But this the Germans refused to do, thus cutting short this first peace move. There were others, notably one inaugurated by Pope Benedict XV in August 1917. All these peace efforts failed. Both sides wanted peace, but neither side wanted it badly enough to make any real concessions.

The United States Enters the War

The stalemate of the first years of the war was broken early in 1917 by America's entry into the war. The United States at first had made every effort to remain neutral. Isolationism was still a strong force; and while there were many Anglophiles in the East, there were also large numbers of German-Americans in the Middle West. America's abandonment of neutrality had several causes. Effective Allied propaganda was one. Another was the growing financial involvement of many Americans in the Allied cause. But more important than either of these factors was Germany's resumption of unrestricted submarine warfare early in 1917.

Unrestricted Submarine Warfare

The decision to step up Germany's submarine campaign was reached after the German peace move of December 1916 had failed. Germany's civilian authorities opposed unrestricted submarine warfare, fearing that it might bring America into the war. But the real power now lay with the military. With time on the Allied side, Hindenburg and Ludendorff felt that only drastic submarine action could still win the war. They realized that this might lead to American intervention, but they thought England would be defeated long before such intervention would become effective.

Unrestricted submarine war began on February 1, 1917. America broke off diplomatic relations with Germany on February 3. As German submarines began sinking American ships, public opinion became more and more interventionist. The publication of the intercepted "Zimmerman Telegram," a note sent by Germany's foreign secretary urging Mexico to make war on the United States, did the rest. On April 6, 1917, Congress declared war on Germany.

The Russian Revolution

America's entrance into the war was made more urgent by recent changes in Russia that weakened the Allied cause. Events there had long been pointing toward a major domestic upheaval. At first the Russian people had loyally supported their government's war effort. But the sufferings of war soon dampened their spirit. With insufficient arms and a chronic shortage of munitions, the army lost more than 3 million men during the first year of the war. While the armies lacked essential materials, the civilian population suffered from food shortages, despite the fact that Russia's economy was primarily agrarian. The blame for all these ills was rightly placed on the inefficiency and corruption of the government. The elected assembly, the *Duma,* repeatedly urged the adoption of reforms; but the tsar continued to meet discontent with repression.

The "February Revolution" and Provisional Government

The overthrow of the tsarist regime was the climax of a gradually mounting wave of popular protest. By 1917 more than a million soldiers had deserted the armed forces; in the cities, food shortages led to repeated strikes and riots; and in the countryside, landless peasants began to seize the land of their noble landlords. In early March street demonstrations broke out in Petrograd (the name given to St. Petersburg at the beginning of the war). In the past the government had always been able to use the army against such disturbances. But the troops now fraternized with the rioters. From the capital, insurrection spread to the provinces. On March 12—or February 27 in the Russian calendar, hence the term "February Revolution"—the *Duma* established a Provisional Government under the premiership of a liberal aristocrat, Prince George Lvov. Three days later, Nicholas II abdicated. He and his family were later moved to Siberia, where they were murdered by the Bolsheviks in the summer of 1918.

The new Provisional Government was faced with problems for which it was completely unprepared. To meet the discontent of the masses some immediate reforms were introduced, but these did not go far enough. The situation was complicated by the existence of a rival government, the Petrograd Soviet (that is, Council) of Workers' and Soldiers' Deputies, consisting of Socialist Revolutionaries, Mensheviks, and

Lenin

November 7, 1917

It was just 8:40 when a thundering wave of cheers announced the entrance of the presidium, with Lenin—great Lenin—among them. A short, stocky figure, with a big head set down in his shoulders, bald and bulging. Little eyes, a snubbish nose, wide, generous mouth, and heavy chin; clean-shaven now, but already beginning to bristle with the well-known beard of his past and future. Dressed in shabby clothes, his trousers much too long for him. Unimpressive, to be the idol of a mob, loved and revered as perhaps few leaders in history have been. A strange popular leader—a leader purely by virtue of intellect; colourless, humourless, uncompromising and detached, without picturesque idiosyncrasies—but with the power of explaining profound ideas in simple terms, of analysing a concrete situation. And combined with shrewdness, the greatest intellectual audacity.

From John Reed, *Ten Days That Shook the World* (New York: International Publishers, 1919), p. 125.

some Bolsheviks. Because of its popular support, the Soviet was the more powerful of the two groups.

The Provisional Government's main difficulty arose from its desire to continue the war. In July the new minister of war, Alexander Kerensky, launched a futile offensive against the Austrians in Galicia. Its failure led to further riots in Petrograd. To restore order Kerensky, on July 25, replaced Prince Lvov as prime minister. To strengthen his position, Kerensky appointed as commander in chief General Lavr Kornilov, who was popular with the army's rank and file. Kornilov succeeded in restoring some discipline but was unable to halt a German offensive against Riga. When there were signs that Kornilov wanted to make himself military dictator, he was arrested, and on September 14 Kerensky himself assumed supreme command of the army.

The revolution meanwhile, which thus far had been remarkably free from terrorism, now became increasingly violent, as workers sacked stores, peasants burned manor houses, and soldiers killed their officers. Revolution in the borderlands, furthermore, threatened the unity of the country. Finally, the Petrograd Soviet, which thus far had tolerated the Provisional Government, was gradually falling under the control of its most radical faction, the Bolsheviks.

The "October Revolution"

The exiled Bolshevik leaders—Nikolai Lenin, Leon Trotsky, and Joseph Stalin—had returned from abroad or from Siberia after the victory of the February Revolution. At first they had commanded only a small minority within the Petrograd Soviet. Constantly reiterating their radical program—immediate peace, seizure of land by the peasants and of factories by the workers—the Bolsheviks gradually increased their following within the Soviet and without. Their immediate aim was to gain control of the soviets in Petrograd and elsewhere. Against the do-nothing policy of the Mensheviks and the Socialist Revolutionaries, Lenin advanced his program of

Lenin addressing an outdoor meeting in Moscow, 1917.

"peace and land." As a result, the balance slowly shifted. By September the Bolsheviks controlled the soviets in Petrograd, Moscow, and several other cities.

The only way for the Bolsheviks to gain control of the government was by using force. When Kerensky got wind of the Bolshevik plot and ordered the arrest of their leaders, Bolshevik troops, on November 6, began occupying strategic points in Petrograd. The main fighting took place around the Winter Palace, seat of the Provisional Government. On November 7 Kerensky took flight, first to the front, and later abroad. The same afternoon an All-Russian Congress of Soviets convened. The majority of its delegates were Bolsheviks. As a first move they formed a new executive, the Council of People's Commissars, with Lenin as Chairman, Trotsky as Foreign Commissar, and Stalin as Commissar for National Minorities.

The "October Revolution"—so named because November 7 was the same as October 25 old-style—was only the first stage on the road

to a Bolshevik victory. The followers of Lenin still included only a small percentage of the Russian people. When the constituent assembly was elected in late November, less than one-fourth of the delegates were Bolsheviks. But this was to be the first and last free election in Russia. When the assembly met for the first time in January 1918, it was dispersed by Bolshevik forces.

The Treaty of Brest-Litovsk

The most important immediate result of the October Revolution was to end the war on the eastern front. On December 5, 1917, the Bolsheviks concluded an armistice with Germany, and on December 22 peace negotiations began at Brest-Litovsk. The Bolsheviks wanted "a just, democratic peace without annexations or indemnities." But the Germans were in no mood to forgo their advantages. At one point the Russian negotiators broke off negotiations, whereupon the Germans resumed their advance. On March

3, 1918, the Russians gave in and accepted Germany's terms.

Under the Treaty of Brest-Litovsk, Russia lost a quarter of her European territory, a third of her population, more than half of her coal and iron, and a third of her industry. The Central Powers were now freed from the burden of a two-front war and won access to the vast economic resources of eastern Europe. Their position was further strengthened by a peace treaty forced on Rumania at Bucharest on March 5, 1918, under which Germany received a ninety-year lease of the country's oil wells. The triumph of German expansionist aims served as a warning to the Allies of what to expect in the event of a German victory.

Continued Stalemate in the West, 1917

With the Central Powers victorious in the East, the Allies more than ever depended on aid from the United States. A first small contingent of American troops under General John J. Pershing had landed in France as early as June 1917. But it was not until spring of 1918 that American units took any real part in the fighting. Of far greater importance was America's material aid. To meet the submarine danger, a vast shipbuilding program was initiated. Unrestricted submarine warfare at first was a serious threat to the Allied cause. But in time various ways of countering the submarine menace were devised, notably the convoy system.

While the Allies were holding their own at sea, the Central Powers were successfully resisting Allied attempts to force a decision on land. The campaigns on the western front in 1917 were among the bloodiest in the whole war. Yet the lessons of Verdun and the Somme still seemed to hold true—a decision on the western front was impossible. The Central Powers, meanwhile, scored one of their greatest victories on the Italian front. The battle of Caporetto in October 1917 cost Italy close to half a million men in casualties and desertions. Only French and British reinforcements averted a still greater disaster.

The Decline of Civilian Morale

Continuous heavy losses at the front and deprivations at home caused a serious decline in civilian morale. The British, suffering less than any other people, bore up best. The French, on the other hand, experienced a major military and political crisis. In May 1917 the senseless bloodshed in the West led to open mutiny. The French home front, too, was becoming more and more defeatist. In Italy, where a strong faction had opposed the war from the start, shortages of food and coal brought on a series of strikes. It was only the disaster of Caporetto that made people rally to the support of the government, realizing that the future of their country was at stake.

The Central Powers underwent similar crises. In Germany, differences between civilian and military leaders caused the resignation of chancellor Bethmann Hollweg and the assumption of virtually dictatorial control by Hindenburg and Ludendorff. In Austria the war gave new momentum to the separatist tendencies of the empire's many nationalities. The Czechs and the Yugoslavs set up organizations abroad to work for Allied recognition of their cause, and Polish, Czech, and Yugoslav prisoners in Allied hands now were formed into national legions to fight against their homeland.

The general weariness that affected all the belligerents after three years of war quite naturally gave rise to further peace efforts. Like all the earlier attempts, however, they failed, since neither side was ready to make the necessary concessions. The Bolsheviks now published some of the secret treaties revealing Allied war aims, and western statesmen made highly idealistic pronouncements to counteract these revelations. In January 1918 President Wilson, in an effort to dissociate America from agreements to which she had not been a party, stated his famous Fourteen Points as the basis for a just peace. The Fourteen Points were to play an important role in the later negotiations for an armistice and peace, but for the time being they had little effect. The only way to get a satisfactory peace, leaders on both sides felt, was to win the war. With time running against her, Germany, in the spring of 1918, decided to make her final bid for victory.

The Collapse
of the Central Powers

Ludendorff's plan for a large-scale spring offensive had some chance of success. The Germans were able to move large numbers of troops from the East. The Allies, on the other hand, were still suffering from the heavy losses of their 1917 offensives, and reinforcements from America were only just beginning to arrive in sufficient numbers.

The Last Offensives

The gigantic "Emperor's Battle" was started in March 1918. At first it was disastrously successful. Within three months the German army once again stood on the Marne, only fifty miles from Paris. But despite brilliant victories, the Germans failed to breach the Allied front. On July 15, when the Germans launched their last major drive in the vicinity of Reims, the Allied front was held largely with the aid of American forces.

On July 18, the Allies began their counteroffensive. Ludendorff at first was able to withdraw his forces in good order. But on August 8, the German army suffered its "black day." Using for the first time large numbers of tanks, the British advanced almost eight miles. From here on the Allies never gave the Germans a moment's rest. By the end of September the German army had lost a million men in six months. Morale was low and desertions mounted. Germany's allies, moreover, were showing signs of imminent collapse. On October 4, finally, Germany and Austria appealed to President Wilson for an armistice based on the Fourteen Points.

Chaos in Central Europe

By the time pre-armistice negotiations were completed a month later, all the Central Powers had collapsed. The first to give up was Bulgaria. The Bulgarian lines were broken in late September, and before the month was out the government had sued for an armistice. Next came Turkey. During the last year of the war, British forces had steadily advanced from the Persian Gulf into Mesopotamia and from Egypt into Palestine and Syria. With Bulgaria out of the

President Wilson's Fourteen Points

1. Open covenants openly arrived at . . . diplomacy shall proceed always frankly and in the public view.

2. Absolute freedom of navigation . . . alike in peace and in war . . . .

3. The removal . . . of all economic barriers and the establishment of an equality of trade conditions . . . .

4. Adequate guarantees . . . that national armaments will be reduced to the lowest point consistent with domestic safety.

5. A free, open-minded and absolutely impartial adjustment of all colonial claims based upon a strict observance of the principle that . . . the interests of the population concerned must have equal weight with the equitable claims of the government . . . .

6. The evacuation of all Russian territory . . . and a sincere welcome into the society of free nations under institutions of her own choosing . . . .

7. Belgium . . . must be evacuated and restored . . . .

8. All French territory should be freed and the invaded portions restored, and the wrong . . . of Alsace-Lorraine . . . should be righted . . . .

9. A readjustment of the frontiers of Italy . . . along clearly recognizable lines of nationality.

10. The peoples of Austria-Hungary . . . should be accorded the freest opportunity of autonomous development.

11. Rumania, Serbia and Montenegro should be evacuated . . . Serbia accorded free and secure access to the sea . . . .

12. The Turkish portions of the present Ottoman Empire should be assured a secure sovereignty, but the other nationalities which are not under Turkish rule should be assured . . . opportunity of autonomous development, and the Dardanelles should be permanently opened as a free passage to the ships and commerce of all nations . . . .

13. An independent Polish State should be erected . . . which should be assured a free and secure access to the sea . . . .

14. A general association of nations must be formed . . . for the purpose of affording mutual guarantees of political independence and territorial integrity to great and small States alike.

From President Wilson's Address to the Joint Session of Congress, January 8, 1918.

war, Turkey was now being threatened from the north as well. On October 30 she concluded an armistice.

The Austro-Hungarian Empire, meanwhile, was falling to pieces. On October 21 the Czechoslovaks declared their independence and a week later the Yugoslavs followed suit. On November 1 Hungary established an independent government. Ten days later, Emperor Charles renounced his throne, and by the middle of November both Austria and Hungary had proclaimed themselves republics.

In Germany the government had reformed itself, in the hope of obtaining more favorable armistice terms. But the Allies would have no dealings with the kaiser. On November 3 mutiny broke out among German sailors at Kiel. Within days the revolt spread through most of northern Germany. On November 7 revolution broke out in Munich and the king of Bavaria abdicated. On November 9, finally, revolution in Berlin overthrew the monarchy and a German Republic was proclaimed.

The Allies, meanwhile, had agreed to accept the Fourteen Points as a basis for an armistice. Under its provisions Germany had to withdraw her forces beyond the Rhine; she had to renounce the treaties of Brest-Litovsk and Bucharest; and she had to surrender large quantities of strategic materials. The terms were so designed as to make any resumption of hostilities impossible. Fighting was officially ended on November 11, at 11 A.M.

The war that was to have been over in four months had lasted more than four years. At its height it had involved some thirty nations. It had killed close to 10 million soldiers, wounded twice that number, and caused millions of civilian deaths. Its total cost has been estimated at over $350 billion. It had brought revolution to central and eastern Europe and had swept away the last remnants of autocratic monarchism. The war's initial purpose—to determine the future of Serbia—had long since given way to far bigger aims. Germany had dreamed of hegemony in Europe and perhaps the world. The Allies had hoped to avert that German threat and in the process to round out their own possessions. Only

the United States was seeking no selfish gains. The Peace Conference was to show whether American idealism would prevail against the hard-headed nationalism of the European Allies.

The Paris Peace Conference

The Peace Conference opened on January 18, 1919. All the belligerents were present, except the Central Powers and Russia. As in most major peace conferences, the important decisions were made by the great powers who had contributed most to winning the war. The peace was thus made by a handful of men, the "Big Four": Wilson, Lloyd George, Clemenceau, and Orlando.

The star of the conference was Woodrow Wilson. The favorite aim of the American President was to set up a League of Nations. Wilson's position had been weakened by the return of a Republican majority in the recent congressional elections. Great Britain was represented by Lloyd George, the mercurial Welsh politician. His views on the peace were fairly moderate. But the British prime minister had recently won an election on the promise of a harsh peace—a promise that was to haunt him throughout the peace negotiations. The most impressive figure of the conference was France's Georges Clemenceau. He hated the Germans, and his foremost aim was to protect France by weakening her former enemy in every possible way. Italy's representative, Prime Minister Vittorio Orlando, played only a minor role. Far more important was his foreign minister, Sidney Sonnino, who was determined to hold Italy's allies to the far-reaching promises they had made in 1915.

Problems of Peacemaking

The problems before the Paris conference were without precedent. The last comparable meeting had been held at Vienna a century earlier. But while the Congress of Vienna had been concerned only with reordering the affairs of the Continent, the problems before the Paris conference ranged over the whole world. The

Allies as well as the Central Powers had accepted the Fourteen Points as a basis for peace, but many of Wilson's principles differed from the provisions of the Allies' secret treaties. A further complication arose from the many foreign and domestic disturbances that went on while the conference was in session. If we add the popular clamor in the Allied countries for a speedy settlement, and if we keep in mind the physical and nervous strain under which the delegates labored, we should not be surprised that the peace they made was not perfect.

So long as the victors agreed among themselves, negotiations at Paris went smoothly. But there were several questions on which they did not see eye to eye. The most important were: Germany's colonies, the Rhineland, reparations, Fiume, and the Shantung Peninsula.

The Allies agreed that Germany's colonies should not be returned to her, but they did not agree on what to do with them. Great Britain and her dominions, France, and Japan wanted to annex Germany's holdings. President Wilson, on the other hand, felt that this would violate his Fourteen Points. The impasse was finally resolved by the adoption of the "Mandate Principle," which provided that the German colonies as well as a large part of the Ottoman Empire were to be placed under foreign control, subject to supervision by the League of Nations. This solution was later attacked by Germany as "veiled annexation" and a violation of the fifth of Wilson's Fourteen Points.

The crisis over the future of the Rhineland almost disrupted the conference. The French, for reasons of security, demanded that the left bank of the Rhine be made into an autonomous buffer state. Such an arrangement, however, ran counter to Wilson's principles. The compromise arrived at after long and acrimonious debate called for the permanent demilitarization of the Rhineland and its occupation by Allied forces for fifteen years. In addition, the territory of the Saar was to remain under League administration for fifteen years and France was given the region's coal mines. Finally, Great Britain and the United States promised France an alliance against possible German aggression.

In the discussion of reparations, an argument arose over the extent to which Germany was to make good damages done to the civilian population of the Allies. Wilson finally gave way to the pressure of his European colleagues and agreed that this should include pensions to victims of war and allowances to their families. To justify so vast a claim, the Allies affirmed that German aggression had been responsible for starting the war. The controversial issue of "war guilt" was thus injected into the peace treaty.

The crisis over Fiume arose from Italy's demand that she be given the Adriatic port in place of the Dalmatian coast, which she had been promised in the Treaty of London but which had been incorporated into Yugoslavia. The Yugoslavs, on the other hand, claimed Fiume as an essential outlet to the sea, and in this they found Allied and American support. When Prime Minister Orlando finally left Paris in protest, the united Allied front showed its first open rift. Italy felt that she had been cheated out of her just reward.

The issue of Shantung involved Japan and China. China had entered the war on the Allied side in 1917. Japan's claim to succeed to Germany's former rights in the Shantung Peninsula clearly conflicted with China's own rights and with Wilson's principles. But the President had only just managed to resist French demands in the Rhineland, and the Fiume crisis was still at its height. So he gave in to Japan's demands, for fear that the Japanese might otherwise refuse to join the League of Nations. The Shantung solution was a serious defeat for the American President, and it lost the United States the traditional friendship of China.

While the negotiations at Paris were in their final stages, the German delegation arrived at Versailles. The Germans were handed a draft of the treaty on May 7 and were given fifteen days in which to present their written observations. These resulted in only a few minor changes. The Germans, therefore, charged that this was a dictated settlement. The signing of the treaty took place on June 28, 1919, at Versailles, five years to the day after the assassination of the Austrian archduke at Sarajevo.

Clemenceau, Wilson, and Lloyd George leaving the palace at Versailles after signing the peace treaty.

The Treaty of Versailles

The peace treaty with Germany contained territorial, military, and economic clauses. It also called for the punishment of "war criminals," including the kaiser. Under the territorial terms of the treaty, Germany had to surrender 13 percent of her prewar area and population. This meant a loss of more than 15 percent of her coal, close to 50 percent of her iron, and 19 percent of her iron and steel industry. Besides giving up her colonies, Germany also had to recognize the independence of Austria. This last provision was to prevent a possible *Anschluss,* or union, for which there was much sentiment in both countries.

The military clauses of the treaty called for the reduction of Germany's army to 100,000 volunteers. The German navy was limited to six battleships of 10,000 tons and a few smaller ships. Germany was to have no offensive weapons—submarines, aircraft, tanks, or heavy artillery—and her general staff was to be dissolved. To supervise German disarmament, an Allied Military Control Commission was appointed.

In the economic field, the precise amount of reparations to be paid by Germany was left for a Reparations Commission to decide. In the meantime Germany was to pay $5 billion in cash or in kind. France was to receive large amounts of coal to make up for the wanton destruction of her coal mines by Germany's retreating armies. Britain was given quantities of ships to compensate for the losses she had suffered from submarine warfare. German foreign assets of some $7 billion were confiscated; most of her rivers were internationalized; many of her patents were seized; and she was prohibited from raising tariffs above their prewar level. In short, everything possible was done to avert the threat of a strong and vengeful Germany. The Treaty of Versailles was no worse than the treaties of Brest-Litovsk and Bucharest, which Germany had imposed upon Russia and Rumania. Nor was it much better.

The Treaties with Germany's Allies

The supplementary treaties with the smaller Central Powers were signed in 1919 and 1920. The Treaty of St. Germain with Austria was almost as harsh as that of Versailles. It called for the surrender of large territories to Czechoslovakia, Poland, Yugoslavia, and Italy. Not counting Hungary, the prewar area of the former empire was thus cut to less than one-third and its population to one-fifth. In addition, Austria's army was limited to 30,000 men. She also had to pay large reparations and agree not to become part of Germany.

Hungary, now separated from Austria, signed her own treaty. Because of a brief communist interregnum under Bela Kun, Hungary did not sign the Treaty of Trianon until the middle of 1920. Its territorial provisions were the most severe of all the postwar treaties. After ceding lands to all her neighbors, including Austria, Hungary was left with little more than a quarter of her former territory and a third of her population. She also had to pay reparations and reduce her army.

Bulgaria, in the Treaty of Neuilly, lost the outlet to the Aegean she had gained in 1913, agreed to reparations, and had to cut her armed forces.

Turkey concluded two peace treaties, one at Sèvres in 1920 and a later one at Lausanne in 1923. The first, which called for a virtual partition of the country, need not concern us

The Disillusionment of Peace

We came to Paris confident that the new order was about to be established; we left it convinced that the new order had merely fouled the old. We arrived as fervent apprentices in the school of President Wilson: we left as renegades. I wish to suggest in this chapter (and without bitterness), that this unhappy diminution of standard was very largely the fault (or one might say with greater fairness 'the misfortune') of democratic diplomacy.

We arrived determined that a Peace of justice and wisdom should be negotiated: we left it, conscious that the Treaties imposed upon our enemies were neither just nor wise. To those who desire to measure for themselves the width of the gulf which sundered intention from practice I should recommend a perusal of the several Notes addressed to the Supreme Council by the German Delegation at Versailles. . . . It is impossible to read the German criticism without deriving the impression that the Paris Peace Conference was guilty of disguising an Imperialistic peace under the surplice of Wilsonism, that seldom in the history of man has such vindictiveness cloaked itself in such unctuous sophistry. Hypocrisy was the predominant and unescapable result. Yet was this hypocrisy wholly conscious, wholly deliberate? I do not think so. . . . We did not realise what we were doing. We did not realise how far we were drifting from our original basis. We were exhausted and overworked.

From Harold Nicolson, *Peacemaking, 1919* (New York: Harcourt, Brace & World, 1933), pp. 187–88.

here, since it was superseded by the later agreement. In the interim, a revolution of Turkish nationalists under Mustapha Kemal Pasha completed the revolution begun by the Young Turks in 1908 and overthrew the regime of the Sultan. The Allies favored the dismemberment of Turkey and in 1919 supported the invasion of Asia Minor by Greek forces. But Turkish resistance under Mustapha Kemal finally convinced the powers that their aim was unattainable. The Allies, therefore, revised the earlier peace settlement. Under the Treaty of Lausanne, signed in July 1923, Turkey gave up everything except Asia Minor and a small foothold in Europe. She did

not have to pay any reparations, and the "capitulations"—rights and privileges granted centuries ago to foreign powers—were abolished. The Straits were demilitarized and opened to ships of all nations in time of peace, but they could be closed if Turkey herself was at war. Alone among all the defeated countries, Turkey had thus been able to enforce a radical change in an initially harsh peace settlement. In October 1923 she was proclaimed a republic, with Mustapha Kemal "Atatürk" as first president.

The Aftermath of War

The history of Europe after 1919 was a prolonged effort on the part of all nations to overcome the effects of the war. As might be expected, the defeated countries, foremost among them Germany, were deeply opposed to the postwar settlement. They attacked it not only as too harsh but also as unjust, since it violated several of Wilson's Fourteen Points. In its attempt to sort out the hopelessly intermingled peoples of central

Europe, for instance, the principle of self-determination was as often ignored as adhered to. In countries like Poland, Czechoslovakia, and Rumania, from one-fourth to one-third of the population consisted of alien minorities, mostly Germans or Hungarians. The problem of national minorities, a source of much unrest before 1914, had thus not been solved by the war.

The situation looked more hopeful with respect to another prewar problem: The war, outwardly at least, had brought the victory of democracy. Autocratic monarchy in central and eastern Europe and Turkey had been replaced by popular governments. But since the political changes in countries like Germany, Austria, and Hungary were closely associated with military defeat, democracy in these countries carried a blemish that only time and success could erase. The tense and tumultuous atmosphere of postwar Europe, however, was not conducive to the peaceful consolidation of democracy. The chaos left behind by war and revolution soon proved too much for the new and inexperienced parliamentary governments of central and eastern Europe. In their place there emerged new kinds of dictatorial and totalitarian regimes, better suited, it seemed, to cope with the emergencies of a world in crisis (see Chapter 16).

The first of these authoritarian systems arose in Russia during the 1920's. The victory of communism in that powerful Eurasian country brought an entirely new and disturbing element into international affairs. The founding of the Third Communist International ("Comintern") in 1919 by Lenin's lieutenant, Grigori Zinoviev, seemed to confirm the western fear that communism was not content to confine its influence to one country. Short-lived communist regimes in Hungary and Bavaria at the end of the war showed that communism thrived on domestic disorder. After several further attempts to engineer communist risings in Germany, Lenin finally decided to concentrate his efforts on the communization of his own country. But the threat of communist Russia continued to frighten the statesmen of Europe until it was overshadowed in the late 1930's by the more immediate threat of Nazi Germany.

The tripartite division of Europe into victors, vanquished, and the Soviet Union was the cause of much international unrest. To remedy this situation the Allies had created the League of Nations. Here was something entirely new in European history, a parliament of nations in which international problems could be discussed and solved. That was how the founders of the League had envisaged its mission. But events soon proved otherwise. When the League opened its first session at Geneva in 1921, several of the great powers were missing: Germany was not admitted until 1926, the Soviet Union became a member eight years later, and the United States never joined.

The failure of the United States to ratify the Treaty of Versailles, which also embraced the Covenant of the League of Nations, showed that

National Minorities in Central Europe 1919

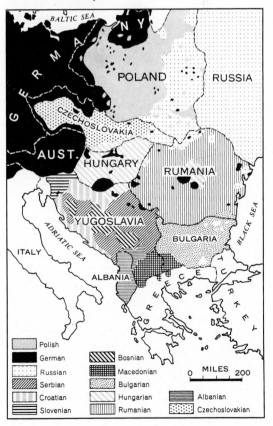

Polish		
German	Bosnian	
Russian	Macedonian	
Serbian	Bulgarian	
Croatian	Hungarian	Albanian
Slovenian	Rumanian	Czechoslovakian

0   MILES   200

Americans were not yet ready to assume the role they were destined to play as the world's most powerful nation. America's absence from the League could not help but have unfortunate results. In an assembly dominated by the European victors, the United States would have served as an impartial arbiter. The League of Nations had many shortcomings; but none was as important as the gap left by America's refusal to become a member.

The League of Nations and Collective Security

The general purpose of the League was "to promote international cooperation and to achieve international peace and security." It was founded on the concept of collective security, under which peace was to be maintained by the community of nations rather than by an uncertain "balance of power." The specific tasks of the League were: to work for international disarmament; to prevent war by arbitration of international disputes; to apply sanctions against aggressors; and to register and revise international agreements. In very few of these tasks was the League successful.

Disarmament

The Treaty of Versailles had stated that the disarmament of Germany was intended "to render possible the initiation of a general limitation of the armaments of all nations." But despite this implied promise, general disarmament was tackled most hesitantly. Only in 1926 did a Preparatory Commission begin discussions of a Disarmament Conference, and the Conference itself did not meet until 1932. Its deliberations at that time proved entirely fruitless.

There were several causes for this failure. Shortly after the war, the Allied Military Control Commission began to report a long series of German violations of the Versailles disarmament provisions. Most important were secret contacts between the new German *Reichswehr* and the Russian Red Army. The evidence of these German violations was sketchy, but it was alarming

enough to keep the Allies from reducing their own military establishments. Another reason for Allied failure to disarm was the difficulty of finding a valid basis for determining a nation's military power. Geographic location, manpower, industrial development, and raw materials, it was felt, were far more important than the actual size of armies. In most of these factors Germany and the Soviet Union excelled, and any general disarmament would have been greatly to their advantage.

Arbitration of International Disputes

The second task of the League was to arbitrate international disputes. Members promised to bring any dispute "suitable for submission to arbitration" before the League Council. Any decision by the Council had to be "unanimously agreed to by the members thereof." If the Council's decision was not unanimous, League members were free to take whatever action they deemed appropriate. Despite the vagueness of these provisions, the League was able to settle a number of international conflicts. Of some thirty cases submitted during the 1920's, the majority were arbitrated. The League was most effective in settling disputes between small powers. As soon as a major power was involved, however, the League proved quite powerless. In the "Corfu incident" of 1923, for instance, when Italy bombarded and occupied the Greek island of Corfu in retaliation for the murder of some Italians, the Italian government refused to acknowledge the League's competency.

Sanctions Against Aggression

The League's procedure in dealing with military aggression was laid down in Article 16 of the Covenant. As major punishment it provided for economic sanctions against the guilty party. This policy, to be effective, needed the cooperation of all the great powers. But since two or more of them usually were outside the League, the application of strict economic sanctions proved impossible. This was to become evident during Japan's invasion of China in 1931 and Italy's war against Abyssinia in 1935. Article 16 also provided for military sanctions, but these were left entirely to individual members. The League itself had no armed forces.

Treaty Revision

The registration and publication of international agreements, called for under Article 18 of the Covenant, was intended to prevent the "secret diplomacy" that Wilson had blamed for helping to start the war. Even so, most serious diplomatic negotiations after the war still went on behind closed doors, and the fear of secret treaties persisted. More significant than the publication of treaties was the provision made in Article 19 of the Covenant for the revision of existing treaties. Here was a possibility for peaceful changes in the peace treaties, once the hatreds of war had cooled down. Had the powers availed themselves of this opportunity, Europe and the world might have been spared the Second World War.

Clearly the League of Nations suffered from many weaknesses. Most of these could have been eliminated had the great powers been ready to do so. But since each of them was primarily concerned with its own selfish aims, the hopeful experiment of the League turned out a failure. Only in fields that involved none of the vital interests of the great powers did the League score any gains. The League's Mandate Commission was able to improve the standard of colonial administration. The International Labor Organization, affiliated with the League, did much to raise the status of workers everywhere. Various other League agencies concerned themselves with matters of health, the illicit drug traffic, the international arms trade, and so forth. These agencies set important precedents for the far-reaching activities of the United Nations.

The "War After the War," 1919–23

For several years after the Peace Conference, Europe underwent so many major and minor international crises that people sometimes wondered if the war had really come to an end. The Allies intervened against the Bolshevik regime in Russia. Poland fought with Lithuania over the town of Vilna, with Czechoslovakia over the region of Teschen, and with Russia over her eastern frontiers. Polish and German irregular forces fought bloody battles over Upper Silesia in 1922. Intermittent conflicts between Italy and Yugoslavia over Fiume lasted until 1924. The Greeks invaded Turkey between 1919 and 1922 and almost came to blows with Italy in 1923. Austria and Hungary clashed over the Burgenland region in 1921. And in 1923 Germany's default in reparation payments led to the invasion of her key industrial region, the Ruhr district, by French and Belgian troops. These were only the more noteworthy among an unending series of international incidents during the early postwar period.

The French Search for Security

The greatest danger to peace was Germany's desire to escape the restrictions of Versailles. This worried the French in particular. The alliance between France and the Anglo-Saxon powers that had been discussed at the Peace Conference failed to materialize when America withdrew from the peace settlement. Since Germany was still far superior in human and industrial resources, the French felt that their security demanded the strictest fulfillment of the peace terms. But this insistence on fulfillment caused a growing rift between France and Great Britain. The British were trying to dissociate themselves from continental affairs and to devote their attention to overseas interests. Germany was no longer a serious economic and naval rival; and since she had been one of England's best customers before the war, Britain wanted her to get back on her feet. Moreover, England felt that a healthy Germany was the best protection against the westward spread of communism. When France invaded the Ruhr in 1923, therefore, Britain expressed her disapproval. She had no desire to see the French assume hegemony over the Continent.

The loss of British support forced France to look elsewhere for security. With Russia disqualified by communism and Italy dissatisfied with the peace settlement, only the smaller

Peace
Settlements

1914	1918 1919	1920	1923	1924	1929
First World War	"War After the War"		French Occupation of Ruhr	"Era of Locarno"	

"succession states" of central Europe were left. In 1921 France concluded an alliance with Poland, in 1926 with Rumania, and in 1927 with Yugoslavia. In addition, Rumania, Yugoslavia, and Czechoslovakia began to organize the so-called Little Entente in 1921. All these countries were interested in maintaining the *status quo,* which was being threatened by the revisionist agitation not only of Germany but of Hungary and Russia as well. Outwardly this French alliance system looked quite impressive. But the total military strength of these small powers was less than a million men, and they required a great deal of French financial aid. As an attempt, furthermore, to isolate Germany, the French system was doomed from the start, for the two outcasts of Europe—Germany and Russia—began to join hands in 1922.

The *Russo-German* Rapprochement

Russo-German relations after the war at first were strained. The Russians still remembered Brest-Litovsk, and the Germans resented Russia's repeated interference in Germany's domestic affairs. Common economic and military interests, however, gradually led to a political *rapprochement.* The first outward sign of this understanding was a treaty of friendship concluded at Rapallo in April 1922. The world was startled and disturbed by what it suspected of being a military alliance. But the Treaty of Rapallo was merely a promise of cooperation between the two partners, important chiefly because it helped Germany escape her diplomatic isolation. There were people in both Germany and Russia who hoped that the treaty would some day develop into something more. But this hope was never fulfilled. Economically the two countries were quite complementary and both stood to gain from mutual trade. But their economic systems were far too different to make such an exchange possible. Despite some later economic and neutrality agreements, Russo-German relations throughout the 1920's remained decidedly cool.

The Ruhr Occupation

The French occupation of the Ruhr in 1923 marked a turning point in the history of postwar Europe. Germany, already suffering from severe inflation, was thrown into an economic crisis, which was made more severe by the passive resistance the people of the Ruhr put up against the French. This resistance, by cutting the coal France hoped to get from the Ruhr, increased French economic difficulties as well. The Ruhr struggle was ended by the German government, which feared for the nation's existence. There were communist disturbances in central Germany and separatist uprisings in the Rhineland. In the South an unknown ex-corporal, Adolf Hitler, was getting ready to make his first try for power. The Ruhr episode taught an important lesson to both French and Germans. It showed that rigid insistence on the fulfillment of the Versailles Treaty on the one hand, and stubborn resistance against such fulfillment on the other, helped neither side. Both, it seemed, had to give way if Europe was to be saved from chaos. For the next six years a group of dedicated statesmen devoted their efforts to bringing about such a compromise.

The "Era of Locarno," 1924–29

The year 1924 saw important political changes in both France and England. In France the rightist cabinet of Raymond Poincaré, known for his vengeful attitude toward Germany, was replaced after the Ruhr fiasco by a left-wing coalition in which Aristide Briand was foreign minister. In England the Labor Party had a brief inning in 1924 but soon gave way to a Conservative government with Austen Chamberlain as foreign secretary. In Germany the direction of foreign policy after the Ruhr crisis was in the hands of Gustav Stresemann. Together, Briand, Chamberlain, and Stresemann brought Europe a brief respite from fear and uncertainty.

The Locarno Pact

Europe's brief return to "normalcy" after 1924 was chiefly due to a more efficient handling of the reparations problem. Without these economic developments, which we will discuss presently, the *rapprochement* between Germany and the western powers would hardly have come about. The first political result of this *rapprochement* was the Locarno Pact.

Under the terms of the Treaty of Versailles, the Allies were to end their occupation of the Rhineland in three phases, beginning in 1925. But since the Allied Military Control Commission had found Germany guilty of disarmament violations, the Allies refused to leave. Stresemann realized that the basic reason for this refusal was France's fear of Germany. To dispel this fear once and for all, he now proposed a treaty by which not only France and Germany, but also England, Italy, and Belgium, would guarantee the *status quo* in western Europe. Such a treaty was signed at Locarno in October, 1925.

To a world torn by international strife for more than a decade, the Locarno Pact came as a harbinger of a new age in which peace and good will rather than war and suspicion would prevail. "We are citizens each of his own country," Stresemann had said at Locarno, "but we are also citizens of Europe and are joined together by a great concept of civilization." This seeming conversion of Stresemann from a rabid German nationalist into a "good European" commanded the admiration of his contemporaries. But Stresemann was less of an idealist than people thought. He was every bit as eager to abolish the restrictions of Versailles as were his nationalist compatriots. Where Stresemann differed was in his realization that the revision of Versailles could not be achieved by force but only through patient negotiation, once Germany had regained the confidence of the world.

The *rapprochement* between Germany and the West, meanwhile, was causing growing apprehension in the Soviet Union. Despite Russia's resumption of diplomatic relations with France and England in 1924, she had remained an outsider in international affairs. England in particular resented the propagandist activities of

Locarno

The Locarno treaties and Germany's entrance into the League have often been described as the apogee of the international system of 1919. In reality Locarno did not create a secure foundation of a European peace. It covered up certain deep cracks that had appeared in the building, but failed to repair the structural weaknesses. It would have been desirable, and in any case unobjectionable, to make concessions to Germany between 1924 and 1930 in such matters as the occupation of the Rhineland and reparations. Probably much more should have been done to enable the young German democracy to develop under favorable conditions. But it was absolutely essential for Britain and France to keep control of any changes in Germany's position in Europe. A revision of the Versailles Treaty should have been sought by procedures of international law and multilateral agreement and by the determined refusal of unilateral *faits accomplis*. It was a tragic fallacy to believe that eastern Europe could be neglected politically and economically without courting the gravest dangers. Even worse was the unfounded belief that international conflicts would dissolve if the states scuttled their armaments.

From Hajo Holborn, *The Political Collapse of Europe* (New York: Knopf, 1954), pp. 131–32.

the Comintern, and in 1927 she once again severed her connections with the Soviets. What Russia feared most was that Germany, as a member of the League, might some day be forced to participate in sanctions against the Soviet Union. To quiet these Russian fears Stresemann, at Locarno, had obtained a modification of Article 16 of the League Covenant, allowing Germany to abstain from participating in any sanctions that endangered her own security. When this still did not satisfy the Russians, Stresemann in April 1926 signed a treaty of neutrality with them. There were some who saw in this Treaty of Berlin an attempt on Germany's part to play a double game between the East and the West. But there is no doubt that Stresemann's foremost concern was always for closer and stronger relations between Germany and the West.

German Foreign Minister Dr. Gustav Stresemann on the occasion of Germany's admission to the League of Nations, September 10, 1926.

The Kellogg-Briand Pact

The efforts of the powers to guarantee Europe's security by treaties that would bolster the collective security system of the League found their climax in the signing of the Pact of Paris, or Kellogg-Briand Pact, in August 1928. Its sixty-two signatories, which included the United States, promised "to renounce war as an instru-ment of national policy." Nothing was more characteristic of the spirit of hopefulness that pervaded the world after Locarno than this attempt to banish war simply by signing a treaty. The Soviet Union was the only major power not present in Paris, but she joined the pact soon thereafter. If security depended on treaties, the world had nothing more to fear.

The Economic Consequences of the War

The economic consequences of the war were even more serious than its political aftermath. The territorial losses of Germany and the dismemberment of Austria-Hungary by themselves caused a major economic shock among the Central Powers. The Allies added to their distress by making seemingly limitless demands for reparations. But the victors, too, found the going far from easy. In the West, France and Belgium suffered from the devastation of their industrial regions. In eastern Europe, lack of seed, fertilizers, and agricultural implements resulted in a marked decline of farm production. All the powers, England in particular, had lost important foreign markets. And a general return to protective tariffs retarded recovery everywhere.

The effects of the postwar economic crisis were felt in many ways. Five years after the war Europe's total industrial production was still at only two-thirds of its prewar level. Unemployment, never much of a problem in the past, now assumed alarming proportions. Another repercussion of the crisis was felt in financial matters. All the major countries of Europe suffered from severe inflation. In Germany, Austria, and Russia, this inflation led to total devaluation of the currency.

The Reparations Problem

Much of the responsibility for Europe's economic difficulties rested with the peacemakers of 1919. In their efforts to solve the Continent's political problems, they often ignored the economic effects of their decisions. They carved new states out of old empires without regard to economic consequences. They even failed to examine the probable effects of the purely economic terms of the peace. A member of the British peace delegation, the economist John Maynard Keynes, called attention to these oversights in his book, *The Economic Consequences of the Peace* (1920), which was a sweeping indictment of the Versailles settlement on economic grounds. The most troublesome part of the treaty, as Keynes foresaw, turned out to be the reparations provisions. In order to pay the large sums called for, the Central Powers needed surplus capital. This they could gain only through increased exports. But such exports competed with the very nations who hoped to profit from reparations. The transfer of large amounts of capital, furthermore, had unsettling effects on the economies of debtors and creditors alike. It was easy, in other words, to ask for huge reparations, but it was difficult to devise methods of paying them.

The reparations problem was further complicated by the mutual indebtedness of the victors. The easiest way out would have been the cancellation of all inter-Allied debts. This solution was proposed by Britain and France but was rejected by the United States, who would have ended up paying for the whole war. America's refusal made the European Allies more than ever dependent on reparations.

The main source of reparations was Germany. The total amount of Germany's obligations had been left open at the Peace Conference. It was later settled at $32 billion. From the start Germany fell behind in her payments. The French, who were to receive more than half of the reparations, were adamant in their demands for prompt payment. The climax of France's insistence on fulfillment came with the invasion of the Ruhr in 1923.

The Dawes Plan and the Young Plan

Prior to this time, America had suggested that the whole reparations issue be studied by an international committee of experts. With the failure of the Ruhr venture, such a committee was appointed late in 1923. It worked out a plan, named after its chairman, the American financier Charles G. Dawes, which went into effect in September 1924. Under the Dawes Plan, Germany was to pay gradually rising amounts that were to reach a "standard annuity" in 1929. The Dawes Plan worked well. More than people realized, however, Germany's ability to pay depended on the influx of foreign loans. With the return of general confidence in her economic stability, Germany began to attract large amounts of capital, especially from the United States. This flow continued until 1929, when American investors began to speculate at home. Since at the same time Germany's yearly payments under the Dawes Plan were about to reach the "standard annuity," and since no time limit had been set on such payments, this seemed a good time to reconsider the whole reparations question.

A series of meetings between German and foreign experts during 1929 finally led to the Young Plan, named after the American expert Owen D. Young. It fixed Germany's total obligations at $29 billion, to be paid over fifty-nine years. But the Young Plan never went into effect. As the Great Depression spread from the United States to Europe, Germany ceased her payments altogether. At a final conference in Lausanne in 1932, Germany was relieved of any future obligations. Opinions differ widely on the total amount of reparations actually paid by Germany. A likely estimate puts it at $6 billion. This was not only far less than originally demanded, but in return Germany had received a far larger amount in foreign loans. The history of reparations has been compared to a merry-go-round: Germany borrowed American funds to pay reparations to the Allies, who used the money to repay their debts to the United States, who lent the money back to Germany.

European Recovery

American capital played an important role in the economic life of Europe. Most of America's loans were private and short-term. Their repayment was made more difficult, furthermore, by the American government's tariff policy. Instead of helping foreign debtors to meet their obligations through increased exports, the United States surrounded itself with high tariff walls. This policy soon provoked a worldwide wave of protectionism. Insistent warnings by European economists against such shortsightedness finally led the League of Nations to call a World Economic Conference in 1927. In their final report, the delegates of the more than fifty participating nations urged their governments to lower tariffs as soon and as much as possible. Before this advice was taken, the Great Depression began. Not least among its causes was the protectionist policy of the postwar years.

Except for its warning on tariffs, however, the World Economic Conference was quite optimistic. Europe's economy after 1925 seemed to justify such optimism. France had rebuilt her destroyed regions, had modernized her industry, and had stabilized her currency. Germany had recovered from the shock of inflation and with the aid of foreign loans had improved her industries so that once again she was the industrial leader of Europe. England's recovery was made much slower by her adherence to the gold standard, her antiquated production methods, and the high living standard of her workers. In Italy, the Fascist government of Benito Mussolini successfully raised the nation's food production. Even in Russia the "New Economic Policy," with its partial return to capitalist practices, brought gradual recovery from the aftermath of war and revolution.

But this apparent economic recovery also had its weak points. It was chiefly restricted to industry. Agriculture continued to suffer from overproduction and foreign competition. The resulting decline of rural buying power reacted upon industry. Some producers, tempted by American loans and the example of American mass-production methods, expanded far beyond the need of their markets. When, after the crash of the American stock market in October 1929, new American loans to Europe ceased and old loans were suddenly recalled, Europe's economy, deprived of its lifeblood, collapsed.

Within one decade, Europe had thus come full cycle from despair through hope and back to despair. In the early twenties it had seemed that the German Oswald Spengler had been right in his best-seller, *The Decline of the West* (1918), which predicted the impending doom of European civilization. But then in the mid-twenties a "silver lining" had appeared on the horizon. The optimism of the "Era of Locarno" may appear unjustified in retrospect. But to contemporaries the decrease of international tension, the economic recovery, and the general air of well-being and stability seemed quite real. They were seen as proof that Europe at long last had found the peace it had so long been looking for. We may rightly wonder what would have happened if the recovery of Europe had lasted for another decade. In any attempt to find the causes of the unhappy events of the thirties and forties, the Great Depression will always loom large.

Suggestions for Further Reading

1. General

There are many volumes covering world history since 1914. The most original is C. Quigley, *Tragedy and Hope: A History of the World in Our Time* (1966). Other outstanding contributions are: F. P. Chambers, *This Age of Conflict: The Western World—1914 to the Present,* 3rd ed. (1962); and E. N. Anderson, *Modern Europe in World Perspective* (1950). D. Thomson, ed., *The Era of Violence, 1898–1945* (1960), Vol. XII in the *New Cambridge Modern History* series, has contributions by noted specialists on every facet of European and world history. A. J. P. Taylor, *From Sarajevo to Potsdam** (1966), presents a highly readable survey. The declining influence of Europe in world affairs is the theme of a stimulating book by H. Holborn, *The Political Collapse of Europe* (1954). R. Aron, *The Century of Total War** (1955), is a thoughtful analysis of world events in the twentieth century; and G. Barraclough, *An Introduction to Contemporary History** (1964), presents a provocative discussion of modern issues.

2. The First World War

On the larger issues of the war, see R. Albrecht-Carrié, *The Meaning of the First World War** (1965), and J. J. Roth, ed., *World War I: A Turning Point in Modern History* (1967). The military side is told in B. H. Liddell Hart, *The War in Outline** (1936), and in V. J. Esposito, *A Concise History of World War I** (1964). On the home fronts, see: F. P. Chambers, *The War Behind the War, 1914–1918: A History of the Political and Civilian Fronts* (1939); A. Mendelssohn-Bartholdy, *The War and German Society* (1937); and A. Marvick, *The Deluge: British Society and the First World War* (1965). There is no comprehensive diplomatic history for the war years. The problem of war aims is treated in: F. Fischer, *Germany's Aims in the First World War* (1967); H. W. Gatzke, *Germany's Drive to the West** (1950); and W. R. Louis, *Great Britain and Germany's Lost Colonies, 1914–1919* (1967). The many futile efforts at a negotiated peace short of total victory are summarized in K. Forster, *The Failures of Peace* (1941). America's involvement in the war is discussed in A. S. Link, *Wilson the Diplomatist** (1957), and E. R. May, *The World War and American Isolation* (1959). For a more recent brief assessment, see D. M. Smith, *The Great Departure: The United States and World War I** (1964). To gain a more vivid impression of the war, B. W. Tuchman, *The Guns of August** (1962), and A. J. P. Taylor, *The First World War: An Illustrated History* (1963), are highly recommended.

3. The Russian Revolution

W. H. Chamberlain, *The Russian Revolution, 1917–1921,* 2 vols. (1952), is a standard work. E. H. Carr, *A History of Soviet Russia: The Bolshevik Revolution, 1917–1923,* 3 vols.* (1950–53), is scholarly but controversial. G. Katkov, *Russia 1917: The February Revolution* (1967), is an important study. The background of the revolution is treated authoritatively in A. B. Ulam, *The Bolsheviks: The Intellectual and Political History of the Triumph of Communism in Russia* (1965). The peace negotiations between Russia and the Central Powers are described by J. W. Wheeler-Bennett, *Brest-Litovsk: The Forgotten*

---

* Available in paperback edition.

Peace, March 1918* (1939). Allied intervention is dealt with in detail in G. F. Kennan, *Russia Leaves the War** (1956), and *The Decision to Intervene** (1958). On developments among Russia's national minorities, see R. Pipes, *The Formation of the Soviet Union: Communism and Nationalism, 1917–1923* (1954). O. H. Radkey, *Agrarian Foes of Bolshevism* (1958), deals with the Socialist Revolutionaries during the revolution. Several participants have left their own version of events: L. Trotsky, *The History of the Russian Revolution,* 3 vols. (1932); V. M. Chernov, *The Great Russian Revolution* (1936); A. F. Kerensky, *The Kerensky Memoirs* (1966); and P. T. Wrangel, *The Memoirs of General Wrangel* (1929). A vivid eye-witness account by a young American communist is J. Reed, *Ten Days That Shook the World** (1919).

4. Revolution in Central Europe

The last days of the war are treated in H. R. Rudin, *Armistice, 1918* (1944); F. Maurice, *The Armistices of 1918* (1943); and K. F. Nowak, *The Collapse of Central Europe* (1924). On the overthrow of the Hohenzollern and Habsburg dynasties, see A. J. Ryder, *The German Revolution of 1918* (1967), and Z. A. B. Zeman, *The Break-Up of the Habsburg Empire, 1914–1918* (1961). Both A. Rosenberg, *The Birth of the German Republic** (1931), and O. Jászi, *The Dissolution of the Habsburg Monarchy** (1929), put events in their respective countries into historical perspective. H. Seton-Watson, *Eastern Europe Between Two Wars, 1918–1941** (1945), and S. Borsody, *The Tragedy of Central Europe** (1960), deal with the problems of the small successor states.

5. The Peace Treaties

The standard history of the Peace Conference is H. W. V. Temperley, *A History of the Peace Conference of Paris,* 6 vols. (1920–24). A. J. Mayer, *Politics and Diplomacy of Peacemaking* (1967), is the best general work. F. Czernin, *Versailles 1919** (1966), is a brief recent account. H. Nicolson, *Peacemaking, 1919** (1933), vividly captures the atmosphere of the negotiations. J. M. Thompson, *Russia, Bolshevism, and the Versailles Peace* (1966), deals with a hitherto neglected problem. The classic indictment of the Versailles settlement is J. M. Keynes, *The Economic Consequences of the Peace* (1920). It is ably answered in E. Mantoux, *The Carthaginian Peace, or the Economic Consequences of Mr. Keynes** (1946). P. Birdsall, *Versailles Twenty Years After* (1941), is a judicious reappraisal of the treaty. See also R. B. McCallum, *Public Opinion and the Last Peace* (1944), and the excellent selection of readings in I. J. Lederer, ed., *The Versailles Settlement: Was It Foredoomed to Failure?** (1960). On the peace settlements with Austria and Hungary, see N. Almond and R. H. Lutz, *The Treaty of St. Germain* (1939), and R. Donald, *The Tragedy of Trianon* (1928). America's part in the negotiations is reassessed in T. A. Bailey, *Wilson and the Peacemakers* (1947).

6. The Aftermath of War

An authoritative history of international relations between the two wars is G. M. Gathorne-Hardy, *A Short History of International Affairs, 1920–1939* (1942). See also the brief account by E. H. Carr, *International Relations Between the Two World Wars, 1919–1939** (1947), and the same author's thoughtful analysis of international politics in *The Twenty Years' Crisis, 1919–1939** (1946). On British foreign policy, see F. S. Northedge, *The Troubled Giant: Britain Among the Great Powers, 1916–1939* (1966). Differences between the western powers are treated in A. Wolfers, *Britain and France Between Two Wars** (1940), and in W. M. Jordan, *Great Britain, France, and the German Problem, 1918–1939* (1943). W. J. Newman, *The Balance of Power in the Interwar Years, 1919–1939** (1968), presents a political scientist's analysis. See also L. Kochan, *The Struggle for Germany** (1963). Germany's relations

---

* Available in paperback edition.

with the Soviet Union are covered in K. Rosenbaum, *Community of Fate: German-Soviet Relations, 1922–1928* (1965), and in H. Dyck, *Weimar Germany and Soviet Russia, 1926–1933* (1966). M. Gilbert, *Britain and Germany Between the Wars* (1964), is a brief survey. German agitation over "war guilt" is criticized by L. Fraser, *Germany Between Two Wars: A Study of Propaganda and War Guilt* (1944). On Germany's attempts to evade the disarmament restrictions of Versailles, see H. W. Gatzke, *Stresemann and the Rearmament of Germany** (1954). The reparations problem is surveyed in the book by E. Mantoux, cited in Section 5 above, and in K. Bergmann, *The History of Reparations* (1927). The standard history of the League of Nations is F. P. Walters, *A History of the League of Nations,* 2 vols. (1952).

---

* Available in paperback edition.

16

Democracy in Crisis

As we turn to the domestic affairs of the major powers during the "long armistice" between 1919 and 1939, we find that here, too, the Great War had brought deep changes. Before 1914 the countries of Europe, despite national differences, still had much in common. That feeling of European unity was now gone. The Continent was divided into victors and vanquished, "have" and "have-not" nations. Among the latter were not only the countries that had lost the war but countries, like Italy and Russia, that felt the peace settlements had not achieved all they had hoped for. It was in these "revisionist" powers that a new type of totalitarian government arose which, more than anything else, helped to destroy the traditional unity of Europe (see Chapter 17).

The Continent's unique role in world affairs was also beginning to be challenged. As the United States gradually emerged from its isolation, and as regions that hitherto had been firmly dominated by Europe now began to play a role of their own, Europe's longstanding predominance became a thing of the past. World politics gradually overshadowed European politics.

The Aftermath of War, 1919–29

One of the major war aims of the western powers had been the triumph of democracy over autoc-

Scene from the ballet *The Green Table* by the German choreographer Kurt Jooss. An example of Germany's cultural renaissance after the First World War, the ballet satirized the futile efforts of the diplomats to prevent war by their interminable talks around the conference table.

racy. This aim seemed to have been achieved with the rise of new democratic governments everywhere east of the Rhine. But the war left behind so many unsolved problems that even countries with a democratic tradition, like France and England, found it difficult to return from the semi-authoritarian and efficient conduct of war to the more democratic and inefficient pursuits of peace. It is not surprising, therefore, that some of the new democratic nations found it hard to cope with the aftermath of war and that their new democracy in many cases turned out to be short-lived.

Stability in Great Britain

Among the western powers, Great Britain enjoyed by far the most stable domestic development. Democracy scored a success when Britain's franchise was extended to all adults in two further reform acts. Transition from war to peace was made easier by the re-election of Lloyd George's coalition cabinet in 1918 and by a brief industrial boom. Beginning in 1920, however, England entered upon an extended economic crisis. Its political effect was to shift power away from the Liberals, first toward the Conservatives and later to Labor.

During most of the 1920's Britain was ruled by the Conservatives, who tried valiantly but vainly to tackle the perennial problems of a large deficit and widespread unemployment. In the elections of 1929 Labor finally won its first major victory. But even this did not give it sufficient strength to introduce decisive economic reforms. The solution of England's economic difficulties had to wait until after the end of the Great Depression.

Despite her unsettled economy, Britain had no serious domestic disturbances. There was some unrest among the workers, and in 1926 trouble in the coal mines led to a general strike. But there was no violence. A certain innate moderation seemed to make the average Englishman poor material for radical agitation from either Right or Left. The Labor Party, though accused of being "soft" on communism, was always moderate in its program and policy; and the Conservatives, though eager to curb the power of the labor unions, were sincerely concerned over the workingman's welfare. The government's policy of maintaining a stable currency was detrimental to British trade, since it hampered competition on the world market. But it also saved Britain's middle class from the demoralizing effects of inflation that were felt in most continental countries.

Instability in France

France led a far more hectic existence after the war. She was worse off economically, having suffered greater losses than Britain. Moreover, the French electoral system of proportional representation, introduced after the First World War, aggravated the excessive factionalism of French politics and caused great instability. There were more than forty different cabinets during the interwar period. For the first five years after the war France was governed by a "national bloc" of rightist and center parties, with Raymond Poincaré as the leading figure. In 1924 reversals in foreign policy, notably the Ruhr fiasco, brought to power a "Cartel of the Left," in which Édouard Herriot and Aristide Briand were prominent. The most urgent task before the French government was the reconstruction of the devastated regions along the northeastern frontiers. Since Germany, until 1924, remained behind in her reparations payments, France herself had to pay for this reconstruction. Attempts to raise the necessary funds through increased taxation ran into opposition from the parties of the Right. Only the threat of runaway inflation and the pressure of public demonstrations finally led to drastic action. In 1926 a cabinet of "national union" under Poincaré was able to stabilize the currency and put France on the road to recovery. With reconstruction completed and German reparations coming in regularly, France's economy improved rapidly. By 1928 the budget began to show a surplus, unemployment had vanished, and increased wages together with benefits from social legislation gave the lower classes a greater share than before in the nation's economy. France seemed well on the way toward resolving the long-standing conflicts between her rich and her poor.

The Weimar Republic

The new German republic from the beginning was plagued by disunity and disorder. Early in 1919 a constituent assembly at Weimar had drawn up an admirably democratic constitution. One of its less happy features, however, was the adoption of proportional representation. As in France, this scheme contributed greatly to political instability. During the fourteen years of its existence, the Weimar Republic saw more than twenty different cabinets, although the heavy legacy of war required a government that had the full support of its citizens. Throughout most of its brief life, the Weimar Republic failed to win such support.

The most loyal friends of the republic were the workers who had suffered most from political discrimination under the empire. The German working class, however, was no longer united. It had been split before and during the revolution of 1918 into a moderate majority of Social Democrats and a radical minority that later formed the German Communist Party. The latter openly threatened to overthrow the republic and on several occasions between 1919 and 1923 tried to carry out its threat.

Most of the bourgeois parties of the Weimar Republic professed loyalty to the new regime, although the parties of the Right were known to be hostile to it. This hostility was nourished by nationalist propaganda, which blamed the republic both for Germany's defeat and for the signing of the *Diktat* of Versailles. Soon after the war, rabidly nationalistic groups of "free corps" and veterans' organizations embarked on a series of uprisings against the hated republic.

Considering the many attacks from every direction, it is surprising that the Weimar Republic was able to survive. But even though most Germans were not very enthusiastic about the new state, they were even less enthusiastic about the extremists who threatened to overthrow it. In the early twenties the moderate antirepublican parties of the Right were able to attract almost 30 percent of the votes. But as Germany's economy improved after 1924, the prorepublican parties made significant gains at the expense of the opposition. Had this recovery lasted longer, the Germans might yet have become reconciled to their new republic.

The New Nations of Eastern Europe

If democracy found the going rough in Germany, it faced even greater difficulties in eastern Europe. Most of the states in this area had gained their independence as a result of the war, and most of them faced similar problems. With the exception of Austria and Czechoslovakia, their economy was predominantly agrarian, and the division of large estates among the peasantry had long been a major issue. Where such land reform was carried out successfully, as in the Baltic states, the rise of independent small proprietors contributed a great deal to political stability. In Poland and Hungary, on the other hand, where reform was obstructed by the landed aristocracy, domestic peace remained precarious.

Economic recovery in most of eastern Europe was slow. Widespread illiteracy, antiquated agricultural methods, and lack of capital funds for industrialization were the main obstacles. Efforts at economic collaboration, especially among the Austrian succession states, ran into strong nationalist opposition. Nationalism in eastern Europe was intensified by the problem of minorities. Almost all the new nations included large numbers of foreign nationals.

All the new states started out with modern constitutions and parliamentary governments. But this democratic trend was soon reversed. The first to change was Hungary. After a brief communist interlude under Bela Kun in 1919, order was restored by conservative forces under Admiral Nicholas Horthy, who founded Europe's first postwar dictatorship of the Right. In

Poland the rise of authoritarian rule came with Marshal Joseph Pilsudski's seizure of power in 1926. Elsewhere "strong men" suspended constitutions and silenced political opposition. With no democratic experience and hopeless economic conditions, firm rule seemed to be the only alternative. None of these regimes was as totalitarian as the communist dictatorship in Russia or the fascist dictatorship in Italy. It was only after Hitler's rise in the 1930's, when fascism gained control over most of central Europe, that the rule of these small dictators became increasingly arbitrary (see Chapter 17).

Among the few countries in eastern Europe where democracy took hold after the war, the most important were Czechoslovakia and Austria. Czechoslovakia, ably led by Thomas Masaryk and Eduard Beneš, was generally considered the model among the new democracies. Here land reform was carried out succesfully, and with almost half of Austria's former industry under Czech control the country enjoyed a balanced economy. Czechoslovakia's major problem was

the desire for greater autonomy among her numerous minorities, which amounted to almost one-third of her population. Especially troublesome were the 3 million Germans living in the Sudeten region.

Austria, since the war, had only Germans within her borders. But even so the new republic was deeply divided along social and economic lines between the urban, industrialized, and radical workers of Vienna, and the rural, agrarian, and conservative peasants of the provinces. Economically, Austria suffered greatly from the consequences of partition. In 1922 the situation became so serious that the League had to step in and grant substantial loans for Austrian reconstruction. By 1926 Austria seemed to be out of danger. But the real cause of her difficulties—the loss of her economic hinterland—had not been removed. As the least viable among the new states of Europe, Austria was to be the first to feel the effects of the Great Depression that spread from the United States to Europe during the early thirties.

The Tragedy of Central Europe

There is no ground for revising the well-established unfavourable opinion about the Habsburg rule in Central Europe. There is much reason, however, for reconsidering the sympathetic opinions about the sovereign nation-states which succeeded the Habsburgs. For these nation-states have also failed, like the Habsburgs, to create a new stable order in that dangerous Middle Zone of Europe situated between Germany and Russia. They too have failed in their alleged mission as bulwarks of peace and security—notwithstanding the opinions of nationalists who readily lay the blame for Central Europe's tragedy on each other, or on Hitler and Stalin, or on the West's appeasement policy towards Nazi Germany which led to Munich, or on the West's collaboration with Soviet Russia which led to Yalta, but who will not admit that the nation-states purporting to solve Central Europe's problem deserve more than an equal share of the blame.

From Stephen Borsody, *The Tragedy of Central Europe* (New York: Collier Books, 1962), p. 24.

The United States and Europe

The recovery of Europe, though uneven, seemed well under way by 1929. It would have been still further advanced had the United States been more aware of its new responsibilities as the world's leading economic power. But America at first preferred to keep aloof from international politics.

Isolationism and Nationalism

This policy of isolationism was considered extremely selfish by most Europeans. America, after all, had suffered much less from the war than Europe had. As a matter of fact, the United States had gained from the war economically, not merely by supplying the Allies but by penetrating into regions formerly controlled by European commerce. The least America could do, so many Europeans felt, was to forget the loans she had made to her allies during the war. But this the United States refused to do.

There were other sources of friction between the United States and its wartime friends. The

French resented America's refusal to honor President Wilson's promise for a joint guarantee, together with Britain, of French security; the British were alarmed by America's growing commercial and naval competition; and neither France nor Britain welcomed the evident *rapprochement* between the United States and Germany. A further cause for concern among Europeans was America's obvious intent of isolating itself not only politically but economically. In an effort to protect American industry against the competition of cheap foreign labor, America during the 1920's introduced some of the highest tariffs in its history.

America's isolationism also had repercussions at home in a growing opposition to foreign influences. This American nationalism manifested itself in several ways. The Ku Klux Klan soon after the war claimed wide support for its persecution of racial and religious minorities; fear of radical elements caused a "red scare" that led to the arrest of several thousand suspects; and, most important, restrictions on foreign immigration severely restricted the flow of immigrants from backward and hence less desirable regions.

American Involvement in Europe

But no matter how much the United States tried to isolate itself, its humanitarian conscience and its economic interests could not help but lead to renewed involvement in international affairs. Americans had already proved themselves far from isolationist as far as charity was concerned. Various relief organizations right after the war had dispensed millions of dollars' worth of supplies wherever they were most needed, even in the Soviet Union. Beginning in 1924 American experts also took the lead in tackling the reparations problem. With the return of economic stability, American investors during the next five years lent vast amounts to various European countries, especially Germany, Italy, and the smaller nations of central Europe.

In the political sphere America shared the hope of the rest of the world for peace and security. The warm reception that the American people gave the Pact of Paris for "the outlawry of war" was seen by some as a hopeful sign that America had outgrown its isolationism. But in other respects the country remained aloof. Even though the American public had come to favor the League of Nations, the government refused to participate in any except the League's cultural and social work.

America was also concerned over disarmament, not so much on land as on sea. The rising influence of Japan in the Pacific posed a threat to American interests, and the large increase in Japanese naval expenditure made some limitation of naval forces seem highly desirable. Agreement on this point was reached at a naval conference in Washington in 1921–22. It called for a ten-year naval holiday, the scrapping of large numbers of ships, and a fixed ratio of 5 : 5 : 3 respectively for the capital ships of the United States, Britain, and Japan. Subsequent efforts at Geneva in 1927 to extend the agreement to small ships failed because the British refused to recognize America's claim to parity for all categories. The issue was finally settled to American satisfaction at a third conference in London three years later. Since both Japan and the smaller naval powers, France and Italy, remained dissatisfied with the results, these attempts at naval limitation were only partly successful.

America During the "Roaring Twenties"

Although the United States had come out of the war unscathed, it found adjustment to peacetime conditions far from easy. American industry had expanded far beyond its prewar capacity, and the sudden cancellation of government contracts deeply upset the economy. As European industries resumed production, furthermore, United States exports declined. Attempts to cut production costs by lowering wages met with strong opposition from the workers. Once the wartime ban on strikes was lifted, labor unrest flared up once more.

Return to "Normalcy"

In domestic as in foreign affairs, the American people were looking back with nostalgia to the peace and prosperity they had known before the war. The man who promised a return to such "normalcy" was the Republican Warren G. Harding, who was elected President by a large majority in 1922. It was under Harding's administration that America entered upon the era of hectic prosperity for which the 1920's are best remembered. The heyday of the "Roaring Twenties" came under Calvin Coolidge.

The Republican administration's overriding concern was with aiding the American business community. High tariffs, the repeal of the excess-profits tax, the lowering of taxes on corporations and on high incomes, injunctions against strikes, and even the persecution of "radicals" and the restriction of foreign immigration—all these measures directly or indirectly benefited big business. Much of America's phenomenal business expansion was due to the ample capital resources that were available from all segments of society. Big business, so it seemed, was becoming everybody's business.

It was not quite everybody's, though. Neither the worker nor the farmer was getting his due share of prosperity. Labor had suffered from the postwar depression and from the popular hysteria that equated union protest with communism. As a result, union membership during the 1920's declined from its wartime high. The American Federation of Labor held its own among skilled workers, but there was no similar organization for the mass of unskilled labor. Even so, most workers in time benefited from the nation's rising economy through almost full employment and better wages.

The stepchild of the American boom was the farmer. He, too, had expanded his operations during the war, borrowing large funds to buy additional land and equipment. As a result, America's farm output by 1919 had more than doubled. From then on, as foreign demand decreased and surpluses accumulated, prices dropped. The government tried to help farmers by creating additional credit facilities and encour-

aging cooperatives, but the Republican administration shrank away from anything that smacked of direct subsidies. Protective tariffs, furthermore, raised the price of industrial products needed by the farmer and led foreign countries to retaliate by cutting down their imports of American grain.

The "Jazz Age"

There was an air of restlessness about America's frantic pursuit of business and pleasure during the "Jazz Age" of the 1920's. As is common in periods of rapid economic expansion, America had its share of private and public corruption. The Eighteenth Amendment of 1920, by its rigorous prohibition of alcoholic beverages, almost invited violation of the law by the average citizen. The "speakeasy" and the "bootlegger" became part of American life, and "racketeering" was a common form of crime.

These, unfortunately, were the features that made the deepest impression abroad. Europeans professed to be shocked by the "materialism" of their *nouveau riche* American cousins. But Europe did not remain entirely immune to American influences. American products and production methods found ready imitators abroad, and American styles and American jazz had their admirers among the young. For the first time in history Europe showed signs of becoming Americanized.

The American people themselves seemed well satisfied with their country's apparently endless progress. In 1928 they voted overwhelmingly for another Republican president, Herbert Hoover. There were some developments, however, that should have caused alarm. For some time before 1929, expansion in some basic areas had begun to slow down. Commodity prices had declined steadily from their peak in 1925 and agricultural prices continued to fall. These signs of recession were obscured by a continuing boom on the American stock market. Here prices were bid up by speculation, mostly with borrowed funds, to levels far out of proportion to dividends and earnings. The first danger signals came in mid-September 1929, when stock prices showed some decline. Failures of speculative companies in London later in the month caused some tremors on Wall Street, but still no panic. The collapse of the American stock market came suddenly, on October 23. The next day, "Black Thursday," American investors sold close to 20 million shares at a total loss of $40 billion. The Great Depression had begun.

The Great Depression

With the rise of industrialization, "business cycles"—that is, alternating phases of prosperity and depression—had become a recognized feature of modern capitalism. But there had never been a depression quite so severe as the one touched off by the American stock-market crash. The basic cause of the depression was the world's failure to solve the economic problems inherited from the First World War. As we have seen, neither at the Peace Conference nor afterward was there any real awareness of how interdependent the world had become economically. Industrial expansion continued full force after the war and soon led to overproduction. Beginning in 1924 a brief period of recovery set in. But, as we now know, that recovery was artificial. As neither farmers nor workers really shared in the economic rise, purchasing power failed to keep up with production. In countries like Germany and Austria, furthermore, industrial expansion was largely stimulated by foreign credits. As these credits dried up, recovery ceased and the economy of these nations collapsed.

This, however, did not happen until the spring of 1931. In the meantime the situation in central Europe had become serious enough to demand radical remedies. One solution proposed in early 1931 was for an Austro-German customs union. But this proposal met with strong opposition from the French, who regarded it as a first step toward an eventual political *Anschluss*. To put pressure on the Austrians,

France began to withdraw some of its short-term credits. In May 1931 Austria's largest private bank collapsed. This is generally seen as the beginning of the European phase of the Great Depression. In July the first German bank suspended payments. In September the British government abandoned the gold standard. As other nations followed Britain's example, the only major power to cling to the gold standard was France. Here the depression was not seriously felt until 1932.

Effects of the Depression

It is difficult to convey the staggering economic blow that the world suffered in the brief span of three or four years after 1929. World industrial production declined more than one-third, prices dropped more than one-half, and more than 30 million people lost their jobs. Some countries were harder hit than others. Germany's industrial production declined by almost 40 percent, and at the height of the depression only one-third of Germany's workers were fully employed. In the United States, industrial production and national income by 1933 had decreased more than one-half, and the unemployment figure was estimated at 14 million.

Because of the worldwide scope of the depression, any attempt to counteract it demanded cooperation among all the major powers. As debtor nations began to default on their obligations, President Hoover in 1931 initiated a year's moratorium on all reparations and war debts. But this proved only a stop-gap. A year later an economic conference at Lausanne all but buried the troublesome problem of intergovernmental debts. To save Germany from complete chaos, a "standstill agreement" in 1931 temporarily stopped the panicky withdrawal of short-term loans; but this did not halt the country's economic decline. Finally, a World Economic Conference in London in 1933 sought to stabilize currencies. It failed when America refused to participate.

International efforts to pull the world out of its economic slump thus turned out to be

The Great Depression in the United States: a breadline.

either too little or too late. In the meantime governments everywhere reverted to the same practices that had helped to bring on the depression in the first place. As America raised its tariffs to unprecedented heights, the rest of the powers followed suit, with even Britain abandoning her traditional policy of free trade in 1932. These and other measures of economic nationalism hindered rather than helped the revival of international trade.

The Democracies on the Eve of the Second World War

The Great Depression belonged to both world wars—its roots went back to the First, and its effects contributed to the Second. While govern-

ments were still trying to repair the damages of the upheaval of 1929, clouds were already gathering for the far greater catastrophe of 1939. In this mounting crisis, resolute political leadership was imperative. In countries like Germany and the successor states of central Europe, democratic governments were no longer able to provide such leadership. As authoritarian regimes gained the upper hand in these nations, they were lost to the democratic cause. But even among the western democracies, the crisis of the 1930's called for firm guidance of political and economic affairs. The need for such guidance was felt particularly strongly in the United States.

The "New Deal"

The Hoover administration, unwilling to interfere with free enterprise, had done little to help relieve the economic crisis. Discontent with Republican half-measures was chiefly responsible for the Democratic sweep in the elections of 1932. For more than twelve years thereafter, the United States was guided by Franklin D. Roosevelt. A superb politician and an inveterate optimist, the President's policy of meeting the most difficult domestic and foreign emergencies with boldness and confidence earned him the admiration of the majority of Americans.

Many of Roosevelt's measures were intended for immediate relief and were thus of passing significance, but many others remain in effect to the present day. Republicans at the time charged that government interference with free enterprise, together with vast "give-away programs," tended to corrupt America's pioneering spirit of self-reliance and would ultimately lead to socialism and bankruptcy. In taxing the rich and aiding the poor, America certainly went far toward repudiating its traditional faith in laissez faire. But the rising standard of living of the masses tended to hasten rather than retard the growth of American business; and if the "welfare state" entailed staggering financial burdens, the nation as a whole seemed willing and able to bear them. The unanimity with which the American people supported the country's war efforts during the Second World War was certainly due in no small measure to the peaceful social and economic revolution of the preceding decade.

Great Britain: Slow Recovery

The most successful holding action against the depression in Europe was waged in Great Britain. In the hope of rallying parliamentary support, Ramsay MacDonald in 1931 transformed his Labor cabinet into a national coalition government. Subsequent elections, however, returned overwhelming Conservative majorities, and in 1935 Stanley Baldwin took over as Prime minister. He was succeeded two years later by Neville Chamberlain. As might be expected from a predominantly Conservative regime, Britain sought to solve her economic problems by retrenchment rather than reform. Taxes were raised, government expenditures were cut, and interest rates were lowered. The devaluation of the pound stimulated exports. By the Imperial Duties Bill of 1932 the Conservatives at long last won their battle for protectionism. Subsequent trade agreements with Germany, the Scandinavian countries, and Russia improved British sales abroad. The over-all effect of these measures was a modest but steady recovery. This was due more to the strength of the nation's capital reserves, however, than to any farsighted government policy. The Conservatives were deeply opposed to governmental economic planning. Instead, they preferred to have industry

Roosevelt's New Deal

In our day these economic truths have become accepted as self-evident . . . :

> The right to a useful and remunerative job in the industries or shops or farms or mines of the nation;
>
> The right to earn enough to provide adequate food and clothing and recreation;
>
> The right of every farmer to raise and sell his products at a return which will give him and his family a decent living;
>
> The right of every businessman, large or small, to trade in an atmosphere of freedom from unfair competition and domination by monopolies at home or abroad;
>
> The right of every family to a decent home;
>
> The right to adequate protection from the economic fears of old age, sickness, accident and unemployment;
>
> The right to a good education.

All of these rights spell security. . . . For unless there is security here at home there cannot be lasting peace in the world.

From Franklin D. Roosevelt, message to Congress, January 11, 1944.

Franklin Delano Roosevelt, the man of the hour, at the beginning of his first administration (March 1933), with Mrs. Roosevelt and their son James.

help itself. National income, to be sure, increased; but the basis of Britain's economy, her export trade, did not increase commeasurably.

There were few important events in British politics during the 1930's. The abdication of Edward VIII in 1936, to marry an untitled divorcee, seemed to strengthen the monarchy rather than weaken it. Economic improvement helped to keep labor unrest at a minimum. Britain's main concern was with developments abroad, where Italy and Germany had started on the course of aggression that was to culminate in the Second World War.

France: A House Divided

In contrast to England and the United States, where democracy successfully withstood the severe test of depression, the French Third Republic during the 1930's was shaken to its

French Premier Léon Blum unveiling the Column of Peace in the Place du Trocadero at a time of mounting international crisis.

very foundations. With a high degree of self-sufficiency, a huge gold reserve, and no unemployment to speak of, France until 1932 was an island of prosperity in a sea of economic misery. But when disaster came it struck swiftly. By 1935 French industrial production had fallen almost one-third, exports were declining rapidly, and capital was fleeing the country at an alarming rate. Things looked up briefly after the government devalued the franc in 1936, but the rise in domestic prices soon neutralized any advantage.

It was not so much the severity of the economic crisis as the inability of the French government to cope with it that accounts for the political chaos that ended with the fall of France in 1940. The Third Republic had been deeply divided from the start. As time went on and France became more and more industrialized, economic development accentuated political differences. Workers and petty employees were almost outcasts from normal French society, while the Right-leaning wealthy classes and peasants had little enthusiasm for the Republic. The war had temporarily drawn the nation together, and once the difficult postwar transition had been made French domestic tensions at long last seemed to have eased. But at this most critical point, the depression intervened, reopening wounds that had only just begun to heal.

Discontent with the government's handling of the economic crisis flared up with sudden violence during the Stavisky scandal in early 1934. Rumors that the machinations of an unsavory promoter, Alexander Stavisky, had enjoyed support from persons high in the government touched off a major riot among Rightist elements in Paris. Many of the rioters were members of various fascist leagues, right-wing and royalist organizations, which in aims and tactics were similar to Hitler's storm troopers and Mussolini's black shirts. Fascism, like communism, was a disease apt to strike any country that was weakened by internal discord.

The government's efforts to meet the emergency by rallying the country behind a cabinet of national union, such as Poincaré had formed in 1926, proved fruitless. In 1936 the parties of the Left—Radical Socialists, Socialists, and Communists—became sufficiently alarmed over the fascist threat, both at home and abroad, to bury their longstanding differences. Their "Popular Front" won a decisive popular victory in the subsequent elections.

For almost two years various Leftist coalitions, in which the Socialist Léon Blum was the leading figure, tried their best to halt the disintegration of the Republic. Blum introduced more far-reaching reforms than any government since the war. But to succeed, Blum's program of social reform needed the cooperation of France's businessmen and bankers. And that cooperation was not forthcoming. There were other obstacles to recovery, notably the unsettled state of international affairs, which called for costly rearmament. But the basic reason for Blum's failure was that he was too radical for the Right and not radical enough for the Left. While the Germans were preparing to fight the world, the French were fighting one another. Successive waves of "sitdown" strikes—a French innovation—and a rigidly enforced 40-hour week slowed down industry when it should have been working overtime. In April 1938 a slight shift to the Right brought Édouard Daladier to the premiership, with far-reaching powers to rule by decree. But Daladier could not do what so many able men before him had failed to do: heal the breach between Right and Left, bourgeoisie and workers, capitalists and socialists, rich and poor. It was a deeply divided France that went to war in September 1939, and it was thus that Hitler found her in the spring of 1940.

The Twilight of Imperialism

In our discussion of events between the two world wars, we have dealt thus far only with Europe and the United States. But there were important developments elsewhere in the world that affected especially those countries that had colonial possessions. Beginning with the First World War, western imperialism entered upon a slow but steady decline. Economists had long questioned the advantages of colonies to the mother country, and historians had claimed that colonial rivalry had been one of the major causes of the war. The war itself had lowered the prestige of the great powers and had aroused a feeling of nationalism among the colonial peoples. Just as the desire for independence among European nations had made for international unrest during the nineteenth century, so colonial nationalism was a major cause of international unrest in the twentieth.

The Mandate System

The powers had shown signs of a more enlightened attitude toward colonies at the peace conference, when they made the mandate system part of the League of Nations Covenant. Former German colonies and certain territories taken from Turkey were to be administered by mandatory powers responsible to the League. In theory this first experiment in international supervision over backward regions was a worthy innovation. But in practice the former German colonies became almost indistinguishable from the mandatory powers' own colonies; and of the more advanced Turkish regions that were promised ultimate independence, only Iraq became a sovereign state. Transjordan, under British tutelage like Iraq, was considered too weak to stand on its own feet. The French mandates, Syria and Lebanon, made some progress toward self-government, but the constitutions granted these countries assured continued French control.

A special case among Turkey's former possessions was the British mandate of Palestine. The root of the trouble in that area was the conflicting national aspirations of Arabs and Jews. Nationalism among the Jews went back to the Zionist Organization, founded by Theodor Herzl in 1897 to provide a home for the Jews in Palestine. In 1917 the British government, in the so-called Balfour Declaration, had backed these Zionist aspirations, with the qualification "that nothing shall be done which may prejudice the civil and religious rights of existing non-Jewish communities in Palestine." Both Arabs and Jews at first seemed ready to cooperate in joint plans for the future of Palestine. But as more and more Jews migrated to Palestine, the Arabs feared that the Jews would emerge as the dominant faction. In 1929 the first major riots broke out among Arabs and Jews. With the advent of Hitler in 1933, Palestine became a refuge for thousands of Jews and immigration increased manyfold. The result was further tension and intermittent violence between Arabs and Jews. On the eve of the Second World War, the future of Palestine was still far from settled.

The British Commonwealth

The mandate system was not the only innovation in colonial administration after the First World War. There were also important changes within the British Empire. As we have seen, during the nineteenth century those regions of the empire inhabited chiefly by white settlers had gradually changed from colonies into self-governing dominions. This emancipation from British influence continued after the war. The dominions had served loyally at the side of the mother country during the war. But at the peace conference, on matters concerning their own interests, they had shown considerable independence. When on several other occasions during the 1920's the dominions refused to follow Britain's lead, it became clear that the relationship needed clarification. This was achieved at the Imperial Conference of 1926. The formula agreed upon at that time stated that Great Britain and the dominions were to be completely equal in status, united only through common allegiance to the crown. The British Commonwealth of Nations thus established was officially launched by the Statute of Westminster in 1931. The dominions thus became fully sovereign states, bound to the mother country merely by ties of blood, sentiment, and economic self-interest.

Even so tenuous a relationship, however, was too much for one member of the Commonwealth—Ireland. Efforts to extend home rule to that unhappy island had been interrupted by the outbreak of war in 1914. During the war, the anti-British Easter Rebellion of 1916, spearheaded by the Republican Sinn Fein movement, had been put down with undue severity. From here on, Sinn Fein became the most dynamic force in Irish politics. In 1921 Britain set up the Irish Free State which held dominion status and thus

shared in the transition from Empire to Commonwealth. Yet in the midst of this hopeful development the depression came, and with it a resurgence of radicalism. In the elections of 1932 the Republicans gained a majority and their leader, Eamon De Valera, became president. During the next few years Ireland severed most of its connections with Great Britain. A new constitution in 1937 completely ignored crown and Commonwealth.

India

Another part of the British Empire that was clamoring for independence was India. Like the dominions, India had stood loyally by Great Britain during the war. As a reward for this support, India expected to be given self-government. A new Government of India Act in 1919, however, still fell far short of home rule. The extremists in the National Congress Party, therefore, refused to cooperate. The new leader of the Congress Party was Mohandas K. Gandhi. A lawyer educated in England, Gandhi had supported the British during the First World War, only to become their most persistent foe thereafter. The keynote of his policy was "noncooperation," an attempt to bring about the breakdown of British rule through passive resistance.

There is no need to go into the many fruitless conferences and proposals by which England tried to solve the Indian problem. Since all of them fell short of granting at least dominion status, they were turned down by the National Congress. The claim of the Congress Party that it represented all of India was denied by the Moslem League of Mohammed Ali Jinnah. This religious split was India's most burning problem. But there were others—economic crises, natural catastrophes, riots, strikes, and famines —all of them adding to the country's extreme instability. When war began in 1939, India's entrance into the family of Commonwealth nations seemed as far away as it had been twenty years earlier.

Colonial Nationalism

The colonial nationalism that caused so much trouble in India was felt elsewhere in the British Empire and in the overseas possessions of the other powers. Britain's protectorate over Egypt was officially terminated in 1922, but continued British control over the Sudan and the Suez Canal gave the Egyptian nationalist "Wafd" party ample cause for agitation. France, in theory at least, had for some time granted French citizenship and representation in the French parliament to some of its colonies. But the French method of centralized rule discouraged the growth of colonial self-government. In advanced regions like North Africa and Indochina, native nationalists rebelled against Frenchification and demanded a voice in running their own affairs. A similar trend was evident in the Netherlands East Indies, where a swiftly growing nationalist movement opposed the enlightened but paternalistic rule of the Dutch.

The End of American Colonialism

One country that was really in earnest about abandoning its imperialist practices was the United States. America had only one real colony, the Philippines. After repeatedly promising independence to the islands, Congress in 1934 provided for American withdrawal after a transition period of ten years. In 1946 the Philippines became a sovereign nation. In Latin America, American "dollar diplomacy" continued briefly after the First World War. But in time the United States adopted a more benevolent "good neighbor policy," especially in economic matters. In 1930 the Clark Memorandum abandoned the Roosevelt Corollary to the Monroe Doctrine, which had been used in the past to excuse United States intervention in Latin America.

The Far East: Prelude to War

Almost everywhere in the world, colonialism after the First World War found itself on the defensive against native nationalism. The only region where imperialism still thrived was in the Far East. Here Japan, between the two world wars, embarked on a wholly new phase of expansion, mainly at the expense of China. During the war the Chinese Republic had already felt the threat of its powerful neighbor: The Twenty-one Demands of 1915 had established a Japanese sphere of influence over the mainland

opposite Japan; and Chinese efforts at the peace conference to enlist Allied support in regaining the Shantung Peninsula had proved in vain. Only when the powers realized that Japanese expansion might threaten their own interests did they become alarmed. The Washington Conference of 1921–22, while dealing primarily with naval disarmament, had also discussed the future of China. The powers at Washington reaffirmed the "Open Door" principle and promised to respect China's integrity and independence. In effect things were where they had been before 1914.

China Under the Kuomintang

China's domestic affairs, since the death of General Yüan in 1916, had been chaotic, with powerful war lords ruling the various provinces. The only group that held any promise for the future were the Chinese Nationalists of the Kuomintang. But although their leader, Sun Yat-sen, was elected president in 1921, his influence was restricted to a small region around Canton. His program of freeing China from outside influences needed foreign help. Since he had been rebuffed by the West in the past, Sun Yat-sen in 1923 turned to the Russians for aid. The Soviet Union welcomed the Chinese Republic not only as an ally against Japan but also as a possible convert to communism. A Chinese Communist Party had been founded in 1921. As a result of its collaboration with the U.S.S.R., the Kuomintang, hitherto a small organization, now became a mass movement. To provide the trained military forces necessary to unite China, a military academy was founded under the direction of an able young officer and ardent follower of Sun Yat-sen, Chiang Kai-shek. Sun Yat-sen himself did not live to see the initial success of his movement for unification. He died in 1925 and to this day remains the saint and symbol of the struggle for Chinese unity.

The campaign against the northern war lords was led by Chiang Kai-shek. It began in 1926 and was most successful. By 1929 the Nationalist government controlled the whole country from its headquarters at Nanking. But except for the lower Yangtze region, its control was at best nominal. In the West and North the provincial war lords maintained their power; and to the south, in Kiangsi and Fukien provinces, the Chinese communists under Mao Tse-tung and Chu Teh were busy organizing the landless peasants in opposition to the Nanking regime. The breach between Chiang Kai-shek and the communists had come in 1927 when Chiang, in a sudden purge, had freed himself from Russian and communist influence. Here we have the seeds of the domestic conflict that was to have such serious consequences after the Second World War.

In the meantime the Nationalist regime had begun to tackle the many problems it had inherited from the past. The western powers assisted by making a few concessions, although most of these did not go far enough. In 1929 Chiang Kai-shek terminated unilaterally the obnoxious treaties granting extraterritoriality to western nations. Railroad construction, a uniform currency, legal reform, and an income tax all tried to help overcome the country's regionalism and backwardness. But the failure of the Nationalist government to introduce an effective agrarian program left the Chinese masses discontented and open to communist agitation. Added to domestic discord and disunity was the constant threat of Japanese intervention.

Moderation in Japan

Japan, in contrast to China, had fared well during the First World War. The country had profited economically from the increased demand for Japanese goods; it had gained territorially from the seizure of German colonies; and it had established a veiled protectorate over part of China. Any desire for further expansion among Japan's militarists was checked by Allied resistance at the Washington Conference in 1922. A terrible earthquake in 1923, furthermore, tied down the nation's energies at home. The 1920's, consequently, were taken up chiefly with domestic developments. The outward westernization of Japan continued, especially among the middle class. In 1925 universal manhood suffrage was introduced. Apathy among the voters, however, together with the limited powers of the Diet, retarded further democratic growth.

The comparative moderation of Japan's policy was especially apparent in the country's relations with China. In 1922 Shantung was returned to China, with Japan retaining only its commercial privileges. A number of moderate Japanese premiers recognized China's right to organize its own affairs and did not hinder the Kuomintang's policies so long as they did not affect Japan's interests. Only when Chiang Kai-shek's move into northern China threatened Japan's sphere of interest in Manchuria were Japanese troops once more sent to Shantung. As late as 1930, however, Japan still recognized China's tariff autonomy; and in October of that year the government, over the violent protests of Japanese patriots, ratified the London Naval Treaty, which further limited naval construction. But this was the end of the era of moderation. The depression now was hitting Japan with disastrous results. The need for cuts in military spending particularly alarmed the militarists, who now came to the fore again, advocating their own brand of totalitarianism. In 1931 they urged Japan into the invasion of Manchuria, which touched off the sequence of events that ended in the Second World War.

An Age of Uncertainty

The years from 1919 to 1939 in retrospect appear as a succession of political and economic crises that were almost bound to lead to another world war. There had been a brief return to normality during the 1920's, but even then the world had not regained the feeling of optimism that had characterized the period before 1914. The war and its aftermath had shaken many traditional beliefs and had disappointed many cherished hopes. National self-determination and democracy, it seemed, did not necessarily solve Europe's political problems; nor did rugged individualism and laissez faire provide the answer to the world's economic ills. The hope that human reason would solve the few remaining "riddles of the universe" was being undermined by new scientific discoveries, and the widely held belief in unlimited progress seemed open to serious question. As a result of growing doubts about hitherto accepted values, the intellectual climate during the postwar era changed from its prewar feeling of confidence to one of uneasiness and uncertainty.

Material Progress

Not everyone, of course, was equally sensitive to these changes. The majority of people, once they had overcome the hardships of war, were ready to enjoy the spectacular achievements that engineering science had in store for them. Material progress certainly seemed as promising as ever. Not only were there such new "miracles" as the radio, the talking picture, and ultimately television, but constant improvements in production and marketing made these and earlier inventions, like the automobile, available to the average person. It is unnecessary here to list the veritable avalanche of laborsaving devices and gadgets that combined to make up a "high standard of living." They did not necessarily make life richer, but they certainly made things more comfortable.

There were other technological and scientific achievements that changed man's everyday life. Improvements in the field of transportation virtually eliminated distance as a barrier. The Old World and the New, until recently days apart, soon were separated only by hours. Some of the most spectacular developments took place in medicine. A concentrated attack—through research, public hygiene, and improvements in nutrition—brought some of the most deadly diseases under control. This accomplishment in turn led to a lengthening of the average lifespan in the more advanced countries from less than fifty years at the beginning of the century to almost sixty-five years by 1939. Modern science and industry thus continued to fulfill their promise of enabling people to live both better and longer than at any other time in history.

Critics of Mass Culture

But material progress was not without its drawbacks, as a few social critics were beginning to point out. The growth of population prior to the Second World War was seen as a threat to cultural values rather than to the world's food supply. The Spanish philosopher Ortega y Gasset, in his book *The Revolt of the Masses* (1932), warned that the increase in human beings was so rapid that it was no longer possible to educate modern man in the traditions of his civilization. As a result, the gap between the cultured few and the superficially educated many was wider than ever and becoming more so. And since it was the masses who really exerted political and economic power, their low standards would henceforth be imposed upon society as a whole. Other voices were raised against the dangers of a civilization that envisaged progress entirely in material terms. One of the most perceptive critics was the British novelist Aldous Huxley, who, in his satirical novel *Brave New World* (1932), predicted with uncanny foresight many later "triumphs" of human ingenuity, from tranquilizer pills to brainwashing. The picture Huxley painted was of a well-adjusted society whose members were scientifically conditioned to whatever status they occupied, existing like animals or vegetables on a well-tended experimental farm. Man as a slave to his technological inventions, as a mere cipher in a collectivist society, as a rootless, lonely, and lost being in a world of bewildering complexity—such were the subjects that increasingly occupied social critics, novelists, and poets.

The "Behavioral Sciences"

The study of man, both as an individual and as a member of society, had for some time past been the task of the social sciences. This term had at first been used only for the traditional subjects: history, political science, and economics. But in time the field had been widened to include the new "behavioral sciences": psychology, sociology, and cultural anthropology.

The beginnings of modern psychology are associated with the name of Sigmund Freud, a Viennese doctor who began formulating his theories at the turn of the century. There had been psychologists before him. True to the spirit of materialism that prevailed at the end of the nineteenth century, men like the German Wilhelm Wundt and the American William James had tried to discover the organic roots of human behavior, assuming that the brain, like any other organ, performed purely biological functions. Freud's approach, on the other hand, was radi-

The Freudian Revolution

Freud's extraordinary achievement was to show us, in scientific terms, the primacy of natural desire, the secret wishes we proclaim in our dreams, the mixture of love and shame and jealousy in our relations to our parents, the child as father to the man, the deeply buried instincts that make us natural beings and that go back to the forgotten struggles of the human race. Until Freud, novelists and dramatists had never dared to think that science would back up their belief that personal passion is a stronger force in people's lives than socially accepted morality. Thanks to Freud, these insights now form a widely shared body of knowledge.

In short, Freud had the ability, such as is given to very few individuals, to introduce a wholly new factor into human knowledge; to impress it upon people's minds as something for which there was evidence. He revealed a part of reality that many people before him had guessed at, but which no one before him was able to describe as systematically and convincingly as he did. In the same way that one associates the discovery of certain fundamentals with Copernicus, Newton, Darwin, Einstein, so one identifies many of one's deepest motivations with Freud. His name is no longer the name of a man; like "Darwin," it is now synonymous with a part of nature.

From Alfred Kazin, "The Freudian Revolution Analyzed," *The New York Times Magazine*, May 6, 1956.

cally different. Basic to his teachings was the idea that human behavior is directed by subconscious instincts, or "drives," of which the most repressed is the sexual impulse. These drives are inhibited, usually in early childhood, and such inhibition leads to various degrees of frustration, which in turn may cause serious neuroses. In an effort to cure his patients, Freud developed a technique called "psychoanalysis," which consisted of an extended and deep probing of the patient's mind to get at the subconscious layers ordinarily revealed only in dreams. The purpose of such probing was to make the patient understand the conflicts that caused his abnormal behavior and by such understanding remove the causes of his mental disturbance.

Freud was not the only pioneer in modern psychology; there were others, notably the Russian Ivan Pavlov. All of them tried to discover at long last what made people act the way they did. The knowledge they gained should have been a source of great satisfaction. But actually, in the beginning at least, the opposite was true. Ever since the Age of Enlightenment man had gloried in the belief that he was a wholly intelligent and rational being. Now suddenly he was faced by the realization that he was subject to dark instincts and drives, and that it was these forces rather than his intellect that determined his behavior. Far from increasing man's self-confidence, modern psychology merely added to his feeling of bewilderment and uncertainty.

The second of the behavioral sciences, sociology, had its beginnings in the nineteenth century with men like Auguste Comte, Karl Marx, and Herbert Spencer. But here, too, the twentieth century introduced new methods and provided many new insights. One of the most important modern sociologists was the Italian Vilfredo Pareto, whose *Mind and Society* was published in English in 1935. Pareto accepted the findings of the psychologists that men were swayed by emotion rather than guided by reason. The ideals or rationalizations that social groups set up were to him mere fronts, or "derivations," which screened the basic irrational motives, or "residues," which really moved people to act. Pareto held that any clever leader or any elite capable of seeing through this human self-deception could use the basic aims of their fellow men to gain supremacy and to establish an authoritarian system in which the masses would obey slogans that appealed to their inner instincts. Pareto thus seemed to provide a "scientific" explanation of fascist totalitarianism. His analysis, if correct, certainly held little hope for a rationally ordered, democratic society.

The third behavioral science, cultural anthropology, likewise tried to find answers to the question of what determined human behavior. By carefully studying primitive tribes, chiefly American Indians and the natives of Pacific islands, anthropologists like Ruth Benedict and Margaret Mead hoped to determine what role environment played in shaping a given culture. One of their discoveries was that differences between cultures were due to environmental factors rather than to inherent biological factors, and that there was no basis for the belief—so dear to many people before 1914—in "superior" and "inferior" races. It was one thing, however, to study a small primitive tribe and another to apply the same research techniques to larger and more complex cultures. But here, too, some promising beginnings were made. Students in the field of "human relations," through detailed case studies, were able to gather valuable data on small segments of their own society, in the hope of determining what motivated its members.

Spengler and Toynbee

Most social scientists were concerned with the present rather than the past. Even historians dealing with past events often did so to gain a better understanding of the present. Some of them, notably the German Oswald Spengler and the Englishman Arnold Toynbee, by studying the rise and fall of past civilizations, tried to predict the future of their own civilization. In the past, history had usually been viewed as a linear process, moving onward and upward toward some faraway goal. These historians presented a different view, according to which history seemed to repeat itself. Civilizations, they held, had always risen and fallen in cycles or curves—from birth to death, from spring to winter, from morning to night. These grandiose views of history tried to supply at least some answer to men's anxious questions about where their civilization was going. The answer that they supplied was far from hopeful.

Oswald Spengler's *The Decline of the West* (1918) was written during the First World War. With an immense display of erudition the author compared some twenty past "cultures," tracing each through identical phases down to a final phase which Spengler called "civilization." Europe, according to Spengler, was in the midst of this final phase. And like all other cultures before it, European culture would soon disintegrate and collapse. This prophecy of impending doom held a morbid fascination for the generation between the two wars. Historians, to be sure, warned that this "morphology of cultures" was far too sweeping, based on evidence often

incomplete or incorrect. Yet it could not be denied that in his comparative study of "cultures," Spengler had uncovered many suggestive parallels, and in his predictions of things to come he seemed to be remarkably correct.

It was largely due to Spengler's inspiration that the historian Arnold Toynbee embarked on his own monumental work, *A Study of History* (1934-54). Like Spengler, Toynbee assumes that there are parallel phases in the development of major civilizations. The birth of a civilization Toynbee sees in man's successful "response" to a "challenge," usually supplied by geography or climate. The growth of a civilization consists in man's gradually solving his physical problems, thus freeing his energies for more elevated intellectual and spiritual pursuits. Not every member of society shares in this process. It is rather a creative minority that takes the lead and makes its views prevail over the passive majority. The breakdown of a civilization, according to Toynbee, occurs when this minority can no longer muster enough creative force to meet a particular challenge. Europe, Toynbee said, was in the midst of this final phase, which he called the "Time of Troubles." He thus arrived at substantially the same prognosis as Spengler of what the future holds in store.

The "New Physics"

While the social sciences thus gave little comfort in an age of uncertainty, the natural sciences for some time past had been demolishing the simple, rational, and mechanistic view of nature that had prevailed since the days of Newton. As we have seen, physical science in the late nineteenth century had still viewed the universe substantially in Newtonian terms. Before the end of the century, however, the findings of scientists like Konrad Röntgen, Pierre and Marie Curie, Ernest Rutherford, Max Planck, and others had already raised doubts concerning these hypotheses. They made it clear that a major new explanation, a whole new system of physics and mathematics, was needed to supply the answers to questions on which Newton had been silent. Such a new system appeared in 1905 when the young German physicist Albert Einstein advanced his "theory of relativity."

Albert Einstein (1879–1955) at the age of 24, shortly before he published his paper on the restricted principle that led to the theory of relativity.

According to Einstein's theory time and space were not absolute, as Newton had assumed, but relative to the observer. Later he included gravitation and motion in his calculations. Mass in Einstein's universe was thus a variable. The mass of a body depended on its rate of motion; its mass increased as its velocity increased, with the speed of light as the theoretical limit. It was the velocity of light, therefore, rather than time and space, that now emerged as absolute in the "new physics."

A further radical departure from accepted theory was Einstein's assumption of the equivalence of mass and energy. Experiments in nuclear physics already had shown that the dividing line between mass and energy was far from clear, and that matter slowly disintegrated into energy by way of radiation. The amount of matter thus lost was infinitesimal compared to the resulting energy. Einstein expressed this relationship between mass and energy in his famous formula $E = mc^2$, E being energy, m mass, and c the velocity of light. The implication of this formula was that if a process could be devised by which matter could suddenly be transformed into energy, a small amount of matter could be made to produce a vast quantity of energy. A practical demonstration of the validity of Einstein's for-

mula came with the first atomic explosion in 1945.

These and other revolutionary developments in science did not immediately affect the outlook of the average person. But as scientists began speaking of the "limitations of science," admitting that they no longer knew all the answers, some of their feeling of uncertainty could not help but enter general consciousness. Instead of living in a rational world with few remaining riddles, man, in the words of Britain's astronomer, Sir Arthur Eddington, was faced by a universe in which "something unknown is doing, we don't know what." A mysterious world (as the physicists said it was), inhabited by irrational man (as the psychologists said he was), caught in a civilization predestined for decay and disintegration (as Spengler and Toynbee said our civilization was)—this was a far cry from the happy and confident prospect that had existed only a short time before.

New Trends in Literature and Art

The uncertainty of the age was also reflected in its literature and art. Social criticism among writers was nothing new. But while the Naturalists of the late nineteenth century had hoped to bring about much-needed reforms by their attacks upon society, there was little such hope behind the criticism of the postwar era. Its common denominator was disillusionment. Yet postwar literature, while deeply tinged with frustration, was also immensely creative. The insights of modern psychology into the hidden motives of human behavior proved a boon to writers in their age-old quest for an understanding of human nature. There had been psychological novels before, but it was only in our own century that almost every writer, consciously or unconsciously, came under the influence of modern psychology, and especially of Freud. One of the effects of Freudian psychology was to call attention to the role of sex as a force in man's life. As a result, sexual matters were now written about with far more candor than earlier generations would have thought permissible.

The incongruent mixture of uncertainty and creativity that characterized literature between the two wars also prevailed in painting. Some artists still dealt with recognizable subjects, but more and more of them rebelled against the realism and impressionism of the prewar era. Instead, painters expressed on canvas their inner feelings and impulses, often in styles that reflected the chaotic world in which they lived. These "expressionists," as they were called, in time became so nonobjective and abstract that it was impossible any longer to recognize in them common aims and interests. Each artist had become a law unto himself.

This same creative uncertainty, this search for new means of expression, had its parallel in modern music. Some composers continued to use traditional methods, inspired by the heritage of their various cultural backgrounds. But others departed from familiar forms and in some cases, by adopting new scales and chords, developed a wholly new musical idiom, which sounded dissonant to most of their contemporaries.

Because so much modern art and music was highly individualistic, it appealed to only a few. Modern architecture had a somewhat wider following. Most architecture in the nineteenth century had been a mere imitation or a mixture of earlier styles. New building materials, steel and concrete, had been developed; but except by a few pioneers, the inherent possibilities of these materials had been ignored. All this changed after the First World War. Architects now became increasingly concerned with the function as well as the appearance of their buildings, and by striving for simplicity and utility were able to produce structures of great beauty. It took some time, however, before the general public abandoned its preference for traditional and more ornate styles in favor of contemporary simplicity.

Anti-intellectualism

It is very difficult to gauge correctly the temper of a period as brief as the twenty years between the two world wars. Many of its accomplishments, especially in science, were impressive. But there was a puzzling paradox behind this extension of human knowledge. The more man found out about the world, the more he realized how little he had known before. From a feeling of supreme self-importance at the end of the nineteenth century, man's view of himself was pushed to the opposite extreme: he felt uncertain and insignificant, a creature of instinct, no longer able to shape his own destiny.

It is not surprising that this uncertainty should turn many people against the rationalist philosophy that had prevailed for the past two hundred years. There had been a similar revolt against reason a century before. And like Romanticism then, antirationalism now sprang from the disillusionment that followed a seemingly futile war. Modern anti-intellectualism, as it is called, took several forms. It brought a revived interest in religion, even among scientists, who had not long ago been ardent defenders of materialism. But far larger numbers turned elsewhere for guidance. There were many reasons for the sudden rise of totalitarianism after the First World War. But not the least among them was that it provided its followers with simple beliefs in an age of bewildering uncertainty.

Suggestions for Further Reading

1. Great Britain and France

A. J. P. Taylor, *English History, 1914–1945* (1965), and C. L. Mowat, *Britain Between the Wars* (1955), are the best general books on the subject. R. Graves and A. Hodge, *The Long Weekend: A Social History of Great Britain, 1918–1939** (1940), recreates the moods and manners of British society during the period. The same is done for the British "establishment" in H. Nicolson, *Diaries and Letters,* 3 vols. (1966–68). There are some excellent biographies of the leading political figures:

* Available in paperback edition.

K. Morgan, *David Lloyd George: Welsh Radical as World Statesman* (1963); R. Blake, *The Unknown Prime Minister: The Life and Times of Andrew Bonar Law* (1955); G. M. Young, *Stanley Baldwin* (1952); G. E. Elton, *The Life of James Ramsay MacDonald* (1939); K. Feiling, *The Life of Neville Chamberlain* (1946); and H. Nicolson, *King George V* (1952). C. R. Attlee, *The Labour Party in Perspective* (1949), is a review of the party's development between the wars by its leader. C. F. Brand, *The British Labour Party: A Short History* (1964), is a useful survey. The best introduction to French postwar history is D. W. Brogan, *France Under the Republic** (1940). E. J. Knapton, *France Since Versailles** (1952), is a brief survey; and A. Werth, *The Twilight of France, 1933–1940* (1942), describes the mounting crisis on the eve of the Second World War. D. Thomson, *Democracy in France** (1946), is helpful for understanding French politics. For biographies of major politicians, see: G. Bruun, *Clemenceau* (1943); G. Wright, *Raymond Poincaré and the French Presidency* (1942); V. Thompson, *Briand: Man of Peace (1930)*; and J. Colton, *Léon Blum: Humanist in Politics* (1966).

2. Germany

The best history of the Weimar Republic in English is E. Eyck, *A History of the Weimar Republic,* 2 vols.** (1962). A Rosenberg, *A History of the German Republic* (1936), combines insight with criticism. On the dissolution of the Republic, see A. Brecht, *Prelude to Silence: The End of the German Republic* (1944), and the collection of essays by German scholars entitled *Path to Dictatorship, 1918–1933** (1966). The two leading personalities of the period are discussed in H. Turner, *Stresemann and the Politics of the Weimar Republic** (1963), and A. Dorpalen, *Hindenburg and the Weimar Republic* (1964). F. L. Carsten, *The Reichswehr and Politics, 1918 to 1933* (1966), deals with a significant phase of the Republic's history.

3. The Small Powers

Good general surveys are: H. Seton-Watson, *Eastern Europe Between the Wars, 1919–1941** (1945); R. L. Wolff, *The Balkans in Our Times* (1956); and B. A. Arneson, *The Democratic Monarchies of Scandinavia* (1939). On individual countries, see: M. MacDonald, *The Republic of Austria, 1918–1934* (1946); R. Machray, *The Poland of Pilsudski* (1937); C. A. Macartney, *Hungary and Her Successors* (1937); and R. W. Seton-Watson, *A History of the Czechs and Slovaks* (1943).

4. The United States

Two very good studies of the pre-Roosevelt era are A. M. Schlesinger, Jr., *The Crisis of the Old Order, 1919–1933* (1957), and W. E. Leuchtenburg, *The Perils of Prosperity, 1914–1932** (1958). The Roosevelt years are covered in several excellent works: A. M. Schlesinger, Jr., *The Coming of the New Deal** (1959), and the same author's *The Politics of Upheaval* (1960); D. W. Brogan, *The Era of Franklin D. Roosevelt* (1951); D. Perkins, *The New Age of Franklin Roosevelt** (1957); and J. M. Burns, *Roosevelt: The Lion and the Fox** (1956). E. F. Goldman, *Rendezvous with Destiny: A History of American Reform** (1952), and R. Hofstadter, *The Age of Reform** (1955), deal with the American liberal and progressive movements. F. L. Allen, *Only Yesterday** (1940), and *The Big Change** (1952), are lively social histories of the period. Among memoirs and biographies of New Dealers, the following stand out: R. E. Sherwood, *Roosevelt and Hopkins** (1948); J. M. Blum, *From the Morgenthau Diaries* (1959); R. G. Tugwell, *The Democratic Roosevelt* (1957); and E. Roosevelt, *This I Remember** (1949).

5. The Great Depression

J. P. Day, *An Introduction to World Economic History Since the Great War* (1939), puts the world economic crisis in its long-range perspective. The crisis itself is studied in J. K. Galbraith, *The Great Crash, 1929** (1955). See also D. A. Shannon, ed., *The Great Depression** (1960), and M. J. Bonn, *The Crumbling of Empire: The Disintegration of World Economy* (1938). H. W. Arndt, *The Economic Lessons*

---

* Available in paperback edition.

of the Nineteen-Thirties (1944), is an attempt to learn from the past. A major aspect of the international repercussions of the financial crisis is the subject of E. W. Bennett, *Germany and the Diplomacy of the Financial Crisis, 1931* (1962).

6. The Twilight of Imperialism

Typical of western disillusionment with imperialism are the books by G. Clark, *The Balance Sheets of Imperialism* (1936), and *A Place in the Sun* (1936). The changes in the British Empire and Commonwealth are discussed in K. Robinson, *The Dilemma of Trusteeship: Aspects of British Colonial Policy Between the Wars* (1965). H. Mukerjee, *India Struggles for Freedom* (1948), traces the long road to Indian independence. Earlier stages on this road are related in M. K. Gandhi, *Autobiography** (1948), and in two autobiographical works by J. Nehru, *Toward Freedom** (1941), and *Glimpses of World History** (1942). On events in the Far East, see: A. Iriye, *After Imperialism: The Search for a New Order in the Far East, 1921–1931* (1965); R. Gould, *China in the Sun* (1946); and S. Chen and P. S. R. Payne, *Sun Yat-sen: A Portrait* (1946). The situation in the Middle East is discussed in G. Antonius, *The Arab Awakening: The Story of the Arab National Movement* (1939); and the first stirrings of unrest in Africa are treated in R. L. Buell, *The Native Problem in Africa* (1928).

7. Intellectual History

Books dealing with the intellectual ferment of the "age of uncertainty" are legion. H. S. Hughes, *Consciousness and Society: The Reorientation of European Social Thought, 1890–1930** (1958), is a fine general study. J. Barzun, *The House of Intellect** (1959), covers the more recent period. Other attempts to see the crisis of our civilization in historical perspective are R. Niebuhr, *The Irony of American History** (1952), and R. Williams, *Culture and Society* (1958). J. Ortega y Gassett, *The Revolt of the Masses** (1932), is a classic criticism of our mass society. The modern trend toward conformity is analyzed in: W. H. Whyte, *The Organization Man** (1956); V. O. Packard, *The Status Seekers** (1959); and A. C. Valentine, *The Age of Conformity* (1954). Other dangers to democratic freedom are pointed out by F. A. Hayek, *The Road to Serfdom** (1944), and K. R. Popper, *The Open Society and Its Enemies** (1950).

The basic work on Freud and psychoanalysis is E. Jones, *The Life and Work of Sigmund Freud,* 3 vols.* (1953–57). See also G. Costigan, *Sigmund Freud: A Short Biography* (1965). The wide impact of Freudianism is treated in P. Rieff, *Freud: The Mind of the Moralist** (1959), and F. J. Hoffmann, *Freudianism and the Literary Mind** (1957).

New trends in the social and behavioral sciences are exemplified in: T. Parsons, *The Structure of Social Action* (1949); E. Fromm, *Escape from Freedom** (1941); C. Kluckhohn, *Mirror for Man** (1949); B. L. Cline, *The Questioners* (1965); and in the studies of American society by D. Riesman, *The Lonely Crowd** (1953) and *Individualism Reconsidered** (1955). For the influence of science on society, see: B. Barber, *Science and the Social Order** (1952); B. F. Skinner, *Science and Social Behavior** (1956); J. Russell, *Science and Modern Life* (1955); and W. Esslinger, *Politics and Science* (1955).

The "prophets of doom" are evaluated in H. S. Hughes, *Oswald Spengler: A Critical Estimate** (1952), and in M. F. Ashley-Montagu, *Toynbee and History* (1956). On the scientific revolution of our century, see L. Infeld, *Albert Einstein** (1950); L. Barnett, *The Universe and Dr. Einstein** (1952); W. Heisenberg, *The Physicist's Conception of Nature* (1958); and M. Planck, *Scientific Autobiography and Other Papers* (1949).

Modern literature is covered in M. Colum, *From These Roots: The Ideas that Have Made Modern Literature* (1944), and in C. Mauriac, *The New Literature* (1959). On modern art, see: E. Langui, ed., *Fifty Years of Modern Art** (1959); W. Haftmann, *Painting in the Twentieth Century,* 2 vols.* (1965); and J. Joedicke, *A History of Modern Architecture* (1959). P. Collaer, *A History of Modern Music** (1961), is an introduction to the subject.

---

* Available in paperback edition.

17

The Rise of Totalitarianism

The communist and fascist regimes that arose in Europe and Asia during the years between the two world wars have been variously described as autocratic, authoritarian, dictatorial, and totalitarian. These terms do not all mean the same thing. There had been autocratic and authoritarian regimes in the past, most recently in tsarist Russia and imperial Germany; and there have been dictatorships from ancient times to the present. But none of these deserves to be called totalitarian. What we mean by a totalitarian regime is a regime in which a determined minority, by use of threat or force, imposes its will upon the total life of a society. The aims of this ruling clique are usually rooted in some all-embracing ideology. The beginnings of totalitarian ideologies go back at least to the nineteenth century, with the appearance of the two creeds that contributed most to totalitarianism: socialism and nationalism. Their growth and spread were aided by industrialism, which gave birth to the mass society in which totalitarianism thrives, and which provided the technical means

whereby total domination by a ruling clique is made possible.

There were many ideological differences between the totalitarianism of the Right and the Left—fascism and communism. Communism owed much of its successes to the fervor that Marxian doctrine inspired among its followers. There was no room for nationalism in Marxism, although nationalism in time became an ingredient of communism. Fascist ideology, by comparison, was less coherent. A mixture of warmed-over nineteenth-century ideas—Romanticism, worship of the state and war, Social Darwinism, racialism, and so forth—its outstanding characteristic was nationalism. Fascism, too, professed a belief in socialism, but it was an extreme state socialism rather than the Marxian concept of socialism.

Despite these ideological differences, fascism and communism were alike in many ways. Both exercised the most minute control over the life of every individual; both ruled through a mixture of propaganda and terror; both segregated and persecuted their opponents in concentration and slave-labor camps; and both sought to extend their power abroad through force or subversion. Why should totalitarian regimes have arisen at the time and in the countries they did? As we shall see, the circumstances differed considerably

Hitler's SS troops at the yearly Nazi rally in Nuremberg, September 1938. The SS (*Schutzstaffel*), an elite formation of carefully selected Nazi fanatics, had its own fully militarized units, the *Waffen* (Weapon) SS.

from country to country, but there were also certain similarities. Totalitarianism arose only in nations with little or no democratic tradition. Most of these countries had been in the throes of lengthy domestic crises caused by the First World War or the Great Depression. In all cases a resolute minority, posing as saviors, initiated changes amounting to a revolution. And as a rule this minority was headed by a leader with great demagogic gifts.

Communism in Crisis, 1917–28

It took several years for communism to gain full control in Russia. As we have seen, a Bolshevik minority under Lenin had seized power in the "October Revolution" of 1917. The initial difficulties faced by the new Soviet Republic were so severe that its survival seems almost miraculous. What the Bolsheviks lacked in numbers they made up in revolutionary zeal. To create a new world they tried to make a clean sweep of the old.

"War Communism" and Civil War

In a series of decrees, "War Communism" became the order of the day. It called for the socialization and complete control of the nation's economy, enforced, if necessary, through terror. From the very start the new secret police, or *Cheka,* became a deadly, efficient instrument of Bolshevik rule. The revolutionary fervor of Bolshevism was also reflected in its foreign policy. Revolution in Russia, Lenin felt, was but the prelude to world revolution; and the success of the latter was necessary to guarantee the survival of Bolshevism at home. Sporadic communist uprisings in Budapest, Vienna, Munich, and Berlin led to the founding, in March 1919, of the Soviet-controlled Third Communist International (Comintern), as a permanent agency devoted to world revolution.

These Bolshevik attempts to conquer Russia and the world simultaneously, however, soon turned out to be premature. "War Communism," far from bringing relief, actually brought further economic misery leading to unrest and civil war.

Opposition to the new regime was helped by Allied intervention. Its chief motive was to revive Russian resistance against Germany. During the spring and early summer of 1918, Allied forces landed at various points in Siberia. A Czech legion, made up of prisoners of war, simultaneously fought communist forces along the Siberian railroad. The Germans, still in control of much of Russia, encouraged separatist movements in the Ukraine and along the Baltic. And to complete the troubles of the Bolsheviks, the Allies imposed a tight naval blockade.

As the antirevolutionary White armies converged on the Soviet heart of Russia, the sphere of Bolshevik influence shrank to the region around Moscow and Petrograd. Yet despite terrific odds, the Bolsheviks were able to survive. The main reason for their survival was the weakness and dispersion of their opponents. Allied intervention, at best, was half-hearted. The White armies lacked popular support, since they were suspected of trying to restore the old order. The fact that the Whites enjoyed Allied support further weakened their cause, since it enabled the Reds to pose as champions of national resistance against foreign intervention. The White armies, finally, operated on widely separated fronts and under divided leadership. For all these various reasons, the White armies were no match for the newly created Red army. By the beginning of 1920, the Bolsheviks had defeated all the White forces except those in southern Russia under General Wrangel.

At this point a new danger suddenly arose. The Poles, who wanted to extend their frontier eastward beyond the Curzon Line, the boundary assigned to them at the Peace Conference, now joined forces with Wrangel in a concerted drive against the Red army. This was no longer a civil but a national war, and in an upsurge of patriotism the Russian people rushed to the defense. In a brilliant counterattack, the Polish army was driven out of Russia and pushed back to the gates of Warsaw. Poland was saved in part by French aid. In the "Miracle of the Vistula," in August 1920, the Red army was halted and thrown back. Under the subsequent peace of Riga, Poland advanced her borders some 150 miles eastward into regions inhabited chiefly by Russians. Another "minorities problem" had been created.

Lenin's "New Economic Policy"

The end of civil and foreign war did not relieve Russia's domestic misery. To add to the nation's calamities, drought and crop failures in 1920–21 brought one of the worst famines in Russian history. The desperate situation called for drastic measures. In March 1921, therefore, Lenin initiated his "New Economic Policy," or NEP, which amounted to a radical departure from War Communism and a partial return to prewar, capitalist practices. Lenin's more orthodox comrades, notably Trotsky, were against such a retreat from Marxian doctrine. But as it turned out, Lenin's policy was justified by its results. In the seven years during which NEP was in effect, agriculture and industry returned to their 1913 levels. As a result, the average Russian was able to get at least the food and clothing he needed and to enjoy a slight rise in wages and standard of living.

The moderation of Soviet policy at home had repercussions abroad. The failure of communist uprisings in central Europe had shown that the coming of world revolution was not as imminent as the communists had hoped. And with Russia's economic recovery depending heavily on foreign trade and foreign capital, the Soviet Republic was eager to resume normal relations with the rest of the world. In this respect the New Economic Policy proved helpful, since it was interpreted abroad as a sign that the Bolsheviks had begun to see the error of their ways and in time would abandon their communist "experiment." There was no reason, therefore, why foreign interests should not avail themselves of the opportunities offered by Russia's vast market and resources. Economic *rapprochement* between Russia and the West began in 1921. By 1925 diplomatic recognition had been granted the Soviet Union by all major powers except the United States.

But despite such hopeful beginnings relations between Russia and other countries never became really close. The major obstacle to Rus-

sia's reintegration into the international community was the well-founded suspicion that the Soviets had not really abandoned their aim of world revolution. As repeated incidents during the 1920's showed, the Comintern was merely marking time.

Lenin did not live to see the results of his New Economic Policy. In 1922 he suffered a paralytic stroke and in 1924, at the age of fifty-three, he died. He had been a remarkable man, with a great mind and superior talents as an agitator and organizer. In his unaffected manner he differed from most other dictators. With a rare mixture of fanaticism and realism, he had always known how to adjust his policy to changed circumstances. Without his leadership it is doubtful that the revolution would have succeeded.

Stalin Versus Trotsky

The death of Lenin brought into the open a struggle for power that had been going on behind the scenes for some time. The two chief protagonists were Trotsky and Stalin. In their aims they were not unlike: Both looked forward to the ultimate victory of world communism. Where they differed was in the policy they advocated. Trotsky believed that Bolshevik Russia could not survive unless the rest of the world became communist too. Russia, therefore, should concentrate on fomenting and supporting revolutions elsewhere. Stalin, on the other hand, felt that communism should first gain a firm hold in Russia and only then should pursue its goal of aiding communist movements elsewhere.

In the struggle that developed between Trotsky and Stalin, the personality and tactics of the two turned out to be decisive. Both men had served the revolution well. But while Trotsky's importance as Commissar of War declined once victory had been won, Stalin's influence continued to grow. His most important position he won in 1922, when he became general secretary of the Communist Party. This gave him control over the entire party machinery. Trotsky's doctrine of "permanent revolution," meanwhile, found little response in a nation exhausted by foreign and civil war. And while

Joseph Stalin, 1879–1953.

Trotsky's often high-handed manner offended his comrades, Stalin was careful to make friends with such "Old Bolsheviks" as Kamenev, the party's chief ideologist, and Zinoviev, the head of the Comintern.

In 1925 Stalin's policy of conciliation and cunning succeeded in forcing Trotsky to resign from the Ministry of War. Soon thereafter, Kamenev and Zinoviev quarreled with Stalin and joined Trotsky in opposition. But Stalin proved the stronger. Allying himself with two other Old Bolsheviks, Rykov and Bukharin, he had the "Trotskyites" expelled from the leadership of the party and ultimately from the party itself. Trotsky was banished, first to Siberia and after 1929 abroad. He was assassinated in Mexico in 1940. In the meantime Stalin, in 1929, had ousted Rykov and Bukharin, whose gradualist approach to socialization no longer fitted into his plans. With the last of his potential rivals thus out of the way, Stalin had emerged supreme.

Communism Triumphant, 1928–41

The Soviet government in 1928 was already a highly complex structure. It received its final form under the "Stalin Constitution" of 1936. The Soviet Union was a federation of states, their number increasing from four in 1922 to sixteen in 1941. Each state retained a large measure of cultural autonomy but was under the strict political control of the Supreme Soviet in Moscow. The Supreme Soviet consisted of two chambers, the Soviet of the Union and the Soviet of Nationalities. When they were not in session, their functions were exercised by a Presidium of some twenty-seven members. More important, however, in directing national affairs was the Council of People's Commissars, also appointed by the Supreme Soviet.

Actual power rested in the hands of only a few people. But a multiplicity of local, regional, and provincial soviets, together with the Supreme Soviet, gave at least an appearance of representative government. Other features of the Russian constitution were also intended to make it appear democratic. The franchise was universal, and a bill of rights guaranteed all sorts of rights and freedoms. The only trouble was that these rights had to be exercised "in the interests of the working people." And the agency that interpreted what these interests were was the Communist Party.

The Communist Party

The membership of the Russian Communist Party in 1918 was estimated at 200,000. Ten years later, it had increased to over a million. But while it continued to grow, it never became a mass party. Its function was rather to serve as an elite, "the vanguard of the working class." Undeviating faith in Marxian doctrine as interpreted by the party's leaders, together with blind obedience to orders from above—these were the basic demands made of all party members. Party organization resembled the structure of the Soviet state, from "cells" at the bottom to the All-Union Party Congress at the top. The Congress selected the Central Committee as the chief policy-making organ, and the Central Committee in turn delegated power to the Politburo, the party's highest authority.

The self-abnegation demanded by party membership was highly rewarded by the Soviet state. All the leading positions in the bureaucracy went to party members, and they alone could hold political office. The upshot of this system was the growth of a new ruling caste of communist functionaries. With the Communist Party as the dominant force in Soviet life, control of the party ensured domination of the state. It was to his leading role in the Communist Party rather than to any governmental position that Stalin owed his absolute power. And beginning in 1928 he used this power to carry the communist revolution to its final triumph.

The Five-Year Plans

In order to survive in a hostile world of capitalist powers, Stalin felt the Soviet Union had to realize as rapidly as possible its inherent productive strength. Stalin hoped to achieve this goal in three Five-Year Plans. Their aim was the large-scale development of basic industries and the increase of agricultural production through collective farming.

The first Five-Year Plan was launched in 1928. Even if we discount the exaggerations of communist propaganda, the achievements of Stalin's policy were most impressive. Between 1928 and 1940 Russia's industrial output grew more than sevenfold. On the eve of the Second World War, the Soviet Union had become one of the leading industrial powers of the world.

Collectivization, the agricultural counterpart to industrialization, was less successful. Agriculture in Russia was hampered by small holdings and antiquated methods. The solution to the problem was seen in large-scale farming and mechanization. But the conservative Russian peasant was opposed to any drastic changes and resorted to passive resistance. To break this opposition, the authorities used force. Executions and deportations, added to a severe famine in 1932–33, caused the death of some 4 million people. But even strong-arm methods did not bring the desired results. While by 1940 most of Russia's land had been converted into collec-

tive farms, the problems of Russian agriculture had by no means been solved.

Stalin's Five-Year Plans completed the victory of communism in Russia. But the victory was won at the price of untold sacrifices on the part of the Russian people. Millions perished, others languished in labor camps, and the rest led a regimented and drab existence, spurred by alternate waves of propaganda and terror. The lot of the average Russian seems to have gradually improved before the war. Free medical care and other social services, together with full employment, provided the Russian worker with security at the expense of freedom. At the same time some of the changes introduced shortly after the revolution were now abandoned. The family, at first de-emphasized, now again became the basis of society. Education became less progressive but more universal. Religion, once persecuted, was again tolerated. One of the most surprising reversals of the Stalinist era was the renewed veneration of Russia's past. During the Second World War in particular this new Russian nationalism turned for inspiration to the great events of Russian history, thus ignoring Marx's admonition that the proletariat had no fatherland. Stalin's motive in blending the old with the new seemed to be to strengthen his regime by rooting it more firmly in the past.

The Sabotage and Treason Trials

While communism under Stalin thus appeared to have a firm hold in Russia, there were nevertheless frequent signs of internal unrest. Among the manifestations of this unrest were the so-called sabotage trials of 1928–33 and the treason trials of 1934–38. The sabotage trials involved several groups of Russian and foreign engineers who were accused of sabotaging Russia's industrial efforts. The foreigners in each case denied these charges, but the Russian defendants readily confessed their guilt. The opinion outside Russia was that these trials were staged by the government to try to hide or excuse the many instances of waste and inefficiency revealed during the early years of the Five-Year Plans.

The same explanation, however, does not hold for the treason trials. These amounted to a major purge of thousands of leading figures of the Soviet regime. The reason given for the Great Purge was an alleged conspiracy, instigated by Hitler and Trotsky and ultimately directed at Stalin. The purge was touched off by the assassination of Sergei Kirov, party chief of Leningrad, in December 1934. In January 1935 Zinoviev and Kamenev were accused of conspiracy in the murder and were sentenced to imprisonment. They were condemned to death, together with fourteen other "Trotskyites," in 1936. Many others followed, including Rykov and Bukharin. In 1937 the purge spread to the Red army. It was also extended throughout the entire Soviet hierarchy. Tens of thousands were arrested, executed, or exiled.

Khrushchev on the Great Purge

Stalin originated the concept "enemy of the people." This term automatically rendered it unnecessary that the ideological errors of a man or men engaged in a controversy be proven; this term made possible the usage of the most cruel repression, violating all norms of revolutionary legality, against anyone who in any way disagreed with Stalin, against those who had bad reputations. This concept "enemy of the people" actually eliminated the possibility of any kind of ideological fight or the making of one's views known on this or that issue, even those of a practical character. In the main, and in actuality, the one proof of guilt used, against all norms of current legal science, was the "confession" of the accused himself; and, as subsequent probing proved, "confessions" were acquired through physical pressures against the accused. This led to glaring violations of revolutionary legality and to the fact that many entirely innocent persons, who in the past had defended the party line, became victims.

From *The Crimes of the Stalin Era: Special Report to the 20th Congress of the Communist Party of the Soviet Union* by Nikita S. Khrushchev, ed. by Boris I. Nicolaevsky (New York: The New Leader, 1956).

Foreign observers were bewildered and horrified by this spectacle of the revolution "devouring its children." The tendency was to see the Great Purge as a sign of Russian weakness. The significance of the fact that the Soviet state was strong enough to survive so tremendous an upheaval was overlooked at the time. That there was opposition in Russia can hardly be doubted. In spreading his net as wide as he did, Stalin destroyed any possible danger of a future conspiracy. This may well have assured the survival of the Soviet Union in the Second World War.

Russia and the West

Prominent in Stalin's repressive policy at home was the fear of possible intervention from abroad. The memory of such intervention during the revolution was never forgotten. Outwardly, Russia's relations with the West improved markedly during the 1930's. The Soviet Union was the only major power not affected by the Great Depression, and the Russian market offered commercial opportunities that existed nowhere else. The rising threats of Nazi Germany in Europe and Japan in Asia established a further bond of interest between the Soviet Union and the democracies. In 1933 the United States finally recognized the U.S.S.R.; the following year Russia was admitted to the League of Nations; and in 1935 the Soviets joined France and Czechoslovakia in military agreements against Germany. But despite this apparent *rapprochement*, Russia continued to distrust the West and the West continued to distrust the Russians. This mutual suspicion was to have tragic consequences on the eve of the Second World War.

The Fascist Revolution in Italy

The rise of fascism, first in Italy and later in Germany, was in part a reaction to the real or imaginary threat of communism. But even without such a threat, conditions in Italy after the First World War made major changes imperative. The Italian people had been divided about intervention in the war. But once the nation had joined the Allies, hopes for territorial rewards had run high. Such expectations had been bitterly disappointed at the Peace Conference. Popular discontent was heightened by postwar economic problems. Riots and strikes, together with a sharp increase in the Socialist vote, made Italy's propertied elements fear that a communist revolution was at hand. Various democratic governments tried to cope with this hopeless situation but with little success. Parliamentary democracy, as we have seen, had never worked well in Italy. Here, then, was a situation in which some unscrupulous demagogue could come along and promise a solution to Italy's problems. The man who saw and seized this opportunity was Benito Mussolini.

Benito Mussolini

It has been said that Mussolini was fascism personified, and the movement certainly would have been unthinkable without him. Born in 1883, son of a socialist blacksmith, Mussolini himself had become a socialist in his youth. He had worked abroad as an agitator, had been jailed in 1911 for opposing Italy's war with Turkey, and in 1912 had become editor of *Avanti*, Italy's leading socialist newspaper. When war broke out in 1914, Mussolini was still a pacifist. But he soon changed and advocated Italian intervention on the Allied side. Here we have the first of many radical reversals in the life of this accomplished opportunist.

Mussolini's first *Fasci di Combattimento*, or "groups of combat," were formed in the spring of 1919. They were made up chiefly of discontented veterans. Their name was derived from the old Roman fasces, a bundle of rods symbolizing unity and authority. The number of these "Black Shirts" rapidly increased from a few hundred to many thousands. Their aims were mostly negative: they were against the monarchy, the Church, the socialists, and the capitalists. In the elections of 1919 the fascists failed to get a single seat. But two years later they won

Benito Mussolini, 1883–1945.

thirty-five. Capitalizing on the fears of the middle class by posing as the defender of law, order, and property, Mussolini was able to seize power in the fall of 1922.

The "March on Rome"

Mussolini's boast of having saved Italy from the danger of a communist revolution was false. That danger, if it ever existed, had run its course by 1922. In the meantime, the Black Shirts were waging a virtual civil war against socialists and labor unions, and Mussolini was mending his fences in preparation for his *coup*. First he changed his revolutionary movement into a regular political party. Then he proclaimed his loyalty to the monarchy and the Church. And finally he made certain that the army would not oppose him. When everything was ready, in October 1922, Mussolini mobilized his Black Shirts for a dramatic "March on Rome." But King Victor Emmanuel had been well prepared and gave way easily. On October 29, 1922, Mussolini was invited to form a new government, and the following day he made his triumphal entry into Rome.

The change from democratic to totalitarian rule in Italy took several years. At the start, Mussolini was given full emergency powers for only one year. He used these powers to tighten fascist control. To make certain of a fascist victory in future elections, a new electoral law in 1923 provided that any party which gained a plurality of votes would automatically receive two-thirds of the parliamentary seats. Even so, opposition in the Chamber continued. In June 1924 one of Mussolini's most fearless critics, the socialist leader Giacomo Matteotti, was kidnapped, "taken for a ride," and murdered. At first it seemed as though popular indignation would sweep the fascists from power. Mussolini, pretending to be deeply shocked by the crime, promised severe punishment of the guilty. But when he realized how little united his opponents were, he reversed his course. A new secret police, the OVRA, was founded, and in a wave of persecution enemies of the state were brought before a special tribunal and sentenced to prison or exile. Nonfascist members of the cabinet were dismissed, and Mussolini was once again given power to rule by decree. In 1926, finally, all opposition parties were outlawed. The Matteotti affair, far from bringing about the fall of fascism, had thus served to complete its victory.

The Fascist State

Like communism before it, fascism created its own system of government. Political power, in Mussolini's "corporative state," was vested in some thirteen "syndicates." These confederations, which included both workers and employers, were initially organized to regulate labor conditions. Strikes and lockouts were declared illegal, and the final word in labor disputes rested with the government. Beginning in 1928 this corporate system was made the basis of Italy's political organization. Under a new electoral law, the syndicates drew up a list of candidates for the Chamber of Deputies. Their final selection, however, rested with the fascist Grand Council, a body of some twenty party leaders appointed by Mussolini. As under communism, the party thus wielded complete political control. Parliament, under this new system, lost most of its former functions. In 1938 even the outward forms of democracy disappeared when the Chamber of Deputies was replaced by a new Chamber of Fasces and Corporations. Since all its members were appointed, there was no longer any need for elections.

The Fascist Party, again like its communist counterpart, considered itself an elite. Its membership in 1934 was about 1.5 million. Its leader, or *Duce,* was Mussolini. Fascist youth organizations took care of indoctrinating the young. The press, radio, and movies were under strict censorship, and every facet of intellectual and artistic life was made to fit in with fascist propaganda. Only in his relations with the Church did Mussolini show a certain leniency. One of the major achievements of his regime was the Lateran Treaty of 1929, which settled the long-standing feud between the Italian government and the papacy.

The major efforts of Mussolini's policy at home were aimed at improving Italy's economic position. Reduction of government spending, suppression of strikes, and increased taxation brought some initial relief and helped Italy share in the general recovery of the late twenties. The Great Depression, however, put an end to this. Even though the Italian government by now had assumed full control over economic affairs, its policy was far less successful than Russia's planned economy under the Five-Year Plans. Not only was Mussolini less ruthless than Stalin, but Italy lacked the Soviet Union's vast natural resources. Beginning in 1935, furthermore, Mussolini embarked on a series of costly wars, the burden of which had to be borne by the Italian people.

One sure way of diverting domestic discontent is through a strong and successful foreign policy. Mussolini first tried this remedy in 1923, when he ordered the Italian navy to bombard the Greek island of Corfu. But, as we have seen, his ardor had been somewhat dampened by the protest of the great powers. For the next ten years, therefore, Italy was careful not to appear too aggressive. She concluded treaties of friendship with a number of countries, especially those which, like Austria and Hungary, shared Italy's opposition to the peace treaties. In 1924 Yugoslavia, in return for concessions elsewhere, agreed to Italy's annexation of Fiume. Relations with Germany, even after Hitler's rise to power, remained cool, chiefly because of Germany's desire for *Anschluss* with Austria. Mussolini's restoration of domestic order, meanwhile, endeared him to foreign visitors; his opposition to communism made him appear the ally of anticommunists everywhere; and his improved relations with the Church won him Catholic support. As a result, the new Italy and its leader commanded considerable respect abroad, at least until 1935. Only then did the world wake up to the danger that fascism posed to world peace.

Fascist Ideology

When Mussolini founded his movement in 1919 he had, by his own admission, "no specific doctrinal plan." He was, as has been said, a born opportunist. In his formative years, Mussolini had come under the influence of a variety of writers, from Machiavelli to Pareto, including Nietzsche, Sorel, and even Marx. Fascism also had its own philosophers, men like Giovanni Gentile and Alfredo Rocco. But we look in vain for an exposition of fascist doctrine as clear as that provided for communism by Marx or even

as rambling as that provided for Nazism by Hitler. Fascism was a dynamic movement, devoted to action rather than thought. Its motto was "Believe, Obey, Fight." Fascism's beliefs covered a wide range of romantic ideals, from the glories of Rome to the irrational creed of modern nationalism. To obey meant subjection to the authority of the state and its leader, the *Duce*. But to fight was the noblest aim of all. War alone, Mussolini said, "puts the stamp of nobility upon the people who have the courage to meet it." This belief in war for war's sake was the essence of fascism.

The Rise of National Socialism in Germany

Mussolini's success in Italy was observed with keen interest in Germany, where a movement akin to fascism had been active since the early twenties. Its leader was an obscure Austrian rabble-rouser, Adolf Hitler, the moving spirit behind the National Socialist German Workers' Party (NSDAP). The members of the party—or "Nazis," as their opponents called them—were similar to Mussolini's first Black Shirts. Most of them were disgruntled war veterans. Like their Italian counterparts, they hoped to seize power by a *coup d'état.* But their Munich *Putsch* in November 1923 had failed. For the next few years Adolf Hitler all but disappeared from the public eye.

Adolf Hitler and His Aims

The man who was soon to determine the fate of the whole world was still not taken very seriously outside the Nazi movement. Born in 1889, the son of an Austrian customs official, Hitler had not gone into politics until after the First World War. Considering his humble background and haphazard education, his subsequent rise to power was remarkable. Circumstances played their part, but even they needed a master. The *Führer,* or leader, of the Nazi Party was neither physically nor intellectually impressive. Yet he had certain qualities and abilities that enabled him to subject to his power first a whole

The Genius of Hitler

Before the war it was common to hear Hitler described as the pawn of the sinister interests who held real power in Germany, of the Junkers or the army, of heavy industry or high finance. This view does not survive examination of the evidence. Hitler acknowledged no masters, and by 1938 at least he exercised arbitrary rule over Germany to a degree rarely, if ever, equalled in a modern industrialized state. . . . Luck and the disunity of his opponents will account for much of Hitler's success—as it will of Napoleon's—but not for all. He began with few advantages, a man without a name and without support other than that which he acquired for himself, not even a citizen of the country he aspired to rule. To achieve what he did Hitler needed—and possessed—talents out of the ordinary which in sum amounted to political genius, however evil its fruits.

From Alan Bullock, *Hitler: A Study in Tyranny* (London: Odhams Press, 1952), p. 735.

people and ultimately a whole continent. One hesitates to use the word "great" in connection with someone so evil. But there was a certain diabolical greatness about this monstrous man. Rarely has anyone inspired such extremes of hatred and adulation as did Adolf Hitler.

As far as Hitler's aims are concerned, National Socialism, in contrast to fascism, had a detailed, if internally contradictory, program. Its twenty-five points offered something to everyone: The worker was promised a share in the profits of industry and the nationalization of the big trusts; the peasant was tempted by land reform and the scrapping of mortgages; and the rest of the people were told to look forward to "the creation and preservation of a healthy middle class." German national honor was to be avenged by breaking the fetters of Versailles. The country was to be strengthened by the union of all Germans in a Greater Germany. The Jews were to be excluded from political life. The parliamentary system was to be abolished. And "positive Christianity" was to replace religious diversity. This program, of course, was never realized, and

provisions that might scare off prospective supporters were soon explained away. Yet with its pan-German nationalism, its anti-Semitism, and its opposition to democracy, it clearly foreshadowed future Nazi policy. A still more important prediction of things to come was given in Hitler's autobiography, *Mein Kampf* (My Battle), which he began in 1924. Besides Judaism and Marxism, Bolshevism now emerged as his major target, and Russia was singled out as the chief victim of future German expansion.

Much of Hitler's ideology, especially its racism and pan-Germanism, had its roots in nineteenth-century Austrian and German thought. Because of such antecedents, and because Hitler's policy, notably in eastern Europe, seemed like a continuation of earlier trends in German history, the rise of National Socialism has been seen as a natural, inevitable, and peculiarly German development. There can be no doubt that Germany's past and the characteristics of her people help to explain the rise of Hitler. But of equal if not greater significance were the evil genius of Hitler himself and the specific circumstances in the early 1930's that made his victory possible.

Hitler's Rise to Power

We have already seen the disastrous effect that the Great Depression had on Germany. Before the nation had found time to recover from the results of a lost war and a runaway inflation, it was plunged once more into a major economic crisis. With millions of unemployed barely existing on a meager dole, political extremism flourished. Between 1928 and 1932 the number of Nazi delegates in the *Reichstag* rose from 12 to 230, and communist strength increased from 54 to 89. This radicalization made the orderly conduct of government by moderate parties impossible. Democracy, which never had taken firm hold in Germany, thus broke down. Economic and political chaos, the threat of communism, and the ever-present nationalist agitation against the Peace Treaty—these were the elements that helped prepare the ground for the rise of dictatorship in Germany, just as they had done ten years earlier in Italy.

Hitler's actual assumption of power was through perfectly legal means. Like Mussolini before him, he was asked—on January 30, 1933—to form a coalition government. The men who thus helped Hitler gain power—the aged President von Hindenburg and his political advisers—felt confident that they would be able to use the Nazi movement to achieve their own ends: the establishment of a conservative and authoritarian regime. They failed to realize that Hitler was not the man to let himself be used.

To strengthen his position, Hitler first held new elections for the *Reichstag*. But despite the intimidation of political opponents, only 44 percent of the German people voted National Socialist. As a next step, Hitler now asked the *Reichstag* to pass an Enabling Act that gave the government full dictatorial powers for four years. These powers were then used to prohibit those political parties that did not dissolve themselves. By July 1933 the National Socialists had emerged as the only legal party in Germany. The following November a solidly Nazi *Reichstag* was elected. In the meantime, Hitler had changed his cabinet to include mostly National Socialists. President von Hindenburg, who became increasingly senile toward the end, died in August 1934. Hitler now combined the office of president with that of chancellor, assuming the title of *Führer und Reichskanzler,* leader and chancellor. The transition from democracy to dictatorship was complete.

National Socialism in Power

Unlike communist Russia and fascist Italy, Nazi Germany did not introduce any sweeping constitutional changes. The *Reichstag* continued to meet, though infrequently, to endorse all measures put before it. There were no more elections, but occasionally the German people were asked in a plebiscite to support an act of the *Führer's*. Needless to say, they always did so by a rousing majority. The organization of the civil service was maintained, though it was purged of Jews and political opponents. The legal system was overhauled, and traditional concepts of law were abandoned in favor of a new kind of justice that elevated the welfare of the people and the state above the rights of the individual. To ferret out enemies of the state, a secret police, the Gestapo, was given the power of arrest and investigation.

Nazism at Home

As was the case in other totalitarian states, the Nazi Party in Germany controlled every aspect of national life. In his struggle for power Hitler had been aided by a number of capable lieutenants. These were now rewarded with leading positions in the government. But some of Hitler's old comrades failed to get what they expected. And others felt that Hitler had broken his word by not carrying out some of the more radical promises of the early Nazi program. To forestall any "second revolution" on the part of these malcontents, Hitler, on June 30, 1934, instituted a major "Blood Purge." In a lightning move several hundred of the *Führer's* possible opponents were arrested and summarily executed.

With the government and the party now under his firm control, there remained only one sphere in which the *Führer* did not wield complete authority, and that was the military. The armed forces had sworn personal allegiance to him after Hindenburg's death, and Hitler's renunciation of the disarmament clauses of the Peace Treaty in March 1935 had further enhanced his standing with the army. But it was not until 1938, after a thorough-going purge of the army's top echelons had removed the generals about whose political leanings Hitler felt uncertain, that the *Führer* felt he had a force on which he could fully rely. Henceforth Hitler himself was to be commander-in-chief of all of Germany's armed forces.

The same process of *Gleichschaltung,* or "coordination," that we saw in government, party, and army extended to every other phase of German life. In many of his innovations, Hitler consciously imitated Mussolini. This was true not only of the symbols and ceremonies of the "Third Reich" but of many of its policies. Like Mussolini, Hitler tried to make his country's economy as strong and self-sufficient as possible.

Hitler speaks.

The most spectacular sign of German recovery was the reduction of unemployment. Public works, rearmament, and military conscription ultimately created an actual labor shortage. In 1934 the *Führer* launched the first of two Four-Year Plans to prepare Germany's economy for war. To finance such costly ventures, huge funds were needed. These were raised through increased taxation, special levies, and rigid control of prices and profits.

The main sufferer of this policy of "guns instead of butter" was the German worker. His wages were low, his hours long, and his movements restricted. A German "Labor Front" took the place of the former unions. Like the Italian "corporations," it included both workers and employers. Strikes were forbidden, and all labor relations were controlled by the state. The farmer fared somewhat better. He was given various kinds of subsidy and was protected against foreclosure. Food production increased, although Germany did not become self-sufficient. One of Hitler's aims was a large and healthy rural population. In Nazi mythology "blood and soil" were considered the source of a nation's strength. Artists and writers, regimented like everyone else in Germany's totalitarian society, were called upon to glorify the "nobility of labor," and Nazi propaganda urged each and every German to place the welfare of the community before the good of the individual.

The majority of Germans readily complied with this appeal to make personal sacrifices and to work hard. Not that there was no opposition to the Nazi regime—the thousands of prisoners in the concentration camps testified to that.

Hitler's efforts to force all Protestants under the control of a "German Christian" church, and his evasion of the concordat he had concluded with the Catholic Church in 1933, brought strong and courageous protests from religious leaders of both confessions. There were other circles of resistance. But these groups were only a minority. This did not mean that the rest of the German people were all ardent Nazis. The Nazi Party, like its counterparts in Russia and Italy, considered itself an elite, and its membership was limited. The average German was, in his own words, *unpolitisch* ("nonpolitical"). He welcomed what he considered the "positive" features of the Nazi regime, and he secretly grumbled about the things he did not like. Moreover, before the outbreak of the Second World War, Hitler also had many admirers abroad. Like Mussolini the *Führer* was praised for the miraculous improvements he had brought about, and in particular for the firm stand he had taken against communism at home and abroad.

Anti-Semitism

There was one aspect of Nazi policy, however, which from the start caused deep indignation among observers abroad, and that was the persecution of the Jews. Anti-Semitism had been one of Hitler's earliest obsessions, and it was the aim that he pursued most persistently and ruthlessly to the bitter end. The first measures against Germany's Jews—fewer than 600,000, or 1 percent of the population—were taken shortly after the Nazis came to power. In April 1933 all Jews were excluded from the civil service, and a national boycott was imposed on Jewish businesses. Soon thereafter the Jews were excluded from the universities, and lawyers and doctors were barred from practice. The next major step came with the "Nuremberg Laws" of 1935, which deprived all Jews of their citizenship and forbade their marriage to non-Jews. As a result of this "cold pogrom," many Jews went into exile. But worse was yet to come. In November 1938 the assassination of a German diplomat in Paris by a young Polish Jew was made the occasion for a "spontaneous" demon-stration against the Jews. Synagogues were burned, shops looted, Jewish homes invaded and their occupants beaten up or killed. Jews henceforth had to wear the yellow star of David and had to live in segregated ghettos.

The intensification of Jewish persecution in 1938 was merely another sign that Hitler was getting ready for war. Most of Germany's domestic policies since 1933 had been geared to that purpose, no matter how ardently the *Führer* might proclaim his peaceful intentions. Hitler's ultimate aim was a "New Order" for Europe, under which the German people would expand into the unlimited *Lebensraum* ("living space") of the East and rule over the "inferior" Slavic peoples of that region. It was the unbounded ambition of Hitler's megalomania that plunged the world into the most frightful war it has ever seen.

The Spread of Authoritarianism

One of the dangers of totalitarianism, in the eyes of the free world, was its tendency to spread to nations that had been weakened by economic crises and political unrest. The rise of communism was generally considered the greater threat, and many a dictatorship of the Right gained power in order to prevent a dictatorship of the Left. The Soviet Union tried its best, with the aid of the Comintern, to help communist parties abroad. But its numerous attempts at fomenting leftist uprisings in central Europe and in the Far East remained unsuccessful. Nowhere outside the Soviet Union did communism gain a decisive victory during the interwar period.

Authoritarianism in Europe

Efforts to set up rightist dictatorships, on the other hand, proved more successful. We have already seen the rise of strong men in most of the smaller nations of central Europe during the aftermath of the First World War. Similar regimes arose in Spain and Portugal. In some countries—Yugoslavia, Albania, Bulgaria, Greece, and Rumania—kings turned into dictators. In others—Hungary, Poland, and Spain—

power was wielded by an alliance of military and agrarian groups. In still others—Austria and Portugal—authority rested with parties supported by the Catholic Church. As in the case of Russia, Italy, and Germany, all these small nations lacked a strong democratic tradition. Their new regimes were authoritarian rather than totalitarian. In some instances Germany and Italy tried to aid the rise of such authoritarian regimes. In Austria a Nazi *Putsch* in July 1934 failed, and Nazi victory was postponed until the *Anschluss* four years later. In Spain, on the other hand, General Francisco Franco defeated the republican government with the help of Italy and Germany. Like communism, fascism had followers in the democracies as well. But with the exception of France, these native fascist parties never posed a serious threat. It was only during the Second World War that the fascist "Fifth Column" became a real danger.

Japanese Fascism

In one nation outside Europe—Japan—economic crisis, rabid nationalism, and the failure of democracy gave rise to a totalitarian regime. The impact of the Great Depression on that heavily industrialized nation had increased the smoldering discontent with the government's inefficiency at home and moderation abroad. The opposition in Japan was centered in the army, particularly among its junior officers. Their aims were expressed in the writings of a young radical, Ikki Kita, who opposed the big industrialists and their political allies and advocated an almost socialist program: restriction of private property, nationalization of industries, and virtual abolition of parliamentary government. With the empire thus revolutionized, he envisaged Japan taking the lead in a crusade against western imperialism and ultimately extending her influence throughout Asia. The military clique itself had no clear program of action other than to gain control of the government. This they hoped to achieve through pressure, mainly by assassinating moderate politicians. Early in 1936 these activities culminated in a mutiny and the murder of several high officials. The army high command took energetic countermeasures and

executed the ringleaders. But at the same time the government made a number of concessions that assured the domination of the military in national affairs. In November 1936 Japan joined Germany and Italy in a treaty against communism, the Anti-Comintern Pact. Fascism had thus founded its own "International."

Japanese fascism differed in several respects from its European counterparts. It was not a well-organized movement under a single leader but rather a small pressure group; and it did not attempt to change the existing system of government but rather to dominate it. Yet in its demands for the subjection of the individual to the state, and in its veneration of tradition as embodied in the person of the emperor, Japan's militarism showed definite fascist traits. Most pronounced was the resemblance among the foreign policies of the three powers. Each sought solution of domestic difficulties through foreign expansion; each based the right to such expansion on claims of inherent superiority; and each looked to a special sphere of influence beyond its frontiers. In the case of Japan that sphere was the mainland of China.

The March of Fascist Aggression, 1931–37

The series of international crises that culminated in the outbreak of the Second World War began as far back as 1931 in the Far East.

Japan Against China

Japan, for some time past, had been trying to gain control over Manchuria, China's border province in the northeast. The region was rich in iron and coal; it adjoined Korea, where a Japanese protectorate had been established in 1907; and it was not under the direct control of Nationalist China. In September 1931 the Japanese army, using a minor incident along the South Manchurian Railway as an excuse, seized the Manchurian city of Kirin and surrounding territory. Local Chinese forces proved no match for the aggressors, and within a few months most of Manchuria had come under Japanese domination. In 1932 the victors renamed their conquest Manchukuo and declared it a Japanese protectorate.

The Chinese government meanwhile protested to the League of Nations and to the United States against this Japanese act of force. The League appointed a special commission of inquiry under Lord Lytton, onetime viceroy of India. Its report condemned Japan's aggression and proposed the establishment of an autonomous Manchuria under Chinese sovereignty. The United States stated that it would not recognize any changes made by force of arms. This was as far as the powers were prepared to go. Under the League Covenant they could and should have taken more drastic action. But China seemed far away, and sanctions might prove costly at a time when most of the world was in the throes of depression. So nothing was done. Japan, to have the last word, withdrew from the League of Nations in 1933.

Hitler Against Versailles

The moral of the Manchurian story was that if an aggressor acted quickly enough, nobody would dare stop him. This lesson was not lost on Adolf Hitler. In a series of dramatic moves between 1933 and 1936, he freed Germany from the most onerous restrictions of the Peace Treaty. In October 1933 the Germans withdrew from the Disarmament Conference and the League of Nations. In January 1935 the Saar region voted to return to Germany. Two months later Hitler denounced the disarmament clauses of the Versailles Treaty and Germany began to rearm openly.

In order to forestall any opposition to his unilateral policy, Hitler was careful at every step to stress Germany's peaceful intentions. In January 1934 he signed a nonaggression pact with Poland. This was seen as a sign that the Germans had become reconciled to their eastern frontiers. In the spring of 1935 Hitler quieted Britain's fears of German rearmament by concluding an Anglo-German naval agreement. The British thus joined the *Führer* in violating the Treaty of Versailles and added considerably to France's feeling of insecurity. It is hardly surprising,

therefore, that France should have sought help elsewhere. In May 1935 she concluded an alliance with the Soviet Union. But this merely gave Hitler the pretext he needed for his next major *coup.*

On March 7, 1936, Hitler ordered the German army to march into the demilitarized zone of the Rhineland. It was the *Führer's* most daring move to date. Had he been forced to back down at this crucial point, the future would doubtless have been far different. But again nothing happened. The French were afraid to act without the British. The British government officially criticized Germany's act. But the general

Hitler's Visitors

Lloyd George visited Hitler in September 1936, discussed world affairs, and came away convinced that Hitler was a reasonable man with acceptable aims and no desire whatsoever to plunge Europe into war. Conservatives, Liberals, and Socialists alike sought out the Führer, and were mesmerized by him. Even Arnold Toynbee was reported to have been won over at his interview to a belief in Hitler's genuine desire for peace in Europe "and close friendship with England." George Lansbury, a pacifist, and earlier leader of the Labour Party, was convinced after their personal encounter that Hitler "will *not* go to war unless pushed into it by others." Lord Allen of Hurwood told the *Daily Telegraph* on his return from Germany that "I watched him with the utmost vigilance throughout our lengthy conversation, and I am convinced he genuinely desires peace." Halifax recorded after his own visit to Berchtesgaden: "He struck me as very sincere, and as believing everything he said." But all Hitler did at these meetings was to repeat to each visitor the same dreary monologue about the insults of Versailles, the need for German unity on an ethnic basis, the evils of communism which he as a German could appreciate more than they could, the stubbornness of the Czechs, the pugnacity of the Poles, and the long-suffering innocence of the Germans. . . . But . . . when Lord Allen of Hurwood, with greater courage than most of his fellow-visitors, raised the issue of Jewish persecution, Hitler had nothing to say.

From Martin Gilbert, *The Roots of Appeasement* (London: Weidenfeld and Nicolson, 1966), pp. 164–65.

feeling in England was that the Germans had merely done what any people would have done under the circumstances—namely, to establish mastery over their own territory. The far-reaching implications of Germany's action were overlooked. If in the future she should ever want to move quickly, as she had done in 1914 and was to do again in 1940, there was no longer any protective belt to save the Lowlands from German invasion.

Mussolini Against Ethiopia

One reason why Hitler was able to get away with his daring move was that it coincided with a serious international crisis elsewhere. On October 3, 1935, an Italian army had invaded the Kingdom of Ethiopia, or Abyssinia, in northeastern Africa. The isolated and backward region had somehow escaped the scramble for colonies among the European powers before 1914. Once before, in 1896, Italy had tried to invade Ethiopia but had been repulsed. This humiliation was never forgotten. In his desire to increase his nation's power and glory, Mussolini now hoped to join Ethiopia with the existing Italian colonies of Eritrea and Somaliland into a sizable imperium. It was for reasons of prestige, therefore, that the fascist dictator embarked on his anachronistic venture into colonial imperialism.

The Ethiopian war did not last long. Italy's forces were too powerful for the antiquated armies of Emperor Haile Selassie. On May 9, 1936, Mussolini proclaimed the annexation of Ethiopia to Italy. Meanwhile the League of Nations, for once, had not been idle. After declaring Italy an aggressor, it had instituted a program of economic sanctions. But such a program, to be effective, had to be airtight. With several major powers remaining outside the League, it could not be. Still, it might have been possible to stop the Italians if oil had been included in the list of embargoes. But the fear that a ban on oil might lead to a general war made both France and England hesitate to take such a step. The French, who looked upon Italy as a possible ally against Germany, did not wish to endanger their friendly relations with Mussolini. The British feared that their navy would

have to bear the major burden of a possible conflict, and such a risk seemed "unrealistic" over an issue as insignificant as Ethiopia. Without the support of its two most powerful members, the League was powerless to act.

The results of the Ethiopian war were of the greatest significance for the future. Once again the western powers, instead of supporting collective security, had preferred to buy peace by making concessions at someone else's expense. But such concessions, as the next few years were to show, merely whetted the appetites of the dictators. Prior to this time, relations between Hitler and Mussolini had not been very close. Hitler's designs on Austria worried Mussolini, who was himself interested in the Danube region.

Guernica (1937), by Pablo Picasso. This large mural expresses the Spanish artist's nightmare vision of modern war. Guernica, a small, defenseless town in the Basque country, was wiped out in a single air raid by Hitler's Condor Legion during the Spanish Civil War. The Museum of Modern Art, New York.

But with the conquest of Ethiopia Italy's energies had found an outlet elsewhere, and Germany's friendly attitude during the conflict had further paved the way for closer collaboration. In October 1936 the two powers concluded a formal agreement to coordinate their foreign policies. This "Rome-Berlin Axis" was later joined by Japan.

War in Spain

The fateful significance of the "Rome-Berlin Axis" became evident in connection with the Spanish Civil War. Spain had long been a deeply divided country. Although a republic since 1931, the traditionally pro-monarchist forces—clergy, army, and aristocracy—still wielded considerable

power. The republican regime had been unable to cope with the economic consequences of the Great Depression. In contrast to the right-wing opposition, the republican Left was far from solid. In the elections of 1936 Republicans, Socialists, Syndicalists, and Communists buried their differences long enough to form a "Popular Front," and as a result they won a majority. But this Republican victory merely hastened the inevitable clash between Nationalists and Republicans. In July 1936 Spanish army units in Morocco, led by General Francisco Franco, rebelled against the Republic. The Spanish Civil War had begun.

Had the Spaniards been left alone, the war would hardly have become the major tragedy it turned out to be. But the war was not to remain a purely Spanish affair. Both Hitler and Mussolini were quick to recognize General Franco and to send men and materials to the Nationalists. The Russians in turn gave material and ideological support to the Republican, or Loyalist, side. But the communists alone were incapable of matching the aid supplied by the fascists. To assure the survival of the Republicans, the wholehearted cooperation of the democracies was needed.

The democracies were no more willing to risk a general war over Spain than they had been to become involved in a war over Manchuria or Ethiopia. Public opinion in general supported the Republicans, but the governments were more cautious. In September 1936 a Nonintervention Committee of some twenty-seven nations—including Germany, Italy, and the Soviet Union—met in London. But the committee could not prevent German and Italian "volunteers" from fighting on Franco's side. In an effort at neutrality, President Roosevelt invoked the Neutrality Act of 1935, prohibiting the export of arms and munitions to both sides in the conflict. But this move hurt only the Loyalists, since Franco continued to receive supplies from Germany and Italy.

The Spanish Civil War lasted for almost three years and caused more than 700,000 deaths. By the time the last Republican forces surrendered in Madrid on March 28, 1939, events in Spain had long been overshadowed by more important developments elsewhere. But Hitler's policy of bloodless expansion in central Europe was doubtless aided by the diversion provided by the slow death of democracy in Spain.

The Road to War

We thus come to the last two years of mounting international crises that finally led to the Second World War. Except for the Civil War in Spain,

the international situation at the beginning of 1937 seemed quite hopeful. But this impression was mistaken. The preceding years had been a crucial time of preparation for the new German *Wehrmacht,* when determined outside opposition might still have put a stop to Hitler's plans for aggression. But from now on the balance of military power began to turn more and more in Germany's favor. In June 1937 Hitler's Minister of Defense issued the first specific directive to prepare for a future war. Five months later Hitler met with his top advisers to present an outline of his strategy. First Germany would seek control over Austria and Czechoslovakia. Then she would be ready to pursue her major aim of eastward expansion to win the living space that the German people were entitled to.

War in the Far East

While Hitler was thus making his plans in Europe, open warfare had already broken out in the Far East. In July 1937 a minor incident near Peking touched off an undeclared war between China and Japan that lasted until 1945. By the end of 1938 the Japanese were in control of most of northwestern China as far west as the Yellow River and as far south as the Yangtze and Hangchow. Still farther south, Japan had seized the city of Canton and surrounding territory. In March 1938 the Japanese set up a "Reformed Government of the Republic of China" at Nanking.

The government of Chiang Kai-shek, meanwhile, had taken refuge in the interior province of Szechwan, with its capital at Chungking. The Chinese armies, though superior in numbers, were woefully short of equipment. To fight the invaders more effectively, Chiang Kai-shek and the Chinese communists agreed to bury their differences. A "scorched earth" policy and constant guerrilla warfare kept the Japanese from consolidating their gains. But despite the determined resistance of the Chinese, their ultimate survival depended on outside aid.

Chinese protests to the League of Nations brought little more than verbal condemnation of Japanese aggression. The French feared that resistance to Japan might lead to a Japanese attack on the French colony of Indochina. And Britain hoped that by appeasing Japan she might save her commercial interests in China. The United States, too, was careful at first not to antagonize Japan. Only when it became clear that the "Open Door" policy in China was being threatened did the United States begin to aid the Chinese. Of all the major powers, only the Soviet Union supported the Chinese from the beginning of the war. But the aid which thus

Europe Before the Second World War 1930–39

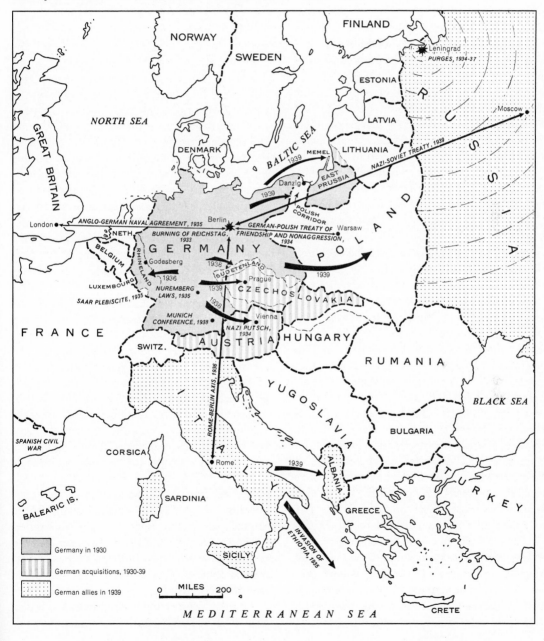

reached China was not sufficient to halt the Japanese advance. Beginning in the spring of 1938, furthermore, attention came to be diverted from Asia to Europe, where Hitler now embarked on his systematic policy of eastward expansion.

The Austrian Anschluss

First on the list of Hitler's victims was the small Republic of Austria. The Austrian *Anschluss* had always been a major Nazi aim. Efforts at a Nazi *Putsch* in 1934, as we have seen, had failed. But this did not end the Nazi conspiracy. In January 1938 the Austrian government uncovered evidence of another Nazi plot. In the hope of removing the tension resulting from this latest incident, Austria's chancellor, Kurt von Schuschnigg, accepted Hitler's invitation to come to Berchtesgaden in early February. Here he was presented with a set of demands the fulfillment of which would have made Austria a virtual German protectorate. Refusal to accept, Hitler made clear, would result in a German invasion of Austria.

Faced with these alternatives, Schuschnigg had little choice but to give in. But in March he decided to make one final attempt to save his country by appealing directly to the Austrian people in a plebiscite. Hitler's reaction was swift. Once more threatening invasion, he forced Schuschnigg to call off the plebiscite and to resign. On March 11 an Austrian Nazi, Seyss-Inquart, was made chancellor. On March 12, German troops crossed the Austrian frontier "to help maintain order." On March 13, Austria was incorporated into the Greater German Reich.

The ultimate success of this latest act of aggression again depended on the attitude of the great powers. As on all earlier occasions, there were loud protests but no action. The French were in the midst of one of their innumerable governmental crises and looked to the British to take the lead. But Britain, while deploring Hitler's methods, saw nothing wrong with an Austro-German *Anschluss*, so long as both peoples wanted it. And Italy, long a champion of Austrian independence, was by now squarely on Germany's side. There was also the hope, of

course, that Hitler would be satisfied, now that his dearest wish had been fulfilled. And the *Führer* did his best to confirm that hope by making his usual promises of peaceful intentions. The Soviet Union came forth with suggestions for a collective stand, warning that Czechoslovakia was next on Hitler's list; but these proposals were considered premature.

The Conquest of Czechoslovakia

The pretext for Germany's intervention against Czechoslovakia was provided by the German minority in the Czech border regions. The three million Sudeten Germans, as they were called, had long been a source of trouble to the Czech government, especially since Hitler's rise to power. Beginning in 1936 their leader, Konrad Henlein, had begun to collaborate secretly with the Nazis; and as Germany's power in Europe increased, the demands of the Sudeten Germans became louder. In April 1938, after the fall of Austria, Henlein demanded complete autonomy for the Sudetenland. This demand was immediately taken up by Nazi propaganda. The climax of Germany's campaign against the Czech government of President Beneš came with Hitler's address to the annual party congress at Nuremberg on September 12, 1938, in which he threatened German intervention on behalf of the Sudeten Germans.

Hitler's threat was no empty boast. The German army had been spending the summer of 1938 in feverish preparation for the invasion of Czechoslovakia. The French and British, meanwhile, had been trying desperately to effect a compromise solution of the Sudeten problem. But the Czechs proved adamant, trusting in their own military strength and the support of their French and Russian allies. When Hitler's speech intensified riots in the Sudetenland, the Czech government proclaimed martial law. War, it seemed, was imminent. It was narrowly averted by the action of Britain's prime minister, Neville Chamberlain, who now initiated a series of last-minute conferences with Hitler that sealed the fate of Czechoslovakia.

At the first meeting in Berchtesgaden, Hitler seemed to be satisfied with "self-determination"

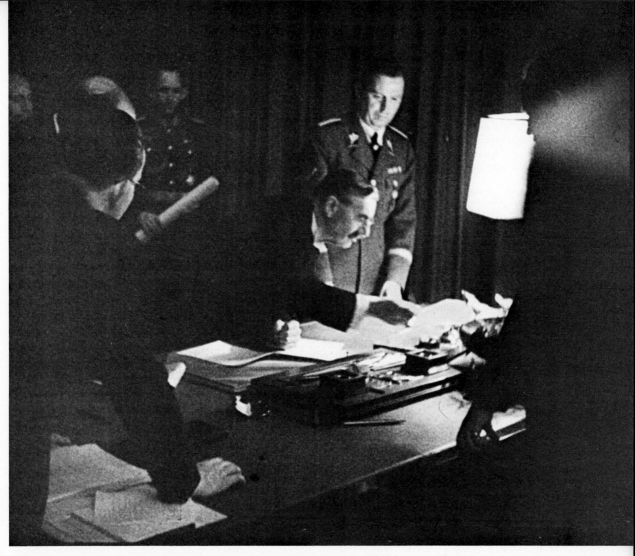

Prime Minister Neville Chamberlain signs the Munich Pact, September 30, 1938.

for the Sudeten region. But when Chamberlain returned a week later for a second meeting, at Godesberg, the *Führer* upped his demands. He now asked for the immediate surrender of the Sudetenland. This the Czechs declared unacceptable. But their protests were ignored at the final meeting in Munich on September 29–30. Hitler and Chamberlain, together with Mussolini and French Premier Daladier, now agreed on the Godesberg terms. In a separate agreement, Great Britain and Germany promised to renounce war in settling their national differences. "Peace for our time," as Chamberlain hopefully put it, seemed to have been assured.

The first reaction of the world, when the Munich decisions were announced, was one of relief. But it was not long before the criticism started. Deprived of her fortifications and most of her heavy industries, Czechoslovakia, the last outpost of democracy in central Europe, had been lost forever. The Russians, to be sure, insisted to the end that they would stand by their treaty obligations. But the strength of the Red army was not rated very high, and there was always the fear that the Soviet Union might try to embroil the West in a war with Hitler and then sit back. The French, in betraying their faithful Czech ally, had assumed a major share of the

The House of Commons Debate on Munich

Mr. Churchill: . . . I will begin by saying what everybody would like to ignore or forget but which must nevertheless be stated, namely, that we have sustained a total and unmitigated defeat, and that France has suffered even more than we have.

Viscountess Astor: Nonsense!

Mr. Churchill: When the noble lady cries "Nonsense," she could not have heard the Chancellor of the Exchequer admit in his illuminating and comprehensive speech just now that Herr Hitler has gained in this particular leap forward in substance all he set out to gain. The utmost my right hon. friend, the Prime Minister, has been able to secure by all his immense exertions, by all the great efforts and mobilization which took place in this country, and by all the anguish and strain through which we have passed in this country, the utmost he has been able to gain—

Hon. Members:—is *peace!*

Mr. Churchill: I thought I might be allowed to make that point in its due place, and I propose to deal with it. The utmost he has been able to gain for Czechoslovakia and in the matters which were in dispute has been that the German Dictator, instead of snatching his victuals from the table, has been content to have them served to him course by course.

Debate in the House of Commons, October 5, 1938.

On the eve of Munich Hitler had promised that the Sudetenland would be his last territorial claim in Europe. But even before the year was out directives had been issued for the final liquidation of Czechoslovakia. In March 1939 the blow was struck. On March 15 German army units crossed the Czech border, and the next day Hitler proclaimed a German protectorate over the Czech regions of Bohemia and Moravia. Slovakia was to become an "independent" German satellite.

The final dismemberment of Czechoslovakia was an important turning point. Up to this time, "Pan-Germanism," the desire to unite all German-speaking peoples, had seemed to be the motive of Hitler's expansionist policy. Now suddenly the world recognized his real aim: to gain living space and to subjugate foreign peoples. It was this latest act of Hitler's that brought about a decisive change in the attitude of the western democracies. On March 31, 1939, Great Britain promised the Poles all possible support in resisting any threat to their independence. And in April both England and France gave similar assurances to Rumania and Greece. What the western powers did not know was that on April 3, 1939, a secret directive had been issued to the German army ordering preparations for war against Poland so that operations could start any time after September 1, 1939.

The Eve of the Second World War

That Hitler should turn against Poland next is hardly surprising. Of all the territorial provisions of Versailles, the loss of the Polish corridor and the city of Danzig had been the most bitter for Germany. But while the world had still not recovered from the dismemberment of Czechoslovakia, the fascist powers made two more quick moves: on March 21, 1939, Lithuania, in compliance with Hitler's demands, returned to Germany the small territory of Memel; and on April 8, 1939, Mussolini sent his troops to occupy the Kingdom of Albania, which had hitherto been an Italian protectorate. A month later, Germany and Italy converted their Axis into a full-fledged alliance, the "Pact of Steel."

In late May 1939 Hitler informed his generals that war with Poland was inevitable. The

responsibility. But how could they have acted differently without the support of Great Britain? And the British, government and people alike, were neither morally nor materially ready for war. Appeasement, ever since Munich, has been an ugly word. But as we have seen, the purchase of peace at the expense of smaller or weaker nations had been going on for some time. The fundamental cause of the Czech disaster was the failure of the democracies all through the 1930's to understand the true aims of fascist aggression. Even at Munich these aims were not yet fully understood. It took one more of Hitler's moves to bring home once and for all the futility of appeasement.

fact that France and Great Britain had promised to protect Poland's independence was denounced by Hitler as an incitement to violence against the German minority in the Polish corridor. On August 22 Hitler held another of his briefing conferences. The *Führer* still hoped that France and Britain might decide not to fight. Not that he feared their intervention. The western powers, he said, were completely unprepared. As a final surprise, Hitler then told his generals: "A few weeks from now I shall, on the common German-Russian border, shake hands with Stalin and carry out with him a redistribution of the world."

The Nazi-Soviet Pact

What the *Führer* was referring to was an agreement between Germany and the Soviet Union to which the finishing touches were then being put in Moscow. The role of Russia in a future war, needless to say, was of major interest and had concerned Germany and the western powers for some time. Since April 1939 Russia had been engaged in negotiations with both sides. But France and Britain were unable to overcome their fundamental distrust of the Russians; and they had little faith in the Red army, especially after the recent purges. Still more significant, the western powers were unwilling to concede to Russia the predominance in eastern Europe which Stalin demanded. The Germans, on the other hand, had no hesitation in making concessions in the East if it meant gaining a free hand in the West. The Russo-German talks did not enter their decisive phase until mid-August. From then on events moved swiftly. On August 23 the two powers signed a nonaggression pact. Its most weighty part was a secret protocol that divided eastern and southeastern Europe into respective spheres of Russian and German influence.

The Nazi-Soviet treaty came as a terrible blow to the West. Two powers who, because of their rival ideologies, had heretofore appeared as irreconcilable enemies, now had suddenly buried their differences and established a common front. The advantages of the Russian pact for Germany were obvious: it saved the *Wehrmacht,* once Poland had been disposed of, from having to fight a war on two fronts. Russia's motives in making a deal with Hitler were less clear. According to Stalin, the Soviet Union had long been afraid that the West was trying to turn Nazi aggressiveness against communism. But it has also been argued that Stalin, by supporting Hitler, hoped to embroil Germany in a war with the western powers. Such a conflict might so weaken both sides that Russia would emerge as the decisive factor in the international balance of power.

With the signing of the Nazi-Soviet pact, the stage was set for the outbreak of war. It was still not clear whether the French and British would keep their word and come to Poland's aid. Negotiations for a last-minute compromise continued, and Hitler at one point postponed the start of hostilities to allow the West one more try at appeasement. But the lessons of the last few years had at long last been learned. On September 3, 1939, three days after the German invasion of Poland, England and France declared war on Germany. The Second World War had begun.

Suggestions for Further Reading

1. General

The totalitarian ideologies of the interwar years are presented in A. Zimmern, *Modern Political Doctrines* (1939), and M. Oakeshott, *Social and Political Doctrines of Contemporary Europe* (1939). H. Arendt, *The Origins of Totalitarianism** (1951), and E. Fromm, *Escape from Freedom** (1941), attempt to explain the roots and appeal of totalitarianism. The development of communist theory from Marx

---

* Available in paperback edition.

to Stalin is surveyed in R. N. Carew-Hunt, *The Theory and Practice of Communism** (1963). Other important books on communism are C. Black and T. Thornton, eds., *Communism and Revolution: The Strategic Uses of Political Violence* (1964), and J. C. Clews, *Communist Propaganda Techniques* (1964). The fascist brand of totalitarianism is dealt with historically in F. L. Carsten, *The Rise of Fascism* (1967), and ideologically in E. Nolte, *Three Faces of Fascism** (1966). See also H. Rogger and E. Weber, eds., *The European Right: A Historical Profile** (1965). Life under totalitarianism is described from personal experience by W. Leonhard, *Child of the Revolution** (1967), and by C. Milosz, *The Captive Mind** (1953). G. Orwell, *1984** (1949), presents a perceptive fictionalized account.

2. Communist Russia

F. Borkenau, *European Communism* (1953), and *World Communism** (1939, 1962), are standard works by a former member of the party. The most comprehensive history of the Soviet Union is E. H. Carr, *A History of Soviet Russia* (1950–64), of which seven volumes have appeared thus far. An excellent brief history is D. W. Treadgold, *Twentieth Century Russia* (1959). T. H. von Laue, *Why Lenin? Why Stalin?: A Reappraisal of the Russian Revolution** (1964), is a judicious reassessment. F. B. Randall, *Stalin's Russia: An Historical Reconsideration* (1965), is factual and objective. See also W. Laqueur, *The Fate of the Revolution: Interpretations of Soviet History* (1967). H. Schwartz, *Russia's Soviet Economy* (1954), is a good introduction. S. Swianiewicz, *Forced Labor and Economic Development: An Enquiry into the Experience of Soviet Industrialization* (1965), is more specialized. M. Fainsod, *How Russia Is Ruled* (1963), discusses the constitution and functioning of Soviet government. L. B. Schapiro, *The Communist Party of the Soviet Union** (1960), is the standard work on the subject. Soviet foreign policy before the Second World War is treated in L. Fischer, *The Soviets in World Affairs** (1951), and M. Beloff, *The Foreign Policy of Soviet Russia, 1929–1941,* 2 vols. (1947–49). For briefer treatments, see G. F. Kennan, *Soviet Foreign Policy, 1917–1941** (1960), and *Russia and the West under Lenin and Stalin** (1960). The most recent and best account is A. Ulam, *Expansion and Coexistence: The History of Soviet Foreign Policy, 1917–1967** (1968). The following are good monographs on various aspects of Soviet history and society: J. Erickson, *The Soviet High Command* (1962); N. Leites and E. Bernaut, *Ritual of Liquidation: The Case of the Moscow Trials* (1954); C. Brandt, *Stalin's Failure in China, 1924–1927* (1958); D. J. Dallin and B. I. Nicolaevsky, *Forced Labor in the Soviet Union* (1947); and L. B. Schapiro, *The Origins of the Communist Autocracy** (1955). The best biographies of the communist leaders are: L. Fischer, *Lenin* (1965); L. Schapiro and W. F. Reddaway, eds., *Lenin: The Man, the Theorist, the Leader: A Reappraisal* (1967); I. Deutscher, *Trotsky,* 3 vols.* (1954–65); and by the same author, *Stalin: A Political Biography** (1949).

3. Fascist Italy

The early years of fascist rule are discussed in A. Rossi, *The Rise of Italian Fascism, 1918–1922* (1938). G. Salvemini, *Under the Axe of Fascism* (1936) and *Prelude to World War II* (1954), are authoritative studies of Italian domestic and foreign policy by a leading antifascist Italian historian. Other good accounts are H. Finer, *Mussolini's Italy** (1935); R. Packard and E. Packard, *Balcony Empire: Italy under Mussolini* (1943); and H. L. Matthews, *The Fruits of Fascism* (1943). On foreign policy, see L. Villari, *Italian Foreign Policy Under Mussolini* (1952). The structure of Mussolini's government is treated in H. Steiner, *Government in Fascist Italy* (1938), and W. Ebenstein, *Fascist Italy* (1939). C. Hibbert, *Benito Mussolini* (1962), and I. Kirkpatrick, *Mussolini: Study of a Demagogue* (1964), are recent biographies of the Italian leader.

4. Nazi Germany

Among the many books dealing with the roots of Nazism, G. L. Mosse, *The Crisis of German Ideology: Intellectual Origins of the Third Reich** (1964), is one of the most stimulating. See also F. Stern,

---

* Available in paperback edition.

*The Politics of Cultural Despair** (1961), and H. Rauschning, *The Revolution of Nihilism* (1939). The debate surrounding Hitler's rise is summed up in J. L. Snell, ed., *The Nazi Revolution: Germany's Guilt or Germany's Fate?** (1959). The most complete account in English of the Hitlerian period is W. L. Shirer, *The Rise and Fall of the Third Reich** (1960). For a briefer survey, see H. Mau and H. Krausnick, *German History 1933–1945** (1953). The best biography of Hitler is A. Bullock, *Hitler: A Study in Tyranny** (1964). Hitler's aims are stated in A. Hitler, *Mein Kampf** (1939), and more openly in *Hitler's Secret Conversations, 1941–1944* (1953). See also *Hitler's Secret Book** (1961). The early events of Nazi Germany are made plausible in W. S. Allen, *The Nazi Seizure of Power** (1965).

The government of the Third Reich is discussed in W. Ebenstein, *The Nazi State* (1943), and in E. Kogon, *The Theory and Practice of Hell** (1958). The fateful role of the army in German politics before and during the Hitler years is described in J. W. Wheeler-Bennett, *The Nemesis of Power: The German Army in Politics, 1918–1945** (1953). On the treatment of the Jews, see G. Reitlinger, *The Final Solution** (1953).

Other important works on various phases of Nazi rule are: D. Schoenbaum, *Hitler's Social Revolution, 1933–1939** (1967); E. K. Bramsted, *Goebbels and National Socialist Propaganda, 1925–1945* (1965); G. Lewy, *The Catholic Church and Nazi Germany** (1964); B. H. Klein, *Germany's Economic Preparations for War* (1959); and A. Schweitzer, *Big Business in the Third Reich* (1964). On the various resistance efforts against Hitler, see T. Prittie, *Germans Against Hitler* (1964), and H. C. Deutsch, *The Conspiracy Against Hitler* (1968). The final act of the Nazi drama is told in H. R. Trevor-Roper, *The Last Days of Hitler** (1947).

5. The Road to War

The definitive history of the diplomatic background of the Second World War remains to be written. A. J. P. Taylor, *The Origins of the Second World War** (1961), is stimulating but thoroughly unreliable. F. Gilbert and G. A. Craig, eds., *The Diplomats, 1919–1939** (1953), includes profiles of the major diplomatic figures of the age of appeasement. Several books discuss Germany's relations with individual countries during the Nazi era: R. W. Seton-Watson, *Britain and the Dictators* (1938); E. Wiskemann, *Czechs and Germans* (1938) and *The Rome-Berlin Axis: A History of the Relations between Hitler and Mussolini** (1949); C. A. Micaud, *The French Right and Nazi Germany, 1933–1939* (1943); and E. Presseisen, *Germany and Japan* (1958). The following works dealing with British foreign policy in the thirties are all severely critical of appeasement: M. Gilbert, *The Roots of Appeasement* (1966); W. R. Rock, *Appeasement on Trial: British Foreign Policy and Its Critics* (1966); and M. George, *The Warped Vision: British Foreign Policy, 1933–1939* (1965). American diplomacy in the late thirties is analyzed in detail by W. L. Langer and S. E. Gleason, *The Challenge to Isolation, 1937–1940** (1952). On the major crises fomented by Hitler, see: G. Brook-Shepherd, *The Anschluss* (1963); J. W. Wheeler-Bennett, *Munich** (1964); and H. Noguères, *Munich: "Peace for Our Time"* (1965). The best book on the Civil War in Spain is G. Jackson, *The Spanish Republic and the Civil War, 1931–1939* (1965). Also very good is H. Thomas, *The Spanish Civil War** (1961). The diplomacy of the Ethiopian War is covered in G. W. Baer, *The Coming of the Italian-Ethiopian War* (1967). The best brief account of the events preceding the outbreak of the Second World War is C. Thorne, *The Approach of War, 1938–1939** (1967).

---

* Available in paperback edition.

18

The Second World War
and Its Aftermath, 1939–1950

The Second World War, in its origins and major events, was quite different from the First. While the question of responsibility for the First World War has caused much controversy, there can be no doubt that the responsibility for the Second rests heavily on one country, Germany, and on one man, Adolf Hitler. Still, it might be argued that Hitler would never have been able to go to war if the western Allies had stopped him in time. To that extent England and France, too, may bear some responsibility. And then, of course, Russia's pact with Hitler made the war well-nigh inevitable.

The war of 1939, far more than the war of 1914, was a world war. Japan had been fighting China for more than two years, and before long the war was to spread to other parts of Asia and to Africa. The earlier war had been largely a war of position. The Second World War was a war of almost constant movement. New weapons, already known but little used in the First World War, were chiefly responsible for the greater speed and mobility of the Second. The airplane in particular revolutionized warfare on land and sea. Its use against civilian targets, furthermore, eradicated all differences between the fighting and the home fronts. The Second World War was a truly total war.

The Axis Triumphant

Since he had planned his war at long range, Hitler at first enjoyed all the advantages of the aggressor. He expected the war to be short. Even

Hitler's Europe: massacred civilians in Russia.

though England and France had honored their pledges to Poland, he did not believe they would fight.

Blitzkrieg in Poland

Germany's forces crossed the Polish border on September 1, 1939. Everything went according to plan. The Poles were no match for the crack Nazi troops, and the main fighting lasted less than four weeks. During that time the *Wehrmacht* took more than 700,000 prisoners at the cost of only 10,000 German dead. The Germans obviously had lost none of their skill at making war.

The world was stunned by Germany's rapid success. Even the Russians were hardly ready to avail themselves of the spoils that had fallen to them as a result of their recent deal with Hitler. It was not until the end of September 1939 that a treaty of partition was signed between the Reich and the Soviet Union. Under its provisions Poland was wiped off the map, Germany taking the western and Russia the eastern half. This operation completed, Germany and Russia announced to the world that there was no longer any reason for Britain and France to continue the war.

War at Sea

This appeal for ending the war was directed primarily at France. The French, as Hitler gauged correctly, were neither enthusiastic nor confident about the war. The French army had dutifully occupied the fortified Maginot Line along France's eastern frontier, but there it sat and waited in the "phony war," as the war in the West came to be called. The British took matters more seriously, expecting a German air attack at any minute. But so long as Hitler thought that his friend Chamberlain might be made to give up the fight, the German air force remained grounded. It was at sea that England felt the first effects of the war. On September 17 the aircraft carrier *Courageous* was torpedoed off the southeastern coast of Ireland, and in mid-October a German submarine sank the battleship *Royal Oak* at its home base of Scapa Flow. It was not until December 1939 that the British scored their first naval victory, against the German battleship *Admiral Graf Spee* off the coast of South America.

The Russo-Finnish War

The next aggressive act on the European continent did not come, as was generally expected, in the West, but in the East. And this time it was not the Germans but the Russians who took the initiative. No sooner had the Soviets shared in the Polish loot than they began to put pressure on the small republics of Estonia, Latvia, and Lithuania to sign "mutual assistance" pacts allowing the Red army to occupy strategic bases along the Baltic coast. The only country to resist was Finland. So on November 30, 1939, Russia renounced a seven-year nonaggression pact with Finland and crossed the Finnish border at eight points. But this was to be no *Blitzkrieg*. The Finns were finally beaten, in March 1940. But in the meantime the Russian armies suffered serious losses and showed themselves woefully unprepared. In protest against Russia's attack on Finland, the League of Nations excluded the Soviet Union from membership, the first major power to be thus censured. But attention was soon diverted away from Finland as the Germans embarked on a second round of aggression against the small nations on their periphery.

Germany Turns North and West

Both Norway and the Low Countries were of great strategic importance to Germany. Possession of Norway would extend Germany's narrow coastline, giving her submarines a wider field of action; and the Low Countries, besides providing a protective glacis for Germany's industrial heart—the Ruhr—would offer the necessary base for operations against France and England. Reports in the fall of 1939 that Britain might occupy Norway made Hitler decide to move. In mid-December he ordered preparations for the northern war. Operations began on April 9, 1940. Simultaneously with their invasion of Norway, the Germans occupied Denmark. The British had been forewarned of the German move against Norway but failed to intercept the German invasion fleet. The main fighting in

Norway took only a few days. Some pockets of resistance held out until early June, but by that time the Germans had already turned their attention elsewhere.

The war in the West was launched on May 10, 1940. It was one of the most breathtaking and frightening military performances ever witnessed. As spearheads of tanks and armored vehicles drove relentlessly forward, bridges and airfields behind the Allied lines were seized by parachute troops, civilian objectives were gutted by air raids, and the endless columns of helpless refugees were strafed by dive bombers. It took the Germans less than a week to overrun the Netherlands and little over two weeks to defeat the Belgian, French, and British forces in Belgium. The remains of the Allied armies, more than 300,000 men, were evacuated to England from Dunkirk on the Channel coast. The Allied cause had suffered a resounding defeat.

On the day the Lowlands were invaded, Chamberlain resigned. He was succeeded by Winston Churchill, sixty-five years old and already a famous man, although his greatest contributions still lay ahead. It was Churchill who inspired the British people to their heroic resistance during the "Battle of Britain."

The Fall of France

There was no one to do for France what Churchill did for England. The man who was pushed into the limelight in the hope that he would unite the French people was Marshal Henri Philippe Pétain. Once before, in 1916, he had been the symbol of his country's resistance in time of national emergency (see p. 397). But in 1940 the old marshal was less concerned with continuing the war than with making peace. France, he felt, had been betrayed by the radical Left and deserted by her British allies. Why not try and save from the wreckage what could be saved by giving in to Hitler?

As the German armies reached the Channel coast in late May 1940, Hitler was faced with a major decision: Should he invade England, or should he complete the conquest of France? He decided to do the latter, mainly because he was still hoping to reach a compromise with the British and thus did not want to antagonize them unnecessarily. There is no need here to go into

Hitler's dance of victory.

the melancholy details of the "Fall of France." It was no longer a war, since there was hardly any resistance. When the French were at their lowest and German victory was beyond a doubt, Italian troops invaded southeastern France. Mussolini had stayed out of the war thus far, claiming that he was not ready for it. But the collapse of France was too good an opportunity to miss.

The official French surrender to Germany took place on June 21, 1940, at Compiègne. Under the terms of the armistice Germany occupied three-fifths of France, including her entire coast. The French also had to pay occupation costs of 400,000,000 francs per day. There were no final territorial provisions; these were to await a later peace conference. The unoccupied, southern part of France chose as its capital the town of Vichy. Besides Pétain, the leaders of the Vichy government included Pierre Laval and Admiral Darlan. The United States recognized the new regime and used its influence to bolster Vichy efforts to keep its fleet and overseas possessions out of German hands.

The Battle of Britain

With France out of the war, Great Britain now stood alone. Her most immediate fear was of a German invasion. But Hitler lacked the necessary equipment to launch his "Operation Sea Lion," and besides, he never gave up hope that England would capitulate without fighting to the finish. To break down British resistance, the German *Luftwaffe,* in July 1940, embarked on all-out air offensive. The Battle of Britain lasted through the rest of the year. Several times the British reached the limits of their reserves in planes and pilots. But they did not give in. Meanwhile, halfhearted preparations for "Operation Sea Lion" continued. But Hitler assumed that to be successful an invasion of England required complete control of the air, and that the Germans never achieved. In the fall of 1940, invasion plans were postponed and Hitler decided to strike elsewhere.

War in North Africa and the Balkans

An empire as large as that of Britain was vulnerable in many places. The British possession most coveted by Hitler was Gibraltar. To take this strongly fortified gateway to the Mediterranean, however, Germany needed the support of Franco's Spain, and that she failed to get. Another important British region was Egypt. The task of ousting the British from there was given to the Italians. In September 1940 an Italian army invaded Egypt from Libya. It was stopped almost immediately by a far smaller British force, which then drove the Italians back into Libya. A major Axis defeat was avoided only by the timely intervention of the German *Afrikakorps* under General Erwin Rommel. By early April 1941 the Axis forces had regained the initiative and were once again on Egyptian soil.

The Italians, meanwhile, had become involved in another venture, this time without even consulting the Germans. In October 1940 Italian troops crossed from Albania into Greece. After some minor gains, they were soon pushed back again into Albania. Once more the Germans had to intervene and thus open another major front. Bulgaria and Hungary were already on the side of the Axis. Yugoslavia was quickly overrun by German, Bulgarian, and Hungarian troops. Greece was defeated and occupied, and the island of Crete was taken by a German air-borne invasion. In the spring of 1941 it seemed that Germany was looking still farther afield, beyond the Balkans, toward the Middle East. But before the *Führer's* schemes went very far, he became occupied with more important objectives in eastern Europe. Combined British and Free French forces were able, therefore, to keep the upper hand in the strategically vital eastern Mediterranean.

There were some other hopeful developments in the spring of 1941, while Britain was still fighting with her back to the wall. The United States was constantly increasing its aid to Great Britain, and ultimate American involvement in the war appeared a definite possibility. The British navy, meanwhile, won a major victory when it sank the German superbattleship *Bismarck* on May 27. And, most important, there were persistent rumors that relations between Germany and Russia were rapidly deteriorating.

Hitler's Russian Gamble

Russo-German relations since the outbreak of the Second World War had been far from smooth. Two totalitarian countries, each bent on expansion, could not possibly avoid for long getting in each other's way. To be sure, the two partners maintained a mutually beneficial economic exchange. But on the diplomatic front Russo-German interests were far less complementary. Hitler was disturbed by Russia's expansion along the Baltic, and Stalin was taken aback by Hitler's unexpected successes in the West. More serious still were the differences between Russia and Germany over the Balkans, where no clear line of demarcation had been worked out. Efforts to clarify these and other matters were made in November 1940 at a conference in Berlin. But the attempt failed, partly because of Russia's far-reaching demands for the control of eastern and southeastern Europe, partly because Hitler had already decided to attack the Soviet Union.

The German Invasion of Russia

There were obvious reasons for Hitler's Russian gamble: He wanted *Lebensraum,* and he hated communism. But there was still another reason why he decided to strike at Russia. The stubborn resistance of the British, he felt, was due chiefly to their hope that Germany might ultimately become involved in a war with the Soviet Union. To attack and defeat Russia while she was still weak from the Finnish War, therefore, was the best way of inducing Britain to surrender. The first preparations for the invasion of Russia were made as early as July 1940. The final directives were issued the following December. The *Wehrmacht* struck on June 22, 1941.

The German armies at the start were disastrously successful. During the first weeks of fighting, hundreds of thousands of Russian soldiers were killed, wounded, or captured. But the Russians seemed to have inexhaustible manpower. What was surprising was how the Russian people rallied to their country's defense. Stalin emerged as a great national leader, and opposition to his ruthless regime disappeared in the face of foreign aggression. One of Hitler's gravest errors, next to invading Russia in the first place, was not to have posed to the Russian people as a liberator from communist oppression. Instead, the *Führer* ordered Russian prisoners to be herded into vast camps where they died of starvation, or else had them transported to Germany as slave labor.

The Russian war helped close overnight the gap between the East and the West. Great Britain now offered Stalin a military alliance, and the Americans included the Soviets in their program of lend-lease. While the East and West were thus joining forces, the Germans were encountering unforeseen difficulties. The winter of 1941 came unusually early, and the German army was not prepared for it. When Germany's commanders wanted to halt their advance, Hitler relieved them and took over himself. The Germans suffered terrible hardships, but they continued their advance. In the fall of 1942 Hitler's generals once again urged him to shorten his lines to more defensible proportions. But the *Führer* remained unyielding. Since August, large German forces had been engaged in the siege of Stalingrad on the lower Volga. The battle of Stalingrad has been compared to the battle of Verdun in the First World War. Both were fought with unusual ferocity and both entailed terrific losses. A German victory at Stalingrad would have given Germany control over the rich oil fields of the Caucasus. But instead of ejecting the Russians from Stalingrad, the Germans were caught in the pincers of a Russian counter-offensive and suffered a major defeat.

The battle of Stalingrad was not the first defeat the Nazis had suffered. As we shall see, the western allies were simultaneously advancing in North Africa. But the disaster in Russia was a decisive event. In a gradually mounting offensive, the Russians now began to push Hitler's armies back across the plains of eastern Europe. It took almost two more years before the fighting reached German soil. Meanwhile the expansion of Japan in the Far East had also been halted in the winter of 1942–43, and the Japanese were being driven back to their home bases. By the spring of 1943, fascist aggression had thus reached its farthest extent and the tide of the war now began to turn.

Hitler's "New Order"

Before we discuss America's role in the Second World War and events in the Far East, we must briefly consider the fate of those areas that for several years suffered under German occupation. There was never any master plan for Hitler's "New Order," since the future depended on the final outcome of the war. Few of the territories under German domination were annexed outright, although the degree to which some of them were being Germanized left no doubt about their ultimate fate. The war had done its share in decreasing the population of eastern Europe. In addition, more than 7 million foreign workers were forced to work in German factories. Into the areas thus vacated, ethnic Germans, mostly from outside the Reich, were sent as pioneers of Hitler's Germanization policy.

But Hitler was not content merely with taking land away from other peoples. The most frightful deed committed in the name of his "New Order" was the willful extermination of from 6 to 8 million people, most of them Jews. Wherever the German armies went, Hitler's private army, the elite SS (*Schutzstaffel*) followed to see that the party's racial policies were carried out. At first there was merely persecution of the Jews, and in this the local populations often participated. But in time more drastic measures were adopted. Hitler's so-called Final Solution called for nothing less than the complete extermination of all Jews. This was carried out by means of gas chambers in special extermination camps. There were several such camps, not only for the extermination of Jews but for the "mercy killing" of the incurably ill and insane, and for the liquidation of political prisoners. These were only the more gruesome acts committed by the Nazis. Additional millions were kept in concentration, slave-labor, and prisoner-of-war camps, where many died more "normal" deaths of starvation. A great many Germans were involved in these crimes; yet after the war almost no one would admit having known of what went on behind the barbed wire of these camps.

The New Order

The following is part of a confidential address given by Heinrich Himmler to his S.S. officers on October 4, 1943.

What happens to a Russian, to a Czech, does not interest me in the slightest. What the nations can offer in the way of good blood of our type we will take, if necessary by kidnaping their children and raising them here with us. Whether nations live in prosperity or starve to death like cattle interests me only in so far as we need them as slaves to our *Kultur*; otherwise it is of no interest to me. Whether 10,000 Russian females fall down from exhaustion while digging an antitank ditch interests me only in so far as the antitank ditch for Germany is finished.

From *Nazi Conspiracy and Aggression* (Washington: U.S. Government Printing Office, 1946), Vol. IV, p. 559.

America Enters the War

America's involvement in the war was a gradual process. The United States government had followed a policy of strict neutrality during the various acts of fascist aggression prior to the Second World War. The question was whether this attitude of aloofness could be maintained in a war between the major European powers. As one country after another fell victim to fascist aggression, America's role in the war became of crucial importance. Axis domination of western Europe and North Africa, once firmly established, would have posed a serious threat to the United States. It was in a spirit of self-preservation, therefore, that America entered upon the road from neutrality to belligerency.

Benevolent Neutrality

As early as November 4, 1939, Congress passed a revised Neutrality Act that lifted the embargo on all implements of war and put all maritime trade on a "cash and carry" basis. This move tended to favor the country with the largest funds and the strongest navy, Great Britain. But Britain's enormous need for material aid made her dollar credits dwindle rapidly. The two governments tried to overcome this difficulty in several ways. One was the "destroyer deal" of 1940, when the United States gave Britain some fifty ships in return for a lease of certain British-held naval bases in the Western Hemisphere. Another way for America to help her future allies was through the Lend-Lease Act of 1941. It gave the President power to provide goods and services to any nation whose defense was considered vital to the United States.

The Lend-Lease Act was an important step away from neutrality. There were other signs that America was getting off the fence. But in August 1941, when Congress was asked to extend the Selective Service Act of the preceding September, the measure was passed only by the slimmest margin. The American people, it seemed, were perfectly willing to go to any limit in helping the antifascist cause so long as they did not become involved in the war themselves. It took the Japanese attack on Pearl Harbor to push the United States across the line from nonintervention to belligerency.

War with Japan

The United States, for some forty years past, had stood in the way of Japan's major aim: to dominate China and extend her power over the trading area of southeastern Asia and the neighboring Pacific. Especially since the start of the Sino-Japanese war in 1937, Washington had been concerned over Japan's violations of the "Open Door" policy in China. To put pressure on the Japanese, the United States, in July 1939, ended its thirty-year-old commercial treaty with Japan and subsequently imposed an embargo on certain strategic goods. By the middle of 1941 the Japanese were becoming seriously affected by the embargo. Tokyo's demand for the cessation of United States restrictions were met with American counterdemands for Japan's withdrawal from China. As far back as January 1941 the Japanese

Pearl Harbor, December 7, 1941.

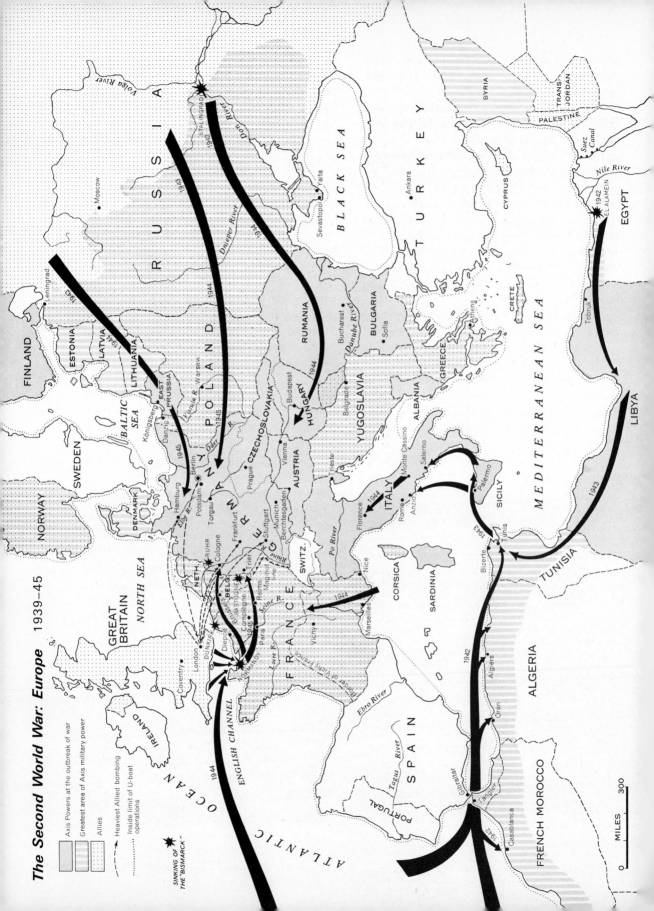

The Second World War: Europe 1939-45

Key:
- Axis Powers at the outbreak of war
- Greatest area of Axis military power
- Allies
- - - - Heaviest Allied bombing
- ········ Inside limit of U-boat operations
- ✴ SINKING OF THE 'BISMARCK'

Scale:
MILES
0 — 300

ATLANTIC OCEAN

IRELAND

GREAT BRITAIN

NORTH SEA

Coventry
London

ENGLISH CHANNEL

NORWAY

SWEDEN

FINLAND

BALTIC SEA

DENMARK

Leningrad 1943

Moscow

R U S S I A

Volga River

Don River

STALINGRAD 1942

Dnieper River

Don River

ESTONIA 1941
LATVIA 1941
LITHUANIA 1941

EAST PRUSSIA
Königsberg
Danzig

Vistula R.

Warsaw

P O L A N D

Oder R.

Berlin
Potsdam
Torgau
Hamburg
Elbe R.

Cologne
RUHR
Frankfurt
Trier
Stuttgart

NETH.
BELG.
BASTOGNE
Maginot Line
Rhine
Rhine

DUNKIRK
Dieppe
NORMANDY
Paris
Compiègne
Reims
Seine R.

F R A N C E

Loire R.

Vichy
Border of Vichy France

Nice
Marseilles

SPAIN

PORTUGAL
Lisbon
Tagus River

Ebro River

Gibraltar
Tangier
Casablanca 1942

FRENCH MOROCCO

ALGERIA
Oran
Algiers 1942

TUNISIA
Bizerte
Tunis 1943

SARDINIA

CORSICA

SICILY
Palermo

ITALY
Florence
Po River
Rome
Anzio
Salerno
Monte Cassino
1944

Munich
Berchtesgaden
SWITZ.
AUSTRIA
Vienna
Prague
CZECHOSLOVAKIA

G E R M A N Y

HUNGARY
Budapest
1944

Trieste

YUGOSLAVIA
Belgrade
Danube River

RUMANIA
Bucharest
1944

BULGARIA
Sofia

ALBANIA

GREECE
Athens

CRETE

MEDITERRANEAN SEA

LIBYA
Tobruk
1943

EGYPT
EL ALAMEIN 1942
Nile River

TURKEY
Ankara

BLACK SEA
Sevastopol
Yalta

CYPRUS

SYRIA

PALESTINE
Suez Canal

TRANS-JORDAN

1943
1944
1945

government had begun to prepare for an armed showdown. The final decision to strike was made on December 1.

When the Japanese air force staged its sneak attack against Pearl Harbor, on December 7, 1941, it caught the American forces entirely unprepared. With more than 3,000 casualties and heavy material losses, the United States suffered one of the greatest defeats in its history. Yet terrible as the catastrophe of Pearl Harbor was, it had one good effect—it cut short the debate between isolationists and interventionists. As Italy and Germany now declared war on the United States, the American people rallied behind the war effort of its government. With the world's mightiest nation thus fully committed, the outcome of the war looked decidedly more favorable for the antifascist powers.

The Defeat of the Axis

In discussing the defeat of the fascist aggressors, we shall deal with each major field of operation separately, keeping in mind, however, that the war was now being fought on a global scale. The European Allies were worried at first that America's involvement in the Pacific would prevent her from continuing her aid to Europe. The Russians in particular kept up a nagging insistence on the immediate opening of a second front on the Continent. Before such an operation could be thought of, however, large numbers of American troops had to be shipped overseas. And this step was possible only after the threat from Germany's submarine fleet had been overcome.

On the eve of the war the total tonnage of Allied merchant shipping amounted to about 25 million tons. Of this total, 21 million tons were lost, mostly to submarine action. The final victory over the submarine menace was due in part to the convoy system and to improved methods of detecting submarines. But the victory at sea could not have been won without the "battle of the shipyards," in which American workers built ships faster than the Germans could sink them. By the middle of 1943 Allied shipping had regained its prewar level and the worst of the danger was past.

The Invasion of North Africa

The first involvement of American ground forces in the war against the Axis took place in North Africa. On November 8, 1942, an Anglo-American invasion force, commanded by General Dwight D. Eisenhower, landed at Casablanca in French Morocco and at various points in Algeria. The purpose of the North African invasion was to eliminate the crack Axis forces in that area. Allied intervention in North Africa was made easier by the collaboration of the French forces stationed there. The leading French representative in Morocco and Algeria at the time was Admiral Darlan. It was due to his cooperation that Allied losses during the landing were kept to a minimum. The fact that Darlan had in the past been decidedly profascist caused some embarrassment. But the situation solved itself when the Admiral was assassinated by a follower of General de Gaulle. The North African campaign ended on May 13, 1943, with the Allied capture of Tunis and Bizerte. The total losses of the Axis in three years of North African fighting had come close to a million men.

In the meantime, the German people were also feeling the effects of American intervention nearer home. Almost daily, large fleets of United States and British bombers penetrated the anti-aircraft defenses of the Reich, bringing death and destruction to industrial centers and strategic objectives. The much-advertised *Luftwaffe* of Reichsmarshal Göring, which had earlier failed to bomb the British into submission, now proved equally ineffective in defending German soil.

The Allied Invasion of Italy

With North Africa in Allied hands, the next objective was to win control of the rest of the Mediterranean. The invasion of Sicily and southern Italy was launched in the summer of 1943. Resistance in Sicily collapsed in mid-August, and on September 2 British and American troops landed on the Italian mainland. The campaign in Italy lasted until the end of the war, slowing down as the emphasis shifted to the northern theater of war. Nevertheless, the war in Italy played a vital part in the final victory, since it helped tie down large German forces that might otherwise have been used on Hitler's two other fronts. But the Italian war also caused one of the first major crises between the Anglo-Saxon powers and their Russian ally.

Stalin had long been annoyed with the West for not opening what he considered a real second front. The invasion of Italy gave new cause for such annoyance. During the Sicilian campaign in July 1943, a number of high officials within the Italian Fascist Party staged a *coup d'état* and forced Mussolini to resign. The new Italian government under Marshal Badoglio asked the Allies for an armistice. While this made the subsequent invasion of the mainland much easier, the agreement with the fascist Badoglio further aroused the anger and suspicion of Stalin. What he feared was that the West might conclude a separate peace without the Russians.

"Operation Overlord"

The delay in opening a second front was partly due to differences within the western camp on where the attack against Hitler's "Fortress Europe" should be launched. Winston Churchill favored the Balkans. Not only did he expect fewer losses from striking at the "soft underbelly of Europe"; he wanted to keep the Russians out of that important peninsula. President Roosevelt and his advisers, on the other hand, saw France as the more suitable terrain for a second front mainly for strategic reasons. It was the American view that prevailed.

The final decision for "Operation Overlord," as the liberation of France was called, was made at a conference of the "Big Three" at Teheran in December 1943. The supreme command was entrusted to General Eisenhower; the scene of the landing was to be the coast of Normandy; and D-day was to be June 6, 1944. Since the Germans had expected the invasion nearer Calais, the Allies were able to establish a firm beachhead. Within three weeks more than 2 million men had been landed on the Continent. After three months of fighting, the Allies had driven the Germans out of northwestern France. On August 15 a second amphibious operation landed on the French Mediterranean coast and within a month

D-Day. The invasion of Normandy, June 6, 1944.

made contact with the main invasion forces in the North. In mid-September the first American forces crossed the German frontier. Here they were halted by the strongly fortified German "Siegfried Line."

The German *Wehrmacht,* while on the run, was still far from beaten. This was shown during the week before Christmas 1944, when Hitler staged his last big offensive of the war. Under cover of fog and snow and in the difficult terrain of the Ardennes, eight German armored divisions drove a deep salient into the Allied lines. This "Battle of the Bulge" proved a costly failure for the Germans, but for a brief moment it threatened to reverse the Allied victory in the West.

Germany Invaded from East and West

The Russians, meanwhile, had been pressing slowly but steadily westward. At the end of January 1945 the Red army stood on the Oder River, less than a hundred miles from Berlin. These were terrible months for the Germans, who now felt what it was like to be the victims of invasion. As the fortunes of war turned, sporadic German opposition to Hitler gathered sufficient strength for a final attempt to rid the country of its tyrant. But the plot of July 20, 1944, miscarried, and the *Führer* took horrible vengeance. Thousands of upright men and women, who might have played a leading role in the postwar reconstruction of Germany, were now put to death. The rest of the German people were urged on into suicidal resistance, especially since the Allied demand for "unconditional surrender" seemed to leave no alternative.

Early in 1945 the Allies stood poised along the western borders of the Reich, ready for the final phase of the European war. The invasion of the Rhineland was launched on February 8, 1945. From here on events happened with lightning speed. By the end of March the Rhine had been crossed, by the middle of April the Ruhr district had been taken; and on April 25 the first American and Russian patrols met on the Elbe River. On April 30, while the Russians were fighting their way into the center of Berlin, Adolf Hitler committed suicide. On May 7, 1945, at the headquarters of General Eisenhower at Reims,

The Red Flood

Columns of marching soldiers, dirty, tired, clad in ragged uniforms—tens and hundreds of thousands of columns . . . columns of women and girls in military grey-green uniforms, high boots and tight blouses, with long hair greased with goose-fat . . . children, mainly small boys; the *bezprizorni* from burned-out villages and towns. . . . Behind the first spearheads drive the staff; they drive in German luxury cars . . . cars with their secretaries and secretary-girl friends and secretary companions . . . cars with war-booty, cases of china, kilometres of textile materials, fur coats, carpets, silver. . . . Cars of the Agitprop Brigade with broadcasting apparatus and theatrical properties . . . lorries belonging to the Political Commissariat, the staffs and motorised units of the NKVD . . . lorries with tons of Russian delicacies, caviar, sturgeon, salami, hectolitres of vodka and Crimean wine. . . . Behind the staffs more marching columns, without a beginning and without an end . . . finally the rearguard; miles and miles of small light cars drawn by low Cossack horses . . . as the Tartars used to drive centuries ago . . . a flood from the Steppes, spreading across Europe. . . .

From J. Stransky, *East Wind over Prague* (London: Hollis and Carter, 1950), pp. 22–25.

a German military delegation signed the terms of Germany's unconditional surrender. May 8, 1945, was officially proclaimed V-E Day, victory day in Europe.

The War in the Pacific

The war against Japan was primarily a naval war in which the United States carried the major burden. Considering America's losses at Pearl Harbor and its heavy commitment of men and material in Europe, the victory in the Pacific was a magnificent achievement. This was particularly true considering the extent of Japanese expansion. A few days after Pearl Harbor, the Japanese overran America's outposts at Guam and Wake Island. Early in 1942, they invaded the Philippines. The Dutch East Indies, the Malay Peninsula, and Burma went next. By May 1942 the whole area east of India and north of

The Second World War: The Pacific 1939–45

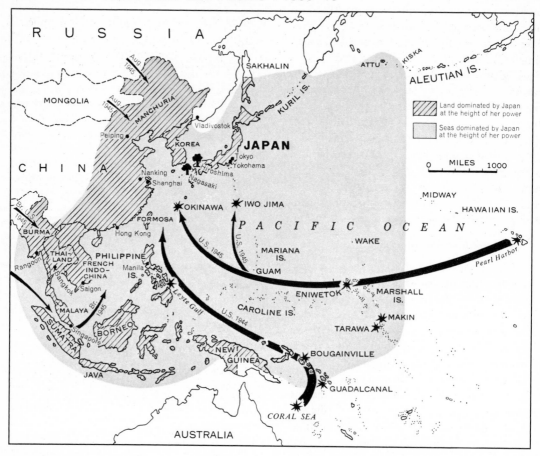

Australia, except for the southern part of New Guinea, had fallen into Japanese hands.

American Naval Victories

It was over the Japanese attempt to force the Allies out of New Guinea and to gain a base for the invasion of Australia that the first major naval battle was fought between United States and Japanese forces. The battle of the Coral Sea in May 1942 brought heavy American losses but it kept the Japanese from their objective. A still more decisive naval battle took place a month later at Midway Island, northwest of Hawaii. The engagement was deliberately sought by the Japanese, who hoped to annihilate the smaller United States fleet and thus open

the way to Hawaii. But the Americans anticipated the enemy's move and the battle of Midway brought a resounding Japanese defeat. For the first time America now held a slight naval margin in the Pacific. The Japanese achieved some last successes when they occupied Attu and Kiska in the Aleutian Islands. But with the landing of United States marines in the Solomon Islands in August 1942 Japanese expansion was halted, and soon the tide began to turn.

The Turn of the Tide

In 1942 United States naval supremacy was established in the Pacific; the next year brought the first breaks through the outer perimeter of Japan's defenses. Beginning with the battle of

Guadalcanal, one after another of Japan's island outposts were retaken in some of the war's bloodiest fighting. Places most Americans had never heard of—Tarawa, Makin, Eniwetok, Iwo Jima, Okinawa—now suddenly became headlines. Meanwhile, United States submarines were taking a heavy toll of Japanese shipping, and the Japanese islands were put under a blockade. In June 1944 American superfortresses began their first bombing raids on Japan. In October 1944 United States forces under General Douglas MacArthur began their reconquest of the Philippines. And in Burma British imperial forces under Lord Louis Mountbatten, supported by Americans and Chinese, were rounding up the Japanese invaders.

The End of the War

The climax of the war in the Pacific came on October 21–22, 1944, with the battle of Leyte Gulf in the Philippine Sea, one of the greatest naval battles ever fought. Japanese losses were such that their navy, henceforth, was no longer a factor in the war. As Allied successes in Europe mounted, more and more strength could be diverted to the Pacific theater. In the spring of 1945 America's commanders in the Pacific were asked to prepare plans for the invasion of Japan. But while these preparations were still under way, on July 16, 1945, the first atomic bomb was successfully exploded at Los Alamos, New Mexico. It was the atomic bombing of Hiroshima and Nagasaki that led to the surrender of Japan on August 14, 1945, and to the end of the Second World War.

The decision to use this terrible new weapon was not an easy one. Should not efforts be made to lay siege to Japan first? But President Truman and his advisers felt that an early surrender of Japan without invasion was most unlikely. And an invasion of Japan, it was estimated, would cost more than a million Allied casualties and at least again that many Japanese. It was thought preferable, therefore, to bring the war to a quick, though horrible, end: 78,000 people were killed at Hiroshima and 50,000 at Nagasaki. The Atomic Age had begun.

The Search for Peace

Considering the tremendous political upheaval resulting from the Second World War, it is surprising how little advance thought had been given to the problem of peace. There had been some general pronouncements, especially the Atlantic Charter, which President Roosevelt and Prime Minister Churchill had issued in August 1941. But this idealistic blueprint for the future, which aimed at a world free from want and fear, was drawn up before the harsh realities of the postwar situation were known. Several conferences during the war—between Roosevelt and Churchill at Casablanca and Quebec, and between the two western leaders and Stalin at Teheran—had dealt primarily with immediate military matters and only incidentally with

Hiroshima

At about 0815 there was a blinding flash. Some described it as brighter than the sun, others likened it to a magnesium flash. Following the flash there was a blast of heat and wind. The large majority of people within 3000 feet of ground zero were killed immediately. Within a radius of about 7000 feet almost every Japanese house collapsed. Beyond this range and up to 15,000–20,000 feet many of them collapsed and others received serious structural damage. Persons in the open were burned on exposed surfaces, and within 3000–5000 feet many were burned to death while others received severe burns through their clothes. . . . The people appeared stunned by the catastrophe and rushed about as jungle animals suddenly released from a cage. Some few apparently attempted to help others from the wreckage, particularly members of their family or friends. Others assisted those who were unable to walk alone. However, many of the injured were left trapped beneath collapsed buildings as people fled by them in the streets. Pandemonium reigned as the uninjured and slightly injured fled the city in fearful panic.

From "The Effects of Atomic Bombs on Health and Medical Services in Hiroshima and Nagasaki," *The United States Strategic Bombing Survey* (Washington: U.S. Government Printing Office, March 1947), p. 3.

The Yalta Conference. Churchill, Roosevelt, and Stalin pose for an official picture with their advisers. President Roosevelt clearly shows the strain of the meeting. He was to die exactly two months later, on April 2, 1945.

long-range political questions. It was not until the final months of the war that the larger issues of the future became the subject of top-level discussions. These took place at two conferences at Yalta and Potsdam, in February and July 1945.

The Yalta Conference

To understand the concessions made at Yalta to the Soviet Union, we must remember that Russia was still an ally of the West and that the expansionist aims of communism were not yet fully understood. Some of Stalin's claims, furthermore, especially in the Baltic, in Poland, and in the Balkans, had already been recognized, at least by implication. And the fact that all these regions were already occupied by the Red armies gave added strength to Soviet arguments. Most important, finally, was the conviction of western military leaders that Russia's continued contribution to the common war effort was essential to ensure an early victory.

The main issues discussed at Yalta dealt with the future of Germany, Poland, the Far East, and the United Nations. So far as Germany was concerned, the meeting achieved very little. The only firm agreement dealt with the postwar division of the country into four occupation zones, administered by an Allied Control Council. The city of Berlin, likewise, was to be divided into separate occupation zones.

A great deal of time at Yalta was spent in trying to determine the future frontiers of Poland

and to agree on the composition of its government. On both points the Russians scored a major victory. Poland's border was moved westward to the "Curzon Line," where it had been fixed briefly after the First World War. Russia thus received almost 47 percent of Poland's prewar territory. The powers agreed, however, that in return for its losses in the east, Poland should receive compensations in the north and west. The new provisional government of Poland, meanwhile, was to be drawn from the Soviet-sponsored Committee of National Liberation rather than from the Polish government-in-exile, which the western powers had favored. To make sure that Poland was ruled democratically, "free and unfettered elections" were to be held.

The Far Eastern decisions made at Yalta caused little difficulty at the time, but they have come in for a great deal of criticism since. In return for Stalin's promise to participate in the Pacific war, the Soviet Union was granted large concessions at the expense of both China and Japan. Most of these made up Russia's losses in the Russo-Japanese War of 1904–05 (see p. 336).

The problem that most concerned the American delegation at Yalta was to get American and British agreement to final plans for a United Nations organization. Most of the details for such an organization had already been worked out, except for two important points: the extent of the great powers' veto in the Security Council and the number of seats each was to hold in the UN Assembly. Both points were satisfactorily settled, a fact that greatly contributed to the success of the conference in American eyes. There had been some hard bargaining at Yalta, but on the whole the atmosphere had been friendly. It remained to be seen whether the powers could carry over their wartime unity of purpose into their postwar search for peace.

The United Nations

The first problem tackled after Yalta was the drafting of a Charter for the United Nations. This was done at the San Francisco Conference in the spring of 1945. The main purposes of the United Nations are: to maintain peace; to develop friendly relations among nations; and to help solve economic, social, and cultural problems. Any peace-loving nation may become a member if sponsored by the Security Council and a two-thirds vote of the Assembly, and a state may be expelled for violating the provisions of the Charter.

Charter of the United Nations

PREAMBLE

We, the peoples of the United Nations

Determined to save succeeding generations from the scourge of war, which twice in our lifetime has brought untold sorrow to mankind, and

To reaffirm faith in fundamental human rights, in the dignity and worth of the human person, in the equal right of men and women and of nations large and small, and

To establish conditions under which justice and respect for the obligations arising from treaties and other sources of international law can be maintained, and

To promote social progress and better standards of life in larger freedom, and for these ends

To practice tolerance and live together in peace with one another as good neighbors, and

To unite our strength to maintain international peace and security, and

To insure, by the acceptance of principles and the institution of methods, that armed force shall not be used, save in the common interest, and

To employ international machinery for the promotion of the economic and social advancement of all peoples, have resolved to combine our efforts to accomplish these aims.

Accordingly, our respective governments, through representatives assembled in the city of San Francisco, who have exhibited their full powers found to be in good and due form, have agreed to the present Charter of the United Nations and do hereby establish an international organization to be known as the United Nations.

The launching of the UN, as seen by *Punch*.

As these provisions suggest, the United Nations owes much to its predecessor, the League of Nations. Like the League, the UN, at least at the start, was entirely dominated by the great powers among its members. The most important agency of the UN is the Security Council, five of whose seats are permanently assigned to the United States, Great Britain, the Soviet Union, France, and Nationalist China. Since each of these powers has an absolute veto, the effectiveness of the UN has been seriously hampered. The chief task of the Council is to maintain peace and security. Like the Council of the League of Nations, it can recommend peaceful arbitration or measures short of war, such as economic sanctions. But unlike the League, the Security

Council may also take "such actions by air, sea, or land forces as may be necessary to maintain or restore international peace."

The Potsdam Conference

While the San Francisco Conference was still in session, the end of the war in Europe called for another top-level conference to settle the future of Germany. In the meantime, Russia's unilateral actions in eastern Europe, notably in Rumania and Poland, had already called forth repeated western protests. When the powers assembled at Potsdam, therefore, in July 1945, the cordiality that had prevailed at Yalta had given way to coldness. The United States, after President Roosevelt's death in April 1945, was represented by President Truman; and Great Britain, after Churchill's defeat at the polls, was represented by Prime Minister Clement Attlee. This left Stalin as the only original member of the Big Three.

The main differences between the East and the West at Potsdam arose over the eastern borders of Germany and over German reparations. As compensation for the territories she had lost to Russia at Yalta, Poland had occupied about one-fifth of Germany, east of the Oder and Neisse rivers. Against Stalin's insistence that these lands become permanently Polish, the western powers at Potsdam won a postponement of any final decision until a later peace conference. As for German reparations, the Soviet Union held on to the high demands it had made at Yalta. But the West got Stalin to agree that Germany was to be left with sufficient resources to support herself and that she was to be treated "as a single economic unit." Here were several causes for subsequent friction among the victors.

During the closing days of the Potsdam Conference attention shifted to the Far East, where the war with Japan was drawing to a close. At the last minute, the Soviet Union entered the war by invading Manchuria. As soon as the fighting had stopped, Russia took possession of the rights and territories she had been promised at Yalta. Control over Japan itself was claimed by the United States. The Korean peninsula was occupied jointly by Russian and American forces. Here was another potential source of conflict.

Peace with the Axis Satellites

With the war finally over, peace negotiations could now begin. The peace conference of the twenty-one nations that had fought against the Axis met in Paris in July 1946. Many of its decisions had been made beforehand by the foreign ministers of the great powers. The peace treaties with Italy, Rumania, Hungary, Bulgaria, and Finland were signed in February 1947. Italy, in spite of her fascist past, was let off remarkably easily. She lost some territory to France, Yugoslavia, and Greece; her colonies were put under the trusteeship of the UN; and she had to pay reparations. The settlements with the rest of the powers were similar. Since, with the exception of Finland, these countries were already under Russian domination, the details of the peace terms are not very important. The Soviet Union in each case got a major share of the reparations and she also took extensive territories from Finland and Rumania. Like the Baltic states and eastern Poland, which the Soviets had annexed earlier, these lands had formerly belonged to tsarist Russia. Russia's aim, it seemed, was to restore the border that had been hers before the advent of communism.

The Problem of Germany

With the signing of the Paris treaties, peacemaking ended for the time being. Treaties with Japan and Austria were not signed until several years later, and there is as yet no final settlement with Germany. It was over the issue of Germany that the East and West had their first real falling-out.

Germany, at Potsdam, lost about one-fourth of the territory she had held in 1937, before Hitler embarked on his eastward expansion. But she still had almost 70 million people, and her industrial resources were considerable. There could be little doubt, therefore, that the former Reich would continue to be a vital factor in world affairs. Beginning in 1946, Russia and the western powers tried to reach an agreement on the future of Germany. But it soon became clear that they did not see eye to eye on many crucial points. What each side hoped was to create a united Germany in its own image. And when this proved impossible, the East and West proceeded to reorganize their respective zones, eventually creating a divided Germany.

The Division of Germany

The first disagreements arose over economic matters. The division of Germany into occupation zones proved a serious obstacle to economic recovery. Any western proposals for economic unification, however, were met by Russian counterproposals for political unity first. Since it had been agreed at Potsdam that Germany was to be treated "as a single economic unit," the western powers, in December 1946, merged their zones economically. West Germany's economy was then given considerable American aid. The result was a miraculous turn for the better. By 1950 the industrial output of West Germany had climbed back to its 1936 level.

While the West was thus integrating its two-thirds of Germany into the economy of western Europe, the Russians began the thoroughgoing "sovietization" of their eastern zone. We need not review the various steps by which these diverging policies finally led to partition. At one point, in 1948–49, the Soviet Union tried to force the West out of the former German capital by imposing a blockade on the Allied sectors of Berlin. But a gigantic western airlift foiled Russia's scheme. In May 1949 a West German Parliamentary Council adopted a constitution for the Federal Republic of Germany, with Bonn as capital and with Konrad Adenauer as its first chancellor. In East Germany a communist-dominated "German Democratic Republic" was founded in October 1949. By 1950 the struggle between East and West over Germany had thus resulted in the political division of the country, each part refusing to recognize the other and claiming to speak for the whole.

The Beginning of the Cold War

To understand the growing tension between the western Allies and the Soviet Union, we must realize the fundamental difference of their aims.

The West envisaged the postwar world largely in prewar terms. The United Nations was to continue the work of the League of Nations, without the latter's shortcomings; and it was hoped that in due time the idealistic principles of the Atlantic Charter would be put into effect. The Soviet Union, on the other hand, endeavored to use the chaos of the postwar world to further its own aims: the extension of Soviet power and the spread of communism.

The Spread of Communism

The communization of eastern Europe was a gradual process. The region had been "liberated" by the Red army, which had then stayed on. At first some outward show of democracy was maintained, with "popular front" governments and "free" elections. But gradually the noncommunist members were ousted from the various coalition governments. By 1947 this policy was causing deep concern in the West. Poland, Rumania, Yugoslavia, Albania, and Bulgaria all had either communist or pro-communist regimes, and the trend in Czechoslovakia and Hungary was in the same direction. The only way to halt this creeping expansion of communism, it was felt, was to meet force with force. The occasion to proclaim such a policy of "containment" came in the spring of 1947, when Russia began to extend her influence over the region surrounding the entrance to the Black Sea.

The Truman Doctrine and the Marshall Plan

In Greece, a small communist minority, supported by communists in neighboring countries, was waging a civil war against the government. The British, after the war, had supplied the Greek monarchy with aid. But Britain had serious economic problems at home, and she was also supporting Turkey's resistance to Soviet demands for concessions. In the spring of 1947, Great Britain announced that she could no longer give aid to Greece and Turkey. It was at this point that the United States took over. In a message to Congress on March 12, 1947, President

Territorial Adjustments After the Second World War   1945

NORWAY

SWEDEN

FINLAND

To Russia

Lake Ladoga

Leased to Russia until 1955

Leningrad

NORTH SEA

DENMARK

B A L T I C   S E A

ESTONIA
To Russia

LATVIA
To Russia

LITHUANIA
To Russia

EAST PRUSSIA
To Russia

R U S S I A

NETH.

U.S.

Berlin

BRITISH ZONE

RUSSIAN ZONE

Occupied by Poland

Occupied by Poland

To Russia

BELG.

FRENCH ZONE

G E R M A N Y

UNITED STATES ZONE

P O L A N D

CZECHOSLOVAKIA

NORTHERN BUKOVINA

F R A N C E

FRENCH ZONE

U.S. ZONE

RUSSIAN ZONE

Vienna

U.S. ZONE

From Hungary to Czech.

SUBCARPATHIAN RUTHENIA

BESSARABIA
To Russia

SWITZ.

FRENCH ZONE

AUSTRIA

BRITISH ZONE

BRATISLAVA BRIDGEHEAD

H U N G A R Y

R U M A N I A

VENEZIA GIULIA
To Yugoslavia

Trieste

Y U G O S L A V I A

DOBRUJA

To Bulgaria

I T A L Y

ADRIATIC SEA

BULGARIA

B L A C K   S E A

ALBANIA

GREECE

The boundaries shown on this map date from the beginning of World War II.

MILES
0   200

DODECANESE IS.
To Greece from Italy

Axis nations after World War II

Lands which changed hands after World War II

Truman called for American support to "free peoples who are resisting attempted subjugation by armed minorities or by outside pressures." Such support, the President added, was to be primarily economic. A comprehensive scheme for American aid was announced three months later by Secretary of State George C. Marshall. By fighting the economic and social conditions that gave rise to communism, the United States hoped to contain it.

The Cominform and the Molotov Plan

The Truman Doctrine and the Marshall Plan opened a wholly new phase in United States foreign policy. America had broken with its isolationist past and had assumed the leadership of the free world. The significance of this break

The Coup d'État in Prague

Letter from President Beneš to the Presidium of the Communist Party:

. . . You know my sincerely democratic creed. I cannot but stay faithful to that creed even at this moment because democracy, according to my belief, is the only reliable and durable basis for a decent and dignified human life.

I insist on parliamentary democracy and parliamentary government as it limits democracy. I state I know very well it is necessary to social and economic content. I built my political work on these principles and cannot—without betraying myself—act otherwise. . . .

Reply by the Presidium of the Communist Party:

The Presidium of the Central Committee of the Communist Party acknowledged your letter dated February 24 and states again that it cannot enter into negotiations with the present leadership of the National Socialist, People's and Slovak Democratic Parties. . . .

Massive people's manifestations during the last few days clearly have shown our working people denounce, with complete unity and with indignation, the policy of these parties and ask the creation of a government in which all honest progressive patriots devoted to the republic and the people are represented. . . .

Being convinced that only such a highly constitutional and parliamentary process can guarantee the peaceful development of the republic and at the same time it corresponds to the ideas of a complete majority of the working people, the Presidium of the Central Committee hopes firmly after careful considerations that you will recognize the correctness of its conclusions and will agree with its proposals.

From H. L. Trefousse, *The Cold War—A Book of Documents* (New York: G. P. Putnam's Sons, 1965), pp. 109–12.

was not lost on the Soviet Union. Secretary Marshall had included all European nations in his plan, but any country in the Russian orbit that tried to participate was prevented from doing so by the Soviets. To tighten her control over eastern Europe, the Soviet Union had already concluded mutual assistance pacts with most of her satellites. In order to coordinate the efforts of European communism, the Russians, in 1947, founded the Communist Information Bureau (Cominform), as successor to the Comintern, which had been dissolved in 1943. In the economic field, finally, the Russians announced their own "Molotov Plan," as counterpart to the European Recovery Program initiated by Secretary Marshall.

The Communist Coup in Czechoslovakia

While East and West were thus consolidating their positions, the Russians scored another victory in the Cold War. Among the occupied nations of eastern Europe, Czechoslovakia alone had been able to maintain some of her democratic freedoms. But these were gradually undermined by the usual infiltration tactics of native communists with Russian backing. By early 1948 the country was ripe for a *coup d'état*. In March, Foreign Minister Jan Masaryk, a friend of the West, was driven to suicide; and in June, President Beneš gave way to communist leader Klement Gottwald. Except for Finland, all of eastern Europe was now under communist rule.

The North Atlantic Treaty

The communist seizure of Czechoslovakia dramatized the need for military as well as economic integration of western resources. Great Britain and France had already concluded the Treaty of Dunkirk in 1947. As an additional safeguard, they now asked the Benelux countries —Belgium, the Netherlands, and Luxembourg—to join them in the Brussels Pact. But the nations of western Europe realized that effective resistance to Russia required the help of the United States. There were still isolationists in America who warned against a military alliance, but the majority of Americans agreed with their government that the only language Russia seemed to understand was the language of force. So on April 4, 1949, the United States joined the members of the Brussels Pact, together with Italy, Portugal, Denmark, Iceland, Norway, and Canada, in the North Atlantic Treaty. These twelve powers were joined later by Greece and Turkey (1951) and by West Germany (1955). The gist of the treaty was contained in Article 5, which stated that "an armed attack against one or more" of its signatories "shall be considered an attack against them all." A North Atlantic Council was set up to direct the formation of the North Atlantic Treaty Organization (NATO).

The United Nations in the Cold War

The growing tension between the East and West was also felt within the United Nations. As long as one of the major powers, through its veto in the Security Council, could prevent joint action, the effectiveness of the UN was limited. Only when international disputes did not involve the interests of a major power could the United Nations make its influence felt. It was thus possible to stop the fighting between Dutch and native forces in Indonesia and between India and Pakistan over Kashmir. In trying to keep Russia from meddling in the affairs of Iran, however, or in calling a halt to the civil war in Greece, United States aid was more important than UN pressure. The United Nations did score one major success before 1950: the founding of the state of Israel. But this was possible only because it was supported by both the Soviet Union and the United States.

The Founding of Israel

We have already discussed the intermittent clashes between Arabs and Jews in Palestine before the Second World War. When the British after the war found it increasingly difficult to keep peace within their mandate, they decided to withdraw. At this point, in 1948, the UN stepped in, hoping to bring about a peaceful partition of Palestine. The Jews proclaimed the independent state of Israel, which was immediately recognized by the United States and the Soviet Union. But the Arabs, who opposed this solution, resisted. In the ensuing war the Israeli forces proved superior. UN efforts for an armistice finally succeeded in 1949. But peace remained precarious and full-scale war was resumed in 1956.

Other UN Activities

The United Nations had other tasks besides settling international disputes. In some of these economic, social, and cultural activities carried on by special agencies, the UN was highly successful. In December 1948 the General Assembly adopted an ambitious program of technical assistance for underdeveloped areas. Much of the necessary money and personnel were made available by the United States under the Point Four program proclaimed by President Truman in January 1949.

Far more important than these economic and social problems, however, was the need for some regulation of international armaments. And here the United Nations made little headway. The main concern was over the control of atomic weapons. In 1946 America proposed the establishment of an International Atomic Development Authority to which the United States would transfer its atomic knowledge and facilities. The Authority was to be given the right of inspection to prevent the secret manufacture of atomic bombs. Since America still had a monopoly in the atomic field, this proposal was most generous and it was endorsed by an overwhelming majority of the General Assembly. But the Soviet Union vetoed the American proposal, objecting in particular to its provisions for inspection. In July 1949, after three years of fruitless debate, the Atomic Energy Commission adjourned. Two months later, Russia announced the first successful explosion of its own atomic bomb.

The Cold War in the Far East

Our discussion of postwar events thus far has dealt mostly with Europe. But the most momentous changes after 1945 took place in other parts of the world. The emancipation of former colonial regions from foreign rule transformed the hitherto passive masses of Asia and Africa into active participants in international affairs. The most important change of all was the emergence of Red China as a major force in the world's balance of power.

Postwar Japan

Because of its leading role in the occupation of Japan, the United States after the Second World War was more deeply involved in Far Eastern affairs than at any other time in its history. Since there was no rivalry among occupying powers, and since Japan's governmental machinery was left intact, the transition from war to peace went more smoothly in Japan than in Germany. A democratic constitution, in May 1947, transferred sovereignty from the emperor to the people. The Japanese army and navy had already been dissolved, patriotic organizations were banned, and education was reformed along democratic lines. In the economic sphere, the changes were less drastic. Plans to break up the large industrial and financial combinations of the *zaibatsu* were abandoned when they were found to interfere with Japan's recovery. Most of the large holdings of absentee landlords, on the other hand, were divided among tenant farmers. Despite these and other reforms, economic revival was slow. Only the war in Korea provided the

The Far East After the Second World War 1945–69

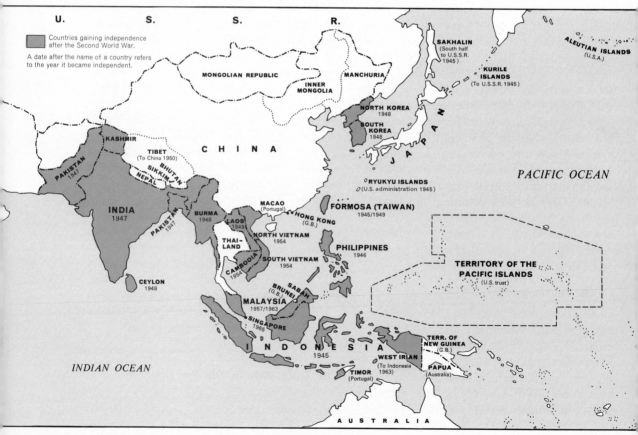

stimulus for Japan's economic recovery during the 1950's.

By 1951 the occupation of Japan had accomplished most of its aims and it was time to think of a peace settlement. The rift between the United States and Russia, however, made a peace conference impracticable. America therefore assumed the chief responsibility for drafting the treaty. Peace with Japan was signed at San Francisco on September 8, 1951. The treaty was generous, restoring full Japanese sovereignty but permitting the United States to maintain military bases in Japan. America and Japan also concluded a defense agreement which ultimately became an alliance.

Communist Victory in China

While events in Japan went largely according to American wishes, developments on the Chinese mainland were far from satisfactory. The end of the war found China still divided between the government forces of Chiang Kai-shek and the communist armies of Mao Tse-tung. Chiang had the backing of Chinese business and banking interests, while Mao's program of land reform brought him the support of the landless masses. Both sides now began a fight for the regions held until recently by Japan. In this contest the communists proved the more successful. By the end of 1948 most of northern China was in communist hands. The United States had given large amounts of financial and military aid to Chiang Kai-shek. But as the Nationalist government failed to introduce much-needed reforms, United States aid was curtailed and finally cut off. In the spring of 1949, Chiang Kai-shek began to withdraw his forces to the island of Formosa. By early 1950 the whole Chinese mainland was in communist hands. On October 1, 1949, the People's Republic of China was officially proclaimed at Peking, with Mao Tse-

tung as president. The Soviet Union immediately recognized the new regime whereas the United States continued to recognize the Nationalist government of Chiang Kai-shek.

The East-West Conflict over Korea

The victory of communism in China radically changed the balance of power between East and West. The effects of this change were felt almost immediately, as events in Korea transformed the Cold War in that country into an armed conflict. The Korean peninsula, at the end of the war, had been divided into American and Russian zones of occupation. Just as in Germany, this temporary partition gradually resulted in two quite different regimes. In 1948, elections in the United States-occupied southern part of Korea resulted in the founding of the Republic of Korea, with Dr. Syngman Rhee as president. The Russians thereupon sponsored their own communist-dominated northern People's Democratic Republic.

Late in 1948 the Soviet Union and the United States began to withdraw their troops from North and South Korea. A UN commission remained behind, trying to prevent a possible conflict between the two parts of Korea. Its efforts, however, proved in vain. On June 24, 1950, North Korean forces crossed the thirty-eighth parallel to "liberate" South Korea. Since Russia at the time was boycotting the Security Council, the United Nations was able to act without being hindered by a Soviet veto. When North Korea refused to halt its aggression, the Security Council asked the members of the UN to go to the aid of South Korea. The United States had already decided to intervene and was soon joined by small contingents from other countries. For the first time, the United Nations had gone to war. The Cold War had turned hot.

Suggestions for Further Reading

1. General

The most vivid and monumental history of the Second World War is W. S. Churchill, *The Second World War,* 6 vols.* (1948–53). An admirably comprehensive treatment is L. L. Snyder, *The War: A Concise History, 1949–1945* (1960). C. Wilmot, *The Struggle for Europe* (1952), is brilliant but controversial. Among general military accounts, the following stand out: H. Baldwin, *Battles Lost and Won: Great Campaigns of World War II* (1966); B. Collier, *The Second World War: A Military History* (1967); and P. Young, *World War, 1939–1945* (1966). D. Flower and J. Reeves, eds., *The Taste of Courage: The War, 1939–1945* (1960), successfully recaptures the atmosphere of the war at the fronts and at home.

2. The War: Military and Naval

The most detailed coverage of the major engagements may be found in the multi-volume series dealing with America's armed forces in the Second World War: Office of the Chief of Military History, *United States Army in World War II* (1947–); S. E. Morison, *History of United States Naval Operations in World War II,* 14 vols. (1947–60); and W. F. Craven and J. L. Cate, *The Army Air Forces in World War II,* 7 vols. (1948–53). Phases of the war not covered in the above are treated in: M. Bloch, *Strange Defeat* (1949), on the fall of France; A. Johnson, *Norway: Her Invasion and Occupation* (1948); R. de Belot, *The Struggle for the Mediterranean, 1939–1945* (1951); A. Clark, *Barbarossa: The Russian-German Conflict, 1941–1945* (1965); and K. Wierzynski, *The Forgotten Battlefield: The Story of Finland* (1944). For some of the war's more dramatic stories, see: R. Grenfell, *The Bismarck Episode* (1949); D. Young, *Rommel: The Desert Fox* (1950); C. V. Woodward, *The Battle for Leyte Gulf* (1947); W. Ansel, *Hitler Confronts England* (1960); and J. Hersey, *Hiroshima* (1946). Most of the war's leading military figures have written their memoirs. Of special interest are D. D. Eisenhower, *Crusade in Europe* (1948); Viscount Montgomery, *Memoirs* (1958); C. de Gaulle, *War Memoirs,* 3 vols.* (1960); M. Weygand, *Recalled to Service* (1952); J. Stilwell, *The Stilwell Papers* (1948); and J. Wainwright, *General Wainwright's Story* (1946). For the German side, see: H. R. Trevor-Roper, ed., *Blitzkrieg to Defeat: Hitler's War Directives, 1939–1945* (1964); B. H. Liddell Hart, *The German Generals Talk* (1948); and S. Freidin and W. Richardson, eds., *The Fatal Decisions* (1956).

3. The War: Political and Economic

J. L. Snell, *Illusion and Necessity: The Diplomacy of Global War* (1963), is a concise and readable introduction. The gradual involvement of the United States in the war is competently treated in W. L. Langer and S. E. Gleason, *The Undeclared War, 1940–1941* (1953). The best account of the diplomatic background of the war with Japan is H. Feis, *The Road to Pearl Harbor* (1950). For a highly critical view of Roosevelt's foreign policy, see C. C. Tansill, *Back Door to War* (1952). Other aspects of American foreign policy are discussed in H. Feis, *The China Tangle* (1953), and in W. L. Langer, *Our Vichy Gamble* (1947). The controversial story of the Vichy regime is told by P. Farmer, *Vichy: Political Dilemma* (1955). The relations among the Allies are reviewed in H. Feis, *Churchill, Roosevelt, Stalin* (1957), and in M. Viorst, *Hostile Allies: FDR and Charles De Gaulle* (1965). R. E. Sherwood, *Roosevelt and Hopkins* (1948), E. L. Stimson, *On Active Service in Peace and War* (1948), and R. Murphy, *Diplomat Among Warriors* (1964), give valuable insights into American policy-making. Explanations of Hitler's fateful decision to invade Russia are provided in A. Rossi, *The Russo-German Alliance* (1951), and in G. L. Weinberg, *Germany and the Soviet Union, 1939–1941* (1954). The Soviet Union's harsh wartime experiences are related in A. Werth, *Russia at War* (1964). Hitler's attitude toward the United States is analyzed in: A. Frye, *Nazi Germany and the American Hemisphere, 1933–1941* (1967); S. Friedländer,

---

* Available in paperback edition.

Prelude to Downfall: Hitler and the United States, 1939–1941 (1967); and J. V. Compton, *The Swastika and the Eagle* (1967). Relations within the Axis are the subject of an excellent study by F. W. Deakin, *The Brutal Friendship: Mussolini, Hitler, and the Fall of Italian Fascism,* 2 vols.* (1966). J. M. Meskill, *Hitler and Japan: The Hollow Alliance* (1966), tells a story of failure. Spain's role in the war is the subject of H. Feis, *The Spanish Story: Franco and the Nations at War** (1948). On the economic aspects of the war, see D. M. Nelson, *Arsenal for Democracy* (1946), and D. L. Gordon and R. Dangerfield, *The Hidden Weapon: The Story of Economic Warfare* (1947). Germany's economic war effort is treated in A. S. Milward, *The German Economy at War* (1965), and in B. A. Carroll, *Design for Total War: Arms and Economics in the Third Reich* (1968).

4. Hitler's "New Order"

The best general account of Europe under Hitler's rule is A. Toynbee, ed., *Hitler's Europe* (1954). See also R. Lemkin, *Axis Rule in Occupied Europe* (1945). A. Dallin, *German Rule in Russia, 1941–1945* (1957), is an excellent monograph. The large-scale popular migrations during the war are treated in E. M. Kulischer, *Europe on the Move: War and Population Changes, 1917–1947* (1948). On German use of slave labor, see E. L. Homze, *Foreign Labor in Nazi Germany* (1967). The more horrible aspects of Hitler's tyranny are told in L. Poliakov, *Harvest of Hate* (1954), and G. Reitlinger, *The Final Solution** (1953), which deal with the extermination of the European Jews. On the concentration camps, see: R. Hoess, *Commandant of Auschwitz** (1959); B. Naumann, *Auschwitz* (1966); and Lord Russell of Liverpool, *The Scourge of the Swastika: A Short History of Nazi War Crimes** (1954).

5. The Search for Peace

The plans made during the war for a postwar settlement are discussed in R. Opie, *et al., The Search for Peace Settlements* (1951), and more briefly in W. L. Neumann, *Making the Peace, 1941–1945* (1950). Separate phases of the problem are treated in J. L. Snell, *Wartime Origins of the East–West Dilemma over Germany* (1959), and in E. F. Penrose, *Economic Planning for the Peace* (1953). See also L. W. Holborn, *War and Peace Aims of the United Nations,* 2 vols. (1948). The conferences at Yalta and Potsdam are described by some of the leading participants: E. R. Stettinius, *Roosevelt and the Russians* (1949); H. S Truman, *Memoirs,* Vol. I, *Year of Decisions** (1955); J. F. Byrnes, *Speaking Frankly* (1947); and W. S. Churchill, *Triumph and Tragedy** (1953). For an evaluation of the Yalta agreements, see J. L. Snell, ed., *The Meaning of Yalta* (1956), and R. F. Fenno, ed., *The Yalta Conference* (1955). H. Feis, *Between War and Peace: The Potsdam Conference** (1960), is the best study of the subject.

6. The Cold War

A good general account of the early postwar years is M. F. Herz, *Beginnings of the Cold War* (1966). On events in Germany, see A. Grosser, *The Colossus Again: Western Germany from Defeat to Rearmament* (1955), and L. D. Clay, *Decision in Germany* (1950). Austria is treated in W. B. Bader, *Austria Between East and West, 1945–1955* (1966). H. Seton-Watson, *The East European Revolution* (1951), treats the victory of communism in that area. The communist seizure of individual countries is told in: S. Mikolajczyk, *The Rape of Poland* (1950); H. Ripka, *Czechoslovakia Enslaved* (1950); and for Hungary in F. Nagy, *The Struggle Behind the Iron Curtain* (1948). Developments in the Far East are analyzed by: H. Feis, *The China Tangle** (1953); H. M. Vinacke, *Far Eastern Politics in the Postwar Period* (1956); A. S. Whiting, *China Crosses the Yalu: The Decision to Enter the Korean War* (1960); and H. Feis, *Contest over Japan* (1967). For the first years of the United Nations, see C. M. Eichelberger, *UN: The First Ten Years* (1955), and T. Lie, *In the Cause of Peace: Seven Years with the United Nations* (1954). J. Kimche and D. Kimche, *A Clash of Destinies: The Arab-Jewish War and the Founding of the State of Israel* (1960), and E. Berger, *The Covenant and the Sword: Arab-Israeli Relations, 1946–1956* (1965), deal with postwar events in the Middle East.

---

* Available in paperback edition.

19

From Cold War
to Coexistence

In the past a war like the one in Korea might easily have sparked a third world war. That the conflict remained localized was in large measure due to the deterrent effect of the atomic bomb. With both the United States and Russia accumulating huge stockpiles of nuclear weapons, the fear that some incident or accident might upset the precarious "balance of terror" between the East and the West became a dominant factor in world affairs. Gradually the latent crises of the Cold War gave way to a state of watchful coexistence between the communist and non-communist worlds.

The years since 1950 have seen other significant changes. In its early phases, the Cold War was primarily a conflict between two super-powers, the United States and the Soviet Union. Europe, which in the past had occupied the center of the stage, seemed to have been relegated to a mere supporting role. In recent decades, however, the old continent has staged a remarkable comeback. At the same time the rise of the former colonial regions—notably China—to independence and influence has injected a wholly new element into the international balance of power. Most problems of our day are truly

The Brandenburg Gate, once the heart of Berlin, now marks the border between East and West.

worldwide, and history, to be meaningful, must be viewed on a global scale.

There are other problems facing us today which, though not new, have suddenly become terribly urgent. Foremost among them is the "population explosion." Demographers estimate that by the end of this century 7 billion people will be alive, twice as many as in 1969. Scientists assure us that the development of existing resources, especially atomic power, could provide ample livelihood for these vast masses. But even in an age of coexistence, much wealth and energy continue to be diverted to military rather than civilian uses. It seems that the alternatives we face are either to risk, through a nuclear arms race, the possible destruction of all mankind, or to ensure, through peaceful effort, a good life for all. It is this alternative between general chaos and general contentment that makes ours both a fearful and an exciting age in which to live.

The Decline and Rise
of Europe

The decline of Europe's role in world affairs had already set in during the First World War, when only the intervention of the United States had enabled the Allies to win. For a brief span between the two wars, a semblance of the old

European system of great powers was resurrected. But as a result of the Second World War, the pre-eminence of Europe came definitely to an end.

The postwar problems facing the nations of Europe were alike in many ways. All the major powers of western Europe suffered territorial losses, either in Europe or overseas, and several of them were threatened by communism from without or within. The one concern shared by all countries, big and small alike, was to recover from the economic effects of the war. In trying to cope with these problems, the nations of free Europe were forced to modify somewhat their economic and political nationalism and to attempt some measure of economic, if not political, union. European recovery was retarded by the fact that the Continent continued to be divided into communist and noncommunist spheres. We are here concerned only with the regions west of the so-called iron curtain. But, as we shall see, the gulf that the Cold War had created between the two halves of Europe in time grew narrower. As both eastern and western Europe recovered from the war and as tentative bridges between the two were built, the reunion of the European continent appeared once more a possibility.

Great Britain: European or World Power?

Great Britain after the Second World War had to cope with two related problems: economic recovery and the loss of most of her empire. In 1945 the British electorate for the first time returned a Labor majority. Under the leadership of Clement Attlee, the government embarked on a program that was denounced as outright socialism by the Conservatives under Winston Churchill. But this opposition was vociferous rather than deep. Most of the enterprises that were nationalized—railroads, airlines, utilities, coal mines, and the Bank of England—remained so even after the Conservatives returned to power in 1951. The most far-reaching measures introduced by the Labor government were the various Social Welfare Acts which aimed at equality of opportunity for all citizens.

The tendency of these measures to make British society more egalitarian was enhanced by the drastic program of austerity by which the government hoped to balance the budget and regain Britain's former position in world trade. Under Conservative rule from 1951 to 1964, the country experienced a temporary economic recovery. In 1964, however, dissatisfaction with a weak policy abroad and renewed economic stagnation at home once more brought a Labor victory. The second Labor cabinet was no more successful in overcoming Britain's economic paralysis than the first one had been. When foreign loans, heavy taxation, and reduced government spending failed to improve matters, the government of prime minister Harold Wilson in 1967 finally devalued the pound. It was hoped that this drastic measure, by discouraging imports and boosting exports, would help correct Britain's unfavorable balance of trade and pull the country out of its perennial depression.

One of the causes of that depression was the rapid shrinking of Britain's empire after the war. Wherever colonial peoples became restive and demanded independence, British interests were almost always involved. Most of the resulting new states remained within the "Commonwealth of Nations" (as the former "British Commonwealth" was called). But the ties of this elusive organization grew weaker over the years, partly as a result of divergent political interests, partly because of the racial policies pursued by such countries as South Africa and Rhodesia. Britain in the past had committed sizable forces to help keep peace in outlying spheres of British interest. Because of economic pressures back home, most of Britain's foreign bases had to be abandoned; the remaining ones—in Singapore and the Persian Gulf—were to be evacuated by 1971. Within less than a generation, the once mighty British Empire thus virtually melted away.

One way of improving its position would have been for Britain to draw closer to those continental nations that had joined forces in the European Economic Community, or Common Market. But the island kingdom was reluctant to abandon its traditional policy of splendid isolation. In the military field precedent was broken when Britain entered into a series of continental alliances that culminated in the North Atlantic Treaty Organization in 1949. But a similar economic *rapprochement,* it was feared, might conflict with its Commonwealth obligations. It was not until 1963 that the country was ready to enter the Common Market. At that time it was barred by the veto of France's President de Gaulle, who asserted that Britain was not ready to assume the full obligations of membership. Subsequent efforts to overcome French opposition failed. Meanwhile Britain remained in by now unenviable isolation—not yet exclusively a European and no longer a true world power. For a great and proud nation, this was an unhappy situation.

France: Search for Lost Grandeur

In France economic recovery was retarded by political instability at home and continued colonial wars abroad. To make a clear break with the past, the French in 1946 gave themselves a new constitution. But the Fourth Republic was little different from the Third. As old enmities persisted and new ones arose, the traditional bickering among numerous small parties and interest groups soon dominated the political scene once again. The chief beneficiaries of this confusion were the French communists, who until 1958 were the leading party in the National Assembly. Only in foreign policy did the new republic show some consistency, chiefly as a result of the efforts of foreign ministers Georges Bidault and Robert Schuman.

France, like Great Britain, found it difficult at first to regain its economic health. French financial problems were staggering, and their solution required drastic taxation and a stable currency. But reluctant taxpayers, creeping inflation, and incessant strikes counteracted the beneficent effects of American Marshall Plan aid. In 1954 the war in Indochina, which had caused a steady financial drain back home despite American aid, came to an end; but at the same time fighting in Algeria gained momentum. It was not until President de Gaulle began to dominate the national scene in the late fifties that a broad

austerity program, combined with careful economic planning, put France back on the road to prosperity.

Another problem that France shared with Britain concerned the future of its colonial empire. In 1946 the Fourth Republic, in an effort to maintain some control over its overseas holdings, founded the French Union. This federation, however, was far too centralized to satisfy the more advanced territories, and a number of them—Syria, Lebanon, Morocco, and Tunisia—demanded, and were given, their independence. In the case of two other possessions—Indochina and Algeria—such independence was won only after drawn-out and costly fighting. In 1958 the French Union was transformed into the French Community, which included France proper, her few remaining overseas possessions, and some of the new African nations that formerly made up French Equatorial and West Africa. The Community was a loose federation whose main significance lay in whatever prestige it held for the mother country of a once great empire.

Prestige was the main concern of the man who assumed direction of French affairs in 1958. Charles de Gaulle, leader of the Free French forces in the Second World War, had served briefly as provisional president in 1945 but had retired before the domestic confusion that reigned at that time. He was recalled in 1958 at the height of the national crisis caused by the war in Algeria. Under de Gaulle's direction a new constitution was adopted that, in an attempt to ensure greater political stability, vastly increased the power of the president. In December 1958 General de Gaulle was elected first president of the Fifth Republic.

From 1958 on, the general's towering figure dominated the French scene. De Gaulle's most important achievement was the solution of the Algerian problem. In 1962 an agreement between French and Arab representatives, endorsed by the French electorate, gave Algeria her independence. Elsewhere, in Europe and overseas, de Gaulle tried to recapture for France some of the "grandeur" that once was hers. To strengthen France's position in Europe, de Gaulle maintained close ties with West Germany and cemented relations with the communist powers, notably the Soviet Union. To counteract Anglo-Saxon influence, he took France out of NATO and barred Britain from membership in the European Economic Community. Along similar lines he drew closer to Communist China, criticized American involvement in Vietnam, and even encouraged separatist sentiment among French Canadians. Supporters of de Gaulle defended his obstructionist policies as a reassertion not merely of French influence but of European influence as well against the growing encroachment of the United States. His critics, on the other hand, charged that when the general said Europe, he meant France; and when he said France, he meant de Gaulle.

In France itself, moreover, de Gaulle's preoccupation with foreign at the expense of domestic concerns gave rise to a wave of discontent that almost led to revolution in 1968. As on earlier occasions when his authority had been challenged, the general was able to maintain his hold and to win a crucial election. But he was able to do so only in return for promises of political and economic reform so far-reaching that his opponents doubted they could be kept.

West Germany: "The Second Republic"

The most spectacular rise from rubble to riches in postwar Europe occurred in West Germany. We have already discussed the partition of the former Reich in 1949 as a result of the Cold War. During the 1950's the western Federal Republic experienced a veritable "economic miracle." In contrast to the nationalization measures adopted by Great Britain and, to a lesser extent, France, Germany followed a more traditional policy of laissez faire. With a favorable balance of trade, a freely convertible currency, and hardly any unemployment, Germany's "free-market economy" aroused the admiration and envy of her neighbors.

Politically, developments in West Germany were remarkably steady, especially compared to

the turbulent years after the First World War. The constitution of the Federal Republic was framed to avoid some of the mistakes of the Weimar Republic. The country was fortunate in having as its first chancellor Konrad Adenauer, a conservative opponent of Nazism and a sincere friend of the West. The "old man" virtually dominated German politics until his retirement in 1963. His successor, Ludwig Erhard, was a man of lesser stature who did not command the respect Adenauer had enjoyed. In 1966 the middle-of-the-road Christian Democratic Union (CDU), which hitherto had dominated the government, had to share power with the moderately leftist Social Democratic Party (SPD), with Kurt Georg Kiesinger of the CDU as chancellor and Willy Brandt of the SPD as foreign minister. Since the aims of the coalition partners were quite similar, continuity of policy was not seriously affected by the change.

Next to economic development, the two most vital issues before the West German government were reunification and rearmament. To reunite not only East and West Germany but the region beyond the Oder-Neisse line (a region that Poland had occupied in 1945) was the fervent wish of every German. Repeated proposals of the western powers to achieve German unity through free general elections invariably met with Soviet opposition. Meanwhile the West German Federal Republic refused to recognize the East German Democratic Republic. As time went on, however, and as each section of Germany developed along widely divergent lines, a growing number of Germans became reconciled with the thought that they might not live to see their country reunited. The continued partition of Germany constituted one of the gravest dangers to world peace, but responsible leaders in both East and West Germany realized that reunification by force would be suicidal folly.

The issue of German rearmament caused considerable debate in the 1950's. As the Russians began training a German military force in East Germany, the western powers decided to permit the limited rearmament of West Germany. Under an agreement ratified in 1955, West Germany was to contribute a maximum of 500,000 men to the common defense of the West under NATO. In return, the Federal Republic was granted complete sovereignty in domestic and foreign affairs.

There was some fear, both in Germany and outside, that rearmament would cause a revival of German militarism and nationalism. But such fears proved groundless. The German government in its foreign policy gave ample proof of its peaceful intentions. Relations with Germany's "traditional enemy" France were better than they had ever been, leading to a treaty of friendship in 1963. Collaboration with the Anglo-Saxon powers was close, and during the 1960's contacts were also resumed with some of the eastern communist states. In its domestic policy, West Germany showed that it had made a sincere break with the Nazi past. There were a few incidents of neo-Nazism, and in 1967 a new right-wing group, the National Democratic Party, gained some ground in local elections. But the majority of Germans clearly endorsed the moderate and peaceful course of their government. Democracy, to all appearances, had taken firm root in Germany.

Italy: From Poverty to Riches

Italy emerged from the Second World War with its already backward economy in a dismal state. After a slow start, however, the nation staged a remarkable recovery. By 1965 Italy's industrial production had increased fourfold, and the nation's per capita income had doubled. With economic improvement came political stability. The new Italian republic was launched successfully in 1946 under the capable leadership of Alcide de Gasperi and his Christian Democratic Party. But with the coming of the Cold War, the government came under increasing attacks from a stong Communist Party on the left and a growing neo-Fascist movement on the right. Only when the Christian Democrats, beginning in 1962, began to ally themselves with the moderate Socialists on their left did some measure of political calm return.

Even so, the fact that one out of every four Italians continued to vote communist showed that all was far from well. While there was prosperity, poverty persisted, especially in the agricultural South. Even in the North real wages did not keep up with the general rise in the economy, and the distribution of income remained uneven. More crucial than these economic inequities was the failure of the new republic to break with some of the authoritarian practices of Italy's past, especially in the bureaucracy and the judiciary, and to bring about a more egalitarian social structure. Italy's emerging industrial society, it seemed, had yet to find a suitable political and social framework. Here was the underlying cause of much of the discontent that found its outlet in the communist vote.

The Quest for European Unity

Given the similarity of problems faced by the nations of western Europe, especially in the economic field, it was only natural that they should try to devise means for common action. The Marshall Plan had shown that lasting recovery could be won only through economic cooperation; and the Brussels Pact, besides calling for a military alliance, had also stressed the need for collaboration in economic, social, and cultural affairs. The major instance of such collaboration was the Schuman Plan, which established the European Coal and Steel Community (ECSC). In 1952 France, Germany, the Benelux countries, and Italy agreed to merge their resources of coal and steel in a common western European market. By 1957 enough progress had been achieved to make it possible to extend the common market to other goods, through the European Economic Community (EEC). In a further attempt at integration, the six members of ECSC and EEC founded the European Atomic Energy Community (Euratom) to promote peaceful atomic research and development.

The European Economic Community was not a closed organization; any country could apply for membership. And the country that stood to profit most from joining was Great

Britain. Initially the British had remained cool toward EEC, preferring instead to form their own European Free Trade Association (EFTA) with some of the small peripheral nations of Europe. As the advantages of EEC became obvious, however, Britain changed its mind—only to be barred by President de Gaulle's vetoes. The hope that ultimately all western Europe might become economically united thus proved premature.

Plans for European political union, furthermore, which had got off to a good start with the founding of the Council of Europe at Strasbourg in 1949, never went beyond the paper stage. As Europe recovered economically, and as the threat of Soviet expansion diminished, national differences once again came to the fore.

The hope that NATO would in time become more than a purely military alliance likewise proved false. Yet despite these disappointments, the trend toward European unity after the Second World War was unmistakable. The European powers realized that the only way in which they could wield any real influence in world affairs was by joining forces and forgetting the divisive issues of the past.

The Americas After the Second World War

To the rest of the world the United States in 1945 appeared to be a country of unbelievable wealth, untouched by the hardships of war. But to Americans themselves the picture looked quite different. Price controls, wage controls, real or artificially induced shortages of essential goods, incessant waves of strikes, and signs of widespread corruption—these were some of the problems faced by the Democratic administration. The government's attempts to deal with the situation by means of further legislation found little public or congressional support. It seemed that the country was tired of government controls and of a social service state that to most Republicans smacked of socialism.

The Truman Era

President Truman was re-elected in 1948 chiefly because of his foreign policy. We have already discussed the crucial decisions that the President had to make during the first phase of the Cold War: the Truman Doctrine, the Marshall Plan, the Berlin air lift, the North Atlantic Treaty, and the intervention in Korea. At the time, these measures were applauded by a majority of Americans. Isolationism, of course, did not vanish overnight. But the fact that a Republican administration after 1952 continued substantially the same policy showed that the shift from isolationism was a matter not so much of choice as of necessity.

One aspect of American involvement abroad that was not universally popular was the foreign-aid program. During the first fifteen years after

---

MacArthur States His Case

Our Victory [in Korea] was complete and our objectives within reach when Red China intervened with numerically superior ground forces. . . . While no man in his right mind would advocate sending our ground forces into continental China . . . the new situation did urgently demand a drastic revision of strategic planning if our political aim was to defeat this enemy. . . .

1. The intensification of the economic blockade of China.
2. The imposition of a naval blockade against the China coast.
3. Removal of restrictions on air reconnaissance of China's coastal areas and of Manchuria.
4. Removal of restrictions on the forces of the Republic of China on Formosa with logistical support to contribute their effective operations against the Chinese mainland. . . .

It has been said in effect that I was a war-monger. Nothing could be further from the truth. I know war as few other men living know it, and nothing, to me, is more revolting. . . . But once war is forced upon us, there is no other alternative than to apply every available means to bring it to a swift end. . . . War's very object is victory, not prolonged indecision. In war there is no substitute for victory. . . .

From General MacArthur's address to a joint session of Congress on April 19, 1951.

A unique photograph of the four men who occupied the American presidency between 1945 and 1968. The occasion was the funeral of House Speaker Sam Rayburn in 1961.

the war, United States economic and military aid amounted to more than $75 billion. Much of it was given in a spirit of genuine helpfulness. But foreign aid was also an important weapon in the Cold War, especially after 1955, when the Soviet Union began stepping up its own foreign-aid program.

In American domestic affairs, one of the major issues at the time was the fear of communist infiltration. This fear arose shortly after the war, gained momentum as the communists scored more and more triumphs in Europe and Asia, and reached its climax during the Korean War. Chiefly because of the agitation of Wisconsin's Senator Joseph McCarthy, the American public was led to believe that its government

had allowed communists to get into key positions in the State Department and the Army. The careless methods used in many congressional investigations did much to harm the reputation of innocent people and led to charges abroad that America was trying to combat totalitarianism by totalitarian methods.

The reality of the communist threat, meanwhile, was brought home by events in Korea. As the war there bogged down in a bloody stalemate, critics of the administration demanded an escalation of the war, including the bombing of communist bases in China. Foremost among these critics was America's commander-in-chief in Korea, General Douglas MacArthur. When efforts to silence him failed, President Truman saw no alternative but to relieve the general of his command. The ensuing crisis was the most serious the United States had faced since 1945. Together with a mounting wave of government scandals and continued suspicion of communist influence in the government, the Korean War was a major cause of the Democratic defeat of 1952.

The Eisenhower Years

The victories of Dwight D. Eisenhower in 1952 and 1956 were as much personal as partisan. During his two administrations, bipartisan majorities collaborated on much valuable social legislation, especially for federal aid to education. The nation's economy continued to flourish, except in the agricultural sector, where overproduction posed a serious problem. The administration's attempts to reduce price supports and to return to a free market in agricultural products incurred the opposition of farm groups; this opposition was one of the reasons for the overwhelming victory of the Democrats in 1958. Other reasons were the temporary economic recession of that year and the antagonism that the Republican administration had aroused among organized labor.

One of the major issues that came to the fore during the Eisenhower years was desegregation. In 1954 the United States Supreme Court ruled that American Negroes had the right to attend the same schools as whites. While in most states integration proceeded smoothly, in the Deep South every possible means was used to prevent desegregation. In 1957–58 President Eisenhower had to send federal troops to enforce integration in Little Rock, Arkansas. But this was only the beginning of a drawn-out crisis, as Negroes now demanded that desegregation be extended to other fields. The resistance of die-hard "white supremacists" to these demands, meanwhile, did much to tarnish America's image abroad.

From Kennedy to Johnson

With the victory of John F. Kennedy in 1960, a fresh and youthful note was injected into

John Fitzgerald Kennedy, 1917–63.

American politics. His administration got off to a promising start when Congress approved a series of social service measures chiefly designed to aid the poor. When the President began to tackle the touchy subject of civil rights, however, he lost the support of southern Democrats and his domestic program came to a halt. Some improvement in the Negro's status was made under pressure of nonviolent protests directed by able black leaders. But as police in the South met peaceful demonstrations with violence, the situation became increasingly explosive. Much of President Kennedy's attention was taken up with foreign affairs, where he faced several severe crises. In his efforts to stand up to communist threats in Southeast Asia, Cuba, and Berlin, the President generally found the support that Congress withheld from his domestic program.

President Kennedy was assassinated in Dallas, Texas, on November 22, 1963. His sudden death came as a shock to the nation and the world. A major crisis was avoided chiefly because of the firm manner in which his successor took charge. Where Kennedy had labored in vain against congressional opposition, Lyndon B.

Johnson was able to achieve some notable successes. By 1964 the new President had gained sufficient popular support to win a landslide victory.

From then on, however, President Johnson found the going more and more difficult. Civil rights by now had become the key issue in American politics. The Civil Rights Act of 1964 was the most sweeping legislation of its kind ever enacted. But its provisions were still disregarded in many parts of the South. Meanwhile Negro protests spread to the North, where the demand was for greater equality in employment, housing, and education. Demonstrations that hitherto had been orderly now became increasingly violent as bloody riots swept through major American cities and as advocates of "black power" preached the use of force. To cope with the economic roots of Negro discontent, the Johnson administration stepped up the anti-poverty programs initiated under Kennedy. But while the "war on poverty" called for vast amounts of money, more and more funds were being diverted to another kind of war that American forces were fighting in Vietnam.

The war in Vietnam proved the most divisive issue in American politics during the last two years of the Johnson administration. With "hawks" (advocating war to the bitter end) ranged against "doves" (favoring American dis-

engagement), many young Americans chose to go to prison rather than to fight an "unjust" war. The cause of the moderates suffered a major loss with the assassination, in June 1968, of Senator Robert F. Kennedy, a leading Democratic contender for the presidency. Racial unrest, meanwhile, had flared up anew after the murder of the Reverend Dr. Martin Luther King, outstanding figure in the nonviolent civil rights movement. It was a deeply disturbed and divided nation that gave the Republican candidate, Richard M. Nixon, a narrow victory in November 1968. The new president's task of reuniting the country was made more difficult by continued Democratic control of Congress.

The United States and Its Neighbors

Since the contest between communism and capitalism was a global one, the maintenance of harmony within the Western Hemisphere was of major concern to every administration after 1945. Relations with America's northern neighbor were, on the whole, cordial. Because of its unprecedented economic growth, Canada ranked as one of the world's leading industrial and commercial powers. United States capital played an important part in this expansion, and the resulting American influence caused some resentment among Canadian nationalists. Military

Richard M. Nixon accepts his party's nomination.

relations between the two countries were close, both within NATO and without. Continued membership in the (British) Commonwealth saved Canada from becoming too dependent on her powerful neighbor, although ties with Great Britain grew noticeably weaker.

Relations between the United States and its southern neighbors were far more complicated. The twenty republics of Latin America differed vastly in size and significance, and the absence of a strong democratic tradition made many of them easy targets for communist propaganda. The most pressing problem of the whole area was its alarming rise in population. Latin America had great economic potentialities, but financial and technical assistance were needed to develop them. This aid the United States was expected to supply. Prior to 1960 very little such aid found its way to Latin America, and as a result anti-American feeling was strong. Since then a number of ambitious development schemes have been launched, notably the Alliance for Progress, proclaimed by President Kennedy in 1961. In 1967 a "Declaration of the Presidents of the Americas" called for the creation of a common market for Latin America to present the rest of the world with a common economic front.

The United States was also concerned with building a united military front against the threat of communism in the Western Hemisphere. In 1947 the Latin American nations and the United States signed the Rio Treaty, which called for mutual assistance in case of war. Subsequent agreements arranged for the exchange of United States arms against strategic raw materials. The most important agency of inter-American cooperation was the Organization of American States (OAS), founded in 1948. It originally included all nations of the Western Hemisphere except Canada, but Cuba was expelled in 1962. The Charter of the OAS proclaimed the equality of its members and laid down the principle of nonintervention in their external and internal affairs. The OAS proved of great value as a stabilizing influence, especially in the Caribbean, where Castro's Cuba posed the most serious threat to hemispheric peace.

The overthrow of Cuban dictator Fulgencio Batista by Fidel Castro's rebel forces in 1959 at first was hailed in the United States as elsewhere as a victory of democracy. It was only when Castro's regime revealed itself as an outpost of communism that the United States broke off relations with Cuba and then, in 1961, supported an ill-fated invasion attempt by anti-Castro forces. Meanwhile Castro had established close ties with Communist China and the Soviet Union. The latter's attempt to use Cuba as a base for ballistic missiles clearly directed against the United States led to a major showdown between the Soviet Union and the United States in which the Russians had to give way. The United States in its various conflicts with Castro took care at every point to obtain the support of the OAS. This was invariably given, though not always unanimously. The OAS also played a major role in mediating a crisis between the United States and Panama over the Panama Canal in 1964.

The Communist World

For almost two decades after 1945, while the Cold War lasted, the communist world appeared to be a monolithic bloc directed from Moscow. It took the rest of the world some time to realize how much the influence of the Soviet Union depended on one man. In retrospect, the death of Soviet Premier Joseph Stalin on March 5, 1953, was a major event in world history. It spelled the end of an era, not only for Russian communism but for world communism.

Russia Under Khrushchev

We have already discussed the main features of the Stalinist era, which reached its high point during the years after 1945. To repair the staggering damages of the war, two new Five-Year Plans called for a new round of industrialization and collectivization. Simultaneously, strictest orthodoxy remained the keynote of Soviet political and cultural life. The slightest deviation from Stalinist-Marxist theory brought imprisonment, slave labor, or death. In a famous speech before the twentieth Party Congress in 1956, Khrushchev charged that Stalin, "a very distrustful man, sickly suspicious," had planned even to liquidate his most intimate political associates.

The reign of terror came to a sudden end with Stalin's death. At first "collective leadership" was instituted. But it was only a matter of time before one of the most ruthless members of the group, Nikita S. Khrushchev, emerged as the recognized leader of the Soviet Union. As Stalin had done a generation earlier, Khrushchev used his key position as Secretary of the Central Committee of the Communist Party to rid himself of his associates. The only novelty was that his rivals were not killed but merely ousted. Here was one example of the "new look" in Soviet policy.

However, Khrushchev, a career party functionary, never really achieved the absolute power that Stalin had wielded before him. Russia under Stalin underwent not only an economic but a social revolution. From a nation of illiterate peasants, the Soviet Union had become a nation of educated workers. And although the basic Marxian concept of state ownership of the means of production remained in force, the concept of a classless society had been far from realized. Instead, there had grown up a substantial upper class: the party elite, the top echelons of the vast political and economic bureaucracy, managerial personnel, technical experts, scientists, and the like. The Soviet Union, in other words, had become a far more complex nation than it had been at the start. To run such a nation by regimentation based on terror was no longer possible. Nor was it even desirable, since blind obedience in the long run killed initiative and made for inefficiency.

The most dramatic change in the life of the average Russian came with the retreat from terror after Stalin's death. This did not mean that there were no longer any political prisoners. But it did mean that the number of punishable political crimes became smaller than it had been under Stalin. Henceforth it became possible to criticize certain aspects of the regime without risking persecution.

The liberalization of Soviet life made itself felt in other ways. In factories and on collective farms the strict discipline of the past was relaxed. Consumer goods became more plentiful, and the housing shortage was reduced. Education was broadened to admit more students to secondary schools and universities. With the easing of travel restrictions, the Russian people for the first time came in contact with the outside world. In Russian art and literature, the orthodox emphasis on "socialist realism" gave way to tolerance of modern trends. Initially, these changes were seen by outside observers as signs that Russia had abandoned its unbending opposition to the West. But Soviet leaders made no secret of the fact that the "new course" was merely a change in methods and that their aim remained what it had always been: the overthrow of capitalism.

"Collective Leadership"

The return to virtual one-man rule under Khrushchev was suddenly reversed in October 1964 when the Russian leader was purged by his party's Central Committee and his double role as premier and party secretary was divided between Alexei N. Kosygin and Leonid I. Brezhnev. The main reasons for Khrushchev's dismissal appeared to be domestic, notably his failure to live up to his boastful economic promises. From now on the trend was once again toward "collective leadership." Economic growth continued, though at a slower rate than expected, especially in the agrarian sector.

In November 1967 the Russian people celebrated the fiftieth anniversary of the revolution that had given birth to the Soviet Union. With increased material gain, however, came signs of spiritual unrest. The younger generation especially, the "grandchildren of the revolution," seemed less and less willing to accept the intellectual restrictions of their totalitarian regime. In this respect they were no different from their contemporaries elsewhere in the communist world, where opposition to the Russian brand of communism had been gaining ground for some time.

Unrest Among the Satellites

The effects of the post-Stalin "thaw" in Russia were also felt among the satellite nations of eastern Europe. The first defection from the Soviet bloc had occurred as early as 1948, when Marshal Tito of Yugoslavia, preferring "Titoism" to "Stalinism," had struck out on his own. By 1956, Stalin's successors had made peace with Tito and had acknowledged that there were "various roads to socialism." But the satellites were not satisfied with mere promises. In the fall of 1956, revolts against Soviet domination broke out first in Poland and later in Hungary. Both countries were motivated by ardent nationalist sentiments. In addition, the Hungarian uprising was strongly anti-communist. For that reason the Hungarian revolution was brutally suppressed by Russian intervention, while Poland's communists, under Wladyslaw Gomulka, were given greater autonomy from Russian control.

There were no further attempts to resist Russian domination forcefully. But the nations of eastern Europe were now enjoying far greater freedom of action than they had ever had under Stalin. From mere satellites they were gradually becoming junior partners of the Soviet Union. In 1961 growing tension between Russia and Albania over the latter's continued adherence to Stalinism led to an open break. In 1964 Rumania declared her virtual independence from Soviet influence and, like Yugoslavia before, drew closer to the West. Intermittent unrest in Poland came to a head early in 1968 and brought some easing of restrictions. The most drastic changes, however, occurred in Czechoslovakia, where, as a result of a peaceful revolution in the spring of 1968, the country regained many democratic freedoms. The Soviet Union's armed intervention in Czechoslovakia emphasized the threat that these liberalizing tendencies posed to Russia's leadership in the communist world.

"Socialist Pluralism"

The unity that once had prevailed among communists had thus given way to diversity, or even disunity. A communist world conference in 1968 was attended by only half the world's ruling Communist parties, and even among those present there were wide differences on many key issues. Instead of a monolithic communist bloc directed from Moscow, there now existed a plurality of socialist states divided into several factions.

The most important split within the communist camp had developed between Moscow and Peking. While Stalin was alive, the potentially powerful People's Republic of China had not contested Russia's claim to leadership. But after 1953 the Chinese gradually began to assert themselves. At first it seemed as though China's influence was to be on the side of moderation. Beginning in 1957, however, Peking showed signs of a new, "hard" line. The Sino-Soviet dispute was initially ideological, each side accusing the other of deviating from true "Marxism-Leninism." Yet in time there arose a number of specific issues. Following the principles of Mao Tse-tung's "great proletarian cultural revolution," China's left-wing ideologists preached "liberation" of peoples everywhere through "armed struggle" rather than through peaceful competition, as advocated by Moscow. As the debates between the two contestants became more and more vituperative, Communist China asserted that the center of world revolution and the leadership of world communism had shifted from Moscow to Peking. Most of Asia's Communist parties, together with Cuba and Albania, were found on Peking's side.

The End of Colonialism in Asia

One of the most revolutionary developments of recent decades has been the liberation of virtually all the world's former colonial territories. This independence movement had already begun in the years between the two world wars. It was stimulated by the weakening of the mother countries in the Second World War and the subsequent rivalry between the free and communist worlds. Although the various native revolts differed from country to country, they all had one thing in common: intense opposition to any kind of colonialism. Some of the new nations took sides in the Cold War, but most of them preferred a "neutralist" stand. The most urgent need for all was economic and technical assistance. At first, most of this aid came from the United States. But in time the Soviet Union, and even Communist China, began to compete for the allegiance of these uncommitted regions.

India and Pakistan

The first major additions to the community of free nations came with the partition of the subcontinent of India in 1947 into the independent states of India and Pakistan. Although both were republics, they continued to be members of the British Commonwealth. India was predominantly Hindu and Pakistan predominantly Moslem. In the process of separating the two religions, many bloody riots broke out. India and Pakistan also clashed repeatedly over the northern state of Kashmir, to which both laid claim. In addition, there were intermittent border incidents between India and Red China.

The Union of India, with a population of more than 500 million in an area one-third the size of the United States, was by far the more important of the two states. The country suffered a tragic loss in 1948, when Mohandas K. Gandhi was assassinated by a religious fanatic. The task of guiding the new nation through its formative years thus fell to Gandhi's disciple, Jawaharlal Nehru, leader of the ruling Congress party. India's main problems were economic. The only way to support its huge population was through long-range development of the country's abundant natural resources with outside aid. India's dependence on such aid from all sides, together with her closeness to the centers of communism and her recent experience with western imperialism, led to a neutralist stand on most international issues. With Nehru's death in 1964, domestic affairs became less stable, especially under his daughter, Mrs. Indira Gandhi, who became

Colonial Nationalism

The West, having sown its own national wild oats in the past, is now sometimes inclined to look with a combination of dismay and superior wisdom on the upstart countries which assert an allegedly anachronistic desire to follow the same course. . . . However great the disenchantment of Europe with nationalism, the colonial nationalist is little likely to be persuaded by an argument so easily identifiable with the interest of the West in maintaining some facsimile of its older relationships in a world swiftly sliding out of its grasp. . . . Even if it be conceded that nationalism fails to furnish the foundations for an acceptable world order and has outlived its usefulness for the advanced, thoroughly "nationalized," countries of the West . . . it has by no means exhausted its contribution to the development of the non-Western peoples. Nationalism . . . has a chronology of its own derived not from the calendar but from the stages of the gradually spreading impact of the revolution which originated in Western Europe. . . . One can plausibly argue that in the different but related stages of the cycle in which Asia and Africa are now engaged nationalism intrudes itself not only with an aura of inevitability but also as the bearer of positive goods.

From Rupert Emerson, *From Empire to Nation* (Cambridge, Mass.: Harvard U. Press, 1960), p. 379.

prime minister in 1966. Yet despite widespread famines and unrest, communism never became a serious threat. India was easily the most successful experiment in democracy on the Asian continent.

In Pakistan democracy was less successful in striking roots. Like India, the country suffered a serious loss in 1948 when its outstanding leader, Mohammed Ali Jinnah, died. Pakistan was divided in two parts, separated by 1,000 miles of Indian territory. Its economy was mainly agricultural, and trade with India, its natural market, suffered from political tensions. Economic difficulties in turn led to political instability. When democracy was no longer able to cope with bureaucratic corruption and inefficiency, the head of Pakistan's armed forces, General Ayub Khan, took over as virtual dictator in 1958. Pakistan's foreign policy at first was firmly pro-western, but during the 1960's its leaders became increasingly neutralist in an effort to attract aid and trade from both sides. The economic results of the shift were gratifying, and the autocratic rule of President Ayub, while it lasted, assured political stability as well.

Communist China

The most unsettling development in Asia after 1950 was the emergence of Communist China as a great power. We have already discussed the founding of the People's Republic of China in 1949. Its government was closely modeled on that of the Soviet Union. As in Russia, all power in China rested with the Communist Party and its leader, Mao Tse-tung. Under the constitution of 1954, the main task of the state was "to bring about, step by step, the socialist industrialization of the country." This goal was to be achieved in several Five-Year Plans. As was the case in other backward nations, the rapid increase in China's production resulted in some impressive achievements. Symbolic of the country's scientific and technical advances was the detonation of its first atomic bomb in 1964, followed in record time by its first hydrogen bomb in 1967. Such remarkable achievements, however, did not mean that Communist China had become a first-class industrial power. The backbone of her economy was still agriculture.

Yet in the long run it was only through industrialization that China could solve her most pressing problem of "too many people, too little land." With an estimated yearly population growth of more than 16 million, the 1-billion mark would be reached by 1990. Meanwhile the government tried by every possible means to boost agricultural production. The second Five-Year Plan of 1958 called for a "great leap forward" in agriculture and industry. The population was organized in gigantic "people's communes" including as many as 100,000 persons and embracing farms and factories. But the "great leap" not only failed to reach its goals; it actually brought a decline of production all along the line. The cause for this failure was seen in the continued moderation of many leading officials.

To purge Chinese communism of these "revisionist" elements, another sweeping revolutionary movement was initiated in the 1960's, the "great proletarian cultural revolution." Spearheaded by younger elements in the party, the "Maoist" revolution repudiated traditional cultural values, emphasized collectivization and austerity, and elevated the figure of China's leader to unprecedented heights of personal adulation. Through indoctrination, brainwashing, and terror it was hoped to produce in China the most regimented society the world had ever seen. Again, however, these drastic methods aggravated rather than solved China's economic problems.

In foreign affairs, Red China was consistently anti-American. The two countries were on opposite sides in the Korean War and in most other conflicts in Asia, including the conflict in Vietnam. Washington's support of the Nationalists on Taiwan, its alliance with Japan, and its refusal to recognize Peking were major targets for communist attacks. Relations between China and the Soviet Union, initially very close, also grew hostile as time went on, with the Chinese accusing their Russian comrades of revisionist betrayal of militant Marxism. In its dealings with the neutralist countries of Asia, China alternated between threats and kindness. There were repeated clashes along the borders of India, Burma, and Nepal, and Tibetan resistance to communization was ruthlessly suppressed in 1959. If Communist China could spread her influence beyond North Korea and North Vietnam, its position within the communist world would be greatly strengthened and its population pressure relieved. The most promising outlet for Chinese expansion was Southeast Asia, and it was here that the Chinese communists concentrated their efforts at internal subversion.

Southeast Asia

The region east of India and south of China saw more political changes after the Second World War than any other part of Asia. Prior to 1945 only Thailand was fully independent. In the years that followed, the Philippines, Burma, Indonesia, Vietnam, Laos, Cambodia, and Malaysia gained their sovereignty. Southeast Asia was a wealthy region, producing five-sixths of the world's natural rubber, more than half of its tin, and 60 percent of its rice. Like all underdeveloped areas, Southeast Asia was predominantly agricultural; but, except for Indonesia, it did not suffer from overpopulation. Despite its natural resources, the living standard of the region was very low. What Southeast Asia needed most was to develop a better-balanced regional economy with more varied commodities and increased industrialization.

With the exception of Thailand, every country of Southeast Asia experienced communist revolts of varying severity. In the case of North Vietnam, communist conquest was actually successful. Burma, Malaysia, Indonesia, and the Philippines, on the other hand, were able to crush communist rebellions that flared up in the fifties and early sixties. In the countries that formerly made up French Indochina—Laos, Cambodia, and particularly South Vietnam—the threat of communism remained strong, leading to a drawn-out civil war in the latter country. The menace of communism and the general backwardness of the whole area seriously retarded the growth of democracy and encouraged the emergence of strong-man governments.

Asia and the West

The free world, under American leadership, did its best to contain the spread of communism in Southeast Asia and the Far East by providing massive economic aid and by encouraging cooperation among the Asian nations themselves. A start was made in 1950 with the Colombo Plan for Cooperative Development in South and Southeast Asia. In 1961 Malaya, the Philippines, and Thailand formed the Association of Southeast Asia, ultimately to become a free trade area. In the military field, the United States, Great Britain, France, Australia, New Zealand, the Philippines, Pakistan, and Thailand in 1954 established the Southeast Asia Treaty Organization (SEATO) for mutual defense against aggression and subversion. In addition, the United States signed bilateral defense pacts with Taiwan, the Philippines, South Korea, and Japan.

American "Imperialism"

The Americans are no saints, but this you can say of them: as "imperialists" they proved to be more inept than their rivals in the game; they allowed us too many liberties; and now that we are independent, they know better than to disregard our opinions or to ignore our rights. Here is one little interesting detail: You can discuss, argue and talk back to the Americans, as we have discussed, argued and talked back to them during all the years of our subjection, and since then—without being slapped down or getting shot at dawn. One wonders, sometimes, what would happen to a Latvian or an Estonian or a Lithuanian who talked back to Mr. Khrushchev. We know, of course, what happened to the Hungarians who did just that.

From a speech by Francisco A. Delgado, Philippine Representative at the United Nations, delivered at the Fifteenth General Assembly of the U.N., October 5, 1960.

Korea and Japan were the main strongholds of American influence in the Far East. The South Korean army was one of the largest in the world, and the forced resignation of Dr. Syngman Rhee's authoritarian government in 1960 brought the country closer to democracy. American influence in Japan decreased after the signing of the peace treaty in 1951. The renewal of the United States-Japanese security treaty in 1960 ran into considerable leftist opposition, although the Communist Party played only a minor role in Japanese politics. Economically, Japan staged a remarkable come-back, which made her once again one of the world's leading industrial powers. Much of Japan's trade was with the United States, a fact that helped cement further the political and military ties between the two nations.

Western support did much to halt the advance of communist expansion, although, as events in Vietnam showed, the threat of such expansion was ever present. The allegiance of the more than a billion Asians living outside the communist orbit might some day decide the contest between the communist world and the free world. Military force alone, the Vietnam experience proved, was not sufficient to stop communism. To win the friendship of the neutral countries in Asia and elsewhere, ways had to be found to help them keep their freedom and gain political stability through economic security.

Nationalism in the Arab World

One of the most turbulent scenes of rebellion against western influence after the Second World War was the Arab Middle East, the area bridging Asia and Africa, from Iran in the east to Morocco in the west. Most of the region was extremely backward and desperately poor. But it was also of great strategic importance, it contained about half the world's oil resources, and it was the religious center of hundreds of millions of non-Arab Moslems living as far away as Southeast Asia. Outwardly, the Arab world presented a certain unity; but below the surface there were many divisive forces, chiefly due to rivalries among Arab leaders. What united the Arab masses was their opposition to foreign domination and their hatred of Israel.

The Suez Crisis

Before the Second World War the only independent Arab states were Egypt, Saudi Arabia, Yemen, and Iraq. After 1945 all the rest won their freedom. Independence, however, did not solve the age-old problems of poverty and illiteracy. Their eradication required the aid of the very same foreigners whom Arab nationalists hated. The most vociferous proponent of Arab nationalism was President Gamal Abdel Nasser of Egypt. Following a neutralist course, he accepted large-scale aid from the West and East alike. When the western powers in 1956 withdrew their support for the Aswan dam, a gigantic power project on the Nile, Nasser retaliated by nationalizing the Suez Canal. The ensuing invasion of Egypt by England, France, and Israel might have resulted in a major war had not the United Nations insisted on the withdrawal of foreign troops. Meanwhile Egypt was left in control of the Canal.

To present a united front to the outside world, the Arab nations in 1945 organized the Arab League. Behind this front, however, Arab

differences persisted, especially between Egypt on the one hand and Jordan, Lebanon, and Iraq on the other. President Nasser's efforts to increase his influence through union with Syria in a United Arab Republic were only temporarily successful. To meet the threat posed by communist support of Arab nationalism, Great Britain, Turkey, Iran, Iraq, and Pakistan in 1955 signed a mutual assistance treaty, the Baghdad Pact. When Iraq dropped out of the alliance in 1958, a new Central Treaty Organization (CENTO) was formed. It included the United States, which, under the "Eisenhower Doctrine" of 1957, had already promised armed assistance against communist aggression to any nation in the Middle East that requested it.

Arabs Against Israel

The main danger to peace in the Middle East was the intermittent war between the Arabs and Israel. The war started in 1948–49, when Israel's neighbors invaded the newly independent country, only to be beaten and evicted. From here on an uneasy armistice prevailed. The Arabs refused to recognize Israel and hundreds of thousands of Arab refugees, made homeless by the partition of Palestine, helped keep the conflict alive. Full-scale fighting was briefly resumed during the Suez crisis in 1956, when Israeli forces made a quick dash for the Suez Canal. In 1967, in a swift and furious six-day war, Israel occupied the Sinai Peninsula and rounded out its territory on the right bank of the Jordan River, vowing to retain its conquests until a final and stable peace could be agreed upon. In the eyes of the Israelis, they were fighting for the very survival of their nation.

Although most of the unrest in the Middle East stemmed from nationalism, its roots lay in the serious domestic problems of the Arab states. Almost everywhere, Arab society was still sharply divided into tiny minorities of extremely wealthy merchants and landowners and huge masses of the poorest peasants. To change this system, a complete social revolution and sweeping economic reforms were needed. Such reforms, however, could be achieved only with outside help. In the Middle East, as in the Far East, economic aid thus offered the only genuine hope for a viable political future.

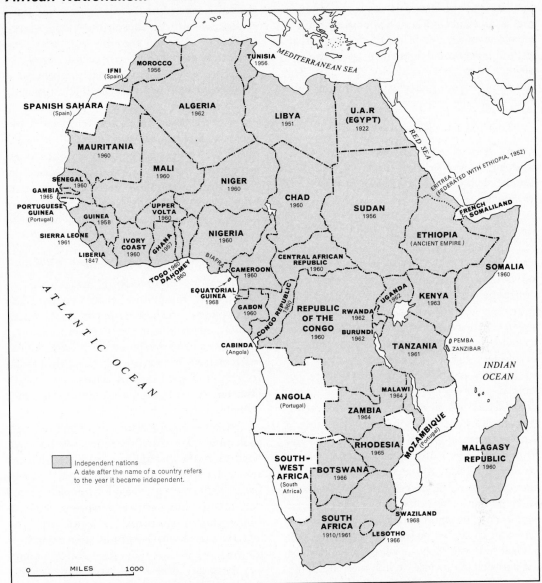

Map legend:
Independent nations
A date after the name of a country refers
to the year it became independent.

MILES 0 — 1000

The Emergence of Africa

The continent of Africa was the last to be swept by the tide of nationalism. From only four sovereign states in 1950, the number by 1968 had grown to thirty-nine. The only important colonies remaining were those of Portugal. The most recent victories of African nationalism occurred in the most backward part of the continent, south of the Sahara, where the native tribes were still primitive, illiterate, and poor. The former colonial powers had virtually eradicated tropical diseases, but the resultant population growth had not been matched by a similar increase in food. Much of Africa, therefore, remained underfed. Added to poverty was extreme diversity, with no tradition of political unity and with some 700 different native dialects. The one sentiment common to all Africans was anticolonialism. Just as it did everywhere else in the world, nationalism in Africa demanded immediate independence, whether people were ready for it or not. This rush into freedom caused severe growing pains for most of the new nations.

Crises in the Congo and Nigeria

All African states were founded as democracies, but lack of political experience and tribal disunity soon gave rise to one-party systems and strong-man rule.

The nation that saw more trouble than any other was the Republic of the Congo. The Belgians had done little to prepare their colony for the independence they were forced to grant in 1960. As a result, order broke down completely, with popular riots, mutinies in the army, and threats of secession in some of the Congo's provinces, notably Katanga. The continued presence of Belgian troops, regulars at first and later mercenaries, further complicated matters. The first premier of the new republic, Patrice Lumumba, was allegedly pro-communist and was removed in 1960 by more moderate elements. He was subsequently murdered, becoming a martyr to anticolonialists within the Congo and without. United Nations troops were able to maintain a measure of order and to prevent the final secession of Katanga. In 1964 the leader of that province, Moise Tshombe, was given the premiership in the hope that he might prove a unifying force. But he was overthrown in 1965 by General Joseph Mobutu, whose pro-Lumumba and anti-Belgian stand gave him a certain popularity. Meanwhile continued mutinies in the outlying provinces showed that the Congo's troubles were far from over.

Another African country troubled by internal unrest was Nigeria. From the beginning of its independence in 1960, Nigeria was beset by festering disputes among its many tribes, especially the poor and backward, but more numerous, Hausa-Fulanis in the North and the more highly educated and advanced Ibos in the South. The fact that the Hausas were Moslems and the

Ibos Christians further accentuated their differences. As time went on and tensions mounted, persecution of the Ibos led to some ghastly massacres. Most of the Ibo population was concentrated in the eastern coastal region. In 1967 this region declared itself independent as the Republic of Biafra. Since Biafra contained most of Nigeria's richest oil fields and installations, government troops intervened and a civil war was on. The new republic had little chance of survival unless it could obtain outside aid. Yet for the rest of the world to recognize one more African nation might encourage secessions from some of the other new states in which hostile tribal groups were living in uneasy coexistence.

Southern Africa: Whites Against Blacks

There was one region in Africa where the native quest for political power continued to be suppressed. In the Republic of South Africa, as in Rhodesia and in the Portuguese colonies of Angola and Mozambique, small white minorities remained in essential control of their country's political and economic affairs. Increasingly, however, this white power came under attack from black nationalism.

In South Africa, where the white minority constituted less than one-fourth of the total population, the government in 1948 introduced a program of strict racial segregation, or *apartheid*. The program provided for complete separation of the races, restricted franchise for nonwhites, forced resettlement of Africans, and separate schools with lower educational standards for African children. The result of this policy was mounting unrest and bloodshed. In 1966 Prime Minister Henrik F. Verwoerd, a leading advocate of *apartheid,* was assassinated. South Africa's racist policies, meanwhile, earned the country the censure of most of the civilized world, including the other members of the Commonwealth. In a show of resentment of such criticism, South Africa withdrew from the Commonwealth in 1961.

In the British dependency of Southern Rhodesia, the ruling white minority amounted to little more than one-twentieth of the total population. When the British government continued to insist on political equality for the black majority as a condition for granting independence to its former colony, the white regime of Ian Smith in 1965 declared the unilateral secession of Rhodesia from the mother country. Subsequent efforts to bring Rhodesia into line through economic sanctions failed, as South Africa and the neighboring Portuguese colony of Mozambique rallied to Rhodesia's support.

To the outside world, Mozambique, together with Angola and Portuguese Guinea, were still "non-self-governing territories," or colonies. In Portuguese eyes, however, they were integral parts of the mother country, overseas provinces whose citizens enjoyed the same rights as those of the mother country. There was little of the racial intolerance in Portugal's colonies that was found in South Africa or Rhodesia. Africans participated in the civil service and married Portuguese, and efforts were made to improve the lot of the poverty-stricken black masses. Yet these efforts were not sufficient to neutralize the appeal of black nationalism which flared up in bloody rebellions, requiring large-scale intervention by Portuguese troops.

The Afro-Asian Bloc

The political emergence of the nonwhite peoples was a worldwide process. While the details of their liberation differed, there were still sufficient similarities to suggest the possibility of collaboration among the many nations that so recently had gained their freedom. As a result, several conferences were held, both among the nations of Asia and Africa and among the nations of Africa alone.

Asian-African Conferences

The first Asian-African conference met at Bandung, Indonesia, in 1955. It was attended by delegates from twenty-nine countries, representing about half the world's population. There were few tangible results, but the meeting registered a common attitude on such basic issues as anticolonialism and censure of racial discrimi-

nation. The next meeting, at Cairo in 1957, was less successful, largely because it was used by communist nations, including the Soviet Union, to advocate a strongly anti-western line. The same held true for some of the subsequent meetings. It was only when the Soviet Union was excluded from the proceedings and when the deliberations shifted to economic problems that these meetings became more businesslike and beneficial. As time went on and most peoples gained their independence, colonialism as a unifying issue lost its importance. Instead, there now were growing differences among the former colonial peoples themselves, as the more radical nations like Communist China and its satellites clashed with moderates like India and Japan. It was due to such differences that the conference scheduled to meet in 1965, on the tenth anniversary of the initial Bandung meeting, was canceled.

The Organization of African Unity

In 1958 the nations of Africa founded their own Conference of Independent African States, which held annual meetings thereafter. As more and more African countries became independent, there arose a need for closer cooperation, especially in economic matters. In the early 1960's a number of regional groupings developed. The next step, obviously, was some wider union of all nonwhite Africa. In 1963 an all-African conference at Addis Ababa, Ethiopia, created the Organization of African Unity (OAU) as a permanent instrument for political and economic cooperation among African states and for the common defense of each member's independence. Progress toward political cooperation was hampered by the large size and great diversity of the continent. In the economic sphere the trend toward regional groupings, such as the East African Economic Community, founded in 1968, was seen as the surest way to overcome Africa's problems. More helpful than economic cooperation among backward countries in Africa and elsewhere, however, was continued aid from the more advanced nations. It was in aiding underdeveloped regions that the free world and the communist world found their most fruitful field for competition.

Delegations from thirty independent African nations sign the charter of the Organization of African Unity at a meeting presided over by Emperor Haile Selassie in Addis Ababa, Ethiopia, in May 1963.

From Cold War to Coexistence

The most clearly discernible trend in international relations after 1950 was the gradual shift away from the angry confrontation of East and West in the Cold War to an equally competitive but more peaceful state of coexistence. Just as the Cold War had developed as the result of a gradually mounting crisis, so the state of peaceful coexistence came only after a decade of intermittent sparring, in which each side felt out the strength of the other. That a major showdown between the East and West was avoided was due mainly to the nuclear balance of power that was reached during the 1950's.

The Korean War

The years immediately after 1950 brought to a climax the international tension that had been building up since 1945. In the fall of 1950,

United Nations forces fought their way into North Korea, close to the borders of Red China. But when victory seemed almost in sight, the Chinese communists intervened and drove the UN armies back into South Korea. By the spring of 1951, the front had become stabilized once more along the thirty-eighth parallel, and there it substantially remained during the bloody stalemate that lasted for two years. Armistice negotiations were begun in 1951 but were not completed until 1953. By that time the war had cost America more than 140,000 casualties and more than $22 billion. The Korean armistice, moreover, merely established an uneasy truce in which North Korean troops continued to face South Korean and American forces across a demilitarized zone.

Escalation in Both Camps

One of the lasting effects of the Korean conflict was a substantial build-up of western military strength. The United States increased its military expenditures fivefold, doubled its armed forces, and extended its network of military bases abroad, and most of America's allies followed suit. It was during the Korean war that NATO perfected its organization and increased its membership by adding Greece and Turkey. At the same time plans were laid for ultimately including West Germany in the western alliance. In 1952, furthermore, the United States exploded its first hydrogen bomb, thus regaining the nuclear lead it had held before the Soviet atomic explosion in 1949.

The change from a Democratic to a Republican administration in Washington, meanwhile, brought to the fore a man who seemed determined to use America's military strength not merely to contain but to challenge communism. Until his death in 1959, the new Secretary of State, John Foster Dulles, was the leading political strategist in the western camp. His policy of "massive retaliation" and "brinkmanship" did not necessarily have the support of America's friends, nor did it have the desired effect of scaring the Russians into making political concessions.

More decisive than the changing of the guard in Washington were the events that took place in Moscow in 1953. We have already discussed the impact of Stalin's death on Russian domestic affairs. While the new Soviet rulers were consolidating their position at home, they adopted a more conciliatory policy abroad. But at the same time the Russian government also announced its first successful testing of a hydrogen bomb. And while the West was rallying its forces behind NATO, the Soviets were lining up their eastern satellites in what ultimately became the Warsaw Pact.

The Search for Coexistence

The first sign that Russia might be willing to negotiate East-West differences was seen in the Korean armistice, which would have been impossible without Soviet acquiescence. In January 1954 the Big Four foreign ministers resumed their talks in Berlin after an interval of several years. In April the Geneva Conference on Far Eastern Affairs, with Communist China attending, temporarily divided Vietnam, where the French had recently been defeated by the Viet-minh communist insurgents. There were to be elections for the whole of Vietnam in 1956, but these were never held. Meanwhile the United States proclaimed its continued concern over Southeast Asia by sponsoring the SEATO alliance.

The culmination of the initial search for coexistence came with the Geneva Summit Conference of 1955. This was the first time since Potsdam ten years earlier that the Big Four had assembled. On the eve of the conference Russia suddenly agreed to an Austrian peace treaty on reasonable terms, another hopeful sign of growing Soviet moderation. Relations at Geneva were cordial, especially between President Eisenhower and Soviet Premier Bulganin, though the results of the conference were disappointing. On none of the major issues—German reunification, European security, and disarmament—was any understanding reached. The only positive achievement was an agreement on cultural exchanges between East and West.

The Cold War Continues

While the "spirit of Geneva" appeared to have dissipated some of the suspicions of the Cold War, events in the Middle East soon showed that war to be far from over. We have already touched on the crisis resulting from President Nasser's nationalization of the Suez Canal in the summer of 1956 and the subsequent attack on Egypt by British, French, and Israeli forces. The withdrawal of these forces under pressure from the UN and the United States was seen as a victory for Nasser and his backers in the communist camp. The Soviet Union's reputation as a champion of anticolonialism, however, was immediately tarnished by its brutal intervention against the uprising in Hungary. Both the Suez crisis and the Hungarian revolution might easily have led to a major showdown had it not been for the fear of a nuclear war.

The year 1957 was relatively peaceful as both East and West tried to repair the damage caused by Suez and Hungary. America's proclamation of the Eisenhower Doctrine served notice that the nation was ready to oppose the spread of Soviet influence in the Middle East. In the Soviet

Union, meanwhile, Khrushchev won final victory over his competitors and emerged as the supreme leader of communism. The most spectacular event of the year, however, was the successful launching of Russia's first earth satellite, Sputnik I, on October 4, 1957. This development proved beyond any doubt that the Soviet Union possessed rockets powerful enough to launch a nuclear attack on the United States. The balance of power in the Cold War had suddenly shifted in Russia's favor.

To the Brink of War

For the next five years the initiative in international affairs remained largely with the Soviet Union. The United States launched its first satellite, Explorer I, in January 1958. But the Russians maintained their lead by placing far heavier satellites into orbit. Continued communist attempts to stir up trouble in the Middle East were foiled by American and British landings in Lebanon and Jordan in 1958. Next came a crisis in the Far East, where Chinese communist attacks on the offshore islands of Quemoy and Matsu were halted only because America stood firmly by her Nationalist Chinese ally. In November 1958 the Soviet Union reopened the German question by once again challenging the western position in Berlin and insisting that the former German capital be made a "free city" within the East German Democratic Republic.

While East-West relations were thus being kept in a state of latent tension, there were feelers from both sides for a second try at summit diplomacy. But the conference finally scheduled for May 1960 in Paris—after an exploratory meeting between President Eisenhower and Premier Khrushchev at Camp David the preceding fall—never materialized. On the eve of the Paris meeting the Russians downed an American U-2 intelligence plane flying over the Soviet Union. Eisenhower's refusal to make amends for this incident led to Khrushchev's withdrawal from the conference before it got under way.

There was much concern and puzzlement in the West over the increasingly aggressive Soviet stance in foreign affairs. Aside from trying to scare the United States into making conces-

sions, Russia's policy was also influenced by the growing rift between Moscow and Peking. The beginnings of this rift, as we have seen, went back to 1956, when the Chinese communists began to criticize Khrushchev's policy of de-Stalinization and his proposed strategy of defeating capitalism through peaceful competition rather than revolution or war. In time, outward signs of the Sino-Soviet split appeared as Russia failed to back the Chinese in their attacks on the offshore islands or to share its atomic secrets with Peking. By 1960 the Soviet Union had drastically cut its material and technical aid, which was essential to China's industrial development. Much of the conflict between Peking and Moscow was over the allegiance of the underdeveloped countries. It was to reassert his claim to leadership over world communism that Khrushchev delivered boastful threats and engaged in bewildering antics in the United Nations Assembly in the fall of 1960.

The advent of the Kennedy administration in 1961 at first seemed to bring a slight lessening of East-West tension. The new President was faced by a bewildering array of foreign problems. In April 1961 the ill-fated Bay of Pigs invasion of Cuba—by anti-communist refugees with American backing—was quickly suppressed by Castro's forces. In South Vietnam, meanwhile, Vietcong guerrillas, supported by communist North Vietnam, were stepping up their "war of liberation." A similar war was going on between the communist Pathet Lao and government forces in Laos. The most serious problem Kennedy inherited, however, was the continued Russian demand for western withdrawal from Berlin.

Kennedy and Khrushchev had a brief impromptu meeting at Vienna in June 1961. Khrushchev already had made some cordial gestures toward the President, and the confrontation was courteous. But shortly after the Vienna meeting the Russians increased their agitation over Berlin, threatening to sign a German peace treaty that would give the East Germans control over access to West Berlin. Only Kennedy's obvious determination to stand firm and go to war rather than give in made Khrushchev finally

The U.S.S. *Barry* (foreground) steams alongside the Soviet freighter *Anosov* during an inspection some 500 miles north of Puerto Rico, just after the Cuban crisis in the autumn of 1962. The *Anosov*, which is leaving Cuba with a cargo of military equipment, appears to be carrying a number of missiles on its deck.

back down. To stop the stream of refugees from East Germany into West Berlin, the communists built the Berlin wall that made East Germany a virtual prison. In October, Khrushchev withdrew his ultimatum on Berlin, thus ending the Berlin crisis, at least for the time being.

There were other signs that negotiations might replace threats in East-West relations. In July 1962 a foreign ministers' conference in Geneva agreed on the formal neutralization of Laos. This, it was hoped, would calm the situation in Southeast Asia. But at the same time the Russians were involved in secret activities in Cuba that soon brought the United States and the Soviet Union to the very brink of war.

The Cuban crisis gained momentum during the summer of 1962 as Washington learned about Soviet Russia's stepped-up military support for Castro. In September a Soviet-Cuban security treaty was announced. In October the United States gained proof that the Soviets had supplied Cuba with missiles capable of delivering nuclear weapons and that launching sites were under construction in Cuba. President Kennedy immediately imposed a strict blockade on further arms shipments to Cuba and demanded that all Soviet offensive weapons be withdrawn and all missile bases dismantled. Faced with pressure from the United Nations and American threats of retaliation, Premier Khrushchev backed down once more, after receiving America's promise not to invade Cuba. The most serious confrontation of the Cold War was over. It had lasted less than two weeks.

Neither War nor Peace

As far back as 1956, Khrushchev had called for "peaceful coexistence between states with differing political and social systems." His subsequent actions belied his words. Besides trying to match Communist China's militant stand against capitalism, the Russians also felt the need for keeping up with the military might of the West. There was much talk in 1960 of a so-called

Khrushchev's Challenge

The coexistence of states with different social systems does not mean that they will only fence themselves off from one another by a high wall and undertake the mutual obligation not to throw stones over the wall or pour dirt upon each other. No! Peaceful coexistence does not mean merely living side by side in the absence of war but with the constantly remaining threat of its breaking out in the future. *Peaceful coexistence can and should develop into peaceful competition for the purpose of satisfying man's needs in the best possible way.*

We say to the leaders of the capitalist states: Let us try out in practice whose system is better, let us compete without war. This is much better than competing in who will produce more arms and who will smash whom. We stand and always will stand for such competition as will help to raise the well-being of the people to a higher level.

From Nikita S. Khrushchev, "On Peaceful Coexistence," *Foreign Affairs,* Vol. XXXVIII (October, 1959), pp. 3–4.

"missile gap," in which the Soviet Union supposedly held the upper hand. It soon became clear, however, that it was the United States that had the lead in the nuclear arms race. To correct that imbalance, Khrushchev embarked on the desperate Cuban gamble. That gamble had failed.

The Cuban crisis, surprisingly, ushered in the first genuine *détente* in the East-West conflict. To reduce the risk of accidental war, Washington and Moscow in early 1963 established a "hot line" of direct communication. In early July 1963 the two powers, together with Great Britain, signed a Nuclear Test Ban Treaty outlawing all but underground tests. There were other agreements on minor issues—East-West trade, increased consular service, a Moscow-New York air link. The relaxation of tension, moreover, did not end with Kennedy's death and Khrushchev's fall from power. In the summer of 1967, at the height of the Middle Eastern crisis, President Johnson and Premier Kosygin held a businesslike conference at Glassboro, New Jersey,

which helped lessen the strain caused by that crisis.

The *détente* between Moscow and Washington, however, did not resolve any of the major issues of the Cold War. The United States and Russia remained opposed on such vital questions as German reunification, general disarmament, the Arab-Israeli conflict, and the unrest in Africa and Asia. The most serious crisis in the late 1960's was the drawn-out war in Vietnam. In an effort to contain the spread of communism in Southeast Asia, the United States poured several hundred thousand men and billions of dollars into a conflict that was in many ways similar to the war in Korea. Just as in that earlier war, the ultimate threat was Red China. But while at the time of Korea the Soviet Union, in its role as leader of world communism, had been instrumental in helping end the war, such mediation was difficult now that Moscow's leadership was being challenged by Peking.

The Vietnam War, while casting a shadow on American-Soviet relations, did not seriously alter the climate of coexistence. One of the more hopeful results of that climate was the Nuclear Non-Proliferation Treaty of 1968, which tried to halt the spread of nuclear weapons. But it was not only the fear of nuclear war that made peaceful coexistence appear preferable to warlike confrontation. Another factor working for coexistence was the loosening of ties within the eastern and western camps and the emergence of the uncommitted and underdeveloped nations as a "third force" in world affairs. We have already noted the dissolution of the once-monolithic communist bloc. Similar changes took place within the western camp, where President de Gaulle tried to create every bit as much trouble for Washington as Mao Tse-tung in the East did for Moscow. The trend toward "polycentrism," or many-centeredness, was also evident in the United Nations, where the new countries of Asia and Africa began more and more to challenge the predominance of the older powers.

As a result of these various realignments, neither the United States nor Russia could any longer count on unquestioning support from their friends and satellites in every crisis. The days of bipolar, East-West, communist-capitalist confrontations were over. The need of the superpowers to solicit the support of a "third world" did much to moderate their international behavior. The shift from Cold War to coexistence did not affect the issues and aims of the East-West conflict, it merely changed the methods used in that conflict. But in an age of nuclear terror, that was no small gain.

Suggestions for Further Reading

1. General

A good general introduction is C. L. Robertson, *International Politics Since World War II: A Short History** (1966). Also useful are: H. Seton-Watson, *Neither War nor Peace: The Struggle for Power in the Postwar World* (1960); D. Rees, *The Age of Containment: The Cold War** (1967); and H. W. Gatzke, *The Present in Perspective: A Look at the World Since 1945,* 3rd. ed.* (1965). E. Luard, ed., *The Cold War: A Reappraisal** (1964), is a symposium of experts. H. L. Trefousse, *The Cold War: A Book of Documents** (1965), is excellent. On American foreign relations, see J. W. Spanier, *American Foreign Policy Since World War II,* 3rd. ed. (1968). Soviet policy is analyzed in M. Mackintosh, *Strategy and Tactics of Soviet Foreign Policy* (1962), and in A. Ulam, *Expansion and Coexistence: The History of Soviet Foreign Policy, 1917–1967** (1968). The effect of the atomic revolution on foreign affairs is weighed by: G. F. Kennan, *Russia, the Atom and the West* (1958); H. M. Kissinger, *Nuclear Weapons and Foreign Policy** (1957); and L. B. Pearson, *Diplomacy in the Nuclear Age* (1959). B. H. Liddell Hart, *Deterrent or Defense: A Fresh Look at the West's Military Position* (1960), evaluates the comparative military strength of the East and West. See also the annual survey published by the London Institute for Strategic Studies, *The Military Balance.* Russian thinking on military matters is discussed in H. S. Dinerstein, *War and the Soviet Union* (1962), and in R. Garthoff, *Soviet Strategy in the Nuclear Age* (1962). For the American side, see H. Kahn, *On Thermonuclear War* (1960). B. Brodie, *Strategy in the Missile Age* (1959), stresses the suicidal dangers of the atomic arms race. Possible alternatives are suggested in T. E. Murray, *Nuclear Policy for War and Peace* (1960), and G. Clark and L. B. Sohn, *World Peace Through World Law* (1960).

2. The Decline and Rise of Europe

The most thoughtful book on this theme is J. L. Lukacs, *Decline and Rise of Europe* (1965). J. Freymond, *Western Europe Since the War** (1964), is more factual and limited in scope. See also S. R. Graubard, ed., *A New Europe?** (1964). The following are among the many books dealing with individual countries: F. Boyd, *British Politics in Transition** (1964); A. Grosser, *French Foreign Policy under De Gaulle* (1967); F. R. Willis, *France, Germany, and the New Europe* (1965); R. Hiscocks, *The Adenauer Era** (1966); and N. Kogan, *A Political History of Postwar Italy* (1966). A. J. Zurcher, *The Struggle to Unite Europe* (1958), is a good introduction to the quest for European unity. U. W. Kitzinger, *The Politics and Economics of European Integration** (1963), presents a sympathetic British view on the Common Market. The key role of France is treated in S. Serfaty, *France, De Gaulle, and Europe* (1967), and in S. N. Fisher, ed., *France and the European Community* (1964).

---

* Available in paperback edition.

3. The Americas

The difficulties of postwar adjustment in the United States are portrayed in E. F. Goldman, *The Crucial Decade: America 1945–1955** (1956). C. Phillips, *The Truman Presidency* (1966), and R. H. Rovere, *Affairs of State: The Eisenhower Years* (1956), deal with the Democratic and Republican periods respectively. On the Kennedy administration, see A. M. Schlesinger, Jr., *A Thousand Days: John F. Kennedy in the White House** (1965); and on Johnson, see R. Evans and R. Novak, *Lyndon B. Johnson: The Exercise of Power* (1966). The economic scene is the subject of J. K. Galbraith, *The Affluent Society** (1958), and of W. Heller, *New Dimensions of Political Economy* (1966). The problems of the Negro and of poverty are discussed in: A. Lewis, *Portrait of a Decade** (1964); L. E. Lomax, *The Negro Revolt** (1963); J. W. Silver, *Mississippi: The Closed Society** (1966); M. Harrington, *The Other America: Poverty in the United States* (1963); and L. Fishman, ed., *Poverty Amid Affluence* (1966). The growing importance of Canada is pointed out in N. L. Nicolson, *Canada in the American Community** (1963), and in J. S. Dickey, ed., *The United States and Canada** (1964). On Latin America's problems, see: M. Eisenhower, *The Wine Is Bitter* (1963); T. Szulc, *The Winds of Revolution: Latin America Today and Tomorrow** (1963); and J. C. Dreier, *The Organization of American States and the Hemisphere Crisis** (1962). One of the best books on the changes in Cuba is T. Draper, *Castro's Revolution: Myths and Realities** (1962).

4. The Communist World

Many of the books cited for Chapter 32 above are also relevant to this latest phase of communism. For the latest general works on Russia, see: H. Seton-Watson, *From Lenin to Khrushchev** (1960); A. Brumberg, ed., *Communism after Stalin** (1960); R. Conquest, *Russia After Khrushchev* (1965); and E. Crankshaw, *Khrushchev: A Career* (1966). On special phases of Soviet life, see: W. W. Kulski, *The Soviet Regime: Communism in Practice** (1963); F. C. Barghoorn, *The Soviet Cultural Offensive* (1960); H. Inkeles and R. A. Bauer, *The Soviet Citizen: Daily Life in a Totalitarian Society* (1959); and M. Djilas, *Conversations with Stalin** (1962). There are several general studies of Russia's satellites: Z. K. Brzezinski, *The Soviet Bloc: Unity and Conflict** (1967); S. Fischer-Galati, *Eastern Europe in the Sixties** (1963); L. B. Bain, *The Reluctant Satellites* (1960); and W. E. Griffith, ed., *Communism in Europe: Continuity, Change, and the Sino-Soviet Dispute*, 2 vols. (1964, 1966). See also W. Z. Laqueur and L. Labedz, eds., *Polycentrism* (1962). On the split between the Soviet Union and Red China, see: D. S. Zagoria, *The Sino-Soviet Conflict, 1956–1961** (1964); W. E. Griffith, *The Sino-Soviet Rift* (1964); and D. W. Treadgold, ed., *Soviet and Chinese Communism: Similarities and Differences* (1967).

5. The End of Colonialism

R. Strausz-Hupé and H. W. Hazard, *The Idea of Colonialism* (1958), corrects some current misconceptions about colonial rule. See also S. C. Easton, *The Twilight of European Colonialism: A Political Analysis* (1960), and R. Emerson, *From Empire to Nation: The Rise to Self-Assertion of Asian and African Peoples** (1962). Changes in the Commonwealth are discussed in Z. Cowen, *The British Commonwealth of Nations in a Changing World* (1965). For the major countries of Asia, old and new, see H. Tinker, *Experiment with Freedom: India and Pakistan** (1967); S. Wolpert, *India** (1965); A. D. Barnett, *Communist China in Perspective** (1962); G. C. Allen, *Japan's Economic Recovery* (1958); N. A. Tarling, *A Concise History of Southeast Asia* (1966); and B. Higgins and J. Higgins, *Indonesia: The Crisis of the Millstones* (1963). On the Middle East, the following are significant: S. N. Fisher, *The Middle East: A History* (1959); G. Lenczowski, *Oil and State in the Middle East* (1960); D. Warriner, *Land Reform and Development in the Middle East* (1962); and T. Little, *Modern Egypt* (1967). African developments are covered in I. Wallerstein, *Africa: The Politics of Independence* (1962), and the same author's, *Africa: The Politics of Unity* (1967). See also C. E. Welch, *Dream of Unity: Pan-Africanism and Political Unification*

---

* Available in paperback edition.

(1966); J. Hatch, *A History of Postwar Africa** (1965); and R. Emerson and M. Kilson, eds., *The Political Awakening of Africa** (1965), selections from speeches and writings of African leaders. The explosive situation in South Africa is examined in N. Phillips, *The Tragedy of Apartheid* (1960). On the attitudes of the two superpowers toward Africa, see R. Emerson, *Africa and United States Policy** (1967), and D. Morison, *The U.S.S.R. and Africa* (1964).

6. From Cold War to Coexistence

Most of the books mentioned in Section 1 above also cover this subject. The following is a selection of individual studies on the major international crises of the fifties and sixties. Each of these crises was a potential cause for a major war: D. Rees, *Korea: The Limited War* (1964); H. Thomas, *The Suez Affair* (1967); J. E. Smith, *The Defense of Berlin* (1963); C. Young, *Politics in the Congo: Decolonization and Independence* (1965); A. J. Dommen, *Conflict in Laos: The Politics of Neutralisation* (1964); A. Abel, *The Missile Crisis* (1966); C. A. Bain, *Vietnam: The Roots of Conflict** (1967); and W. Laqueur, *The Road to Jerusalem: The Arab-Israeli Conflict 1967* (1968). Recent books on American foreign policy include: R. Hilsman, *To Move a Nation* (1967), on Kennedy's foreign policy; P. L. Geyelin, *Lyndon B. Johnson and the World* (1966); and the critical assessment by J. W. Fulbright, *The Arrogance of Power* (1966).

---

* Available in paperback edition.

Epilogue:
The Challenges of Our Time

Looking back over the years since the Second World War, we cannot help feeling that our civilization has entered a wholly new phase. It is difficult as yet to find a name for this new age. Terms like Age of Anxiety, Age of Anarchy, or Age of Uncertainty merely reflect our sense of bewilderment in the face of ceaseless change. We are living in one of those times of which the Swiss historian Jacob Burckhardt wrote: "The historical process is suddenly accelerated in terrifying fashion. Developments which otherwise take centuries fly by like phantoms in months or weeks, and are fulfilled." As students of history we realize that even events that seem sudden have their roots in the past. The nuclear revolution, world communism, colonial nationalism, the "population explosion"—all have their history. But never before have so many crucial developments reached crisis proportions; never before has mankind been confronted with so many changes and challenges. The way in which we meet these challenges will determine not only our own fate but the future of our civilization.

Paris University students occupied the lecture halls of the Sorbonne in May 1968, demanding such reforms as reduced class size, revised examination procedures, permission to carry on political activities at the universities, and the creation of faculty-student committees for the administration of all aspects of university education.

The "Population Explosion"

It is difficult to decide which of our current problems is the most pressing. The one that has been with us longest is the relentless increase of population. At the time it first became noticeable, in the eighteenth century, our optimistic forebears saw it as merely another sign of mankind's steady progress. "Myriads of centuries of still increasing population may pass away," William Godwin wrote in 1793, "and the earth be still found sufficient for the subsistence of its inhabitants." Not long afterward, however, a different voice was heard. "The power of population," Thomas Malthus wrote in 1798, "is indefinitely greater than the power in the earth to produce subsistence for man." The fate of man, Malthus concluded, was not happiness and perfection but sorrow and misery.

For almost a century and a half Malthus' prognosis seemed overly alarmist. World population expanded as never before—from one billion in 1830 to two billion in 1930. But as the number of people increased, so did their supply of food. So long as there were fertile open spaces ready to absorb Europe's surplus millions, and so long as human ingenuity found ways of boosting nature's yield, there was no cause for alarm. All this has suddenly changed. Before the Second World War, advances in medicine and public health had substantially lowered the death rate and prolonged the life span in the more highly developed countries. Since then these blessings have spread to the rest of the world. The result has been a dramatic increase in population. While it took a whole century before 1930 to add one billion to the world's population, present estimates are that the number of people alive at the end of this century will be close to seven billion. The term "population explosion," unknown until a few years ago, has suddenly become an everyday phrase.

Depletion or Abundance?

The possible consequences of this explosion are frightening indeed. Already our natural resources are growing short and the basic elements of our daily existence—water and air—are being polluted. In less than a century, demographers warn us, there may be "standing room only." Yet we have been slow to heed these warnings. It is only within the last year or two that governments have begun to address themselves to the problems of human environment and the blight of large cities. Most countries still consider a rising birth rate a source of pride, and only a few governments have tried to control their population growth. Modern methods of birth control make large-scale population planning easy. Yet age-old prejudices and religious scruples work against such a solution.

Why does this rising tide of humanity not cause more widespread anxiety? One reason is that our scientists assure us there will always be enough food for everyone. The world will be crowded, they say, but it will be comfortable. An intensively cultivated earth and an as yet barely exploited sea will provide man with new foods that will not only taste better but be better for us. Nor will there be any shortage of other necessities. As a matter of fact, life will become easier as technological advancement reduces the need for human labor. Not only industry but agriculture will become increasingly automated. Deserts will bloom, irrigated by water distilled from the sea, and the oceans will yield their riches of food and raw materials to the inhabitants of manmade islands. The power of our planet to produce subsistence, it seems, is as unlimited as the power of mankind to reproduce itself. The only shortage will be of space. And even here a remedy may be at hand.

The Race for Outer Space

Man's first probes into outer space are still so recent that they are hardly a subject for the historian. Yet the year 1957, when the first manmade object went into orbit around the earth, may some day take its place alongside that other memorable date, 1492, when man discovered a whole new world beyond the horizons of the old. The initial motive behind space exploration was scientific curiosity. But as scientists assured their governments that the conquest

Astronaut walking on the moon near the Apollo 11 Lunar Module during extra-vehicular activity, July 16, 1969.

of space was merely a matter of time, individual research turned into government-sponsored space programs.

The race for outer space began when the Soviet Union sent its first Sputnik into orbit on October 4, 1957. The United States launched its first Explorer on January 31, 1958. It was not long before large numbers of manmade satellites were orbiting the earth, the sun, and the moon. The United States held the quantitative and scientific lead in this race, sending up a greater number of objects and gaining more valuable scientific information from such probes. But the Soviet Union orbited heavier space vehicles and scored such spectacular firsts as photographing the far side of the moon and launching a space probe to the planet Venus. Russia's greatest feat came on April 12, 1961, when the world's first "cosmonaut," Major Yuri Gagarin, went into orbit around the earth.

Man on the Moon

As bigger and more sophisticated vehicles carried teams of astronauts on more extended space missions, unmanned satellites made their first landings on the moon, relaying back information in preparation for a manned landing. The great moment came on July 20, 1969, when astronaut Neil Armstrong stepped down a ladder from the Apollo 11 lunar module onto the surface of the moon. "We came in peace for all mankind," a plaque on Apollo 11 proclaimed.

"For one priceless moment in the whole history of man," President Nixon said, "all the people on this earth are truly one."

The implications of the opening up of outer space are tremendous indeed. A second trip to the moon by Apollo 12 in 1970 made what had seemed a miracle appear almost routine. Within the next hundred years, we are told, voyages to the moon will become commonplace, and luxury hotels will cater to travelers who have come to admire the spectacular scenery. There will be large numbers of satellites orbiting the earth, serving as way-stations to the moon and the planets. Population pressure on earth will ultimately be relieved by giant space ships, accommodating thousands of people. To the layman these and other fantastic schemes still belong in the realm of science fiction. But to our scientists, they are quite real.

For the time being, however, we are more concerned with developments closer to home. In the space immediately surrounding the earth, space research may yield important economic and military advantages. Already satellites are being used for communication and reconnaissance. In 1966 the United States and Russia agreed to limit their space exploration to peaceful uses and to ban weapons of mass destruction from outer space. Yet the fact remains that a nation controlling large numbers of manned satellites would gain decisive military and political advantages. In the race for outer space, friendship or enmity between the contestants may thus determine the future peace of the world.

The Nuclear Revolution

The same potential for good or evil prevails in another phase of East-West competition, the nuclear race. Here the immediate stakes are higher and the alternatives more fearful. Atomic power gives twentieth-century man the power to perfect or destroy his civilization.

The nuclear revolution burst upon the world on August 6, 1945, when the first atomic bomb—equivalent to 20,000 tons of TNT—was exploded over the Japanese city of Hiroshima.

This was only the beginning. Seven years later, in 1952, the first hydrogen bomb was exploded over the Bikini atoll in the Pacific. Its power was a thousand times greater than that of the atomic bomb. Even this was not the ultimate. Scientists claim that a country capable of manufacturing megaton bombs, reckoned in millions of tons of TNT, can also produce gigaton bombs, measured in billions of tons. The methods of delivering these frightful weapons, meanwhile, have been perfected until intercontinental missiles, armed with nuclear warheads and traveling at supersonic speeds, can drop their deadly cargoes "on target," thousands of miles away.

For a while after 1945 the United States held an atomic monopoly. But as the Soviet Union developed its own atomic bomb in 1949 and its hydrogen bomb in 1953, America lost its lead. Since then the "nuclear club" has grown to include Britain, France, and Communist China. Other nations will follow. The atomic race between the United States and Russia thus has turned into an atomic free-for-all, in which a nuclear attack might be launched from any quarter at any time. The only sure way of avoiding such catastrophe is through disarmament. But here achievements thus far have been small. A nuclear test ban treaty in 1963 and a nonproliferation treaty in 1968 tried to put limits on the indiscriminate testing and spread of nuclear weapons. But since neither France nor China was a signatory to these treaties, their effectiveness was limited at best.

With efforts being concentrated on atomic armaments, much less was done to develop the peaceful possibilities of the atom. America's Atoms for Peace Program of 1953 was helpful in sponsoring atomic research among friendly nations, and Russia gave similar support to its allies. In 1956 an International Atomic Energy Agency was established at Vienna, with Russia and the United States participating. The purpose of this body was to aid atomic projects in less-developed countries by contributing fissionable materials and nuclear equipment. When it came to implementing this plan, however, Russia and the United States could not agree on the necessary safeguards to make sure that such recipients would not use atomic materials for military purposes. The greatest progress in peaceful atomic development has been in the generation of electric power and the desalinization of seawater. In 1963 the United States and Russia launched a joint nuclear research program calling for limited exchange of scientists and scientific information. Its results, however, were disappointing.

In meeting the challenge of the atom, the East and the West seemed destined to go their own ways. The nuclear race is thus merely part of a general competition between capitalism and communism to determine which side has the more effective answers to the world's economic problems.

Competitive Coexistence

Until ten or fifteen years ago, the economic leadership of the United States and of western Europe was unquestioned. Since then the communist world has begun to challenge this lead. Communism claims that it can defeat capitalism without a war, by peaceful economic competition alone. The Soviet Union has boasted repeatedly that in the foreseeable future it will out-produce the United States and that the communist world as a whole will out-produce the free world. While the timing may be too optimistic, the challenge itself, in the opinion of some experts, is not. Russia has greater mineral resources than the United States; it has a well-trained and disciplined labor force; and it has the necessary knowledge to keep abreast of the latest scientific and technological developments. Thus far the West has been able to hold its own against this communist challenge.

That challenge, furthermore, also has its positive aspects. The economic achievements of communism will be welcomed by anyone concerned with the eradication of poverty the world over. The only danger is that communist successes will appeal to and sway the world's underdeveloped regions. If communism should prove to have an answer for their economic problems, these countries might disregard the lack of personal freedom that communism entails, especially since few of them have ever known such freedom.

The Revolution of Rising Expectations

The population of the underdeveloped countries of Asia, Africa, and Latin America in 1970 was almost three times that of Europe and North America. If present population trends continue, the colored people of the world in the year 2000 will outnumber the whites by almost five to one. Most of the former colonial peoples have only recently won their independence, and the few that have not will do so soon. But these peoples want more than independence; they want to share some of the many benefits that modern civilization has to offer. This revolution of rising expectations, in order to succeed, needs outside help. Most of the new nations of Asia and Africa and the underdeveloped countries of Latin America look for help to the free world. If such help is not forthcoming, they will have to find it elsewhere.

The major share of aid to underdeveloped lands thus far has come from the United States. Since the Second World War, America has spent more than $50 billion helping allied, neutral, and even some communist countries. This foreign aid was a heavy burden on the American taxpayer and in time endangered the country's balance of payments. A few other nations, notably France and Great Britain, joined in helping backward areas. Yet the cost of foreign aid is such that it will have to be borne by all members of the free world.

Meanwhile the leading communist countries made their own contributions to economic aid. The Soviet Union extended its first credits to underdeveloped countries in 1954. In time Communist China, too, began to aid some of its neighbors, although it could ill afford to do so. Most communist aid was given as long-term credits for "trade not aid," a form of assistance preferred by most underdeveloped countries. Although no nation has yet embraced communism as a result of such aid alone, communist support has strengthened anti-western or neu-

Black rally in New York City protesting the arrest of the Panther 21.

tralist tendencies in many countries. To help the underdeveloped nations stand on their own feet and develop a political and economic order suited to their needs is one of the greatest challenges before the world today.

The War on Poverty

The revolution of rising expectations, at first confined to the world's former colonial regions, in recent years has also made itself felt at home. While we were feeding people in faraway lands, millions of our countrymen went hungry; and while our government was helping to improve housing conditions abroad, millions of Americans lived in slums and ghettos. It was primarily among black and Puerto Rican Americans that these economic and social injustices prevailed.

And it was in response to the growing militancy of these minorities that war was finally declared on poverty. It will be a long war with many fronts—from health and housing to education and employment. Like all wars, it will be violent, as impatience with slow progress erupts into bloody riots. Yet victory in the war on poverty is essential to our national survival. Much of racial prejudice is rooted in economic injustice. If we eradicate one, we may overcome the other.

Man in the Nuclear Age

These, then, are some of the challenges before us: the population explosion, the race for outer space, the nuclear revolution, and the revolution of rising expectations, both at home and abroad. Each of these challenges is sufficient to demand the joint efforts of the whole world. Yet in each instance, as we have seen, political and ideological rivalry has prevented cooperation between the East and the West for the good of mankind. Far from making for a happier world, the revolutionary developments of our time have only aggravated existing tensions and fears.

Foremost among our many fears is the fear of war. Ever since the Second World War governments have tried to banish this fear by finding ways of abolishing armaments. They are still trying. Meanwhile, psychologists claim that the ultimate cause of war does not lie in political and economic rivalries but in man himself, in the human tendency toward aggression. Recent discoveries in the study of human relations seem to hold some cause for hope. According to social scientists, within the next hundred years man will learn more about himself than he has in his whole previous history. He will discover not only the causes and cures of his individual neuroses but the causes and cures of mass hatreds leading to war. Thus he may at long last learn how to live in peace with himself and with his fellow man.

The Biological Revolution

While man is learning more about his inner self, he is also learning more every day about his physical being. Biology, the science of life, is busy making discoveries that may deeply affect and alter human existence. Some of these discoveries—artificial insemination, the transplantation of organs, and the use of drugs to control moods and feelings—are already being put to use. Other innovations—test-tube babies, the postponement of death, mind control, even the creation of life from inert materials—are still in the experimental stage. In their sum total, the discoveries that biology holds in store for us amount to a veritable Biological Revolution. The impact of that revolution has been compared with such major stages in human development as the discovery of fire or the wheel, the advent of agriculture, and the development of printing.

The ethical questions raised by discoveries and practices that so completely change the traditional pattern of human life stagger one's imagination. They have led some biologists to question whether man is ready thus to tamper with his heredity. But meanwhile the experiments in the laboratories continue.

The Mind Perplexed

An avalanche of unprecedented changes crowded into a span of less than a generation has left most of us confused and bewildered. In time we will no doubt get used to this new and different world, but for the present we have hardly grasped the meaning of all that has happened so fast. In our search for understanding we turn to a variety of old and new doctrines, none of which gives us the inner security we are looking for. The temper of our time is a mixture of anticipation and apprehension, optimism and pessimism, confidence and anxiety.

The philosophy of existentialism well illustrates this blend of hope and despair. Its antecedents go back to the nineteenth century, but its vogue dates from the Second World War. The existentialist maintains that the individual rather than the abstract concept of humanity constitutes true reality. He affirms the loneliness of man in a strange and hostile world. Such loneliness, far from leading to desperation, is seen as a challenge, a call to action, since "man's destiny is within himself."

While some of us are searching for a new philosophy to fit a new age, others find existing doctrines sufficient to their needs. To the true communist believer, Marxist doctrine still supplies ready-made answers to most problems. He has nothing to fear, his leaders tell him, since history is on his side. There was a time when communism had a large following in the West, especially among intellectuals. But most of these have long since become disillusioned, and new converts to communism in the free world are few. Instead, a modified form of socialism has gained ground among the so-called New Left. Its adherents are equally opposed to American capitalism and the bureaucratized communism of the Soviet Union. Their heroes are Mao

Tse-tung and Fidel Castro, not Brezhnev and Kosygin.

Communism's one-time rival, fascism, also has lost much of the following it once had in the West, although one still finds it in some Latin American and Mediterranean countries. One of its ingredients, nationalism, is still a potent force, especially in the newly independent nations of Asia and Africa. Where it is used by unscrupulous leaders for selfish ends, nationalism rivals communism as a danger to world peace.

Some of the ground lost by communism and fascism has been reclaimed by religion. There are many reasons for this religious revival, foremost among them the widely felt need for some central belief, some principle of authority, in time of great intellectual and emotional stress. The return to religion has taken many different forms and has involved not only a revival of interest in the traditional faiths of the West but a new interest on the part of many westerners for the religions of the East. Among western religions one of the noteworthy trends has been the effort of religious leaders to overcome age-old differences and to work toward religious unity. Reformist tendencies within the papacy have furthered this trend.

The Revolt of Youth

These are some of the ways in which men are trying to cope with their feelings of uncertainty and anxiety. There are others. One large segment of our society—the younger generation—has been particularly shaken by the vicissitudes of a world in the making of which it had no part. During the 1950's, youth everywhere was reproached by its elders for the passivity with which it faced the turmoil of the times. There were some "beatniks" and "angry young men," but they were exceptions in an otherwise "quiet generation." All this changed during the sixties. As students began to rebel against society, not only in the United States but the world over, the older generation was faced with a new cause for concern in an already deeply troubled world.

The revolt of youth against age is nothing new, of course, although there has never been anything quite like the scope and intensity of today's youthful unrest. Most of the unrest was centered in the world's large universities, where huge enrollments, combined with antiquated regulations, tended to dehumanize education.

The Great Debate— Youth against Age

I hope you old . . . die! I hope all you old . . . die. Go ahead and watch us and die!
— Columbia University Student, May, 1968

These students, ill at ease in their factory-like universities and lost in the midst of the lonely crowd, could be compared to the workers in the first factories at the start of the 19th century. The workers destroyed the machines; the students symbolically break their working tools and the instruments of their servitude, the tables and the chairs.
— Raymond Aron, May, 1968

The use of a university is to make young gentlemen as unlike their fathers as possible.
— Woodrow Wilson

The young leading the young, is like the blind leading the blind; they will both fall into the ditch.
— Lord Chesterfield

Almost everything that is great has been done by youth.
— Disraeli

Everyone believes in his own youth that the world began to exist only with his own coming, and that in reality everything exists on his account.
— Goethe

Youth loves honor and victory more than money. It really cares next to nothing about money, for it has not yet learned what the lack of it means.
— Aristotle

In the old there is no taste, in the young no insight.
— Babylonian Talmud

Compiled by Ruth Block, "Now, About That Gap," *The New York Times Magazine*, July 7, 1968, pp. 30–31.

But from the campuses of the "multiversities" the revolt spread to the smaller schools and into the streets. The aims of the youthful rebels differed from place to place; but they were united in their opposition to what they thought their elders stood for—meaningless discipline, social injustice, and senseless wars. Some of the young expressed their protest by withdrawal rather than action, ignoring traditional manners and mores and becoming "hippies" or "flower children." Others believed that only by attacking the existing "establishment" could they find a way to realize the better world of which they dreamed. As student radicals made themselves spokesmen for social ills, especially among underprivileged blacks, what had started as peaceful protest erupted into violent confrontations with the forces of "law and order."

The older generation was put out and perplexed by a movement intent on biting the hand that fed it. Believers in authority hinted at a communist conspiracy and advocated repression. Less alarmist observers pointed out that the rebels, after all, were only a strident minority within the young generation. But like any spontaneous outbreak of protest in the past, the revolt of the young deserved the serious attention it received from their more thoughtful elders. If there ever was a time for a reassessment of values, this was it. Youth may not have a monopoly on idealism, but neither does age have a monopoly on wisdom.

On the other hand, the young do well to remember that age is an inevitable phase in everyone's life and that while the old will not live forever, the young will soon grow old. History may be made by the young, but it is recorded by the old. It remains to be seen how the youth of today will write the history of its revolt years hence. In the long-range perspective of human development, our generation is a mere incident. But in retrospect our age may some day appear as one of the most creative phases of history, when competition between rival ideologies brought forth undreamed-of human progress, and when fruitful debate among generations helped create a just society in which such progress was shared by all.

Source of Illustrations

Prologue
2: Rev. Raymond V. Schoder, S.J. 9: Alison Frantz, Athens. 17: Alinari-ARB. 23: Anne Munchow, Aachen. 27: Librarie Larousse. 34: A. C. Cooper Ltd., in the Library-Inner Temple, London.

Chapter 1
38, 39: RTH. 44: *The Reformation* © 1966, Time-Life Books; © Time Inc. 48: BA. 52: Alinari-ARB. 54: Bildarchiv, ÖNBV. 57: Alinari-Scala (New York/Florence), in the Vatican Museum.

Chapter 2
66: The Toledo Museum of Art. 68: MMA, Harris Brisbane Dick Fund, 1936. 74: BA. 76: Bibliothèque Publique et Universitaire, Geneva. 78, 82: BA.

Chapter 3
86, 87: BA. 91: Philadelphia Museum of Art. 101: The Folger Shakespeare Library. 103: BA. 106: André Held, in the Musée Cantonal des Beaux-Arts, Lausanne.

Chapter 4
110, 111: BA. 112: Rare Book Division, NYPL/ALT. 122: National Portrait Gallery, London. 125: Mansell Collection, London. 128: Rare Book Division, NYPL/ALT. 130: Mansell Collection, London.

Chapter 5
138, 139: Draeger Frères, Paris. 140: Cliches Musées Nationaux, in Musée du Louvre. 149: Prints Division, NYPL/ALT. 156: Photo-Hachette. 159: Rijksmuseum, Amsterdam.

Chapter 6
164, 165: Freeman, in BM. 170: RTH. 171: ms. add. 3965 14, original in the Portsmouth Collection, University Library, Cambridge. 174: Anderson-ARB. 185: MMA, Harris Brisbane Dick Fund, 1932.

Chapter 7
190: Photographie Giraudon. 196: Historical Pictures Service, Chicago. 198: BA. 207: Ullstein, Berlin. 210: Library of Congress.

Chapter 8
214: Robert Descharnes, courtesy of American Heritage Publishing Co., Inc. 216: BA. 219: Cliches Musées Nationaux in Musée de Versailles et des Trianons. 231: RTH. 234: BM.

Chapter 9
238, 239: Prints Division, NYPL/ALT. 240: Historical Pictures Service, Chicago. 245: Manchester Public Library. 247: National Gallery, London. 254: Museo centrale del Risorgimento, Roma.

Chapter 10
264, 265: BA. 269: Authenticated News International. 271: Prints Division, NYPL/ALT. 277: RTH. 281: Sovfoto.

Chapter 11
290: Photo, NYPL/ALT; © *Punch*. 292: Gernsheim Collection, University of Texas. 298: Brown Brothers. 306: BA.

Chapter 12
314: RTH. 317: NYPL/ALT. 321: Library of Congress. 333: Brown Brothers. 336: BA.

Chapter 13
340: Camille Lacheroy, courtesy of Éditions du Pont-Royal, Paris. 342: Gernsheim Collection, University of Texas. 346: Top, Photo-Bulloz; bottom, BA. 357: Sovfoto. 361: American Museum of Natural History.

Chapter 14
368: Photo, NYPL/ALT; © *Punch*. 373: BA. 377: RTH. 380, 387: UPI.

Chapter 15
392: BA. 396: Brown Brothers. 401: BA. 406: Culver Pictures. 414: WW.

Chapter 16
420: Theater Collection, NYPL/ALT. 428: Ewing Galloway. 429: WW. 430: Keystone Press Agency, Inc. 438: Lotte Jacobi.

Chapter 17
442, 446, 449: WW. 454: UPI. 458: The Museum of Modern Art, New York. 463: CBS News.

Chapter 18
468: Sovfoto. 471: WW. 475: U.S. Navy. 478: U.S. Coast Guard. 482: Ewing Galloway. 484: © *Punch*.

Chapter 19
494: Axel Grosser. 501: WW. 502: Stern, Black Star. 503, 514, 517: UPI.

Epilogue
523: AFP from Pictorial Parade. 525: NASA. 528: Hap Stewart.

Index

Index

Page numbers in italics refer to maps or illustrations.

aristocracy (*continued*)
  Russian, 309 (*see also* nobility; social classes)
Aristotle, 10, 167, 169
arithmetic (*see* mathematics)
Arkwright, Richard, 267, 268
armada (*see* Spanish Armada)
Armada, The (Mattingly), quoted,104
Armstrong, Neil, 525–26
army: Austrian, 407; French, 59, 138, 143, 225–26, 228; German, 352, 406, 453; Italian, 41; Japanese, 456; Parliamentary, 129; Prussian, 155, 156, 157, 199, 200, 206–7, 233; Russian, 159, 160; Spanish, 134 (*see also* military power; Navy)
Arnold, Matthew, 365
Arouet, François Marie (*see* Voltaire)
art: baroque, 173, *174,* 175; 18th-century, 184, 185, *185;* English, *128;* French, 142; Greek, 8; Italian, 49–52, *50;* 19th-century, 364–65; Renaissance, 49–50; Romantic, 246, *247;* Russian, 505; 20th-century, 438–39 (*see also* painting; sculpture)
Articles of Confederation, 319
artisans: English, 129; German, 260; and industrialism, 266; in Middle Ages, 167; in 19th century, 256
Artois, Charles Philippe, Count of, 220, 252 (*see also* Charles X)
Asia, 194; imperialism in, 377–79; since Second World War, 506–10 (*see also specific country*)
Asia Minor, 8, 507
Asian-African conferences, 513
Asiento, 146
Association of Southeast Asia, 509
astrolabe, 88
astronauts, 525–26
astronomy, 167–68, 169, 170–71, *170*
Aswan dam, 510
Atatürk, Mustapha Kemal, 407, 408
atheism, 176, 182
Athens, 8; and Sparta, 10
Atlantic Charter, 481, 486
atomic bomb, 438, 481, 508, 526
Atomic Development Authority, 489
Atomic Energy Agency, 526
Atomic Energy Commission, 489
Atoms for Peace Program 526
Attlee, Clement, 485, 496
Attu, 480
Augsburg, League of, 144
Augsburg, Peace of, 76, 87, 132
Augustan Age, 142
Augustenburg, Duke of, 301

Augustine (St.), Bishop of Hippo, 141
Augustus, quoted, 13–14
Augustus (of Poland) the Strong, 154
Aurelius, Marcus, 15
Ausgleich, 299, 311, 353
Austerlitz, battle of, 230
Australia, 307, 326, 327
Austria, in 18th century, 197, 200–201, 203, 207–9; and Habsburgs, 154; and Italy, 146; in 19th century, 258, 259, 270, 291, 295, 296, 298–99, 300–302; and Prussia, 298–99; in 20th century, 423, 424, 427, 462
Austria-Hungary: before First World War, 394–95, 397, 398, 402, 403, 404, 407; in First World War, 353–54, 370, 372–74, 385, 386–87, 388 (*see also* Austria; Austrian Empire; Hungary)
Austrian Empire: in 18th century, 197, 200–201, 203, 207–9; and France, 230–31; in 17th century, 132, 133, 154 (*see also* Austria)
Austrian Netherlands, 243 (*see also* Belgium)
"Authoritarian Empire" (France), 294
authoritarian government, 409, 455–56 (*see also* dictatorships; totalitarianism)
Autobiography (Cellini), 43, 51
Avignon, 53; popes at, 35
Axis, 464, 469–74, 477–79
Ayub Khan, Mohammad, 507–8
Azov, 159, 160
Aztec Empire, 93

B

Babylonian Captivity, 35, 39
Babylonian civilization (*see* Mesopotamia)
Bach, Johann Sebastian, 186
Bacon, Francis, 168, 172
Badoglio, Pietro, 478
Bagehot, Walter, 343, 362
Baghdad Pact, 510
Bahamas, 90
Bakunin, Mikhail, 285, 311, 345
balance of power: in Cold War, 495, 516; in 18th century, 192–93; before First World War, 369; in 19th century, 307, 311 (*see also* Cold War; international relations)
Balboa, Vasco de, 92
Baldwin, Stanley, 429
Balfour Declaration, 431
Balkan League, 386
Balkans, 231, 290, 370–72, *371,* 373,

384, 385, 386–87, 395, 397; in Second World War, 472 (*see also specific country*)
Baltic Sea, *157,* 423
Balzac, Honoré de, 284, 364
Bancroft, George, 316
Bank of England, 115, 151
banking, 59; French, 229; Italian, 42
Baptists, 79, 147
Barbados, 117
barbarians, 17 (*see also* Germanic tribes; Huns)
baroque style, 173, 175
Barras, Paul, 228
Barry, U.S.S., *517*
Bastille, 178; attack on, 219, 220
Battle of the Bulge, 479
Bavaria, 135, 200, 260, 409
Bay of Pigs invasion, 516
Bayle, Pierre, 47, 176–77
bayonet, 143
beatniks, 530
Beauharnais, Josephine (*see* Josephine)
Bebel, August, 353
Beccaria, Cesare di, 181
Becker, Carl L., quoted, 181
behavioral sciences, 435–37
Belamy, Edward, 325
Belgium, 143, 209, 225; in First World War, 389, 395; independence of, 253; in 19th century, 270; in Second World War, 471
Belgrade, 63
Benedetti, Vincent, *292*
Benedict XV (Pope), 399
Benedict, Ruth, 436
Benelux countries, 488, 499 (*see also specific country*)
Beneš, Eduard, 424, 462, 488; quoted, 488
benevolent despotism, 183
Bentham, Jeremy, 273
Bentinck, William, 329
Berchtesgaden, 462
Berchtold, Leopold von, 388
Berlin: airlift to, 486, 500; division of, 482, 486, *491,* 516–17
Berlin, Congress of, *371,* 372
Berlin, Treaty of, 413
Bernini, Giovanni, 175
Bernstein, Eduard, 344
Bernstorff, Johann-Heinrich, Count von, *392*
Berri, Charles, Duke of, 250, 252
Bessarabia, 232, 291, 372
Bethmann-Hollweg, Theobold von, 402

Carnegie, Andrew, 344
Carnot, Lazare, 226
Carolingian Empire, 22–24
carpetbaggers, 323
cartels, 344
Carthage, 13
Cartier, Jacques, 118
Cartwright, Edmund, 267
Casablanca, conference at, 481
caste system (see social classes)
Castiglione, Baldassare, 47
Castile, 60–61, 96 (see also Spain)
Castereagli, Robert, 241, 244
Castro, Fidel, 504, 530
Catalonia, 61
cathedral: Beauvais, 27; Florence, 51;
    St. Paul's, 125
Catherine II (of Russia) the Great,
    198, 199, 204–6
Catherine of Aragon, 80, 81
Catholic Church (see Roman Catholic
    Church)
Catholic League, 106, 110–11, 132,
    133, 134
Catholic Reformation, 96
Cavalier Parliament, 146–47, 148
Cavour, Camillo di, 291, 292, 292, 295,
    296, 297, 298, 306
CDU, 498
Cellini, Benvenuto, 43, 51
censorship, 83, 178, 252
Center Party, German, 352
CENTO, 510
Central Africa, 376
Central America, 92, 325, 379, 380
Central Committee of Communist
    Party, 446
Central Powers, 393–99, 394, 402–4
Central Treaty Organization, 510
Cervantes, Miguel de, 107
Ceylon, 100
CGT, 346
Chamber of Deputies, French, 252, 257,
    349
Chamberlain, Austen, 412
Chamberlain, Joseph, 347, 348
Chamberlain, Neville, 429, 462–63, 463,
    470, 471
Chambers of Reunion, 144
Champaigne, Philippe de, painting by,
    122
Champlain, Samuel de, 118
Charlemagne, 22–24, 36; coronation of,
    22
Charles I (of Austria), 398, 404
Charles I (of England), 127–30, 128,
    131, 152
Charles II (of England), 131, 146–48

Charles VI (of France), 59
Charles VII (of France), 59
Charles VIII (of France), 60
Charles IX (of France), 105
Charles X (of France), 252, 254
Charles IV (Holy Roman Emperor),
    king of Spain, 61, 63, 72, 76, 80, 95,
    98
Charles VI (Holy Roman Emperor), 197
Charles II (of Spain), 145
Charles III (of Spain), 204
Charles XII (of Sweden), 157–58, 160
Charles Albert (of Piedmont), 258
Charles the Bold, Duke of Burgundy,
    60
Charles the Great (see Charlemagne)
Charter: English, 261; French, 252
"Charter Oath," Japanese, 335
Chartist Movement, 26
Chaucer, Geoffrey, 49
Cheap Clothes and Nasty (Kingsley), 284
Cheka, 44
Chesterfield, Philip Stanhope, Lord,
    quoted, 530
Chiang Kai-shek, 433–34, 460, 491
child labor, 272, 277, 277, 351
China: Communist, 490, 491, 498, 506,
    508, 516, 526, 527; before First
    World War, 333–34; in First World
    War, 405; in 19th century, 330–34;
    before Second World War, 433–34,
    456–57; since Second World War,
    490–91, 498, 506, 508; and Soviet
    Union, 506; and U.S., 508 (see also
    Manchu dynasty)
Chinese Republic, 334
Christendom, 72, 135 (see also Chris-
    tianity)
Christian Democratic Party, Italian, 499
Christian Democratic Union, German,
    498
Christian socialism, 284–85, 347
Christianity, in China, 330; early organ-
    ization of, 25; origins of, 362–63;
    in Roman Empire, 14–15, 17–18;
    science and, 172–73, 362–63; spread
    of, 31 (see also Greek Orthodox
    Church; Protestant Reformation;
    Roman Catholic Church; Russian
    Orthodox Church)
churches (see cathedral)
Churchill, Winston, 471, 478, 481, 482,
    496; quoted, 464
Cicero, Marcus Tullius, 44, 177
city-states: 3; Greek, 9–10; Italian,
    40–42, 41, 88; Roman, 14 (see also
    states)
Civil Constitution of the Clergy, 223

civil liberties: British, 150; French, 217,
    229–30; Mill's theory of, 273–74
    (see also liberty)
Civil Rights Act of 1964, 503
civil rights legislation, 322, 502, 503
civil service, in Germany, 453, 455
civil war: American, 316, 317, 321–22;
    in England, 127–30; in France, 104–
    6; in Greece, 486; in Nigeria, 512;
    in Spain, 459–60 (see also American
    Revolution; French Revolution; re-
    bellion; revolution; Wars of the
    Roses)
civilization: definition of, 3; study of,
    437
Civilization of the Renaissance in Italy,
    The, (Burckhardt), 46
Clarendon Code, 147
Clarendon, Edward Hyde, Earl of, 147
Clarendon, George W.F., 292
Clarissa Harlowe (Richardson), 187
Clark Memorandum, 433
class structure (see social classes)
Classical economists, 275–76
classicism, 249
Clemenceau, Georges, 349, 398, 404,
    406
Clement VII (Pope), 35, 56, 80
clergy, English, 81; French, 53, 59,
    121–22; in 19th century, 247; in
    16th century, 67–68; Spanish, 69;
    taxation of, 62 (see also bishops;
    priests)
Cleveland, Grover, 379
Clive, Robert, 202
Coal Mines Act, 277
coal production, 268, 269, 352
Cobden-Chevalier treaty, 294
Code Napoléon (see Napoleonic Code)
coexistence, 495, 515–19, 527
coinage, 8, 44 (see also money)
Colbert, Jean Baptiste, 118, 140
Cold War, 486–89, 495, 515–16; in Far
    East, 489–91, 490; U.N. in, 489
Coligny, Gaspard de, 105
"collective leadership," 605–6
collectivization, 447, 504
Colombia, 380
Colombo Plan, 509
Colonial Reformers, 326
colonies: in Africa, 374–77, 375, 512;
    in Asia, 119–20, 377–78, 506–10;
    Belgian, 376, 512; British, 117, 376–
    77, 378, 381–82, 496; Dutch, 117,
    118–19, 377; French, 117, 118–19,
    202, 203, 294, 374, 375–76, 377, 497;
    German, 376, 378–79, 405; Italian,
    376, 377; in North America, 118–

electoral system: French, 218, 222, 252, 422; Italian, 450; Roman, 13–14 (see also suffrage)

electricity, 169

"Eleven Years' Tyranny," 128

Elizabeth (of Russia), 203

Elizabeth I (of England) 81, 100, 101–4, *101*, 124, 125, 127

Emancipation Bill of *1829*, 254

Emancipation Edict, 309, 311

Emancipation Proclamation, 321, 322

Emerson, Rupert, quoted, 507

"Emperor's Battle," 403

empiricism, 177

Ems dispatch, 304

Enabling Act, 453

enclosure movement, 267

Encyclopedia (Diderot), 179, 180; quoted, 180

Engels, Friedrich, 280, 281, 282, 344; quoted, 272

England, Anabaptists in, 79; Elizabethan, 101–4; in 15th century, 61; in Hundred Years' War, 33; in Middle Ages, 32–33; Norman Conquest of, 25; Puritan Rebellion in, 127–30, *127;* Restoration in, 131–32; in 13th century, 29–30 (see also Great Britain)

Eniwetok, 481

enlightened despotism, 183, 191, 203–9, 229

Enlightenment, 177–84, 246, 247, 266

Entente Cordiale, 383, 389

Erasmus, 47, 70–71, 75, 98; quoted, 71

Erhard, Ludwig, 498

Eritrea, 377, 458

Ermak, 120

escapism, 246

Escorial, 107

Essay Concerning the Human Understanding (Locke), 177

Essay on Population (Malthus), 275, 360

Essay on the Inequality of the Human Races (Gobineau), 362

"establishment," 530

Estates General, 120, 121, 140, 217, 218–19, 220; monarchy and, 62

Estonia, 470

Étatisme, 115

Ethics Demonstrated in the Geometrical Manner (Spinoza), 173

Ethiopia, 458–59

Euclid, 8, 10

Eugene (of Savoy), 145, 154

Euratom, 499

Europe: and America, 315–16; early civilization of, 14; economy of (see economy, European); in 18th century, 191–95, *192;* in 15th century, 39–40, 56–63, *58;* before First World War, 341–47, 369–74, *371;* in First World War, *394;* industrial centers in, *114;* in Middle Ages, 25–26, 28–37; Mongols in, 30; national minorities in, *409;* in 19th century, 238–62, *242,* 255–56, *255, 288,* 289–90, *305,* 315; peace settlements in, *408;* protestantism in, *75;* before Second World War, 408–10, *461;* in Second World War, 468–69, *476;* since Second World War, 487, 495–96; in 17th century, 111–36, *135;* in 16th century, *95;* in Thirty Years' War, 132–36, *135*

European Atomic Energy Community, 499

European Coal and Steel Community, 499

European Economic Community (see Common Market)

European Free Trade Association, 500

European Recovery Program (see Marshall Plan)

evolution, theory of, 359–63

Evolutionary Socialism (Bernstein), 344

existentialism, 529

expansionism, U.S., 316–17, 319, 325 (see also imperialism)

experimentation, scientific, 169–70, 172

exploration: in 15th and 16th centuries, 56, 87–93, *92–93;* Spanish, 90–91 (see also colonies)

Explorer I, 516, 525

expressionism, 439

extermination camps, 474

extraterritoriality, principle of, 330

F

Fabian Society, 344, 348

factory acts, 276–77, 278

factory system, 113, 267–68

Far East, 378, 380, 381, 382, 433–34, 460–62, 483, 485, 489–91, *490* (see also specific country)

farmers: English, 266–67; Indian, 329; Prussian, 206; Spanish, 97; U.S., 323, 324–25, 426 (see also agriculture; peasants)

farming, collective, 447 (see also agriculture)

Fasci di Combattimento, 449

fascism, 424, 430, 443–44, 530; Italian, 416, 448–49; Japanese, 456 (see also Nazism)

Fashoda crisis, 383

February Revolution, 399–400

Fenian Brotherhood, 308

Ferdinand I (of Austria), 259

Ferdinand I (Holy Roman Emperor), 76, 95–96

Ferdinand II (Holy Roman Emperor), 132–33, 134, 154

Ferdinand of Aragon, 60–61, 62

Ferry, Jules, 349

Ferry Laws, 342

feudalism, 24–25; Austrian, 259; Japanese, 334–35; 19th century, 255 (see also serfdom)

Feuerbach, Ludwig, 359

Feuillant Club, 223

Ficino, Marsilio, 46

Fielding, Henry, 185

"Fifth Column," 456

finance (see banking; economy; money; taxation)

Finland, 232, 470, 488

firearms, 57, 93

First Industrial Revolution (see Industrial Revolution)

First International, 345, *346*

First Memoir on Property (Proudhon), 285

"first treaty settlement," 330

First World War, 326, 327, 343, 387–89, 393–99, *394,* 402–4

"Fists of Righteous Harmony," 333

Fiume, 405, 451

Five Ordinances, 252

Five-Year Plans: Chinese, 508; Russian, 447, 504

Flanders, 98, 136 (see also Belgium; Netherlands)

Flaubert, Gustave, 364

Fleury, André de Cardinal, 195

Florence, 40, 42; Cathedral of, 51

Force and Matter (Büchner), 359

foreign aid, 487; Russian, 501, 527; U.S., 500–501, 527 (see also Lend-Lease program; Marshall Plan)

foreign policy: Chinese, 508; English, 102, 126, 127, 147, 149, 196, 230, 244; French, 225, 256, 294, 422; German, 352, 370, 499; of Hohenzollerns, 156; Italian, 451; Pakistani, 508; Russian, 309, 311; U.S., 315, 319, 325, 486–88, 502

Forli, Melozzo da, painting by, *57*

Formosa, 332, 335, 491

Fort Duquesne, 202

Four-Year Plans, German, 454

Fourier, Charles, 280

Gomulka, Wladyslaw, 506
"good neighbor policy," 433
Göring, Hermann, 477
Gospel of Wealth, The (Carnegie), 344
Goths (*see* Germanic tribes)
Gottwald, Klement, 488
government: Austrian, 299, 353; authoritarian, 409; colonial, 119; democratic (*see* democracy); English, 124–31, 347–48; French, 123, 140, 197, 222–23, 293, 295, 349, 430–31; German, 302, 351–52, 453–55; Indian, 328, 329; Italian, 41–42, 298, 354–55, 449–51; Japanese, 335; in Middle Ages, 31–32; Polish, 158; Prussian, 299–300; Roman, 11, 13; Russian, 160, 308, 310, 400, 401, 446; U.S. 323–24 (*see also* monarchy; Parliament *for specific country;* political system; republican government)
Government of India Act, 432
Goya, Francisco de, painting by, *231*
grain trade, 100
Granada, 60, 90, 97
Grand Alliance of the Hague, 145, 147
gravitation, law of, 170, 171–72
Great Britain: in 18th century, 195–97, 199–200, 201, 209–10; before First World War, 347–49, 382–83, 385–86; in First World War 389, 394–95, 396, 397, 398, 402, 403; in Napoleonic Wars, 228, 230, 232, 233; in 19th century, 244, 253–55, 261, 266–67, 307–8, 326–30, *328;* before Second World War, 422, 429–30, 432, 457, 463–64; in Second World War, 470, 472; since Second World War, 496–97; in 17th century, 124–32, *127*, 146–53 (*see also* Commonwealth of Nations; England)
Great Depression, 393, 416, 417, 424, 427–28, *428*
Great Exhibition of *1851*, 264–65, 270
"Great Fear," 220
"great leap forward," 508
Great Mutiny of *1857*, 329
Great Northern War, 160
Great Reform Bill, 254
Great Schism, 35, 39, 53, 67
Greco, El, 107
Greece, 5–11, 515; city-states of, 9–10; communism in, 486; before First World War, 386; in First World War, 395; in 19th century, 251; during Persian Wars, 9–10; in Second World War, 472; in 13th century, 30 (*see also* Athens)

Greek Orthodox Church: and Roman Catholic Church, 28; in Turkey, 291
Greek War of Independence, 251
Greeks, 6–11
Green Table, The (Jooss), *420–21*
Greenland, 88
Gregory VII (Pope), 35
grossdeutsch group, 260
Grotius, Hugo, 177
Guadalcanal, 481
Guadaloupe, 117, 202
Guam, 380, 479
Guarantee of Harmony and Freedom (Weitling), 281
Guérard, Albert, quoted, 293
Guernica (Picasso), *458–59*
Guesde, Jules, 350
Gulliver's Travels (Swift), 185
gunpowder, 57
guns (*see* firearms)
Gustavus III (of Sweden), 204
Gustavus Adolphus, 133–34, 143, 157

H

Habsburgs, 61, 85–96, 104, *110–11,* 122, 123, 132, 133, 134, 145, 154, 155, 200–201, 207, 259, 354
Haeckel, Ernst, 359
Hague Peace Conference, 380
Haile Selassie, 458
Haiti, 91
Halley, Edmund, 171
Halley's comet, *171*
Hals, Frans, 107
Hanbury, Benjamin, quoted, 107
Handel, George Frederick, 186
Hanover, Elector of, 195
Hanoverians, 195, 201
Hanseatic League, 88
Harding, Warren G., 426
Hargreaves, James, 267
Harper's Ferry, 320
Harvey, William, 169; quoted, 169
Hatzfeldt, Count Paul von, *292*
Haugwitz, Count Christian von, 201
Hauptmann, Gerhart, 364
Hausa-Fulanis, 512
Hawaii, 325, 379, 380 (*see also* Pearl Harbor)
Hawkins, John, 103
Hay, John, 380
Hay-Pauncefote Treaty, 380
Haydn, Joseph, 186
Haymarket Square riot, 324
Hebrews, 5
Hegel, Georg Wilhelm Friedrich, 249

Heligoland Treaty, 687
Hellenistic Era, 10–11
Henlein, Konrad, 462
Henry IV (of England), 59.
Henry VII (of England), 61, 62, 102
Henry VIII (of England), 61, 62, 79–81, 84, 102, 126
Henry II (of France), 105
Henry III (of France), 105
Henry IV (of France), of Navarre, 105–6, 121
Henry IV (of Germany), 26
Henry the Navigator, 89–90
Herder, Johann Gottfried von, 186
heresy, 35, 79, 81; in 15th century, 70; Hussite, 54–55, 79
Herriot, Edouard, 422
Herzegovina, 354, 371, 372, 385
Herzen, Alexander, 310, 356
Herzl, Theodor, 431
Hesse, Hans, painting by, *44*
Hetàiria Philikē, 251
Himmler, Heinrich, quoted, 474
Hindenburg, Paul von, 396, 398, 399, 402, 453
hippies, 530
Hiroshima, 481, 526
Historical and Critical Dictionary (Bayle), 176
history: in Age of Romanticism, 247–48; Italian, 45–46; Marxian, 282; 20th-century, 437; U.S., 316
History of Civilization (Voltaire), 179
History of the Decline and Fall of the Roman Empire (Gibbon), 185
History of the Peloponnesian War (Thucydides), quoted, 10
Hitler, Adolf, 49, 412, 424, 430, 431, 451–55, *454,* 457–58, 460, 462–64
Hobbes, Thomas, 112, 131–32, 152, 175; quoted, 131
Hobson, J.A., quoted, 337
Hogarth, William, 186; engraving by, *185;* painting by, *196*
"Hohenzollern miracle," 203
Hohenzollerns, 155, 156, 200, 304
Holbach, Paul d', 182
Holbein, Hans, cartoon by, *68*
Holstein, Freidrich, Baron von, 382
Holy Alliance, 243–44
Holy Roman Empire, 153–54, 231, 243, 305
Home Rule Bills, 347, 348
Homer, Winslow, 325
Homestead Act, 323
Hook, Sidney, 283
Hoover, Herbert, 426, 427

Leninism, 345
Leo X (Pope), 56, *68,* 72
Leo XIII (Pope), 347, 363
Leonardo da Vinci, 51, 52, 167
Leopold II (of Belgium), 376
Leopold I (Holy Roman Emperor), 154
Lepanto, battle at, 97, 98
Le Tellier, Michel, 143
Letter from Sidney (Wakefield), 326
Leviathan (Hobbes), *112,* 131–32; quoted, 131
Leyte Gulf, battle of, 481
Liaotung Peninsula, 332
"Liberal Empire" (France), 294–95
Liberal Party: British, 307, 308, 347, 348, 349; French, 252, 256
liberalism, 242; and economics, 275–76; and education, 278; English, 273–76; French, 276; German, 260, 276, 300, 352; in politics, 274–75; Russian, 251–52
liberty, 181–82, 183–84, 273–74 (*see also* civil liberties)
liberum veto, 159, 205
Libya, 376
Liebknecht, Wilhelm, 353
Lincoln, Abraham, 320, 321, 322
literature: baroque, 175; 18th-century, 184–86; English, 107, 131–32; French, 108, 142–43; German, 186–87; Greek, 8; Italian, 43; Latin, 44; 19th-century, 364; Renaissance, 46–47; Romantic, 246; Russian, 505; Spanish, 107; "Storm and Stress" movement in, 186–87; 20th-century, 435, 436; U.S., 316, 325 (*see also* drama; history; poetry)
Lithuania, 358, 397, 464, 470
Little Entente, 412
Little Rock, Arkansas, 502
Livingstone, David, 376
Livy, 47
Lloyd George, David, 347, 349, 398, 404, *406*
Locarno Pact, 412–13
Locke, John, 124, 152–53, 175, 176, 177, 178, 184, 212, 221; quoted, 152
locomotives, 269
logic, study of, 8
Lollards, 55, 79
Lombards, 20
Lombardy, 296
London: Naval Treaty of, 434; Treaty of, 386, 395, 405
Long Parliament, 128–29
Longfellow, Henry Wadsworth, 316
Lord Protector, 130

Lorraine, 305, 350, 382
Louis XI, 59–60, 61, 62
Louis XIII, 121, 122, 123
Louis XIV, 123, 124, 131, 136, 138–46, *140,* 147, 151, 155, 178, 195
Louis XV, 197, 204, 209, 217
Louis XVI, 209, 216, 217, 218, 220, 221, 222, 223, 224, 225, 241
Louis XVII, 241
Louis XVIII, 235, 241, 250, 252
Louis Napoleon, 258 (*see also* Napoleon III)
Louis Philippe, 252, 253, 256, 257, 277, 278
Louisbourg, 201
Louvois, François, 143
Low countries, 470–71 (*see also* Netherlands)
lower class: English, 182–83; French, 124; and industrialization, 271–72, 276; in 19th century, 256, 261
Loyalists, Spanish, 459–60
Loyola, Ignatius of (St.), 82–83, *82*
Ludendorff, Erich von, 396, 398, 399, 402, 403
Luftwaffe, 472, 477 (*see also* air warfare)
Lumumba, Patrice, 512
Lusitania, 392, 397
Luther, Martin, 59, *66,* 71–77, 83, 84, 98; quoted, 72, 73
Lutheranism, 73–77, 132–33
Lützen, battle at, 134
Luxembourg, 303
Lvov, George, 400
Lyell, Charles, 360, 363
Lyons, 59
Lytton, Lord, 457

M

MacArthur, Douglas, 481, 501–2; quoted, 500
McCarthy, Joseph, 501
MacDonald, Ramsay, 429
MacDowell, Edward, 325
Macedon, 10
Macedonia, 386–87
Machiavelli, Niccolò, 47–49, *48,* 60, 63, 121, 167, 200; quoted, 49
McKinley, William, 379; quoted, 379
McKinley Tariff Act, 324
Madagascar, 377
Madras, 201
Magdeburg, siege of, *110–11,* 134
Magellan, Ferdinand, 92–93
Maginot Line, 470
Magyars, 25, 259, 299, 353, 354; invasions of, 24

Mahommed Jemil Bey, *292*
Maine, U.S.S., 380
Maintenon, Françoise, 142
Makin, 481
Malacca, 100
Malay Peninsula, 479
Malaya, 509
Malaysia, 508, 509
Mallarmé, Stéphane, 365
Malthus, Robert, 275–76, 360, 524
man, Renaissance, 40, 47, 52
Manchu dynasty, 330, 331, 333, 334
Manchukuo, 457 (*see also* Manchuria)
Manchuria, 336, 434, 456–57, 485
Mandate Commission, 411
mandate system, 405, 431–32
Manteuffel, Baron Otto von, *292*
manufacturing (*see* industry)
Mao Tse-tung, 434, *491,* 506, 508, 529–30
March Laws, 259
margrave, 155
Maria Louisa (wife of Napoleon), 233
Maria Theresa (of Austria), *190,* 197, 200, 203, 205, 207
Maria Theresa (wife of Louis XIV), 124, 136, 142
Marie Antoinette, 222, 224
Marks, Erich, quoted, 107
Marlborough, John Churchill, Duke of, 145
Marne, battle of the, 395
Marshall, George C., 487
Marshall Plan, 487, 488, 497, 499, 500
Martin V, 53
Martinique, 117
Marx, Karl, 280, 281–84, *281,* 344, 347, 361, 436
Marxism, 273, 280–84, 344, 345, 356, 443, 529–30
Mary I, 81, 101, 102
Mary II, 148–50, *149*
Mary of Burgundy, 60–61, 98
Mary Stuart (Queen of Scots), 102, *104,* 126
Masaccio, 49
Masaryk, Jan, 488
Masaryk, Thomas, 354, 424
mass culture, 435
mass production, 323, 343 (*see also* industry)
Massachusetts, 211
Massachusetts Bay Company, 119
Masurian Lakes, battle at, 396
materialism, 359, 426
Mathematical Principles of Natural Philosophy, The (Newton), 171

National Assembly, Russian (see *Duma*)

National Association for the Protection of Labour, 279

National Congress Party, Indian, 329, 432

national consciousness, 248 (see also nationalism)

National Convention, French, 225, 226

national debt, English, 151, 195

National Democratic Party, German, 499

National Farmers' Alliance and Industrial Union, 324

National Grange of the Patrons of Husbandry, 324

National Liberal Party, German, 352

National People's Party, Chinese, 333

National Socialist German Workers' Party (see Nazism)

national workshops, 257, 280

nationalism, 284; African, 511–12, *511;* Arab, 510; Asian, 336; Austrian, 253–54, 298, 299; Belgian, 253; Bulgarian, 373; colonial, 432–33; European, 240, 242, 248–49, 255–56, 289; French, 262, 351; German, 262, 300, 423; and Habsburg Empire, 259; "integral," 351; Irish, 348; of Jews, 431–32; and racialism, 362; Russian, 447; Serbian, 487; U.S., 425

Nationalist Party, Irish, 347

Nationalists, Chinese, 133–34, 491

nationalization program, 496, 498

nations, law of, 177

NATO, 488–89, 497, 499, 500, 504, 515

natural law, 177, 180, 182, 183, 273, 274

natural selection, 360

Naturalism, 364

Navarino, battle of, 251

navy: British, 199–200, 385–86, 394, 472; Dutch, 100; in 15th century, 57; German, 386, 397, 406; Japanese, 335, 425, 479–81, *480;* U.S., 325, 479–81, *480* (see also army; ships)

Nazi-Soviet Pact, 465

Nazism, 409, 451–52, 453–55 (see also Germany, in Second World War)

Near East, 290–93, 378, 381, 382, 385 (see also specific countries)

Necker, Jacques, 216, 222

Nehru, Jawaharlal, 507

Nelson, Horatio, 228, 230

neo-Romantics, 365

NEP (see New Economic Policy)

Netherlands, 59, 60, 78, 79, 135, 144, 197; Calvinism in, 99; division of,

99–101, *99;* North American colony of, 100, 118; revolt of, 98–101; in Second World War, 471; in 17th century, 147; Spain and, 96, 98–101, 99

Neuilly, Treaty of, 407

Neutrality Act, 460, 474

New Amsterdam, 100, 118

New Caledonia, 294

New Deal, 428–29

New Economic Policy (Russian), 416, 445

New England, 119

New France, 119

New Guinea, 378, 480

New Harmony, Indiana, 280

new imperialism, 374, 377–79 (see also colonies; imperialism)

New Left, 529–30

New Mexico, 319, 320

New Model Army, 129

"New Order," 474

"new physics," 437–38

New Poor Law, 277

New Rome (see Constantinople)

New Testament (see Bible)

New Zealand, 326, 327

Newcomen, Thomas, 268

Newfoundland, 145

newspapers: 18th-century, 186; 19th-century, 270

Newton, Isaac, 166, 169, 171–72, 177, 178, 179, 363

Nicaragua, 381

Nice, 296

Nicholas I (of Russia), 252, 253, 259, 291, 309, 356

Nicholas II (of Russia), 356, 358, 398, 400

Nicholas V (Pope), 55–56

Nicolaevsky, Boris I., quoted, 448

Nietzsche, Friedrich, 343, 365

Nigeria, 512

Nightingale, Florence, 291

nihilists, 310–11

Nile Valley, 4

Nixon, Richard M., 503, *503*

Noailles, Viscount Louis Marie de, 220

Nobel, Alfred, 343, 344

Nobel prizes, 344

nobility: 18th-century, 191–92; English, 146–47; French, 105, 121, 123, 141, 197, 217, 220; monarchy and, 61–62; Prussian, 207; Russian, 160–61, 198–99, 204, 309 (see also aristocracy; social classes)

nomads (see barbarians)

Nonintervention Committee, 460

Norman Conquest, 25, 29

Normandy, invasion of, 478–79, *478*

Normandy, Duke of, 24

Norris, Frank, 325

Norsemen, 88

North, Frederick, Lord, 211

North Africa, 20, 372, 373, 375–76, 383, 433; in Second World War, 472, 477

North America: Dutch settlement of, 100, 118; English settlement of, 118–19; French settlement of, 118–19; Russian exploration of, 120 (see also Canada; Mexico; United States)

North Atlantic Council, 489

North Atlantic Treaty Organization (see NATO)

North German Confederation, 302

Northmen, 25 (see also Vikings)

Northwest Ordinance, 211

Norway, 62, 77, 470–71

Notebooks (Leonardo da Vinci), 52

Nouvelle Héloïse (Rousseau), 186

Nova Scotia, 145

novels, 185, 186, 354 (see also literature)

NSDAP (see Nazism)

Nuclear Non-Proliferation Treaty, 518

Nuclear Test Ban Treaty, 518, 526

nuclear weapons, 495, 526–27 (see also atomic bomb; hydrogen bomb)

Nuremberg Laws, 455

O

OAS, 504

Oates, Titus, 147–48

OAU, 513, *514*

occupation zones, after Second World War, 482, 483, 485, 486

oceanic commerce, 87, 92–93, 93, (see also exploration; shipping)

Octavian, 13 (see also Augustus)

October Manifesto, 358

October Revolution, 400–401

Octobrists, 358

Of Civil Government: Two Treatises (Locke), 152; quoted, 152

office-holding, in France, 123, 218

oil resources, 510, 512

Okinawa, 481

Old Believers, 158, 159

Old Testament (see Bible)

Olney, Richard, 325

On Liberty (Mill), 273

Roman Catholic Church (*continued*) 62–63; and Mussolini, 449, 450, 451; and Protestantism (*see* Thirty Years' War); reforms of, 69–70, 82–83; and Romanticism, 246–47; in 16th century, 67–68; in Spain, 96; in 13th century, 31–32 (*see also* Catholic League; Christianity; Great Schism; papacy)

Roman Empire, early, 11–19; under Augustus, 13–14; boundaries of, 12; and German frontier, 18–19

Roman Empire, late: under Constantine, 17–18; decline of, 16–19; under Diocletian, 17 (*see also* Holy Roman Empire)

Roman Senate, 13–14

Romanovs, 158

Romanticism, 186–87, 245–49

Rome, 297, 298, 306; Mussolini's march on, 450; sack of, 40, 55, 82 (*see also* Roman Empire)

Rome-Berlin Axis, 459 (*see also* Axis)

Rommel, Erwin, 472

Röntgen, Konrad, 437

Roosevelt, Eleanor, *429*

Roosevelt, Franklin D., 428, 429, 460, 481, *482,* 485; quoted, 429

Roosevelt, James, *429*

Roosevelt, Theodore, 336, *336,* 362, 379, 380, 381, 433

Roosevelt Corollary, 381, 433

Rosen, Baron Roman Romanovich, *336*

Rousseau, Jean Jacques, 183–84, 186, 246; quoted, 184

Rouvroy, Louis de, quoted, 143

Royal Oak, 470

royal prerogative, 126, 127

Royal Society of London, 168, 169

Royalists, French, 252

rubber, production of, 509

Ruhr, 470, 479; French invasion of, 411, 412, 415

"Rules of Reasoning" (Newton), quoted, 172

Rumania, 251, 259, 291, 372, 395, 397, 402, 409, 486, 506

Ruskin, John, 365

Russia, 62, 153; colonies of, 119–20; in Crimean War, 290–91; in 18th century, 198–99, 204–6, *205;* before First World War, 356–57, 370–72, 373, 382, 383–84, 385; in First World War, 389, 395–96, 397, 398, 401–2; and France, 231, 232–35; and Japan, 335–36, *336;* Mongols in, 30; in 19th century, 251, 270, 290–93, 308–11, 316, 322; and Poland, 205–6; in 17th century, 158–61; in 13th century, 30 (*see also* Soviet Union)

Russia Company, 115

Russian Orthodox Church, 158

Russian Revolution, 281, 399–402

Russo-German alliance, 412

Russo-Japanese War, 378, 382

Russo-Turkish War, 370–72, *371*

Ruthenians, 259

Rutherford, Ernest, 437

Rykov, Alexei, 446, 448

Ryswick, Peace of, 144, 155

S

Saar, 405, 457

sabotage trials, 447

Sadowa, battle at, 302, 303

St. Bartholomew's Day Massacre, 105, *106*

St. Germain, Treaty of, 407

St. Helena, 235

St. Ignatius Church, ceiling of, *174*

St. Paul's Cathedral (London), *125*

St. Peter's Cathedral (Rome), 56, 71

St. Petersburg, 161

Saint-Simon, Henri de, 280

Sakhalin, 336

Salisbury, Robert Gascoyne-Cecil, Lord, 347, 382

salutary neglect, 196, 209

Samoa, 325, 379, 380

samurai, 335

San Francisco Conference, 483

San Stefano, Treaty of, 371

Santa Anna, Antonio López de, 326

Sarajevo, 387–88

Saratoga, battle of, 211

Sardinia (*see* Piedmont-Sardinia)

Satsuma Rebellion, 335

Saudi Arabia, 510

Savonarola, Girolamo, 70

Savoy, 146, 296

Saxons (*see* Anglo-Saxons)

Scandinavian kingdoms, 30 (*see also* Denmark; Norway; Sweden)

Scarlatti, Domenico, 175

Scharnhorst, Gerhard von, 233

schism (*see* Great Schism)

Schleswig-Holstein, 301

Schlieffen, Alfred von, 389

Schlieffen Plan, 389, 395

Schoenerer, Georg von, 354

scholarship: in Age of Romanticism, 248; Renaissance, 46–47; 16th-century, 70–71 (*see also* education; Humanism; universities)

scholasticism, 40, 168

Schönbrunn palace, 175

Schoolmen, 46, 177 (*see also* scholasticism)

schools: French, 229; U.S., 502 (*see also* education; universities)

Schulverein, 354

Schuman, Robert, 497

Schuman Plan, 499

Schluschnigg, Kurt von, 462

Schutzstaffel (*see* SS troops)

Schwarzenberg, Felix, 259, 299

science: in Hellenistic Era, 10; 19th-century, 358–59; and religion, 172–73, 362–64; Renaissance, 52 (*see also* astronomy; mathematics; physics; scientific revolution)

scientific method, 166, 168, 172, 181

scientific revolution, 165–73, 184

scientific socialism, 279, 283

Scotland, 102, 128; Calvinism in, 78; in 17th century, 151–52

sculpture: French, 142; Renaissance, 49, 51 (*see also* art)

"Sea Beggars," 101, 104

Sea Dogs, 104

sea power, 130, 151, 199–200, 202, 470; in Second World War, 479–81, *480;* in 16th century, 100, 104 (*see also* navy; shipping)

SEATO, 509, 515

Sebastopol, 291

Second French Empire, 293–95

Second French Revolution, 225

Second Industrial Revolution, 341, 343–44, 359

Second International, 345

Second Reform Bill, 307–8, 311

Second Treatise of Government (Locke) 177

Second World War, 434, 460, 469–81, *476, 480,* 524

secret police: German, 453; Italian, 450; Russian, 444

sectionalism, U.S., 318, 323

secularism: in 15th century, 69; Italian, 43–44

Security Council of U.N., 483, 484–85

seigneuries, 118

Selective Service Act, 475

self-determination, principle of, 409, 434, 462

senatorial class, 13–14

sepoys, 329

September massacres, 225

spice trade, 88, 89, 90, 100
Spinoza, Baruch, 172–73
Spirit of the Laws, The (Montesquieu), 179
spoils system, 318
Sputnik, 525
squires, 124, 129
Srbik, Heinrich von, quoted, 241
SS troops, *442*, 474 (*see also* storm troopers)
stadtholders, 100
Stael, Mme. de, 246
Stalin, Joseph, 358, 400, 401, 445–46, *446*, 447, 448, 473, 478, 481, *482*, 483, *485*, 504–5
Stalingrad, battle of, 473
Stamp Act, 210, *210*
Standard Oil Company, 323
Stanislaus of Poland, *198*, 205
Stanley, Henry Morton, 376, *377*
Star Chamber, 61, 128
state, Hegel's view of, 249
states: French (*see* departments, French); German, 243; North American, 212; papal (*see* Papal States) (*see also* city-states)
states' rights, 319
Statute of Westminster, 432
Statuto, 354
Stavisky, Alexander, 430
steam engine, 266, 268
steamboat, 270
steel production, 323
Steele, Richard, 185
Stein, Heinrich von, 233
Stettin, 156
stock market, 426–27
Stoicism, 11, 14, 15, 177
Stolypin, Peter, 358
Stone Age, 4
"Storm and Stress" movement, 186–87
storm troopers, 430
Stourbridge, Lion, *269*
Strafford, Earl of (*see* Wentworth, Thomas)
Straits Convention of *1841*, 290
Stransky, J., quoted, 479
Strasbourg, 144
Strauss, David Friedrich, 363
streltsi, 159
Stresemann, Gustav, 412, 413, *414*
strikes, 324, 345, 348, 431
Stuarts, 117, 119, 126–30, 151, 152, 195
student uprisings, 530–31
Study of History, A (Toynbee), 437
submarine warfare, 333, 402, 477, 481
Sudan, 376, 381, 382, 433

Sudetenland, 424, 462–64
Suez Canal, 307, 433, 510, 515
Suez Canal Company, 329
suffrage, 129, 341; in Austria, 353, 354; in England, 254, 342, 348; in France, 222, 225, 257, 341–42; in Germany, 342; in Italy, 341–42, 354–55; in Roman Empire, 13; in U.S., 316, 318, 342
"suffragettes," *342*
sugar: production of, 117–18; trade, 201
Suleiman the Magnificent, 63
Sullivan, Louis, 325
Sully, Maximilien, 121, 140
Sun King, 142, 197 (*see also* Louis XIV)
Sun Yat-sen, 333–34, 433
superstition, 176, 177, 178
Supreme Court, U.S., 320, 322, 324
Supreme Soviet, 446
Sweden, 62, 77, 135; in 17th century, 157–58, *157;* in Thirty Years' War, 133–34
Swift, Jonathan, 185
Switzerland, 135, 243, 341; Calvinism in, 77–79
Sybil (Disraeli), 284
"Syllabus of the Principal Errors of Our Times, A," 363
Sylvius, Aeneas, 56
Symbolists, 365
syndicalism, 285, 355
syndicates, 344
Synthetic Philosophy (Spencer), 361
Syria, 20, 431, 497, 510

T

Taff Vale decision, 348
taille, 59, 217
Taiping Rebellion, 330–32
Taiwan, 509
Takahira, Baron Kogoro, *336*
Talleyrand, Charles de, *240,* 243
tank warfare, 403, 471
Tannenberg, battle at, 396
Tarawa, 481
tariffs: Austrian, 354; British, 261; French, 140, 350; German, 352; mercantilism and, 115–16; Prussian, 206; U.S., 318, 319, 324, 379, 425, 426, 428 (*see also* free trade; protectionism)
taxation: Austrian, 208; in Brandenburg, 156; of clergy, 62; colonial, 210; Dutch, 99; English, 127, 128, 196, 261, 349; French, 59, 117, 121, 140, 216, 217; Roman, 19; Russian, 160

Taylor, A.J.P., quoted, 370
tea, Indian, 211
technology: 15th-century, 56; in Middle Ages, 36; U.S., 524 (*see also* science)
Teheran, conference at, 478, 481
telegraph, 270
telescopes, 170, *170*, 173
Tennis Court Oath, 218, *219;* quoted, 218
Test Act, 147, 254
Tetzel, Friar Johann, 71
Texas, 319
textile industry, 58, 113, 355; inventions in, 267
Thackeray, William, 364
Thailand, 508, 509
theology, science and, 172–73; 362–63 (*see also* philosophy)
Theory of the Leisure Class, The (Veblen), 325
Thiers, Adolphe, 304
Third Communist International, 409, 444
Third Estate, 218–19, *219*
Third Reich, 453
Thirty Years' War, *110–11,* 123, 132–36, *135,* 155
Thomas Aquinas (St.), 28
Three Emperors' League, 370, 372, 373
Thucydides, quoted, 10
Thyssen, Fritz, 352
Tibet, 383
Tientsin, Treaties of, 331
Tigris-Euphrates Valley, 4
Tilly, Johan, *110–11*
"Time of Troubles," 437
tin, production of, 509
Tirpitz, Alfred von, 386
Titian, 52
Tito, Marshal (Josip Brozovich), 506
Tito, Santi di, painting by, *48*
Tocqueville, Alexis de, 316, 342; quoted, 257, 316
Tokyo, 334
Toleration Act, 150
Tolstoy, Leo, 364
Tom Jones (Fielding), 185
tool-making, 185
Tordesillas, Treaty of, 91–92
Tories, 148, 149, 150, 195, 211, 254, 376 (*see also* Conservative Party, British)
Torricelli, Evangelista, 169
totalitarianism, 436, 443–65
Toynbee, Arnold J., 88, 437; quoted, 89

trade and commerce: Chinese, 330; and Continental System, 231–32; Dutch, 100; 18th-century, 194; English, 307, 429; 15th- and 16th-century, 56, 59, 89; French, 294, 350; Greek, 7; 17th-century, 112, 115–16; U.S., 324 (*see also* industrialism; industry)

trade routes (*see* shipping)

trade unions (*see* gilds; labor unions)

Trades Union Congress, 279

transatlantic cable, 316

transformism, 355

Transjordan, 431

transportation: 18th-century, 268–69; 19th-century, 269–71 (*see also* railroads; ships)

Trans-Siberian Railway, 356

Transvaal, 377

treason trials, Russian, 447–48

"treaty ports," 330

Treitschke, Heinrich von, 362

Trent, 322

Trent, Council of, 83, 96

Trianon, Treaty of, 407

Triple Alliance, 372–73, 384, 385, 395

Triple Entente, 381, 383–84

Triple Monarchy, 299

Tripoli, 376, 385, 386

Troppau Protocol, 244

Trotsky, Leon, 358, 400, 445–46

True Law of Free Monarchies, The (James I), 126

Truman, Harry S., 481, 485, 489, 500–502, *501*

Truman Doctrine, 486–87, 489, 500

"trusts," 323–34, 344

Tshombe, Moise, 512

Tudors, 61, 101–2, 124, 125–26

Tunis, 477

Tunisia, 497

Turgenev, Ivan, 364

Turgot, Anne Robert, 181, 217

Turin, 295

Turkey, 251, 290–91, *290,* 486, 515; before First World War, 370–72, *371,* 382; in First World War, 395, 403–4, 407–8

Turkish Empire, 97, 376 (*see also* Ottoman Empire)

Turkish Straits, 290, 291, 373, 374, 385, 386, 396, 408

Turks (*see* Ottoman Empire; Turkish Empire)

Turner, Joseph, 246

Twain, Mark (Samuel L. Clemens), 325

Twenty-one Demands, 433

"two-power standard," 326

type, movable, 558–59

tyrannies (*see* dictatorships; totalitarianism)

Tyrol, 154 (*see also* Austria)

Tz'ŭ Hsi, 333, *333*

U

Ulpian, quoted, 16

"Ultras," 252

Ulyanov, Vladimir Ilyich (*see* Lenin, Nikolai)

U.N. (*see* United Nations)

underdeveloped countries, 489, 518, 527, 528

unemployment: in 15th century, 59; in Germany, 452, 454; in 19th century, 280; in 20th century, 427

Union, Act of (*1707*), 152

Union Act (*1840*), 327

Union of India, 507 (*see also* India)

Union of South Africa, 327, 377

unions (*see* labor unions)

Unitarianism, 79

United Nations, 483–85, 486, 489, 510, 512, 514

United Nations Charter, quoted, 483

United Provinces, 99–101, *99* (*see also* Netherlands)

United Socialist Party, French, 350

United States: and Asia, 509–10; and China, 508; in 18th century, 209–12; before First World War, 379–81; in First World War, 309, 402; in 19th century, 270–71, 315–25, *317, 320, 321;* before Second World War, 424–27, 428–29; in Second World War, 474–75, 477, 479–81, *480;* since Second World War, 486–88, 500–504, 527; and Soviet Union, 515–19; space program of, 525–26

universe, concepts of, 166–67, 168, 172–73, 180, 182

universities: Italian, 52; medieval, 167; Russian, 310 (*see also* education; schools)

upper class, Russian, 252 (*see also* aristocracy; nobility)

Urban II (Pope) 26, 28

Urban VI (Pope), 35

urban proletariat, 240, 259

urban renewal program, of Napoleon III, 294

urbanization: European, 115; and industrialization, 343; Italian, 42–46; and lower class, *271,* 272; 19th-century, 239 (*see also* city-states)

Urbino, Duke of, 47

Ure, Andrew, quoted, 272

USSR (*see* Soviet Union)

Utah, 320

utilitarianism, 273–74

Utopia (More), 70, 80

Utopian socialism, 279–80

Utrecht, Peace of, 145–46, 151, 195

Utrecht, Union of, 99 (*see also* Netherlands)

U-2 incident, 516

V

Valla, Lorenzo, 46–47

vassalage (*see* feudalism; serfdom)

vassals (*see* feudalism; serfdom)

Vatican Library, 56, *57*

Vauban, Sebastien de, 143

V-E Day, 479

Veblen, Thorstein, 325

Velasquez, Diego, 107

Venezuela, 380

Venice, 41, 42

Verdun, battle of, 397–98

Verlaine, Paul, 365

Vermeer, Jan, 175

Versailles: palace of, *138–39,* 141, 175, 218, 219; Treaty of, 405, 406–7, 409, 410, 457–58

Verwoerd, Henrik F., 512

Vesalius, Andreas, 167

Vespucci, Amerigo, 91

Vichy government, 472

Victor Emmanuel I, 244

Victor Emmanuel II, 258, 295, 296, 297

Victor Emmanuel III, 355, 450

Victoria, *314,* 347

Victorian Compromise, 307–8

Vienna, 63, 134; Congress of, 241–43, 404; Kennedy and Khrushchev in, 516–17; in 19th century, 259; Peace of, 301; siege of, 154

Vietcong, 516

Vietnam, 498, 503, 508, 509, 515, 516, 518

vikings, 24

Villafranca agreement, 296

villages, emergence of, 4

Virginia Company, 119

virtù, 43, 48, 49

Visconti, Gian Galeazzo, 42

Vivaldi, Antonio, 175

V-J Day, 481

Vladivostok, 378

Voltaire, 47, 154, *164,* 178–79, 181,